THE SACRED ENCOUNTER

· THE ·
SACRED
ENCOUNTER

Jewish Perspectives on Sexuality

Edited by

RABBI LISA J. GRUSHCOW, DPHIL

Foreword by Rabbi David Ellenson, PhD

CCAR Challenge and Change Series

Every effort has been made to ascertain the owners of copyrights for the selections used in this volume and to obtain permission to reprint copyrighted passages. The Central Conference of American Rabbis expresses gratitude for permissions it has received. The Conference will be pleased, in subsequent editions, to correct any inadvertent errors or omissions that may be pointed out.

145 "Created by the Hand of Heaven: Sex, Love, and the Androgynos" by Elliot Rose Kukla in *The Passionate Torah: Sex and Judaism*, edited by Danya Ruttneberg [NYU Press, 2009], pp. 193-203. Used by permission.
247 "Embracing Lesbians and Gay Men: A Reform Jewish Innovation" by Denise Eger in *Contemporary Debate in American Reform Judaism, Conflicting Visions*, edited by Dana Evan Kaplan [Taylor and Francis Group LLC Books, 2001], pp. 180-192. Used by permission.
587 "I Do? Consent and Coercion in Sexual Relations" by Mark Dratch in *Rav Chesed: Essays in Honor of Rabbi Dr. Lookstein*, 2 Vol. [KTAV Publishing, 2009]. Used by permission.

Library of Congress Cataloging-in-Publication Data

The sacred encounter : Jewish perspectives on sexuality / edited by Rabbi Lisa J. Grushcow, DPhil ; foreword by Rabbi David Ellenson, PhD.
    pages cm. -- (CCAR challenge and change series)
  Includes bibliographical references.
  ISBN 978-0-88123-203-5 (pbk. : alk. paper)
  1. Sex--Religious aspects--Judaism. 2. Sex--Biblical teaching. 3. Sex in rabbinical literature. 4. Bible. Old Testament--Criticism, interpretation, etc. 5. Rabbinical literature--History and criticism. 6. Reform Judaism. I. Grushcow, Lisa, 1974-

  BM720.S4S33 2014
  296.3'664--dc23

                            2014000749

10 9 8 7 6 5 4 3 2 1

CCAR Press, 355 Lexington Avenue, New York, NY 10017
(212) 972-3636
www.ccarpress.org

Sacred Encounter Task Force

Rabbi Lisa J. Grushcow, DPhil, Editor

Rabbi Craig Axler

Dr. Carole Balin

Rabbi Denise Eger

Rabbi Michael Latz

Rabbi Michelle Lenke

Rabbi Nancy Wiener, DMin

Rabbi Elizabeth Wood

Rabbi Hara E. Person,
Publisher, CCAR Press

Rabbi Steven A. Fox,
Chief Executive,
Central Conference of American Rabbis

Contents

Acknowledgments

Above all, I want to thank Rabbi Hara Person, Publisher and Director of the CCAR Press, for asking me to undertake this project, and for going above and beyond in working with me to bring it to completion. It has been a pleasure to partner with her, and every page of this book has been improved by her insight and dedication. Many thanks also to the staff of the CCAR, including Rabbi Steve Fox, Deborah Smilow, Ortal Bensky, rabbinic interns Daniel Kirzane and Adena Kemper, college intern Marie Lambert, and copy editor Debra Hirsch Corman. Thanks also to colleagues Rabbi Mary Zamore, Rabbi Amy Schwartzman, and Dr. Carole Balin, who helped cheer us on, suggesting ideas, titles, and writers for the book. We are also very grateful to the Advisory Committee for this volume for their enthusiasm and wisdom, including Rabbi Craig Axler, Dr. Carole Balin, Rabbi Denise Eger, Rabbi Michael Latz, Rabbi Michelle Lenke, Rabbi Nancy Wiener, DMin, and Rabbi Elizabeth Wood. I am grateful to Temple Emanu-El-Beth Sholom, in Montreal, where I have just completed my first year as senior rabbi, and to Congregation Rodeph Sholom, in NYC, where I served as associate rabbi for nine years. Both congregations have shown me the truth of the Rabbinic dictum, "from my students I learn most of all." Moreover, both congregations made the space for me to pursue this project in addition to very full-time pulpit responsibilities. This attests to the value they place on being part of a broader conversation within our Reform Movement, and within Judaism as a whole—as well as respect for the intellectual interests of their rabbi. In the constantly shifting role of the rabbi, this is no small thing, and I thank my congregants and colleagues alike.

On a similar note, I am exceptionally appreciative of all those who contributed to the book, despite competing demands on their time. Many people stretched their own comfort zones to add their voices to this anthology. I appreciate not only the work they put in, but also the risks that they took. We looked for contributors to share an even wider range of perspectives, and sometimes came up short. My hope is that future publications in this area will be able to include even more diversity.

In my own personal and professional life, I continue to be grateful to the Reform Movement and the Hebrew Union College–Jewish Institute of Religion, who took me in when others would not. Being able to study for the rabbinate without being in the closet let me bring my whole self forward, and has made me a better rabbi and a better Jew. I am also profoundly aware of all those who broke ground before me, and whose work and lives make my work and life possible.

Last but far from least, I am grateful to Rabbi Andrea Myers. For over fifteen years, she has taught me that the world is a big, beautiful place, all the more so when we are at home with ourselves. Her love and wisdom have shaped me, and therefore this book, in ways too many to count.

Rabbi Lisa J. Grushcow, DPhil

Foreword

Rabbi David Ellenson, PhD

The famed code of Jewish law the *Shulchan Aruch* has as its frontispiece a passage from Psalm 16:8. The verse states, *"Shiviti Adonai l'negdi tamid*—I have placed God before me always." This is quite purposeful. For the *Shulchan Aruch*, which seeks to govern and direct every aspect of living, is animated by the belief that no dimension of life is or should be devoid or absent of God's presence. It asserts the hope that God is or ought to be present in every detail and encounter of life.

As I read *The Sacred Encounter* and turned its pages, this passage from Psalm 16:8 and its placement at the opening of the *Shulchan Aruch* came to mind over and over again. For this verse from Psalms and its selection as the reading that invites us to enter the premiere code of Jewish law at its very outset reminds us of the aspiration that animates Judaism—the holy can and hopefully will be experienced in every aspect of human existence.

The Sacred Encounter is surely informed by this conviction. Appropriate consideration is paid to classical Jewish sources, both biblical and Rabbinic; and modern literature, both literary and scientific, is well represented. A vast array of topics is explored. Unsurprisingly for a book produced under the aegis of the Central Conference of American

Rabbis on sexuality, significant attention is paid to GLBTQ issues and Jewish attitudes toward non-heterosexual dimensions of human sexuality. However, the book is hardly limited to such concerns. Indeed, *The Sacred Encounter* is comprehensive in its treatment of its subject matter. Eroticisms of all types are addressed, and sexual intimacy as a theological concern, the expression of sexuality at points both young and old in the human life cycle, pornography, cybersex, sexual boundary violations and transgressions, marriage, divorce, breastfeeding and weaning, infertility, dress, and more are among the topics considered. Furthermore, the range of authors is truly impressive. While most of the writers are Reform colleagues, Reconstructionist, Conservative, Orthodox, trans-denominational, and nondenominational rabbis write as well. Voices both scholarly and personal—and sometimes they are both—are also heard. In sum, one should not expect uniformity in this work. Instead, this book displays a diverse and multilayered liberal Jewish ethos regarding the most private and intimate human quality—sexuality. The many voices and attitudes present in the liberal Jewish world on this topic and the dazzling array of opinions and interests that liberal Jews hold on these matters are here on display. That is as it should be. Different persons writing on the same topic have distinct attitudes and viewpoints. The reader will delight in encountering these diverse insights and will be appropriately stimulated and provoked by them.

However, for all the diversity and variety *The Sacred Encounter* evidences on the topic of human sexuality from a liberal Jewish perspective, one theme and attitude is constant. It is that each human being is a person created in the image of God and therefore possessed of dignity and worthy of respect.

To highlight what this means, I would turn to a work written in 1988 by Judith Romney Wegner, a graduate of Harvard Law School who later received her doctorate in Talmud from Brown University. Hers is a classic and erudite book germane to this foreword. In her *Chattel or Person? The Status of Women in the Mishnah*, Dr. Wegner observed that while the *Tannaim*, the rabbis of the first two centuries of the Common Era who wrote the Mishnah, accorded the women of their era status as "persons" in the area of property rights, they failed to do so in the realm of sexuality. In this arena, women were treated as "chattel." Their "sexuality" was owned by men—a father, a brother, or a husband—and could be bartered or traded accordingly.

For all the disparate attitudes and voices in *The Sacred Encounter*, every author writing on each topic rejects the notion that any human being and their sexuality can be regarded as "chattel." Instead, the affirmation of the personhood of every individual and their sexuality so long as it is not exploitative of others is uniformly respected. The authors in this book, building upon yet extending beyond the classical Jewish foundations they have inherited, regard each and every person—straight or gay, young or old—and their expression of sexuality as a God-given expression of their humanity. They accord each expression respect and regard each expression as potentially holy. This ethos serves as the uniform base for the construction of a liberal Jewish approach to sexuality, and this attitude is found on every page of this book.

In Proverbs 3:6, it is written, "*B'chol d'rachecha da-eihu*—In all your ways, know God." *The Sacred Encounter* and its philosophy of respect for human persons as sexual beings will surely allow its readers to reflect on and hopefully encounter God in the most intimate moments of their sexual expression. It is a worthy addition to Jewish literature and teachings in our day.

Introduction:
This Too Is Torah

> Once, Rav Kahana went in and hid under Rav's bed. He heard him
> talking and laughing and doing what he needed. Kahana said, "It
> is as if [Rav] Abba had never before tasted this dish!" Abba said,
> "Kahane, are you here?! Get out, it's not appropriate!" He said to
> him, "This too is Torah, and I need to learn."
>
> (Babylonian Talmud, *B'rachot* 62a)

This Talmudic story, about rabbis who lived eighteen hundred years
ago, is often cited to show Judaism as a sex-positive religion. Understanding sex is shown to be so important that the student is justified
in hiding under his teacher's bed, to listen in on the teacher's intimate
moments with his wife. Strikingly, the phrase used as a euphemism for
Abba, the teacher, having sex ("doing his needs") uses the root of the
same word that Kahana uses: "I need to learn." The story suggests that
the need for sex and the need for knowledge both are part of what it
means to be a human being.

What is less often mentioned is the fact that the story of Kahana
hiding under Abba's bed is in the middle of a section in which students

follow their teachers into the bathroom, to watch them there as well. For the Rabbis of the Talmud, everything needed to be known and discussed. But ever since the Garden of Eden, there has been a particularly strong connection between sex and knowledge. Insofar as Judaism is a religion of laws, part of this connection is the desire to know the right and wrong ways to act, in the sexual arena as in all others. Insofar as Judaism is a religion of stories, the connection between sex and knowledge also has to do with the desire to know ourselves, other people, and God. It is no accident that the word for knowledge (*daat*) is used in the Bible to describe sex. Our ancestors knew, as we do today, that our sexuality is connected to the deepest part of ourselves, and to know someone else through sex can be sacred and profound.

Even as we share certain experiences and understandings with our biblical ancestors and those of Rabbinic times, when we read the Talmudic story about Abba and Kahana, we might have some different questions. For instance, what does Abba's wife think of her husband's student under the bed? How does the idea of *derech eretz*, what is appropriate and inappropriate, change over time? Now that the rabbi who is in bed might be a woman, and her spouse might be of the same sex, is the conversation a different one?

The first book in this Challenge and Changes series, *The Sacred Table: Creating a Jewish Food Ethic*, looked at ancient Jewish teachings on food from a modern, liberal perspective. This book does the same with sex. It is worth noting that when Kahana hears Abba talking and laughing with his wife, he uses an analogy with eating to express his surprise: "It is as if Abba had never before tasted this dish!" Eating and sexuality are similar in that both are ways that we express our identities. But despite the Talmudic story, what we do in bed is more private than what we put on our plates. Other people are often involved. It is a topic of conversation unlike any other. And yet, it is indeed Torah, and we must learn.

In modern Western culture, most associations between religion and sex are negative. Religion is seen as a negative force, suppressing sex and sexuality alike. For lesbian, gay, bisexual, and transgender (LGBT) people, both religious and political authorities have often been a source of persecution. One of the most significant impacts of the modern secular state has been to separate political legislation from the private acts of citizens. As Canadian prime minister Pierre Trudeau famously said in 1967, "There's no place for the state in the bedrooms of the nation." As of the writing of this introduction in the summer of 2013, the Supreme Court of the United States has just decided landmark cases on marriage equality, protecting its LGBT citizens and their rights and setting a positive trajectory.

In the midst of the political debate over marriage in the United States, many conservative religious voices emerged to argue against marriage equality. Religious condemnation—in contemporary debate, and for centuries before—has been particularly hard on many people who are LGBT, leading to internalized homophobia as well as external oppression. As a result, many people who are LGBT have rejected religion entirely. One might think that the best liberal approach to sexuality is one that is entirely secular.

What place, then, for a book on liberal Jewish approaches to sexuality? I would argue: an essential place. Those of us whose religious paradigm is a progressive one have a lot to say about sexuality. In a society where conservative religious voices try to claim a monopoly on social issues, it is especially important for liberal people of faith to present a different view, and not to abdicate our religious approach. As adherents to a religion that is based on interpretation, questioning, and debate, Jews have a special opportunity to show that there is more than one religious perspective on sexuality.

But the approach of this book is not based on a single issue. First and foremost is the insistence that every human being is a sexual being, wherever they are on the spectrum. And so this is not a book simply about LGBT issues, either in terms of textual interpretation or movement policy. The evolution of liberal Judaism in this area over the past decades has been transformative, with wide-ranging impact and implications, and as such is discussed. Ultimately, though, our interest in bringing these essays together is to present a broad and deep exploration of sexuality in all its forms, using a liberal Jewish lens.

The format of the book recognizes that sexuality is a deeply personal issue, as well as an intellectual one. For this reason, each section contains not only essays, but also personal reflections.

Part 1, "In the Beginning: Biblical and Rabbinic Contexts," contains essays focused on interpretation, exploring foundational texts. Special attention is given to the texts traditionally understood to condemn homosexuality, with essays providing close textual analyses and creative new approaches. Other essays ambitiously take on the question of sexuality within the Rabbinic tradition as a whole and ask how ancient texts might inform our modern search for meaning.

Part Two is "God in the Bedroom, God in the Body: Theology and Identity." This section provides multiple perspectives on the intersection of theology, identity, and sexuality. Essays cover topics as varied as how we see our diverse sexual identities reflected in Jewish teachings, the creation of new liturgies, interfaith sexual encounters in Yiddish literature, and the realities of LGBT life in Israel today. The diversity of the essays is indicative of the diversity of the issues. The common thread is the desire to find connections between our most deeply felt experiences and our most deeply held beliefs.

In Part Three, "'A Progressive Religion': Sexuality and the Reform Movement," we take a close look at the approach of the Reform Movement to sexuality, providing an unprecedented historical perspective on the Movement's approach to sexuality, diversity, and inclusion. This section contains essays that praise the groundbreaking steps the Reform Movement has taken, as well as those that are critical of the ways in which work remains to be done. It also includes a fascinating variety of perspectives on the debate over the ordination of LGBT rabbis, with an interview with Rabbi Dr. Eugene B. Borowitz accompanied by two former students' perspectives, complemented by a third piece with a vantage point from Leo Baeck College in London.

Part Four, "Beloved Companions: Jewish Marital Models," examines Jewish perspectives on marriage and how those perspectives have changed over time. In so doing, the section attempts to identify enduring values within marriage, as well as the challenges to making marriage a sacred relationship. The issue of marital infidelity is approached from both a philosophical and a deeply human perspective. Innovative Reform approaches to the idea of family purity and the ritual of divorce also are discussed. Part 4 closes with a timely personal piece on the fight for marriage equality.

Part Five is "Ages and Stages: Sexuality throughout Our Lives." All too often, sexuality is seen as the exclusive territory of young adults. This section expands in two directions, beginning with different models of sexuality education for children and teenagers, and extending through old age, which is being constantly redefined. Within the section, there is considerable debate: Should synagogues teach only about sexuality or also include practical information about sex? How do we approach fertility, both desired and undesired? If a person is married to a spouse with dementia, are there models for sacred relationship that honor this commitment and yet allow for alternative companionship and love? The essays in part 5 range from the practical to the provocative.

Part Six is "There Be Dragons: Issues, Ethics, and Boundaries." This is perhaps the most innovative section of the book and definitely the most diverse. The fundamental question is how Jewish values can be applied in a variety of situations. These essays take us from post-Holocaust DP camps to the contemporary Caribbean, and from the sanctuary to cyberspace. Along the way, we explore issues of consent and desire, lines that should never be crossed, and unexplored territories with unexpected meaning.

As the range of essays suggests, the goal of this anthology is to bring together a variety of voices. My hope is that some of the most fruitful discussions will emerge from differences between essays that are close to one another in their placement, but radically different in their perspective. As such, it should be clear that no single essay represents the official voice of the Central Conference of American Rabbis or of the Reform Movement. Rather, in combination with each other, they give the reader an understanding of the issues at hand for Reform and other liberal Jews.

We begin the book with personal voices, "Short Takes" on the intersection between Judaism and sexuality. With these Short Takes especially, the reader has the opportunity to eavesdrop, like Kahana underneath Abba's bed—but without the intrusion. May *The Sacred Encounter* deepen your own conversations and connections: in the synagogue, in the classroom, and yes, in bed. This too is Torah.

Short Takes

How does Judaism inform your relationship to sex and sexuality?

My freshman year of college, I was offered what seemed like a dream job: teaching fellow students how to have safer, more enjoyable sex. As a student health educator, I gave presentations on many topics, from contraceptive use to pleasure-focused "orgasm workshops."

This new job coincided with my renewed interest in Jewish practice and belief. At first, I did not think that the two were related. But they were. Both related to the agency that we have to beautify our lives and experience joy. Both related to how we conduct ourselves.

At their best, both sex and Judaism are deeply spiritual and spirited.

Rabbi Joshua M. Z. Stanton

*   *   *

Can I turn this question on its head? Because for me, my sexuality has informed my Judaism far more than my Judaism has informed my sexuality. I came out as a lesbian to myself when I was nine and didn't even have a word for it. By the time my thirteen-year-old self asked my

Orthodox-leaning Conservative rabbi (in 1973), "What does Judaism teach about homosexuality?" I was certain of my identity. When my rabbi answered back, "Child, put those thoughts out of your head," I decided to put Judaism away and embrace my sexuality. I never thought I'd be able to live as both a Jew and a lesbian. When, at age twenty-four I found a congregation with an outreach to LGBT Jews, I began to live as a fully integrated person.

Rabbi Robin Nafshi

*   *   *

Judaism provides for me the vocabulary to express the sacred dimension of what might otherwise be described merely as "a long-term monogamous sexual relationship." For almost thirty years, I have not only been married, but I and my husband have been *m'kudashim*—sacred to one another, set apart for one another, existing in a unique relationship to each other unlike the relationship that either of us have with any other man or woman in the world, because we are sexually involved only with each other. Sex is not merely a physical act, it is also an act of *yichud*—of spiritual union and intimacy.

Rabbi Linda Motzkin

*   *   *

> "And God said, 'Let **Us** make humanity in **Our** image
> [*b'tzalmeinu*]. . . .' Thus God created *Adam* ["the human"]. . . .
> [Thus God] created **them** [*otam*]." (Genesis 1:26–27)

God's first act of procreation requires an array of holiness to produce *Adam*, our universal ancestor. *Adam* is neither "he" nor "she" (nor "it"). *Adam* is "they."

Holy creation cannot be reduced to one narrow "he/she/it." Nor can the holiness of human relations.

There is no single proper sexuality. The best we can do is embrace others, celebrating them as uniquely individual embodiments of divine honor and dignity. As Jews, this is our sacred task.

Dr. Andy Dubin

"Many waters cannot quench love." So sings the Song of Songs (8:7), a sensuous and moving celebration of intimacy and devotion. Because of, not despite, its expressive sexuality, the Song is seen by tradition as a holy depiction of the encounter between the Jewish people and God. This intersection between the Divine calling and the human relationship shows that to delight in another person is to find a gateway into what gives the world meaning. The same Divine source that calls me, as a person who is committed to halachah, to be holy teaches me that the holiness of a relationship is based on commitment to fairness and love.

Rabbi Michael Bernstein

*   *   *

I am blessed to have been raised and mentored by open-minded and loving souls, including my parents and four rabbis, who shaped my identity and my commitment to Judaism. Because of these strong roots, I have always felt an undeniable freedom to be a faithful Jewish woman while loving and being sexually involved with whom I choose. For me, that has meant a non-Jewish spouse, and for other Jewish people, it can mean being with someone of the same gender or of a different race, culture, or religion. To me, this freedom serves to strengthen our faith and cultivate peace, understanding, and love.

Leah Barber-Heinz

*   *   *

Growing our children consciously within the framework of *midot*, Jewish values, provides every entry for open, honest, ongoing discussions about sexuality. Modeling in our everyday lives and teaching our children to value and guard their bodies (*sh'mirat haguf*), not to embarrass themselves or others (*lo l'vayeish*), and having the courage to be honest with themselves and others (*ometz lev*) ensures an ongoing conversation that addresses any aspect of our sexuality, not the least of which is puberty.

Our traditions provide a clear pathway for us to raise healthy, happy children, and we must only step onto the road.

Rabbi Amy Weiss

*   *   *

Sometimes teens ask me, "At what age may a person have sex, especially when the couple is in love?"

I respond, "With sexual relationships, age matters, and maturity matters more. Love matters, but love cannot be the only thing that matters. Here's what also matters: health and safety (physical and emotional); trust; modesty and privacy; honest communication; equality; fidelity; responsibility for the risks of sexual activity; a commitment to the relationships' long-term wellbeing. Love is not enough . . . at any age! Any healthy sexual relationship should exhibit these Jewish values in order to be a source of joy and holiness."

Rabbi Jonathan Blake

*   *   *

As a secular Israeli girl growing up in New Bedford, Massachusetts, I dreamed of someday returning to live in Tel Aviv, marrying a tall, dark, and handsome Israeli soldier, and becoming a writer, a professor, perhaps even a Knesset member. Instead, I grew up and moved to Jerusalem but came back to the States, where I married a short American Jewish woman and became a professional queer Jew. What drives me to do this work is the gap between the realities of Jewish life, ranging from intolerance to a basic level of acceptance, to the Jewish world as I believe it should be—communities of genuine inclusion and equality.

Idit Klein

"Is sex dirty?" "Yes, if you're doing it right . . ."

One aspect of Judaism of which I am proudest is that we are not Puritans, *l'havdil*. We do not deny or squelch the carnal aspects of living. When the Sages determined that the Song of Songs not only belonged in the *Tanach* but was in fact its "Holy of Holies" (*Mishnah Yadayim* 3:5), they recognized that sexuality, potentially, is a holy gift.

Sexuality is commonly linked to the *yetzer hara* for a reason. Properly channeled, it is the most godly expression of love. But abused, it humiliates and destroys. The gift of sex is to discover how to channel it in a godly way: namely, in a covenantal relationship of love that ultimately uplifts, rather than degrades, both lovers.

Rabbi Neal Gold

*　　*　　*

There is something very grounded with the Jewish view of life, and that includes sexuality. I knew as a child I was a trans girl. I wandered in the wilderness until I found the Tzitz Eliezer's 1974 responsum accepting trans women into the community. I had found my path back home.

Dana Beyer, MD

*　　*　　*

Traditional Judaism portrays sex and sexuality as a positive and beautiful thing, as long as the sexual act is within the context of marriage. For many of us, myself included, marriage is a long way past puberty, and therefore sex is not always the sweet reward for the act of *kiddushin*.

In the postmodern world in which Reform Judaism evolves and exists, Jews encounter a range of relationships and the boundaries for what is sexually acceptable within them can vary. Keeping in mind that body and soul are uniquely connected—that the use of body can significantly impact the emotional homeostasis within one's soul—is of utter importance. *Parashat T'rumah* comes to mind, "And you shall

overlay [the Ark] with pure gold, inside and outside" (Exodus 25:11).
The point? What you have going on inside should mirror the outside
and vice versa. A sense of integrity is the biggest tool and greatest
strength of one's sexuality.

Rabbi Joui M. Hessel, RJE

*   *   *

There is something comforting about our tradition's acknowledgment
of sex as something that partners should provide for one another—the
idea of sex as a need and an obligation. In a world that often treats sex
as frivolity or transgression, I find it helpful to recognize that my body's
desires are taken into account in Jewish law and practice. Yet the idea
of sex as obligation also troubles me. I would never want to force myself or my partner into participating in sexual acts we didn't want, for
the sake of some legal requirement that reaches into the most private
of moments. I believe I am obligated to honor and love my own and
my partner's desires, not because of some abstract understanding of
what men and women are contractually bound to in a marriage, but
because I honor and love myself and my partner for all that we are in
body and spirit.

Jessica Kirzane

*   *   *

The Jewish concept of *sh'lom bayit*—domestic harmony and good relations between husband and wife—informs my relationship to sex in a
very simple way: I have sex when I don't particularly want to. Sometimes I'm tired, sometimes I have a long list of things I still need to
accomplish, and sometimes I'm just indifferent to the whole process.
But, I still have sex anyway. Because my husband wants to, because it
makes him happy, and because it, honestly, makes dealing with him
for the rest of the day much easier. And more peaceful for both of us.

Alina Adams

A favorite story in the Talmud is about a great sage who is surprised that he has inappropriate sexual temptations. The closing line of the story: "The greater the person, the greater the sexual temptation." I learn from this that having temptations to engage in inappropriate sex (such as adultery) is neither a sign of sickness nor a permission to indulge. My sexuality is a part of who I am and a challenge to motivate me to say no to some things so I can say yes to other, more important things, such as long-term love and moral behavior.

Rabbi Edwin Goldberg

*   *   *

For most first-year rabbinical students, the year in Israel presents the geographical freedom to explore prayer, Torah, and Israeli politics. My year also included the personal freedom to come out as a lesbian, first to myself, then to my classmates, and finally to my family and friends back home. Paradoxically, the hyper-gender-separated environment gave me the opportunity to walk down the streets of Jerusalem with my girlfriend without the fear that may have resulted from coming out in a more familiar community. Eight years later, I am still grateful for the ways that Judaism has shaped my own understanding of my sexuality.

Rabbi Karen R. Perolman

*   *   *

So much of my Judaism is tied to that one, mystifying word: relationship. It is at once a profoundly basic and endlessly unexplainable bond that my wife and I share. We are the descendants of a huddled together Adam and Eve as darkness fell, the children of Isaac and Rebekah at the well. Based on compassion and earnestness, our love is Judaic. My love for God is likewise Judaic. Based on Torah and mitzvot, wrapped up in the awesome stories of our people, it is a love as deep as the loved shared by Abraham and God, Moses and God, my grandparents and God. My love for my work is indeed Judaic, for it is a rabbinic life and, with that, a life that seeks to foster the love that people share with each other, their spouse or partner, and the love people share with our heritage.

Rabbi Benjamin David

*　　*　　*

Before I converted to Judaism, I was involved in some intensely demeaning and dangerous sexual practices, such as sadomasochism. I'm not saying that these practices are demeaning and dangerous for everyone, but I "took them to an unhealthy place" as they say. I needed to be seriously hurt and deeply degraded. As a Jew, I am a member of a holy covenant people. For me, being degraded is no longer appropriate, and amazingly, I no longer need it to feel like a whole person. I have a new self-image now, one of sanctity, not objectification. Of worth, not of trash.

Anonymous

*　　*　　*

While Judaism has never really emphasized "fun," it has always celebrated "joy." Why is that? I think it's because that while fun is certainly fun, joy (*simchah*) elevates us, helps us grow, and builds relationships with others. Yes, sex is fun. But for me, sex isn't just about having fun, it is about creating joy. Yes, sex feels good, but even more importantly, it helps me strengthen my sense of intimacy and closeness with the most important person in my life.

Rabbi Geoffrey A. Mitelman

*　　*　　*

The Hebrew word for weapon is *neshek* and the Hebrew word for kiss is *n'shikah*. When I was a teenager, I was interested in a girl in my youth group. Peer pressure told me to tap her butt every time I saw her as a way of flirting with her. Appropriately, she was incredibly offended and told me so. Judaism reminds us that sex can be one of the most beautiful, meaningful, and sacred experiences two people share, or it can cause tremendous damage. With that duality comes the need for respect, reflection, and restraint.

Avram Mandell

*   *   *

As the president of the National Association of Temple Educators and as the wife of a rabbi, do I need to hold my sexuality in check? While I don't want to invite anyone into my bedroom beyond my husband, I do want others, including my two daughters and son, to see that I embrace my sexuality and that Judaism encourages me to do so. If not, how would I be the mother of three beautiful children? My sexuality is part of my naturally flirty nature and at the core of my being a strong, independent Jewish woman.

Lisa Lieberman Barzilai, RJE

*   *   *

On June 26, 2013, the Supreme Court of the United States over-turned the Defense of Marriage Act (DOMA). Just hours later, the Reform Movement came out with a statement fully supporting this decision. For Reform Jewish gays and lesbians to have the support of our Movement is such a blessing! It is an important reminder that all of us are created *b'tzelem Elohim*, in the image of the Holy One. It raises the sanctity of our sexuality and our partnerships. I am proud that my Movement is now on record as supporting me and the woman I love.

Rabbi Michele Lenke

*   *   *

"All the *K'tuvim* are holy, but the Song of Songs is the Holy of Holies." (Rabbi Akiva, *Mishnah Yadayim* 3:5)

Hands in mine: ample calloused woman hands, lean manicured man hands, stubby sweaty child fingers.

It's a mosh pit, a spiral dance. Round and round we go, circling a missive from our Beloved, gorgeously arrayed. (Simchat Torah, Los Angeles, 5773)

Orthodox Jews have strategies for keeping sexuality in healthy balance. We have ours. We marry as grown-ups for the deep values connection, no sex-starvation to cloud our judgment. Shoulders, elbows, knees, and toes are commonplace and dear and not traps. The libidinous energy of Torah study crackles around old friends; we grin at strangers; keep our heads, go home clean.

Rabbi Robin Podolsky

*   *   *

Judaism doesn't teach us to hate our bodies, to think that our bodies are sinful while our spirits are pure. Judaism doesn't ask us to afflict our bodies. Sure we have the five "afflictions" of Yom Kippur: no eating or drinking, no bathing or anointing, no shoes, no sex. But the Hebrew word for "afflict" in this example might better be translated as "humble." In any case, here we learn that sex, like eating, bathing, protecting our feet from the rough ground, is meant to give us pleasure. It's necessary to life. Between committed partners, especially on Shabbat, it's sacred. Enjoy!

Rabbi Debra Kassoff

*   *   *

The "L" Word in Three Lessons

Lillian. Sixty-year-old Orthodox woman working in a small Reform synagogue. She spoke about the mikveh with a twinkle in her eye, smile upon her face. She embodied that no matter how long she was married, the mikveh made her feel like a bride.

Lilith. Now her very existence was a shock. Judaism and independent women? Power, strength, and opinion? Well-received or not, it existed in my faith.

Lila. Daughter of a colleague from a same-sex marriage. She and her mothers made me most aware that we are all the same.

And all the rest is commentary.

Julie T. Standig

*   *   *

My Judaism does not influence my sexual practice, beyond meeting other Jews at camp and such. The parallel I can draw is that Judaism involves many routines, practices, and rules just as sex should. These include always using proper protection, choosing the right partners, and not rushing into things because of peer pressure or intense but fleeting emotions.

Caleb Price

*   *   *

For me, sexuality is about vulnerability: trusting someone with my sexual self and desires, and being trusted by them in return. The Jewish framework of covenant gives a safe space to take risks with someone who I trust with my love and my life. We are sanctified to each other.

Like the biblical covenant, it is not always equal. We come from different places. But the commitment creates an intimate space, in which there is both refuge and adventure. If the commitment is broken, that space is shattered, like the glass under the chuppah. But at its best, that combination of commitment and safety, openness and risk, is what makes sex sacred; what makes it holy; what makes us whole.

Anonymous

*   *   *

When my high school girlfriend and I became sexually intimate, I felt a gap between the way intimacy felt so right within my relationship and so discordant outside of it. Eventually I started going to Mayyim Hayyim, a progressive mikveh in Newton, MA, as a modified *nidah* practice. Mayyim Hayyim provided me with the spiritual space and ritual practice to integrate my queer and Jewish identities. Yet I was desperate for conversation. I still had neither personal role models nor guidance from the Jewish tradition on how to use, adapt, and/or appropriate Jewish rituals for queer Jews.

Gabriella Spitzer

*   *   *

For so many of us, our first sexual experiences occurred at overnight Jewish summer camp. With echoes in my mind of my father's pre-camp talk about respecting others while respecting myself, I was enthralled by the sexual anecdotes and exploits of my cabinmates. At camp, I could be my most authentic, my most candid and vulnerable self.

When I started working at camp, my peers and I learned on the job how intensely delicate romantic relationships could be in the crucible of the camp setting. And perhaps because the air was charged with hormones, or because of the separation from parents and high school mores, we had the courage to experiment, to open ourselves sexually in a safe and nurturing Jewish environment.

Rabbi Noam Katz

*   *   *

· Part One ·

In the Beginning:
Biblical and Rabbinic Contexts

Torah is our starting point. Jews of all denominations read the same Torah portions in synagogue every week. What we read is more or less the same—allowing for variances in the length of portion and the occasional discrepancies in calendar based on holiday observance. But how we read can be profoundly different.

Leviticus 18:22, with its condemnation of sex between men, would seem the obvious place to start: "Do not lie with a male as one lies with a woman; it is an abomination." I have a vivid memory of reading the Hertz *Chumash* in the seats of my Conservative synagogue as an adolescent and finding this comment: "[*Thou shalt not lie down*] *with mankind. Discloses the abyss of depravity from which Torah saved the Israelite.*" It was not the most inspiring interpretation; with inklings of my own nascent sexuality, I read the words with dread and a deep sense that I did not belong.

As Rabbi Nancy H. Wiener, Rabbi David Greenstein, Rabbi Karen Bender, and Rabbi Jeffrey Brown all acknowledge in their essays, this text—and its classic interpretation—has caused tremendous harm. Wiener ("A Reform Understanding of *To-eivah*") responds to it by exploring the meanings connected with the word *to-eivah*, "abomination,"

3

showing through her analysis how the understanding of the word has changed and should continue to change to have meaning for us as liberal Jews. Wiener's piece shows the possibilities inherent in looking at the text with great breadth and depth. In "'A Great Voice, Never Ending': Reading the Torah in Light of the New Status of Gays and Lesbians in the Jewish Community," Greenstein looks at liberal approaches to understanding the problematic texts, including Wiener's reading of *to-eivah*. He then suggests a new creative reading, based on recognition of the living power of the text alongside our modern commitments and beliefs.

Despite new analyses, the texts have a life of their own. Bender ("How to Respond to Bible-Thumping Homphobia, Or: Judaism as Evolutionary If Not Revolutionary") confronts the challenge of what she calls "selective fundamentalism," arguing that "Bible-thumping homophobia" is the result of a willfully narrow reading of the biblical text, and she suggests that ultimately, we ourselves are defined by how we read and respond. In "Preaching against the Text: An Argument in Favor of Restoring Leviticus 18 to Yom Kippur Afternoon," Brown takes yet another approach, suggesting that Leviticus 18 can be used to start essential conversations about sexuality and sexual ethics, with the model of "preaching against the text."

Each of these pieces, prompted by Leviticus 18 (along with Leviticus 20) and its uses and abuses, makes an important contribution. However, they do not open this section. Instead, we have chosen to begin with Rabbi Amy Scheinerman's discussion of Rabbinic interpretations of biblical texts on human sexuality as a whole ("Sexuality: Human Biology versus Rabbinic Decree"). She includes classic commentaries on topics such as desire, fertility, and relationships of various sorts, concluding that within certain parameters, "human sexuality is to be celebrated as a blessing."

This essay was chosen to begin Part One because it concerns itself not with homosexuality in particular and not exclusively with condemnation; rather, its focus is on sexuality as a topic in itself, replete with holiness and humor, serious limitations and profound potential. In this it reflects the approach of the book as a whole. Following Scheinerman's piece is Rabbi Steven Greenberg's essay, "The Real Sin of Sodom," prompting us to think differently about the story of Sodom and reminding us that sexuality is not always the primary issue; Wiener makes this point as well.

After the essays on Leviticus 18 and 20, Part One closes with a different biblical study: my own piece ("Spirit of Jealousy, Spirit of Holiness: Timeless Insights from a Time-Bound Text") on Rabbinic and modern interpretations of the *sotah*, the suspected wife of Numbers 5:11–31, with a focus on sexual jealousy and the search for resolution. Finally, there are two personal reflections. In "*Kol Ishah*—Sexuality and the Voice of a Woman," Rabbi Judith Z. Abrams explores the origin of the laws around *kol ishah*, limiting a woman's voice on the grounds of sexual distraction, and gives voice to a different point of view. "Why should I have to shut up for the rest of my life," she asks one of her teachers, who defended the restrictions, "just because you used to be fifteen?" Rabbi Andrea Myers ("It Gets Beautiful—One Rabbi's Perspective on Being Jewish and LGBTQ") also makes the case for defining one's own sexuality in a proactive, positive way. She goes far beyond Leviticus, reframing the conversation about sexuality not in terms of what is permitted and forbidden, but rather, what is beautiful. She leaves us with a charge: "to live with dignity and humor, beauty and joy, as you take your place in a Jewish tradition that is thousands of years old."

1

SEXUALITY

Human Biology versus Rabbinic Decree

Rabbi Amy Scheinerman

Questions to Ask

Torah, our master narrative, recognizes two sexes, male and female, as the fundamental biology of humankind. It further acknowledges sexual desire as a basic component of biology. Several questions arise: Is human sexuality good or bad? Does it lead to desirable behavior that promotes family and community or to dangerous behavior that is detrimental to both individuals and society? If sexuality is a matter of innate biology, to what extent is it possible, desirable, or obligatory to limit human sexuality? What does Torah have to say about human sexuality?

In the world of the Rabbis, we can further ask: can textual interpretation considered to be *Torah Sheb'al Peh* (Oral Torah) manipulate and redefine biology? And what is at stake in answering that question? The Rabbis attempt to constrain human sexuality lest it get out of control and lead to egregious violations of halachah (Jewish law), yet there are subtle hints conveyed in narrative passages that they recognize limitations in their attempt to legislate human nature; I suspect these hints are encoded in narrative by the final redactors. Within the confines of Jewish ethical norms, however, sexuality is celebrated.

A Rabbinic Model of the Sexes

The Rabbis sought to reconcile sexuality as they experienced and knew it in this world with the simplistic model of our master narrative, Torah. Torah suggests that humans originally dwelled in an idyllic garden paradise. Once outside the Garden, their urges wrought untold evil. What was the primordial human—the one who could live in peace—like? We find a reflection of this attempt to envision the ideal in *B'reishit Rabbah*[1] 1:54–55, which posits a surprising view of the first human being:

> *And God said: Let us make a human*, etc. Rabbi Yochanan opened: *Behind and before You formed me, and You placed Your hands upon me* (Ps. 139:5).
>
> Rabbi Yochanan said: If a man is righteous, he will enjoy two worlds, for it says, *Behind and before You formed me*; but if not, he will have to account for it, for it says, *and You placed Your hands upon me*.
>
> Rabbi Yermia the son of Elazar said: When the Holy One, Blessed be God, created the first human, God created him androgynous, for it says, *Male and female created God them* (Gen. 1:27).
>
> Rabbi Shmuel bar Nachman said: When the Holy One, Blessed be God, created the first human, God made it two-faced, then God sawed it and made a back for this one and a back for that one.
>
> They objected to him: But it says, *God took one of his ribs* [tzeila] (Gen. 2:21). He answered: [It means] "one of his sides," similarly to that which is written, *And the side* [tzeila] *of the Tabernacle* (Exod. 26:20). Rabbi Tanchuma in the name of Rabbi Banayah and Rabbi Berechiah in the name of Rabbi Elazar [said]: God created him as a golem, and he was stretched from one end of the world to the other, as it says, *My golem which Your eyes have seen* (Ps. 139:16).

Reading Psalm 139 as a commentary on the creation of the first human, we are offered two models. The first model, taught by Rabbi Yermia ben Elazar and buttressed by Rabbi Shmuel bar Nachman, is an androgynous primordial human, both male and female, yet one being. Is the suggestion here that ideally, sexuality of the kind that engenders physical intimacy between two people, and all its concomitant complications, is unnecessary? After all, at least in theory, an androgynous being can reproduce by itself. The second model, offered by Rabbi Tanchuma and Rabbi Berechiah, is an unsexed, undifferentiated primordial human, a golem that fills the world. This creature seems devoid of sexuality, but it is unclear how it would reproduce. Both views are "proved" by Torah (Exod. 26:20 and Ps. 139:16, respectively). The midrash stands in stark contrast with human biology, suggesting that the human ideal from which we are descended neither knows nor requires the sexuality that so defines us.

The ideal model presented in *B'reishit Rabbah* is matched by Rabbinic efforts to "prove" aspects of human sexual biology by citing Torah. Such efforts appear a number of times in Rabbinic literature. Perhaps the most amusing example is found in the Babylonian Talmud, *B'rachot* 51b, in the form of a narrative that appears amid a discussion of *Birkat HaMazon* (Blessing after Meals). The Rabbis are discussing who may participate in, and who may lead, the *m'zuman* (the invitation to join in the blessings). They pause their discussion to tell the story of Yalta, the educated, intelligent, strong-willed wife of Rabbi Nachman.

> Ulla once happened to be a guest at Rav Nachman's house. He ate a meal, led *Birkat HaMazon*, and passed the cup of blessing to Rav Nachman. Rav Nachman said to him: Please pass the cup of blessing (כסא דברכתא) to Yalta.
>
> He [Ulla] replied: This is what Rabbi Yochanan [ben Nappacha] said: The issue of a woman's belly (בטנה) is blessed only through the issue of a man's belly (בטנו), as Scripture says: *God will bless the issue of your [masculine singular] belly* (Deut. 7:13). It does not say "her belly" but rather "your belly." So too a *baraita* teaches: Rabbi Natan said: Where is the proof text in Scripture that the issue of a woman's belly is blessed only through the issue of a man's belly? As Scripture says, *God will bless the issue of your [masculine singular] belly*. It does not say "her belly" but rather "your belly."
>
> When Yalta heard this, she became furiously angry, went to the wine storeroom, and smashed four hundred jars of wine.
>
> Rav Nachman said to Ulla: Please send her another cup. He [Ulla] sent it [with this message]: All of this is a goblet of blessing [*navga d'virchata*]. She sent [this message back to Ulla]: From travelers come tall tales, and from rag pickers lice.

Ulla, a guest in Rav Nachman's house, refuses to abide by the local custom of passing the *kos b'rachah* (cup of blessing) to the (only?) woman at the table. The cup of blessing coming after *Birkat HaMazon* was understood to confer blessings of every kind—health, business success, happiness, successful learning, children, peace—on those who participate. Using texts plucked out of context and unconnected to *Birkat HaMazon*, Ulla argues that the only blessing the *kos b'rachah* confers is that of fertility and that only men receive this blessing. Women conceive and bear children only through the blessings of men. Yalta, understandably infuriated, responds to his words with the physical act of smashing four hundred jars of wine; in short order she destroys the possibility of many cups for a good long time to come. Now who controls the blessing of fertility? Yalta's act of smashing the jars of wine is a frightening and real challenge to halachah and its interpretive methodology that Ulla has exploited to redefine the physical realities of human biology and women's sexuality. Like the Torah's presumption of two sexes only—male and female—the Rabbis presume they can cleverly argue against a biological reality that is, in truth, beyond their control. Yalta's act suggests that those who told the story—or the redactors, who may have purposely placed the narrative here—are subtly acknowledging that they recognize the limits of halachah to define human sexuality and fertility.

What Kind of Sex Does Torah Permit?

If biological sexuality cannot be determined by textual interpretation, it can be constrained by halachah. We find a protracted discussion of sexuality in the Babylonian Talmud, *N'darim* 20, covering what is permitted and what is not. The Gemara[2] opens with a disparate list of things one should not do because they may well lead to serious violations of halachah. Last on the list is speaking with a woman, which might lead to lewdness. This in turn is expanded by the opinion that even looking at a woman is a serious problem. The discussion segues to the centerpiece of the passage, an extraordinarily rigid opinion in the name of Rabbi Yochanan ben Dahavai, who claims to have learned it from the ministering angels:

> People are born lame because they [i.e., their parents] over-turned their table; dumb, because they kiss that place; deaf, because they converse during sexual intercourse; blind, because they look at that place.

In one brief statement, Rabbi Yochanan ben Dahavai promulgates four rules that forbid anal intercourse, oral sex, viewing a woman's genitals, and even conversation between lovers during sexual intercourse. They strike us as standards set by one who fits H. L. Mencken's definition of Puritanism: "The haunting fear that someone, somewhere, may be happy."[3] Yet Rabbi Yochanan ben Dahavai claims to have learned them from the ministering angels. Zeroing in on the claim that conversation during intercourse is not permitted, the Gemara proceeds first to dismantle an acclaimed source and second to demonstrate that respected rabbis permitted this and much more. They tell us that both Rabbi[4] and Rav[5] (covering the *Tannaim*[6] of Land of Israel and the *Amoraim*[7] of Babylonia) affirmed in actual cases that Torah does not forbid *any* sexual practice.

> A woman once came before Rabbi [Y'hudah HaNasi] and said, Rabbi! I set a table before my husband [i.e., I prepared to make love with him], but he overturned it [i.e., wanted to engage in anal intercourse]. Rabbi replied, My daughter! The Torah has permitted you to him. What then can I do for you?
> (Babylonian Talmud, *N'darim* 20b)

The Gemara goes so far as to assert that a man is permitted to fantasize about another woman while making love to his wife, as long as the object of his fantasies is not another one of his wives.[8]

> On the basis of this Rabbi taught: One may not drink out of one goblet [i.e., make love with one woman] and think of another. Ravina said: This is necessary only when both are his wives.
> (Babylonian Talmud, *N'darim* 20b)

The claim being made is that Torah does not regulate private, consensual sex between a husband and wife. This amounts to a wholesale affirmation of a wide spectrum of expressions of human sexuality, though all within the confines of licit marriage.

Torah's concern, the Sages tell us, is attitude: a man may not engage in sexual relations with his wife if it is in the emotional context of fear, pain, neglect, or hate. Sexuality that is an expression of love is lauded.

The Babylonian Talmud, *Eiruvin* 100b, affirms this view: compulsion is evil, but sexual desire is wonderful:

> Rami bar Chama citing R. Assi further ruled: A man is forbidden to compel his wife to the [marital] obligation, since it is said in Scripture, And he who acts impetuously with his feet[9] sins (Prov. 19:2). . . . Rabbi Shmuel bar Nachmani said in the name of Rabbi Yochanan: A woman who petitions her husband to engage in marital relations will have children the likes of whom did not exist even in the generation of Moses.

Sexuality and Procreation

We see a similar pattern in the discussion of the mitzvah of procreation. The attempt to control biology gives way to the blessing of sexuality. *Mishnah Y'vamot* 6:6 begins with the assumption that Genesis 1:28 ("be fertile and increase") is prescriptive.[10] The discussion concerns precisely how many offspring a man is required to have in order to fulfill the mitzvah. Given that the Rabbis have deemed procreation an obligation, they box themselves in attempting to answer the question, what happens if a husband and wife do not have children? The answer is chilling: if, after ten years of marriage and no miscarriages, a couple remains childless, the husband divorces his wife.

> No man may abstain from keeping the law, *Be fruitful and multiply* (Gen. 1:28), unless he already has children: according to the school of Shammai, two sons; according to the School of Hillel,

a son and a daughter, for it is written, *Male and female God created them* (Gen. 5:2).

If he married a woman and lived with her ten years and she bore no child, it is not permitted him to abstain [from fulfilling the mitzvah of procreation]. If he divorced her, she may be married to another and the second husband may live with her for ten years. If she had a miscarriage, the space [of ten years] is measured from the time of the miscarriage.

The duty to be fruitful and multiply falls on the man but not on the woman. Rabbi Yochanan ben Baroka [dissents from this view and] says: Of them both it is written, *God blessed them, and God said to them, "Be fruitful and multiply"* (Gen. 1:28).

Imagine a husband and wife deeply in love. They have a wonderful sexual relationship but have not been blessed with children. Love is a powerful bond. Who would rend it asunder? This is precisely the scenario in *P'sikta D'Rav Kahana* 22:2.[11] Just such a couple comes to Rabbi Shimon bar Yochai because they know halachah requires them to divorce. Rabbi Shimon recognizes that they are very much in love and prescribes the most peculiar "divorce" ritual imaginable: they are to spend their last night together just as they did their first. They are to reenact their wedding night, complete with feasting, drinking, and (we may presume) lovemaking.

A man is under the obligation to fulfill the commandment, *Be fruitful and multiply* (Gen. 1:28), but a woman is under no such obligation. . . . In Sidon it happened that a man took a wife, with whom he lived for ten years, and she bore him no children. When they came to Rabbi Shimon bar Yochai to be divorced, the man said to his wife, "Take any precious object I have in my house—take it and go back to your father's house." Thereupon, Rabbi Shimon bar Yochai said, "Even as you were wed with food and drink [being served], so you are not to separate save with food and drink [being served]." What did the wife do? She prepared a great feast, gave her husband too much [alcohol] to drink, and summoned her menservants and maidservants saying, "Take him to my father's house." At midnight he woke up from his sleep and asked, "Where am I?" She replied, "Did you not say, 'Whatever precious object I have in my house—take it and go back to your father's house?' I have no object more precious than you." When Shimon bar Yochai heard what the wife had done, he prayed on the couple's behalf, and they were remembered with children. For, even as the Holy One remembers barren women, righteous men also have the power to remember barren women.

While the midrash does not explicitly recount their lovemaking, Rabbi Shimon bar Yochai's instructions were abundantly clear, and the reader needs little imagination to fill in the lacuna. In reenacting their wedding night, their feasting would have been followed by lovemaking, after which the husband fell asleep. Their deep love and commitment to one another inspire Rabbi Shimon bar Yochai to extend the ten-year limit and bless them with fertility.

As Yalta pointed out the limitations of halachah when it runs up against biology, Rabbi Shimon recognizes the limitations of halachah—and its injustice—when it interferes with a successful and loving marital relationship. That sexuality is a centerpiece of this midrash is significant. Their love is more important than Mishnah's requirement concerning procreation.

The Sexual Urge: Good or Bad?

The sexual urge, feared and condemned in many Talmudic passages, is exalted and ennobled in others. The Babylonian Talmud, *Yoma* 69b, tells the story of a time when the *yetzer hara* (the evil inclination or urge) for idolatry was banished from the world. Yet the *yetzer hara* for sexual impropriety remained. The people, sensing that God would be especially gracious toward them, fasted for three days and prayed that the *yetzer hara* (in this passage, personified and referred to as "he") be turned over to them. They put him in a lead pot and sealed it, even though he warned them, "Know that if you kill me, the world goes down." In the next three days, while they kept the *yetzer hara* imprisoned, not a fresh egg could be found in the Land of Israel. Without the sexual urge, generativity stops. Life cannot go on. The self-sustaining order of God's creation—as Genesis 1:11–12, 1:22, and 1:28 describe it with respect to plants, animals, and humans—comes to a grinding halt. Thus midrash *Kohelet Rabbah* 3:11 tells us that when Genesis 1:31 says, *And God saw all that [God] had made and it was very good*, "good" refers to the *yetzer hatov*, but "very good" refers to the *yetzer hara*, because without it, "a man would not build a house, marry a woman, or father children."

As productive as the *yetzer hara* can be, it is nonetheless dangerous and needs to be resisted when its drive is *not* toward marriage and family. The Rabbis consider the aggressive urges of men to be potentially dangerous. In a thought experiment found in the Babylonian Talmud, *Sanhedrin* 75b, they posit the theoretical case of a young man who is so consumed with desire for a particular woman that his physical life is endangered. Presumably he will die if he cannot have her. The Rabbis suggest a list of possible interactions to satisfy his lust, ranging from allowing him to have sex with her to having her converse with him from behind a fence blocking her from view. Their conclusion is to disallow even the "mildest" proposal and sagely point out that even marriage would not assuage the passions of such a man. His insatiable desire may threaten his life, but it endangers the object of his passion even more.

Sexual desire can be dangerous, but it can also be sanctifying. In a permitted context, the Rabbis can readily endorse the sexual urge, sexuality, and the pleasure they bring—but only in a permitted context. One of the most delightful expressions of this principle is found in a narrative recorded in the Babylonian Talmud, *M'nachot* 44a. Ostensibly told to demonstrate the reward for obeying the commandment of tzitzit[12] in this world, the story speaks more stunningly to human sexuality and passion. A young scholar's intense sexual desire leads him to the most beautiful and expensive prostitute known. The young man eagerly anticipates his appointment with the prostitute, but just as the moment of consummation arrives—as they lie naked together in her luxurious bed—his tzitzit fly up and slap him in the face. They remind him to suppress his sexual urge.

Once a man, who was very scrupulous about the commandment of tzitzit, heard of a certain prostitute, in one of the towns
by the sea, who accepted four hundred gold [*dinarim*] for her fee.
He sent her four hundred gold [*dinarim*] and made an appointment with her. When the day arrived, he came and waited at her
door, and her maid came and told her, "That man who sent you
four hundred gold [*dinarim*] is here and waiting at the door," to
which she replied, "Let him come in." When he came in, she
prepared for him seven beds, six of silver and one of gold; and
between one bed and the other there were steps of silver, but the
last [steps] were of gold. She then went up to the top bed and lay
down upon it naked. He too went up after her in his desire to sit
naked with her, when all of a sudden the four fringes [the tzitzit
of his tallit] struck him across the face. Thereupon he climbed
down and sat on the ground.

We might think that the story would end here, on the note of
the capacity of tzitzit to control even the most powerful human
urges. But it does not. In fact, this is only the beginning of the
story. The young man and the prostitute begin an emotional relationship—based not solely on sexuality, but certainly with sexuality
as the component that brought them together—that leads to her
t'shuvah and conversion.

She also climbed down and sat on the ground and said, "By the
Roman Capitol, I will not leave you alone until you tell me what
blemish you saw in me." He replied, "By the Temple, never have I
seen a woman as beautiful as you, but there is one commandment
that the Eternal our God has commanded us. It is called tzitzit, and
concerning it, it is written, "*I am the Eternal your God*" twice, signifying: I am the One who will exact punishment in the future, and
I am the One who will give reward in the future. Now [the tzitzit]
appeared to me as four witnesses [testifying against me]. She said,
"I will not leave you until you tell me your name, the name of your
town, the name of your teacher, and the name of your school in
which you study the Torah." He wrote all this down and handed it
to her. Thereupon she arose and divided her estate into three parts:
one-third for the government, one-third to be distributed among
the poor, and one-third she took with her in her hand. The bedclothes, however, she retained. She then came to the *beit midrash* of

Rabbi Chiyya and said to him, "Master, give instructions about me that they make me a proselyte." He replied, "My daughter, perhaps you have set your eyes on one of the disciples?" She thereupon took out the script and handed it to him. He said, "Go and enjoy what you have acquired." Those very bedclothes that she had spread for him for lust she now spread out for him for sanctity.

The couple eventually marries, with the blessing of Rabbi Chiya, the young student's master, and their sexuality is sanctified. The story, brought to illustrate the power of tzitzit to remind one of the mitzvot, concludes, "This is the reward [for obeying the commandment of tzitzit] in this world, and as for its reward in the world-to-come, I do not know how great it is." While this is a fitting conclusion for the contextual conversation about tzitzit, the story itself speaks to the sanctity of sexuality in marriage.

Conclusion

The Rabbis recognize and openly acknowledge the strong biological component of sexuality. They recognize its purpose and potential for good, as well as its danger and potential for harm. Torah places no limits on sexual acts in the bedroom of husband and wife, and by and large the Rabbis do not attempt to do so either. Rather, they are concerned with the attitude one brings to the bedroom; this is what differentiates love from exploitation. Nonetheless, the Rabbis' attempts to impose halachic limitations to constrain and confine sexuality on occasion conflict with biology and human nature. The tradents, or perhaps the redactors, recognized the limits of halachah and subtly affirmed that even with the most clever and erudite scriptural arguments, halachah and its proponents cannot redefine biology and ought not interfere with a loving marital relationship. Confined to safe parameters—affection and not exploitation, love and not abuse—human sexuality is to be celebrated as a blessing.

NOTES

1. *B'reishit Rabbah* (or *Genesis Rabbah*) is a compilation of midrashim on the Book of Genesis believed to have been composed in the fourth and fifth centuries CE, the same period the Babylonian Talmud was taking shape, by the same general communities of scholars.

2. Both the Babylonian and Jerusalem Talmuds are constructed on the foundation of the Mishnah of Rabbi Y'hudah HaNasi, compiled around 200 CE. Gemara is the redacted record of lengthy discussion of mishnah that took place in the academies after the Mishnah was completed. Talmud is the Mishnah together with the Gemara.

3. H. L. Mencken, *A Book of Burlesques* (1916).

4. Rabbi Y'hudah HaNasi, compiler of the Mishnah, second century CE.

5. Rav Abba Arika, third century CE, who established the academy in Sura, was known as Rav.

6. Sages of the Mishnah.

7. Sages of the Gemara.

8. This presumes, of course, polygamous marriage.

9. "Feet" here and elsewhere is a euphemism for male genitalia.

10. A more logical reading is that "be fruitful and multiply" is, in its context, descriptive. Consider Gen. 1:22, which speaks of God's creation as self-sustaining and self-replicating. If Gen. 1:28 is truly prescriptive, why does the obligation devolve only on Jews? Why is it not among the *Sheva Mitzvot B'nei Noach* (the Seven Commandments of the Sons of Noah, the Rabbis' formulation of God's laws for all humanity)? The Rabbis' decision to interpret Gen. 1:28 prescriptively rather than descriptively further points to their attempt to determine human sexual biology through textual interpretation.

11. A parallel version is found in the midrash on Song of Songs, *Shir HaShirim Rabbah* 1:4:2.

12. Ritual fringes on the corners of a garment, as instructed in Num. 15:37–41 and Deut. 22:12.

2

THE REAL SIN OF SODOM

Rabbi Steven Greenberg

In 2006, daily riots erupted in Jerusalem's streets as the *Haredi* (ultra-Orthodox) community violently protested the upcoming Jerusalem Gay Pride march. *Haredi* youths pelted police officers with large stones, blocks, bottles, angle irons, and wood planks. Posters lined the streets promising the payment of thousands of shekels to any zealot who would kill a "sodomite" marching in the parade. The riots were so intense that it became necessary for *Haredi* rabbinic leaders to come to the scene with megaphones and encourage the crowds to disperse. In another act of intolerance, the *Edah Haredit*, a right-wing *Haredi* rabbinical court, pronounced a rabbinic curse—a *pulsa d'nura*—on those organizing the march and against the policemen defending the marchers.

The fear voiced by many religious leaders was that the pride march (which had been originally scheduled for August but postponed due to the war in Lebanon) would turn Jerusalem into Sodom. Indeed, the religious press—Jewish, Christian, and Muslim—was rife with warnings of the dire consequences of abandoning the holy city to the corruptions of Sodom and Gomorrah, cities that were destroyed for their wickedness.

The story of Sodom and Gomorrah is surely the best known of the biblical narratives used to condemn homosexuality. For over a millennium, preachers have employed it—with dramatic effect—to prohibit and punish sex between men. The word "sodomy," invented by an English churchman to describe male intercourse, helped to transform male sexual relations into an unparalleled evil. For generations, men who were accused of sodomy were humiliated, persecuted, tortured, and put to gruesome death in imitation of the violent divine destruction of Sodom. Today, the people who carry placards reading "God hates fags" know this must be so by reading their Bible.

The details of the story in the Book of Genesis, chapter 19, are well known. God knows that the cry from Sodom is great and sends angels to investigate the gravity of the situation. Lot, the patriarch of Sodom's only decent family, ushers the angelic guests into his house. After dinner, the townsfolk of Sodom clamor at the door, demanding that Lot send out the guests "that they might know them."

Despite the common perception that the sin of Sodom was rampant sexual vice, Jewish literature has largely rejected this reading. The prophet Ezekiel locates the sin of Sodom in its inhospitality, its cruelty, and perversion of justice, and not in homosexuality. He describes Sodom as arrogant and insensitive to human need. The residents of Sodom had plenty of bread and untroubled tranquility, yet they refused to support the poor and the needy.

Among early Rabbinic commentators, the common reading of the sin of Sodom was its cruelty, arrogance, and disdain for the poor. The Sages of the Babylonian Talmud also associated Sodom with the sins of pride, envy, cruelty to orphans, theft, murder, and perversion of justice. While the event that sealed the fate of the Sodomites was their demand for Lot to bring out his guests so that the mob might "know" them, this still was not seen so much as an act of sexual excess, but as hatred of the stranger and exploitation of the weak. Midrashic writers lavishly portray Sodom and the surrounding cities as arrogant and self-satisfied, destroyed for the sins of greed and indifference to the poor.

Rabbinic legends about Sodom describe an area of unusual natural resources, precious stones, silver, and gold. Every path in Sodom, say the Sages, was lined with seven rows of fruit trees. Eager to keep their great wealth for themselves, and suspicious of outsiders' desires to share in it, the residents of Sodom agreed to overturn the ancient law of hospitality to wayfarers. The legislation later prohibited giving charity to anyone. One legend claims that when a beggar would wander into Sodom, the people would mark their names on their coins and give him a *dinar*. However, no one would sell him bread. When he perished of hunger, everyone would come and claim his coin. There was once a maiden who secretly carried bread out to a poor person in the street in her water pitcher. After three days passed and the man didn't die, the maiden was discovered. They covered the girl with honey and put her atop the city walls, leaving her there until bees came and ate her. Hers was the cry that came up to God, the cry that inaugurated the angelic visit and its consequences.

Another famous Rabbinic tale mirrors the Greek myth of Procrustes. Both the Jewish and Greek stories are about beds that invert the ethic of hospitality. In Sodom, they had a bed for weary guests upon which they might rest. However, when the wayfarer would lie down, they made sure that he fit the bed perfectly. A short man was stretched to fit it, and a tall man was cut to size. The midrash tells us that Eliezer, Abraham's loyal servant, was once offered to lie upon it, but he declined, claiming that since his mother died, he pledged not to have a pleasant night's sleep on a comfortable bed. In the Greek myth, Procrustes (meaning "he who stretches") kept a house by the side of the road for passing strangers. He offered them a warm meal and a bed that always fit whomever lay upon it. Once they lay upon it, he would likewise cut off the legs of those too long or stretch those too short. Theseus, the hero of the Greek tale, turns the tables on Procrustes and fatally adjusts him to his own bed.

The people of Sodom are not only protective of their wealth and punishing of acts of charity, they are also desperate to force everyone to fit a single measure. They have a well-to-do gated community that makes sure no beggars disturb their luxury and peace. They have zoned out poverty. But what makes Sodom the "right" kind of neighborhood is that no difference is tolerated. "Our kind" of folk are welcomed and protected, while all the rest are excluded or eliminated. It can hardly be incidental that the locus of this one-size-fits-all violence is a bed that serves as a guillotine and a rack. The place of sleep, comfort, and sexual pleasure in Sodom has been transformed into a place of threat and malice, a device of torture for strangers.

Eliezer saves himself from being amputated or stretched by the mourning of his mother. Mourning the dead is a particularly selfless expression of relationship and love. The people of Sodom treat all who are not inside the walls as being as good as dead; Eliezer treats the dead with an honor and presence that make their memory a living reality. Sodom is a place where compassion is punished brutally, as the story of the young maiden suggests. Eliezer is saved from Sodom's evil not by his sword or cunning, as is Theseus in the Greek myth, but by his own loving beyond all boundaries or benefit—by a loving that, like a mother's love, has no reasons.

Without a doubt, Jerusalem is in danger of becoming Sodom. But it will not be made so by gay pride marchers—at least not according to the prophet Ezekiel or the Rabbis. What bought down the wrath of God upon Sodom was not homosexuality, but inhospitality and cruelty, arrogance and greed, callousness, fear of loss, and ultimately, violence against the stranger. Indeed, we cannot let Jerusalem become like Sodom—a city where humiliation and even violence against people who are different are judged to be the epitome of moral decency and religious integrity.

An earlier version of this essay appeared on the Keshet Blog on October 29, 2012.

3

A REFORM UNDERSTANDING OF *TO-EIVAH*

Rabbi Nancy H. Wiener, DMin

In recent years, Jews across the denominational spectrum have invoked the term תּוֹעֵבָה (*to-eivah*) in their discussions of human sexuality. Most often, it has been used as a means to categorically reject the possibility that particular sexual behaviors and members of sexual minorities could be acceptable within an authentic Jewish framework. However, Reform Judaism has taken an inclusive stance toward sexual minorities. In the process, our policies have been interpreted as an indication that we have rendered the category *to-eivah* meaningless and irrelevant in the realm of sexual behavior and values. By adopting the Ad Hoc Committee on Human Sexuality's "Reform Jewish Sexual Values" at its convention in June 1998, the CCAR has actually done the reverse. We have challenged ourselves to ask what meaning *to-eivah* can have in a Reform context today. This is neither merely an intellectual interest nor a polemical goal. We work daily with people whose lives and families are adversely affected, who believe there is no meaningful place for them in the Jewish community because of their (or a family member's) sexual orientation or gender identity. We owe it to them and to ourselves, as their leaders, to answer this question in a thoughtful and thorough manner.

To-eivah in the Ancient Near Eastern Context

In the Hebrew Bible, *to-eivah* is a categorical description of behaviors. The most widely recognized application of this category in the Bible is to "whatever is ritually or ethically loathsome and repugnant to God and men" or to an "offensive violation of established custom."[1] Such a category has antecedents in other ancient Near Eastern cultures. In fact, William Hallo posits that there are functional equivalents in Sumerian and Akkadian.[2] The range of activities discussed in Sumerian and Akkadian texts is extremely broad.

> Summing up the cuneiform evidence, it may be said in general that the divine distaste expressed in this genre of sayings seems, in Sumerian texts of the second millennium, to be reserved for infractions against ethical or behavioral norms, while in Akkadian texts of the first millennium it is extended as well to normally legitimate activities which happen to be conducted on an unacceptable day.[3]

Of particular note here is the possibility for an activity to be categorized as *to-eivah* by some groups and not others, as well as at certain times or under certain situations and not others. Thus a single activity can move in and out of the category depending on circumstances.

To-eivah in the Bible

The root ת-ע-ב (*tav-ayin-bet*) is used over one hundred times in the Bible.[4] It appears most frequently in Deuteronomy, Proverbs, and Ezekiel, with its most common form being תּוֹעֵבָה (*to-eivah*). Its semantic range includes "what gives offense to God or man [*sic*] especially the violation of established custom . . . cults in general . . . child sacrifice . . . imperfect sacrificial victims, sexual irregularities, false weights and measures . . . eating with foreigners."[5]

Its most common translations are "abomination" or "abhorred." According to the BDB, the root itself means "erroneous."[6] Of particular note here is that these three translations or meanings are rarely understood as synonyms in English. Something can be an error without being categorized as morally or ethically offensive. Moreover not everything that is erroneous evokes a strong, negative, visceral response akin to abhorrence.

Interestingly, the range of synonyms that appear in Hebrew underscore the emotional and visceral responses that such erroneous behaviors evoke. They include ל-ע-ג (*gimel-ayin-lamed*) and ז-ר-ה (*zayin-reish-hei*), both of which mean "abhorred" or "loathed"; מ-א-ס (*mem-alef-samech*), "rejected"; פ-ג-ל (*pei-gimel-lamed*), "foul" (such as refuse) or "soft" (as in flaccid); and ש-ק-צ (*shin-kuf-tzadi*), "detested." These responses can be roused by any variety of stimuli. Yet, in the biblical texts in which they are paired with *to-eivah*, they focus attention on the emotional and visceral range of meaning of *to-eivah*. The noun serves as a visceral label. The verb ת-ע-ב (*tav-ayin-bet*) is denominative and means to label something *to-eivah*. The polar opposite, קָדוֹשׁ (*kadosh*), also describes a visceral response. The terms themselves have no inherent content; they are categories whose contents are to be determined. Specific things and behaviors can be placed into these categories.[7]

The activities the Bible describes as *to-eivah* fall into a number of broad categories. Aspects of eating can be described as *to-eivah*—eating certain foods (Deut. 14:3) or eating with certain people (Gen. 43:32). Certain sexual relations are *to-eivah*, such as lying with a man as with a woman (Lev. 18:22, 20:13); remarrying an ex-wife if she has been married in the interim (Deut. 24:4); or taking a son's wives—broadly speaking, sleeping with unavailable women (Ezek. 22:11). Engaging in idolatry is *to-eivah*, with primary examples being bringing images of others' gods into one's home (Deut. 7:25–26), following other gods when you enter into the Land (Deut. 13:15–16), and choosing a false god (Isa. 41:24, 44:19). Engaging in unethical activities such as robbery (Ezek. 18:12), shedding blood / living by the sword (Ezek. 33:26), or rendering an unfair judgment (Lev. 19:15) is *to-eivah*. Mistreating others because of a disrespectful attitude is *to-eivah*, including being greedy for personal gain (Jer. 6:13–15, 8:12) or failing to support the needy due to haughtiness (Ezek. 16:50). Misleading others so that they will interact with you as they would otherwise not normally do, such as by wearing clothes associated with the opposite sex (Deut. 22:5), is *to-eivah*. Finally, engaging in an empty ritual or doing something without the proper intent, such as using incense as part of an empty ritual (Isa. 1:13), praying after turning a deaf ear to instruction (Prov. 28:9), or being wicked and still offering a sacrifice (Prov. 21:27), is *to-eivah*.

In fact, the majority of the above-mentioned activities can be aptly characterized as erroneous. Either one is acting in a way that demonstrates an error in understanding or in adhering to local custom, or one is erroneously identifying a food as unclean when it is clean, erroneously believing magic and divination have power, behaving in morally or ethically erroneous ways, erroneously believing he or she can alter nature, or erroneously attempting to engage the divine through idolatrous practices or through the worship of idols.

Of these, some are described as *to-avat Adonai*, while the majority are described as just *to-eivah*, with no explicit mention of God. The claim that something is *to-eivah* for a particular deity is not peculiar to the ancient Israelites. A Phoenician grave inscription of King Tibnit of Sidon, late sixth century BCE, warns against disturbing his sarcophagus as a *to'abat Ashtart*.[8] In the former category are activities of two kinds: those clearly associated with idolatry and those connected with falsehoods. In the category of *to-avat Adonai* are bringing images of others' gods into one's home (Deut. 7:25–26); offering blemished animals (Deut. 17:1); following the cultic practices of other peoples (Deut. 29–31); engaging in child sacrifice or engaging sorcerers, diviners, necromancers, and so on (Deut. 18:9–12); offering a cultic prostitute's pay in the Temple (Deut. 23:18); making a sculptured or molten image (Deut. 27:15); and making a sacrifice when one is a wicked person (Prov. 15:8).[9]

It is the activities of deception in the category *to-avat Adonai* that give rise to the most diverse examples. The activities of deception that are *to-avat Adonai* are putting on men's apparel if you are a woman and vice versa (Deut. 22:5), employing false weights and measures (Deut. 25:13–16; Prov. 11:1, 20:10, 20:23), having a crooked mind (Prov.

11:20), lying in speech (Prov. 12:22), thinking evil thoughts (Prov. 15:26), being haughty (Prov. 16:5), and acquitting the guilty and convicting the innocent (Prov. 17:15). And people who are understood to be devious or deceptive by nature are consistently deemed *to-avat Adonai*, as are their actions (Prov. 3:32, 15:9).

Interestingly, an antonym for *to-avat Adonai* that appears in Proverbs is רְצוֹנוֹ (*r'tzono*), "in accordance with God's will" or "pleasing to God" (Prov. 11:1: "False scales are an abomination to *Adonai*; an honest weight pleases God"). And the antithesis of the one who acts deceptively or deviously is either a צַדִּיק (*tzaddik*), "a righteous person" (Prov. 11:20: "Those of stubborn heart / crooked mind are an abomination to *Adonai*, but those whose way is blameless please God"), or a מְרַדֵּף צְדָקָה (*m'radeif tzedakah*), "a seeker of righteousness" (Prov. 15:9: "The way of the wicked is an abomination to *Adonai*, but God loves the one who pursues righteousness").

The remainder of actions, including all of the sexual activities, categorized as *to-eivah*, are not *to-avat Adonai*. They are clearly seen as erroneous activities. They break social norms and may evoke strong visceral and emotional responses. But linguistically such responses are not ascribed to God. Moreover, the determination that they belong in this category is not seen as divine. Some, based on their position in the text, seem to be activities associated with foreign cultures and peoples. In a world in which lands, peoples, and cultures were associated with specific gods, these activities were associated with these gods as well. The semantic range for the word most often rendered as "foreign," זָרָה (*zarah*), includes "loathsome," "strange," and "foreign."

Foreign Worship Practices

עֲבוֹדָה זָרָה (*avodah zarah*),[10] literally "foreign or strange worship," is synonymous with idolatry. The Bible clearly rejects a number of activities as כְּמַעֲשֵׂה אֶרֶץ־מִצְרַיִם...וּכְמַעֲשֵׂה אֶרֶץ־כְּנַעַן (*k'maaseih eretz Mitzrayim . . . uch'maaseih eretz K'naan*; Lev. 18:3), activities of foreign groups:

Egyptians and Canaanites. The label "foreign" is not merely descriptive; it is pejorative. Among the foreign cultic practices deemed objectionable by the biblical writers is engaging with male or female prostitutes in heterosexual or homosexual intercourse. In fact, the majority of sexual prohibitions mentioned in Leviticus 18 follow the admonition against engaging in activities of foreign cultures.

Perhaps, like some of the other activities that are in this category, these sexual activities can be understood as doing something with the wrong attitude or with improper intent. Engaging in these activities could be understood by others, as well as by the people themselves, as worshiping the gods of these other lands and peoples. They could be understood as turning away from the practices of one's own people and one's own God. Perhaps they were also understood as expressions of greed or haughtiness in relation to other human beings and before God. In a world in which women were recognized as part of a specific man's domain and holdings, women were sexually off-limits to all other men. In a world in which free men were seen as subjects, not objects, a male having sex with another male was tantamount to treating that male as a sexual object, a woman; it was an act of oppression or degradation.[11] Having sex with another man's woman or with another man could have been understood as adopting an unacceptable attitude or giving in to one's own greed or sense of self-importance, thus diminishing the worth of another human being or his property. A parallel is drawn between illicit sexual relations and *avodah zarah*.

Some Postbiblical, Premodern Considerations[12]

Discussions about *to-eivah* appear in a wide range of postbiblical Jewish writings: midrashic collections, biblical commentaries, and legal codes. They raise numerous concerns, including the term's meaning, the term's relevance in a postbiblical society, and appropriate societal responses to those who engage in what is deemed *to-eivah*. The following paragraphs will highlight and illustrate some of the issues contained in these texts as they, too, contribute to our reexamination of this category.

The Difference between "Laying" and "Being Laid" and the Implications of Intent and Consent

A text in *Sifra* to Leviticus (*K'doshim*, *perek* 10) clearly distinguishes between "laying" and "lying." It also raises concerns about culpability and punishment and their relation to intentionality.

> שתי משכבות באשה[13] (*sh'tei mishkavot b'ishah*): There are two ways of laying a woman (vaginal and anal). Rabbi Yishmael says a verse seeks to shed light on a given subject, but also winds up having light shed on it.[14] Surely they shall be put to death by stoning. You say stoning or by one of the deaths prescribed by Torah. Scripture teaches their blood is upon them. And later it says their blood is upon them. Just as דמיהם (*d'meihem*), "their blood," meant stoning before then, it means the same here.
>
> עונש (*onesh*)—we have derived. Where is the warning? Scripture teaches, ואת זכר לא תשכב משכבי אשה (*v'et zachar lo tishkav mishk'vei ishah*; Lev. 18:22): I only have a warning against laying.
>
> Whence is the prohibition against being laid?
>
> Scripture teaches לא יהיה קדש בבני ישראל (*lo yih'yeh kadeish mib'nei Yisrael*; Deut. 23:18) and it also teaches וגם קדש היה בארץ (*v'gam kadeish hayah vaaretz*; I Kings 14:24).
>
> And Rabbi Akiva says: ואת זכר לא תשכב (*v'et zachar lo tishkav*) read as "lain with."
>
> Rabbi Chanina ben Idi says: משכב זכר והבהמה (*mishkav zachar uhab'heimah* laying or lying with a male or a beast) were within the same category as all the עריות (*arayot*) and behold Scripture pulls them out and calls them תּוֹעֵבָה (*to-eivah*), as these are עֲרָיוֹת (*arayot*), sexual offenses, for which one is liable, when זָדוֹן (*zadon*), intentional, to be כָּרֵת (*kareit*), cut off, and if שְׁגָגָה (*sh'gagah*), unintentional, one makes a sin offering, and for which Canaanites were exiled, so it is with all of the עֲרָיוֹת (*arayot*).[15]

A clear distinction is drawn between initiating sexual contact, "laying," and being the object of another's sexual advances, "being laid." Moreover, if one is "laid," then a secondary issue must be considered in order to determine a just punishment. Were both parties acting willfully and willingly? Even when involved in proscribed sexual activity, one receives a far less severe punishment if he has done so unwillingly, by being forced.

Abraham ibn Ezra focuses his attention on the phraseology of Leviticus 20:13, which states, "If a man lies with a male as one lies with a woman, the two of them have done [an act that is] *to-eivah*." For Ibn Ezra, the two can only be accused of committing a *to-eivah* if there was consent. Otherwise, only the one who has forced the other to engage in sex has committed a *to-eivah*. Ibn Ezra uses the same variables of consent and force to determine if someone is to be punished for the act of revealing a woman's blood flow, discussed five verses later, in Leviticus 20:18. There he states that the meaning of the phrase וְהִוא גִלְּתָה (*v'hi giltah*) means "willingly," because if she were forced, only he would be cut off.

The Fluidity of That Which Is Deemed *To-eivah*

Rashi, commenting on Deuteronomy 14:3, considers the impact of personal and group perception and the contents of the category *to-eivah*. He focuses on the restrictive application of the term *to-eivah*. He writes, "Anything that I have declared to be an abomination to you (which in itself may not be an abominable thing)."

Silberman, elucidating Rashi's comments, explains:

> The term *to-eivah* is a comparative one, for what one person regards as an abomination, another may deem to be perfectly agreeable. . . . For this reason Scripture frequently states that a certain action or person is *to-eivat Adonai*, an abomination unto the Lord. This is the meaning here. . . . Every act that God has forbidden us to do, He has by virtue of that prohibition declared to be abominable.[16]

From this we are reminded that we all react differently to the same stimuli. What we view as erroneous or objectionable or abhorrent may not be viewed as such by others. An odor or taste may be pleasant to one person and offensive for another. The use of the same word in different contexts determines whether or not it is acceptable or abhorrent. In different societies and time periods, men wearing earrings or makeup, women wearing clothing that exposed their arms, face, or feet or covered their legs in something resembling pants, or individuals with tattoos or piercings were either viewed as honored adult members of the society or pariahs. The categorization was determined by divine or human fiat and became binding for and was applied to those who recognized the authority of that source. Genesis 43:32 offers us an opportunity to appreciate how ancient this understanding is: "They served him separately and them separately and the Egyptians who usually ate with him separately, for the Egyptians could not eat food with the Hebrews, since it was an abomination to the Egyptians." Not only ancient Hebrews and Israelites, but the Egyptians as well, had customs and practices that needed to be explained to those from other cultures who would find them unusual and perhaps incomprehensible. So it is today as well; what we choose to do or not to do reflects our own values, our own religious sensibilities, and our own sense of what constitutes an error in judgment or an error in action.

The earliest strata of Jewish legal writings accepted polygamy and two major types of non-marital intercourse—with a concubine or with a maidservant.[17] Each woman was seen as having a clearly understood relation to the man with whom she was having sexual relations. The concubine did not have a written agreement (*ketubah*) nor did she celebrate *kiddushin*, but her children could be acknowledged as legitimate offspring. A concubine became the exclusive sexual partner of a man with whom a verbal agreement was made. That agreement could have certain conditions attached to it. For example, the agreement could include information about frequency (from one time to ongoing until asked to leave) or location (whether she would live among the members of a man's household or separately). A maidservant, in contrast, was merely property, available for her owner to use as he saw fit, with the offspring joining the ranks of his acquisitions. These extramarital relations were understood in context as having clear intent and parameters. Neither was considered *to-eivah*, and both were considered distinct from prostitution, which was categorized as *to-eivah*, a form of idolatry.

Polygamy and concubinage remained part of the social and cultural landscape of Sephardic and eastern Jewish communities well into the modern period. The rabbis of Ashkenaz generally rejected the notions that in a postbiblical context these extramarital liaisons existed or that they could be acceptable. And with the eleventh-century *takanah* of Rabbenu Gershom legislating against polygamy, in stark contrast to the Bible and even earlier postbiblical Jewish communities, all sexual relations outside of a monogamous marriage were deemed unacceptable within the communities of Ashkenaz.

However, the eighteenth-century Ashkenazic rabbi Jacob Emden wrote an unusual responsum in which he deemed permissible certain non-marital sexual relations. He posited that marriage was not required and that one could fulfill the mitzvah of being fruitful and multiplying with a concubine if he has not found a woman to marry him or if his wife has not given birth to his children and he cannot divorce her. He also wrote of how during the periods during which Jewish law prohibited sexual relations with a wife (during the periods of *nidah* and postpartum), it was permissible for one to turn to a concubine. The intent of these non-marital sexual relations was to satisfy a man's sexual needs, and both he and the concubine, and ostensibly the wife, understood this.[18] In all of these cases, the rabbis were concerned in their decisions with the intent behind one's choice to engage in sexual activity. For some, the only permissible intent was fulfilling the mitzvot associated with marriage, within the context of monogamous marriage. For others, non-marital sexual partners were permitted if the intent and parameters of the relationship were clearly understood. A man's intention to satisfy his sexual needs or his desire to fulfill the mitzvah of having progeny could result in his having sexual partners who were not his legal wife. In all cases, both parties who engaged in sexual relations understood the nature of the relationship—what they could expect from the liaison for themselves and their potential offspring.

Intent and Its Consequences

Bar Kapara (Babylonian Talmud, *N'darim* 51a) played with the word *to-eivah*, offering a creative etymology for it. He divided it into the words תּוֹעָה and בה (*to-eh vah*), concluding that a *to-eivah* is something that leads one to err through it. This rendering of *to-eivah* found resonance in later generations as well. Rashi's discussions of intent as it relates to *to-eivah* seem to reflect Bar Kapara's perspective. As Rashi's comments on Deuteronomy 22:5 underscore, to lead another to make an error in judgment or to act in error is also *to-eivah*. Of a woman's wearing male apparel or a man's wearing female apparel, Rashi writes:

> . . . so that she look like a man, in order to consort with men, for this [a man in woman's clothes] can only be for the purpose of adultery נִאוּף (*ni-uf*), unchastity (*Sifrei*; *Nazir* 59a), in order to go and stay unnoticed among women. Another explanation of the second part of the text is: it implies that a man should not remove by a depilatory the hair of the genitals and the hair beneath the arm pit (*Nazir* 59a). כִּי תוֹעֲבָה הִיא (*ki to-eivah hi*), because it is *to-eivah*. This implies that the Torah forbids only the wearing of garb that leads to abomination, unchastity (*Sifrei*).

Sifrei comments in a similar vein:

> כְּלִי גֶבֶר (*k'li gever*) clothing of a man: A woman shall not wear that which pertains to a man. What does the text come to teach us? That a woman will not wear white garments and the man isn't covered in colors. [Rather] the text teaches "תוֹעֵבָה [*to-eivah*]," a thing that brings one to "תוֹעֵבָה [*to-eivah*]," this is the general category of the thing: A woman shouldn't dress in a manner that a man dresses and go among men, and a man should not adorn himself with women's jewelry and go among women. Rabbi Eliezer ben Yaakov says: Whence do we know a woman shouldn't wear armor/arms and go to war? [Because] the text says: A man's garment shouldn't be on a woman, and the man will not adorn himself with women's jewelry. The text says: And a man shall not wear a woman's dress.[19]

How different this is from a general prohibition about all types of clothing! In both references contained in *Sifrei*, the prohibition has to do with the external characteristics of the clothing or adornments. Interestingly, it is the adornments—jewelry or armor—not the garment itself, that could ultimately lead someone to misidentify another person's gender and then engage with that person, based on a false assumption, in an activity that could be considered *to-eivah*. To choose to wear something that you know can lead another astray is an act of will with malevolent intent.

Proper Intent and Attitude

In the *Tosefta*, the range of activities mentioned repeatedly in Proverbs and the semantic range that highlights improper attitudes toward others become the focus:[20]

> The people of Sodom said because food comes forth from our land and silver and gold come forth from our land and precious stones and pearls come forth from our land, we do not need people to come to us—they only come to diminish us. We will arise and forget how things are things are usually done [Neusner].[21] God says to them, By means of the good I've caused for you, you have forgotten, how things are usually done / the law protecting travelers. I will make you be forgotten from the world.
>
> What does it mean פָּרַץ נַחַל (*paratz nachal*)?
>
> Job 28:4: He breaks open a watercourse in a place far from inhabitants, forgotten by foot travelers.
>
> What does it mean לַפִּיד בּוּז (*lapid buz*)?
>
> Job 12:5: Contempt is ready in the thought of him that is at ease, for those that are ruined, that slip with their feet.
>
> What does it mean יִשְׁלָיוּ אֹהָלִים (*yishlayu ohalim*)?
>
> Job 12:6: The tents of robbers prosper, and they who provoke God are secure; they who bring their God in hand.
>
> Thus he says, As I live, declares God, אִם עָשְׂתָה סְדוֹם אֲחוֹתֵךְ (*im as'tah S'dom achoteich*; Ezek. 16:48ff).
>
> Behold this is the sin of Sodom: גָּאוֹן שִׂבְעַת לֶחֶם (*gaon sivat lechem*) pride and surfeit of food, arrogance, prosperous ease, complacency . . . never helped the poor and needy; they were proud and engaged in *to-eivah* in front of me. That is why I have "swept them away" when I saw it.[22]

There is both intra-biblical exegesis and rabbinic support that the sin of Sodom was not homosexual sexual activity. It was the haughtiness and pride, the greed and arrogance of the people of Sodom that led them to treat others poorly, to be inhospitable, and to cut themselves off from others.

A Reform Understanding of *To-eivah*

Throughout the millennia, our rabbinic forebears have visited and revisited the term *to-eivah*, attempting to understand it in the biblical context and to determine its relevance and application for their own times and communities. Their insights into key questions and categories related to *to-eivah* can provide us with a scaffolding for our own exploration into the meaning that the category *to-eivah* might have for us as Reform Jews and, more specifically, how we might understand it in relation to our lives as sexual beings. As Reform Jews, in accordance with "Reform Jewish Sexual Values" adopted by the CCAR (see p. 241), we seek to elevate our sexual behavior from its most bestial level, to set ourselves apart and act in a holy manner. We affirm that "our sexuality and sexual expression are integral and powerful elements in the potential wholeness of human beings. . . . Each Jew should seek to conduct his/her sexual life in a manner that elicits the intrinsic holiness within the person and the relationship."

In his paper "Towards a Taxonomy for Reform Jews to Evaluate Sexual Behaviors," Jonathan A. Stein[23] suggested that we think about our sexual behaviors via categories. He saw the category *to-eivah*, "abhorrent," as an operative category for contemporary liberal Jewish sensibilities when considered in relation to "Reform Jewish Sexual Values." In that context, this category would consist of the most unacceptable behaviors involving sex. In the Ad Hoc Committee on Human Sexuality's early discussions, a suggestion was made that a breach of all of the sexual values including those that involve abuse, violence, and coercion would be included in this category. In his paper, Rabbi Stein added the phrase "or which violate[s] certain historic Jewish and human societal norms." But Rashi's incisive observation that what is acceptable to one may be abhorrent to another is still valid today. Personal, visceral, and emotional responses to certain activities will vary. Using them as criteria is at best limited and at worst faulty. Moreover, many sexual and relational expressions long viewed as violating "certain historic Jewish and human societal norms" are no longer viewed as such. Therefore, we must acknowledge that in the area of human sexuality, activities and interactions that were once understood to be natural for all human beings or divinely ordained, such as heterosexuality, are no longer automatically accepted as such.

Our circumstances and knowledge, our range of experience, are all radically different from those expressed in the Bible, and much like Emden and so many others in generations that preceded our own, we must determine for ourselves what contemporary meaning they have for us. Two clear contemporary examples of Reform Judaism's rejection of long-held Jewish societal norms are our acceptance of ex-spouses remarrying each other, even if they've been married to others in the interim, and our acceptance of adult consensual sex between members of the same gender. Conversely, today we do object to adults engaging in sexual activity with minors, a practice tolerated in biblical and postbiblical Jewish texts. Human beings have always had a wide range of behaviors to express their sexual desires and needs. Other more concrete criteria than that which "violate[s] certain historic Jewish and human societal norms" will better serve us as guides as we explore the range of meaning that *to-eivah* can have for us as Reform Jews.

According to "Reform Jewish Sexual Values," there are ten values that compose a holy relationship:

1. *B'tzelem Elohim* (In the image of God)
2. *Emet* (Truth)
3. *B'riut* (Health)
4. *Mishpat* (Justice)
5. *Mishpachah* (Family)

6. *Tz'niut*   (Modesty)
7. *B'rit*   (Covenantal Relationship)
8. *Simchah*   (Joy)
9. *Ahavah*   (Love)
10. *K'dushah*   (Holiness)

It is interesting to note that the breaches that comprised traditional understandings of *to-eivah* by analogy and through interpretation were deemed objectionable precisely because they did not embody some of these values. The concerns expressed in Prophets and in Deuteronomy and reiterated in *Tosefta* about greed and haughtiness interfering with one's ability to respond to the needy or causing one to put personal gain over other considerations are relevant in the realm of sexual behavior as well. As Reform Jews, we affirm that sexual intimacy should be mutually expressive for those involved. To not consider the needs of a sexual partner, to engage in sexual behavior solely to satisfy one's own needs or to enhance one's position—personally, economically, professionally, or as a means to assert one's power over another—would be to fail to recognize the partner as created *b'tzelem Elohim*, in the image of God. At such times, the intent, the parameters, and the potential outcomes for both parties are not clear. All of these, it can be argued, lack an intent that affirms the "Reform Jewish Sexual Values." They may, in fact, be considered תּוֹעֵבָה (*to-eivah*) because they lead one to err or תּוֹעֶה בָהּ (*to-eh vah*).

According to traditional sources and commentaries, to deceive another, through dress or by false weights and measures, is to commit an act that is *to-eivah*. As the *Sifrei* teaches, to claim to be someone other than who you are to engage in sexual activity is, at the very least, improper. To do so would be a failure of *emet*, truth. Particularly egregious are willful lies related to one's marital status, age, or health status (vis-à-vis STDs and HIV). They deny a prospective partner the possibility of making an informed decision. Such activities may be *to-eivah*.

According to traditional sources on *to-eivah*, the antithesis of acting deceptively is to be a מְרַדֵּף צְדָקָה (*m'radeif tzedakah*), a seeker of righteousness or justice. To be a *m'radeif tzedakah*, according to "Reform Jewish Sexual Values," is "to reach out and care for others, to treat all of those created in the image of God with respect and dignity, to strive to create equality and justice wherever people are treated unfairly." All activities that exploit a power or age differential or in any way compromise the dignity and equality of another are a failure of מִשְׁפָּט (*mishpat*), justice; such activities may be *to-eivah*.

Ideally, all of our sexual relationships should be founded on a בְּרִית (*b'rit*), a covenant. They should be undergirded by mutual esteem, trust, and faithfulness. Moreover, a *b'rit* delineates the roles and responsibilities of the parties who enter into it. As Emden's responsum underscores, no matter the nature of a sexual relationship (marital or non-marital), it is essential to clarify each partner's relationship to the other and the expectations of each, thus defining the terms of the *b'rit*, as it were. A failure to abide by those roles and responsibilities represents a breach of trust and faith, a breach of the *b'rit*. Children believe adults care about their safety and well-being. Spouses believe the same about a partner to whom they have made a loving commitment. Endangering physical or emotional well-being and safety, particularly in the sexual arena, is a breach of trust, a failure to uphold a *b'rit*. Acts that breach both the values of *b'rit*, and *mishpat*, such as child molestation and incest and spousal rape and abuse, are *to-eivah*.

We should also consider a number of other variables. As Ibn Ezra and the text from *Sifrei* advise, we must ask if the people involved are acting with intent/willfully or if there has been coercion. Is one person leading another to believe that there is one intent, while there is actually another? Sexual behaviors that fail to respect the inherent holiness and dignity of a sexual partner, that are built on lies and falsehoods with the express intent of leading someone to act in a way she or he would otherwise avoid, that exploit power differentials, that mistreat or abuse others, and that violate another person's sense of trust, faith, or boundaries may be considered *to-eivah*.

If such falsehoods lead someone to do something that he or she feels is unethical or morally objectionable, it might be considered *to-eivah*.

As the Center for the Prevention of Sexual and Domestic Violence has taught, the violation is determined by the "victim," not the "perpetrator." Only the person experiencing a sense of violation knows it. We all have different things that make us uncomfortable; each of us has the right and the obligation to communicate when something is uncomfortable, and each of us has the right to have such a communication heard and heeded.

Moreover, to act with force is to commit an act that is *to-eivah*. In accordance with Ibn Ezra's methodology, the victim is not to be held responsible, only the perpetrator. A gray area, based on Ibn Ezra's insights and "Reform Jewish Sexual Values," is consensual sadomasochistic or bondage and domination, sexual practices. There are those who would argue that both parties who engage in these behaviors suffer from some sort of pathological disturbance. Others argue that the range of healthy consensual sexual activity in which adults engage is exceedingly broad and that as long as it is truly consensual, it should not be disparaged or rejected by those who do not engage in such practices themselves.

To exploit an age or power differential is *to-eivah*—therefore, child molestation, engaging in sex with a minor, sexual harassment, and engaging in sex with a subordinate at work are all *to-eivah*. Physically or emotionally abusing another while engaging in sexual acts or through references to sexuality is *to-eivah*. Rape, though often thought of as sexual, is widely recognized as an act of violence that involves sexual organs. It is a violent assault perpetrated to assert power over or humiliate another. As violence, as a desecration of the sanctity of another human being, as a blatant disregard for honesty and mutuality, it is *to-eivah*.

Conclusion

As Reform Jews, we take our sexual lives seriously and seek to have our values reflected in our sexual behaviors and sexual relations. By deepening our understanding of the meaning *to-eivah* can have for us as liberal Jews, we can take greater responsibility for the choices we make and help our congregants do the same. For us, as clergy, our enhanced knowledge and sensitivity will redound in our counseling and teaching practices. It will make our welcome more genuine, enabling those who have felt disenfranchised or marginalized to find a place for themselves within the Jewish community. It will also help us clarify the limits that we do recognize in the sphere of sexual expression and identify the values upon which they are based in a clear and cogent manner.

NOTES

1. *The Interpreter's Dictionary of the Bible* (New York: Abingdon Press, 1962), 12–13.
2. William H. Hallo, "Biblical Abominations and Sumerian Taboos," *JQR* 86, no. 1 (July 1985): 21–40.
3. Ibid., 33.
4. (vol. 4, 1980 ,ספר קרית:ירושלים) חדשה קונקורדנציה אברהם, אבן־שושן,
5. *Encyclopaedia Biblica* (London: Adam and Charles Black, 1899), 21.
6. *A Hebrew and English Lexicon of the Old Testament*, ed. Francis Brown, S. R. Driver, and Charles A. Briggs (Oxford: Oxford University Press, 1951), 1072.
7. My thanks to Dr. S. David Sperling for his assistance and insights on these matters.
8. Hallo, "Biblical Abominations and Sumerian Taboos," 34.
9. Note that all but one of these references appear in Deuteronomy.
10. While biblically based, this is a Rabbinic term.
11. In the Middle Assyrian laws, ca. 1076 BCE (law 20), a convicted sodomizer is himself sodomized and then castrated (M. Roth, *Law Collections from Mesopotamia and Asia Minor* [Atlanta: Scholars Press, 1995], 160). In Apuleis's *Golden Ass*, there is a story about an adulterer who is punished by being penetrated by the offended husband.
12. My thanks to Drs. Alyssa Gray and Sharon Koren for their assistance and input on this section.
13. The highlighted phrases from the *Sifra* text are intentionally left untranslated precisely because the discussion is an attempt to clarify their meaning.
14. My thanks to Dr. Michael Chernick for his assistance with the translation for this Aramaic phrase.
15. *Sifra* to Leviticus, *K'doshim perek* 10, verse 11 (ed. Yequtiel Yehudah Waldman).

16. Rabbi A. M. Silberman, *Chumash with Rashi's Commentary* (Jerusalem: Feldheim, 1934), 5:204.

17. Louis Epstein, *Marriage Laws in the Bible and Talmud*, Harvard Semitic Series 12 (Cambridge, MA: Harvard University Press, 1942).

18. *She'elot U'tshuvot, Sh'eilat Yavetz*, vol. 2, no. 15 (New York: Gross, 1961).

19. *Sifrei D'varim, piska* 226.

20. The Hebrew phrases that are highlighted remain untranslated because the *Tosefta* discussion is an attempt to elucidate their meanings.

21. Jastrow 449: law for the protection of travelers/traders.

22. Lieberman, *Tosefta Sotah, perek* 3, *halachah* 12.

23. Jonathan A. Stein, "Toward a Taxonomy for Reform Jews to Evaluate Sexual Behavior," *CCAR Journal*, Fall 2001, pp. 25–33.

4

"A GREAT VOICE, NEVER ENDING"

Reading the Torah in Light of
the New Status of Gays and Lesbians
in the Jewish Community

RABBI DAVID GREENSTEIN, PhD

I

In recounting the revelation at Mount Sinai, Moses recalled to Israel that "it is these things that the Eternal spoke to your entire assembly, at the mountain, from out of the fire, the murky cloud—a great voice, never ending [*v'lo yasaf*]" (Deut. 5:19).

Rabbi Yitzchak of Radvil, an early Chasidic master, comments:

> Any thought that it is only at Mount Sinai that God spoke, as it were, is certainly heresy [*k'firah*]. . . . For the truth is this: that the Will of the Blessed One is not subject to change, for His Will is His Essence, as is written, "I am the Eternal; I have not changed" (Mal. 3:6). Therefore it is impossible to say that at Mount Sinai the Holy Blessed One spoke the Torah, as it were, but beforehand He did not speak it, or that after the Giving of the Torah there was no speaking, . . . for there could be no greater change than this! But, as Rashi explained with his holy spirit, "a great voice, never ending"—"that it did not cease." For this voice continues to this very day. . . . This voice was already [speaking] before heaven and earth were created, and [will continue] to eternity.[1]

As we live through the manifold changes of modern times, changes wrought to our material, intellectual, moral, and spiritual existence, Jews have been confronted with interconnected questions regarding our relationship to the Torah. We must decide whether we understand Torah as a divine voice that is historically rooted in time past, and that ceased long ago, or whether it continues to speak. And, if it continues to speak, is its eternal message unchanging or, precisely because it is eternal, capable of change?

The focus of this short essay[2] will be on the challenges posed as we continue to grapple with new ideas, perceptions, and values regarding sexuality, and specifically with regard to homosexuality.[3]

II

We begin with a declaration of three basic premises. "Premise 1" is that all human beings, whatever their sexual orientation, are equally endowed with the blessing of sexuality and with the obligation to express that blessing in a holy manner.

The question of accepting gays and lesbians into the community, while still a matter of controversy, has taken on a new urgency across the spectrum of the Jewish community. This is a very new development in the social and religious history of the Jews. For those who accept premise 1, this ferment is indicative of a profound forward step in our consciousness. "Premise 2" is that the dawning of this new apprehension has real meaning for religiously committed Jews. It emerges that a basic teaching of the Torah, found at its very beginning—that all human beings are created in God's image (*b'tzelem Elohim*)—has come into fuller recognition over the last generation, in large part thanks to the teachings of Rabbi Irving "Yitz" Greenberg.[4] While this concept has biblical origins, Rabbinic celebrations, and medieval philosophical and mystical explanations, it is not until our own day that *b'tzelem Elohim* has become a watchword and orienting principle in the greater Jewish world. The explicit recourse to this universal concept as a fundamental and orienting principle in Judaism has had significant impact in a number of areas, including interfaith relations.[5] And we have continued to deepen our understanding of this teaching as we embrace the sacred value of our own embodied natures. Our newfound recognition of the full humanity and Jewish status of women comes from our new appreciation of ourselves as gendered beings. Our affirmation of our sexuality as essential—for all of us—to our very selves is another step forward.

We affirm this position not as some concession to "the times," to a secular or liberal agenda, or as some sociopolitical compromise with tradition. Rather, this understanding is a positive religious development whose coming to fruition in this era marks this time as an epoch of major significance in the history of culture and religion in general and of Judaism in particular. In the same way, we see our recognition of the fully equal status of homosexuals—as human beings and as Jews—not as a favor we are doing to the GLBT community or as a capitulation to political correctness, but as our own blessed attainment of a new religious insight.

These two premises prompt us, as faithful Jews, to ask certain difficult questions, but, it will be argued, they also prepare us for how we might hope to look for answers to them.

We must ask: How shall we understand our Torah in light of our affirmation of premise 1? Doesn't the Torah reject homosexuality? And: How does our embrace of premise 2 affect our relationship to our tradition? Is it possible to affirm this second premise without adopting a relativist or supersessionist theology of revelation?

These questions lead us to "premise 3." It states a fundamental conviction: that the Torah must still be able to speak to us in a meaningful and authoritative voice, that the Torah's voice never ceases. Can we embrace premise 3 as we reject those Torah texts that seem to be founded on older views of human reality?

This essay will briefly explore how others have grappled with these questions, and then it will suggest that our initial premises can help us adopt a new, different, and more fruitful approach.

III

As the straight and gay communities interact more and more—in all segments of the Jewish community—we are witnesses to a profound change of thinking and feeling, wherein the idea of healthy homosexuality—once considered inconceivable and unacceptable—has now become increasingly accepted, while the idea that homosexuality is abhorrent and that homosexuals are to be condemned has itself become increasingly an abhorrent and unacceptable idea. This is so even among many Orthodox Jews.

While homophobia, sometimes ostensibly justified by biblical warrant, exists in all groups, it is Orthodoxy that has long been unapologetic about its rejection and denigration of homosexuality. This group accepts that the Torah, as it has been understood for generations, condemns the act of sexual intercourse between two males as a capital offense (Lev. 18:22 and 20:13). It affirms subsequent Rabbinic tradition that expanded the prohibition to include same-sex erotic activity between females.[6] Homosexual intercourse is called *to-eivah*, "an abomination," in those biblical verses, and the sense of disgust for the act was internalized so as to include both the very idea itself and any people who might not be deterred by such an idea.

Therefore, until recently, it has been acceptable in this community to voice utter disgust with regard to homosexuals, for they were people who were not deterred by what this community deemed to be an outrageous and hateful idea. The great contemporary halachic decisor Rabbi Moshe Feinstein, for example, was quite explicit in his visceral rejection of homosexuals as people.[7] But this approach is no longer exclusively regnant. As one rabbi writes, "While Orthodoxy cannot permit homosexual sex, there is a range of opinion today on several issues regarding a homosexual person."[8]

Yet, though the divine image of the homosexual person has become more evident, nevertheless the power and inviolability of the Torah's words are taken for granted. Thus, that same rabbi, in compiling a bibliography of articles on the Orthodox position regarding homosexuality, writes, "I disqualified as non-Orthodox any articles that claim the prohibition no longer applies."[9]

A unique voice in the Orthodox world has been Rabbi Steven Greenberg, who, after years of struggle, finally openly identified as a gay person and has written and spoken extensively about finding alternative ways to maintain Orthodox commitments and nevertheless accept homosexuality as having the potential for holiness. He has dared to claim that the Torah's verses can be read differently. His reading is significant in that it attempts to read the verse as a condemnation of acts of sexual humiliation. It is this aspect of violence and degradation that is prohibited as an abomination, rather than the physical sex act itself.

Such a reading has been suggested by others who have tried to find ways to respond positively to homosexuality.[10] But there seems to be an insurmountable flaw to this reading. For, were the prohibition limited to acts of homosexual rape, it would make no sense that the Torah, at Leviticus 20:13, would require that both parties involved in the act be punished with death. Why should the two of them be put to death when only one of them is a willing participant in the act?

Thus, the standard Orthodox reading must be rejected as incompatible with our basic premises, and the valiant attempt offered by some traditionalists to read the verses as applying exclusively to coercive sex is inadequate to the text itself. Nevertheless, Rabbi Greenberg's insistence on a broader consideration of sexual ethics, one applicable to both men and women, is a major step forward.

IV

All the non-Orthodox movements, on the other hand, have more or less agreed to welcome homosexuals as full participants in Jewish religious life, accepting gays as spiritual leaders and as eligible for some sort of committed, loving partnership.[11] Nevertheless, it can be argued that none has succeeded in articulating a reading of the Torah's verses that preserves their coherence while satisfying our basic premises.

The Reconstructionist Movement officially accepted homosexuals into its seminary in 1984. The rabbinic manual of the Reconstructionist Movement includes provisions for a Jewish marriage ceremony for same-sex couples, to be used at the discretion of the individual rabbi. How has this approach been squared with the Torah's verses? In 1993 the Movement declared, "We regard the Jewish values that affirm the inherent dignity, integrity and equality of human beings as having primacy over historically conditioned attitudes based on . . . texts that condemn homosexuality as an abomination."[12] In other words, in the name of the core Jewish values of justice and human equality, the Torah's prohibitions against homosexuality must be overruled. The voice speaking through those verses has been silenced.

The Reform Movement has included views supportive of the homosexual community for decades. In 2000, the Central Conference of American Rabbis (CCAR) resolved that each rabbi would have the power to decide whether to perform a Jewish ceremony of marriage for same-sex couples.[13] Nevertheless, this resolution was adopted in the face of the CCAR's own Responsa Committee's decision, in 1998, that refused to allow the traditional concept of Jewish marriage—*kiddushin*—to be applied to same-sex unions.[14] Among many problematic elements in the responsum, we find this statement: "While it may be true that we as a community no longer look upon homosexual behavior, as we once did, as a revulsive act, the fact remains that no Jewish community has ever gone so far as to sanctify as marriage a sexual relationship which the Torah defines as *ervah*. Not even we, with all our liberality, have ever done this before."[15] The deep ambivalence of this responsum is obvious. That it was subsequently overruled through a resolution is a welcome development. But it must be noted that in doing so, the Reform Movement gave up trying to deal with the issue in terms of concepts of Jewish law and sought a political solution instead. It was a tacit admission that they had not succeeded in answering the question: how do we read the Torah now?

The Conservative Movement has fared no better. Fifteen years after reaching a consensus affirming that homosexuality was forbidden by the Torah and the tradition, the Conservative Movement struggled anew with this issue. In 2006 the Committee on Jewish Law and Standards adopted three *t'shuvot* (responsa) as legitimate, though the responsa reached almost opposite conclusions.[16] Two of the responsa declared that there was no reason to overturn the settled law of traditional halachah. They affirmed that while sensitivity to homosexual individuals was imperative, there were no permissible ways for homosexuals to realize their desires in a sexual fashion. Shamefully, one responsum embraced the value of "reparative therapy"! Clearly, these responsa must be rejected as incompatible with our premises.

The third opinion[17] was hailed as permissive and became the basis for allowing gays to be accepted as Conservative clergy. Yet this opinion affirmed that the Torah does, indeed, prohibit the act of anal homosexual intercourse. It viewed all other prohibitions to be of Rabbinic status, to be set aside today, since their enforcement today impugns the human dignity of homosexuals. This responsum is fundamentally wrong. It fails to meet the basic standard of premise 1. The ancient Rabbis recognized that sex acts could not be selectively prohibited or permitted with regard to heterosexuals. The same truth applies to homosexuals. But this responsum assumes that for gays, and for gays only, sexuality can be divided up into discrete activities. It declares that homosexuality can be affirmed as a legitimate variety of sexuality while, at the same time, declaring a biblical prohibition of a sex act—anal intercourse—that is completely legitimate for heterosexuals.[18] We are again left without a way to read the Torah's verses.

V

The difficulty of sustaining, rereading, or dismissing a Torah law seems to be exacerbated here because of our deeply ambivalent thoughts and emotions regarding sexuality. And these conflicts are further sharpened by the Torah's emotionally charged word *to-eivah*, "abomination," which draws our focus hypnotically. It alerts us that if we choose to disallow homosexual acts, we are inexorably drawn into an ugly set of attitudes. Rabbi Joel Roth, who insists on the full prohibition of homosexuality, works hard to neutralize the force of the term *to-eivah*. He maintains that there is no emotive message of disgust or condemnation to the term.[19] But this seems to deny what we know of language, emotions, and history.

Ironically, liberal voices, while rejecting the Torah's prohibition, have sought to salvage meaning from the Torah's emotive language of condemnation. They seek to discover whether a liberal approach to sexual ethics can retain a sense of outrage and condemnation for some kinds of sexual sins.

Studying the use of the term in key biblical texts,[20] Rabbi Seth Goldstein, a Reconstructionist rabbi, concludes that the term's basic meaning, retained throughout its history, relates to "violations of a socially constructed boundary."[21] He claims that sexual offenses were never the term's focus. Its application to homosexuals was an error. However, the concept of *to-eivah* is meaningful as a condemnation of that which threatens the Jewish people, their identity and values. "What threatens Judaism and Jewish practice can be maintained as an 'abomination,' but what does not threaten Judaism and Jewish practice can no longer be considered an 'abomination.'"[22]

Rabbi Nancy H. Wiener offers "A Reform Understanding of *To-eivah*"[23] (see pp. 23–42). Rabbi Wiener rejects applying this term to homosexuality. Her study leads her to define it as referring to violations of the core "values that comprise a holy relationship."[24] The use of force, manipulation, or deceit makes an act a *to-eivah*. Indeed, such an act is not to be viewed as a sexual act at all, but "as an act of violence that involves sexual organs. It is a violent assault perpetrated to assert power over or humiliate another. As violence, as a desecration of the sanctity of another human being, as a blatant disregard for honesty and mutuality, it is *to-eivah*."[25]

It is noteworthy that this explanation of the term by a Reform rabbi discovers that it represents the violation of the core values of her movement, much as the Reconstructionist rabbi's study offered evidence to show that the term referred to violations of his movement's core values.

But it emerges, thus far, that modern readers cannot seem to keep the Torah's verses intact as a meaningful message. For the liberal position, the first half of the verse must be ignored or nullified, while the last term may be imbued with continued relevance. For the traditionalist-restrictive position, the first half of the verse is as meaningful as ever, while the last half must be deprived of any real force.

VI

I believe that the failure to hold fast to all three of the premises outlined at the start of this essay has led to a failure to make coherent sense of the Torah in this instance. Either we are uneasy with our acceptance of the essential quality of human sexuality, or we see our new values as external to our religious traditions, or we are convinced that the Torah's voice has been frozen as a past historical phenomenon. But should we embrace the force of all these premises together, we might discover a new way to hear the Torah's verses.

Leviticus 18:22 can be broken down into three components. It mentions (a) persons for whom certain (b) actions are prohibited, and it characterizes such prohibited acts as (c) *to-eivah*. Leviticus 20:13 adds another component, the punishment of death for both persons involved in the sinful act.

We may begin with the problematic concept of *to-eivah*. It is not necessary to account for all instances of the use of this term through the Bible in order to offer a possible understanding of its use here. The very first occurrence of the concept in the Torah is in the Joseph story. Joseph, viceroy of Egypt, has ordered that his brothers (who do not as yet recognize him) dine with him. The Torah tells us, "They served him [Joseph] separately and them separately and the Egyptians who usually ate with him separately, for the Egyptians could not eat food with the Hebrews, since it was an abomination [*to-eivah*] to the Egyptians" (Gen. 43:32).

Many have explained that this text indicates that *to-eivah* may indicate a socially conditioned revulsion. We must understand what act or concept was considered offensive here. All parties are expected to eat a meal. There is nothing offensive about that. What is offensive is the inclusion of alien elements into the acceptable group. Hebrews can eat by themselves without offending Egyptians. But they cannot eat along with Egyptians. What is offensive is to ruin a situation that is innocuous in itself by introducing an unwelcome element.[26]

What acts are forbidden by these verses in Leviticus? The strange term *mishk'vei ishah* is used here, a *hapax legomenon* that appears nowhere else in Torah. Until now it has been understood to refer to homosexual relations. Yet, in subsequent, Rabbinic literature, the term for homosexual intercourse is, rather, *mishkav zachar*, based on the meaning of this term in the Torah, where it, indeed, means cohabitation with a male. But it refers to a *woman* cohabiting with a male. When the Israelite army returns from battle with the Midianites, an irate Moses exclaims, "Slay also every woman who has known a man carnally; but spare every female dependent who has not had carnal relations with a man" (Num. 31:17–18). The term *mishkav zachar* is twice used here to refer to a *woman* engaging in sexual relations with a *man*. If we return to the Levitical phrase, *mishk'vei ishah*, we may conclude, by analogy, that the term must refer to a *man* having sexual relations with a *woman*. The acts forbidden by the Torah are not homosexual acts at all! Furthermore, unlike in Numbers, the term in Leviticus has been rendered in the plural. What is that prohibited act or set of acts?

We turn to the first part of the verse, the part that mentions the persons involved in the forbidden act: "And with a man"—*v'et zachar* (Lev. 18:22). The particle *et* may indicate the object of an action. This is its meaning from the start of the Torah: "In the beginning God created [*et*] the heavens and [*et*] the earth" (Gen. 1:1). The first place where the word *et* is unambiguously used in another way is in Genesis 5:24, "Enoch walked with [*et*] God."[27] Here it is clear that the particle does not signify an object indication. Rather it means "along with." Until now Leviticus 18:22 has been read to mean that a male is prohibited from making another man the object (*et*) of his sex act. But now we may read the verse very differently:

> *V'et zachar*—*And along with* another male
> *lo tishkav*—you shall not lie
> *mishk'vei ishah*—in sexual intercourse *with a woman*;
> *to-eivah hi*—it is abhorrent.

There is no prohibition of homosexual acts of any kind. Rather, the Torah prohibits two males from joining together to engage in intercourse with a woman. This is a *to-eivah* because the introduction of the second man completely transforms the act from a neutral act into a manipulation that degrades the act of intercourse and makes the woman subject to objectification that may become violent.

Previous commentators' intuitions that what is meant here is some form of coercive sex act were correct. *But the act is heterosexual, not homosexual.* Thus, we can now understand Leviticus 20:13 in a simple way. The penalty prescribed by the Torah is for the two men who force themselves upon the woman. The *perpetrators are guilty*; not the victim.

VII

It is important to understand what this reading purports to be and what it does not purport to be, what it accomplishes and what it does not accomplish. This reading does not purport to present what the original intent of the verse might have been. On the contrary, it claims that whatever previous readings of the verse may have been considered normative in the Jewish community, the time has now come to leave them aside and offer a new reading. More to the point, it seeks not a new "reading" of a static text, but a *new hearing of the Torah's voice.*

It hears no condemnation of homosexuality from the Torah. Rather it expands the sexual ethics of the Torah to include one case of prohibition against coercive sex, heretofore never explicitly forbidden, but, as we have seen, urgently required by our own sense of justice.[28] It does not complete the task of treating all problematic verses in the Torah. It merely recoups certain approaches, exegetical and theological, that have been discarded (albeit, for understandable reasons) but that offer much promise for the future, if we are willing to place our efforts and our faith in them.

Rabbi Yitzchak of Radvil posited that our failure to hear the continuing voice of God must be attributed to our early sexual pollution by the serpent in the Garden. I believe it is fitting, now, that our recuperation of a healthier sense of our sexuality has impelled us to hear the never ceasing voice of the Torah once more.

NOTES

1. *Or Yitzhaq* (Brooklyn, 2009), 188, 261–62.

2. For a fuller discussion of many points raised here, please see my essay, "*Pithu Li Sha`arei Tzedeq*—Open the Gates of Righteousness for Me: An Opening Toward a New Reading of the Torah in Light of the New Status of Gays and Lesbians in the Jewish Community," first published in the *Journal of the Academy for Jewish Religion* 3, no. 1 (2007): 1–21, and available at their website, http://ajrsem.org/teachings/journal/journal5767/, or at my synagogue website, http://www.shomrei.org/media.asp?catid=16&showdetails=1.

3. For convenience, this essay will use the term "homosexual" to apply to both males and females whose sexuality is most fully realized in relation to another person of the same gender.

4. For an accessible statement on the centrality of this concept, see *Living in the Image of God: Jewish Teachings to Perfect the World—Conversations with Rabbi Irving Greenberg*, by Shalom Freedman (Northvale, NJ: Jason Aronson, 1998), esp. 31–43. Greenberg's influential teaching has had its greatest impact outside the Orthodox community with which Greenberg identifies.

5. See, e.g., Rabbi Irving Greenberg's collection of essays, *For the Sake of Heaven and Earth: The New Encounter between Judaism and Christianity* (Philadelphia: Jewish Publication Society, 2004).

6. See, e.g., Maimonides, *Mishneh Torah, Hilchot Isurei Biah* 21:8.

7. See Rabbi Steven Greenberg, *Wrestling with God and Men* (Madison: University of Wisconsin Press, 2004), 135–44. A survey of Orthodox responsa with their varying attitudes toward homosexuality may be found in Ze'ev Schweidel,

"(Br)Others in Our Midst: On the Place of Religious Homosexuals in Religious Society" [in Hebrew], *Akdamot* 17 (2006): 81–110.

8. Rabbi Uri C. Cohen of ATID, www.atid.org.

9. Ibid.

10. See, e.g., Rabbi Bradley Artson, "Judaism and Homosexuality," *Tikkun* 3, no. 2 (March/April 1988): 52–54, and other writings. He also authored a responsum submitted to the Rabbinical Assembly's Committee on Jewish Law and Standards (CJLS) in 1991, but it was not accepted. For an early intuition that coercion may be involved in the biblical concern about homosexuality, see the comments by Ibn Ezra to these verses in Leviticus and to Deut. 27:15–25.

11. For my own analysis of the need for an egalitarian wedding ceremony, equally applicable to gays and straights, see "Equality and Sanctity: Rethinking Jewish Marriage in Theory and in Ceremony," first published in *G'vanim* 5:1 (2009): 1–35. It is available at the AJR website, http://ajrsem.org/uploads/docs/greenstein69.pdf, or at my synagogue website, http://www.shomrei.org/media.asp?catid=16&showdetails=1.

12. From http://www.religioustolerance.org/hom_jother.htm. "Homosexuality and Judaism: The Reconstructionist Position," quoted in http://www.jewishrecon.org/resource/becoming-kehillah-mekabelet

13. Resolution on Same Gender Offication. http://ccarnet.org/rabbis-speak/resolutions/2000/same-gender-officiation/

14. "On Homosexual Marriage," *CCAR Journal: A Reform Jewish Quarterly*, Winter 1998, 5–35.

15. Ibid., 17. For subsequent discussion see, out of many examples, the essay by Rabbi Peter S. Knobel, "*Kiddushin:* An Equal Opportunity Covenant, Not Only for Heterosexuals," *CCAR Journal*, Fall 2005, 20–34. On pp. 24–25, he endorses Rabbi Steven Greenberg's reading of the verses in Leviticus.

16. The responsa are available at the CJLS website, http://www.rabbinicalassembly.org/law/new_teshuvot.html.

17. "Homosexuality, Human Dignity and Halakhah," by Rabbis Elliot Dorff, Daniel Nevins, and Avram Reisner. There were two other permissive *t'shuvot* that were not accepted by the committee as legitimate positions because they were deemed *takanot* and did not receive the requisite number of votes, though they may have passed had they been deemed to be mere responsa. The two *t'shuvot* are "A New Context: The Halakhah of Same-Sex Relations," by Rabbis Myron Geller, Robert Fine, and David Fine, and "Halakhic and Metahalakhic Arguments concerning Judaism and Homosexuality," by Rabbi Gordon Tucker. For discussion of the strengths and weaknesses of those responsa, see my more extensive essay, cited above.

18. Indeed, the permissibility of anal intercourse for straights was not obvious to the rabbis, since it involved a clearly non-procreative act. They deduced its legitimacy from none other than the verse that, according to Rabbis Dorff, Nevins, and Reisner, prohibits anal intercourse for gays—Leviticus 18:22! See Babylonian Talmud, *Sanhedrin* 54a, and S. Greenberg, *Wrestling*, 284, n. 30.

19. This topic is treated in his earlier *t'shuvah* "Homosexuality," in *Responsa: 1991–2000*, Committee on Jewish Laws and Standards of the Conservative Movement, ed. Kassell Abelson and David J. Fine (New York: Rabbinical Assembly, 2002), 613–75. On p. 615 he writes, "The term *to'evah* in the Torah does not refer to an

inherent quality of an act. Acts are *to'evah* because the Torah calls them *to'evah*. 'Abhorrence' is not an inherent quality of the act, it is an attributed quality."

20. Seth Goldstein, "Reading *Toevah*: Biblical Scholarship and Difficult Texts," *The Reconstructionist* 67, no. 2 (Spring 2003): 48–60.

21. Ibid., 55.

22. Ibid., 57.

23. *CCAR Journal*, Fall 2005, 5–19.

24. Ibid., 16.

25. Ibid., 18.

26. A similar argument can be made for the use of the term in Deut. 25:13–16. For a fuller discussion, see my earlier essay, as mentioned above.

27. See also Gen. 6:9 (and Gen. 4:1).

28. See Rachel Adler, *Engendering Judaism: An Inclusive Theology and Ethics* (Philadelphia: Jewish Publication Society, 1998), 105–67, for a forceful discussion of the lacunae and shortcomings of the Torah's code of sexual ethics when the Torah is limited to a traditional reading.

5

HOW TO RESPOND TO
BIBLE-THUMPING HOMOPHOBIA
OR:
JUDAISM AS EVOLUTIONARY
IF NOT REVOLUTIONARY
Rabbi Karen Bender

What is it about feelings toward homosexuality that suddenly and situationally transform some people into fundamentalists? Those who do not consult biblical texts for any other decisions in life will cite Leviticus to support anti-homosexual views. Many people who knowingly choose to violate scores of laws from Torah will treat Leviticus 18 and 20 as authoritative in defining the homosexual act as an abomination.

Their argument feels strong because it seems grounded in Torah. Regardless of how we may feel about this subject today, one cannot deny that Jews and Christians have referenced Leviticus 18 and 20 as the basis for formulating their anti-gay views for millennia. That is to say, to use Leviticus 18 and 20 as a basis for forging a Jewish view against gays and lesbians is hardly radical. On the contrary, until recently, it has always been normative to do so. You could even argue that there has been a Jewish tradition against homosexuality since the time the Torah was written and that until very recently Jewish leaders have never refuted the prohibitions against homosexuality.

Then how should those of us who embrace homosexuality as natural and valid respond to such Bible-thumping homophobia? We must respond by refusing to begin the discussion where the homophobes wish to begin the discussion. They want to begin with the prohibitive texts of Leviticus. There is always room to address the Levitical prohibitions later. We must insist instead on beginning with philosophy instead of text, with reason instead of emotion, with the history of Jewish process instead of the history of Jewish discrimination.

Instead of addressing Bible-based homophobia with a response to Leviticus 18 and 20, begin with the assertion that Judaism is evolutionary. Judaism has evolved since its inception, changing and adapting to modernity, cultures, and discoveries in science. When necessary, Judaism has been not just evolutionary, but revolutionary. Begin with the notion of *takanah*, because the very existence of *takanah* in Jewish history proves that Judaism evolves. Judaism has never been rigid or set in stone, but malleable rather, like the parchment of a scroll.

Consider the meaning of the word *takanah*. Its root is *tav-kuf-nun*, which means "repair." How fascinating that the Rabbis, in naming revolutionary revision in halachah (Jewish law), did not choose a word such as *shinui* (change) or *hafichah* (reversal). They chose the word *takanah*. The very term *takanah*, as opposed to a term like *shinui* or *hafichah*, implies that the halachah is somehow flawed and in need of repair.

Take, for example, the *takanah* of Rabbeinu Gershom, the tenth-century head of the Talmudic academy of Mainz. Modernity had determined that the biblical allowance of men marrying up to four wives had become untenable, unfashionable, or perhaps even immoral by the standards and norms of that time. Rabbeinu Gershom issued a *takanah* against polygamy, practiced by some Jewish communities up to that time, legislating a *cherem* (ban) on Jewish men marrying more than one woman. A less known *takanah* of Rabbeinu Gershom, though just as interesting, was his elimination of a husband's right to divorce without his wife's consent. Previously, unilateral divorce was permitted. Gershom's "repair" of the law included wives in the process of divorce.

While the term *takanah* is often translated as "ordinance," a more literal understanding of the term is that it is a repair of the law. Halachah, then, is sometimes in need of repair.

Even before *takanot* had begun to be instituted, Jewish tradition asserted its ability to override and reverse its own decrees, laws, and precedents. Deuteronomy 23:4 states, "No Ammonite or Moabite shall be admitted into the congregation of the Eternal; none of their descendants, even in the tenth generation, shall ever be admitted into the congregation of the Eternal." And yet we know from the Book of Ruth that Ruth is a Moabite and a convert, even the progenitor of King David and thus progenitor of the Messiah! The fact that the Book of Ruth reverses the law against intermarriage with Moabites is one example of the ways in which Judaism has evolved. This proves that Jewish authorities have not historically felt bound to blindly enforce prior norms. Rather, they felt free to effect change so that Judaism could change and thrive.

The first Jewish step in responding to Bible-thumping homophobia is thus to establish and demonstrate that Judaism is a living, dynamic religious system. In so doing, one can dislodge oneself from feeling bound to early texts that are anti-homosexual.

Another method of confronting anti-gay Bible thumpers who insist on the authority of biblical texts is to challenge them with texts that undermine the use of Torah to marginalize homosexuals. Turn, for example, to Leviticus 19:18, which says, "Love your neighbor as yourself," and explain that Bible-based rage toward homosexuals violates Leviticus 19:18. Explore Genesis 1:27, where we learn about all human beings created in "the image of God," and help the Bible-thumping homophobe understand that homosexuals are made in God's image too.

Once you have cited loving texts from the Torah, it is important to identify the pathology of the homophobe, as opposed to the pathology of the homosexual or the abomination of the homosexual act. To do so, there is value in consulting contributions from the modern philosopher Jean-Paul Sartre, who took upon himself the task of understanding anti-Semitism from the anti-Semite's point of view. Though Sartre is neither a rabbi nor a Jewish scholar, his analysis is remarkably applicable and useful.

Jean-Paul Sartre's book *Anti-Semite and Jew* is a great tool in demonstrating this point because of the fascinating parallel between

Bible-thumping homophobia and early twentieth-century European anti-Semitism. Sartre asserts that anti-Semitism was erroneously perceived in France to be a normal and even dignified form of thinking among French Christians. "A man may be a good father and good husband, a conscientious citizen, highly cultivated, philanthropic, *and* in addition an anti-Semite."[1] According to Sartre, hatred toward Jews by Christian Frenchmen was as socially acceptable and legitimate as having an affinity toward one political party or another.

Sartre further explains that for most French gentiles, Jews were physically and emotionally revolting. In fact, it was common to feel repulsed by Jews:

> There is a disgust for the Jew, just as there is a disgust for the Chinese or the Negro among certain people. Thus it is not from the body that the sense of repulsion arises, since one may love a Jewess very well if one does not know what her race is; rather it is something that enters the body from the mind. It is an involvement of the mind, but one so deep-seated and complete that it extends to the physiological realm, as happens in cases of hysteria.[2]

But Sartre concludes that Jews are ultimately not the problem. Rather, anti-Semitism is. "I do not say that these . . . conceptions are necessarily contradictory. I do say that they are dangerous and false."[3] In other words, anti-Semitism is the pathology, not Jewishness. This is Sartre's epiphany, which he wants to share with an anti-Semitic France in the aftermath of the Holocaust and France's willing participation in eliminating Jews.

Similarly, homophobia places the homosexual in a pathological light. Considering the Sartre lens, this notion needs to be turned on its head. Homosexuality is not the pathology; homophobia is. Homosexuality is not the sin; homophobia is the sin.

In the concluding pages of his book Sartre writes, "Richard Wright, the Negro writer, said recently: 'There is no Negro problem in the United States, there is only a White problem.' In the same way, we must say that anti-Semitism is not a Jewish problem; it is *our* problem."[4] Homophobia, Bible-based or not, is not a gay problem; it is a straight problem. Homophobia today is also a Jewish problem, because the organized Jewish community and Jewish authorities are obligated not only to be tolerant, but to compensate for early Jewish texts that are hostile toward homosexuality and can be used against GLBTQ people today.

Having demonstrated that Judaism is evolutionary, if not revolutionary, having considered Torah texts that command us to love one's neighbor and to love the stranger, and having compared anti-gay sentiment to anti-Semitism, one can turn to the fateful texts of Leviticus that the Bible-thumping homophobe considers to be central and authoritative. Those of us who apply the evolutionary nature of Judaism to the modern understanding of homosexuality do not like these texts, but we cannot avoid them. In fact, we must address them.

Leviticus 18:22 reads, "Do not lie with a male as one lies with a woman; it is an abhorrence." And Leviticus 20:13 states, "If a man lies with a male as one lies with a woman, the two of them have done an abhorrent thing; they shall be put to death—and they retain their bloodguilt." For the anti-gay fundamentalist, these two texts prove their point of view. Case closed—the Torah does not accept homosexuality. In fact, the Torah finds it abhorrent!

There are multiple weaknesses in this argument. First, from a Jewish perspective, Judaism is fundamentally non-fundamentalist. The Karaites attempted to propagate a fundamentalist approach to Judaism, and they were unsuccessful. Had the Karaites been successful, then they would be thriving today. But instead, Rabbinic Judaism, with its acceptance of multiple and conflicting interpretations of Torah, is the Judaism that took hold and is the basis for modern Jewish living. That is because authentic Judaism is Torah with commentary.

Next, the act forbidden in Leviticus seems to be anal intercourse. Could two men engage in sexual activity that does not include anal intercourse and even get married without violating Leviticus 18 and 20? There is nothing stated in the Torah forbidding other acts between men, and there is nothing stated in Torah forbidding lesbian sexuality whatsoever. Would the Bible-thumping homophobe, who uses Leviticus 18 and 20 as proof of God's or Judaism's prohibition of homosexuality, be willing to agree that the Torah does not forbid lesbianism or gay marriage or other sexual acts between men? Would he or she then agree that these other acts are acceptable?

Furthermore, do people who reference Leviticus 18 and 20 as proof that homosexuality is wrong also accept as binding and authoritative all of the other positive and negative commandments found in Torah? Do they believe in the enforcement of Exodus 31:14, "You shall keep the Sabbath, for it is holy for you. One who profanes it shall be put to death"? Do they believe in the enforcement of Exodus 21:17, "One who insults one's father or mother shall be put to death"? How about Deuteronomy 21:18–21, "If a parent has a wayward and defiant son, who does not heed his father or mother and does not obey them even after they discipline him, his father and mother shall take hold of him and bring him out to the elders of his town at the public place of his community. They shall say to the elders of his town, 'This son of ours is disloyal and defiant; he does not heed us. He is a glutton and a drunkard.' Thereupon the residents of his town shall stone him to death"? Do they believe in Deuteronomy 22:28, "If a man comes upon a virgin who is not engaged and he seizes her and lies with her, and they are discovered, the man who lay with her shall pay the girl's father fifty [shekels of] silver, and she shall be his wife. Because he has violated her, he can never have the right to divorce her"?

If the Bible-thumping homophobe holds Leviticus 18 and 20 as authoritative proof against homosexuality but does not agree that Exodus and Deuteronomy are proof that violators of Shabbat and defiant children should be killed or that rape victims are required to marry their rapists, then they are engaging in selective fundamentalism. Selective fundamentalism is the act of holding as authoritative biblical verses that you like, but rejecting as irrelevant biblical verses that you don't like.

The question is, who gives anyone the authority to impose selected biblical verses on other people but not all verses upon themselves?

How does a Bible-thumping homophobe defend such selective fundamentalism and inconsistency of biblical authority?

And are so-called Torah-true Jews or fundamentalists consistent, or are they practicing selective fundamentalism as well?

Jews who cite Leviticus as a basis for heterosexism do have the added support of later halachic passages that even further restrict homosexuals and add lesbianism to the list of forbidden conduct. While on the face of it one might think that this substantiates the use of Leviticus for an anti-gay Jewish perspective, in fact the *Shulchan Aruch* and other texts that deal with homosexuality are addressing homosexuality in their time as a modern reality. Therefore, the rabbis who expanded restrictions on homosexuals in their texts during their times ironically invite modern Jewish leaders to also apply modern sensibilities to the issue of homosexuality.

There is also value in noting that the authors of Torah could not have imagined what we would today consider to be constitutional homosexuality. They could not have conceived that some people are born with an attraction to members of the same sex that is akin to the attraction that heterosexuals feel toward members of the opposite sex. In their world, everyone was heterosexual, and so homosexual acts were perceived as unnatural, cultic, and violating societal norms. It is impossible for us to know what their views and laws would have been had they enjoyed the psychological insights of today. But one could assume that the biblical writers, who were so devoted to justice, charity, and compassion, would certainly have written Leviticus 18 and 20 differently had they understood, as we do, constitutional homosexuality—had they understood that homosexuality is natural for a certain segment of the population.

The final question to address on the subject of responding to Bible-thumping homophobia is how does Jewish tradition feel about differences in the human family? Two types of texts speak directly to this question. The first is the multiplicity of occurrences in the Torah of quotes like "You must love the stranger, for you were strangers in the land of Egypt" (Deut. 10:19). The stranger is referenced as having a special entitlement to our love. Why? Because we were hated strangers in Egypt and we have a collective memory of that pain, a collective empathy for the plight of the one who is different and unwelcome. Texts like Deuteronomy 10:19 speak not of mere tolerance but of love for the one who is so different that he or she makes us uncomfortable.

Also germane to the question of how Jewish tradition addresses differences in the human family is a relatively unknown text from the Jerusalem Talmud: "One who sees a black-, a red-, or a white-skinned person, or a hunchback, or a midget says, 'Blessed [are You, Eternal our God, Ruler of the universe,] who diversifies [*m'shaneh*] the creatures" (*B'rachot* 9:1).

Here is a powerful expectation from the Rabbinic tradition. This is not asking us, as Torah does, to love or to feel a certain way toward the stranger. Rather, we are asked to make an affirmative blessing upon seeing someone who is different from us, a blessing that praises God for making people dissimilar from each other. We bless God for having created human diversity.

The Jerusalem Talmud states, "From a person's blessings one can tell whether he is a boor or a disciple of sages" (*B'rachot* 1:4). We define ourselves by the blessings we offer in the world. Many are bent on cursing those who are different. Many are determined to use biblical texts as a justification for cursing those who are different, in particular homosexuals, who would today be called members of the LGBTQ community. But the truth is that we do not define homosexuals by the curses or blessings that we bestow upon them, by the tolerance we grant, or the love we withhold. On the contrary, by the curses or blessing we choose to bestow upon others, we define ourselves.

NOTES

1. Jean-Paul Sartre, *Anti-Semite and Jew* (New York: Schocken Books, 1995), 8.
2. Ibid., 11.
3. Ibid., 9.
4. Ibid., 152.

6

PREACHING AGAINST THE TEXT

An Argument in Favor of Restoring Leviticus 18 to Yom Kippur Afternoon

RABBI JEFFREY BROWN

This essay will seek to argue for the restoration of Leviticus 18 to its traditional place as the Torah reading during our Yom Kippur *Minchah* services. To be sure, at first glance this will be a most unpopular idea. There is, after all, much that is strongly objectionable about the contents of this infamous chapter. This author is cognizant of, and particularly interested in, the tragic and painful history surrounding Leviticus 18:22 and its problematic and complicated impact on Western and Jewish sexuality.

It would be easy (and politically correct) for us[1] to designate Leviticus 19 (or another appropriately themed passage) as the proper reading instead. Nonetheless, I shall seek to argue that doing so would constitute a missed opportunity for our communities and their GLBTQ constituents/allies.

Introduction

Baruch Levine sums up the chapter in question as follows:

Chapter 18 is the most systematic and complete collection of laws within the Torah dealing with the subject of incest and other forbidden sexual unions. It outlines in detail which unions among relatives within the ancient Israelite clan are forbidden on grounds of incest, adultery, and so on; and in so doing, it indirectly defines the limits of the immediate family.[2]

Our halachic tradition reads the verses of this chapter as the foundation for the set of prohibitions known as *gilui arayot* (uncovering of nakedness).

Our more particular concern, here, is 18:22. In some parts of the Conservative[3] and Orthodox worlds today, that verse's prohibition against gay male sex still carries the weight of law to varying degrees. Thus, ArtScroll notes, in absolute terms:

> The chapter of [sexual] immorality ends with two forms of sexual perversion: homosexuality and bestiality. The harshness with which the Torah describes them testifies to the repugnance in which God holds those who engage in these unnatural practices. . . . None of the relationships given above are described with this term of disgust, because they involve normal activity, though with prohibited mates. Homosexuality, however, is unnatural and therefore abominable.[4]

It need not be stated here, in this forum, that the Reform Movement's modern understanding of sexuality and sexual orientation diverges from the traditional Jewish view. We have sought to position ourselves at/near the forefront of the gay rights movement within the wider Jewish community. As early as 1977, the UAHC resolved to support equal rights for gays and lesbians, and to work against discrimination aimed at the gay community.[5]

In that spirit, it is not surprising to find such a different reading of Leviticus 18:22 in the URJ/WRJ's *The Torah: A Women's Commentary:*

> In the early 21st century, this is one of the most misinterpreted, abused, and decontextualized verses in the Torah. This verse, ripped from its place in the system of levitical laws, is often mobilized to justify discriminatory legislation and behavior against

homosexuals and their families. While the act of anal intercourse would present a problem to the person who organized his life according to the levitical laws, it has no place in judicial systems not governed by the total system of Leviticus—and does not cohere with contemporary sexual notions of mutual consent and sexual preference.[6]

Those of us (and our communities) who agree with this approach (and who, by extension, seek to lift up those who identify as GLBTQ) face a unique problem. How are we to navigate the annual question of whether or not to read Leviticus 18 on Yom Kippur afternoon, as Jewish tradition indicates? How do we resolve the tension between honoring the tradition that has been passed down to us, on the one hand, with our contemporary interpretation of that tradition, on the other?

Why Do We Traditionally Read Leviticus 18 on Yom Kippur Afternoon? Do Any Non-Orthodox *Machzorim* Still Follow the Custom?

The custom of reading Leviticus 18 on Yom Kippur afternoon comes to us from the Babylonian Talmud. *M'gilah* 31a notes, "On [the morning of] the Day of Atonement we read from the section that begins with *acharei mot*. . . . At *Minchah* we read the *arayot*."

Why was Leviticus 18 chosen for the afternoon service? Rashi, commenting on *M'gilah* 31a, implies that Yom Kippur reminds us of all of the prohibitions that we are supposed to follow. Yet, at the same time, he highlights sexual transgressions. For Rashi, there is something unique (and threatening) about the ability of a person's "carnal desire" to "overwhelm" his ability to make good choices. This, according to Rashi, explains the Rabbis' choice of a Torah reading that is aimed at convincing people to refrain from the particular prohibitions of Leviticus 18.

Steinsaltz echoes Rashi by noting, "These readings are meant to arouse the sinners to repentance, and to evoke feelings of remorse among those who have not yet sinned, but who may yet be carried away by the desires of their hearts."[7]

Quoting *Otzar HaGeonim* (an early twentieth-century anthology of geonic Talmud commentary),[8] Agnon offers a similar explanation for the reading:

> The reason why the section about incest [Leviticus 18] is read during the Afternoon Prayer on Yom Kippur is because there is no atoning for sins on Yom Kippur until one has turned in Teshuvah. Hence, we read the section about incest so that if, God forbid, one of the children of Israel shall have broken the prohibition against incest, he will remember his transgression as soon as the prohibition is read before him, and will turn in Teshuvah, that he may be forgiven.[9]

Like Rashi, *Otzar HaGeonim* privileges sexual ethics above the rest of the values that constitute Jewish morality. Both believe that if there is one subcategory of transgressions that is especially problematic—one kind of sin that Judaism should specifically convince violators to stop committing—then this is the one. And our sources imply that the best way to do that is by shining the proverbial spotlight on this sin: by reading Leviticus 18 on Yom Kippur afternoon.

There are several other, perhaps less convincing, explanations as to why the Rabbis chose Leviticus 18 as the *Minchah* reading:

1. It seems that some of the Rabbis were convinced that service attendees would leave the synagogue after the conclusion of Yom Kippur and proceed directly to an illicit sexual encounter! Thus, *Mishnah Taanit* 4:8:

   > Rabban Shimon ben Gamliel used to say: The happiest days [on the Jewish calendar] for Israel were the fifteenth of Av and the Day of Atonement. For on those days the daughters of Jerusalem would go out dressed in white. . . . And what did they used to say? "Young man, lift up your eyes and select for yourself [a wife]."

1. According to this text, Yom Kippur afternoon was a time of intense joy and celebration. For the Rabbis of the Mishnah, it was

natural to celebrate the joy of the conclusion of Yom Kippur by encouraging young people to go out into the hills of Jerusalem to meet each other. Therefore *M'gilah* 31a indicates Leviticus 18 as the *Minchah* Torah reading: as a reminder to those revelers about boundaries not to be transgressed.[10]

2. Bernard Zlotowitz, writing in *CCAR Journal* in 1975, creatively argues that Leviticus 18 and the rest of the High Holy Day scriptural readings might be understood in the context of a commentary on Christianity. Zlotowitz asserts:

> The Rabbis included *arayot* [and the other High Holy Day scriptural readings] primarily as an attack against Christianity. Paul had taught that once Jesus came, the Law was no longer obligatory. Such rituals as circumcision, dietary laws, and Sabbath need no longer be observed. But certain early Christians, in their zeal to overthrow the Torah, rejected the moral as well as the ceremonial law. . . . Under the circumstances, what would be more natural as a Scripture lesson for Yom Kippur than *arayot* as an anti-Christian polemic? Proper sexual behavior was the very foundation of Jewish family survival. . . . In the context of the times, this passage was certainly another natural refutation of Christianity.[11]

3. Ismar Elbogen, in a footnote buried in the back of his *Jewish Liturgy: A Comprehensive History*, explains, "They would read Lev. 18 as a continuation of the morning pericope [Leviticus 16]."[12] Plainly, he observes that the Rabbis of *M'gilah* 31a designated Leviticus 18 as the Torah reading on the afternoon of Yom Kippur because they saw it as the logical "continuation" of that which had been read in the morning.[13]

Now that our survey of traditional explanations for Leviticus 18 is complete, let us survey the non-Orthodox *machzorim* of the last century to witness how those who came before us chose to navigate this question. To begin with, let us note how indebted we are to Zlotowitz[14] for his comprehensive survey of liberal liturgies through the mid-twentieth century. The chart on the next page summarizes his findings with regard to Yom Kippur afternoon Torah readings:

Machzor Title	Year Published	Location	Torah Reading
Seder HaAvodah[15]	1841	Hamburg	Lev. 18
Olath Tamid (Einhorn)	1858	USA	Lev. 19:1–37
Minhag America (Wise)	1866	USA	Exod. 32:11–14; 34:1–10
Avodath Israel (Szold and Jastrow)	1873	USA	Lev. 19:1–18
Seder HaAvodah	1904	Hamburg	Lev. 19:1–18
Seder T'filah	1908	Stuttgart	Lev. 18
Gebetuch fuer die Neue Synagogue	1922	Berlin	Lev. 19:1–18
Union Prayer Book	1922	USA	Exod. 33:12–34:10
Liberal Jewish Prayer Book	1923	London	Lev. 19:1–4, 19:9–18
Forms of Prayer	1929	London	Deut. 30:1–20
Union Prayer Book	1945	USA	Lev. 19:1–4, 19:9–18, 19:33–37

Unfortunately, there are few sources at our disposal that indicate *why* these *machzorim* made the choices that they did. We can only speculate that the content of Leviticus 18 was not edifying[16] in some way to the nine communities who chose to indicate new Torah readings.

The inclination to ignore *M'gilah* 31a and its advice about Leviticus 18 is a trend that has persisted in all of the following liberal *machzorim* of the last few decades:

- Our own *Gates of Repentance* (1984) offers only one choice for the reading (largely following the *Union Prayer Book* of 1945): Leviticus 19:1–4, 9–18, 32–37. Although *Gates of Repentance* does not include marginalia/commentary within the book itself, we do have access to Lawrence Hoffman's *Gates of Understanding 2* for context on how some of the key editing decisions were made. Regarding the issue before us, Hoffman writes:

We saw above that Reform practice prefers Torah and Haftarah readings with themes appropriate to the spiritual expectations of modern worshippers. On Yom Kippur morning, for example, we read Deuteronomy 29–30, on human responsibility, rather than the traditional selection, Leviticus 16, which describes sacrifice. Here, too, it has been customary for us to replace the traditional reading of Leviticus 18 with selections from Leviticus 19, which is part of what Bible scholars call the Holiness Code. It details a series of ethical actions entailed in our striving for holiness.[17]

Note that *Gates of Understanding 2* does not specify which of the many problematic elements of Leviticus 18 fail to meet the "spiritual expectations of modern worshippers" threshold.[18]

- For its Yom Kippur afternoon Torah reading, *Forms of Prayer* (Reform Synagogues of Great Britain, 1985) follows in the footsteps of its forebears by choosing Deuteronomy 30:8–20.[19]

- *On Wings of Awe* (B'nai B'rith Hillel Foundations, 1985), edited by Richard Levy, denotes Leviticus 18 as the primary reading and Leviticus 19:1–18, 32–37 as an "alternative reading."[20]

- *Kavvanat HaLev* (IMPJ, 1988–1989) offers Leviticus 19:1–18. And *Kol HaNeshamah: Prayerbook for the Days of Awe* (Reconstructionist Press, 1999) indicates the same reading, with the caveat: "Some communities that have not read *Nitzavim* (Deut. 29:9–30:20) in the morning may choose to substitute it here."

- *Machzor Ruach Chadashah* (Liberal Judaism [UK], 2003) suggests the same reading as *Gates of Repentance*. The editors explain their reasoning in the Notes section at the back of the prayer book: "In common with many Progressive *machzorim*, we replace the traditional reading from the Torah for YK afternoon, Lev. 18, with this selection from that section of Leviticus known as the Holiness Code, whose moral *dicta* are so appropriate to this day."[21]

Breaking the Silence

A few words must be offered here as to why this author believes that the liturgical strategy of simply offering an alternative Torah reading is inadequate on Yom Kippur afternoon. To be sure, I would generally affirm the longstanding Reform practice of choosing liturgical/ lectionary selections that meet the "spiritual expectations of modern worshippers" (as Hoffman puts it). As a proud Reform clergyperson, that methodology is an important part of my rabbinate.

I would argue here, however, that Leviticus 18 (on Yom Kippur afternoon) is an extraordinary example of a reading that cannot be washed away so quickly. We are faced with a double challenge: an occasion that demands that we be even more mindful than usual of our liturgical choices; and a confrontation with the subject of homophobia, and the intolerance that it has engendered over two and a half millennia.

To read an alternate selection of Torah without explaining why the alternate reading was chosen (which is exactly what *Gates of Repentance* and all of the rest of the *machzorim* cited above do) is problematic. To do so is to argue with the Torah: in silence, and from silence. And this argument from silence, like so many others, is not convincing. It simply ignores the pain of our GLBTQ friends by pretending that Leviticus 18:22 does not exist,[22] and it does not address the problems that the text raises.

Some of my colleagues will suggest that the exact opposite is true: that choosing an alternative reading on Yom Kippur afternoon in the twenty-first century does in fact address the problem at hand. For they would argue that an alternative reading is done, *davka*, out of respect for our GLBTQ friends and their allies (so as to shield them from the pain that might be caused by having to listen to Leviticus 18). But I would humbly and respectfully disagree with this assertion. To do an alternative reading without acknowledging why—without critiquing 18:22 out loud—is to miss an opportunity to do more substantial *tikkun*: to redeem our sacred but flawed Torah and bring a small measure of healing to the members of our community who have suffered under the heterocentrism of our Jewish and secular cultures. Steven Greenberg articulates this so much more effectively, when he writes:

> But while I do not wish to minimize the pain of the thousands before us who were tormented by these bits of ink and parchment, I believe these words to be a site of reckoning and of potential re-demption. The Hebrew name of the Book of Leviticus, Vayikra, roughly means, "And the Lord called." So, let us imagine that we are now all called upon to stand before the open scroll, to read, and to be read.[23]

To seek "reckoning" and "potential redemption"—isn't that what Yom Kippur is all about? How does silently acquiescing to a more tasteful Torah reading bring that about? Wittgenstein postulated that "what we cannot speak about we must pass over in silence." That may be true. But we *can*, and must, speak about Leviticus 18. We must speak the truth and call the Torah what is: a holy but imperfect document.[24]

A minimalist approach to this strategy might mimic the practice of Congregation Beth Chayim Chadashim (BCC), a URJ-affiliated synagogue that seeks to sustain "a Jewish community for gay, lesbian, bisexual and transgender Jews, while welcoming all who wish to make community."[25] Lisa Edwards reports that it is BCC's practice to read Leviticus 19, but to "always" mention the traditional practice of read-ing Leviticus 18 on Yom Kippur afternoon.[26] Even as BCC follows *Gates of Repentance* in not reading Leviticus 18, they have broken the silence by offering a soft rebuke of it.

Plaskow, Not *P'shat*

Two recent non-Orthodox *machzorim* choose a more aggressive ap-proach. They have both designated Leviticus 18 as the primary To-rah reading. But, to accompany those readings, these *machzorim* offer commentaries and marginal notes. Their pairing of Torah text with modern commentary asserts that it is possible to read Leviticus 18 on Yom Kippur *and* be sensitive to the needs of our GLBTQ members and their allies at the same time.

Mahzor Hadesh Yameinu (Ronald Aigen, 2001) is one such example. The *machzor* was written by the rabbi of Canada's oldest Reconstructionist synagogue (Congregation Dorshei Emet). There we find that the primary Torah reading for Yom Kippur afternoon is Leviticus 18. An alternate reading (Lev. 19:1–18) is also offered.

Leviticus 18 might seem like a surprising choice, given the Reconstructionist Movement's long history[27] of welcome/openness to lesbian and gay congregants. Note, however, how the *machzor* seeks to offer an alternative understanding of Leviticus 18. Here is what Aigen writes for the explanatory note that accompanies 18:22:

> The term *to'eivah*, "abhorrence," is used in the Torah to describe a wide variety of objectionable practices, from forbidden eating practices (Genesis 43:32); to the prohibition of remarrying a divorced wife if she had subsequently married and been divorced from a second man (Deuteronomy 24:4); as well as the proscription against using unjust weights and measures (Deuteronomy 25:16). In all these cases, the term *to'eivah* refers to behaviors which are assumed to be learned and volitional. The biblical view of homosexuality did not share the contemporary understanding of sexual orientation, whether heterosexual or homosexual, as a biological given. It is on the basis of this understanding of homosexuality that contemporary liberal communities have declared that the biblical category of *to'eivah* should no longer apply in this case. Homosexual males and lesbian females ought not to be condemned for who they are, but rather fully included in the life of the community together with their partners and children.[28]

A similar strategy of printing progressive commentary on the margins of the traditional lectionary reading can be found in *Machzor Lev Shalem* (Rabbinical Assembly, 2010). In addition to appropriate historical and anthropological explanations of Leviticus 18, the *machzor* quotes a passage by Elliot Dorff on the connection between our own individual (sexual) choices and the way that those ethical choices reflect on the rest of the Jewish people: "In this, as in other areas of life, our actions should be a *kiddush hashem*, a sanctification of God's name."[29] The *machzor* then goes out of its way (like *Hadesh Yameinu*) to address 18:22

and the overriding question of the status of lesbians and gays by offering two important pieces of commentary contributed by Judith Plaskow.

Here, we must note the significant influence that Plaskow's 1997 article "Sexuality and *Teshuvah*: Leviticus 18"[30] had on the editors of both *Hadesh Yameinu*[31] and *Machzor Lev Shalem*.

Plaskow begins that piece by situating herself:

> As someone who has long been disturbed by the content of Le-viticus 18, I had always applauded the substitution of an alternative Torah reading—until a particular incident made me reconsider the link between sex and Yom Kippur. After a lecture I delivered in the spring of 1995 on rethinking Jewish attitudes toward sexuality, a woman approached me very distressed. She belonged to a Con-servative synagogue that had abandoned the practice of reading Leviticus 18 on Yom Kippur, and as a victim of childhood sexual abuse by her grandfather, she felt betrayed by that decision. While she was not necessarily committed to the understanding of sexual holiness contained in Leviticus, she felt that in quietly changing the reading without communal discussion, her congregation had avoided issues of sexual responsibility altogether.[32]

Plaskow goes on to argue that Yom Kippur is an occasion for Jewish communities to "connect the theme of atonement with issues of behav-ior in intimate relationships." Like Rashi, Plaskow privileges sexual acts by putting them into a category that deserves special attention on our Day of Atonement. All of this in the hope of bringing a greater sense of healing to victims, perpetrators, and our communities.

Plaskow suggests that Leviticus 18 can be a valuable teaching tool. The text, she argues, has the ability to prompt important and frank conversations. For Plaskow, the possibility of these conversations is not limited to sexual abuse; rather, she reminds us that Leviticus 18 can be a useful opening for reflections on sexuality and on sexual eth-ics in general. Each in their own way, *Hadesh Yameinu* and *Machzor Lev Shalem* (as well as Levy 1985, through his translation of 18:22) have sought to do this. Using strategically chosen commentary (in *Lev Shalem*'s case there are two selections[33] borrowed from Plaskow's article), the editors of these *machzorim* have indicated to worshipers that the Torah text has something to offer us that goes beyond the offensive and problematic *p'shat*.

Plaskow reminds us that we have a choice. We need not avoid Leviticus 18 for fear of making our communities uncomfortable. For our tradition doesn't just give us permission to read this difficult text out loud. It also empowers us to *use* it: for our purposes and our agenda.

Plaskow suggests one possible use: coupling the reading with a conversation about sex ethics. To illustrate her vision, she appends a document to her article that summarizes her own *chavurah*'s values on this important topic. Selections from "The Su Kasha Ethic"[34] can be used as a study text in communities that might be open to that kind of creative discussion experience on Yom Kippur afternoon.

To take up Plaskow's suggestion (as *Lev Shalem* in particular has done)[35] would be a noble and worthwhile expression of *tikkun* and *t'shuvah* in and of itself. When we use Leviticus 18 for our purposes (rather than the purposes that are implicit in the *p'shat* reading of the text) we begin to redeem a broken and shameful text.

It is this author's contention, however, that *Hadesh Yameinu* and *Lev Shalem* could have gone further. The commentaries and marginal notes that they include do not adequately express the pain and hurt that so many generations of our gay and lesbian ancestors have suffered because of the close-mindedness of this text.

Thus, we are presented with an opportunity. As our new CCAR *machzor* is drafted, and as we come together to reimagine newly relevant, challenging, and uplifting High Holy Day worship, we don't just have the chance to follow in the worthy footsteps of *Hadesh Yameinu* and *Lev Shalem* by opening a conversation on Yom Kippur about Jewish sex ethics in general. We can also take up *Hadesh Yameinu* and *Lev Shalem*'s cause and move it one step forward: by having our new *machzor* instruct (or by worship leaders enabling) our communities to actively preach against the text.

Plaskow Redux: Preaching against the Text

Preaching against the text, by actively asserting that the Torah is (occasionally) wrong, is an approach that my homiletics teachers advised against at Hebrew Union College–Jewish Institute of Religion. At the time, it never occurred to me to question their advice. But since my ordination, I have come to conclude that there are many legitimate uses for such a methodology. First among them is an awareness on my part that preaching against the text affirms my progressive identity. Divine or Mosaic authorship are notions that are outside of my own theology. To assert human authorship of the Torah (as I do) is to admit that our text is sometimes flawed, just as we are.

I know that I am not alone in these beliefs among my Reform colleagues. Many, if not most, of my friends in the Reform rabbinate take these same principles for granted. Yet, how many liberal colleagues take the "risk" of preaching against the text when it violates an obvious core belief? All too often, we choose another part of the *parashah* to preach on instead, or cite a Rabbinic text[36] that tries to make something terribly problematic just disappear.[37]

There is an established discourse on these matters in liberal Christian circles. For example, consider the work of the late Peter Gomes. Citing Roland Bainton, Gomes warns against "Protestant America's bibliolatry, the worship of the text of scripture and its elevation as the sole norm of faith and practice."[38] Gomes goes on to write:

> In addressing a moral issue with both public and personal implications on the basis of Christian principles derived from a reading of the Bible, rather than simply on the basis of biblical practice and precedent, Bainton liberates us from a simpleminded bondage to texts whose context may be unrelated and unhelpful to our own. *In other words, to be biblical may well mean to move beyond the Bible itself to the larger principles that can be derived from Christian faith of which the Bible is a part, but for which the Bible cannot possibly be a substitute. To determine with what Christian principles one reads the Bible is to undertake an enterprise that requires more rather than less engagement with the Bible and with the cultures of its interpretation. It involves a*

rather daunting effort to see beyond the diversions of text and context, and of precedent and practice, and into the far more complex landscape of principle and teaching by which the whole is made considerably larger than the sum of its parts. Contrary to popular thinking, this invariably means giving more attention to the Bible, and more rather than less care to its study and interpretation.[39]

Even though Gomes is writing from a Christian perspective, his teaching can easily be applied to our own faith. Note with care how he gently reminds us that our traditions and beliefs—our ultimate values—are bigger than the words of a single verse!

We know that to be true of our own Reform Judaism. We can easily articulate the Jewish values that inform our own sense of welcoming lesbian and gay Jews: a passionate belief in *b'tzelem Elohim* (being created in the image of God), the value of hospitality, and the notion of "loving our neighbors as ourselves" (to name a few).

Gomes argues that even as we would see that "the whole is made considerably larger than the sum of its parts," we must have more, rather than less, "engagement" with the text. I would suggest that the most effective way to engage a problematic text (like 18:22) is to critique it, or to preach against it. Doing so allows us to engage with it, and see beyond it, at the very same time.

An authentically Jewish discourse on this aspect of homiletics is virtually nonexistent. Indeed, I initially failed to turn up a single reference to a source that explores a Jewish notion of "preaching against the text." My findings were confirmed by two experts in the field.[40]

I subsequently was able to identify one article on the subject. It, too, was authored by Judith Plaskow.

Her article, adapted from the 1997 ordination sermon that she delivered in Cincinnati, is aptly titled "Preaching Against the Text."[41] In it, she addresses the question of why a *darshanit* (one delivering a sermon) might choose to speak against a problematic piece of Torah, instead of "emphasizing the positive." She writes:

My first answer to this question is that it is intellectually dishonest to focus simply on the positive aspects of tradition. Individual religious ideas and values have contexts; they are connected to other ideas. They are parts of systems that seek to express and establish particular worldviews. Why engage with tradition if we're not prepared to look at the ways it shapes us for good and for evil? . . . To wrench what we like out of context and ignore the rest is to engage in a kind of pretense, to act as if we were deriving our values from tradition when what we are actually doing is seeking support for our own convictions.

Such intellectual dishonesty might be excused were it to serve a spiritual purpose. But I would argue that failure to grapple with the hard parts of tradition is spiritually and socially corrosive because it leaves destructive ideas intact to shape our consciousness and affect our hearts and minds.[42]

Plaskow goes on to spell out the relationship between preaching against the text and bringing about a sense of healing:

Remaining silent about the negative aspects of tradition not only leaves them to do their work in the world, it also deprives us of an important spiritual resource. In congregations, in Hillels, and in other places rabbis serve, many Jews are in pain. Sometimes they are in pain and feel they have been wounded directly by some aspect of Jewish tradition. More often, they have been hurt by injustices or abuse described and sometimes reinscribed by tradition, but not immediately attributable to its influence. In either case, what they frequently need and seek are not simply spiritual ideals they can counterpose to the bitterness of their experiences, but places to name and explore the contours and causes of their pain. . . . Viewed in this light, acknowledging those aspects of tradition that need to be repudiated and exorcised is a necessary moment in the process of creating something new.[43]

Conclusion

Our movement is engaged, at this very moment, "in the process of creating something new." Our colleagues on the *machzor* editorial committee are doing this formally, as they toil to produce a new text for us. But the impending arrival of the new *machzor* means that we are newly empowered as well to wonder: what liturgical changes might we be moved to make on a local basis, to reflect the ultimate values of the institutions and communities that we are associated with?

Our liberal colleagues of decades and centuries past chose an alternative path for Yom Kippur afternoon by designating Torah readings from outside of Leviticus 18. Imagine how much more powerful our Yom Kippur afternoon services might be if we made a different choice: by reading Leviticus 18 (and verse 22 in particular) precisely so that we might preach against it. What might this look like, practically speaking? We might consider using the marginalia of our new *machzor* (or the creative handouts that some of us use on the High Holy Days) not just to put Leviticus 18 in its proper context, but also to grant permission to our communities to do any/all of the following:

1. Read/chant Leviticus 18 (or just 18:22) *sotto voce*. There is ample precedent in our tradition for adjusting the way we chant biblical text based on its content (and our interpretation of it). Just as we try to speed through the list of Haman's ten sons on Purim,[44] so too should we change the tone of our chanting here to reflect our objection to the words. Alternatively, we might chant the reading according to the trope of Lamentations to signify the "gloom and despair"[45] that we associate with the historical implications of 18:22's edict.

2. Arrange for an openly gay or lesbian member of the congregation/staff to chant the reading. Before or after the reading, we might give them the opportunity to say a few words about their journey and the context in which they continue to be drawn to Torah and Jewish life, even as we struggle with 18:22.

3. Empower a clergyperson or a respected lay leader to preach against the text by delivering a *d'rash* that would explicitly critique the biblical author for 18:22 and name the pain and hurt that our GLBTQ friends and relatives have suffered because of its hatefulness.

This approach will not be right for every Reform synagogue. But for those of us who are comfortable doing so, wouldn't this homiletic strategy be the one that would allow us to be most welcoming of GLBTQ Jews and their allies? Doesn't this strategy, more than the other two discussed here, enable us to clarify our values and begin to fix a text that seems inherently broken?

I conclude as Plaskow did, as she faced my colleagues who were ordained in 1997: "Confronting the hard places in tradition and in our lives is neither comfortable nor easy. But it is a necessary step in shaping a Judaism that is inclusive and life-giving, in continuity with tradition and yet responsive to the contemporary world."[46]

That confrontation is the challenge that lies before us. Let us pray that we might all, each in our own ways and communities, find the wisdom and courage to face it.

NOTES

1. On a micro-level, every local *sh'liach tzibur* or rabbi is empowered to decide the Torah readings for their respective communities. On a macro-level, though, we acknowledge the unique influence that our CCAR *machzor* editorial committee wields, as it makes its own decision on this matter, thereby setting a "default" tone for the rest of the Movement. As of the writing of this article in the spring of 2011, the editorial committee had not begun discussing the Yom Kippur afternoon Torah reading in earnest (e-mail from Rabbi Edwin Goldberg on May 1, 2011).

2. Baruch A. Levine, *The JPS Torah Commentary: Leviticus* (Philadelphia: Jewish Publication Society, 1989), 117.

3. See Isaac Klein, *A Guide to Religious Practice* (New York/Jerusalem: JTSA, 1992), 380–88. Note how Klein omits all reference to homosexual intimacy and/or relationships (the aspect of Leviticus 18 that this paper is primarily concerned with). Compare that with the December 2006 CJLS-approved responsum/*takanot*: Elliot Dorff, Daniel Nevins, and Avram Reisner, "Homosexuality, Human Dignity & Halakhah: A Combined Responsum for the Committee on Jewish Law and Standards"; Myron Geller, Robert Fine, and David Fine, "A New Context: The Halakhah of Same-Sex Relations"; and Gordon Tucker, "Halakhic and Metahalakhic Arguments Concerning Judaism and Homosexuality." All are posted on the "Jewish Law" section of www.rabbinicalassembly.org (viewed July 27, 2011).

4. Nosson Scherman, ed., *The Chumash: The Stone Edition* (Brooklyn: Mesorah Publications, Ltd., 1993), 653.

5. Resolution entitled "Human Rights of Homosexuals," 45th General Assembly of the Union of American Hebrew Congregations, as posted on www.urj.org (viewed April 1, 2011). See also the resolution entitled "Rights of Homosexuals" passed at the 1977 CCAR Convention, as posted on www.ccarnet.org (viewed April 1, 2011).

6. Tamara Cohn Eskenazi and Andrea L. Weiss, eds., *The Torah: A Women's Commentary* (New York: URJ Press and Women of Reform Judaism, 2008), 692.

7. Adin Steinsaltz, *A Guide to Jewish Prayer* (New York: Schocken Books, 2000), 208.

8. Nahum Rakover, *A Guide to the Sources of Jewish Law* (Jerusalem: The Library of Jewish Law, 1994), 59.

9. S. Y. Agnon, ed., *Days of Awe: A Treasury of Jewish Wisdom for Reflection, Repentance, and Renewal on the High Holy Days* (New York: Schocken Books, 1995), 262. See also Lawrence A. Hoffman, *Gates of Understanding 2: Appreciating the Days of Awe* (New York: Central Conference of American Rabbis, 1984), 145: "Why this [Leviticus 18] should have become the reading for Yom Kippur is unclear, but a traditional view, offered, for example, in 1917 by J. D. Eisenstein, is this: 'On Yom Kippur even the most profligate sinners come to synagogue, those who do not come again all year round, so that they must be warned against illicit sexual relations.'"

10. Dr. Richard Sarason cautions that we not read too much into the possible relationship between the *Taanit* mishnah and the *M'gilah* gemara. The author(s) of the mishnah were recalling a pre-70 CE practice (of going out into the hills on Yom Kippur). According to Sarason, it would be historically inaccurate to presume that that practice was still occurring during the amoraic period (e-mail from Dr. Richard Sarason, May 25, 2011).

11. Bernard M. Zlotowitz, "The Torah and Haftarah Readings for the High Holy Days," *CCAR Journal* 91 (Fall 1975): 102–3. Reprinted in Hara E. Person and Sara Newman, eds., *Machzor: Challenge and Change* (New York: CCAR Press, 2010), 137–49.

12. Ismar Elbogen, *Jewish Liturgy: A Comprehensive History*, trans. Raymond P. Scheindlin (Philadelphia and New York/Jerusalem: JPS and JTSA, 1993), 423n72. Similarly, the 2007 edition of *Encyclopaedia Judaica* (vol. 5, p. 489) notes, "During the afternoon service three men are called to the reading of the Torah of Leviticus 18, which deals with incest prohibitions (and which is a continuation of the morning reading of the Torah according to the ancient custom which still exists in Italy)."

13. The choice of Leviticus 16 for the traditional Yom Kippur morning reading makes much more sense: Leviticus 16 contains the details of the ancient cultic observance of Yom Kippur. In my research, I did not encounter any sources to explain why (according to this explanation) Leviticus 17 would be omitted from Yom Kippur Torah readings.

14. Zlotowitz, "The Torah and Haftarah Readings," 95–98. Sarason adds to this data: "High Holy Day scriptural readings were not altered in the earliest European Reform prayer books (Hamburg, West London, Geiger), excepting that of the radical Berlin *Reformgemeinde*; that began in the 1850s in America. The traditional readings are also kept in most Conservative *machzorim* (although the Jules Harlow *machzor* of 1972 gives Lev. 19 as an alternative reading in the afternoon!)" (e-mail from Dr. Sarason, May 25, 2011).

15. Zlotowitz omits *machzor* title. See instead Michael A. Meyer, *Response to Modernity: A History of the Reform Movement of Judaism* (Detroit: Wayne State University Press, 1988), 422n61.

16. As Hoffman points out, there are plenty of aspects of Leviticus 18 that are problematic, outside of the sphere of our GLBTQ concerns. This project, however, is devoted to addressing GLBTQ concerns in particular.

17. Hoffman, *Gates*, 145.

18. According to an e-mail conversation with Hoffman (April 12, 2011), no one on the *Gates of Repentance* editorial committee ever seriously considered including Leviticus 18 as the Yom Kippur afternoon Torah reading. In his words: the issue "was moot from the start." To them, it seemed obvious that the reading shouldn't be included. Furthermore, Hoffman indicated that GLBTQ concerns were not a factor in their decision-making process: "I do not, however, recall much (or any, for that matter) concern altogether re GLBTQ back then. This was a time when feminism was still sexist language, for goodness sake, because too many people thought God talk still had to be masculine and hierarchical. GLBTQ was an acronym no one had heard of."

19. Jonathan Magonet and Lionel Blue, eds., *Forms of Prayer for Jewish Worship: Prayers for the High Holydays* (London: the Reform Synagogues of Great Britain, 1985), 976–85. Note from the Editors' Introduction: "While this liturgy was being revised, another revision was taking place in the attitudes of the society which it serves, concerning sexual injustice in general and women's rights in particular" (pp. ix–x). To what extent did these societal "revisions" make it easier for the editorial committee of *Forms of Prayer* to ignore Leviticus 18? The *machzor* does not say.

20. Richard N. Levy, *On Wings of Awe: A Machzor for Rosh Hashanah and Yom Kippur* (Washington, DC: B'nai B'rith Hillel Foundations, 1985), 414–19. See especially p. 417 for Levy's thoughtful translation of Lev. 18:22, in which he seeks to offer both a literal *and* interpretive take: "You shall not lie with a man as with a woman; it is an abhorrence (or, an emulation of the practices of pagan religion)." This article would be incomplete without also acknowledging the recent revision (after this article was written) of Levy's *On Wings of Awe* (Jersey City, NJ: Ktav Publishing House, Inc. in association with Hillel: The Foundation for Jewish Campus Life, 2011). Interestingly, Leviticus 18 is not offered as an option in the revised edition. Instead, worshipers are directed to read Leviticus 19:1–18, 32–37 (pp. 510–12). In a private e-mail exchange, Levy reflected on Leviticus 18: "I included it in the original edition because the book was intended to be used by Hillel students from a variety of backgrounds, including those which customarily read that chapter in the afternoon, but in revising the book I felt that encountering Leviticus 18:22 can be taken as an insult by LGBTQ students, their friends, family, and supporters." In our exchange, Levy went on to argue that Yom Kippur is not an appropriate day to do the kind of *tikkun* that this author calls for here. Levy wrote, "To turn our attention from work on ourselves to critiques of others distracts us from the *tikkun* we need to do with our own souls. Yom Kippur is also a day when we need to re-commit ourselves to the study and practice of Torah—and to embark on a critique of Torah distracts us from the commitment as well" (e-mail from Rabbi Richard Levy on December 12, 2011).

21. *Machzor Ruach Chadashah* (London: Liberal Judaism, 2003), 499, with thanks to Sheryl Stahl of HUC's Los Angeles library for helping me to track down this text.

22. I wonder if this argument from silence does not also run the risk of unintentionally ignoring GLBTQ Jews. Yes, our alternative reading is not explicitly offensive to gays and lesbians. But it also ignores the reality of gay life in our communities.

23. Steven Greenberg, *Wrestling with God and Men: Homosexuality in the Jewish Tradition* (Madison: University of Wisconsin Press, 2004), 76.

24. See, for example, Neil Gillman, *Sacred Fragments: Recovering Theology for the Modern Jew* (Philadelphia: Jewish Publication Society, 1990), 31–32: "As for revelation, if we are serious in affirming that no myth is a fiction, then we have in the same breath affirmed both the principle and the fact of revelation. . . . The thesis that Torah contains the classic Jewish mythic explanation of one community's experience of the world, is clearly still a third version of what we have called the middle option on revelation. . . . In this extended sense, myth and *midrash* share many characteristics. Both are culturally conditioned, human renderings of realities that lie beyond direct human apprehension. Both exhibit startling continuities and equally surprising discontinuities as they move through history. As long as the community that shapes them remains vital, it will determine what it wishes to keep and what it prefers to discard and reshape in the light of its ongoing experience." Like so many of my Reform colleagues, I agree that 18:22 should be "discarded." I believe, admittedly paradoxically, that the best way to do that is by reading it out loud on Yom Kippur afternoon: to affirm the (whole) myth of our people, and to "discontinue" a part of that myth at the very same time (by publicly critiquing it).

25. http://www.bcc-la.org/content/about/ (viewed May 10, 2011).

26. E-mail correspondence with Rabbi Lisa Edwards (April 8, 2011).

27. See the "JRF Homosexuality Report and Inclusion of GLBTQ Persons," http://jrf.org/node/1742 (viewed April 13, 2011).

28. Ronald Aigen, *Mahzor Hadesh Yameinu: Renew Our Days—A Prayer-Circle for Days of Awe* (Hampstead, Quebec: Ronald Aigen, 2001), 666.

29. Edward Feld, ed., *Mahzor Lev Shalem* (New York: The Rabbinical Assembly, 2010), 363.

30. Judith Plaskow, "Sexuality and *Teshuvah*: Leviticus 18," in *Beginning Anew: A Woman's Companion to the High Holy Days*, ed. Gail Twersky Reimer and Judith A. Kates (New York: Touchstone, 1997), 290–302. Reprinted in Judith Plaskow, *The Coming of Lilith: Essays on Feminism, Judaism, and Sexual Ethics, 1972–2003*, ed. with Donna Berman (Boston: Beacon Press, 2005), 165–77. Citations below will reference the 2005 edition.

31. Aigen, *Hadesh Yameinu*, 656. With thanks to Rabbi Aigen for directing my attention to his introduction to the *Minchah* service (e-mail with Rabbi Ron Aigen, April 14, 2011), which invokes some of Plaskow's themes.

32. Plaskow, "Sexuality," in *The Coming of Lilith*, 166.

33. Feld, *Machzor Lev Shalem*, 363–64.

34. Plaskow, "Sexuality," in *The Coming of Lilith*, 175–77.

35. Feld, *Machzor Lev Shalem*, 364.

36. For example, Rabbi Shimon's comment (Babylonian Talmud, *Sanhedrin* 71a) regarding the wayward and rebellious son: "In truth, the rebellious and defiant son never existed and never will exist. Why, then, was the account about him written? So that you will expound the possible reasons for such misconduct and receive a reward for doing so."

37. There are exceptions to this generalization, of course. We might situate certain aspects of Jewish feminism (to name a recent example) within this phenomenon. And if we are seeking individual colleagues who embrace this methodology as a regular homiletic approach, I would name Dr. Marc Saperstein as a noteworthy example. See some of his writing on the website of Leo Baeck College: http://lbc .reformjudaism.org.uk/SermonsPapers/ sermons-a-papers.html, especially his 2010 and 2011 Shabbat Zachor sermons, as well as the one entitled "My Least Favourite Biblical Verse" (e-mail correspondence with Dr. Marc Saperstein, April 14, 2011) (sermons viewed on May 4, 2011).

38. Peter J. Gomes, *The Good Book: Reading the Bible with Mind and Heart* (New York: William Morrow and Company, Inc., 1996), 81. I am grateful to Professor Barbara Lundblad of Union Theological Seminary for her reference to Gomes.

39. Ibid., 82 (emphasis added).

40. E-mail correspondence with Dr. Marc Saperstein (April 14, 2011) and Rabbi Margaret Moers Wenig (April 15, 2011).

41. Judith Plaskow, "Preaching Against the Text," in *The Coming of Lilith*, 152–56.

42. Ibid., 155.

43. Ibid., 155–56.

44. Joshua R. Jacobson, *Chanting the Hebrew Bible: Student Edition* (Philadelphia: Jewish Publication Society, 2005), 165.

45. A. W. Binder, *Biblical Chant* (New York: Sacred Music Press / HUC-JIR School of Sacred Music, 1959), 100, with thanks to Cantor William Tiep for referring me to Binder.

46. Plaskow, "Preaching," in *The Coming of Lilith*, 156.

I thank my teacher Dr. Richard Sarason for kindly reviewing an early draft of this article prior to submission. Any errors that remain are my own.

7

SPIRIT OF JEALOUSY, SPIRIT OF HOLINESS

Timeless Insights from a Time-Bound Text

RABBI LISA J. GRUSHCOW, DPHIL

"If any wife has gone astray and broken faith with her husband"—so begins the biblical passage pertaining to the *sotah*, the suspected wife. In Numbers 5:11–31, we are introduced to a situation in which a man suspects his wife of adultery. It is possible that she has indeed strayed, as the opening verses suggest, but it is also possible that she is innocent. It is the uncertainty about the wife's guilt or innocence that defines the situation, distinct from a clear-cut case of adultery. The husband is jealous, and his jealousy may or may not be founded in fact: "a spirit of jealousy comes upon [the husband] and he is jealous of his wife and she is defiled; or if a spirit of jealousy comes upon him and he is jealous of his wife and she is not defiled" (Num. 5:14).

What is to be done? Here is where the biblical passage shows its premodern origins. The law is not in any way egalitarian, nor should we expect it to be. The husband is jealous, but there are no witnesses to his wife's alleged infidelity. He expresses his jealousy and brings his wife to a priest, along with a meal offering of barley as a *jealousy offering* and as a *memorial offering remembering sin*. The priest brings the woman forward, mixes holy water with dust from the floor of the Tabernacle, uncovers her hair, and places the offering in her hands.

He speaks to her about her actions and makes her swear, telling her that God will make her a curse and an oath among her people; if she is innocent, she will be clean from the water, but if she is guilty, it will make her thigh fall and her belly swell. These words are written on a scroll and blotted out in the water, which the woman is made to drink. The meal offering of barley is offered. After the woman drinks, if she is defiled, she faces the consequences described; but if she is pure, she is acquitted and conceives.

Modern scholars disagree on everything from the actual physical consequences of the ordeal to whether it should even be called an ordeal,[1] and no one knows whether the ritual ever actually took place.[2] Moreover, in all the Rabbinic discussions of the topic—and these are extensive, as there is an entire tractate of the Mishnah, *Tosefta*, and Palestinian and Babylonian Talmuds dedicated to this ritual, as well as a number of halachic and aggadic midrashim—there is very little resolution. The more the Rabbis examined the details of the rules, the more uncertainty emerged. A ritual that was intended to determine guilt or innocence and eliminate doubt did nothing of the sort, at least in its interpretation; and in the absence of actual practice, interpretation was all our ancestors had. Finally, the Rabbis of the Talmud recount that Yochanan ben Zakkai put an end to the ritual toward the end of the first century CE.

Modern scholars disagree about the various details of the biblical passage and its interpretation, but overall they fall into two camps. The first camp argues that the *sotah* ritual is an example of the worst kind of Rabbinic misogyny, as seen in the expanded details of the *sotah*'s humiliation and exposure. Conversely, the second camp argues that the ritual is an example of Rabbinic proto-feminism, evidenced by the delimitation of some of its aspects, and its ultimate disappearance.[3] My own reading of the texts suggests that the Rabbinic material shows two major, and sometimes contradictory, approaches: first, we see the imposition of rules and procedures on an unusually extra-legal process; and second, we find an expansive, impassioned condemnation of adultery and sexual wrongdoing.[4] This means that in some interpretations, we see the arguments for delimiting the ordeal, for example, by requiring the husband to declare his jealousy before witnesses (*kinui*), and for witnesses to see his wife seclude herself with the man against whom she has been warned (*s'tirah*). Other times, we see an extreme focus on the measure-for-measure punishment of the *sotah*, which depends on a presumption of guilt. Some of these differences of approach can be connected with the different times and places in which they were written. For the most part, though, they reflect two separate overarching Rabbinic impulses: to make laws normative and fair, and to condemn sexual sin.

All this shows the complexity with which our ancestors treated these themes. For a modern reader, though, what insights—if any—can be gained from this ancient ordeal and its interpretation?

The first insight is a simple one: the recognition of the reality of jealousy in human relationships in general and sexual relationships in particular. Jealousy is an ancient and powerful emotion, which can define the nature of a relationship. On this theme, there are two fascinating teachings that are woven into the discussions of *sotah*, both involving Rabbi Meir, who lived in the second century BCE and was known for his marriage to Beruryah. We find the following teaching as part of a discussion of the husband's suspicion of his wife:

> Rabbi Meir would say: [A man's] taste in eating is like his taste in women. You have a man who, when the fly alights in his cup, puts it aside and does not taste from it. This one is a bad lot for women, for he looks to divorce his wife. You have a man who, when the fly takes up residence in his cup, throws it out and does not drink from it—like Papos ben Y'hudah, who shut his wife in the house, and went out. And you have a man who, when the fly falls into his cup, he throws it out and drinks from it. This is the quality of every man, who sees his wife speaking with her neighbors and with her relatives, and leaves her be. You have a man who, when the fly falls into his meal, he picks it up and sucks it, and throws it away and eats what was in it. This is the quality of an evil man, who sees his wife going out with her head uncovered, going out with her shoulders uncovered, arrogant before her manservants, arrogant before her maidservants, spinning in the marketplace, bathing, and

being flirtatious with everyone—it is a commandment to divorce
her, as it is said, "If a man should take a wife and marries her . . ."
[Deut. 24:1, re: divorce].

(*Tosefta Sotah* 5:9; parallels in Jerusalem Talmud, *Sotah* 1:7;
Babylonian Talmud, *Gittin* 90a–b; and *B'midbar Rabbah* 9:12)

This passage is striking in that it acknowledges that some types
of jealousy are warranted and some are unwarranted. A man who
becomes jealous too easily, who looks too closely to find any fault
in his wife's behavior, is "a bad lot for women." On the other hand,
a man who sees his wife acting inappropriately and does nothing
also is doing wrong.

Here, we might think of the origins of the term *kiddushin*, "marriage," and its connection to the idea of separation. In other words, the
relationship between spouses is meant to be an exclusive one. And, in
a world in which not only the couple but the society as a whole has a
stake in the relationship, there are certain norms to be followed. Papos
ben Y'hudah is condemned for locking his wife in the house for fear
of infidelity. The wife who is too flirtatious in public is acting inappropriately. There is no escaping the text's assumptions about gender
or propriety. Still, the fundamental idea that there should be limits to
behavior within marriage, but also a foundation of commitment and
trust, is relevant to relationships today.

A second text involving Rabbi Meir is intriguing, and relates to the
theme of jealousy in the life of a marriage:

Rabbi Zabdai the son-in-law of Rabbi Levi would tell this story:
Rabbi Meir would go and expound in the synagogue of Hammata
every night of the week. There was a woman who came to hear
him. One time, the lesson lasted longer than usual. She went to
her house and found the light had gone out. Her husband said to
her, "Where were you?" She said to him, "Listening to the lesson
of the teacher." He said to her, "[May God do] such-and-such [to
me] if this woman comes into her house until she goes and spits in
the face of this teacher!" Rabbi Meir intuited by the Holy Spirit
and pretended to have a pain in his eye. He said, "Any woman who
knows how to speak [a charm] over an eye, come and speak." Her

neighbors said to her, "This is your chance to return to your home. Pretend to be a charmer and spit in his eye!" She came to him, and he said to her, "Do you know how to speak over an eye?" Out of her fear, she said, "No." He said, "They spit in it seven times, and it is good for it." When she had spat, he said to her, "Go and say to your husband, you told her once, and she spat seven times!" His students said to him, "Rabbi, do we disgrace the Torah like this? If you had only told us, would we not have brought in benches and straps, and hit him and reconciled him to his wife?" He said to them, "The honor of Meir is not like the honor of his creator. And if Scripture says that the holy name, which is written in holiness, should be erased in water to make peace between a man and his wife, should not the honor of Meir be [erased] all the more so?"

(Jerusalem Talmud, *Sotah* 1:4)

The resolution of this story refers to the part of the *sotah* ritual in which God's name is dissolved into the water that the suspected wife is made to drink. However, there are a number of aspects that also connect the story to issues surrounding jealousy. First, the husband forbids his wife from his house, a euphemism for sexual relations, just as the husband of the *sotah* does by his *kinui*, his initial warning. Second, he criticizes her for entering (and staying late in) the house of study, though elsewhere in the Jerusalem Talmud (*Sotah* 1:2), it is stated that a husband cannot forbid his wife from being in the presence of many men at once in a synagogue; this suggests that such prohibitions were conceivable and also that they were condemned. Third, the situation is revealed to Rabbi Meir by *ruach hakodesh*, "the spirit of holiness," which could be introduced as a contrast to *ruach kinah*, "the spirit of jealousy"; here, Meir models holy, reasonable behavior, in stark contrast with the irrationality of the husband.

Then, as now, jealousy could lead to conflict and estrangement, within a marriage and even beyond. This story is often cited in relation to *sh'lom bayit*, the importance of making peace in the home. But it is worth noting that the wife is not simply instructed to return to her husband and submit to his accusations; rather, the husband is sent a message about appropriate and inappropriate behavior. From a modern vantage point, we may wish that Rabbi Meir had told the woman to divorce her husband, but that was rarely a viable or desirable option at the time. What might resonate more strongly is the implication that jealousy or even actual infidelity need not be the death of a relationship. At its best, this passage tells us something about models of intervention when jealousy corrodes the foundation of a relationship. Rabbi Meir is personally involved—and, in a somewhat less subtle way, his students are willing to be involved as well.

Our second insight, then, is that emotions and actions within a marriage can affect a community outside the walls of the marital home and that external parties can intervene to support a relationship. The isolation in which modern relationships exist is not always to our benefit. Sometimes, outside help is required, to transform the spirit of jealousy into the spirit of holiness.

The third insight that we can find in the biblical and Rabbinic texts on *sotah* is an insistence on the power of ritual. The narrative of why the *sotah* ritual ended in Second Temple times is a complicated one, seemingly unrelated to the destruction of the Temple in 70 CE. It is safe to say that it was not intended as a radical, ethical, proto-feminist move; in fact, as with many developments described in Rabbinic literature, it seems to be an ex post facto explanation of a change that had already occurred.[5] The ritual may never have existed in practice, and even in theory, it eventually disappeared. But the initial impetus behind the ritual—namely, the resolution of uncertainty—did not disappear. And so we find that it continues in the imagination of Jews and non-Jews. The Dead Sea Scrolls include fragments that seem connected to the *sotah*'s ordeal.[6] The nascent Christian community also made reference to the *sotah* ritual to prove Mary's innocence in a fascinating, noncanonical second-century text, the Protevangelium of James.[7]

Centuries later, two fragments in the Cairo *Genizah* attest to continued interest in the biblical ritual.[8] They fall into the category of magical texts, with an emphasis on the permutations of the divine name as it is used in the proceedings. Amidst these fragmentary interpretations, we find a tantalizing line: "And this is the manner of taking which we do today, in the matter that we have no priest or holy water, and no tabernacle."⁹ It goes on to describe how a righteous man could take water from a spring and dust from the corners of the ark in which the Torah was kept, and mix it with the dissolved words from the oath as described in the biblical text. This mixture could then be administered to the suspected wife and would take immediate effect. Whether this modified ritual was ever implemented, we do not know. Nor would we recommend it. But it attests to a continued interest, and a continued desire to resolve a situation that is by definition elusive: an accusation based on suspicion, in the absence of proof.

Finally, there is a notable modern attempt to bring the practice to our own times. In a volume of contemporary commentaries on the Torah, *Beginning the Journey*, there is an attempt to create an egalitarian ritual, loosely based on the *sotah*'s ordeal, to reestablish trust when a relationship has been damaged by jealousy or infidelity.¹⁰ Like the biblical and Rabbinic descriptions and the fragments from the Cairo *Genizah*, the actual usage of the ritual is not attested. But as in the ancient texts, this innovation bears witness to a deep human desire to establish certainty—if not certainty about what has happened in the past, certainty about a commitment to the future.¹¹

Our most intimate relationships are sometimes our most vulnerable. Sexuality, uncertainty, and jealousy are a volatile combination. It is easy to feel, like the man in Numbers, overtaken by a spirit beyond the self, motivating irrational action—and there are many real reasons for a relationship to be under strain. In response, the Torah and Rabbinic commentaries, alongside modern interpretation, can help us. We acknowledge the power of jealousy, and we seek to find resolution and healing. Some of our most time-bound texts, when we look closely, can be timeless.

NOTES

1. Lisa J. Grushcow, *Writing the Wayward Wife: Rabbinic Interpretations of Sotah* (Leiden and Boston: Brill, 2006), 125. This essay draws on the book, itself based on my doctoral dissertation (Oxford University, 2003).

2. Ibid., 2.

3. Ibid., 19–31.

4. Ibid., 264–71.

5. Ibid., 233–63.

6. Ibid., 279–81.

7. Ibid., 292–94.

8. Ibid., 297–300.

9. JTSL ENA 3635.17, 17c lines 17–19. Parallel with the Cambridge collection, T.-S. K 1.56.

10. Kay Greenwald, Lisa Langer, Laura Novak Winer, "A Ritual for Rebuilding Trust," in *Beginning the Journey: Toward a Women's Commentary*, ed. Rabbi Emily Feigenson (New York: Women of Reform Judaism, 1999).

11. Greenwald, Langer, and Winer express this aspiration in their ritual: "In the Torah we read of an ordeal of broken trust. For our ancestors, the culmination of the ordeal lay in the drinking of water. Today, you will share a cup of water. For our ancestors, that water was made bitter. Today, the water reminds us of the bitterness you have overcome. Yet, water is also a symbol of life. In drinking this water, you reclaim your hopes for your life together."

PERSONAL REFLECTIONS

PERSONAL REFLECTION

Kol Ishah—Sexuality and the Voice of a Woman

Rabbi Judith Z. Abrams, PhD

One of the ways women's voices are literally silenced in the Orthodox world is through the notion of *kol ishah*, that is, the idea that a woman's voice is so alluring that it constitutes a distraction to the men who hear it and interferes with their ability to concentrate in prayer. It is one of the means by which women are deprived of the opportunity to lead services. Even in secular settings (e.g., modern popular music), Orthodox men do not listen to women singing, again, because the sound of their singing is so alluring that it might lead them to sinful thoughts. We might expect such a far-reaching ban on women's expression might have solid grounding in our traditional texts. Not only would we be wrong in that assumption, but a look at the texts proves the opposite point: women sang officially, publicly, and liturgically for most of our people's existence.

I remember when I first seriously looked into the textual basis of *kol ishah*. I used my computer concordance of all of Rabbinic literature (here defined as Mishnah, *Tosefta*, Jerusalem and Babylonian Talmuds, and midrash collections) to look for the term. I expected to find a long list of sources. I found only three hits. I thought, "Well, I must have looked it up wrong." So I tried *kol ha-ishah*, *kolot nashim*, and other variations. No matter what I tried, I still I came up with just three hits in all of Rabbinic literature. And each of those citations is a repetition of just one statement. So the prohibition comes down to this single statement:

> If one gazes at the little finger of a woman, is it as if he gazed at her secret place? No, it means in one's own wife, and when he recites the *Sh'ma*.
>
> Rav Chisda: A woman's leg is a sexual incitement, as it says, "Uncover the leg, pass through the rivers" (Isa. 47:2), and it says afterwards, "Your nakedness shall be uncovered, yea, your shame shall be seen" (Isa. 47:3).
>
> Shmuel said: A woman's voice is a sexual incitement, as it says, "For sweet is your voice and your countenance is comely" (Song of Songs 2:14).
>
> Rav Sheshet said: A woman's hair is a sexual incitement, as it says, "Your hair is as a flock of goats" (Song of Songs 4:1).
>
> (Babylonian Talmud, *B'rachot* 24a; Babylonian Talmud, *Kiddushin* 70a; Jerusalem Talmud, *Challah* 2:1; Shmuel's saying)

This passage talks about things that might distract a man while reciting the *Sh'ma*. I think reasonable minds would agree that a man might be distracted by seeing his wife naked before him while he was attempting to recite the *Sh'ma*. But what comes next is, in essence, a list of what different sages find most enticing about women . . . a sort of sidebar to the main conversation. Since Shmuel's statement is included in this sidebar, later generations took it to mean that hearing a woman's voice is as distracting as having one's wife sit naked before him.

When I realized this, I contacted one of my mentors and asked, "Is this really the entire basis for not allowing women's voices to be heard?" He told me it was. I must admit, I was flabbergasted. We had been hung out to dry on the flimsiest of pretexts. I asked a fellow teacher what he thought of this and he said, "Well, when I was fifteen, I'd have been distracted by a woman's voice." To which I replied, "Why should I have to shut up for the rest of my life just because you used to be fifteen?"

The prohibition is all the more surprising because Scripture and Rabbinic literature assume that women sing publicly. Of course, Miriam and the women sing at the shores of the sea (Exod.15:20–21). Women take part in loud public rejoicing (Neh. 12:43). When Jeremiah wants to mourn, he does not call on male singers, he calls for women to sing:

> Summon the dirge-singers [*lam'kon'not*], let them come. Let them quickly start a wailing for us, that our eyes may run with tears, our pupils flow with water. . . . Hear, O women, the word of the Eternal, let your ears receive the word of God's mouth, and teach your daughters wailing and one another lamentation.
>
> (Jer. 9:16, 19)

In the Mishnah, it is assumed that women sing professionally, publicly, and liturgically:

> Women may raise a wail during the festival [week] but not clap [their hands in grief]; Rabbi Yishmael says, those that are close to the bier clap [their hands in grief]. On the days of the New Moon, of Chanukah, and of Purim they may raise a wail and clap [their hands in grief]. Neither on the former [i.e., the festival week] nor on the latter occasions do they chant a dirge. After [the dead] has been interred they neither raise a wail nor clap [their hands in grief]. What is meant by "raising a wail"? When all sing in unison. What is meant by a dirge? When one leads and all respond after her. As it is said, "And teach your daughters wailing and one another [each] lamentation" (Jer. 9:19). But as the future [days] to come, [the prophet] says, "God will destroy death forever, and the Eternal God will wipe away tears from off all faces" (Isa. 25:8).
>
> (*Mishnah Mo-eid Katan* 3:9;
> Babylonian Talmud, *Mo-eid Katan* 28b)

So, weighing our evidence, we have biblical, Mishnaic, and Talmudic testimony that women sing publicly and liturgically as opposed to a single statement by one sage that does not, in context, ban women's voices at all. I believe there is far more textual support affirming the right of women to sing in public and at services than there is for banning it. "May the sounds of joy and salvation be heard in the tents of the righteous" (Ps. 118:15)!

PERSONAL REFLECTION

It Gets Beautiful—
One Rabbi's Perspective on
Being Jewish and LGBTQ

RABBI ANDREA MYERS

When I was living on Long Island as a sheltered teenager in the 1980s, the term "lesbian" might as well have been a country in the Middle East, somewhere in the Interzone between Mesopotamia and Bilitis, due south of the Well of Loneliness.

That was a long time ago. I came out in college and am now married to my partner of fifteen years. All told, we are officially married in Canada, officially domesticated in New York City, and religiously married by a rabbi with a proud history of civil disobedience—and we have the requisite assortment of children and cats. While some might stereotype my life as being heteronormative, I am an unapologetic queer, who has never been either heterosexual or normative.

I am also a rabbi. I grew up as a Lutheran, went to Brandeis (not knowing it was Jewish), discovered Judaism there, studied and converted in Israel, and was ordained by the Academy for Jewish Religion in New York City. By some accounts, the different aspects of my identity should be in tension with each other: a rabbi with non-Jewish parents, someone who is both religious and gay. In reality, though, all these elements are integrated and related. An essential part of my theology is that God wants us to live fulfilling, joyous lives. "Choose life," we are told in the Torah, "so that you and your descendants may live" (Deut. 30:19).

For too long, discussions of Judaism and LGBTQ life have focused on what is permitted and not permitted, and on how to make room for oneself within the limits of the tradition. Specifically, the prohibition in Leviticus (Lev. 18:22, 20:13) is cited again and again, as the starting point for any conversation about Judaism and sexual identity.

But I am a liberal rabbi, and I believe strongly that traditions can and must change. I want to share a different way to think about what it means to be a LGBTQ Jew, based on the premise that God made us who we are. There is a concept in Judaism known as *hiddur mitzvah*, which means taking something that is commanded and making it beautiful. The idea is based on a biblical verse, Exodus 15:2: "This is my God who I will glorify." Rabbi Yishmael asks, "Is it possible for a human being to add glory to the Creator? What this really means is: I shall glorify God in the way I perform mitzvot [commandments]" (*M'chilta, Shirata* 3).

So when I think about being both gay and Jewish, the question I ask is not, "Is my life and are my actions prohibited by the biblical text and Rabbinic tradition?" The questions I ask instead are these: How can I live my life in a way that is beautiful? How can I actively choose the life that is mine to live?

My partner and I got married in October 2001, a month after 9/11. We briefly considered calling the wedding off; it didn't feel like the right time to celebrate. But then we realized that there is no better way to fight terrorism than a big gay Jewish wedding in New York City. And if we were going to do it, we wanted to do it right. We wanted to make it beautiful. For my side of the family, an open bar was critical. For me and my partner, the focus was on a custom *ketubah* (Jewish marriage contract) with language and artwork that reflected our theology and hopes—and our shared fascination with the art of medieval Jewish illumination. The point of all of it was *hidur mitzvah*.

Ultimately, that is what I want to convey to anyone trying to figure out the synergy of their Jewish and LGBTQ identities: how to live with dignity and humor, beauty and joy, as you take your place in a Jewish tradition that is thousands of years old. It is easy to feel scared and marginalized as a queer person in a straight world, and especially one that uses the language of religion to exclude. Within the LGBTQ community, it is easy to feel lost in the ever-shifting alphabet soup of sexual and gender identifying labels. The Torah tells us that all of us were made in God's image (Gen. 1:27), so wherever you are on this particular rainbow, there is something in you that is divine. If it's good enough for God, it should be good enough for your fellow human beings, *kal vachomer*, all the more so, for your fellow Jews. Your life shouldn't look like mine or your parents' or your neighbor's; it should look like your own, and whatever you dream it to be. As Herzl said, *Im tirtzu, ein zo aggadah*, "If you really want it, it is no dream."

Moved to action by a series of tragic suicides of gay youth and the epidemic of bullying in our nation's schools, Dan Savage and Terry Miller started the important "It Gets Better" campaign. The idea was to encourage LGBTQ people and allies to share stories about how life got better for them. I am blessed and lucky that it got better for me too. But the phrase "It Gets Better," essential as it is, leaves me wanting more. It shouldn't just get better. Colds get better. Life should get beautiful—and I hope, sometimes, hilarious.

Part Two

God in the Bedroom,
God in the Body:
Theology and Identity

In Part Two, we move from biblical and Rabbinic texts to reflections based on those texts and others as they shape our theologies and our identities—namely, our understanding of God and ourselves.

Sexuality touches on the most intimate parts of our selves. A helpful metaphor is that rather than being like a separate room in a house that can be closed off, sexuality is like the floorboards, running throughout the structure. This section shows the truth of that insight. Sexuality, theology, and identity intersect in these essays, reflecting a search for integration.

Rabbi Marc Katz's opening essay, "The *Kavanah* of the Bedroom: Sex and Intention in Jewish Law," considers Jewish laws about sex and intentionality; in his words, "Jewish law places a premium on where one's thoughts go in bed." From this premise, Katz explores various Rabbinic and medieval theological perspectives on how sex can be approached with sacred intention. This is followed by Rabbi Daniel A. Lehrman's piece, "Alone Together," which posits that before we can approach sexual union with another human being, we need to develop the integrity of our individual identities. In a world shaped by technology and constant connection, the ability to be alone is fundamental as a prerequisite for bringing our whole selves to an intimate connection with another. Lehrman cites Jacob's encounter with God—and his brother—after wrestling with the angel as a model for this creative tension between the ability to be alone and the ability to connect on the deepest level. The juxtaposition of Katz and Lehrman's essays leads to a fascinating question: how do our modern challenges of approaching sex with intentionality compare with those faced by our ancestors?

"'Your Love Is Sweeter Than Wine': Erotic Theology in Jewish Tradition" by Rabbi Geoffrey W. Dennis, delves deeper into the issue of sex and the sacred. Surveying Jewish thought from the ancient Near East, through Rabbinic and mystical literature, and into the world of modern Reform Judaism, Dennis suggests that there is a long tradition of comparing the relationship between God and Israel to a sexual connection, in which we find "[the] use of sexuality as a theological metaphor." Drawing on this tradition, he identifies features of our erotic theology that let us develop new perspectives on both our sexuality and our faith.

The diversity of Jewish thought is also explored in "'Created by the Hand of Heaven': Sex, Love, and the *Androgynos*." Here, Rabbi Elliot Kukla suggests that in some ways, the religious authorities of the past were more open than many people today regarding the spectrum of gender and sexual identities: "Our Rabbis took people as they really were and went on from there." Kukla's essay points to the power of recognizing one's own identity in Jewish sacred texts—and along the way, suggests a thought-provoking interpretation of Leviticus 18. The discussion of identity continues with Rabbi Jane Rachel Litman's creative glossary of bisexuality and other elements of sexuality and gender identity ("'Bisexual' Identity: A Guide for the Perplexed"). The individual entries combine, in Litman's words, "to construct a Jewish theological argument in critique of sexual and gender determinism, while presenting some useful information about current thinking on Jewish, gender, and sexual identity along the way." Like Kukla, Litman emphasizes the shortcomings of a binary approach to identity (male/female, gay/straight).

Thinking about the intersections of theology, identity, and sexuality does not simply mean making room for a variety of identities under the big tent of Judaism. Rather, it has implications not only for how we think about ourselves, but how we think about God. Rabbi Nikki Lyn DeBlosi makes this case in "Blessed Is God Who Changes Us: Theological Que(e)ries." Recognizing the gender and sexual diversity that Kukla and Litman discuss, DeBlosi argues that a shift is required: from seeing "different" sexualities as something to be tolerated as long as they are not chosen, to a celebration of the diversity of humanity, as created by God.

"All true theology must finally be personal." These words from Rabbi Lawrence Kushner form the opening of Rabbi Camille Shira Angel's essay "Crafting an Inclusive Liturgical Mirror" about the liturgical expression of queer theology. In writing about the ground-breaking prayer book that she and her LGBTQ congregation have created, she emphasizes the importance of liturgy in which the individual and community can see themselves reflected. Outlining some of the principles behind the prayer book and giving examples of what was included and excluded, Angel shows how *Siddur Sha'ar Zahav* "is located at the intersection of sexuality and liturgy and offers us language for living our complicated lives with passion and an attitude of thanksgiving."

The last two essays in Part Two consider the complexity of identity and sexuality in two very different contexts. In "What Kind of a Man Are You?: Interethnic Sexual Encounter in Yiddish American Narratives" Jessica Kirzane analyzes interethnic sexual encounter in Yiddish American narratives, exploring how Jewish identity was shaped—at least in literature—by sexual encounters with non-Jews. Then, in *"Between Sodom and Eden* + 13: A Bar Mitzvah Look Back and Ahead," Lee Walzer provides a vantage point on the history of the LGBT community in Israel and the complex factors shaping contemporary realities. Along the way, he makes a valuable contribution to the "pinkwashing" debate and provides a thoughtful analysis of why "Israel continues to be an LGBT success story," even as work remains to be done. These two contexts—the world of Diaspora Yiddish literature and modern

Israeli society—evoke issues of sexuality that stretch beyond theology to touch on culture, ethnicity, and other aspects of Jewish identity.

The personal reflections that close Part Two speak to two very different embodied experiences. In the provocatively titled "The Problem with *Tz'niut*—How Are Women (Not) Like Pastries?," Rabbi Dalia Marx critiques the ultra-Orthodox stance on modesty in Israel, arguing that it focuses inappropriate attention on the sexuality of women and girls. Her essay speaks both to diverse Jewish identities in the State of Israel and to the issue of what it means to have one's sexual identity defined by an external gaze. Rabbi Lisa Hochberg-Miller's "This Is the Way the World Ends" sheds light on the transformation of a synagogue's culture. She points to a moment in which a family's identity, shaped by sexuality, is recognized in a way that is welcoming rather than limiting.

Even as our sexuality is essential to who we are, it is not always the most relevant factor. As Hochberg-Miller shows, an earlier emphasis on heterosexual models in synagogue life caused an inappropriate focus on gender roles and sexuality, perhaps just as the emphasis on women's dress in Israel causes an inappropriate focus as well. My own experience is that as liberal as our synagogues may be, our discourse often assumes heterosexuality—whether it is expressed through mothers lighting candles and fathers doing *Kiddush* or through opposite-sex matchmaking for babies, only partly in jest. To move away from these models opens new possibilities for all of us in our relationships with ourselves, with each other, and with God.

8

THE *KAVANAH* OF THE BEDROOM

Sex and Intention in Jewish Law

RABBI MARC KATZ

In her recent controversial book *Unorthodox: The Scandalous Rejection of My Hasidic Roots*, Deborah Feldman writes about a problem she and her husband, Eli, were having in the bedroom. The two often argued in the evening. Since according to Jewish law, they were not permitted to have sex in a state of anger or frustration, Feldman would use these arguments to effect periods of abstinence.[1] Sex, in their understanding of Jewish law, was sacred enough that a negative attitude during it would corrupt the act.

In describing her marriage and sex life, Feldman identifies a key characteristic in Jewish law: that one's state of mind during sex matters. While Feldman's is a somewhat extreme case, Jewish law has not shied away from examining what constitutes bad intent and sinful thoughts during a sexual act. In some cases, according to traditional sources, one's mind-set may invalidate a sexual act altogether, while in others, it may have a eugenic effect, bringing curses on children born from that union.

In exploring the roots of the Jewish laws regarding sex and intentionality, it is important to note that the texts considered were written by heterosexual men. Their context is male-centered and hetero-normative. It is therefore a challenge to extrapolate lessons for our day, and one must be careful in drawing broad conclusions.

One of the earliest examples of the Rabbinic attempt to define what constitutes "intentional" sex is found in *Mishnah K'ritot* 2:6, in a larger discussion about the difference between the penalties associated with sleeping with a betrothed free-woman or with a betrothed slave-woman. At issue is whether in each case, the act is considered a sin punishable by either *kareit*, an early death at the hands of heaven, or by needing to bring a sin offering. The mishnah reads:

> With respect to all forbidden unions:[2] [if one person] was an adult and one was a minor, the minor is not liable. If one person was awake and one was asleep, the one who was sleeping is not liable. If one was an inadvertent transgressor and one was a deliberate transgressor, the inadvertent transgressor brings a sin offering, and the deliberate transgressor is liable to *kareit*.
>
> (*Mishnah K'ritot* 2:6)

The first two cases in the mishnah teach that to be liable for sexual sins, one must first have the faculties to understand the correct approach to sex. In this case, neither a minor nor someone who is asleep can fulfill this requirement. They fall under the category of an *anoos*, someone who acts under coercion. Therefore, they are not held liable for their actions.

Although the application of the *anoos* category may not seem out of the ordinary here—of course a forced sexual encounter is not held to the same standards as one that is not—it is used here as a foil to how the term appears in *Mishnah Y'vamot* 6:1. To understand this mishnah, a little background is necessary. The Bible requires that when a woman's husband dies without offspring, that woman, called a *y'vamah*, should marry the brother of her husband in the hope that the union will produce a surrogate child and heir to the dead brother. This is known as levirate marriage and appears in Deuteronomy 25. One way that the two become married is through sex. The following mishnah defines what can be considered "valid and intentional" sex in the case of levirate marriage and in the case of forbidden sexual encounters like adultery:

> One who cohabits with his *y'vamah*, whether by mistake or on purpose, whether by coercion (*anoos*) or willingly . . . whether one begins sex or completes it, in all these cases he has acquired [the *y'vamah* as his wife]. . . . And so it is with one who has sex with any *arayot* [i.e., any forbidden union found in Leviticus 18].
>
> (*Mishnah Y'vamot* 6:1)

How can sex "count" and be punishable when one is an *anoos* in *Mishnah Y'vamot*, while not counting in *Mishnah K'ritot*? According to the Rabbis, the difference between these rulings lies in one's intent. They write that if a man does not want to have sex but is threatened with bodily harm if he does not engage, his act, while forgiven, *is* considered sex.[3] However, if he does not intend to have sex in the first place, for example, he is walking on the roof, slips, falls, and penetrates a woman, his act is legally meaningless. They have not had sex. While fantastical (and funny), this exchange in the Gemara makes an important claim. Penetration alone does not define sex. One must bring both an awareness and an intent for sex to occur.

However, even when both parties do bring this awareness and intent, not all sex is considered equal. Perhaps the most famous discussion of the importance of one's intention during sex appears in the Babylonian Talmud, *N'darim* 20b. There we find a discussion by Rabbi Levi of nine characteristics that taint one's offspring. In other words, if someone is in one of nine states during sex, they will curse their seed, making children produced from that sexual encounter into "rebels" and "transgressors."[4] These nine characteristics include at least six that speak directly to the role of one's intent in the sexual act:

- *Eimah* (**sex when one partner is afraid**): The Rabbis long ago forbade a husband from forcing his wife to have sex with him (see Babylonian Talmud, *Eiruvin* 100b); however, the Talmud warns against nonphysical coercion as well. If a husband imposes fear on his wife so that her heart is not fully in the sexual encounter, sex is forbidden.

- *S'nuah* (sex when partners hate one another): There is little agreement among the medieval commentators about why this category is so problematic. For some, it is because hate means the absence of love. For others, it may cause a husband to think about another woman during sex, an act that is forbidden, as we will see below.

- *T'murah* (sex when a husband thinks he is sleeping with someone else during the act): Earlier in Tractate *N'darim*, Rabbi states, "One should not drink from this cup while setting his eyes on another cup." Therefore, Jewish law condemns those having sex while thinking of someone else. *T'murah* is an extreme case of this, because a man falls into this classification when in the dark he actually sleeps with the wrong partner!

- *M'rivah* (sex during an argument): According to a number of medieval commentators, love and harmony are important prerequisites to a marital sexual encounter. Arguments disrupt that harmony and affect the balance in a relationship.

- *Shichrut* (sex while drunk): Classical Jewish law prohibits drunken sex even if only one member of a couple is drunk. Here, "drunk" means that one consumes alcohol to a point where his or her thought processes are impaired or confused.[5]

- *G'rushat haleiv* (sex between a husband and wife when divorce is imminent): On the surface this ruling seems superfluous since one may not have sex with a partner who is "hated" or with whom he is angry. Nevertheless, classical Jewish law compels divorce in a number of cases that do not involve emotion—for example if a husband can no longer provide financially for his wife. Even here, where a husband still cares deeply for his spouse, he may not have sex with her if he intends to divorce her.

It is important to note that the Rabbis and later commentators were writing for their time. Clearly this list is male-centric because of the milieu in which these texts were written. However, living in a modern egalitarian society, we can apply these prohibitions to all sexual encounters. Jewish law places a premium on where one's thoughts go in bed. While few commentators agree on the ideal mind-set during sex (we will come back to this), tradition has set up boundaries to ensure that a sexual encounter does not become spiteful (as in the case of a hateful encounter), hazy (as in the case of a drunk encounter), or devious (as in the case of a sexual encounter when divorce is imminent).

In fact, even the intention one brings to foreplay is legislated by Jewish law. In the same Talmudic passage (*N'darim* 20a–b) where we find the nine characteristics that can taint offspring, we find a debate between two Rabbinic sages. One sage, Rabbi Yochanan ben Dahavai, states that children risk ending up "mute and deaf" if their parents "converse at the time of cohabitation." Here the punishment fits the crime. Since parents sin by listening and speaking, their children are affected with an inability to do either. However, immediately following this comment, the Talmud brings the case of Ima Shalom, whose children were exceedingly beautiful. When asked what she did right, one of her answers is that her husband "converses with her . . . in the middle of the night," which in turn causes him to turn into a "demon" in the bedroom. While the medieval commentators debate the meaning of this transformation, many agree that turning into a demon is a good thing.

Faced with this contradiction—Yochanan ben Dahavai condemning conversation in the bedroom, and Ima Shalom lauding it—the anonymous editor of the Talmud develops a compromise so that there is no contradiction. Ima Shalom's statement deals with conversations about sex itself, while Yochanan ben Dahavai refers to conversations about other things. Here, intimate speech is encouraged in the bedroom if the point is to enhance the sexual experience of the two. The problem, however, is when the talk moves away from the act itself and into the mundane. Talk of chores, errands, and finances deserves a place in the household, but, the Talmud warns, it has no place in the bedroom.

As we have seen, both sections from *N'darim* 20a–b speak emphatically about the need to avoid certain conversations, thoughts, and states during sex. However, the Talmud avoids a prescriptive conversation about what a good, intentional sexual encounter looks like. Should one have a conversation or thought in the bedroom, what would that ideally be? For this answer, we must turn to the medieval commentators. What we find when we do is that there is little agreement about what one should be thinking about during sex. We will examine three thinkers, Moses Maimonides (Rambam, twelfth-century North Africa), Abraham ben David of Posquieres (Raavad, thirteenth-century France), and the mystical work *Igeret HaKodesh*, pseudepigraphically attributed to Moshe ben Nachman (Nachmanides, thirteenth-century Spain), in hopes of answering this question.

Of these three thinkers, Maimonides takes the most restrictive view of one's motivations during sex. For Maimonides, who was a philosopher and legalist inspired by Aristotle, sex was necessary but not the ideal. In his famous philosophical work, *Guide for the Perplexed*, he lauds "the knowledge of God, the formation of ideas, the mastery of desire and passion, [and] the distinction between that which is to be chosen and that which is to be rejected"[6] as parts of one's form, one's heavenly endowed gifts from God. However, "eating, drinking, sexual intercourse, excessive lust, passion, and all vices" are hazards of having a body. A person's goal is to have "form subdue the body, refuse the fulfillment of its desires, and reduce them, as far as possible, to a just and proper measure." Sex is a product of being human, but the higher purpose of humanity is to subdue those desires so one can better connect with God.

With this in mind, there is little question why Maimonides wrote in his magnum opus the *Mishneh Torah*, "Although a man's wife is permitted to him at all times, it is fitting that a wise man behave with holiness. He should not be found frequenting his wife like a rooster. Rather each Shabbat eve, only, he should approach her, if he has strength."[7] Therefore, when he does have sex, his mind-set should be similarly restrained. He writes, "He should not be too frivolous, and shouldn't disgrace his mouth with obscene nonsense even if it is just between the two of them." For Maimonides, talk should be simply a way to get a

partner in the mood; "he should laugh, just a little with her so she re-
laxes, and he should have sex with a little embarrassment and without
boldness, and should withdraw from her immediately."[8]

According to Maimonides there are two reasons why a human being should engage in sexual relations. He writes, "He should only have
sex to keep his body health and preserve the human race [lit., his seed].
Therefore, he should not engage in intercourse whenever he feels an
urge, but only when he knows that he needs to spill his seed for medical
purposes or in order to preserve the human race."[9] This view comports
with other statements, where Maimonides writes, "This act [i.e., sex]
was only given for the sake of procreation."[10] Perhaps the most telling
of his statements appears in his commentary on *Mishnah Sanhedrin* 7:3:

> The intent of sexual relations is the preservation of the species
> and not only pleasure. The aspect of pleasure was introduced only
> to motivate the created beings toward that ultimate goal. . . . The
> proof of this is that desire and pleasure cease after ejaculation; this
> was the entire goal for which our instincts were aroused. If the goal
> were pleasure, satisfaction would continue as long as man desired.[11]

What we see from these statements is that Maimonides has a hi-
erarchal approach to sexual intent. Because sex is a necessary evil, its
main purpose is procreation. Should one need sex for health benefits,
then this also acceptable. However, sexual pleasure is a means to fulfill
one's conjugal obligation. It is not an end in itself. One's mind should
be turned toward the mitzvah, not the feeling, during sex.

Abraham ben David of Posquieres, the Raavad, views sex with a very
different outlook. In his work *Baalei HaNefesh* (Masters of the Soul)
written in 1180, the Raavad outlines four intentions one may have
during sex: (1) he is fulfilling the commandment to procreate found in
Torah (Gen. 1:28); (2) he is benefitting the health of a fetus, since he
believed that sex during the second and third trimester was beneficial
to the well-being of the future child; (3) he may have sex with the sole
intent to please his partner; or (4) sex may be used as a tool to calm his
desires and hold back a person's evil inclination (*yetzer hara*).[12]

However, for the Raavad, not all of these intents hold equal ground. He writes in his preface that the first three constitute the "greatest reward" and in the body of his work explains that the first rationale, procreation, is "the most proper of them." Although many recent scholars have found a clear ascetic sentiment in other sections of his work, paralleled in medieval Christian writing of the time,[13] it is clear from the above list that Abraham ben David displays a significant departure from Maimonides. Where the former understood sexual satisfaction as a necessary evil, the Raavad held up satisfaction as a significant aspect of sex and a valid intention one may bring to the sexual act. Interestingly, while love does not appear in this list, it does appear later in the chapter. In an extended commentary to the nine characteristics in *N'darim* 20b, Ben David cites the absence of love as the reason why scornful and drunken sex are condemned. True, one may have sex for procreation and pleasure, but it *must* contain love.

Perhaps the broadest list of intentions appears in the mystical work *Igeret HaKodesh*. In addition to many of the intentions outlined by Ben David, namely the importance of pleasure, the author of this work added a number of his own. First, the author believed that one's thoughts during sex could positively affect a fetus's disposition when he or she eventually matured. Taking into account a midrash where a queen gave birth to a black child even though both she and the king were white, because the queen used to ruminate on the black designs in the ceiling,[14] the author of the work reminds his reader that one's thoughts during sex are passed on to one's children. Therefore, if one concentrates on the holiness of the act during sex, one will produce holy offspring. He writes, "When a man unites with his wife, if his imagination and thoughts concentrate on matters of wisdom and understanding, good and worthy qualities, those thoughts have the power to create an image in the drop of sperm."[15] For the author of *Igeret HaKodesh*, the intent to procreate wasn't the end goal, as it was for Maimonides; rather the goal is to enter sex in the state of mind that will produce holy and wise offspring.

The second major addition of the work is the return of God back into the bedroom. For the mystical author, one should direct one's attention to God in addition to the intentions of passion, procreation, and desire. David Biale, author of the book *Eros and the Jews*, writes, "In kabbalistic terms intercourse is the uniting of the male and female aspects of God, rather than a merely physical act. In fact, for an esoteric point of view, the secret (*sod*) meaning of carnal knowledge (*daat*) is kabbalistic knowledge. When a man understands the mystical meaning of intercourse, he transforms the act into communion with the divine: the physical becomes epistemological."[16] In other words, one's bedroom becomes a microcosm of God. Just as the mystics believed that God had male and female aspects, which under the right circumstances unite—think, for example, about the Shabbat bride, the marriage between God's masculine and feminine features—the author of *Igeret HaKodesh* believed that the coming together of male and female during sex could mimic God, drawing down holiness from heaven and creating a sort of mini-cosmos in the bedroom. Therefore, he believed, anyone engaged in a sexual act should keep in mind this cosmic significance.

Although there are many more approaches than these three, Maimonides, the Raavad, and *Igeret HaKodesh* demonstrate just how varied the Jewish approach can be to the optimal intent one may bring to sex. Each agrees that there are things to avoid, namely the nine pitfalls found in *N'darim* 20b. But while drunken, spiteful, or aloof sex is understood as inappropriate by all the thinkers cited here, there is little agreement about exactly what is the appropriate intention to bring into the bedroom. Maimonides may advocate for a narrow approach to sex, but if one takes the author of *Igeret HaKodesh* at his word, there is much room for imagination and play. Our thoughts should be "holy," but exactly how that is defined is open to interpretation.

At root in all of these texts is the idea of *kavanah*, or sacred intention, which plays out in any number of spheres in Jewish practice. We close our eyes when we say the *Sh'ma* so that our thoughts can focus on the meaning of the words. If we were simply proofreading a Torah scroll and we got to the verses of *Sh'ma* (Deut. 6:4 and following) and didn't focus on the prayer itself, the act of reading it would not count toward our daily prayer requirement. Likewise shaking the *lulav*, wrapping *t'fillin*, and lighting the Shabbat candles all require a certain level of concentration and intention. If the Rabbinic and medieval discussion of sex shows us anything, it is that sex is no different. Like prayer and other sacred acts, sex is something special and should not be approached lightly in either action or thought. The specific conclusions of which acts and thoughts one should avoid in the bedroom and which one should pursue is less important than the fact that these things have been debated. By including sex in the wider discussion of intention, our ancestors have elevated one of most instinctual and secular of acts into an element of the sacred conversation of how we can be more holy in the world.

NOTES

1. Deborah Feldman, *Unorthodox: The Scandalous Rejection of My Hasidic Roots* (New York: Simon & Schuster, 2012), 227.

2. Here the Hebrew reads *arayot* and refers to all forbidden unions found in Leviticus 18, including adultery, incest, and homosexuality.

3. See Babylonian Talmud, *Y'vamot* 53b. The Gemara was speaking only about the case of a man. The violation of women has a long and complicated history in the Jewish tradition, and it would be unfair to extrapolate lessons from what will turn into an absurdist text and apply them to this.

4. Proof text from Ezek. 20:38.

5. *Mishnah B'rurah* 240:18.

6. *Guide for the Perplexed* 3:8, M. Friedlander, trans. (London: Routledge, 1904).

7. *Mishneh Torah, Hilchot Dei-ot* 5:4.

8. Ibid.

9. Ibid., 3:2.

10. *Mishneh Torah, Hilchot Isurei Biah* 21:9.

11. Translation found in Maimonides, *Mishneh Torah*, vol. 19, *Issurei Biah*, trans. Eliyahu Touger (New York: Moznaim, 2002).

12. For a full translation of this section see Jeremy Cohen, "Rationales for Conjugal Sex in RaABaD's *Ba'alei ha-Nefesh*," *Jewish History* 6, nos. 1–2 (1992): 65–78.

13. See David Biale, *Eros and the Jews: From Biblical Israel to Contemporary America* (New York: Basic Books, 1992), 96, 263n50.

14. *Midrash Tanchuma, Naso* 7.

15. Quote found in Biti Roi, "Iggeret Ha-Kodesh," in *Jewish Women: A Comprehensive Historical Encyclopedia*, http://jwa.org/encyclopedia/article/iggeret-ha-kodesh.

16. Biale, *Eros and the Jews*, 105.

9

ALONE TOGETHER

RABBI DANIEL A. LEHRMAN, NCPsyA, LP

Benjamin arrives for therapy having just returned from a trip to his parents' home, where he spent Rosh HaShanah with them and his two sisters. Three years have passed since the whole family was together. "It's just unbelievable!" he reports. "The minute I walk into that kitchen it's like I'm ten again! All the stuff we've worked on here—my mother with her sarcastic judgments every second, my sister acting like a baby to win the approval of my dad, me feeling like I'm not protecting my other sister from my mom's passive-aggressive crap—I'm yanked right back into it all again! I ended up slamming the porch door before I'd been there an hour! It's embarrassing! For the whole first day, I just wanted to get out of there."

Benjamin is caught up in the struggle of being at once connected with his family yet also separate from them. One step through the door and he feels engulfed in the *meshugas*, in a vortex of resentment, guilt, rage, need, and hurt, that completely takes control over him. His responses are not responses at all, but simply reflexes, automatic reactions he cannot manage. In the language of neuroscience, he was thrust into the limbic system of his brain, the zone of roiling emotions and the survival instincts of fight or flight ("I just wanted to get out of there"). He had no access to his neocortex, the more evolved part of his brain that could help him to regulate his emotions, bring some perspective and reason into the moment, and give him some space in which to gain hold of himself so as to respond and interact as the mature thirty-four-year-old man he has become.

In relationship, we need our own space and we yearn to be connected—a complementary tension, like the north and south poles of a magnet. The ratio of these needs varies enormously from person to person, but the presence of them is in everyone. Arthur Schopenhauer, in a fable that struck a chord with Sigmund Freud, tells of a troop of porcupines lumbering around in the cold. Seeking warmth, they draw close. But once in contact, they start to poke each other with their quills! So they spread out again, only to shiver in the cold. Back they waddle in search of one another, now stung but together and warm, now safe but freezing and alone.[1] What does it take to be both a "Me" and a "We" without causing undue pain to oneself or the other?

Childhood dramatizes the struggle. Ethan, at age four, is laughed at one day by his lunchtime tablemates for having a lunchbox that appears to have a flower on it. "That's a *girl's* lunchbox!" and Ethan goes home weeping to declare he can never again appear in public with the detestable object. In that moment, Ethan was so delicately permeable to his classmates that he was unable to hold on to a stable sense of self that could survive the onslaught of criticism. Similar moments will of course recur at every stage and turn of growth, as will others of the opposite tendency—the adamantine rigidity, for example, of the mother and daughter locked in a power struggle, equally unbudgeable in their frigid standoff that may take days to thaw. We might say here that each has become wholly *impermeable* to the other, absolutely insusceptible to any give-and-take. Rabbi Hillel was a pithy psychologist: "If I am not for myself, who will be for me? If I am for myself alone, what am I?"[2] Too pliant and I lose myself. Too rigid and I lose my partner.

Sexuality ups the ante of the lifelong challenge we are describing, since in a sexual relationship the partners become permeable to each other in such manifold and unique ways. Indeed, we might describe sexual desire itself as a desire to *be* permeable to another person and to experience another's permeability. Psychologist David Schnarch draws a distinction that is useful for exploring such desires. He calls *intimacy need*, "the degree of desire to engage and disclose core aspects of oneself to one's partner." *Intimacy tolerance*, on the other hand, is "the unilateral ability to maintain a comfortable and clearly defined identity as one (and one's partner) discloses core aspects of self."[3] We have a need for togetherness, but we can tolerate only so much of it. We have a hard time tolerating our own needs.

Between the poles of need and tolerance, we enact in sexual intimacy many intertwined questions: *How much do I want to let my partner in? How much am I able? How much do I want to be let in by my partner? What do we do when our needs and tolerances differ? If intimacy is about opening parts of myself to my partner, how much access do I myself even have to such "core aspects" of myself? Am I willing to risk meeting some aspects of both self and other in moments of physical relating?* We will explore some of these dynamics of emotional and sexual intimacy as they are highlighted within a contemporary cultural context.

In our texting, cell-phoning, e-mailing, Skyping, Facebooking, Twittering culture, we live in a constancy of interpersonal contact that only a decade or two ago was unimaginable. Mundane daily tasks that used to be done alone—grocery shopping, driving to work, going for a jog—can now be accomplished to the accompaniment of conversation, including even live video, with anyone anywhere on earth. To call this a transformation in our means of communication is an understatement that does not describe how it has reshaped the very texture of interpersonal contact and, in particular, the experience of aloneness.

I see acute forms of such changes among some young adults who have been immersed in our culture of constant contact throughout their formative years. Some have scant experience of being alone at all. Certainly they have been out of physical proximity to other people, but being alone is a different matter. Those countless nighttimes when a teenager used to enter a zone of solitary self-reflection behind the shut door of his or her bedroom—for many young people, such hours scarcely exist. The airwaves are carrying messages from behind that door to the four corners of the earth, no matter how firmly it was slammed. One may be studying, buying bagels, working out, riding a horse, sitting on the toilet—anything—and be seldom more than minutes, even seconds, away from communicating with somebody, or trying anxiously to do so. Some report a near-constant craving for input and for validation. To rest content in a private state of being can feel intolerable. A disorienting helplessness may be brought on if an Internet connection or cell phone becomes unavailable, like losing track of your group while hiking in unfamiliar woods.

There is even a handy acronym for one variety of this unsettling experience: FOMO, "fear of missing out." It refers to "the blend of anxiety, inadequacy, and irritation that can flare up while skimming social media," according to one young woman who is well acquainted with it.[4] The syndrome she describes is surely shared by millions daily. She is sitting happily alone at home with a movie when she gets alerts from a half-dozen friends telling her of the cool things they are doing. Some are out at a live-music venue; others send pictures of themselves slurping fancy milkshakes at a trendy restaurant. "Suddenly, my simple domestic pleasures paled in comparison with the things I could be doing. The flurry of possibilities set off a rush of restlessness and indecision."[5] The pleasure of being simply and satisfyingly alone snuck up on her one evening, and suddenly, the experience became suspect. Her own enjoyment of it became insufficient; a gratifying inner state of being was no longer self-validating. "Is being by myself okay?" she implicitly asks herself. "Is there something wrong with me that I am not with others?" Such acute forms of discomfort with aloneness may well be most prevalent among young adults, but this group's experience highlights a more general cultural condition in which loss of connectibility often triggers anxiety. My eighty-four-year-old relative is hardly the only senior who would be pacing the living room floor if his three children were not at all times available at the press of a speed dial—and he has owned a cell phone for but a tenth of his life.

What is it to be alone? To be alone is certainly not simply to be in the absence of other people. As put by Donald Winnicott, an influential psychodynamic theorist and clinician, "A person may be in solitary confinement, and yet not be able to be alone."[6] In Winnicott's view, not everyone has developed a capacity for aloneness. It is, rather, an achievement and "one of the most important signs of maturity in emotional development." A capacity for aloneness begins to develop in a surprising way, namely, when one is not alone: "The basis of the capacity to be alone is a paradox; it is the experience of being alone while someone else is present." Winnicott is speaking here of an infant and parent or other caretaker, and he is imagining a scene such as the baby lying in his crib watching shadows change on the ceiling while Mommy or Daddy is washing dishes or folding laundry. There must be a "sufficiency of this experience" over time, because in it, the infant builds up a feeling of safety. It is an experience of being watched over, but without impingement. Only with repeated experiences of such security and "holding" does one come to "build up a belief in a benign environment." In the terms of Erik Erikson, "basic trust" has been established so that one may experience aloneness as an opportunity for reverie and pleasure more than as a zone of danger.

The safe space of being alone is closely related for Winnicott to "relaxing," to a "sufficiency of living," and to being able "to rest contented even in the absence of external objects and stimuli." To be alone is "to be in a state in which there is no orientation, to be able to exist for a time without being either a reactor to an external impingement or an active person with a direction of interest or movement."[7] An "internal world has become possible."[8] There is a self-validating sufficiency in being able to be alone, a simple contentment, such as the young woman felt while sitting at home watching a movie. It is a feeling that I don't need constant reassurance from others of my adequacy; my "internal world"—the mere being of my own self—is okay, more than okay, beautiful. To be able to be alone is thus for Winnicott crucial to becoming a mature person—an individuated, autonomous, self-initiating human being, who can feel her own feelings because she has access to her "internal world" and can therefore experience her own desires and take steps toward her own goals.

How is this capacity for feeling contented in our own company important for emotional sexual intimacy? The word "intimacy" itself opens for us a doorway. From Latin *intimus*, a superlative form meaning "innermost," it is related to words in a variety of languages meaning secret, deep, and private. In its verb form, as in "He intimated to me that we should speak separately after the meeting," it means "to put into, drive or press into, to make known." This cluster of words and meanings calls up whole tableaux of sexual images and associations, from the depths and caverns of the body to the secrets and mysteries of arousal and desire. Memories of initial attraction and the beginnings of a sexual relationship call up the thrill of inviting someone, and of being permitted, "behind the scenes," past the curtain of social boundaries, into interior realms not accessible to just anyone. Thus did Isaac bring Rebekah into the tent of his mother Sarah, and he took Rebekah as his wife (Gen. 24:67). Thus does Bruce Springsteen sing, "She'll let you deep inside, but there's a secret garden she hides."

In bringing someone into our tent, we traverse a distance—more than a spatial distance, of course—an emotional, psychical distance, from You and Me, to We. We begin to become naked to one another —how much, who knows? At first, the desire to become a We can feel all-consuming, devouring. But then it can get scary. *Will I expose myself and be accepted? Will I find comfort? Disapproval? Ridicule? Will I want him more than he wants me? Will I feel repulsed? Will she? Will I feel trapped? Endangered?* Before long, and sometimes right away, we are in the thick of our needs and tolerances and their pulls and pushes. "Because the full emotional responsiveness of the other can never be taken for granted," writes psychoanalyst Stephen A. Mitchell, "sexual encounters always contain elements of risk and implicit drama."[9]

For plunging into so much unknown, it helps to have developed some self-trust, some experience of an internal world that can tolerate the elements of risk. Schnarch's *intimacy tolerance*—"the unilateral ability to maintain a comfortable and clearly defined identity as one (and one's partner) discloses core aspects of self"—might better be called "intimacy courage." This is the courage to say, *I can afford to take the risk of connection, because if I reach out and do not find the embrace I seek, I will be okay; I will be able to try again. I may be hurt, but I will not be ruined.* Courage does not mean one is fearless. It means one can move into the fear and through it. A comfort with aloneness as Winnicott describes it is a secure base that enables one, whether for the first time or the thousandth, to make this venture.

A momentous turning point in the life of Jacob resounds with the themes we are delving into. While the connection is not sexual, it is transformingly intimate. Jacob is about to meet Esau, the brother whom he had tricked out of their father Isaac's blessing twenty years earlier and from whom he fled because their mother Rebekah was terrified of Esau's vengeful homicidal rage. It is the night before the fateful meeting. We might expect Jacob in his anxiety to huddle up and take comfort with his large family. Instead he makes a surprising move. He decides to separate himself. He sends his two wives, his eleven children, his two maidservants, and all his possessions across the river Jabbok while he stays on the other side. "And Jacob was left alone" (Gen. 32:25). He sought solitude—a good thing, since otherwise the family would have had little rest. All night until the break of dawn, Jacob wrestled. With what? His guilty conscience? His terror of his brother's revenge? Fear of his own brutal instincts? The parts of him that could not muster the courage he needed to face his wronged sibling? However we understand Jacob's wrestling partner, some quantum change occurred that night, an identity-changing leap, marked by a new name. Without so much as a text sent to a wife across the Jabbok, Jacob became Israel.

Like Moses later, who, alone, "came near to *Adonai*" (Exod. 24:2), Jacob, alone, meets God face to face (Gen. 32:31). In solitude, the soul metabolizes and synthesizes experience. Winnicott observes that once the alone state is entered into, "the stage is set for an id experience."[10] Here, "id" denotes far more than "erotic." It refers to the bottomless well of energy springing from the unconscious. "In the course of time," he continues, "there arrives a sensation or an impulse. In this setting the sensation or impulse will feel real and be truly a personal experience."[11] Jacob certainly needed to feel real. When he sent his retinue across the Jabbok, he must have intuited that only authenticity would do for the next day's meeting, when Esau would surely see through any remnant of guile. So he'd better gain access to his deepest self. His transformative id experience became possible when he decided to spend a night alone. In solitude Jacob became capable of bringing forth all of himself—far more than his wives, children, and servants, and his hundreds of animals as offerings—to meet Esau. Having stripped himself of his emotional armor, he could step forward into that wonderful moment when his brother receives him, falls on his neck, kisses him, and they weep (Gen. 33:4).

Jacob needed courage on both sides of the river Jabbok. He expected danger in meeting Esau, but in fact his injury was sustained before he crossed, when he met himself. The socket of his hip was strained that night, leaving him with a limp (Gen. 32:26). Where Winnicott stresses the trust and safety of aloneness, Jacob reminds us not only that in being alone we are not alone, but that dangers do reside on both shores, in relationship and also in solitude. For intimate relating–and perhaps for sexual intimacy above all—we need the trust and safety, but not as end points or the final goal, rather as a place from which to reach out toward connection, with all its risks. Sex therapist Esther Perel, among others, notes that we must not just *tolerate* our separateness, we *need* the separateness if we want a relationship to flourish. "To sustain an elan toward the other, there must be a synapse to cross," she writes. Eroticism "thrives in the space between the self and the other."[12] The goal, then, is not to collapse the distance between oneself and one's partner. "Our ability to tolerate our separateness—and the fundamental insecurity it engenders—is a precondition for maintaining interest and desire in a relationship."[13] Insecurity as elan: this may be a much needed counterpoise to the familiar view of coupledom as permanent security. We need to be a little bit off-balance, not on completely sure footing, if we wish to maintain and cultivate erotic connection. Stephen A. Mitchell writes of our "conflictual longings for certainty and permanence,"[14] of how safety and predictability become stultifying in a relationship, and of how these qualities are not even real. For we cannot truly "fix the fluidity and multiplicity of the other into a predictable pattern" because life itself, if we are awake to it, is too much in motion. If we think we have the other person figured out, then perhaps we ought to look at our own need to close down and shut out the unknown, the mystery and risk of relationship. Thus Mitchell observes that the "habituation that often, perhaps usually, dulls romantic love is not intrinsic to the nature of love itself but is a protective degradation, a defense against the vulnerability inherent in romantic love."[15] Vulnerability and insecurity: we may be accustomed to thinking of them as feelings that an intimate relationship puts an end to. Could they or some forms of them be the very soil from which erotic intimacy draws its vitality?

Let us conclude with a thought-provoking observation of Winnicott's about what happens after sex: "It is perhaps fair to say that after satisfactory intercourse each partner is alone and is contented to be alone. Being able to enjoy being alone along with another person who is also alone is in itself an experience of health."[16] Here we come full circle. We started with the paradox that the way we learn to be alone is through not being alone, but rather by being in the presence of a loving caretaker who can help us to build trust in a safe environment and therefore in a safe inner self. Such a safe inner self permits us the confidence to reach out toward another. Having connected, we are then able to share some of the interior worlds of our aloneness, as in the intimacy of sexual relations. And then we can relax back into our internal space—in our private solitude if we wish, or even while still in the presence of our partner, in what Rilke calls, in *Letters to a Young Poet*, "the love that consists in this: that two solitudes protect and touch and greet one another." Being with another enabled solitude, and solitude enables a deep *being* with another. Thus can a human being be in solitary confinement, yet not be able to be alone, or in closest proximity with another, snuggled up in bed, and be alone—together.

NOTES

1. Recounted in Deborah Luepnitz, *Schopenhauer's Porcupines* (New York: Basic Books, 2002), 2.

2. *Pirkei Avot* 1:14.

3. David Schnarch, *Constructing the Sexual Crucible: An Integration of Sexual and Marital Therapy* (New York: W.W. Norton, 1991), 183.

4. Jenna Wortham, "Feel Like a Wallflower? Maybe It's Your Facebook Wall," *New York Times*, April 9, 2011.

5. Ibid.

6. Donald Winnicott, "The Capacity to Be Alone" (1958), in *The Maturational Processes and the Facilitating Environment: Studies in the Theory of Emotional Development* (London: Hogarth Press / Institute of Psycho-Analysis, 1965; New York: International Universities Press, 1965; repr. London: Karnac Books, 1990), 29–36.

7. Winnicott's description here of some of the qualities of aloneness is strikingly similar to Erich Fromm's description of "being" in his distinction between the two modes "being" and "having." Fromm further describes Shabbat (striking some Heschelian notes, whose *The Sabbath* Fromm had doubtless read) as a prime example of the "being" mode. See Erich Fromm, *To Have or To Be* (New York: Continuum, 1976), 48ff.

8. Winnicott, 33.

9. Stephen A. Mitchell, *Relational Concepts in Psychoanalysis: An Integration* (Cambridge, MA: Harvard University Press, 1988), 105.

10. Winnicott, 34.

11. Ibid., 34.

12. Esther Perel, *Mating in Captivity: Unlocking the Erotic and the Domestic* (New York: Harper Collins, 2006), xv.

13. Ibid., 65.

14. Stephen A. Mitchell, *Can Love Last? The Fate of Romance Over Time* (New York: W.W. Norton, 2002), 51.

15. Ibid., 45.

16. Winnicott, 31.

10

"YOUR LOVE IS SWEETER THAN WINE"

Erotic Theology in Jewish Tradition

Rabbi Geoffrey W. Dennis

"Erotic theology" is not a term we use much in the Reform Movement, even among our theologians. In this respect, we Reformers are very much the children of medieval rationalist philosophers like Saadyah Gaon and Maimonides, whose argument that God has neither body nor passion—is in fact devoid of any quality that can be construed as "human"—has come to permeate Reform thinking.[1] Consequently when Jews describe God, we characterize God as a purely spiritual entity that transcends gender, without a hint of anything that can be remotely associated with sexuality.[2] In fact—as the sentence above reveals by its avoidance of a familiar pronoun—we today even hesitate to refer to God as "He." Thus, when we Reform Jews discuss God's relation to gender, we tend to focus on questions of liturgy and how best to achieve a "gender neutral" language for expressing our thoughts on divinity.

Yet even a casual examination of Jewish writings about God reveals this attitude to be but one voice among many. There are other ways to think about God and God's relationship to creation, humanity, and Jews in particular. In reality, we have used erotic metaphors and even the language of sexuality to describe our God and have done so with considerable consistency across time.

Broadly speaking, the term "erotic theology" is most often associated with texts and ideas we today identify as "mystical." For some scholars, eroticizing divinity is the very definition of mysticism.[3] Yet much more of this erotic discourse is hiding in plain sight, appearing in the Hebrew Scriptures, the Talmud, the midrash, and other fundamental and authoritative Jewish sources.

God and Israel in Ancient Near Eastern Context

To grasp our tradition of erotic theology, it is useful to first consider the mythic and religious milieu in which Israelite religion and monotheism emerged.

For virtually all peoples of the ancient Near East, divinity was characterized in gendered terms—gods and goddesses. Gender and sex were cosmic, meta-divine realities; the gods did not select or control their gender—it was assigned to them by a higher fate.[4] That being said, the partnership of the gods was fundamental to the cosmos, creating and sustaining it. Referred to by academics as a *syzygy* (a yoked pair), or in more expressly sexual form a *heiros gamos* (sacred coupling), this complementary gender structure of divinity was thought to give birth to the world, perpetuate the seasons, and fructify the earth. It was an important feature in all the known religions of the ancient Mediterranean basin and the Near East.[5] The particularly sexual aspect of the gods' *heiros gamos* was often forefront and explicit in pagan religious literature of the ancient Near East.[6]

Intuitively, this kind of sexual theology works best in a polytheistic context. This being so, it is logical to think, as many readers of the Bible have, that once the Israelites settled upon the proposition that "our God is one" (Deut. 6:4), any notion of God engaging in cosmic sexual acts to perpetuate the world would be rendered nonsensical; in the absence of a corresponding consort goddess, divine asexuality would seem to be a logical corollary. Yet a careful reading of the Hebrew Scriptures reveals that even in the monotheistic context of

Israelite religion, the concept of *syzygy*, of divine partnership, is actually displaced rather then dispensed with.

To understand how the sexual life of the God of Israel was reconceptualized in Israelite thought, we begin with a text that is itself utterly without erotic overtones: the Israelite Creation narrative of Genesis 1:1–2:3. In it, God forms the cosmos via a series of speech-acts, progressively dividing up the watery primordial chaos into binary groupings: heaven and earth, sea and dry land, plants and animals. At the conclusion of this project, following the creation of binary humanity, whom God declares to be made in His image,[7] God takes time to rest and designates that day of rest, the Shabbat, a sacred day. In contrast to many polytheistic cosmogonies, where some aspect of the universe is formed by means of divine birth, the God of Israel creates only via words. Any notion of cosmic partnership, let alone sexuality, is absent in this account; sex is a feature of Creation ("Be fruitful and multiply") but not of the Creator.

Here is where awareness of the cultural and literary context of Scripture becomes critical to understanding this Hebrew Creation myth. Scholars of the ancient Near East recognize that the Creation account in Genesis is partly a monotheistic variation on a Babylonian creation myth, the *Enuma Elish*. In this myth, the world is created, not by birth, nor by divine fiat, but as the aftermath of a cosmic battle. The god Marduk is offered dominance in the divine *syzygy* by the other gods and goddesses if he will do battle against the sea/chaos monster Tiamat. Marduk defeats the creature and then divvies up its corpse to construct the cosmos, in a pattern similar to the one described in Genesis. At the culmination of the process, Marduk creates humanity from Tiamat's blood with the express purpose that man will "bear the god's burden, that those [the gods] may rest." The gods who sided with Marduk enjoy with him the privilege of cosmic governance and conclude the process of creation in festive rest.[8] This feature of the *Enuma Elish*, the theme of a supremely powerful deity being in partnership with other, lesser gods, is the feature that is of interest to us, while the idea of divine rest is the key to understanding it.

For the Babylonian account, "rest," one of the privileges of cosmic authority, is vouchsafed only to divine things: Marduk and his partner gods and goddesses. In the Genesis account, by contrast, the singular God rests alone—but only for a while. For when God chooses Israel to be "His people" at Mount Sinai, God includes the commandment to the Israelites to "remember the Sabbath day and keep it holy. Six days you shall labor and do all your work, but the seventh day is a Sabbath of the Lord your God. . . . For in six days the Lord made heaven and earth and sea—and all that is in them—and He rested on the seventh day" (Exod. 20:8–11). In essence, by bringing Israel into covenant with divinity, God elevates the people Israel to a status analogous to that of a minor deity in *Enuma Elish*. While it is subtle, it is nonetheless the case that the biblical writers revived and reworked the pagan theme of *syzygy* to assert that Israel has become God's consort; this move exalts Israel over other peoples by making it alone God's sacred partner.

"Your Time for Love Had Arrived": Erotic Rhetoric in the *Tanach*

While the texts we've discussed so far remain bereft of any erotic connotations, elsewhere in Scripture it becomes clearer that the covenant at Sinai is more than a mere contract between a patron god and a vassal people; it is a wedding covenant, and Israel has become God's bride. Thus several of the prophetic writers speak of the relationship of God and Israel as that of a husband and wife: "I accounted your favor, the devotion of your youth, your love as a bride" (Jer. 2:2). Israel's lack of devotion to the exclusive worship of God is likened to marital infidelity (Isa. 54:6; Jer. 3:1). Marriage also stands as the metaphor for describing Israel's reconciliation with God:

> On that day—declares Adonai—you will call Me *Ishi* [literally, "my man," but idiomatically, "my husband"], and no longer call Me *Baali* [another term for "my husband," related to the word "Baal," an alien god]. . . . I will betroth you to Me forever; I will

> betroth you to Me in righteousness and justice, in steadfast love
> and compassion. I will betroth you to Me in faithfulness, and you
> shall know[9] the Lord.
>
> (Hos. 2:18; 2:21–22)

In deploying this image of God and Israel as partners in a sacred marriage, the biblical authors generally eschew the kind of raw, explicitly sexual imagery that we can find in Egyptian and Mesopotamian mythologies. But as the Hosea passage demonstrates, the sexual dimension of this relationship is never far below the surface, and in one text, Ezekiel 16:7–8, overtly sexual rhetoric bursts forth in a vivid and startling graphic passage.[10] The point is made: the love that God has for Israel is a kind of erotic love. Israel is expected to reciprocate that love with equal passion and desire.

While the prophets envisioned Israel as God's lover, even to the point of comparing God's desire for a relationship as analogous to that of a sexual partner, what we do not see in the Hebrew Scriptures is a theology of *heiros gamos*—the idea that the harmonious "union" of God and Israel is a matter of creative/cosmic import in a way analogous to the pagan theologies we have already mentioned. Whether this lacuna is a result of Israelite writers refusing to make this connection or whether later editors of the Scriptures, offended by this erotic strain of Israelite theology, censored it is not known.[11]

"I Am My Beloved's and His Desire Is for Me": Embracing the Metaphor in Rabbinic and Mystical Literature

This use of sexuality as a theological metaphor continues, unabated, throughout later Jewish teachings. The Jewish mystical project probably emerged in part with the decision that the book *Shir HaShirim* (Song of Songs) be included in the biblical canon.[12] According to the Talmud, Rabbi Akiva, a Rabbinic figure widely identified with the esoteric, was shocked when he learned that the inclusion of that book had once been controversial to sages a century before him. He is said to have remarked, "For all the Writings are holy, and the Song of Songs is holy of holies" (*Mishnah Yadayim* 3:5).

Akiva could assert this because the early Jewish mystics understood that book, which poetically narrates the love and desire felt between a woman and a man, to be the internal musings of God; Song of Songs lays bare divine desires for Israel during the Exodus. For Akiva and those who thought like him, no conception of the covenant was more central than this one (Babylonian Talmud, *Eiruvin* 21b; *Shir HaShirim Rabbah* 3:15–19).

The canonization of Song of Songs—its acceptance as authoritative—served to affirm and reinforce the trope characterizing God and Israel's relationship as that of lovers. The dominant tenor of this image is emotional. But the Song of Songs' extravagant imagery of the lover's world and its constant use of metaphors from both nature and human physical desire also invite the interpreter to see God's universe as erotically charged. In such a cosmos, it is easy to imagine that sexual union is indispensable to the balance and harmony of all things. In this way of thinking, male and female come to symbolize the polarities of existence that live in constant tension, while sexuality is the necessary recurrent mechanism that reintegrates those polarities into a unity. What eventually emerged (or reemerged) from this was a belief that sexuality is the force that sustains existence at all levels. For our mystics in particular, being male and female come to be regarded as more then merely part of the divine plan; they become the essential dynamo of the universal order, and unpacking these conjugal mysteries reveals the mind of God.

But not just for mystics. There are multiple reiterations of the marriage motif in Talmud, midrash, and medieval commentaries: "Already the groom wishes to lead the bride to the bridal chamber. . . . And [at Sinai] the Holy Blessed One went forth to meet them like a bridegroom who goes forth to meet the bride, so the Holy One went forth to meet them and give them the Torah" (*Pirkei D' Rabbi Eliezer* 41; see also Babylonian Talmud, *P'sachim* 106a–b). The meeting at Sinai is one that culminates in a spiritual consummation: "God became wedded to the Jewish people at the time of the Exodus and through the giving of the Torah. The consummation took place when God's Presence enveloped them" (comment of Eleazar Rokeach, on Talmud, *Kiddushin*; see also Rashi's comment on Song of Songs 3:11). The motif of marriage was also extended to the principal symbols and institutions of Judaism. Thus, the Torah becomes a *ketubah* (marriage contract) (*Sh'mot Rabbah* 46:1; *D'varim Rabbah* 3:12), the Sabbath is a reiteration of the wedding (*B'reishit Rabbah* 11:8; *P'sikta Rabbati* 23:6), and while it stood, the Temple in Jerusalem was perceived as the bridal chamber (*Eichah Rabbah* 4:11) where Israel and God enjoy their most perfect union (*Midrash Tanchuma* [Buber], Numbers 17a).[13]

Like the Bible, Rabbinic literature rarely elaborated on this motif in an expressly sexual fashion. Exceptional is this Talmudic passage discussing the meaning of the *k'ruvim* (sphinx-angels) statues that decorated the Ark of the Covenant kept inside the Holy of Holies (the innermost chamber) of the Temple:

> Rav K'tina said: When Israel would ascend [to the Temple] on the Festival, they [the priests] would open the curtain for them, and show them the cherubs, who were entwined in [sexual] embrace. They would then tell them, "Behold how beloved you are of God, like the love of man and woman."
>
> (Babylonian Talmud, *Yoma* 54a–b)

Here one sage describes these two cherubs, one apparently representing God, the other Israel, as actually coupling like two lovers. In the subsequent narrative, some colleagues were scandalized by this story, but another prominent sage, Resh Lakish, rallies in defense of this claim.

Among the mystics it was taught that the *k'ruvim* in the Temple were representations of the *merkavah*, the "chariot" of God, an idiom that was taken to embody the divine order.[14] For some like, Rav K'tina, the cherubs personified their belief that Eros was the driving force of creation.

For centuries this deeper erotic theology remained a largely esoteric idea—that is, until the great kabbalistic flowering of the thirteenth century. It is in *Igeret HaKodesh*, a medieval mystical sex manual, that a case for the metaphysical significance of coitus is fully articulated:

> Such is the secret of man and woman in the ways of Kabbalah. Thus, this [human sexual] union is a matter most elevated [when] it is done properly, and the greater secret is that the *merkavot* [also] unite, this one to that, in the manner of male and female.
>
> (*Igeret HaKodesh* 1:49)

As said earlier, the *merkavot* (chariots) mentioned in this passage is a mystical term, borrowed from the Bible (Ezekiel 1 and 10), for the structure of the godhead. So what the author of the *Igeret HaKodesh* is conveying is that our division into male and female is a reflection of the larger cosmic structure, and when humans unite in sex, the act is a mimesis of what happens within the divine realms (*Sefer HaYichud*, 33c–d; *Or HaChamah* 1:186a). Just as important, human sexuality becomes, in a sense, a substitute for the function of the ancient Temple in maintaining cosmic harmony.[15]

Meanwhile, in another thirteenth-century masterwork of classic Kabbalah, *Sefer HaZohar*, the belief that there is a sexual dynamic operating, not just within the world, but *within* God, is made fully explicit.[16] In the Zoharic theology of the *s'firot*, a flow chart of ten divine emanations, these divine forces are divided into male and female quantities, and it is the ongoing union of these attributes that enlivens and sustains our material universe. In particular, the *Zohar* emphasizes the importance that two particular *s'firot*, *Tiferet*, representing the transcendent (masculine) aspect of God, and *Shechinah*, signifying the immanent (feminine) divine presence in creation, be constantly brought together. And since *Shechinah*'s alternate mystical identity is *K'neset Yisrael* (Assembly of Israel), Jewish mysticism takes the further step of elevating an abstracted, idealized notion of Jewish peoplehood closer to quasi-divine status, making Israel an integral part of the godhead (*Zohar, Mishpatim* 2:126a).[17]

From the time of the *Zohar* on, this conjugal theology became more visible, aspects of it became well-known, and erotic metaphors were expansively applied to describe the Jewish people's passionate relationship with its God. This is especially evident in our siddur (prayer book), where liturgical poems such as *Anim Z'mirot, Y'did Nefesh*, and *L'cha Dodi* address God in the language of desire. Prominent mystics, such as Moses DeLeon, Isaac Luria, and the Baal Shem Tov, held that much of the worship service is a means for us to "adorn" the feminine aspect of God in preparation for its union with its masculine counterpart.[18] Chasidism even compares the prayer experience to sexual ecstasy.[19]

Without question, even the most traditional Jew understood this erotic imagery to be, on some level, figurative. Yet it was always taken seriously. The consequence of esoteric theology is that in Jewish tradition human sexuality became seen as an especially exalted, sanctified, and potentially enlightening aspect of the human experience. More than that, sex potentially takes on divine qualities—through it we are deeply integrated into the causality of the universe and how *we* use *our* sexuality has cosmic consequences, effecting the larger creation, and even divinity itself.

This theology of erotic mysteries reverberates in complex ways on subsequent Jewish attitudes toward the concrete realities of sex. On one hand, it elevates the status of the human body (*Igeret HaKodesh* 1:6). On the other hand, having raised the status of sex so high, it also means that sexual behavior that is considered transgressive is much more consequential. In traditional circles, permitted sexual acts, performed with the correct intention, are conduits of divine blessing, harmonizing divine forces, and even enhancing divine power. Conversely, inappropriate sexuality (generally coinciding with the biblical and Rabbinic categories of forbidden unions and acts) undermines the cosmic order and weakens divine power in creation. Jewish mysticism consequently views human sexuality as a portal to both holy and demonic realms.[20]

Carnal Israel: Reclaiming a Spirituality
of Sexuality in Contemporary Reform

Yet this erotic theology, influential as it has been, has become invisible to most liberal Jews. The bulk of Jewish thought that has passed through the crucible of modernity has embraced the rational philosophic traditions in Judaism that eschew ascribing any "human" qualities to God and consequently finds the language of desire an awkward way to relate to deity.[21] Partly as a result of this, and partly as a result of the larger compartmentalization of religion in the West, sexuality has been both thoroughly secularized and radically privatized, to the point where the suggestion that religious norms might delimit sexual behavior is seen as either quaint or intrusive by many Reform Jews.

Thus there exists a "meaning gap" between traditionalists and modernists. This tension, even polarity, about the sacred meaning of sex contributes to contemporary conflicts about sexual mores. For those who cleave to these traditions, who regard Israel as a cosmic force in God's order, the contemporary disregard of such customs as *nidah* (family purity rules), sexual continence outside of marriage, and the acceptance of homosexuality are matters of grave consequence. For those of us who have largely secularized the meaning of sex—or even have a more generalized sense of Judaism's positive perception of sex—the strictures and prudishness of traditional Jewish communities are both stifling and incomprehensible. Both sides value sexuality, but for very different reasons.

It does not have to be so, of course. The Talmud generally treated the pragmatics of human sexuality and the erotic relationship of God and Israel as complementary, not conflicting subjects. Certainly being passionate about God is not alien to the spirit of Reform Judaism. As Rabbi Eric Yoffe has observed, "Reform Judaism . . . began as a God-intoxicated movement."[22]

And there are ample ideas to draw on from our tradition with which we Reformers can reenvision a Jewish way that strikes a simultaneously moral and compassionate balance between radically traditional and radically secular approaches to sexuality.

The contemporary theologian Jay Michaelson rightly observes that Judaism is a "religion of boundaries."[23] As we have seen, for traditionalists, many expressions of human sexuality that we liberal Jews recognize as legitimate, especially queer sexuality, are "out of bounds." As Reform Jews, however, I believe we are uniquely positioned to lead our fellow Jews toward a new and fruitful synthesis between sexuality and spirituality, one that still recognizes the continuing value of boundaries, while inclusively redefining those boundaries to encompass, for example, the value of interfaith marriage or the rightness of GBLT sexuality. Our heritage of erotic theology, especially, provides us with some tools for this new synthesis. Notions of God's androgyny, for example, or that God is simultaneous a Deity of laws and *Ein Sof*, divinity without boundaries, allow us to imagine how the image of God still applies to those whose sexual boundaries differ from our own. Or consider that erotic theology allowed the androcentric culture of Judaism to imagine itself as the "female" partner in the divine-human *syzygy*,[24] thus breaking the boundaries of what we think of as Judaism's conventional gender and sexual essentialism. All these features of our erotic theology offer us starting points within our tradition from which we can begin to construct a simultaneously inclusive, healthy, and moral model of sexuality for our times.

Erotic theology invites us, as liberal Jews, to think about sex as central, rather than peripheral, to the concerns of Torah—a positive corollary to a life-affirming religion. It is at the intersection between tradition and modernity, between the poles of the reconditely mystical and the utterly utilitarian, that contemporary Reform Jews should look to locate how our faith and our sexuality can once again be harmoniously joined.

This article is an adaption of an earlier essay by the author, "The Bride of God: Jewish Erotic Theology," in *Jews and Sex*, ed. Nathan Abrams (London: Five Leaves Publishing, 2008).

NOTES

1. Saadyah ibn Yusuf, *The Book of Beliefs and Opinions*, trans. Samuel Rosenblatt (New Haven: Yale University Press, 1989), 93; Moses Maimonides, *Guide for the Perplexed*, trans. Shlomo Pines (Chicago: University of Chicago Press, 1963), 1:59. See also Moshe Idel's discussion in *Kabbalah and Eros* (New Haven: Yale University Press, 2005), 8–11.

2. While Maimonides is the most prominent proponent of this position, it is the result of a long Jewish campaign, already initiated by some biblical authors, against all anthropomorphic interpretations of deity. See Abraham Joshua Heschel, *The Prophets* (Peabody, MA: Hendrickson Publishing, 2007), 269–78; and Louis Jacobs, *A Jewish Theology* (West Orange, NJ: Behrman House, 1973), 25–31. Today the position that God is pure spirit without any meaningful embodiment or physical attributes enjoys wide affirmation among all branches of Judaism, excepting Kabbalah-centered Chasidic and *Haredi* communities. Examples of such doctrinal affirmations in the Reform Movement include the 1937 Columbus Platform. The Orthodox world is not given to umbrella statements of belief, but modern Orthodox attitude toward the incorporeality of God is exemplified in such works as David Bleich's *With Perfect Faith: Foundations of Jewish Belief* (New York: Ktav, 1986).

3. Cameron Afzal, in "Early Jewish and Christian Mysticism: A Collage of Working Definitions" (paper presented at the 2001 Conference of the Society of Biblical Literature), 3.

4. Yehezkel Kaufmann, *The Religion of Israel* (New York: Schocken Books, 1972), 21–23.

5. Most readers will be familiar with the sexual escapades of the Greek gods and goddesses or may even know the sex-and-death myth of Egyptian deities Osiris and Isis. Sexually explicit myths of creation, fertility, and rebirth also fill the less familiar sacred literature of Sumerian, Assyrian, and Babylonian civilizations.

6. W. W. Hallo and K. W. Younger, *The Context of Scripture* (Leiden: Brill Publishing, 2003), 1:280–81. There are also examples of gods who create the cosmos via an act of auto-eroticism (the myths of Atum and Ra), but that is taking us even further afield.

7. I use "His" here because that's how the text reads in Hebrew. I will continue that convention throughout the chapter. The masculine pronoun reflects the nature of Hebrew, in which all pronouns have gender, and in most cases in the Bible, the gender language of God is masculine. Its use here, and in other translations in this chapter, simply reflects the biblical wording, rather than the opinion of the author. It is, however, also an inescapable aspect of our discussion that when the tradition uses erotic language to denote the relationship between God and Israel, God is most often cast as the male in the male-female dyad. Later we will note where this rigid gender characterization of divinity varies, and even breaks down, in some mystical rhetoric.

8. Hallo and Younger, *Context of Scripture*, 400. See also Thorkild Jacobsen, "The Battle between Marduk and Tiamat," *Journal of American Oriental Studies* 88 (1968).

9. The Hebrew verb translated here as "know," *yod-dalet-ayin*, also carries the denotation of "have intercourse," a double entendre that the biblical writer consciously deploys.

10. God addresses Israel: "Your breasts became firm and your [pubic] hair sprouted. You were still naked and bare. Again I passed by you and saw that you were now old enough for love. So I spread the corner of My cloak over your nakedness; I swore an oath to you and entered into a covenant with you; you became Mine, says the Eternal God" (Ezekiel 16:7–8). The act of a man spreading his cloak over a woman signified his "honorable intentions," that the coitus about to be initiated is for the purpose of marriage (see Ruth 3:9). See David Biale, *Eros and the Jews* (Berkeley: University of California Press, 1997), 114; Howard Eilberg-Schwartz, *God's Phallus* (Boston: Beacon Press, 1994), 111.

11. We do have evidence that some Israelites at some point believed the God of Israel had a consort goddess. Examples of sacred graffiti, probably dating from the eighth century BCE, have been found with pictures and words praising *YHVH* and "his *asheirah (tzeirei).*" We even see that that idea may have been included in the formal Israelite cult at different times (I Kings 15:13; II Kings 21:7; 23:7). To learn more, see William Dever's, *Did God Have a Wife? Archaeology and Folk Religion in Ancient Israel* (Eerdmans Press, 2005).

12. See Arthur Green, "The Song of Songs in Early Jewish Mysticism," *Orim* 2 (1987): 49–63.

13. As it appears in Idel, *Kabbalah and Eros*, 34. Notice the reiteration of the sexual commandment "Be fruitful and multiply" (Gen. 1:28) in the context of the Temple.

14. Using the expression *merkavah* as shorthand for the celestial order is derived from the Book of Ezekiel, chapters 1 and 10, in which the prophet experiences an apocalypse of God enthroned upon a supernal chariot formed of numinous beings.

15. Idel, *Kabbalah and Eros*, 33.

16. This idea does not start with the *Zohar*, however. Similar notions concerning the "higher" and "lower" Glory of God appear in the writings of the German Pietists. A number of the strange parables in *Sefer HaBahir* also hint at an intra-divine sexual dynamic.

17. Arthur Green, *Guide to the Zohar* (Stanford, CA: Stanford University Press, 2003), 51–52; also see Idel, *Kabbalah and Eros* (New Haven: Yale University Press, 2005), 140. It is also intriguing that in passages where Israel is "wed" to the *Shechinah* or Shabbat, there is a metaphoric gender-reversal occurring, with the people Israel taking on the masculine role, while the immanence of God is feminized.

18. Lawrence Fine, *Physician of the Soul, Healer of the Cosmos: Isaac Luria and His Kabbalistic Fellowship* (Stanford, CA: Stanford University Press, 2003), 224–25. See also Elliot R. Wolfson, *Circle in the Square: Studies in the Use of Gender in Kabbalistic Symbolism* (Albany: State University of New York Press, 1995), 112–13.

19. "Prayer is union with the Divine Presence. Just as two people will move their bodies back and forth as they begin the act of love, so must a person accompany the beginning of prayer with the rhythmic swaying of the body. But as one reaches the height of union with the Presence, the movement of the body ceases" (Arthur Green and Barry W. Holtz, *Your Word Is Fire* [Woodstock, VT: Jewish Lights, 1993], 80). Note that in this image, the worshiper is in union with the feminine aspect of divinity ("Divine Presence" is a translation of *Shechinah*). In the *Zohar*, the devotee is often cast as the female partner to God imagined as male. This remarkable facility for both gender and sexual role reversal in Jewish erotic theology seemingly undermines how we should think about God and ourselves.

20. Just as modern Jews are unacquainted with pre-modern Jewish notions of gender embedded in divinity, they may also be unaware of the long Jewish tradition of demonology. See Geoffrey W. Dennis, *The Encyclopedia of Jewish Myth, Magic, and Mysticism* (Woodbury, MN: Llewellyn, 2007), 65–67. The linking of sexual transgression with evil spirits is almost as old (Babylonian Talmud, *Eiruvin* 18b, *Sotah* 9b, and *Shabbat* 196a; *B'reishit Rabbah* 20:11; *Avot D'Rabbi Natan* 1:4). The idea that certain illicit behaviors undermine God's power and reinforce the realm of the demonic is a prominent feature in the sexual ethics of kabbalistic works such as the *Zohar* (1:55a, 1:57a, 2:231b, 3:76b). Also see Fine, *Physician of the Soul*, 173–74.

21. In fact kabbalists do not ignore the anti-anthropomorphic arguments of the philosophers, at least insofar as they agree with the rationalists that the essence of God, the *Ein Sof*—the highest, incomprehensible, absolute reality of God—is beyond all discussion of gender or sex. Yet despite this concession, Kabbalah gives its greatest attention to the claim that within those aspects of the godhead that interface with creation, this male-female complex is the organizing principle of the divine order. Thus the mystics found no contradiction in affirming a sexless (indeed, featureless) divinity, while still envisioning God as the "lover of Israel."

22. Eric Yoffie, "A Reform View of Mitzvot," in *Duties of the Soul*, ed. Niles Goldstein and Peter Knobel (New York: URJ Press, 1999), 28.

23. Jay Michaelson, "Boundaries and the Boundless: Homosexuality, Liminality, Judaism," in *Jews and Sex*, ed. Nathan Abrams (Nottingham, UK: Five Leaves, 2008).

24. *B'reishit Rabbah* 13:13; *Zohar* 1:60b.

11

"CREATED BY THE HAND OF HEAVEN"

Sex, Love, and the *Androgynos*

RABBI ELLIOT KUKLA

> An *androgynos* is in some respects legally equivalent to men, and in some respects legally equivalent to women, in some respects legally equivalent to men and women, and in some respects legally equivalent to neither men nor women. . . . How is the *androgynos* legally equivalent to men? The *androgynos* conveys impurity with white [penile discharge] like men, dresses like men, marries but is not taken in marriage like men.
>
> *(Mishnah Bikurim 4:1–2)*

"The *Androgynos* Marries"

The first time I read this text I was stunned. I was stunned because the question was not *if* the *androgynos* could marry but *how* the *androgynos* marries. Not only is a person who is neither male nor female allowed to be a fully sexual being worthy of companionship in Jewish sacred texts, the *androgynos* is *presumed* to be one. The inclusion of transgender and gender nonconforming people within loving relationships, community, and family life is still a hotly contested issue in the twenty-first century, but the Rabbis of the Mishnah writing in the first century CE were merely debating the details!

The Rabbis of the Mishnah identify at least four possible genders/sexes:[1] the *zachar* (male) and the *n'keivah* (female), as well as two sexes that are beyond male and female: the *tumtum* and the *androgynos*. The Talmud sees the *tumtum* as a person whose genitals are obscured, making it difficult to discern whether he/she should be classified as male or female. The *androgynos* is a person who has both male and female sex traits. All these sexes appear frequently in classical Jewish texts[2]—the *androgynos* appears over one hundred times in the Babylonian Talmud alone.

The *tumtum* and *androgynos* are usually used to bolster a fairly rigid and hierarchical binary gender system. However, they are also always seen as fully human and integrated into the social life of the Rabbis. *Mishnah Bikurim* chapter 4 explores the various civil and ritual laws that apply to the *androgynos*. Throughout this chapter care is taken to describe the ways in which the *androgynos*'s life is protected, sanctified, and embedded within Jewish communal life.

At the end of this chapter of Mishnah, Rabbi Yossi offers the startling opinion that the *androgynos* is: "*B'riah bifnei atzmah hu.*" This phrase is hard to translate into English, but the best equivalent is probably "*he* is a created being of *her* own." This Hebrew term blends male and female pronouns to poetically express the complexity of the androgynos's identity. The term *B'riah bifnei atzmah* is a classical Jewish legal term for exceptionality. The *koi*, an animal that is neither wild nor domesticated, is referred to by the same phrase (*Tosefta Bikurim* 2). Rabbi Yossi is a minority opinion in the Mishnah, but his view that the *androgynos* is a unique being of its own, beyond male and female categories, frequently guides the way the *androgynos* is treated in later Talmudic and halachic texts (see, for example, Babylonian Talmud, *Y'vamot* 83a).

The fact that the *androgynos* marries in the Mishnah is no small matter. It raises a series of questions that the twenty-first century is just beginning to tackle.[3] If the *androgynos* is a created being of its own and not (or not only) a male being, then how does the *androgynos*'s presence in marriage impact the way we have understood the gender hierarchy between husband and wife in traditional Judaism? Once the *androgynos* marries a woman, does that mean that the couple is permitted to engage in all forms of sexual intimacy, with all possible combinations of genitalia? If so, how does this impact Jewish law prohibiting homosexuality? More generally, how does the presence of a gender nonconforming sexual being disrupt the heterosexual and misogynist assumptions underlying a traditional Jewish view of sex and love?

The Disappearing Hermaphrodite

Over the past few years I have had the opportunity to offer workshops about gender diversity in Jewish sacred texts at a number of synagogues, universities, and communal organizations. I have found that progressive people are often (quite rightly) offended by the lower-class and ambiguous status that the *androgynos* seems to hold in ancient society. It is certainly true that the *androgynos* is not afforded the same rights and privileges as men and denied some of the protections of women. However, it often takes someone of transgender or intersex experience to get the radical meta-point—our existence is recognized. We are seen as full human beings in Jewish sacred texts!

Sadly, the humanity of people who do not fit into binary genders is not nearly so clear in our time. Each year, upwards of thirty transgender and gender nonconforming people are murdered worldwide, and most of these crimes go unsolved and unpunished.[4] Not only is the *androgynos* protected from violence in Jewish texts, but the *androgynos* is presumed to be a part of loving family and community life. The sexuality of the *androgynos* in Jewish texts is troubling and difficult to classify, but never effaced. This is a very uncomfortable fact for a modern society that denies the very existence of gender multiplicity, much less acknowledging that we might be desirable loving partners. The first time I encountered the *tumtum* and *androgynos* in a text I was learning in an ultra-Orthodox yeshiva. My teacher told me that they were mythical creatures, kind of like a unicorn.

Modern society holds that there are two (and only two) ways of being human. From before we are born people ask, "Is it a boy or a girl?" From the moment of birth onward, most facets of our life—the clothes we are told to wear, the activities we are supposed to like, the careers and hobbies we are encouraged to pursue, the loving relationships we are expected to have—are guided by the answer to this crucial question.

The past few decades of feminist organizing have deeply questioned whether we can (or should) see gender as an essential way to divide up humanity. And yet most of us twenty-first-century people have still been raised to believe that whether we are a girl or a boy is a simple, and unchangeable, fact. The less than two centimeters of body tissue that lies between a medically "acceptable" clitoris and a passable penis will still consign you to a life of earning less on the dollar, a one in three possibility of being sexually abused, as well as a very rational fear of walking home alone at night. "If three decades of feminist theorizing about gender has thoroughly dislodged the notion that anatomy is destiny, that gender is natural, and that male and female are the only options," asks the contemporary queer theorist Judith Halberstam, "why do we still operate in a world that assumes that people who are not male are female, and people who are not female are male (and even that people who are not male are not people!)?"[5]

According to the Intersex Society of North America, the primary organization that advocates for intersex people, one in every one to two thousand infants is born with physical traits that cannot be easily classified as male or female.[6] Many more people discover at the onset of puberty that they have ambiguous hormonal or chromosomal status. Intersexuality is quite common. But the twenty-first century (from locker rooms to census forms) is structured to allow two, and only two, sexes. In our times, if visible anatomy does not identify the sex of a baby, in most cases a surgeon operates to transform the infant into an unambiguous boy or girl. If an individual's body takes an alternate route to maturity at puberty, we offer hormone therapies, to stimulate conformity.

The exceptional bodies that richly populate the Mishnah, as well as the Hellenistic ancient world, have almost vanished in modernity. This is not because sex is any less variable in twenty-first-century United States then it was in first-century Palestine, but because cultural authority figures such as doctors, scientists, and scholars have found ways to make individuals who don't conform to binary sex assignment disappear.

Michel Foucault argues that in modernity human sexual embodiment changed.[7] Until that point, sex difference was generally seen through the prism of a single normative sex. Galen, a second-century-CE Greek physician, held that women were simply men who lacked an essential form of inner heat. This coolness led women to be less perfectly formed than males. Hence, organs that reached their full external development in the male remained "inverted" in the female.[8] This single-gendered view of sexual embodiment persisted in colloquial speech even after it had begun to be replaced by the modern science of binary sex assignment. A nineteenth-century doggerel verse betrays traces of this sentiment when it rhymes: "Though they of different sexes be / Yet on the whole they are the same as we / For those that have the strictest searchers been / Find women are but men turned outside in."[9]

A single-gendered view of human sexuality persisted through the medieval period. Maleness represented the pinnacle of human perfection, with femaleness as its nadir. This framework is certainly misogynist and hierarchical; however, it allowed for the open, if begrudging, social acknowledgment of sexual individuality. As Anne Fausto-Sterling has described in her book, *Sexing the Body: Gender Politics and the Construction of Sexuality*, throughout medieval and early modern Europe, determining the sex of a body rested on the authority of religious institutions, thus differing religious concerns led to divergent approaches to gender variance. Referring to a number of case studies of hermaphrodites in the early modern period, Fausto-Sterling writes: "The Italians seemed relatively nonplussed by the blurring of gender borders, the French rigidly regulated it, while the English, although finding it distasteful, worried more about class transgressions."[10] What all these approaches have in common is their recognition of gender diversity, regardless of their responses to it.

Rigid binary categories for the human experience grew in popularity in the eighteenth and nineteenth centuries, as a way to regulate and control society. The Victorian science of difference discovered "evidence" of dichotomous physiological differences between men and women, working and owning classes, white people and people of color. This evidence was used to justify and reinforce fundamental social and economic hierarchies at a time when these power structures were under siege by various emancipation movements.[11] "People of mixed sex all but disappeared," writes Fausto-Sterling, "not because they had become rarer, but because scientific methods classified them out of existence."[12]

Beyond Binary

Jewish sacred texts speak in a different voice. Although Jewish Sages often tried to sort the world into binaries, they also acknowledged that not all parts of God's creation can be contained in orderly boxes. Distinctions between Jews and non-Jews, Shabbat and the days of the week, purity and impurity, are crucial to Jewish tradition. However, it was the parts of the universe that defied binaries that interested the Rabbis of the Mishnah and the Talmud the most. Pages and pages of sacred texts are occupied with the minute details of the moment between fruit and bud, wildness and domestication, innocence and maturity, the twilight hour between day and night.

The Mishnah and the *Tosefta*, compiled in the first few centuries of the common era, explore all the ways that genders beyond male and female fit into all aspects of civil and community life including in regard to inheritance, purity, earning a livelihood, and ritual participation, as well as sex and love.[13] The Sages of the Talmuds, dealing with the *tumtum* and *androgynos* nearly five hundred years later, also see them as persons who are fully integrated in society, including as sexual beings. In the Babylonian Talmud we learn the story of a *tumtum* who becomes a parent of seven children (Babylonian Talmud, *Y'vamot* 83b). In the same tractate the radical claim is made that the first ancestors of the Jewish people—Abraham and Sarah—were actually originally *tumtumim*. According to this text they only later transitioned genders to become male and female (Babylonian Talmud, *Y'vamot* 64a).

These texts reveal a tension in classical Jewish thought. Homosexuality between men is prohibited, and a gender hierarchy that places men above women is fundamental to human relations and Jewish law. However, the openly acknowledged presence of gender nonconforming figures in sex and marriage implicitly questions the solidity of both compulsory heterosexuality and the subjugation of women. This tension is particularly clear in a fascinating text in *Y'vamot* that deals with the (in)famous verse: "A man should not lie with a man as he would with a woman" (Lev. 18:22). In modern Western culture this is perhaps the most common verse used as a weapon against the LGBT community and interpreted as a blanket ban on queer sex of all varieties. In Jewish tradition this verse has primarily been understood much more narrowly as a prohibition on anal intercourse between men.

In an obscure passage of Talmud this verse is understood as even more specific: "Said Rava: 'Bar Hamduri used logic to explain to me the verse: *A man should not lie with another man in the lying-places of a woman* (Lev. 18:22). Who is this man who has within him two-lying places? Aha . . . that is the *androgynos*!" (*Y'vamot* 83a). In this text the Hebrew word for "lying-places" is understood literally to mean orifices capable of receiving penetration. Who is this male-like person (i.e., someone with a penis), they ask, who has two orifices? The answer is the *androgynos*—who can be penetrated both anally and through a vagina. In other words, according to Rava / Bar Hamduri's reading this verse is not referring to male homosexuality at all! Instead it is specifically teaching that men are forbidden to have vaginal sex with the *androgynos*, as this is the "lying-place" of women. This often ignored little text destabilizes one of the most central Torah bases for prohibiting homosexual sex.

The majority of the Sages in this debate reject Rava and Bar Hamduri's narrow reading of the verse from Leviticus. Instead, they understand it as referring to sex between men. However, they go on to discuss whether men are liable to death by stoning for sex with an *androgynos* just as they would be for sex with another male. The opposing view is put forth that a man incurs the penalty for lying with a man only "when he comes upon the *androgynos* in the way of males, but if he does not come upon him in the way of males, he is not liable."[14] In other words, according to the majority opinion, only receiving penetrative anal sex with the *androgynos* is prohibited.

This text is certainly homophobic: it reinforces the penalty of stoning for homosexual acts. It also reinforces Rabbinic misogyny, as the central concern seems to be treating a person with a penis in a "feminine" and therefore degrading fashion. However, by including the *androgynos*—who is understood in this text as neither male nor female—in the conversation, it also (perhaps unintentionally) undermines the a priori assumptions of heterosexuality and gender hierarchy. The openly acknowledged presence of a gender nonconforming person within sexual acts makes it clear that it is much harder to define the line between sexes than we might have thought. And it challenges the law's capacity to describe the limits around sanctioned heterosexuality.

Despite the problematic nature of this perplexing text it can be seen as a significant disruption of normative understandings of gender and sexuality. The feminist theorist Judith Plaskow, in an article called "Dismantling the Gender Binary Within Judaism: The Challenge of Transgender to Compulsory Heterosexuality" writes that the very existence of the *tumtum* and *androgynos* potentially destabilizes gender binaries, and hence heterosexuality within Judaism. She writes:

> The figure of the hermaphrodite plays a paradoxical role in rabbinic thought, as it does in other cultural contexts. On the one hand, the hermaphrodite poses a problem that binary gender logic must find a way to erase; it is a "necessary irritant" that ultimately serves to consolidate and stabilize the two-gender system. On the other hand, the hermaphrodite is the "vanishing point" of the gender binary; it embodies the dissolution of male and female as absolute categories.[15]

The presence of gender nonconforming partners in sex and marriage makes it clear that the line around sex differences and the boundaries around sexual identities are constantly shifting and difficult to define. Therefore, it is far more difficult than most of us have supposed to make sweeping statements about the dominance of "men," the subjugation of "women" in traditional Jewish sexual relations, or the compulsory nature of heterosexuality in classical Jewish life and law.

Contemporary Implications

The boundaries around sexual identities have shifted throughout history. Names for gender and sexual identities cannot be translated between languages and eras without also importing an entire set of preconceptions. An exact equivalence cannot be made between pre-modern gender diversity and contemporary transgender and intersex identities; however, it is important to note that bodies and identities beyond male and female have existed across millennia and discussions of pre-modern gender diversity can inform and enrich contemporary gender nonconforming lives.

The *androgynos*'s presence in Jewish sacred tradition as a "uniquely created being of its own" intertwined in loving sexual relationships makes it clear that sex is complicated. Today, we confront those who don't "fit" into binary sex assignment and endeavor to change them. Our Rabbis took people as they really were and went on from there. There are many ways to read these texts, and the Sages' approach is very far from perfect. They certainly do not advocate the overthrow of binary systems; they do not argue for sex and gender liberation, as some of us might wish that they had. But they also never question whether gender diversity really exists or whether gender nonconforming people should be included in romantic and social life. They do not advocate operations to transform an infant's body to better fit a gender category or assume that transgender adults are the objects of fetish, but never genuine love.

The inclusion of the *androgynos* in discussions of sexuality and love in Jewish sacred texts opens more space in society for men, women, transgender, intersex people, and everyone else. The image of the *androgynos* as a lover, partner, and parent forces the tradition to acknowledge that not all of creation, and not all of our relationships, can be understood within binary systems. It is also a theological statement—it is a proclamation that God creates a diversity of bodies and an abundance of desires that is far too complex for human beings to understand. It conveys an understanding that all people are created *al y'dei shamayim* (*Maggid Mishneh* on Rambam, *Hilchot Shofar*)—by the hand of heaven; and that every divine creation is entitled to be seen, loved, and desired.

Most of these ideas and many of these sentences were written in collaboration with my *chevruta* (study partner) Rabbi Reuben Zellman. Thank you!

NOTES

1. The term "gender" has been used to denote social roles and behaviors, while "sex" indicates physiological differences. Both sex and gender can be complex for transgender and gender nonconforming individuals. In recent years theorists such as Michel Foucault and Judith Butler have pointed to the shifting nature of sex, as well as gender, across lines of history and geography. Butler and other contemporary feminists have suggested that the borders around sex have been drawn and redrawn in various times and places to meet a variety of social and cultural needs. This view posits that the sexing of our bodies, as much as the gendering of our roles, is culturally and historically construed. This contemporary feminist position is where I situate myself. I do not mean to deny that there are sexual characteristics that unite and divide bodies in every epoch, but I believe that it is impossible to say anything about sex difference that does not also encode messages about gender relations and power. For more information see Judith Butler, *Gender Trouble: Feminism and the Subversion of Identity* (New York: Routledge, 1990); Michel Foucault, *The History of Sexuality*, trans. Robert Hurley (New York: Vintage Books, 1985).

2. The *tumtum* appears 17 times in the Mishnah; 23 times in the *Tosefta*; 119 times in the Babylonian Talmud; 22 times in the Jerusalem Talmud; and hundreds of times in midrash, commentaries, and halachah. The *androgynos* appears 21 times

in the Mishnah; 19 times in the *Tosefta*; 109 times in the Babylonian Talmud; and countless times in midrash and halachah.

3. In 1978, the Union for Reform Judaism (URJ) passed a very lukewarm responsum allowing transsexuals to marry, but it explicitly excludes individuals whose gender is not clearly established and only permits marriage between individuals where it is clear "that this in no way constitutes a homosexual marriage." See "Conversion and Marriage after Transsexual Surgery," CCAR Responsum 5750.8.

4. For a complete list of the victims of hate crimes against gender nonconforming individuals each year, see http://www.gender.org/remember/index.html.

5. Judith Halberstam, *Female Masculinity* (Durham: Duke University Press, 1998), 20.

6. www.isna.org.

7. This position, which is followed by Laqueur and others, is most fully associated with the work of Foucault. See Foucault, *History of Sexuality*.

8. See Galen, *De semine*, 2.1, in *Opera omnia*, ed. William Teffler (Philadelphia: Westminster Press, 1955).

9. Cited in Thomas Laqueur, *Making Sex: Body and Gender from the Greeks to Freud* (Cambridge: Harvard University Press, 1992), 6.

10. Anne Fausto-Sterling, *Sexing the Body: Gender Politics and the Construction of Sexuality* (New York: Basic Books, 1990), 35.

11. For a fuller discussion of the nineteenth-century science of difference and the enforcement of social power, see Fausto-Sterling, *Sexing the Body*, 30–45.

12. Ibid., 39.

13. See *Mishnah Bikurim* 4; *Tosefta Bikurim* 2; *Tosefta M'gilah* 2, *Tosefta Rosh HaShanah*, chapter 2.

14. For more on this topic, see "Stoning the Androginos: The Laws of *Mishkav Zachar* and the Penetration of Masculinity," a dissertation in process by Max Strassfeld for a PhD at Stanford University, under the direction of Charlotte Fonrobert.

15. Judith Plaskow, "Dismantling the Gender Binary Within Judaism: The Challenge of Transgender to Compulsory Heterosexuality" in *Balancing on the Mechitza: Transgender in Jewish Community*, edited by Noach Dzmura (Berkeley, CA: North Atlantic Books, 2010), 199.

12

"BISEXUAL" IDENTITY

A Guide for the Perplexed

RABBI JANE RACHEL LITMAN

Rabbis are asked a lot of questions; that's part of the job. From "What direction do you light the Chanukah candles?" to "How do I talk to my friend who was just diagnosed with cancer?" to "Can I be pro-Israel and pro-peace?" rabbis hear and respond to the ongoing search for answers that is deeply embedded in Jewish existence and meaning. Jewish textual references to rabbinic responsa date as far back as the *Tosefta* (c. 200 CE), and the process continues to this day.[1] Within this markedly Jewish form of inquiry and reflection, individual rabbis sometimes develop a specific expertise.

I have served gay outreach congregations for most of my pastoral rabbinate and personally identify as queer, so in addition to the usual subjects, I tend to hear a lot of questions about sexuality and gender identity. As a consequence, I've framed this essay about "bisexuality" in the form of a glossary—answers to a set of implied questions—in order to add another chapter to the Jewish responsa canon. However, the essay is not a true glossary in that the "entries" are not designed to stand alone, but to construct a Jewish theological argument in critique of sexual and gender determinism, while presenting some useful information about current thinking on Jewish, gender, and sexual identity along the way.

Bisexuality: Our culture presents a binary view of gender identity—that people are either male or female—and of sexual identity—that people are attracted to either the same gender (homosexual) or the opposite gender (heterosexual). The truth is that many people do not conform to these dichotomous categories either in terms of gender identity or sexual identity. Rather than black and white, people's sexual identities are a rainbow of colors. In terms of sexual identity, people who do not conform to the hetero/homo categories are often called "bisexual." However, the term "bisexual" is a misnomer, since the defining feature of bisexuality is that bisexual people are *not* binary in their sexual attraction, but rather universal, loving their partners without regard to gender. For most people, qualities such as intelligence, kindness, romantic appeal, and so forth are likely to be the guides for sexual attraction; for bisexual people, a potential partner's gender is not on that list. A better term might be "unisexual" or just "sexual"; however, for the sake of clarity, I will continue to use the term "bisexual" in this essay.

Ironically, the existence of "bi"sexual people is threatening to the "bi"nary model. Therefore bisexual people are frequently subject to erasure: bisexual people in same-gender relationships tend to be named as gay or lesbian, and bisexual people in mixed-gender relationships are named as heterosexual.

Compulsory Heterosexuality: Writer and poet Adrienne Rich coined the term "compulsory heterosexuality" to describe the way that our society rewards heterosexuality and punishes and silences alternatives.[2] Her insight provides a framework for understanding sexual identification in contemporary society. In the 1950s, sex researcher Albert Kinsey developed a scale of sexual identity ranging from zero to six, zero being entirely heterosexual and six being entirely homosexual. It is obvious that a linear scale with gradations of zero to six could as easily have gradations of zero to seven billion, with each individual living person on earth lined up in a row according to the intensity of her/his attraction to people of the "opposite" or "same" gender (assuming that there are only two genders—see the entry "Gender Identity" below). Compulsory heterosexuality pushes everyone in the lineup to cluster at zero or as close to it as possible. According to Rich, if society did not compel heterosexuality, the seven-billion-person lineup would appear different from the current heterosexual congestion.

In our world, it is conceivable that the most "homosexual" people (those who would be classified as sixes on the Kinsey scale) for whatever reasons of personality, biology, or culture are those most able to resist the heterosexual compulsion and claim their authentic expression of sexual identity. Perhaps the experience of many homosexually identified people that they were "born that way" is reflective of the deep-seated drive necessary to claim a gay or lesbian identity in such a heterosexually compulsory world. Perhaps billions of bisexual people who do not have this deep-seated attraction to the same gender or personal strength of will or other determinative factor, but who would be perfectly happy if the right same-gendered person appeared in their lives, are imagining themselves as heterosexual because they have been deprived of meaningful choice in the matter due to compulsory heterosexuality.

Determinism: Horace Kallen, the originator of the theory of cultural pluralism, made the oft quoted remark that "men may change their clothes, their politics, their wives, their religions, their philosophies, to a greater or lesser extent; they cannot change their grandfathers."[3] Kallen reiterates this deterministic view of Jewish identity: "An Irishman is always an Irishman, a Jew always a Jew. . . . Irishman and Jew are facts in nature; citizen and church-member artifacts in civilization."[4] Kallen viewed ethnicity as a biologically determined "fact in nature." There is a certain irony that Kallen, the secular son of a rabbi, who only later in life reaffirmed his Jewish identification, viewed ethnic identity as a biologically determined given.

Determinists postulate many kinds of causal imperatives beyond Kallen's now anachronistic view of biologically determined Jewish identity as a fact in nature. Theological determinism proposes that the existence of an all-knowing God mandates human predestination. In the modern world, various theorists have proposed genetic determinism, environmental determinism, and cultural/social determinism. The issue of whether sexual/gender identity is predetermined (and the mechanism for this determination) is a subject of debate.

Free Will: Jewish thought emphasizes human free will, as described in Torah: "I have put before you life and death, blessing and curse. Choose life" (Deut. 30:19). Judaism teaches that education, introspection, and self-discipline, forces controlled by the ever-emerging self, can be more powerful than external deterministic forces. What does this mean in terms of identity and choice?

Contrary to Kallen's determinist view, professors David Hollinger[5] and Werner Sollors[6] evaluate ethnic identity in contemporary North America as a matter of "consent" or free choice. According to Hollinger and Sollors, Americans are increasingly multiracial and multicultural. The heirs to a number of cultural heritages, post-ethnic Americans make the choice, that is, "consent," to emphasize or diminish the significance of particular ethnic and other identifications as they construct a sense of self.

Similarly, sexual theorists critique the idea of an essential sexual identity. French philosopher Michel Foucault[7] understands sexuality as a cultural construct rather than a natural phenomenon. Foucault explains that until the late nineteenth century there could be no such thing as a homosexual identity because the very idea didn't exist. Until that time there were certain homosexual or heterosexual behaviors, and a variety of social meanings were interpreted from the behaviors. Foucault shows that the definition of homosexual *identity* as it is currently commonly understood in North America—that is, a sense of the nature of self and commonality with a group—was a product of social forces, mostly a result of the emerging medical establishment.

According to cultural anthropologist Gayle Rubin,[8] people "self-express" their gender and sexual identities in relation to cultural possibilities of identifications. As more culturally constructed possibilities emerge, so do more individual self-expressions of identity. In this context, "self-expression" is equivalent to ethnic "consent," choice, and free will.

Gender Identity: Feminists of the 1970s critiqued the limited gender roles available to people, particularly women, but also men. Since that time, the primary goal of those who promote gender egalitarianism has been to expand the roles available to women and men. However, in recent times, those who critique the limitations of historical male and female gender roles have come up with a new strategy. In addition to expanding the roles of the binary categories of female and male, contemporary gender theorists propose that there are more than two gender categories available. Not all people need identify or express as "male" or "female."

Though most people's sex chromosomes are either XX or XY, this gene pair is only one of twenty-three human chromosome pairs and need not be elevated to a definitional or essential status, any more than genetic eye or hair color essentially defines the social role or self-expression of a human being. A percentage of people also have sex chromosomes other than XX and XY. In addition, factors beyond genetic material contribute to gender identity, including hormonal makeup, cultural norms, behavioral choices, and inner sense of self. Some people who identify as trans or gender queer see themselves as neither male nor female.

Of interest to a Jewish perspective on gender identity are a number of Talmudic texts that conceive of at least four (and perhaps as many as six or seven) "genders," with specific characteristics and legal rights and disabilities. Two of these "genders" are male and female, but the others have no obvious English equivalents. It is tempting to wonder if—like the proverbial story of the Eskimo language's multiple ways of describing snow—the Rabbinic linguistic richness in regard to gender indicated something about contemporaneous Jewish culture. It is not entirely clear if the Talmud describes only individuals who are biologically/genetically neither male nor female or also discusses those of variant social gender status, people who might currently be called "butch" or "effeminate." The Rabbinic Hebrew terms *androgynos* and *tumtum* may deal with those whom our society describes as "intersex" or may describe people who don't fit male and female heterosexual identities. They might also refer to people who do not fit societal gender roles, or they reference some mix of all of the above. One thing is clear: the Talmud's gender categories differ from those of mainstream contemporary society. In fact, the Talmudic text itself quotes Rabbi Yosei as saying, "An *androgyne, he* is a creation unto *herself*, and the Sages could not decide whether it is a man or a woman" (*Mishnah Bikurim* 4:11).

Heteronormativity: Social theorist Michael Warner explains that society poses certain statuses as normative and others as deviant. The normative status has greater privileges and "rights" than the deviant status, which is stigmatized. In our North American society, male is normative. Protestant is normative. White is normative. Heterosexual is normative. Able-bodied is normative. People who do not fall into normative categories are subtly (and not so subtly) erased from public discourse, making it more difficult for them to achieve authentic self-expression. Heteronormativity creates a ranking of both family structures and sexual practices in addition to sexual and gender identities. LGBT family structures, including adoption, foster parenting, and conceiving children through use of donors and surrogates, are not created though heteronormative processes and are subject to delegitimation and explicit discrimination legally, socially, and even in terms of Jewish religious practice.

Jewish Identity: Despite Kallen's deterministic assertion that "a Jew [is] always a Jew," Jewish identification in contemporary North America is largely a matter of choice. Jews are multiracial and multicultural. There is no single "Jewish gene," and therefore no one is born genetically Jewish. Children born into Jewish families need to be educated and socialized into Judaism in order to create a meaningful Jewish identity. Then, as adults, they engage in a process of self-construction and self-expression in relation to Judaism. A commonplace of modern Jewish life is that "all modern Jews are Jews by choice." There are ways in which Jewish identity is similar to sexual/gender identity and ways in which it is different.

Love and Marriage: Sexual identity is not only about sex. People's sexual identity informs how they will make choices about families, communities, and values. People who identify as other than heterosexual are just as likely to be members of committed love relationships, caring families, and decent communities as heterosexual people. Like Jews, LGBT people are personally confronted with the realities of being a minority. Like Jews, LGBT people tend to value tolerance for others and broadly based civil rights.

Performativity: Feminist and gender theorist Judith Butler describes performativity as the ability of words and speech to create phenomena through repetition.[9] Butler particularly focuses on gender and explains that people are not gendered in and of themselves, but rather "do" or "act" gender through a series of discrete performances. The collective society agrees to see the discrete performances of gender as a seamless narrative whole. People who disrupt the performance either as actors or audience are punished, and according to Butler, the normative social response to poor gender performance is silence. Butler encourages gender and sexual nonconformists to mindfully disrupt their own performativity by staging acts of gender disruption such as wearing drag clothing. Butler's view of gender and sexual identity as iterations and actions rather than as a static state of being allows for gender and sexual fluidity over time. Someone may be "doing" straightness at one point in his or her life and "doing" drag queen at another, depending on her or his performativity.

Queer: Like the word "Torah," the word "queer" has both a general and a more specific sense. It can be employed as an umbrella appellation for all LGBT people, providing a sense of inclusivity and broad-based acceptance. Yet the term is also used in a more narrow way to highlight the rejection of contemporary social norms.

In terms of the general umbrella usage, historically there have been political tensions between some gay/lesbian and bi/trans people. The existence of gay and lesbian people does not disrupt the binary mythos, but the existence of bi/trans people does challenge the binary, a fact that can create different perspectives and agendas. In addition, bisexual and transgender people can be subject to less overt discrimination depending on life choices. For example, a bisexual person who marries a person of the "opposite" gender is much less likely to face ongoing overt discrimination, though erasure and invisibility also take a toll. There are also tensions within the trans community between people who wish to conform to the gender binary and merely switch genders and those who wish to disrupt the binary altogether. Some LGBT people prefer to identify as queer as a way of addressing and overcoming historical tensions. Queer also has a specific transgressive quality and conveys a social/political perspective that critiques heteronormativity.

Strategic Approaches: One common political strategy of contemporary gay, lesbian, and trans rights advocates is to maintain that people who are variant from the norm in their sexual or gender identities are "born that way" and have no volition in the matter. This determinist strategy is a response to years of oppressive theory that pathologizes LGBT identity as an illness or—worse still—vilifies it as a sin. Some homophobes (those who hold negative attitudes toward LGBT people) assert that if variant sexual/gender identity is understood as an illness, it can be "cured," and if it is conceptualized as a sinful lifestyle choice, it can be repented. Psychologically healthy LGBT people do not want to be "cured" or "redeemed." A number of studies have shown that presenting gender/sexual variance as a condition determined from birth is a convincing response to such homophobic arguments. These studies provide political justification for the determinist strategy; in North America, voters who believe that gay people are "born that way" are much more likely to support gay rights ordinances.

Most bisexual activists think that the doctrine that gender/sexual identity is invariably determined (how is unclear) at birth has unintended and detrimental consequences for both the movement for gender/sexual identity freedom and for queer people themselves. Though many queer people experience themselves as born gay, others, particularly many bisexual people, do not.

Is oppression only unacceptable if it is in relation to an inherent status? Let us turn to Jewish identity. Since Judaism is a choice, and any Jew could theoretically choose to become Christian, the deterministic political argument suggests that it might be acceptable to discriminate against Jews since they choose their own deviant condition. Such a position is a throwback to the medieval disputations and pogroms. People have free will to choose their religious affiliation, communal memberships, and sexual/gender expressions and should not be subject to discrimination as a result of free choice.

Theological Implications: The Bible and many generations of Jewish and majority culture religious authorities have privileged procreative unions composed of male and female dyads (marriage between one man and one woman). It is no wonder that Jews who identify as other than heterosexual might look to a determinist philosophy in order to avoid direct confrontation with Torah, Jewish tradition, and mainstream religious culture. However, Judaism is not a fundamentalist faith. Our heritage is one of ongoing interpretation. In this way, we are able to cherish our heritage but not remain frozen in history. As Mordecai Kaplan is often quoted as saying, "The past has a vote, but not a veto." It is time for liberal Jews to say that heterosexuality is not morally superior to other sexual identities. What is ethically superior is authenticity. As long as anyone is maintaining a false identity in order to conform to heteronormativity, he or she is doing spiritual damage to herself or himself and others.

Midrash (*Mishnah Sanhedrin* 4:5) teaches that in the government mint all the coins are the same, but in God's mint each coin is different. When non-hetero-sexual/gender identity is viewed as a difference rather than an illness or a sin, it is clear that Jewish tradition supports that pursuit of authentic selfhood rather than conformity to majoritarian demands. Indeed, Jewish identity itself is a choice supporting diversity.

Martin Buber summed up the situation well: "Every person born into this world represents something new, something that never existed before, something original and unique. It is the duty of every person in Israel to know and consider that he/she is unique in the world in her/his particular character and that there has never been someone like him/her before, for if there had been someone like her/him before, there would be no need for him/her to be in the world. Every single person is a new thing in the world and is called upon to fulfill his/her particularity in the world."[10]

NOTES

1. For Reform responsa, see http://ccarnet.org/rabbis-speak/reform-responsa/.

2. Adrienne Rich, "Compulsory Heterosexuality and Lesbian Existence," *Signs* 5, no. 4 (Summer 1980), 631–60.

3. Horace M. Kallen, "Democracy Versus the Melting-Pot," *The Nation*, February 1915, 217–18.

4. Horace M. Kallen, *The Structure of Lasting Peace* (Boston: Marshall Jones, 1918), 122.

5. David A. Hollinger, *Postethnic America: Beyond Multiculturalism* (New York: Basic Books, 2005).

6. Werner Sollors, *Beyond Ethnicity: Consent and Descent in American Culture* (New York: Oxford University Press, 1987).

7. Michel Foucault, *The History of Sexuality* (New York: Pantheon Books, 1978).

8. Gayle Rubin, *Deviations* (Durham, NC: Duke University Press, 2011).

9. Judith Butler, *Gender Trouble: Feminism and the Subversion of Identity* (New York: Routledge, 1990).

10. Adapted from Martin Buber, *The Way of Man and Ten Rungs* (New York: Citadel Press, 2006), 12.

13

BLESSED IS GOD WHO CHANGES US

Theological Que(e)ries

RABBI NIKKI LYN DEBLOSI, PHD

As a college student, I was dragged from the closet by my insightful and loving mother. When she turned to me saying, "I have to ask you something," I didn't need her to specify the question; I immediately replied, "I'm gay." My mother's initial acceptance hinged on a truth she embraced: sexual orientation is not a choice. I remember feeling incredibly grateful and blessed at her reaction; and yet, I was saddened, too. To accept gay, lesbian, bisexual, and transgender individuals solely because we do not "choose" our identities implies that we would, if we could, change—that our lives are less than ideal. But my life certainly does not feel like a consolation prize. Queer theory[1] can provide an ethical and a theological challenge to a limited and limiting conception of human sexuality, gender identity, and gender expression that implies queer folks live lives less valuable.[2]

Like Rachel Adler's feminist intervention into Judaism, a queer theological intervention begins from the assumption that ethics demand the practical inclusion of GLBTQ folks in Jewish ritual and religious life. Such an intervention acknowledges the importance of tactical strategies to increase "equal access to the rights and responsibilities of Jewish religious life" for previously marginalized communities—but does not stop there.[3] Adler calls us to "engender" Judaism: to analyze, re-create, renew, and rethink both our "classical texts" and "the lived experiences of the people Israel" as affected by changing notions of gender and sexuality.[4] Those of us deeply concerned with the full inclusion of LGBTQ Jews call our community to "queer" Judaism. Queering Judaism—like engendering Judaism—does not shun the risk of changing Judaism. But those of us committed to a continually relevant and ethically responsible Judaism must be willing to risk change, just as our Reform predecessors willingly risked the changes that the inclusion of women would bring. The Judaism we will bring about will remain deeply linked to our ancient covenantal tradition—a meaningful form and expression of Judaism—but it must reflect and shape the valuable lives of each of the members of our diverse communities.

If Judaism takes queer theory—and the personal narratives of LGBTQ individuals[5]—seriously, it will not stop at the occasional synagogue-sponsored booth at the local Pride festival or grudging openness to their rabbis' performing commitment ceremonies for LGBTQ couples. Instead, it will take on the more difficult project of "raising fundamental questions about a heterosexist, patriarchal social order, about gender roles, and about the fluidity and nature of human sexuality."[6] Disagreement abounds on these issues;[7] for progress to be made, we must engage more fully with the claims (forwarded not only by queer theorists but also as articulated in the personal statements of queer individuals) that sex, gender, and sexuality are at least in part socially constructed, mutable, and complex.[8] Unlike political or tactical arguments for the inclusion of gays and lesbians in political and public life, queer theory acknowledges that truly accepting LGBTQ people into contemporary society might well require the utter overhaul of "the way things are."[9] Similarly, the full inclusion and acceptance of LGBTQ Jews will require at the very least a deep theological examination of "the way things are" Jewishly. What does it mean, for example, to be created in the image of God, and how ought that theological truth affect Judaism's approach to LGBTQ individuals? Are we created only "male and female"? What do those labels mean for our range of gender expression? How can we create and sustain a system of belief about God that includes God's relationship to those of us the Bible ostensibly condemns as *to-eivah* ("abomination"; Lev. 18:22)? What theological changes will the full inclusion of LGBTQ Jews demand?

Like Jewish feminist work, writing at the intersection of queer theory and Judaism has moved from an early focus on tactical issues to a critical attention to the limitations of that approach to a subsequent theological intervention. Willingness even to open a dialogue on LGBTQ inclusion emerges from an acknowledgment of a changed reality: homosexuality is no longer universally considered a "sin" or a "disease"; in nearly all circles, sexual orientation is now recognized as an integral part of a person's psychological makeup.[10] Moving forward from this basic assumption, much writing on LGBTQ issues focuses on practical consequences like halachic adaptation (or its impossibility), equal access, and inclusion in existing rituals and institutions.

Writing focused on inclusion displays a range of interpretations of the prohibition in Leviticus 18:22 and contemporary conceptions of human sexuality. All the major movements in Judaism currently acknowledge that sexual orientation (and, in some movements, gender identity) are part of God's creation. Differences emerge when we begin to consider how Judaism ought to reflect that creation in practice—the "acts-versus-identity" distinction: Can we prohibit homosexual acts without prohibiting homosexual identity?[11] If we answer "yes," we must address the psychological damage and imbalance that results: why would God create homosexuals and then condemn them "to live a life of total celibacy and sexual abstention"?[12] If Judaism acknowledges sexuality and sexual expression as part of God's plan for human beings, how can it simultaneously mandate for some Jews "permanent social and sexual loneliness"?[13] Are only certain sexual acts prohibited? For example, one Conservative position on homosexuality views halachah as banning anal sex between men, and Judaism generally as discouraging sexual experimentation and promiscuity—but as otherwise accepting of LGBTQ sexual expression.[14] In the Reform Movement, whose positions on LGBTQ issues vary because of a policy of pluralism in terms of the practice of individual rabbis, the notions of *b'tzelem Elohim* and human dignity influence its theological and practical approach toward queer inclusion in Jewish life and ritual. Despite its longstanding condemnation of discrimination against gays and lesbians in housing and employment (1977) and its call "to treat with respect and to integrate fully all Jews into the life of the community regardless of sexual orientation,"[15] the Reform Movement struggles over the long Jewish tradition of honoring only "heterosexual, monogamous, procreative marriage" as "the ideal human relationship for the perpetuation of species, covenantal fulfillment, and the preservation of the Jewish people."[16] The burden has been on the LGBTQ community to prove that it can fulfill such lofty values—that LGBTQ individuals can simply be "stirred into" existing institutions, that no fundamental change of those institutions is necessary (theologically or ethically as well as practically).[17] While the Reform Movement endorses civil marriage for gays and lesbians, it does not mandate that its rabbis consider LGBTQ Jews equally capable as heterosexuals of entering a relationship marked by *k'dushah* (holiness).[18] And, of course, even this characterization will inevitably be out of date, perhaps is already out of date, given the relatively rapid pace of cultural change, both within and outside the Reform rabbinate, around sexuality issues. As a new generation of Reform rabbis and cantors are ordained, we may be seeing a groundswell of support for fuller inclusion of LGBTQ concerns into clergy's approach to, for example, *all* marriages, as is reflected in the CCAR Press's updated wedding preparation publication *Beyond Breaking the Glass* (2012).

Including LGBTQ people in unchanged Jewish institutions and rituals does not represent "queering Judaism." While asserting that sexual orientation is part of what it means to be a human being created in God's image does represent a theological intervention, simply including more types of people under a particular theological umbrella does not lead irrevocably to a questioning of that umbrella's structure—the kind of questioning queer theory deems crucial. Like feminist theory, queer theory argues that gender and sexuality are socially constructed. In her foundational article "Thinking Sex," Gayle Rubin offers a succinct formulation of the ideological assumptions that queer theory exposes, among them "sexual essentialism." Our dominant cultural narrative deems sex "a natural force that exists prior to social life and shapes institutions," "eternally unchanging, asocial, and transhistorical."[19] The work of queer theorists, historians, and scientists like Michel Foucault, David M. Halperin, John Boswell, Anne Fausto-Sterling, and others belies the truth—that "sexuality is constituted in society and history, not biologically ordained."[20] These assertions parallel feminist theories about gender roles.[21] Queer theory begs us to ask different questions about Judaism. Must we accept wholeheartedly and without reservation thousands of years of Jewish insistence that the only ideal life for human beings (intended by God) is heterosexual marriage and family? If we truly believe that all human beings are created *b'tzelem Elohim*, then, indeed, as Jay Michaelson argues, "Why does God make some people gay?" is a theological question.[22]

The message that our humanity, including our sexual orientation, is "a reflection of the divine" bolsters LGBTQ Jews.[23] *B'tzelem Elohim* becomes a theological bedrock for ethical and religious change: "We too deserve respect as God's own handiwork. Our sexual orientation is part of creation's original design. We are as much a reflection of God as any straight person may claim to be. We are entitled to as much dignity, as many rights, and as much happiness as any other child of God."[24] How will Judaism help us to shape and to acknowledge that happiness? Queer theory demands that we move the discussion of LGBTQ Jewish marriage from the realm of the political to the realm of the theological and the ethical. As we examine the relevance or applicability of *kiddushin* to LGBTQ marriage, should we not also examine its continued relevance or applicability to straight marriage? Ought we not, as Rachel Adler does, question the very moral, ethical, and theological underpinnings to *kiddushin* (marriage)—an institution founded upon *kinyan* (acquisition) and on a strict gender binary between men and women? The nitty-gritty, risky attention to queer theological concerns may very well lead to a broad reexamination that might lead to a ritual and practical reinterpretation of Jewish marriage that more broadly acknowledges the full humanity of us all.[25]

Such a rethinking can seem scary. In a debate with Judith Plaskow, Tamar Ross exposes the real "threat" of queer theory: a challenge to the hierarchy of sexual norms bolstered by a gender binary. According to Ross, queer theorists conclude that "because sexual roles are learned and vary across cultures, they are arbitrary. This leads to the problematic conclusion that there are no socially or morally compelling reasons for culturally imparted conceptions of how sexuality ought to be conceived."[26] Ross's anti-relativist argument represents a common response to queer theory's insistence on questioning the status quo. Few queer theorists, however, argue that morality and standards are meaningless.[27] Ross argues that there are "deeply ingrained, rational bases for gendered practices" and accuses queer theorists of ignoring those in favor of "emphasiz[ing] their contingency."[28] On the contrary, the "bases" Ross articulates are among those some queer theorists—myself included—would gladly challenge, including a narrowly defined version of the "family" that requires a masculine/male father and a feminine/female mother.[29] Ross implies that, without the sexual binary, all human beings would be "the same." We would cease to learn from difference, which promotes "altruism," a tenet "fostered by the need to overcome difference and respond to the Other."[30] Queer theory suggests that allowing for *more* difference only increases our opportunity to reach out and respond to many Others.

While some writers criticize queer theory for ignoring the "reality" of sexed and gendered bodies, such criticisms misread queer theory's deconstructionist claims. Particularly in post-1990s queer theory, authors acknowledge that some aspects of our selves are "given" and unchangeable—like our anatomies.[31] It is the value-laden system that sutures a certain sexual anatomy to a certain kind of desire for a certain kind of sexual object that is culturally proscribed and changes over time. It is the insistence that sex and gender exist only in a binary (two and only two options) that queer theory troubles.

Queer theory promotes a sexual ethics based on diversity that refuses to concede "that if being gay could be shown to be learned, chosen, or partly chosen, then it could be reasonably forbidden."[32] To accept LGBTQ people as full human beings deserving of full lives *only if* our sexuality is proved immutable is to send the message that to be lesbian, gay, bisexual, transgender, or queer is to be less of a human being.[33] Queer theory insists that sexual diversity can be a value.[34] Much Jewish writing on LGBTQ issues reflects both changed knowledge about sexual orientation and the influence of queer theories that dismantle the gender binary. Though many interpreters have seen in Genesis a theological basis for the subjugation of women and a religious mandate for heterosexuality, Judaism does offer a richer conception of humankind than a rigid gender binary. As Rabbis Ayelet Cohen, Margaret Wenig, and Elliot Kukla (among others) assert, the Rabbis of our tradition admitted diversity in sex and gender, naming not only the categories "male" and "female" but also "*tumtum*" and "*androgynos.*"[35] Queer theory, and the experience of LGBTQ Jews, has motivated these writers to highlight and reclaim the gender diversity apparent in Jewish texts that challenges the notion that "there are two (and only two) ways of being human."[36] The Torah can be a source of new ways of thinking about gender, sexuality, and belonging in the Jewish people. In mining Rabbinic readings of the prohibition against cross-dressing, Rabbis Kukla and Zellman conclude, "The Torah is asking us not to misrepresent our gender, which we can understand as using external garments to conceal our inner selves," offering a *nechemta* for gender-nonconforming Jews today.[37] Responding to Genesis, Rabbi Wenig reads the *zachar un'keivah* (male and female; Gen. 1:27) of the Creation story not as a description of a gender binary but as "a merism"—from *zachar* to *n'keivah* God created us, and all in between.[38]

A strategy of reinterpreting potentially harmful and exclusionary texts invites some critics to accuse LGBTQ readers of interpreting anachronistically or simply ignoring particularly troubling texts. Rabbis David Ellenson and Gordon Tucker each propose a methodological alternative providing theological grounding for LGBTQ inclusion.[39]

Responding to *Parashat Mishpatim*, Rabbi Ellenson insists that "any passage of Scripture that diminishes the humanity of another ought to be questioned altogether."[40] Seeking corrective verses elsewhere in Torah, Ellenson proposes that we employ "overarching principles," like those found at Exodus 22:20 and 23:9 enjoining us not to oppress the stranger, to balance against the rules and regulations of halachah.[41] Taking his cue from legal scholar Robert Cover, Ellenson calls us to formulate a theology based not only on rigid rules but on flexible, lasting values. [42] Ellenson's methodology requires careful attention and an open mind. If we follow Ellenson, "the experience of oppression demands sensitivity and response on the part of Jews to the needs of others," including the needs of LGBTQ Jews for full inclusion and acceptance.[43] Rabbi Tucker similarly relies on Cover's legal theory to challenge the "theological claim" that Leviticus 18:22 unambiguously condemns all expressions of sex and intimacy between persons of the same sex.[44] Tucker's overarching principles emerge from aggadic texts demonstrating that "God is more accepting, more empathetic, more compassionate than we are, and that God provides freely for the needs of all creatures."[45] These texts demonstrate God's compassion for the daughters of Zelophehad, excluded by the ancient Israelite system of inheritance, or for the *mamzer* (bastard), shut out of Jewish life. God *acts* on this compassion to repair oppression and damage inflicted by human beings—even by Jewish human beings, even by rabbis, even by the Sanhedrin itself.[46] Tucker urges us to turn

> to all the texts (and there are many) that tell us that humans were meant to live in loving partnership, to all of the narrative texts (and there are many) that have progressively forbidden us to exclude and stigmatize people for conditions that they did not choose or control, and to the text in *Leviticus Rabbah* that depicts God as a greater source of compassion for the unjustly excluded than the Sanhedrin itself. These *aggadot*, and others, as well as the more recent compelling personal narratives of Jewish gays and lesbians, must be culled together to provide an authentic reading of the Torah and our tradition that will enable us to approximate even more closely the will and the image of our compassionate God.[47]

Tucker's and Ellenson's interventions represent an emerging theological contribution that could queer Judaism: a heuristic "attentive to potential resources in its immediate environment, imaginative about combinations, and flexible about the structure of the recipe"—though confident that the outcome will increase dignity for all human beings.[48]

Two key questions underlie much debate on LGBTQ issues: What *kind of* difference is queerness? What difference does queerness make? Rabbi Steven Greenberg highlights two blessings over difference: *Dayan ha-emet* and *m'shaneh hab'riyot*.[49] The first acknowledges God as "the true Judge," while the second praises God as one "who differentiates creatures." A Talmudic discussion in *B'rachot* 58b debates which kinds of human "distinction" prompt which blessing, reflecting the value judgments of its time. For example, differences "from birth" are benign differences, but differences that represent a change in a person's status (from seeing to blind, for example) represent a lamentable turn of events. And yet, only "in relation to people," Greenberg points out, were the Sages "not certain when a difference was to be blessed and when it was to be mourned."[50] "Strange" animals (an elephant or a monkey) always prompt us to acknowledge God as *m'shaneh hab'riyot*. Is queerness a difference to be lamented or celebrated?[51] "Pro-gay" arguments that rely too heavily on a born-that-way model tread dangerously close to reciting *Dayan ha-emet* upon seeing a queer person: it is a wish that the world could be otherwise, and a promise that one accepts the way things are, however difficult or imperfect. In some instances, such a blessing might be as painfully meaningful as reciting those words upon hearing of the death of a loved one. Applied to human beings whose lives can be just as rich and fulfilling and blessed as any "unblemished" person, the blessing can hurt.[52] Rabbi Harris Goldstein sees the diversity in Creation as a theological mandate to us that we must respect and celebrate that difference. Rabbi Goldstein cites the story of Rabbi Shimon ben Elazar, who was chided for calling a man ugly.[53] The story's moral? "We have to accept, welcome, and love that diversity God created, or else take those issues up with the Creator, not with the person who was created."[54]

Emerging queer theologies, particularly writing by Rabbi Elliot Kukla and by Jay Michaelson, begin from the position that, because God's Creation is so miraculously diverse, we ought to value difference, not demonize it. Despite its emphasis on separations and distinctions described by two (and only two) terms (male and female, light and darkness, holy and ordinary), Judaism does make room for difference, for "exceptionality," for "the possibility that uniqueness can burst through the walls that demarcate our society."[55] Recognizing difference might simply prompt a call for tactical inclusion. Queer theory urges us to ask: does being queer make a difference to Judaism? Or, as Jay Michaelson phrases it, "Is being gay like having brown eyes—a biological quirk of no religious significance? Or, given the central status in Judaism of procreation, family, patrimony, and gender binarism, is there something more theologically significant about people who . . . defy the traditional constructions of each?"[56] A tactical approach to LGBTQ inclusion would reassure the dominant culture that "adding queers and stirring" will not change much of anything; Michaelson rejects such an approach in favor of a theological exploration of how sexuality and sexual orientation will change and expand Judaism. Queer experience causes us to think about God and about love differently and guides us to read old stories with new twists. Rigorous theology turns away from reified notions of God in favor of more expansive and transcendent models. Michaelson argues that queer experience, unfettered by dominant binary categories, helps us reach a theological goal: "The farther we get from our preconceived notions of what 'identity' is supposed to be and the more open we are to categories beyond our imagination or experience, the closer we are to realization" of the spiritual and the divine.[57] Both Michaelson and Kukla see redemptive possibilities in the difficult work of coming out—an affirmation of life in the face of a culture that demands conformity.[58] Holiness (*k'dushah*)[59] emerges not only from strict separation but also from the in-between— the twilight in Creation, the moments and the beings that "we might have thought . . . dangerous and forbidden" that turn out to be "the best times for prayer."[60]

From tactical efforts to stretch the Jewish umbrella so that it shelters more people to emerging queer theologies that suggest we might find holiness in diversity—and diversity already embedded in traditional Jewish texts—my exploration of how contemporary writers are "queering" Judaism is not simply a theoretical or intellectual exercise. As so many of the writers I encountered stress, the stakes for this project are incredibly high. Will Judaism respond to the cry of the oppressed, the marginalized, the victimized? Will we, its leaders, turn to all available methods and narratives while yet honoring a tradition that begins with revelation and continue to our contemporary moment? The theological consequences of our answers affect us all. I am greatly angered by responses to queer efforts to engage with Judaism that imply these issues are "merely" marginal. For example, Tamar Ross exclaims, "In order to accommodate the left-handed exceptions to the rule, do we really need to go to the length of doing away with all distinctions between the rule and the exception?"[61] Queer Jewish theology responds affirmatively, but with a difference: We need not do away with distinctions altogether, but we certainly must treat "exceptions" not as anomalies, but as fully human, created *b'tzelem Elohim*, and worthy of a place in Jewish tradition that considers them central and essential to God's vision. It matters little whether queers represent 10 percent of the population or a tenth of a percent. As Rabbi Tucker eloquently reminds us, "Their [i.e., queer Jews'] numbers are not insignificant, but in another sense, the numbers are far less relevant than one's knowledge—unshakable, intuitive knowledge—about a single person."[62] I am reminded of a Talmudic injunction: "It is *forbidden* to count Israel,"[63] the Rabbis note, for did not the prophet say, "The number of the people Israel shall be like the sands of the sea, not to be measured or counted" (Hosea 2:1)?[64] Let us count each one, and let each one count—and let us honor the diversity and difference that each one represents. Let our beliefs guide and expand our practice, queering Judaism.

Blessed are You, God, Sovereign of the universe, who changes Your creatures.

NOTES

1. Over the past several decades, the trend in critical, deconstructionist, and post-modern theory has been a move from the more particular and limited terms "gay" and "lesbian" toward the more inclusive term "queer"—flexible not only because of its common use as an "umbrella" term for anyone outside the heterosexual norm (anyone whose biological sex, gender identity or expression, or sexual orientation does not conform to the dominant model in which, for example, "masculine" men desire "feminine" women), but also because of its potential use as a verb. The term "queer" tends also to be favored by youth who see sexuality and gender (and their expression) as flexible over time (so that one person may identify or be perceived more closely as a "gay man" at one point in time or as a "trans man" at another point in time). The term and its usage are complicated and embroiled in identity politics as well as deep personal emotion. To provide a complete bibliography of authors who employ the term "queer" as a verb is beyond the scope of this paper, but some helpful writers include Judith Butler, Laurent Berlant, Michael Warner, Ann Pellegrini, Jose E. Munoz, Elizabeth Freeman, Judith Halberstam, and Michel Foucault. I will employ the term "queer" to indicate this inclusive use.

2. See, e.g., Michael Warner, *The Trouble with Normal: Sex, Politics, and the Ethics of Queer Life* (Cambridge, MA: Harvard University Press, 1999); Janet R. Jakobsen and Ann Pellegrini, *Love the Sin: Sexual Regulation and the Limits of Religious Tolerance* (New York: New York University Press, 2003); and Lauren Berlant, *The Queen of America Goes to Washington City: Essays on Sex and Citizenship* (Durham, NC: Duke University Press, 1997). Such theorists argue that LGBTQ folks ought not be required to be "like heterosexuals" to be considered worthy of dignity, respect, or political rights. Judith Plaskow addresses a similar phenomenon in the Jewish world when she addresses gradual-change approaches to LGBTQ inclusion that "[assume] an assimilationist model of homosexual identity in which gays and lesbians are normalized through acceptance of dominant values" (Judith Plaskow, *The Coming of Lilith: Essays on Feminism, Judaism, and Sexual Ethics, 1972–2003*, ed. Judith Plaskow and Donna Berman [Boston: Beacon Press, 2005], 180–81).

3. Tamar Ross and Judith Plaskow, "The View from Here: Gender Theory and Gendered Realities: An Exchange between Tamar Ross and Judith Plaskow," *Nashim: A Journal of Jewish Women's Studies and Gender Issues* 13 (Spring 2007): 215. Judith Plaskow acknowledges a second tactical strategy, namely, rediscovering and revaluing "the neglected particularities of women's experience" (ibid.). The limitations of these strategies for ensuring real and lasting change increasingly have become clear to feminists, particularly feminists outside the Orthodox Movement (who are constrained by halachah and "tradition" in a different way). Plaskow has warned that attending to "the fruits but not the bases of discrimination" will leave untouched an underlying "assumption of women's Otherness" that has theological, spiritual, and practical consequences (Judith Plaskow, "The Right Question Is Theological," in *On Being a Jewish Feminist: A Reader*, ed. Susannah Heschel [New York: Schocken Books, 1983], 224). Plaskow's warning mirrors my concern about claims for LGBTQ acceptance that rely too heavily on a "born that way" logic. Rachel Adler also addresses the dangers of focusing only on "the problems of inclusion" and thereby neglecting to "transform the androcentric texts, categories, and structures that exclude

. . . women" (Rachel Adler, *Engendering Judaism* [Philadelphia: Jewish Publication Society, 1998], xix).

4. Adler, *Engendering Judaism*, xiv. Adler's analysis focuses on women's inclusion, though she does at several points ask the question about queer inclusion as well.

5. The edited collection *Queer Jews* (David Shneer and Cayrn Aviv, eds. New York: Routledge, 2002) presents personal narratives of LGBTQ individuals; the recent Torah study companion *Torah Que(e)ries*, whose title obviously inspired this author, also comments on the personal stakes for LGBTQ Jews of a successful theological intervention. These anthologies prove that "Queer people . . . have important—*essential*—things to say about what life is really like that the Tradition needs to hear" (Benay Lappe, "The New Rabbis: A Postscript," in *Torah Queeries: Weekly Commentaries on the Hebrew Bible*, ed. Gregg Drinkwater, Joshua Lesser, and David Shneer [New York: New York University Press, 2009], 311).

6. Plaskow, *Coming of Lilith*, 184.

7. See, e.g., the debate between Judith Plaskow and Tamar Ross in which Ross criticizes queer theory ("The View from Here,"); or Rachel Adler's essay "A Question of Boundaries: Toward a Jewish Feminist Theology of Self and Others" (*Tikkun*, May/June 1991), in which she chides critical theory for its jargon and inaccessibility. An engagement with, and partial rejection of, theories of human sexuality from the late nineteenth and early twentieth centuries (including Sigmund Freud's groundbreaking *Three Essays on the Theory of Sexuality*) appears in Roth's Conservative *t'shuvah*, among other evidence of dialogue among differing viewpoints.

8. See, e.g., Ann Pellegrini in *Judaism Since Gender*, ed. Miriam Peskowitz and Laura Levitt (New York: Routledge, 1997). At its core, queer theory claims that there are many more ways to live a meaningful life than are described and prescribed by the dominant narrative, which claims that gender and sexual expression are limited to an inevitable division between "male" and "female" that maps onto the similar distinctions of "masculine" and "feminine." Even something seemingly as small and innocuous as the traditional parents' blessing for children participates in the dominant narrative: why do we send the message that our antatomically male children can identify only with our anatomically male ancestors? When I bless my young son, I ask God to help him to emulate not only Ephraim and Menasseh, but also Sarah, Rebekah, Leah, and Rachel.

9. See Michel Foucault, "Friendship as a Way of Life," in *Foucault Live: Collected Interviews, 1961–1984*, 2nd ed., ed. Sylvère Lotringer (New York: Semiotext[e], 1996), 308–12; Judith Butler, *Gender Trouble: Feminism and the Subversion of Identity* (New York: Routledge, 2006); and Warner, *Trouble with Normal*.

10. See, e.g., Elliot N. Dorff, Daniel S. Nevins, and Avram I. Reisner, "Homosexuality, Human Dignity and Halakhah: A Combined Responsum for the Committee on Jewish Law and Standards," Rabbinical Assembly, December 6, 2006, http://www.rabbinicalassembly.org/sites/default/files/public/halakhah/teshuvot/20052010/dorff_nevins_reisner_dignity.pdf; Joel Roth; and Gordon Tucker, "דרוש וקבל שכר": Halakhic and Metahalakhic Arguments Concerning Judaism and Homosexuality," Rabbinical Assembly, December 6, 2006, http://www.rabbinicalassembly.org/sites/default/files/public/halakhah/teshuvot/20052010/tucker_homosexuality.pdf. The argument that homosexuality be considered an illness rather than a sin appears as early as Havelock Ellis's 1897 medical treatise on homosexuality. (For more on the

history of homosexuality, see David M. Halperin, "Is There a History of Sexuality?" in *The Lesbian and Gay Studies Reader*, ed. Henry Abelove, Michele Aina Barale, and David M. Halperin (New York: Routledge, 1993) 416–31.

Let me be clear: acknowledging that sexual orientation, gender identity, and gender expression are an integral part of a human being's psychological makeup does not require that all calls for LGBTQ political, social, or religious inclusion must cling to the notion that we do not "choose" to be gay. Whether or not it is "chosen" sidesteps the crucial issue: whether or not our lives remain *valuable* and *valid* if we are gay. The fact that I "chose" Judaism does not mean my religion can be changed as easily as my clothing.

Much of the debate on homosexuality does engage in a debate about the nature and limits of homosexuality as a category or expression of identity. David Brodsky argues that the injunction in Leviticus has been "mischaracterized as a prohibition against homosexuality" when rather it prohibits only "some specific forms of male same-sex intercourse and not homosexuality as a category of identity" (David Brodsky, "Sex in the Talmud: How to Understand Leviticus 18 and 20: *Parashat Kedoshim* [Leviticus 19:1–20:27]," in *Torah Queeries: Weekly Commentaries on the Hebrew Bible*, ed. Gregg Drinkwater, Joshua Lesser, and David Shneer [New York: New York University Press, 2009], 157). His analysis here relies on the work of Michel Foucault and of Halperin, who argue that "homosexuality" as a category of *identity* emerged only in the nineteenth century.

The view that "reading our notions of identity into earlier texts that mention sexual acts is problematic and misleading" both helps and hurts the project for LGBTQ inclusion (see ibid.). For example, saying that we cannot impose contemporary notions of sexual identity onto an ancient Israelite context allows us to reinterpret the Leviticus prohibition; it simply does not refer to the kinds of people and acts (in a particular context) that we mean today when we say "homosexuality." On the other hand, saying that we cannot impose contemporary notions of sexual identity onto an ancient Israelite culture would prevent us from, as many queer writers do, reclaiming the stories of same-sex intimacy, affection, and love that we see in the Torah (or in other Jewish texts; see, e.g., Steven Greenberg's chapter on David and Jonathan in *Wrestling with God and Men: Homosexuality in the Jewish Tradition* (Madison: University of Wisconsin Press, 2004) or his writing on Andalusian Jewish poetry. Indeed, Joel Roth rejects the Foucauldian approach to the history of sexuality, saying that there is "not one shred of evidence" that the Leviticus prohibition targets anything other than homosexual activity (Roth, "Homosexuality Revisited," 2). Indeed, he cites an alternative historical model, one that seeks to reclaim and revalue different forms of intimacy and affiliation in history (John Boswell's *Same-Sex Unions in Premodern Europe*). This research, along with other textual evidence, Roth argues, proves that the ancient Israelites did not know only a coercive form of homosexuality (as Greenberg argues), that "the Bible itself recognizes the possibility of a loving relationship between equals" as between David and Jonathan, and that the Leviticus prohibition does not "refer to humiliation and denigration, as a woman" (Roth, "Homosexuality Revisited," 4–5).

11. For some Jewish writers, like David Brodsky, the issue for Jews is *which* acts are prohibited according to Leviticus (and its Rabbinic interpreters). He argues that "the rabbis prohibited only anal penetration between men" (Brodsky, "Sex in the

Talmud," 157). He argues that in order to avoid prohibiting all physical contact between males as strictly as the tradition prohibits physical contact between men and
women (which would present inconveniences and problems for daily Jewish life), the
Rabbis were more lenient than we might have assumed concerning physical (even
intimate) contact between males that did not involve anal penetration (which the
Rabbis see as warranting the death penalty according to Leviticus) (ibid., 160–65).
Brodsky's view reflects a more common assertion by contemporary Conservative
writers on this topic, who argue that Leviticus only explicitly forbids anal sex (see
Dorff et al., "Homosexuality, Human Dignity and Halakhah"). Brodsky also notes
that Maimonides brought an "innovation" into the halachic discussion, forbidding
any male-male "nonpenetrative sexual/sensual activities" only if accompanied by
"desire" (Brodsky, "Sex in the Talmud," 165).

Most writers on this topic stress that the Bible itself does not condemn desire
but "only" acts (see, e.g., Greenberg, *Wrestling*, 85). But, as many queer theorists
have noted, granting the permission to "be" gay without the permission to "act" gay
ultimately amounts to granting no permission at all. Michael Warner notes that such
an argument, even when advanced by queer people (gays and lesbians who argue
that our identity is "not about sex," implying that sex is always and only trivial or
deviant), "implicitly confirm[s] the dominant assumption that homosexuality is itself
unworthy" (Warner, *Trouble with Normal*, 47). Janet Jakobsen and Ann Pellegrini
call for "equal rights for gay people"—rights that "would have to protect not just
homosexual identity, but also homosexual conduct in all its rich and various forms"
(Jakobsen and Pellegrini, *Love the Sin*, 37). They (following a related argument by
law professor Janet Halley) suggest a new analogy; rather than arguing that homosexuality is "like race" (biologically determined, immutable, genetically encoded),
Jakobsen and Pellegrini say that sexual orientation is "like religion": changeable over
time, but constitutive of our identities, and deeply cherished. Generally speaking,
we deplore coercion and forced conversion in religion. And, as the authors note,
"religion is never a matter solely of text and belief, but crucially involves—we could
even say is instantiated by—practice" (ibid., 99). This claims rings particularly true
for the Jewish people, who responded to God's call with *naaseh v'nishma* (Exod. 24:7).

12. Chaim Rapoport, *Judaism and Homosexuality: An Authentic Orthodox View*
(London: Vallentine Mitchell, 2004), 21. This is a particular dilemma, Orthodox
rabbi Chaim Rapoport notes, for Jews, who do not generally endorse celibacy. The
first biblical commandment, after all, is *p'ru ur'vu*, "Be fruitful and multiply" (Gen.
1:28).

Rapoport also urges for change on an individual—and not an institutional—level.
For example, it would be one thing to be compassionate or tolerant of a person who
transgresses kashrut and another to endorse an Orthodox pork barbeque restaurant
(ibid., 86). Far better than the view that homosexuals ought to be cut off from the
Jewish community and mourned as dead, Rapoport's view at worst suggests that homosexuality is a challenge or a burden or a test to be withstood or overcome; at best,
Rapoport calls for private, individual tolerance for gay and lesbian Orthodox Jews,
who must at least strive to be celibate.

The position of gay Orthodox rabbi Steven Greenberg, outlined in *Wrestling
with God and Men*, represents a slightly different approach, though Greenberg certainly also argues that gays and lesbians are created in God's image—a belief that

has consequences for how we treat LGBTQ individuals in our Jewish communities. The focus of Greenberg's argument, however, is on the rationales for the prohibition against homosexual sex or intimacy. Greenberg sidesteps the theological implications of LGBTQ inclusion (e.g., will it or should it change how we view *k'dushah* or *mishpachah*?) and instead proposes possible rationales against the prohibition in order to give gays and lesbians more options for expressing their sexual orientation in the context of a loving relationship.

Greenberg argues that one rationale might have been that such acts, in an ancient Israelite context, always indicated "subjugation and domination" (Greenberg, *Wrestling*, 65). The Torah might also have intended, Greenberg speculates, to alleviate "category confusion"; homosexuality blurred the lines between male and female because it involved penetration of the "wrong" kind of body (ibid., 175–91). Greenberg's analysis relies on his translation and interpretation of *mishk'vei ishah*, "the lyings of a woman" (Lev. 18:22). If such activity puts a man in the position of a woman, then (in the hierarchical ancient Israelite society) homosexuality represents humiliation and domination (Greenberg, *Wrestling*, 202). Today, Greenberg argues, we know that gay and lesbian people can have loving intimate relations, without domination or humiliation (ibid., 202–6).

Greenberg's interpretation suggests an underlying misogyny in the Jewish concept of sexual relations (it is always humiliating to be in the position of a woman, unless one is "naturally" suited to that position—i.e., for women, penetration does not necessarily mean humiliation, but only because women are seen as properly occupying the "bottom" position in a dyadic power structure). David Brodsky addresses this misogyny in his short *d'rash* on Leviticus in *Torah Que(e)ries*, citing *B'reishit Rabbah* 63:10, which implies that "the male who is penetrated is equal to a woman and is viewed as inferior" (Brodsky, "Sex in the Talmud," 158).

13. Dorff et al., "Homosexuality, Human Dignity and Halakhah," 3. Note that Conservative rabbis Elliot Dorff, Daniel Nevins, and Avram Reisner still argue that the Torah prohibits certain sexual acts, i.e., anal intercourse between men (ibid., 5). Additionally, they rely so heavily on the notion that homosexuality is not chosen that they encourage (stopping short of actually mandating) bisexuals to act only on their heterosexual desires (ibid., 3).

14. Ibid., 3–4. Their mention of promiscuity and experimentation does not echo the common charge that all homosexuals are promiscuous, but reflects awareness of some of the more flexible and "sex-positive" attitudes observable in the queer community today. In such circles, limits and guidelines still exist (against coercion, e.g., and for self-determination), but sexuality is seen more on the side of virtue (a good for human beings) than of vice. For more on this topic, see the works of Ann Pellegrini and Samuel Delany. Roth disagrees with Dorff, Nevins, and Reisner in their interpretation of the biblical ban as encompassing *only* anal intercourse between men. The Talmud, they note, ranks human dignity so highly that it can override some obligations and commandments (in one place, they suggest, the Talmud even states that human dignity can override a negative Torah commandment, but later this revolutionary statement is severely limited)—but ultimately not "an explicit biblical rule" (ibid., 10).

15. Central Conference of American Rabbis, "Report of the Ad Hoc Committee on Homosexuality and the Rabbinate," Resolution Adopted by the CCAR, 1990, http://ccarnet.org/rabbis-speak/resolutions/1990/homsexuality-and-the-rabbinate-1990/.

16. Ibid.

17. In the realm of sanctified relationships, the Reform Movement shows no unity of position, either. Rabbis are, of course, free to officiate (or not) at commitment ceremonies or weddings for gay and lesbian couples and are free to dub them (or not) *kiddushin*.

18. See Central Conference of American Rabbis, "On Gay and Lesbian Marriage," Resolution Adopted by the CCAR, March 1996, http://ccarnet.org/rabbis-speak/reolutions/1996/on-gay-and-lesbian-marriage-1996/; and Central Conference of American Rabbis, "Same Gender Officiation," Resolution Adopted by the CCAR, 2000, http://ccarnet.org/rabbis-speak/resolutions/2000/same-gender-officiation/.

19. Gayle Rubin, "Thinking Sex: Notes for a Radical Theory of the Politics of Sexuality," in *The Lesbian and Gay Studies Reader*, ed. Henry Abelove, Michele Aina Barale, and David M. Halperin (New York: Routledge, 1993), 9.

20. Ibid., 10.

21. See, e.g., Betty Freidan's *The Feminine Mystique* (New York: Norton, 1963) and Simone de Beauvoir's *The Second Sex* (New York: Vintage Books, 1952).

22. Michaelson , 2010.

23. Greenberg, *Wrestling*, 41.

24. Margaret Moers Wenig, "'Male and Female God Created Them': *Parashat Bereshit* (Genesis 1:1-6:8)," in *Torah Queeries: Weekly Commentaries on the Hebrew Bible*, ed. Gregg Drinkwater, Joshua Lesser, and David Shneer (New York: New York University Press, 2009), 11.

25. Indeed, some rabbis in the Reform Movement have argued for such a reexamination, along Adler's lines, including Peter S. Knobel, who writes, "Gay and lesbian relationships give us a unique opportunity to indicate our changed understanding of marriage by using a new ceremony and symbolizing the partnership aspects of marriage, rather than the property transfer aspects of marriage, and encouraging all couples to use it" (Peter S. Knobel, "*Kiddushin*: An Equal Opportunity Covenant, Not Only for Heterosexuals," *CCAR Journal* (Fall 2005): 23.

26. Ross and Plaskow, "View from Here," 219.

27. See, e.g., Jakobsen and Pellegrini, *Love the Sin*. Furthermore, when queer theory "meets" Judaism, Judaism's own moral and ethical claims come into play.

28. Ross and Plaskow, "View from Here," 219.

29. See ibid., 222.

30. Ibid., 221.

31. See, e.g., Judith Butler's *Bodies That Matter: On the Discursive Limits of "Sex"* (New York: Routledge, 1993), a work that addresses the many misreadings that followed her *Gender Trouble: Feminism and the Subversion of Identity* (New York: Routledge, 1990). Of course, the possibility of sex reassignment surgery and hormone therapy challenges even the fixity of our bodies.

32. Warner, *Trouble with Normal*, 9.

33. So many "coming out" stories include the tale of the reaction of some well-meaning friend or relative who says, "Of *course* you didn't *choose* to be this way." When "this way" means the way I understand myself, relate to others, love, and make a family—and when I experience those things as good—to hear such a reaction implies that the life I lead is lesser, undesirable, a consolation. I received a similar

reaction when I told some people of my decision to convert to Judaism: "Who would *choose* such a life?"

34. See, e.g., Eve Kosofsky Sedgwick, "How to Bring Your Kids Up Gay," *Social Text* 29 (1991): 18–27; and Jakobsen and Pellegrini, *Love the Sin*.

35. See Ayelet Cohen, "Liberation and Transgender Jews: Passover," in *Torah Queeries: Weekly Commentaries on the Hebrew Bible*, ed. Gregg Drinkwater, Joshua Lesser, and David Shneer (New York: New York University Press, 2009), 304; Wenig, "Male and Female," 13–15; Elliot Kukla, "Created Beings of Our Own: Toward a Jewish Liberation Theology for Men, Women, and Everyone Else," in *Righteous Indignation: A Jewish Call For Justice*, ed. Or. N Rose, Jo Ellen Green Kaiser, and Margie Klein (Woodstock, VT: Jewish Lights Publishing, 2008); Elliot Kukla, "'Created by the Hand of Heaven': Sex, Love, and the Androgynos," in *The Passionate Torah*, ed. Danya Ruttenberg (New York: New York University Press, 2009), 193–202; Elliot Kukla and Reuben Zellman, "To Wear Is Human, To Live—Divine: *Parashat Ki Tetse* (Deuteronomy 21:10–25:19)," in *Torah Queeries: Weekly Commentaries on the Hebrew Bible*, ed. Gregg Drinkwater, Joshua Lesser, and David Shneer, 254–58 (New York: New York University Press, 2009). Kukla mentions also the *saris* and the *alyonit*. As Plaskow acknowledges, the *tumtum* and the *androgynos* serve as limit cases for the Rabbis in making halachic determinations; these unusual and perhaps fictional (in the Rabbis' minds) individuals served to "sharpen and reinforce gender-bifurcated halakhic norms" (Ross and Plaskow, "View from Here," 212). For those versed in queer theory who are concerned with sexual ethics, these possibilities of human sexual existence offer a much broader view of what it means to be created *b'tzelem Elohim* than the gender binary could ever provide. Still, we ought to take seriously Kukla's warning against quickly claiming "an exact equivalence . . . between premodern gender diversity and contemporary transgender and intersex identities" (Kukla, "Created by the Hand of Heaven," 200).

36. Kukla, "Created Beings," 215. See also Anne Fausto-Sterling, *Sexing the Body: Gender Politics and the Construction of Sexuality* (New York: Basic Books, 2000).

37. Kukla and Zellman, "To Wear Is Human," 256.

38. Wenig, "Male and Female," 16.

39. Hints of this methodology already appear in some Rabbinic interpretations of the Torah. Writing in relationship to the ban on anal sex between males, Dorff, for example, notes, "The Jewish tradition has interpreted and narrowed many other morally problematic verses in the Torah, making the death penalty virtually inoperative" (Dorff, "How Flexible," 151). Balanced against these narrow readings are "expansive" readings, through which "the Rabbis expanded the many Torah verses that give us valuable moral norms" (ibid.). Kukla and Zellman, like Dorff and others, cite the verse mandating the death penalty for a rebellious son, noting that, despite such a "straightforward" mandate, "Judaism has not carried out the extremely harsh practice that the Torah would seem to require" (Kukla and Zellman, "To Wear Is Human," 254).

40. David Ellenson, "Laws and Judgments as a 'Bridge to a Better World': *Parashat Mishpatim* (Exodus 21:1–24:8)," in *Torah Queeries: Weekly Commentaries on the Hebrew Bible*, ed. Gregg Drinkwater, Joshua Lesser, and David Shneer (New York: New York University Press, 2009), 99.

41. Ibid., 100.

42. Ibid.

43. Ibid., 99.

44. Tucker, "Halakhic and Metahalakhic Arguments," 5.

45. Ibid., 28. The texts to which Tucker turns include *Sh'mot Rabbah* 32 and *Sifrei Pinchas* 133, as well as other texts from from Torah, Rabbinic literature, the codes, and the contemporary narratives of LGBTQ individuals.

46. *Vayikra Rabbah* 32.

47. Tucker, "Halakhic and Metahalakhic Arguments," 29.

48. Adler, *Engendering Judaism*, xxiii–iv.

49. Greenberg, *Wrestling*, 190.

50. Ibid.

51. I am grateful for conversations with my colleague Rachel Grant Meyer on this issue. The concept of difference without judgment or hierarchy is one I explored at length in my dissertation. For more on this issue outside Judaism, see Martha Nussbaum, *Frontiers of Justice* (Cambridge, MA: Belknap Press of Harvard University Press, 2006); and Martha Minow, *Making All the Difference* (Ithaca, NY: Cornell University Press, 1990).

52. Some communities have begun to teach about the blessing *m'shaneh hab'riyot* as a way to think about disability in the Jewish community.

53. Harris Goldstein, "Understand What It Means to Be Created in the Image of God," in *The Body*, January 1995, http://www.thebody.com/content/art13149.html, citing Babylonian Talmud, *Derech Eretz* 4.

54. Ibid.

55 Kukla, "Created Beings," 220. See also Kukla, "'Created by the Hand of Heaven': Sex, Love, and the *Andrygonos*," reprinted in this volume.

56. Jay Michaelson, "Toward a Queer Theology," *Sh'ma: A Journal of Jewish Responsibility*, December 2005, http://www.shma.com/2005/12/toward-a-queer-jewish-theology/.

57. Ibid.

58. Jay Michaelson, "On the Religious Significance of Homosexuality; or, Queering God, Torah, and Israel," in *The Passionate Torah*, ed. Danya Ruttenberg (New York: New York University Press, 2009), 218.

59. Kukla translates *k'dushah* as "out of the ordinary" (Kukla, "Created Beings," 219).

60. Ibid.

61. Ross and Plaskow, "View from Here," 238.

62. Tucker, "Halakhic and Metahalakhic Arguments," 18.

63. Babylonian Talmud, *Yoma* 22b.

64. These sentiments also appear in my sermon "*Ahat, Shteim, Shalosh* . . . (A Sermon on *Parashat Bamidbar*)" (Congregation Kol Ami, White Plains, NY, May 27, 2011).

14

CRAFTING AN
INCLUSIVE LITURGICAL MIRROR

Rabbi Camille Shira Angel

> All true theology must finally be personal. God meets one of
> us. And we in turn are compelled to tell a story from which
> no objective theological truth can be distilled. For this reason
> authentic God talk must always begin with the introduction
> *maaseh sh'hayah*, "it once happened."
>
> *Rabbi Lawrence Kushner*[1]

Maaseh sh'hayah, "it once happened," that a group of three knowledge-able Jews, who knew themselves to be gay, decided to organize a gay, Jewish gathering for Shabbat. It was San Francisco and the year was 1977. With the backdrop of the 1960s, the sexual revolution, feminism, and the civil rights movements, gathering a group of gay Jews for Shabbat seemed like a compelling idea. Little could those men have imagined that they were at the forefront of liturgical innovation. The "gayby boom" was impossible to imagine, not to mention marriage equality. Civil marriage for homosexuals? Beyond belief. But gathering for social purposes and reflexive purposes didn't seem that unusual. No one could have predicted that by the age of retirement the original conveners would have lived to see their efforts bear fruit and multiply, not only for themselves, but for future generations.

In 1977, I was twelve years old. The only time I had ever encountered the word "homosexual" in a Jewish book was when I snuck my father's copy of *Love, Sex, and Marriage: A Jewish View*, written by Rabbi Roland Gittelsohn and published by the Union of American Hebrew Congregations in 1976. On the verge of puberty, I was seeking language to help define my budding sexuality, only to find confusing messages, at best.

> We do not really know what causes homosexuality. According to one theory, it results from chemical imbalances. Another explanation is that it comes from unhealthy and unhappy relations between opposite sexes. Another explains that masturbation either signals or causes homosexuality. If, however, a young person has persistent and gnawing fears that he or she is homosexual he or she need not worry. Homosexuals manifest no greater number of serious personality problems than one would expect to find in the normal population.[2]

We know that words can create and destroy whole worlds—and from that day forward, seeds of internalized homophobia were sadly implanted in my Jewish heart. For years while participating in Jewish settings like camp, *beit sefer* (religious school), youth group, I felt awkward and like a misfit because I harbored an unseemly secret about myself. I wanted to belong but in order to do so, I had to learn to compartmentalize my sense of self and thus compromise my integrity. The possibility of feeling blessed by God as being created just right seemed unfathomable.

Between then and today, tectonic cultural and ideological plates have shifted, and the sex-positive language and discourse now available reveal a liberating new landscape. Today a young Jew can do an Internet search for "Judaism, Gays, and Lesbians" and instantaneously find many positive references and resources celebrating and sanctifying same-sex desire and love.

My congregation, Sha'ar Zahav in San Francisco, has been a pioneer. In 1982 our first prayer book, *Siddur Sha'ar Zahav*, appeared, and since then we have a tradition of creating liturgy that reflects who we are. One of my favorite readings, one that I wish I had read as an adolescent, is entitled "Remembering the Bar/Bat Mitzvah Problem":

> Today I am a man.
> Today I am a woman.
> Today I am mortified.
> Bad enough to be growing into this body, but a public celebration of the fact?
> Maybe all *b'nei mitzvah* struggle with identity, rules, clothes, traditions, expectations.
> But can anyone see who I am, hidden by make-up, or by a crew cut and tie?
> Years and years later, I can say:
> Today I am who I am.
> Surely Adonai understands that.[3]

Here, the author's message of God's acceptance conveys to the reader the divine ideal, of authenticity, which we aspire to imitate.

When I experience people of all ages and backgrounds encountering these words, I witness what is for me a corrective on the historical Jewish (and Judeo-Christian) damnation of same-sex erotic desire and relationships. *Siddur Sha'ar Zahav* is located at the intersection of sexuality and liturgy and offers us language for living our complicated lives with passion and thanksgiving.

I am inspired to believe that change for the better *is* possible each time I hold this heavy prayer book in my hands. Sha'ar Zahav's elegant, "homemade" siddur represents the creativity of gay, lesbian, bisexual and transgender, straight and queer people, giving voice to our tradition's ancient words and sanctifying the contemporary realities with new poems of praise and petition.

What are the relevant intersections between sexuality and liturgy? Our foundational guiding principles include ensuring that the language we use expresses feminist sensibilities, celebrates human sexuality, does not use disability as a metaphor, and includes references to our varied sexual and gender identities.

For the first time in Jewish history, gay and lesbian, bisexual and transgender human beings, our friends, families, and allies are the audience. We created this prayer book and chose to publish it at our expense for our own benefit. Yes, we had others in mind, and we care about history's sake, but predominantly we endeavored on behalf of our inclusive Sha'ar Zahav community, in the here and now.

What we chose to call ourselves in print evolved over many years and many hot debates, many *machlo-kot l'shem shamayim*, arguments for the sake of a better way. To figure out inclusive language—how to name ourselves, to honor our diversity and our semantic, not only sexual, preferences—has been a uniquely challenging process.

When I first arrived at Sha'ar Zahav as the rabbi in 2000, I was handed a piece of protocol entitled "The Use of the Word 'Queer'"—which plainly stated that no one was to use this word to describe our community in public, from the bimah or in the press. How far we've come in such a short amount of time in order to embrace new ideas, new language and trends, and the next generation. "When you use the word 'lesbian,' I think of my mother. I am not a lesbian. I am queer!" offered a twentysomething, second-generation member in our community.[4]

When it came time to publish the siddur, we wrote the following inclusive statement in the introduction:

> *Siddur Sha'ar Zahav* endeavors to respect the varied, and at times contradictory, sensibilities of our people and our congregation. Our goal is for all of us...to see ourselves reflected in our liturgy, so that none of us experience the invisibility and exclusion we have historically encountered. . . . While we know that not every reading will speak to each of us, we hope that in these pages all of us will find a point of departure for prayer, and for dialogue with the Source of creation.[5]

Siddur Sha'ar Zahav makes explicit that all people are created *b'tzelem Elohim*, with divine intention and love, as it says in our "A Queer *Amidah*":

God of Oneness, infinite, eternal
How very queer of You to have created anything at all.
God of queerness in whom are united all separations
we stand before You now
queer ourselves,
made of heaven and earth,
day and night
female and male,
together
all of us
within Your awesome holy Oneness.

. . . . And together
in our many different ways
we express our innate fruitfulness
varied as the colors of Your rainbow
refractions of one sacred light
we join together in community
united in heartfelt prayer
in awe of Your creation
and its manifest paradoxes.[6]

We found that the more members we could enlist to help create an authentic and meaningful prayer book, the more inclusive it became. Just by saying that you are welcoming does not make it so. Nothing makes someone feel more connected and a part of something greater than being listened to and known. At the heart of inclusivity is the sense of belonging. When I open *Siddur Sha'ar Zahav*, I know I belong to this specific group as well as to a larger group, the Jewish people, and even more grandly, to peoples everywhere.

Our history as a community became part of our prayer book. *Siddur Sha'ar Zahav* was composed by a community with an intimate knowledge of illness gained by experiencing the effects of AIDS on our community. My teacher and colleague Rabbi Sharon Kleinbaum describes our education eloquently in her introduction to *Siddur B'chol L'vav'cha*, the siddur of her congregation in New York, Congregation Beit Simchat Torah:

> We learned that we were powerful and we learned the limits of our power. ACT UP and GMHC are emblems of our power. The families of choice we fashioned, who cared for and mourned for and comforted so many who were sick, are emblems of our power. The Americans With Disabilities Act is an emblem of our power. Yet still no cure for HIV/AIDS has been found, no vaccine has been developed, and AIDS is raging through Africa, affecting millions more. . . . Our poems and prayers reflect a full range of feelings in the face of illness and loss.[7]

My teacher and colleague Rabbi Laura Geller, one of the first pioneer women rabbis, applied the feminist hermeneutical lens to Jewish liturgy and observed the absence of blessings to mark the powerful events in a woman's life. She began to catalogue all the moments in her life that had gone unblessed. She and others began to write new material with emotional resonance and power to sanctify women's experiences. And from one generation to the next, feminism led the way to liturgical and ritual innovation for all of us.

It was important to me as a rabbi that a book of Jewish prayer offer words of praise for realities and moments that are not always acknowledged in a prayer context or that have not historically been understood as worthy of blessing. With that in mind, *Siddur Sha'ar Zahav* includes prayers thanking the Divine Spirit for the experience of being single, for donor fathers and surrogate mothers, for letting go of having a biological child, for those without children, and for questioning sexuality. Radical inclusivity means that we include prayers to be said when transitioning genders, when mourning the death of a newborn child, or when someone has died and left us angry. And yet we chose to exclude a memorial prayer for a pet, a prayer to be said at a covenantal ceremony for a new baby, which may or may not include traditional *b'rit milah*, and a prayer entitled "For Anonymous Sex."

We have insinuated a female messiah in our *Havdalah* prayers, a queer *Al HaNisim* for the miracles for Chanukah, and a list of Jewish queer *ushpizin* and *ushpizot* from history to invite into our festival sukkot. These passages are not "sexual" in the sense of erotic or sensual in content, yet they are "LGBTQ" in orientation as they offer different entryways to connect to Jewish tradition.

Every time I hold *Siddur Sha'ar Zahav* in my hands, I encounter the Divine. Before I've even opened the cover, I consider with awe the Mysterious Power and Creative Force in the universe, who empowers the oppressed to make our lives a blessing.

Praying with a siddur that names, honors, and reflects the divine image in which I've been created is for me a spiritual gift with profound healing properties. The communal experience of writing and using liturgy that reflects the diversity of human sexuality and that represents themes and issues of special relevance in our lives is invigorating, inspiring, and for many, a first.

Riv-Ellen Prell, professor of religious studies and an expert in the field of feminism and American Judaism, writes:

> Prayer is both "social," enabling individuals to join together in community, and "reflexive," creating a mirror for personal experience. Prayer expresses the collective identity of a group, differentiating that group from all others, but particularly those close at hand, by ritualizing "perceptions of time" and articulating shared experience.[8]

Our siddur offers just this with new liturgy and new holy days meant to integrate our LGBTQ and Jewish identities, calendars, and sensitivities. We have Shabbat Freedom on Gay Pride weekend, when we sing a full *Hallel* of psalms; we have Transgender Day of Remembrance in conjunction with the national day of memorial for those transgender victims of hate and violence; and we have suggestions for marking World AIDS Day.

Perhaps the sweetest and juiciest section of liturgy is our *b'rachot*, our blessings for relationships, which include such blessings as "For the

First Kiss," "For Lovers," "For Unexpected Intimacy," "For Friends, Partners, Parents, and Family," and "For Making Love." This last blessing reads as follows:

> Thank You, Source of Life and Wonder, for the delight of human touch, for the laughter, for the unexpected, for all the blessings You bestow.[9]

May our dreams and our particular aspirations and desires be for us and peoples everywhere an enduring legacy of blessing.

NOTES

1. Lawrence Kushner, *Honey from the Rock: Ten Gates of Jewish Mysticism* (Woodstock, VT: Jewish Lights, 2000), 16.

2. R. Bertram Gittelsohn, *Love, Sex, and Marriage: A Jewish View*, rev. ed. (New York: Union of American Hebrew Congregations, 1976), 131ff.

3. Ray Bernstein, "On the Bar/Bar Mitzvah Problem," in *Siddur Sha'ar Zahav*, ed. Michael Tyler and Leslie Kane (San Francisco: Congregation Sha'ar Zahav, 2009), 49.

4. Ruby Cymrot-Wu, in conversation with author, 2007.

5. *Siddur Sha'ar Zahav*, ix.

6. Maggid Andrew Ramer, "A Queer *Amidah*," in *Siddur Sha'ar Zahav*, 260.

7. Rabbi Sharon Kleinbaum, ed., *Siddur B'chol L'vav'cha* (New York: Congregation Beit Simchat Torah, 2008), 23.

8. Riv-Ellen Prell, "Liberal Liturgy," *Tikkun* 5, no. 2 (March/April 1990): 116.

9. Andrea Guerra, "For Making Love," in *Siddur Sha'ar Zahav*, 25.

15

"WHAT KIND OF A MAN ARE YOU?"

Interethnic Sexual Encounter in Yiddish American Narratives

JESSICA KIRZANE

In the modern era, representations of Jews as essentially different from non-Jews have always been located at the intersection of ideologies of race, gender, and religion. Each of these separate realms of thought have come together to form ideas and representations of Jews that have varied across time and space. Representations of Jewish difference have not simply been limited to non-Jews who were afraid of or repulsed by what they understood as Jewish difference—Jews themselves understood their Jewishness as something that set them apart, and they spoke of themselves in terms borrowed and developed from the same gendered, racial, and religious notions that their non-Jewish neighbors used. For much of European and American history, both Jews and non-Jews have drawn upon contemporary anthropological, biological, and philosophical ideas to represent Jewish religious practices and Jewish bodies as outside of the perceived norm of white, European heterosexuality.[1]

This essay examines the way that Yiddish writers in America represented Jews as different from non-Jews by looking at narratives of interethnic sexual encounter. It considers how Jewish writers accepted and rearticulated contemporary discourses of Jewish sexual and racial difference in their fictional works. It also considers how these authors represented members of other racial groups as sexual beings, how they drew upon and developed stereotypical ideas about the sexualities of non-Jewish groups.

This is far from an exhaustive study of interethnic sexual encounter in Yiddish American literature; rather it is meant as a thematic sampling that will illuminate the ways that some Yiddish writers use fictionalized sexual experiences to situate Jewish Americans in American society. I have chosen to present three examples of Yiddish writers describing sexual encounters between Jewish men and non-Jewish women. I find these stories particularly illuminating because together they demonstrate how Yiddish American writers use non-Jewish women as foils to demonstrate the social and cultural anxieties facing modern Jewish men through the trope of sexual attraction and restraint. The Jewish men in these stories are consistently sexually hesitant and concerned with morality and discretion, while the non-Jewish women, though they are each very different in their background and social position, are sexually available in ways that highlight the Jewish male's sexual desires and anxieties. These non-Jewish women serve to provoke the Jewish man's contemplation about what it means to be both a Jew and a man, to be an outcast and yet to have sexual needs and desires. They also provoke Jewish readers to consider where Jews fit into burgeoning American categories of race and ethnicity.

Yiddish fictions about interethnic sexual encounter are not straightforward realistic narratives; interethnic sex in Yiddish fiction is never only and simply about sex itself. These sexual encounters bear the symbolic weight of anxieties and hopes of assimilation, of fears about Jewish difference and inferiority, of fantasies of conquest, and of questions about Jewish particularity and human universality. Representations of interethnic sexual encounter in Yiddish literature demonstrate the "fantasy and projection"[2] that Jewish writers and their Jewish characters place on the idea of the non-Jew. These representations emphasize the idea of the non-Jew as something forbidden, exotic, and profoundly different. Descriptions of non-Jews in Jewish literature often tell us as much about what Jews believed was the opposite of Jewish as they tell us about what Jews thought of non-Jews themselves. Because erotic relations between Jews and non-Jews appear "momentous and threatening,"[3] these narratives draw attention to and secure the boundaries between Jew and non-Jew. Yet, at the very moment that these narratives articulate difference, by bringing Jews and non-Jews together in (potential) sexual union, these stories also contest these boundaries by demonstrating their fluidity and the ambivalent position of the Jew among American racial binaries.[4] These representations variously position Jewish men as alienated and homeless in a world of absolute racial dichotomies in which they don't fit, and they depict Jewish men undergoing change through intercultural encounter and readjusting to new ideas of separateness and universality, of restraint and desire.

Borukh Glozman's "In the Fields of Georgia" ("Af di Felder fun Dzshordzshiye"): The Loneliness of Pious Jewish Sexual Restraint

Borukh Glozman, born in 1893 in the town of Mazyr in what is now Belorus, immigrated to the United States in 1911. After working in several different trades, he attended Ohio State University and served in the U.S. Army during World War I. His integration into American culture created for him a sense of estrangement from Jewishness, while his choice to write in Yiddish and his loyalty to the Jewish language and people left him feeling out of place in America. Whether based in America or abroad, this sense of alienation was a major undercurrent in Glozman's writing. He employed a variety of strategies to address this concern, among them an engagement with erotic relations that emphasized the distance between love and desire, women and men. His stories representing interethnic desire further accentuate the distance between the Jewish man and the object of his desires, so that the man ultimately retreats into himself and his loneliness.[5]

In his story "In the Fields of Georgia" (1927), the Jewish male figure's sexual restraint when presented with a seductive black woman is
part and parcel of his alienation as a Jew in a foreign landscape and the
impossibility of his ever finding a home, sexual or otherwise.[6] In the
absence of whiteness, Jewishness becomes the opposite of blackness,
and sexual transgression for the Jew is impossible. This sexual restraint
forces the Jew into isolation by virtue of his own adherence to religious
and moral taboos.

The protagonist of "In the Fields of Georgia" is an unnamed
Jew, a traveling salesman who is situated in exile from his wife and
children, a Jewish community, and a home. Walking on a sandy
road toward Jacksonville, Florida, "his wagon, laden with various
small articles of clothing and merchandise, plods along toward the
south, but his mind, laden with longing, is drawn northward."[7] His
perpetual movement nevertheless indicates an underlying stagnancy—
ever pulled in two directions, the Jew remains fixed at this crossroads
of duty and desire. Trapped in a lonely existence, he visits his wife
only once a year, all "for the sake of livelihood."[8] When the Jew
knocks on a door to see if he can find a night's lodging, he is greeted
by "a fleshy, heavy Negress," who opens her home to him.[9] Like
the Jew, the black woman is also completely alone and defined by
her longing. She lives by herself in a home set back from the road
and on this Christmas night has set the table for two, expecting no
second guest to appear. Eager to make the Jew feel welcome, the
woman suggestively slices open a melon "like a heart cut in two and
opened up with red blood pouring out" to signal the availability of
her own warm body as sustenance to the weary traveler, reminding
him that Abraham himself had taken a black wife, Hagar.[10] But the
Jew refuses the much-needed pleasures of both her unkosher food
and her unkosher body.

The Jew and the black women disappoint one another through
their competing notions of masculinity and sexuality. To the Jew, the
black woman signifies only the act of sex itself—she is all juiciness and
fleshiness, an overabundance of availability and desire, representations

that draw upon tropes of the corporality and primitiveness of black bodies. The Jew wishes to build "a fence, a *mekhitse*" between himself and the hypersexualized black woman in order to maintain the sexual purity his religious tradition dictates.[11] He is tempted and excited by the idea of physical closeness with the woman, but he holds himself back, courageously fleeing the seductive trap.

Meanwhile, the narration shifts perspectives so that the reader comes to learn that the black woman is not acting out of unthinking physical impulses and unharnessed libido. Rather, she sees in the Jewish man the potential to give her life meaning and emotional fulfillment by impregnating her. The black woman sees the Jewish man as a potential gift from God. She believes the visitor may ease her loneliness, and perhaps even provide her with a child, and she prays to her God, a carnal God who fathered a son himself, to persuade the Jew to sleep with her.[12] For the black woman, having sexual relations with the Jew would not be a sin. Rather, sex could be for them a holy, God-sanctioned act of reproduction. When the omniscient narrator enters into the woman's mind and expresses the purity and religiosity of her sexual intentions, he opens the Jew's sexual restraint to critique—the Jew's very masculinity and sexual drive are called into question. "What kind of a man is he, anyway?" the woman, and alongside her the reader, asks.[13] From the black woman's perspective, the Jew's religious commitment to sex segregation (the *mekhitse*) is an indication of his effeminacy and cowardice, and the restraint he shows in leaving before she is able to enter his bed is charged with her interpretation that he has abandoned her and left her childless and alone.

The simple binary between Jew and non-Jew and the contradistinction between the Jew and the black woman's interpretations of their potential sexual encounter calls into question the value of the existential position of the wandering, alienated Jew. The story is ultimately about the tension between the desire for assimilation into and separation from American society. If the Jew would just co-mingle with the black woman, who herself is on the margins of society, he would not need to feel so alienated in the American world. He would have a partner in his separateness, a fixed and grounded home to abate his wandering. The black woman, though herself marginal, is very much located within the American landscape, and impregnating her would give the Jew and his progeny a clear place in the American social fabric. It is his own obstinate clinging to his faraway wife that denies him pleasure, comfort, and family. His separateness is not placed upon him from the outside; it is the price of his remaining (sexually) moral according to his own Jewish metrics in a foreign land. His righteousness is his own curse, even as it gives him the blessed knowledge that he has maintained his values and been true to his wife, a representative of pure, unadulterated Jewish tradition and values. The Jew's anti-assimilationist tendencies win out in the end—he leaves without having slept with the black woman. But with the black woman's mournful cries as its parting sound, the story calls into question the value of this eternal Jewish separateness.

Isaac Bashevis Singer's The Slave (Der Knekht): Loneliness as Both Cause and Effect of Interethnic Sexual Encounter

In his writing, the famed, Nobel Prize–winning Yiddish author Isaac Bashevis Singer is notorious for deploying erotic themes together with religious motifs to produce a variety of effects.[14] Isaac Bashevis Singer's *The Slave* (1961) is situated among the author's many considerations of religious taboo, sexuality, and the limits of Jewish identity and community. Although it is set in thirteenth-century Poland after the Chmielnicki massacres, the novel presents a dilemma parallel to the one in "In the Fields of Georgia."[15] In *The Slave*, the protagonist, Jacob, faces the same challenge that the unnamed Jew of "In the Fields of Georgia" encounters: competing values of sexual restraint and of companionship. Jacob's loyalty to Jewishness and to the possibility of a wife he has long not seen comes into competition with his desire for a sexually available lonely Polish woman who is forbidden not only because Jacob is married (though he does not know if his wife is still living) but also because she is situated across inviolable cultural and ethnic barriers. Although he tries to resist the Polish woman, his sexual and emotional needs prevail over his religious stringency. The novel becomes a narrative not about Jacob's restraint and the maintenance of these barriers but about what happens when the barriers are crossed, about the existential loneliness and impossibility of dwelling in the space between accepted identities, without the conventional supports of community.

In the novel, Jacob, a Jewish man who has been sold as a slave to peasant farmers, lives on top of a mountain alone. He separates himself from the society of the Polish peasants in an effort to maintain a Jewish praxis and identity in an aggressively foreign atmosphere. To avoid eating nonkosher meat, he becomes a vegetarian, refusing to eat forbidden food even when the non-Jews try to force it into his mouth, and he tries to keep track of the Jewish calendar and observe Shabbat and holidays to the best of his ability. He also avoids sexual contact with non-Jewish women, even when they conduct themselves "no better than animals," exposing themselves to him and calling, "Come and lie with me."[16] Wanda, a tall, gentle, attentive young woman, develops an attachment to Jacob as she sees to his needs and tries to help him fulfill his religious obligations. Jacob is attracted to her but inflicts on himself a restraint so harsh as to be a self-punishment. He draws a false contrast between sexual love for Wanda and his spiritual love for God and feels that to consummate his desire for Wanda would be to relinquish his Judaism.[17] He can't stop thinking about Wanda: "He knew well that he wasn't permitted to look at her, but he saw everything: her eyes, which were sometimes blue and sometimes green, her full lips, her gracefully long neck, her round bosom," yet he forces himself to "try to strangle his love for her."[18] He fantasizes about her in dreams and wakes up with his heart pounding.[19] She offers her body to him, and he craves her physically and emotionally, though he consistently resists her advances. It seems that she is the key to ending the torment of his loneliness and to rebuilding his life and creating a family, yet he cannot bring himself to transgress the hard-and-fast line between Jew and non-Jew.

Ultimately, however, that line itself proves to be more complex than the initial binary of Jew and Pole. In his time among the Polish peasants, Jacob gradually loses his memories of the markers of cultural distinctiveness that helped him to uphold his identity. He becomes more comfortable speaking Polish than Yiddish and is unable to remember and write down all of the commandments. Likewise, Wanda transgresses the line between Jew and Pole as she helps Jacob to maintain his religious practice and as she learns about his God through asking him questions about the meaning of life. When Wanda and Jacob finally succumb to their desires, their union obscures the stark division between Jew and Pole—both have become something between these separate identities, and therefore neither fully has a place in a world in which the division between Jew and non-Jew is absolute.

When Jewish men from Jacob's hometown pay ransom and bring Jacob back to his Jewish community, Jacob finds that he cannot return to his old patterns of Jewishness and does not belong among the other Jews. Jacob, disgusted by a hypocritical Jewish community that does not meet the expectations of his memory of Jewish piety, returns to Wanda, who has been hiding in the woods, apart from her peasant community, hoping for his return. The two find a town of Jews where Jacob won't be recognized, where they can live as a Jewish couple, Jacob and Sarah. Separate or apart, in Jewish or Polish settings, both Wanda/Sarah and Jacob are estranged from the supports of community, fearlessly bucking conventionality as they find love and comfort with one another. Jacob and Wanda/Sarah remain an uncomfortable third term, forever alienated from Jewish and Polish life, living their private lives in secret and set apart from the Jewish community in which they live.

The novel frames sexual restraint as a Jewish value, as part of the stringency of a Jewish lifestyle. When Jacob relinquishes his "Jewish" self-restraint and gives in to the "primitive" desires of the flesh, he relinquishes something of his own Jewish identity as well. He is ever after skeptical of Jewish religious law and of his own place within it, as someone who has violated its strictures. Likewise, in joining with Jacob, Wanda/Sarah loses much of herself, including her own name. For both Jacob and Wanda/Sarah, the radical communal departure that constitutes their love is ruinous to their social existence; it transforms them into beings that have no place in their world as it is legally and socially constituted. Wanda/Sarah must be silent in public so that her Polish accent does not reveal her origin to the Jewish community, and when she dies, she cannot be buried in a Jewish cemetery. Although she lived as a Jewish woman, following the commandments, because her secret becomes known her son is not accepted as a Jew. Wanda/Sarah is socially outcast from the Jewish community, just as Jacob is theologically outcast, understanding his partnership with Wanda/Sarah to be a sin that has forever altered his relationship to God. Without God or humanity, Wanda/Sarah and Jacob are "alone together."[20]

Although they are separated in life when Wanda/Sarah dies in childbirth, the couple is united in death, buried together both within and without the Jewish community—in a grave that, at the time of Wanda/Sarah's burial, was located outside the Jewish cemetery, but with the growth of the cemetery comes to be situated within its bounds. While this seems to be a resolution that posthumously provides the couple with a religious community and social place, this tacit acceptance of the couple as Jewish, belonging in the Jewish cemetery, also erases the hybridization and transformation Jacob and Wanda/Sarah both experienced as they together formed an entity outside of the Jewish-Polish dichotomy. It is both a reconciliation between the Jewish community and its transgressor and an acknowledgment that such a reconciliation is never truly possible when the physical space of Jew and Pole lacks a literal middle ground in which to lay the couple's remains. Enveloping Wanda/Sarah and Jacob into the Jewish cemetery in death erases the transgression they represented in life and does not address the ultimate question they posed for the community about the value of the communal divisions themselves. It is an unsatisfying resolution that hides the complicated alienation that defined the lives of Jacob and Wanda/Sarah, the dislocation that their relationship represents, and the ambiguity that they draw to the question of who belongs within the Jewish community.

Lamed Shapiro's "New Yorkish": Transnational Jewish Racial Identity and the Complexity of Jewish Interethnic Encounter in America

Lamed Shapiro's story "New Yorkish" (1931) presents a complicated picture of the in-between status of the Jew in a racially stratified society.[21] Lamed Shapiro (1878–1948) is best known for his graphic depiction of anti-Jewish brutality, though his writing also extended into the realm of American Jewish life, always focusing on the "struggle of the modern Jew thrust into a desperate search for meaning at the very moment when the traditional community is decaying from within and threatened by destruction from without."[22] His story "New Yorkish" follows these broader concerns by meditating more narrowly on the Jew's position within American consumer culture and the struggle for real human relationships beyond monetary exchange and the artifice of popular culture's renditions of ethnic identity. The story describes a sexual encounter between an Americanized East European Jewish immigrant and a Spanish American prostitute in the ethnically diverse and capitalist-driven New York City. The protagonist, Lakritspletsl (who calls himself Manny), spends an evening with a Spanish woman, Jenny, whom he insists on renaming Dolores. Lakritspletsl's insistence that Jenny be called Dolores places the two characters on equal footing as "ethnics" in contradistinction to American whiteness and to the images of blackness they consume as theater-goers at a blackface performance. While Lakritspletsl's desire for Jenny is an exoticizing desire, which he further emphasizes by his fascination for her dark hair, this desire also reinscribes Lakritspletsl as a racialized other in relation to the Spanish woman, harkening back to a time when Jews were persecuted by Spanish authorities. His desire to name Jenny/Dolores as Spanish references his complicated racial positioning as a potentially white American and as a European other.[23]

Shapiro's "New Yorkish" also emphasizes the racialized difference of the Jew through his ambivalent relationship to sexuality itself and to the idea of exchanging money for sex. Lakritspletsl's sexual hesitation, his insistence that taking a woman home is "not his way," is a mark of his Jewishness.[24] He is positioned between European decorum, in his hesitation at sleeping with a prostitute, and a racialized underworld of sexual impropriety, which he participates in by buying the prostitute's time for an evening of company. His sexual restraint also recalls tropes of Jewish effeminacy and lack of sexual drive or ability. His hesitancy leads Jenny/Dolores to ask, "What kind of a man are you?" questioning his masculine sexual impulses.[25] This is the same question uttered by the women in "In the Fields of Georgia" and *The Slave*—the sexual hesitancies of Jewish men with regard to non-Jewish women place Jewish men in a separate category of maleness, a category outside of conquest and desire. The question draws attention to the gendered and racial differences imagined onto Jewish bodies and also to the moral and cultural differences that lead these Jewish men to express ambivalence about their sexual liaisons.

When the couple finally does go back to his apartment, it is not a typical exchange between a prostitute and a client. They climb the stairs "like a married couple coming home late at night from a party at the home of good friends" and spend the night together, waking up in each other's arms.[26] Lakritspletsl does not know how to express the desire and affection he feels for the woman but is repeatedly surprised that "bought love is also love."[27] Moreover, in his musings, Lakritspletsl compares compensating a prostitute to paying a child a shekel to recite a psalm, Judaizing his sexual exchange and equating it with religious piety—"the psalm is genuine" even if paid for.[28] His surprise, and the genuineness of his feelings beyond sexual desire, demonstrate that his sexual drive is different from the typical client's objectification and consumption of the prostitute's body for sexual release. There is something more dignified (and more Jewish?) than the base economic exchange as compensation for the sexual act.

Lakritspletsl negotiates his encounter with Jenny/Dolores by first exoticizing her as a racial other and then domesticating her as a wifely figure. He knows consciously that both of these conceptions are products of his own desires more than they are built of reality, but he persists in them because they fulfill his needs. Being with Jenny/Dolores allows Lakritspletsl to reinvent himself as a white American in comparison with an ethnic other and as a moral, compassionate partner rather than a consumer of female bodies. Yet both of these self-definitions fail within the context of the story. Lakritspletsl, with his unpronounceably Jewish name, is no more a member of white American society than is Jenny/Dolores, and when he pays for the services of Jenny/Dolores as a prostitute, he finds that his experience of love is implicated in monetary exchange. In both cases, there seems to be an opportunity to acknowledge that Lakritspletsl and Jenny/Dolores are not so different, that both are outside of the mainstream of white American culture but trying to understand how to be a part of it, and that both are engaging in love through the marketplace—Lakritspletsl by paying for restaurants and entertainments in order to find love, and Jenny/Dolores by accepting money for sex—but both are also longing for something deeper than economic exchange. Yet Lakritspletsl seems to find no way to express his connections to Jenny/Dolores and allows her to leave with much yet unsaid. When Lakritspletsl cries out at the story's end, "My God! What happened? What was all of this?" he expresses confusion about himself and his relation as a Jew to love and sentiment, sex and the body, and monetary exchange in a world in which ethnic identities and the role and character of the Jew, among others, is in flux.[29]

Conclusion

These three selections certainly do not give a comprehensive view of the representation of interethnic sexual encounter in Yiddish literature, but they gesture toward the sexualized representation of the Jewish self and the ethnic other in Yiddish literature. From these stories we can draw several generalizations. In all three narratives examined in this study, Jewish male sexuality and the sexuality of female ethnic other are deployed to signal and articulate Jewish racial difference and to characterize the nature of Jewishness in a racialized world. Whether sexually passive and piously restrained, as in *The Slave* and "In the Fields of Georgia," or moderately sexually permissive in negotiation between a variety of racial and sexual options, as in "New Yorkish," the Jewish men in these interethnic sexual encounters face temptation and the possibility of pleasure and companionship; however, each of them finds himself ultimately alone (whether "alone together" with a displaced partner, as Jacob in *The Slave*, or alone on his own) in a modern world that has no place for him. The Jewish men in these stories crave the comfort of racial belonging, of homeland, of sexual pleasure and release, but find themselves, whether the relationship has been consummated or not, in a position of in-betweenness, on the road between desire and obligation, past and present, white and black, Jew and non-Jew, pulled in both directions, such that actual movement and redemption are impossible.

NOTES

1. For examples, see Ann Pellegrini, "Whiteface Performances: 'Race,' Gender, and Jewish Bodies," in *Jews and Other Differences: The New Jewish Cultural Studies*, ed. Jonathan Boyarin and Daniel Boyarin (Minneapolis: University of Minnesota, 1997), 108–75; John M. Efron, *Defenders of the Race: Jewish Doctors and Race Science in Fin-de-siècle Europe* (New Haven: Yale University Press, 1994).

2. Biale, David. *Eros and the Jews: From Biblical Israel to Contemporary America* (New York: Basic Books, 1992), 230.

3. Ibid, 230

4. For a more extended discussion of the "interarticulation" of race and gender, see Judith Butler, *Bodies That Matter: On the Discursive Limits of "Sex"* (New York: Routledge, 1993).

5. See Aaron Bekerman, *Barukh Glozman: A Monografing Mit a Bibliografiye fun Zayne Verk* (New York: *Ivangoroder br. 130. A.N.A.P*, 1944).

208 · THE SACRED ENCOUNTER

6. Barukh Glozman, "Af di Felder fun Dzshordzshia," in *Geklibene Verk fun Barukh Glozman*, vol. 5 (Vilna: Vilner Farlag fun B. Kletskin, 1927), 7–18.

7. Ibid., 8.

8. Ibid.

9. Ibid., 10.

10. Ibid., 15, 13.

11. Ibid., 14.

12. Ibid., 16.

13. Ibid.

14. See Leonard Pragar, "Ironic Couplings: The Sacred and the Sexual in Isaac Bashevis Singer," in *Recovering the Canon: Essays on Isaac Bashevis Singer*, ed. David Neal Miller (Leiden: Brill, 1986), 66–75.

15. Yitzchok Bashevis Singer, *Der Knekht* (Tel Aviv: Y.L. Peretz Farlag, 1980).

16. Ibid., 13.

17. Bonnie Lyons, "Sexual Love in I. B. Singer's Work," *Studies in American Jewish Literature* 1 (1981): 70.

18. Singer, *Der Knekht*, 17, 20.

19. Ibid., 36.

20. Lyons, "Sexual Love," 72.

21. Lamed Shapiro, "Nyuyorkish," in *Nyuyorkish un Andere Zakhn* (New York: Lamed Shapiro Farlag "Aleyn," 1931), 7–35.

22. Leah Garrett, "Introduction," *The Cross and Other Jewish Stories* (New Haven: Yale University Press, 2007), ix.

23. Hana Wirth Nesher, "Rereading Jewish American Literature," CUNY Lecture Series, October 4, 2007 (podcast), http://www1.cuny.edu/mu/podcasts/2007/10/04/rereading-jewish-american-literature/.

24. Shapiro, "Nyuyorkish," 24.

25. Ibid., 25.

26. Ibid., 27.

27. Ibid., 32.

28. Ibid.

29. Ibid., 35.

16

BETWEEN SODOM AND EDEN + 13

A Bar Mitzvah Look Back and Ahead

LEE WALZER

Two scenes from twenty-first-century life in Israel: The hip presenters on *Arutz ha-Y'ladim*, Israel's children's channel, breathlessly shout, "And here she is with her summer smash hit, 'Love Boy.' Welcome to Dana International!" Out comes Israel's popular transsexual singer through a beaded curtain to cheers from the preteen audience as she sings, "Chocolate six-pack abs. Says he's from France, but seems Moroccan. All day long at the gym, so no need to check his straightness. He doesn't use words. He talks with his hands, burns with his eyes. When he says, 'Let's start,' my heart dances in circles."

For International, who catapulted Israel to international fame with her 1998 victory representing Israel with her catchy, kitschy hit "Diva" in the Eurovision Song Contest, the children's circuit is nothing new; she's been singing on kids' programs for years.

Too outré? Then consider the recent campaign "The Right to a Family." Started by an Israeli gay couple, Yuval and Liran Altman-Kaduri, frustrated in their efforts to start a family by Israeli laws barring domestic surrogacy (at the present time) for same-sex couples, the campaign went viral on Facebook. Their page, *Anachnu Rotzim Yeled* (We Want a Child), contained photos of Israelis and even Hollywood star Joan Rivers brandishing signs that said in Hebrew and English, "They Deserve a Child Too." They got a pop group to record a remake of a well-known Israeli song, "If I Have a Child." They organized a star-studded evening at a Tel Aviv club featuring some of Israel's most famous singers, actors, and entertainers. The gay news portal on Mako, an Israeli entertainment company, noted that to their sorrow, as well as the sorrow of many gays and lesbians, in Israel they're allowed to give but not get. They can serve in the military, pay taxes, contribute to society—but not be parents or marry. Even in 2013, the state prevents gays and lesbians from establishing families, adopting children, or using the services of a surrogate. Those who succeed in becoming parents through surrogacy abroad face illogical difficulties, bureaucracy, and roadblocks imposed by the state afterward.

A bar mitzvah ago in years (thirteen), I published a look at Israel's LGBT community, *Between Sodom and Eden: A Gay Journey through Today's Changing Israel*, examining the political, legal, and social progress of Israeli LGBTs and the social-political background to that progress. A look back at that time, and forward since then, shows how Israel has embraced, on the surface, equality for Israeli gays and lesbians. The progress stands out in light of Israel's not-so-favorable treatment of other minority groups, including Reform Jews and the country's Arab citizens.

This essay will highlight major milestones in the history of the Israeli LGBT community and then will examine how it succeeded and what that success says about Zionism, Judaism, and new dynamics in Israeli society.

Milestones

Although gay and lesbian activism in Israel formally dates to the 1970s when the Society for the Protection of Personal Rights was established, this was in a period when homosexual acts were still illegal and gays and lesbians were barred from serving in certain military units.

In 1987, the Knesset voted to repeal Israel's seldom-enforced sodomy law, a relic of the British Mandate in Palestine, after years of effort by progressive members of Knesset (MKs). The repeal set off a decade-plus of rapid change that reflected wider changes in Israeli society—the decline of the collective mentality of Israel's founders and the legitimization of individualism; the growth of a consumer society; and the transition from the New Jew envisioned by the socialist pioneers and its replacement with a cacophonous debate (which continues to this day) about what it means to be an Israeli.

Following the repeal of the sodomy law, the Knesset in 1991 amended the country's Equal Workplace Opportunities law to include sexual orientation. A year later, the Knesset Committee on the Status of Women, chaired by then-MK Yael Dayan, held the first-ever hearing in Israel on gay issues. The hearing itself was a big deal, but it became a sensation when Tel Aviv University professor (and future Member of Knesset) Uzi Even told of how he was removed from his work in a top-secret military unit (reputedly dealing with Israel's nuclear weapons program) because he was gay. The late Prime Minister Yitzchak Rabin told his cabinet a week later that he saw no reason to discriminate against gay and lesbian soldiers, and within a few months, the old, discriminatory regulations were gone.

The first mass gay and lesbian pride event occurred a year later in 1993, followed by the first Pride Parade in 1998.

Since 2000, the progress has not been as dramatic as during that thirteen-year period between 1987 and 2000, but the community has continued to build on its previous successes. The Inheritance Law began treating same-sex and heterosexual couples equally in 2004. Israel recognized same-sex marriages conducted abroad in 2006, after Israeli same-sex couples married in Canada and returned to demand recognition of these marriages, as had long been the case for civil marriages entered into by Israelis abroad.

Moreover, the political and legal progress begat social progress. Nitzan Horowitz, a former *Haaretz* reporter and foreign editor for *Channel 10 News*, became Israel's first openly gay elected member of

Knesset in 2009. Horowitz announced in May 2013 that he was running for mayor of Tel Aviv.

Culturally, the music closet burst open with some of Israel's most popular singers—Korin Allal, Ivri Lider, Yehudit Ravitz, and Yehuda Poliker—all coming out of the closet. It's not an exaggeration to say that Israeli gays and lesbians have an outsized influence on the Israeli media; both print and TV coverage of community issues is sympathetic, even laudatory, and the media has played a significant role in changing public attitudes.

Amid this progress was the horrific attack on an LGBT youth group called Barno'ar on August 1, 2009. A masked gunman burst into the offices of the Association of LGBTs (Aguda) in Tel Aviv and fired indiscriminately, killing one of the youth group counselors and a sixteen-year-old girl. The attack brought a wave of support from Israeli politicians across the political spectrum, including from Likud Prime Minister Benjamin Netanyahu. It also deeply shook the community, which had never faced such a deadly and mysterious hate crime. It took until June 2013 for the Israeli police to crack the case, and the shock waves are still being felt, with new revelations and twists coming out every day.[1]

Why the Change?

As noted above, the road toward equality for Israel's LGBT community stems from several wider changes in Israeli society. First, during the period of rapid gay and lesbian advances in the 1990s, Israeli society completed a transformation from a collectivist society with norms imposed from above to a society that first made room for and then embraced individualism. The Zionist movement that laid the groundwork for and later governed the State of Israel was highly ideological and collective in its outlook. The goal of Zionism was not only the establishment of a state for the Jews, but also the creation of a New Jew—a Jew who would be connected to the land, at remove from religion, and a warrior. In other words, this New Jew was to be the total opposite (from the standpoint of early Zionist theorists) of the Diaspora Jew that Zionism sought to supplant. It goes without saying that the New Jew would also be heterosexual.

The vision of the founders endured for the first three decades after Israel's rebirth, but the seeds of individualism began to sprout, both ideologically and for individuals. Thus, the verities of Zionism and the New Jew faced growing questions and criticism, and new identities began to supplant the New Jew—reflected in the emergence of Mizrachi Jews, the growth of Jewish religiosity, the birth of an Israeli feminist movement, and the increased assertiveness of Palestinian citizens of Israel.

In tandem with the gradual emergence of these previously suppressed voices, Israeli society underwent a transformation from a socialist economy to a consumer society. Whereas the kibbutz, with its collective ownership of goods, was a potent symbol of the Zionism of Israel's early years as a state, that gave way during the years of Menachem Begin's premiership to consumerism, with access to previously out-of-reach material goods such as color televisions, private automobiles, and increased travel abroad, as well as to increased privatization within the kibbutzim.

The religion and state conundrum also played an unexpected role in the Israeli LGBT community's progress. First, while gay advances have faced often shrill opposition from Israel's religious political parties, rarely have they used their political muscle to thwart legislative advances. The reasons for this reflect both their political calculations and ideology. At the *tachlis* (practical) level of politics, religious parties have proven able to rationally weigh how much this issue mattered to them, and the answer, in many cases, was not much. Proponents of pro-LGBT legislation would call votes when they knew that religious Knesset members would be absent due to a fast day, or they would arrange for middle-of-the-night votes with their implicit consent. In addition, however, gay civil equality was much less of a problem for religious parties than ensuring funding for their religious institutions, maintaining control of personal status issues such as marriage and "who is a Jew?," or ensuring their vision of the Jewish character of the state—by retaining the ban on public transportation during Shabbat, for example.

At the ideological level, two different currents have ensured that LGBT rights did not become a major focus of the religious parties in Israel. First, Orthodox Jewish attitudes toward homosexuality, while condemnatory, have never been an obsession the way that has become the case for many conservative Christian denominations. In *Between Sodom and Eden*, I posited that this was the case because (1) Judaism in general has been sex-positive, even if the confines for acceptable sexual expression are tightly drawn in Orthodox Judaism; (2) the companion belief that few Jews were homosexual; (3) the Jewish approach to mitzvot, under which doing a mitzvah is good in its own right, and recognition that all Jews are striving to fulfill as many mitzvot as possible, even amid the difficulty in fulfilling all 613 mitzvot; and (4) the *Kulanu Y'hudim* (We're all Jews) ethos of Israeli Jewish society, which creates a sense of solidarity and common destiny even in the face of the various divides and fissures in Israeli society.

Finally, when one examines the conduct of the ultra-Orthodox religious parties such as Shas and Yahadut HaTorah (as opposed to Orthodox parties such as the National Religious Party), one cannot ignore ultra-Orthodox ideology concerning Zionism and the State of Israel. While most Jews today view the rebirth of Israel with joy, the ultra-Orthodox are at best ambivalent. Most view Zionism as religious heresy and view the State of Israel as an unpleasant fact that must be dealt with. The ultra-Orthodox political parties likely view the Israeli LGBT movement and Israeli society's increased acceptance of the LGBT community as further proof of the corruption of the Zionist enterprise.

Conversely, much of the nonreligious Jewish public in Israel is happy to use the LGBT community, at some level, as a way to provoke the religious parties, whose control over aspects of public life in Israel it strongly resents. When Dana International was chosen to represent

Israel in the 1998 Eurovision Song Contest and brought home first prize for Israel, secular politicians could not resist using the transsexual International as a means to insult the ultra-Orthodox. Her victory came a few weeks after the ultra-Orthodox forced the organizers of a gala pageant celebrating Israel's jubilee to cancel a planned dance number by the Batsheva Dance Company called "Echad Mi Yodei-a" (after the Passover song of the same name) in which dancers clad in ultra-Orthodox garb were going to strip down to their undergarments. The cancellation outraged many Israelis and led to some greeting religious politicians with cries of "Good morning, Iran," which was a hit song at that time by Israeli rock's then–*enfant terrible*, Aviv Geffen.

Against that backdrop, Israel TV's lively, often raucous *Popolitika* program took on the meaning of International's victory, with host Tomi Lapid (father of the current head of the Yesh Atid party, Yair Lapid) and supportive journalists and gay activists gleefully ganging up on the lone ultra-Orthodox panel member, Yonatan Shreiber. Lapid Sr. told Shreiber in a line I have often heard in Israel, "If I had to choose between a gay son and one like you [an ultra-Orthodox one], I'd choose the gay son."

Finally, the LGBT community proves the centrality of the "We're all Jews" ethos that still holds sway among Israeli Jews. While individualism as a value has gained a foothold in Israeli society, it is still seen in some circles as negative. The group individualism of Mizrachim, the Russians, the religious, and, most certainly, Palestinian citizens of Israel is viewed by many as threatening. As Devora Ezra, the then-director of secondary education in the Haifa municipal government, told me back in 1998, "Any public that wants a culture or community of its own, that's fine, so long as it doesn't hurt the security of the state and so long as it's not anti-Zionist." By fitting into the Israeli consensus, save for the difference of sexuality, the Israeli LGBT community was able to gain support and growing acceptance.

Rather than demand recognition of the distinct characteristics/outlook of sexual minorities, Israeli gay and lesbian activists emphasized their desire for equal responsibilities, like serving in the Israel Defense

Forces (IDF). Their critique of Israeli society's homophobia did not extend to Zionism or Israeli society's treatment of minorities in general; rather than critique the New Jew of the founders, Israeli LGBT activists created a new gay version of the same: two IDF combat unit veterans living happily ever after with two children. The push for recognition of LGBT families likewise safely fits into Israeli society's consensus—having children contributes to keeping Israel demographically Jewish and comports with the mitzvah to be fruitful and multiply.

A Look Back and Forward

In the thirteen years since *Between Sodom and Eden*, there have been several phenomena of note—some that were not certain at the time the book appeared and others that the book already foresaw.

One question that was unclear thirteen years ago was whether a community, with strong institutions, would develop or, alternatively, whether a more assimilationist model would hold sway, with Israeli gays and lesbians being indistinguishable from their heterosexual counterparts, save for their sexual orientation. The answer has turned out to be both. The most recent issue of *F.O.D.*, a glossy gay quarterly, answered that first question with an article titled "History as We've Forgotten It." The article examined efforts in the community to better preserve and commemorate the Israeli LGBT community's history. The fact that a magazine is examining whether the Israeli LGBT community could better preserve its history ipso facto suggests that there is indeed a community, with institutions and individuals who should be remembered for their contributions.

The evolution of the Hebrew language also provides support for the notion that a vibrant LGBT community today exists. The writing of this article coincided with Pride Month, and the Israeli media, as usual, went into celebratory overdrive to mark the occasion. What stood out in broadcasts and newspaper articles is how the country's media have adopted "gayspeak." In the 1970s, the Israeli press described those with same-sex attractions as *homosexualistim*. By 2013, the mainstream Israeli media, including the state-operated Israel Broadcast Authority, were routinely using terminology that originated within the community, including *hak'hilah hagei-a* ("the gay community," based on the word *g'ei*, "proud"), and *hak'hilah halehabatit* (*lehabatit* being a spoken acronym for *lesbiot, homo'im, transjenderim, v'biseksualim*, or "the LGBT community").

And yet, even in 2013, the LGBT community has to struggle with the still-popular view of "Why do you need a community? Why do you want to separate yourself?" An Israel Radio talk show host asked these very questions to a representative from HOD, a group for religious gay men, on June 7, in the midst of the Pride Celebration taking place that afternoon in Tel Aviv.

Queer Studies

While LGBT political activism in Israel has been moderate and strategic, its very successes have created the space for more critical voices to emerge. Israeli academics and activists have written sophisticated scholarship on LGBT Israeli history and queer interpretations of sexuality (especially the work of Amalia Ziv for the latter[2]). The emergence of queer studies, apart from enriching knowledge of sexuality and sexual minorities, has enriched the community by casting a critical eye on a generally celebratory narrative of the development of the Israeli LGBT community.

Law professor Aeyal Gross recently published a critique of Israeli LGBT politics titled "The Politics of LGBT Rights: Between (Home) Normativity and (Homo) Nationalism and Queer Politics."[3] Gross calls gay rights a "fig leaf for Israeli democracy" and notes that the promotion of Israel's record on LGBT rights is designed to "to present Israel as a liberal democracy, in contrast to its neighbors and especially the Palestinians and Iran," an accusation often known as "pinkwashing." He also offers a critical take on gay political strategy, quoting longtime activist and now-academic Amit Kama's critique of the long-standing mainstream political strategy as "selling cellophane-wrapped gays." Gross takes the critique further, noting the embrace not only of the mainstream by Israeli LGBT organizations but also of the Israeli nationalist narrative (which he labels "the new homonationalism"), accompanied by the separation of LGBT rights from the wider context of democracy and human rights.

The emergence of critiques of the meaning of Israel's record on LGBT rights and of community strategy is a healthy development for the community. As has been the case in the United States, it takes both mainstream approaches and more critical ones to effect social change.

LGBT Rights and *Hasbarah* (Lobbying/Public Diplomacy/Marketing)

Speaking of selling "cellophane-wrapped gays," successive Israeli governments in recent years have marketed Israel's generally impressive record on LGBT rights abroad, to generate greater support for Israel among liberal and progressive groups in the United States and Western Europe, to highlight more progressive elements of Israeli life and politics as a hedge against the light being shone on ultra-Orthodox efforts to restrict women's equality, and as an economic boon to Israel.

These efforts got their start in the 1990s, when progressive (or at least practical) Israeli consuls general in San Francisco and New York began targeted outreach at American LGBT leaders and promoting Israeli LGBT culture (cinema, writers, and artists) in the LGBT community.

The initial outreach turned into an integral part of Israeli *hasbarah davka* under Likud Prime Minister Benjamin Netanyahu. Netanyahu, whom many Republican Party leaders would love to run for president here in the United States, has touted Israel's LGBT community before a rapturous Republican-dominated U.S. Congress, as well as at the United Nations. What this nice Jewish (and generally liberal) writer has wondered is how Netanyahu's highlighting of Israel's LGBT record plays among his adoring GOP and evangelical fans in the United States. On the one hand, he in particular—and Israeli governments generally—presumably want to prove Israel's progressive bona fides as a bastion of democracy in an otherwise autocratic or Islamist Middle East, which certainly fits with how the Republican Party and evangelicals view both Israel and its neighbors. On the other hand, one wonders why these constituencies in American politics don't recoil from a record on LGBT rights that would provoke their anger domestically.

While this writer personally sees nothing wrong with so-called pinkwashing—public diplomacy is all about successful marketing after all—Israeli academics such as Aeyal Gross have highlighted in their writings just how cynical a Likud government's LGBT *hasbarah* can be. LGBT Israeli successes have often come from court rulings or shrewd maneuvering by progressive politicians; some of these measures faced opposition from Likud governing coalitions, including within the Likud party itself. To highlight, in the international arena, measures and issues that, at best, it was lukewarm toward in Israel indeed constitutes impressive political contortionism.

Mishpachah (Family)

While critical voices have emerged from the community, the mainstream, integrationist approaches still dominate. Nowhere is this clearer than in Israel's gayby boom. Present even during my writing of *Between Sodom and Eden*, the gayby boom has taken off in recent years, with surrogacy agencies establishing offices in Israel and increased numbers of Hebrew children's books[4]—both original and in translation—featuring gay and lesbian families.

The phenomenon has become so prominent that Avner Bernheimer, former editor of *Yediot Achronot*'s "7 Days" weekend section who, perhaps influenced by his years in Los Angeles while his partner pursued an advanced degree at UCLA, branched into screenwriting.

His new, semi-autobiographical series *Ima v'Abaz* (Mom and Dads) features a gay couple that has a child with a close woman friend of theirs. Unlike the cuddly *Modern Family* here in the United States, *Ima v'Abaz* is simultaneously funny, dramatic, and serious (not to mention sexually explicit).

It would exaggerate the situation to say that parenthood is now expected for Israeli gays and lesbians, but not by much. The *New York Times*, in an article about *Ima v'Abaz*, noted that Tel Aviv's LGBT community center faces stroller gridlock most evenings, and the Israeli Ministry of Health has recommended that domestic surrogacy be allowed for gay men, rather than forcing them to travel abroad to the United States or India, as a number of my friends and acquaintances have done.

As such, the "We Want a Child" campaign launched by the Altman-Kaduris does speak to some of Israeli society's core values, and the road to parenthood is likely to get easier in the years ahead for Israeli lesbians and gay men.

Conclusion

Israel continues to be an LGBT success story, even if that success raises uncomfortable questions about how Israel handles other civil and human rights issues. In a quarter century, Israeli sexual minorities have made the journey from the margins to substantial legal rights and increased social visibility. While social acceptance is still fragile, the community has been able to consolidate its legal and political victories and created in their aftermath community institutions and models for living an open life as sexual minorities. The use of the LGBT community for purposes of *hasbarah* abroad underscores the extent to which the community has entered the Israeli consensus.

NOTES

1. At the time of this writing, three suspects have been arrested, and the motive appears to have been revenge—against a fourth individual, Shaul Ganon, a prominent gay community leader who helped organize the Agudah's youth outreach. Ganon stands accused of interfering with the police investigation because of an alleged sexual relationship with one of the suspects, fifteen years old at the time. This, according to press reports, prompted relatives of the youth to seek revenge. Ganon has denied the accusations and has been released to house arrest, while the other three suspects remain jailed and the investigation continues.

2. Amalia Ziv, *Machshavot Mini'ot: Tei'oriya Qvirit, Pornografia, v'ha-Politika shel ha-Mini'ut (Sexual Thoughts: Queer Theory, Pornography, and the Politics of Sexuality)* [in Hebrew] (Tel Aviv: Resling, 2013).

3. Aeyal Gross, "The Politics of LGBT Rights: Between (Homo) Normativity and (Homo) Nationalism and Queer Politics," *Maasei Mishpat* 5 (2013): 101–41 (Hebrew).

4. See, e.g., Doron Braunstein, *L'Dani Sh'nei Avot (Danny Has Two Dads)* [in Hebrew] (Tel Aviv: Maya Miya, 2011); Smadar Shir, *Kol Tzivei HaKeshet (All the Colors of the Rainbow)* [in Hebrew] (Tel Aviv: Yediot Achronot, 2010) (about diverse families, including gay and lesbian ones).

PERSONAL REFLECTIONS

PERSONAL REFLECTION

The Problem with *Tz'niut*— How Are Women (Not) Like Pastries?

Rabbi Dalia Marx, PhD

What should my children, growing up in the Jerusalem, make of the images of women sprayed over with black ink on advertisements in the streets of the capital of the State of Israel? What should they understand from the threats of ultra-Orthodox leaders to boycott public national events where a woman sings? What should they think about the seven-year-old girl who was spat upon by a *Haredi* man in the town of Beit-Shemesh because her socks did not reach all the way to her skirt? How should they understand the explanation of that man's neighbor who supported the act, saying that "healthy men" should not be exposed to such temptation? All these matters and many more teach my children that women are a threat, that they are nothing but a temptation and therefore an obstacle, that they need to be controlled, and that in order to do so, one may erase their face, their voice, and their public presence.

We can assume that my great-grandmothers, daughters of the Old City of Jerusalem during the pre-Zionist period, occasionally disagreed with their parents and teachers about such things as the style of their dresses or the length of a skirt. But they were not greeted every morning by bright, gigantic posters or tattered announcements in the streets warning them, as daughters of Jerusalem, not to cause temptation to passersby with inappropriately thin stockings, or by uncovered arms, or by hair that was not adequately tucked out of sight. And even if my female forebearers had some formal education, it is unlikely that they heard daily lectures about modesty. Does this mean that they were less modest than the women of today?

A male teacher at an ultra-Orthodox school for girls in Israel entered his classroom of adolescents holding a platter of steaming warm raisin pastries in his hand. He took a piece of pastry, said the appropriate blessing, and in front of his amazed students he bit into one of the cakes. "This arouses your appetites, doesn't it?" he asked. "And that's how I feel when you all don't dress appropriately."

What can we imagine is the lesson that the young students learned from such a creative example rendered by their imaginative teacher? They will learn that, like pastries, they exist only to provide pleasure to others. They will learn that, like pastries, if they appear in ways deemed stimulating, they are likely to cause temptation and even sin. They will learn that men are weak and that women are objects of men's sexual urges, and as such are responsible for protecting the men from these urges.

The concept of *kol b'ishah ervah* (a woman's voice is immodest) is an exaggerated interpretation of a Talmudic dictum that a man should not recite the *Sh'ma* in the presence of a singing woman, lest he be distracted (Babylonian Talmud, *B'rachot* 24a). It was later expanded to exclude women from singing in public or on the radio so as not to arouse men. Literally the term means "woman's voice is nakedness." *Tz'niut*, the Jewish value of dressing and behaving modestly, and the related concept of *kol b'ishah ervah* teach women that they are constantly being scrutinized by males and are to be constantly subjected to male control over their appearance. This obsessive attention to modest dress and to women's comportment compels women to be vigilantly attentive to their bodies, to the way they walk, their attire, and so forth.

There are those who say that if we loosen up the standards and bare-bellied young girls go out in the streets, it will be necessary to raise a greater consciousness about *tz'niut*. According to this view, *tz'niut* acts as a shield against excessive and wanton behavior.

But I would contend that the more these walls of protection are erected, the greater becomes the problem created by the attention to *tz'niut*, and it testifies to the ineffectiveness of those walls. *Tz'niut* becomes a monster that feeds on itself—the more limitations and religious instruction are created to enforce it, the more women become aware of the very thing they are supposed to be on guard against—both their physicality and their sensuality. In other words, it has the opposite effect from what is intended—all this attention places *more* focus on the very thing that is supposed to be concealed from the eye and mind.

When strict rules about *tz'niut* are imposed from the outside related to what women may and may not wear, how they must act in public, and other similar issues, many women adopt the external trappings of the value without taking the inner value of humility seriously. Take, for example, the rules that hair must be completely covered on married women, resulting in an industry of expensive custom-made wigs made of human hair. Rather than thinking seriously about what *tz'niut* means in relation to one's whole way of behaving and relating to other people and to God, all the focus gets placed on external concerns related to men's perceptions of women's sexuality, with rules against wearing sleeves that don't cover the elbow, having to wear thick, opaque stockings that don't reveal any bit of the ankle or leg, and a prohibition against wearing bright colors.

Please do not get me wrong. I am not in favor of revealing and exceedingly sexy clothing, which can actually be equally offensive to women. Paradoxically, *tz'niut* when it is understood as attention only to the appearance of women, and *p'ritzut* (the opposite of *tz'niut*, the danger of exceeding promiscuity) when it is defined as wearing revealing clothing, are really two sides of the same coin. On the one hand, the result is an enforcement of unreasonable covering up (just imagine having to be completely covered up during the Israeli summer), and on the other hand, unrestricted bodily exposure in order to cause sexual incitement. They are both a consequence of the same approach that sees women as only that which is provocative and dangerous. Concerns about both *tz'niut* and wanton behavior reduce women to mere sexual objects, a commodity.

It is not that *tz'niut* has nothing to teach us. Micah, the prophet, teaches that God requires three things of human beings: "It has been declared to you, O mortal, what is good, and what the Eternal requires of you: to do justly, and to love mercy, and to walk humbly with your God" (Micah 6:8).

Micah's charge to "walk humbly with God" suggests a requirement that has no limit. It certainly cannot be measured in centimeters as one would measure a garment. It doesn't depend on the color of buttons or the length of a skirt, but it is a call for leading a life of value and intentionality—both for men and women—in relationship to the Divine. If we really pay attention to the prophet's words, we will find that Micah sets forth a rigorous requirement exceeding those of any *pashkvil* (public announcement on the walls of the ultra-Orthodox neighborhoods). As for the true meaning of *tz'niut* itself, this is an ongoing challenge to which we must constantly respond as part of our human heritage.

The call for *tz'niut*, in the profound sense of the matter, is really a call for operating in the world conscientiously and with attention, conducting oneself with awareness, and recognizing what the "I" needs, while at the same time limiting the ego's needs. We do not require policing from outside, as is suggested in some parts of the Jewish world; on the contrary, the work is ours to do. Each of us bears the task of seeking a life of holiness.

The relatively recent refusal of Israeli Jews to tolerate religious coercion and to reject demands posed by *Haredi*'s leaders regarding the public sphere in Israel has yielded some interesting results. For the first time in the history of the State of Israel, more and more Israelis are embracing their Jewishness and feel empowered enough to choose their personal paths within it. They are not willing to succumb to non-egalitarian and exclusionary forms of religious behavior, and at the same time they do not wish to throw away their heritage. In fact, the struggle in Jerusalem against the exclusion of women has been so fierce that there has been a backing away from some of the extremism that threatened to take over our city in the recent past. This gives me hope that my children will merit growing up in a better Jerusalem and a better Israel, one in which the focus will be not on the control of women's choices and visibility, but rather on living a life of meaning and connection with the Divine, and on developing a relationship with the true meaning of *tz'niut*.

With thanks to Rabbi Bill Cutter for help with the translation.

PERSONAL REFLECTION

This Is the Way the World Ends

Rabbi Lisa Hochberg-Miller

> This is the way the world ends
> This is the way the world ends
> This is the way the world ends
> Not with a bang but a whimper.
> *(T. S. Eliot, "The Hollow Men," 1925)*

I remember the Erev Shabbat that the congregation's gendered tradition crumbled into the dust. As I stood on the bimah, the final words of T. S. Eliot's famous poem echoed in my mind, but the truth was, there was not even a whimper. Not even a whisper.

It was the Erev Shabbat of Michal Merraro's bat mitzvah, and the tradition at Temple Israel of Long Beach, in 1994, as it was in most other Reform congregations in the country, was that the mother of the bat mitzvah would kindle the congregation's Shabbat candles on the bimah, followed by the father chanting the *Kiddush*. But Michal didn't have a mother and a father . . . Michal had two mothers.

The service began. The organ played the opening hymn. The senior rabbi called the family forward. Michal—bright eyes behind gold-framed glasses, blonde curly hair, smiling and glowing with the excitement that it was *her* bat mitzvah—stepped to the *Kiddush* table, surrounded by her two mothers. Her mother read an opening prayer, then reached forward, kindling the first candle, followed by the second. And then seamlessly, Michal's other parent, her mom, lifted the *Kiddush* cup and began to chant. The congregation was standing, all voices joined together. This is how the world ends, this is how the world ends, I thought to myself. To this day, nineteen years later, I still remember that Shabbat well. Not with a bang, a tradition dies with a silent whimper. Without debate, without discussion, without angst. Without committee discussion, without a board vote, it was just a quiet moving forward from what the tradition had been to what the future must be. For the first time, two mothers were side by side on the bimah, the congregation's representatives in welcoming Shabbat. Not with a bang, but in ancient chant, a gendered tradition based on assumptions about sexuality, marriage, and family had died, and a new door had opened. And like that, the place of this family of three women in our congregation was validated.

Part Three

"A Progressive Religion":
Sexuality and
the Reform Movement

In 1885, the founders of American Reform Judaism penned the Pittsburgh Platform and adopted principles that defined their approach. They wrote, "We hold that all such Mosaic and rabbinical laws as regulate diet, priestly purity, and dress originated in ages and under the influence of ideas entirely foreign to our present mental and spiritual state." In that single sentence, they asserted their independence from ritual biblical rules—particularly those pertaining to food, clothing, and the priestly cult—and asserted the relevance of their own time and place. One's "present mental and spiritual state" was profoundly important to how one was to live a Jewish life.

From the very first section of this book, we have seen the liberal Jewish openness to new ways of interpreting ancient texts. But the history of the Reform Movement on sexuality is a story that encompasses far more than textual interpretation. In some ways, the place we have reached is very far from what the authors of the Pittsburgh Platform would have imagined; our contemporary conversations about what happens in our beds might have them rolling in their graves. At least equally possible, however, their progressive approach would have allowed them to be open to new issues and ideas. Our current challenge, as the authors in Part Three show, is to do the same: to be willing to do the hard work of constantly reexamining how our values shape our practices. In their words, "we recognize in Judaism a progressive religion, ever striving to be in accord with the postulates of reason."

As part of this ongoing effort, the various branches of the Reform Movement have been explicitly discussing issues of sexuality since the 1970s (the reader is referred to *Kulanu*, a sourcebook published by the Union for Reform Judaism (2007), for documentation of this history). Part Three opens with two excerpts from the work of the Central Conference of American Rabbis (CCAR) Ad Hoc Committee on Human Sexuality, which did its work in the 1990s. As in Part One of this book, the opening focus is not on LGBTQ sexuality specifically, but rather on the phenomenon of sexuality as a whole. This reflects the approach of the Ad Hoc Committee; although homosexuality (in the language of the time) was the issue that prompted the group's formation, their charge was to look at human sexuality more broadly in the light of Jewish tradition and Reform Jewish values. In keeping with this approach, they begin with the following statement: "As liberal Jews, we seek to understand human sexuality and sexual expression in a religious context. . . . It is our belief that Reform Judaism can speak meaningfully to all aspects of our lives, including intimate human relationships."

We then turn to the history of the Reform Movement on LGBTQ issues, starting with Rabbi Denise Eger's essay, "Embracing Lesbians and Gay Men: A Reform Jewish Innovation." Eger traces the developments within different Reform decision-making bodies, painting a picture of key debates and arguing that overall, "Reform Judaism in the latter half of the twentieth century became a welcoming haven for gay men and lesbians who wished to be an active part of the Jewish community. . . . there will be no going back into the closet." As part of her piece, she includes powerful quotations from Rabbi Alexander Schindler, *z"l*, a prophetic figure in this history, and describes the courageous role of the Women's Rabbinic Network (WRN). In "To Ordain or Not to Ordain: The Tale of the CCAR Committee on Homosexuality and the Rabbinate," Rabbi Michal Loving focuses on one of the many issues summarized by Eger—namely, the question of ordination and the work of the CCAR Ad Hoc Committee on Homosexuality and the Rabbinate, which met from 1986 to 1990. This important historical essay provides a window into the debate, showing, on the one hand, how far the committee came, in the face of ambivalence and opposition; and on the other hand, how dated its decisions now seem. It is a fascinating study in how change happens. One day, perhaps Loving's essay will be part of an interfaith comparative study, exploring when and how different religious denominations came to their decisions on this issue (perhaps mapped onto earlier debates about the ordination of women).

Toward the end of her essay, Eger expresses the hope that "the commitment to the inclusion of Jewish gay men and lesbians within the Movement continues to be a priority within the congregational arm of the Movement." In "Assessing Lesbian, Gay, Bisexual, and Transgender Inclusion in the Reform Movement: A Promise Fulfilled or a Promise in Progress?" Dr. Joel L. Kushner asks whether the promise of the Reform Movement's leadership on LGBT issues has been fulfilled. Kushner argues that despite significant efforts, "there is . . . a wide gap between the desire to be inclusive and taking the everyday actions that are required to manifest that stated desire. . . . As a Movement, we may not be doing as well as we think." The theoretical model and case studies that he discusses challenge us not to rest on the laurels of past achievements, but rather to ask ourselves whether our actions are as progressive as our ideology aspires to be.

The next piece in Part Three is an interview with Rabbi Dr. Eugene B. Borowitz, a leading Reform theologian and the influential teacher of generations of rabbis. The interview gives Dr. Borowitz the opportunity to explain his own changed position on the ordination of LGBT rabbinical students. This interview, together with the two personal reflections by Rabbi David Adelson and Rabbi Molly G. Kane on Borowitz's decisions, provides a Rashomon-like perspective on the many ways in which a single story can be told. It is a reminder that, as Part One shows, Judaism is an interpretive religion, and even recent events can be experienced differently by different people. Above all, though, these accounts show the truth of the phrase "Reform is a verb."

Following these perspectives is a personal reflection ("This Other Eden—Personal Reflections on Sexuality in the UK") by Rabbi Dr. Deborah Kahn-Harris, principal of Leo Baeck College in London. She provides yet another vantage point from across the ocean, attesting to the ways that "time moves many things on." Or, as Kane attests, "liberation comes in stages and . . . we are not there yet, but someday soon we could be."

17

MISSION STATEMENT

CENTRAL CONFERENCE OF AMERICAN RABBIS
AD HOC COMMITTEE ON HUMAN SEXUALITY

As liberal Jews, we seek to understand human sexuality and sexual expression in a religious context. While we are aware that at this point in our history the value systems of many liberal Jews are based upon contemporary secular norms, it is our belief that Reform Judaism can speak meaningfully to all aspects of our lives, including intimate human relationships. In framing a religious value system that can guide all of us in making decisions about our sexuality, we utilize religious principles derived from our Reform predecessors. These principles are based upon the threefold approach that Reform Judaism has developed in the course of its history: universalism, particularism, and contemporary knowledge. This threefold approach can be expressed through the following guiding principles:

1. *B'riah* (The Created Universe). We exist as part of a vast and varied world fashioned by a purposeful Creator. "When God created humanity, God made man in the Divine image—male and female—and God found it very good" (Gen. 1:27–28, 1:31). Creator and creature are bound together through this intentional act. *B'riah* reminds us that our human uniqueness and

diversity, including our sexuality, are ultimately derived from the conscious Divine act of creation and as such are purposeful and positive.

2. *Am B'rit* (People of the Covenant). As Jews we also exist as part of a particular people that has a unique and holy relationship with God. After entering into covenant with God at Sinai, our people responded by saying, "All that the Eternal God has spoken we will faithfully do" (Exod. 24:7). Each generation, like the first one at Sinai, is committed to responsible action, the essential confirmation of belief. We share a special mandate to preserve this relationship through the Jewish generations of history. We weigh the many voices of our tradition as we seek to find ways for modern Jews to express themselves as sexual beings in an authentically Jewish manner.

3. *Daat* (Contemporary Knowledge). Yosef Albo, a noted medieval Jewish philosopher, wrote, "It is impossible that the law of God shall be complete, so that it will be adequate for all times, because the novel conditions that constantly arise in the affairs of men, in laws and in deeds, are too numerous to count" (*Sefer Halkarim*, discourse #3, chapter 23). We draw upon secular knowledge as we engage in holy endeavors. In an age of rapidly expanding information and understanding, to grasp fully human sexuality and its expressions, we believe it is necessary to gain insight and guidance from contemporary knowledge in related fields.

Originally published in *CCAR Journal*, vol. XLVIII/4, Fall 2001, pp. 7-8.

REFORM JEWISH SEXUAL VALUES

CENTRAL CONFERENCE OF AMERICAN RABBIS
AD HOC COMMITTEE ON HUMAN SEXUALITY

RABBI SELIG SALKOWITZ, DMIN

Jewish religious values are predicated upon the unity of God and the integrity of the world and its inhabitants as Divine creations. These values identify *sh'leimut* as a fundamental goal of human experience. The Hebrew root *sh-l-m* expresses the ideal of wholeness, completeness, unity, and peace. Sexuality and sexual expression are integral and powerful elements in the potential wholeness of human beings. Our tradition commands us to sanctify the basic elements of the human being through values that express the Divine in every person and in every relationship. Each Jew should seek to conduct his/her sexual life in a manner that elicits the intrinsic holiness within the person and the relationship. Thus can *sh'leimut* be realized. The specific values that follow are contemporary interpretations of human *sh'leimut*:

1. *B'tzelem Elohim* ("in the image of God"). This fundamental Jewish idea, articulated in Genesis 1:27, "And God created humankind in the Divine image—male and female," is at the core

of all Jewish values. *B'tzelem Elohim* underscores the inherent dignity of every person, woman and man, with the equal honor and respect due to each individual's integrity and sexual identity. *B'tzelem Elohim* requires each of us to value one's self and one's sexual partner and to be sensitive to his/her needs. Thus do we affirm that consensuality and mutuality are among the values necessary to validate a sexual relationship as spiritual and ethical and, therefore, "in the image of God."

2. *Emet* ("truth"). Authentic and ethical human relationships should be grounded in both truth and honesty. "These are the things you are to do: speak the truth to one another, render true and perfect justice in your gates" (Zech. 8:16). People can only truly know each other and appreciate the Divine in all people when they come to each other openly and honestly. Both partners in an intimate relationship should strive to communicate lovingly. They should tell each other what gives them pleasure and what does not, and should honestly share their love as well as the challenges that their relationship presents. However, honesty that is destructive of the relationship lacks the quality of *rachamim*, "mercy." "Mercy and truth shall meet, justice and peace shall embrace" (Ps. 85:11). For that reason, intimate partners should be mindful that there might be moments when they are better served by not being totally candid with each other. In addition, falsehood that manipulates is sinful. Dating partners must not lie to each other in order to mislead the other into a sexual relationship. Neither partner should use the other as a sexual object. Finally, parents should learn how to teach their children both the facts and the physical, emotional, and spiritual consequences of sexual behavior. Parents should then use that teaching to help their children face the realities of the contemporary world.

3. *B'riut* ("health"). Our tradition enjoins upon us the responsibility to rejoice in and to maximize our physical, emotional, and spiritual health. "Blessed is our Eternal God, Creator of the

Universe, who has made our bodies with wisdom, combining veins, arteries, and vital organs into a finely balanced network" (*Gates of Prayer*, p. 284). Reform Judaism encourages adults of all ages and physical and mental capabilities to develop expressions of their sexuality that are both responsible and joyful. The abuse of human sexuality can be destructive to our emotional, spiritual, and physical health. We have a duty to engage only in those sexual behaviors that do not put others or ourselves at risk. In our age of HIV/AIDS and epidemic sexually transmitted diseases, irresponsible sexual behavior can put our lives and the lives of others at risk. We must act upon the knowledge that our sexual behavior is linked to our physical health.

4. *Mishpat* ("justice"). Judaism enjoins upon us the mandate to reach out and care for others, to treat all those created in the image of God with respect and dignity, to strive to create equality and justice wherever people are treated unfairly, to help meet the needs of the less fortunate, and to engage in *tikkun olam*, "the repair of God's creation." The prophet Amos exhorts us to "let justice well up as waters, righteousness as a mighty stream" (Amos 5:24). As a people who have historically suffered at the hands of the powerful, we must be especially sensitive to any abuse of power and victimization of other human beings. According to the sages, *yetzer hara*, through its sexual component, may sometimes lead to destructive behavior and sin. All forms of sexual harassment, incest, child molestation, and rape violate the value of *mishpat*. Our pursuit of *mishpat* should inspire us to eradicate prejudice, inequality, and discrimination based upon gender or sexual orientation.

5. *Mishpachah* ("family"). The family is a cornerstone of Jewish life. The Torah, through the first mitzvah, *p'ru ur'vu*, "be fruitful and multiply" (Gen. 1:28), emphasizes the obligation of bringing children into the world through the institution of the family. In our age, the traditional notion of family as being two parents and children (and perhaps older generations)

living in the same household is in the process of being re-defined. Men and women of various ages living together, singles, gay and lesbian couples, single-parent households, and the like, may all be understood as families in the wider, if not traditional, sense. "Family" also has multiple meanings in an age of increasingly complex biotechnology and choice. Although procreation and family are especially important as guarantors of the survival of the Jewish people, all Jews have a responsibility to raise and nurture the next generation of our people. The importance of family, whether biologically or relationally based, remains the foundation of meaningful human existence.

6. *Tz'niut* ("modesty"). Nachmanides' classic *Igeret HaKodesh*, "The Holy Letter," sets forth the Jewish view that the Holy One did not create anything that is not beautiful and potentially good. The human body in itself is never to be considered an object of shame or embarrassment. Instead, "it is the manner and context in which it [i.e., the body] is utilized, the ends to which it is used, which determine condemnation or praise." Our behavior should never reduce the human body to an object. Dress, language, and behavior should reflect a sensitivity to the Jewish respect for modesty and privacy. As Jews we acknowl-edge and celebrate the differences between public, private, and holy time as well as the differences between public, private, and holy places.

7. *B'rit* ("covenantal relationship"). For sexual expression in hu-man relationships to reach the fullness of its potential, it should be grounded in fidelity and the intention of permanence. This grounding mirrors the historic Jewish ideal of the relationship between God and the people Israel, with its mutual responsi-bilities and its assumption of constancy. The prophet Hosea wrote, "I will betroth you to Me forever; I will betroth you to Me in righteousness and justice, in love and compassion; I will betroth you to Me in everlasting faithfulness" (Hos. 2:21–22). A

sexual relationship is covenantal when it is stable and enduring and includes mutual esteem, trust, and faithfulness.

8. *Simchah* ("joy"). Human sexuality, as a powerful force in our lives, has the potential for physical closeness and pleasure, emotional intimacy and communication. The experience of sexual pleasure and orgasm, both in relationships and individually, can greatly delight women and men. Our tradition teaches that procreation is not the sole purpose of sexual intimacy; it not only recognizes but also rejoices in the gratification that our sexuality can bring to us. As an expression of love, the physical release and relaxation, the enjoyment of sensuality and playfulness that responsible sexual activity can provide are encouraged by our Jewish tradition. The sages teach that the *Shechinah*, the "Divine Presence," joins with people when they unite in love, but add that if there is no joy between them, the *Shechinah* will not be present (*Shabbat* 30b, *Zohar* 1). Judaism insists that the *simchah* of human sexual activity should be experienced only in healthy and responsible human relationships.

9. *Ahavah* ("love"). The mitzvah from Leviticus 19:18, "You shall love your neighbor as yourself; I am Adonai," serves as an essential maxim of all human relationships. The same Hebrew value term, *ahavah*, is used to describe the ideal relationship between God and humanity as well as that between people. The Jewish marriage ceremony speaks of *"ahavah v'achavah, shalom v'reiyut,"* "love and affection, wholeness and friendship," as ideals that should undergird holy relationships. For Jews, *ahavah* is not only a feeling or emotion, but also the concrete behaviors we display toward God and our fellow humans. *Ahavah* implies "self-esteem," the internal conviction that each of us should appear worthy in our own eyes. To be loved, one must consider oneself lovable; without regard for self, one can hardly care for others. *Ahavah* forbids any abuse or violence in sexual or any aspect of human relationships. *Ahavah* should be expressed through behavior that displays caring, support, and empathy.

10. *K'dushah* ("holiness"). This value comes from the meaning of the Hebrew root *k-d-sh*, "distinct from all others, unique, set apart for an elevated purpose." The Torah instructs us: "You shall be holy, for I, Adonai your God, am holy" (Lev. 19:2). Holiness is not simply a state of being; rather, it is a continuing process of human striving for increasingly higher levels of moral living. In a Reform Jewish context, a relationship may attain a measure of *k'dushah* when both partners voluntarily set themselves apart exclusively for each other, thereby finding unique emotional, sexual, and spiritual intimacy.

Our Torah teaches that, on the eve of Jacob's meeting and reconciliation with his brother Esau, he wrestled with a manifestation of Divinity and was wounded. The text continues: *"vayavo Yaakov shaleim,"* "and Jacob arrived *shaleim*" following his struggles with himself and others. Thus did he become known as Yisrael, the one who wrestles with God. We, too, as *B'nei/B'not Yisrael*, the spiritual descendants of Jacob, as human beings and as liberal Jews, wrestle with ourselves and our lives to achieve a measure of *sh'leimut*. It is hoped that the sexual values described in this statement serve as a source of guidance that leads us to a life of holiness.

Originally published in *CCAR Journal* vol. XLVIII/4, Fall 2001, pp. 9-13.

19

EMBRACING LESBIANS AND GAY MEN

A Reform Jewish Innovation

RABBI DENISE L. EGER

Part I: 2001, A Reform Jewish Innovation

Reform Judaism has been responsible for several revolutions within the ancient traditions. Perhaps the most visible, and one of the main principles upon which it was founded, has been the assertion of the absolute equality of men and women in religious obligations.[1] Out of this conviction came the notion of women as rabbis. Although it took well over one hundred years to actualize, the ordination of women as rabbis and their acceptance as cantors were two of the many factors that have allowed gays and lesbians to be welcomed and returned to the Jewish community through the Reform Movement. The notion of the liberation of women, so fervent in the late 1960s and early 1970s, was a part of the larger picture of the so-called sexual revolution of the era. By bringing women into the circles of decision making, as well as smashing our notions of God and gender, the atmosphere was ripe for other innovations as well.

The women's liberation movement gained strength with the African-American civil rights movement. Thus the notion of equality between blacks and whites also gave strength to the notion of equality between men and women.

A second factor in the return and welcome of gays and lesbians to Jewish life was Reform Judaism's emphasis on the concept of prophetic Judaism. This ideal of championing the cause of the widow, orphan, and stranger gave grounding to the heavy involvement of both Reform rabbis and laity in issues of social justice. For many years, social action in Reform Judaism meant involvement in the African-American struggle for civil rights. Many Reform rabbis and the Union of American Hebrew Congregations (UAHC) were deeply involved in supporting the march for justice by our African-American neighbors. So, as the gay rights movement grew, Reform Jews could understand the struggle for civil rights and freedom from discrimination that gays and lesbians sought.

A third factor that made Reform Judaism receptive to welcoming gay men and lesbians was the prevalence of both Jewish psychiatrists and psychologists. Many had become familiar with the groundbreaking study of Dr. Evelyn Hooker. Funded by the National Institute for Mental Health and presented in 1956 to the American Psychological Association, Dr. Hooker's revolutionary study was titled "The Adjustment of the Male Overt Homosexual." Her very controversial findings, which were widely publicized, concluded that gay men were as well adjusted as straight men.[2] This rocked the psychiatric world. Since early in the twentieth century, homosexuality had been classified as mental illness, psychopathology, as well as criminal offense. Finally, in 1973, the American Psychological Association dropped homosexuality from its official list of mental illnesses.

Thus the combination of these three notions—the equality of women, civil rights involvement, and Dr. Hooker's groundbreaking research—helped pave the way for the inclusion of gays and lesbians in Jewish life through the Reform Movement.

While the modern gay rights movement often claims the Stonewall riots of the summer of 1969 as its beginning, gay men and lesbians formed their first organizations throughout the 1950s and 1960s.[3] One of those groups, formed in Los Angeles in 1968, was the Metropolitan Community Church (MCC). Founded by the Reverend Troy Perry, a former Pentecostal minister, MCC was a church by and for gays and lesbians. Perry's organization quickly grew and became a central organizing force for the gay and lesbian community. Many Jews came to the activities of the church and were supporters of the church but not members. Out of this group of people came the idea for their own place of worship. Thus the Metropolitan Community Temple was born in 1972.

Support from the UAHC and CCAR

The Metropolitan Community Temple sought assistance from the local UAHC office in helping to form their group and eventually applied for membership status in the UAHC. Rabbi Erwin Herman and Southern California UAHC lay president Norm Eichberg carried the group's banner throughout the UAHC.[4] The group Hebraicized its name to Beth Chayim Chadashim, and after much controversy, Beth Chayim Chadashim was finally admitted in 1973 as a full participating congregation in the Reform Movement. But this was just a beginning.

Even prior to this start, sermons had been given calling for police to stop the harassment of gay people and for the extension of the basic protections of laws as guaranteed in the Bill of Rights.[5] The Central Conference of American Rabbis (CCAR) and the UAHC both had committees that debated the acceptance of a gay congregation into the UAHC. Following the successful defeat of the Briggs Initiative in 1978 in California, Rabbi Allen B. Bennett came out publicly as a gay man. This brave act gave a public face to Jewish gays and certainly to the fact that rabbis were among those who needed the acceptance, love, and support of the Reform Movement.

In 1975 at the UAHC Biennial Convention, a strong resolution calling for full civil rights for homosexuals in the civic arena was passed. This was followed in 1977 by another resolution at the UAHC Biennial calling for the same civil rights. By 1977, other gay synagogues had formed, and several had become members of the UAHC, including those in San Francisco, Miami, and Philadelphia.

The UAHC continued throughout the 1980s to keep gay rights on its agenda. In 1987, the UAHC passed yet another resolution, this time to "encourage lesbian and gay Jews to share and participate in the worship, leadership, and general congregational life of all synagogues." This resolution also urged the employment of synagogue personnel "without regard to sexual orientation." However, the specific issue of the ordination of gays and lesbians was referred to the second Ad Hoc Committee on Homosexuality of the CCAR.

Also in the 1980s, the UAHC confronted the AIDS crisis in a very strong way. It published outstanding teaching materials, including an AIDS curriculum for the supplemental religious school setting and study guides for some of the early television programs that dealt with AIDS. These materials took Jewish values and placed them in the context of the AIDS crisis, making it possible for Jews to be challenged to care for those with HIV disease. In the early 1980s, there was much religious hysteria, especially from Christian fundamentalists about AIDS being God's punishment for homosexuality. Each of the UAHC's publications helped to strongly convince not only the Jewish community but also other religious communities of the fallacy of these fundamentalist ideas.

By 1987, the UAHC Biennial even had Surgeon General Everett Koop address the plenum about AIDS and HIV. The Union established a separate AIDS Committee that prepared many materials, including a 1987 issue of *Keeping Posted* magazine for youth that was devoted entirely to the issue of AIDS. Rabbi Alexander Schindler, then president of the UAHC, spoke eloquently about the plight of people with AIDS at a UAHC-sponsored community service. In the sermon, he not only identified with the struggle of gay people but stated, "I declare myself the compassionate ally of every person heterosexual and homosexual, Jew and non-Jew, who is wrestling with the shame, the confusion, the fear, the endless torment involved in the inner struggle for sexual identity. It is, when all is said and done, a struggle for the integrity of selfhood."[6]

The UAHC's AIDS Committee also made a quilt piece for the NAMES Project AIDS quilt for all of the many Jews who had died from complications of AIDS. This piece of the quilt traveled to many UAHC congregations before being placed in the larger quilt.

Also in 1989, Rabbi Schindler expanded his comments from the March AIDS service sermon to include in his Biennial address to the Sixtieth Assembly of the UAHC an entire section about including gay and lesbian Jews. He expanded on themes from his March address:

> Yes, our resolutions express our resolve to act. There is one realm, however, in which our resolutions have been forthright, but our actions considerably less so. I speak now of the plea of gay and lesbian Jews for fuller acceptance in our midst. . . . To be sure, many of us feel pity for gays and lesbians, and we agree, intellectually, that it is a grievous wrong to stigmatize them, to ostracize them, to hold them in moral disdain. But something more than a grasp of the mind is required; there is a need for a grasp of the heart. Something different from pity is called for; we need, as a community to cross those boundaries of Otherness, those fringed boundaries, where compassion gives way to identification. . . . We who were marranos in Madrid, who clung to the closet of assimilation and conversion in order to live without molestation, we cannot deny the demand for gay and lesbian visibility![7]

His words did not go unnoticed. Out of his address another resolution was passed at the 1989 UAHC Biennial on visibility for gays and lesbians within the Movement. These resolutions translated into further concrete action taken by the UAHC Commission on Social Action, which promoted equal employment opportunities in the Reform Movement,[8] opposed discrimination against gays in the military,[9] and responded to anti-gay-rights referenda.[10] In 1992, Rabbi Schindler challenged the Boy Scouts of America for its stand against gay men and homosexuality.[11]

The UAHC continued to lead the way on gay and lesbian issues, including resolutions in 1993 for recognizing lesbian and gay partnerships and for supporting the participation of the Commission on Social Action in the 1993 Gay and Lesbian March on Washington. Further, staff from the Religious Action Center of the UAHC testified before Congress and spoke forcefully against the Defense of Marriage Act, which defined marriage as an institution of heterosexual privilege.

The UAHC also created a Task Force on Lesbian and Gay Inclusion, which in 1996 published a workbook distributed to all UAHC congregations. This workbook, called *KULANU (All of Us)*, is a booklet of programs to help congregations welcome and include gays and lesbians in their midst.

The CCAR has also dealt with and passed a number of resolutions of strong support for civil rights for homosexuals. In 1977, the CCAR passed a resolution that called "for the decriminalization of homosexual acts between consenting adults and prohibits discrimination against them as persons."[12] In 1981, the Task Force on Jewish Sexual Values of the Central Conference of American Rabbis was formed. During that conference, Dr. Sol Gordon presented a workshop on homosexuality, one that widely influenced many who attended. His thesis was based on the idea that one's sexual orientation is determined before the age of five years, and therefore, it is beyond the ability of the adult individual to change.[13]

HUC-JIR Policies

In 1986, a resolution was introduced to the CCAR by Rabbi Margaret Wenig and Margaret Holub, then a rabbinic student, calling for the ordination of openly gay and lesbian individuals as rabbis as well as revisions of the admission policy of the CCAR and the placement policy of the Rabbinical Placement Commission. The policy of Hebrew Union College–Jewish Institute of Religion, the Reform Movement's seminary, had been to deny ordination to anyone who was openly gay. This resolution was referred to committee for study. After four years of deliberation and study, the "Report of the Ad Hoc Committee on Homosexuality in the Rabbinate" was accepted by the plenum of the conference in June 1990 in Seattle, Washington. The report of the committee continued to affirm civil rights for gays and lesbians and the "efforts to eliminate discrimination in housing and employment." Further, the report repudiated hate language and physical abuse toward gays and lesbians.

The document affirmed "monogamous heterosexual marriage as the ideal human relationship for fulfilling the perpetuation of the species and covenantal fulfillment and the preservation of the Jewish people." However, it did note that a minority of the committee affirmed the equal possibility of covenantal fulfillment in homosexual relationships.

During the four years of deliberation of this task force, the HUC-JIR further clarified its admission policy. By the time the report of the committee was issued in 1990, President Alfred Gottschalk of HUC-JIR had set forth written guidelines concerning sexual orientation. The school considers the sexual orientation of an applicant only in the context of a candidate's overall suitability for the rabbinate, his or her qualifications to serve the Jewish community effectively, and his or her capacity to find personal fulfillment within the rabbinate.[14] The acceptance of this report was a hallmark in the spiritual struggle for equality by gays and lesbians. A major mainstream religious tradition had placed no bar on the ordination of gays and lesbians—a major milestone in the struggle for equality.

The CCAR continued to stand for the civil rights of gays and lesbians, including taking a stand against the Boy Scouts of America position excluding gay Scouts and Scout leaders. Also, in 1993, the CCAR resolved not to hold regional or national meetings in any state, province, or municipality that had passed a law after January 1, 1995, denying gays and lesbians legal protection of their civil rights. This resolution was in protest of many of the antigay ballot initiatives that had been forced on voters, especially in Colorado and Oregon. In 1996, the CCAR also endorsed civil marriage for gays and lesbians, acknowledging that this "is separate from the question of rabbinic officiation at such marriages."

Following this resolution in 1996, the CCAR formed another committee to look at issues of human sexuality, but once again, at the urging of the CCAR president, the committee's first task was to look at the issues of gay and lesbian wedding ceremonies. While the CCAR had taken a position to endorse civil marriage, the status of a religious ceremony was still left open to debate. In part, the divisive nature of the debate at the CCAR Convention that year over the civil marriage resolution led the CCAR leadership to form a committee to examine this issue.

The Ad Hoc Committee on Human Sexuality, after two years of deliberation and study, concluded "that *k'dushah* may be present in committed same-gender relationship between two Jews." The report further concluded that gay and lesbian relationships could serve "as the foundation of stable Jewish families, thus adding strength to the Jewish community." Thus, the report states that gay and lesbian relationships are "worthy of affirmation through appropriate Jewish ritual." However, the committee was not prepared to state that this ceremony of affirmation was on a par with *kiddushin* and further left it up to each rabbi to decide about the issue of officiation according to "his or her own rabbinic conscience." Of course, this leaves the door open for rabbis not to officiate as well.

Concurrent with the work of the Ad Hoc Committee on Homosexuality, the Responsa Committee of the CCAR also entertained the question of whether a Reform rabbi may officiate at a wedding or commitment ceremony and whether or not gay and lesbian unions qualify as *kiddushin*. The majority opinion concluded that a rabbi should not officiate. A vocal minority of this committee indicated that they disagreed, holding that a Reform rabbi may officiate at the wedding or commitment ceremony between two Jews of the same gender.

The Quandary

How can two committees of the same organization deal with an issue and yet come to diametrically opposite opinions? This is a quandary felt by many members of the CCAR and particularly gay and lesbian rabbis. The issue of marriage, which is the final spiritual hurdle of reconciliation of gay men and lesbians, continues to be divisive within the Movement in the same way it is divisive within the larger cultural context.

For those in our culture, whether Jewish or not, who believe homosexuality is a sin and aberrant behavior, there is no option for discussion. For those of us who believe that homosexuality is one of the varieties of human expression of love and an innate and unchanging mode of being, then homosexuality, homosexual relationships, and equality flow naturally in the scheme of things. The Responsa Committee's report documents this quite well. It states, "In trying to talk to each other about this question, we discovered that we as a Committee had ceased to share the most elemental kinds of assumptions necessary for a common religious conversation. We were speaking different languages, languages that used similar words and terminology but which defined them in starkly and irreconcilably different ways."[15] The Reform Movement that had seemingly championed the rights of gay and lesbian people from a secular and civil rights perspective seems to have gotten hung up in the theological realms. This discussion becomes so explosive when discussed that it has the potential to divide the entire Reform Jewish enterprise.

It was precisely this fear that led to the acceptance of both reports, that of the Ad Hoc Committee on Human Sexuality and that of the Responsa Committee. It was this fear that prevented the Ad Hoc Committee on Human Sexuality from moving forward with a resolution to the floor of the plenum of the CCAR at the June 1998 Convention in Anaheim, California. Despite the fact that a third of the membership of the CCAR signed on to a statement that they would officiate or had already officiated at a ceremony of commitment between two Jews of the same gender, the CCAR leadership was petrified of the possible schisms between those who supported gays and lesbians in their quest for spiritual fulfillment beneath the chuppah and those who opposed this idea.

These two reports were not the final word on this topic. The CCAR has appointed a Task Force on Gays and Lesbians in the Rabbinate. This committee task force created workshops and study sessions on the marriage topic for Reform rabbis all across the country, and it will also deal with issues of placement for lesbian and gay rabbis in conjunction with the Joint Placement Commission. Further, this task force is charged with finding support mechanisms for gay colleagues within the CCAR.

A resolution on same-sex ceremonies passed overwhelmingly at the March 2000 CCAR Convention calling for Reform rabbis to have the option of performing such ceremonies. While each Reform rabbi already has the right to follow his or her own conscience, and many rabbis had already been officiating at gay and lesbian wedding ceremonies, this resolution helped to give strength to gay and lesbian Jews around the world in their quest for spiritual fulfillment beneath the chuppah. The resolution affirmed that "the relationship of a Jewish same gender couple may be worthy of affirmation through appropriate ritual sanctification."[16]

The resolution was introduced by the Women's Rabbinic Network (WRN), the organization of Reform women rabbis, once again highlighting the link between the ordination of women as rabbis and gay and lesbian issues. Many members of the WRN were frustrated by the events in the CCAR during the spring of 1998. The opportunity to vote on the Ad Hoc Committee on Human Sexuality was no longer an option. The WRN voted at its March 1999 Convention to urge the CCAR to take up the issue of same-gender ceremonies at its Pittsburgh Convention. However, the only issue debated at the Pittsburgh Convention was the new Pittsburgh Platform. Thus, in the summer of 1999, the WRN introduced an initial resolution to the CCAR for consideration at the Greensboro 2000 Convention. Again, there was a year of discussion at every rabbinic regional convention on the language of the resolution and need for such a resolution.

In the months and weeks leading up to the March 2000 CCAR Convention, the resolution was debated hotly over the Internet in rabbinic e-mail discussions and in person. It was a debate that was not among the Movement's shining moments. There were many hurtful and ad hominem attacks made, and the WRN was attacked. The misogyny present in these discussions by Reform rabbis was somewhat surprising and somewhat predictable. The WRN was accused of being run by a group of lesbians. It was as if the women rabbis of the CCAR and members of the WRN were out to destroy the safe haven for certain male members of the CCAR. The very existence and need for the WRN was questioned as some kind of rabbinic cabal against the CCAR. The attacks were made as if women rabbis weren't legitimate members of the CCAR.

The leadership of the CCAR had changed at the Pittsburgh Convention. Rabbi Charles Kroloff became president of the CCAR, and he was willing and determined to have the issue of officiation at same-gender ceremonies debated under his watch. In addition, Rabbi Paul Menitoff, the executive director of the CCAR, gave his full backing and support to the idea of bringing the topic before the plenum of the CCAR.

One area of concern was the Israeli Reform Movement. In 1998, when the Ad Hoc Committee on Human Sexuality's report was to be presented, the Israeli Reform Movement was adamantly against a resolution of support for officiation at same-gender ceremonies. In fact, MARAM, the Israeli Reform rabbinic organization, will not permit its members to officiate at same-gender ceremonies. This is in part because of the precarious situation of the Reform rabbinate in Israel.[17] During the spring of 1998, the Reform Movement was in delicate negotiations with the Chief Rabbinate in Israel on issues of conversion. One of the many reasons the original resolution of the Ad Hoc Committee on Human Sexuality was pulled from the table was because of concern for the Reform Movement in Israel. Thus, for the WRN resolution to be successful, the Israeli Reform Movement had to be consulted.

In October 1999 I met with the top leaders of Israeli Reform rabbis, Rabbi Meir Azari and Rabbi Yehoram Mazor, the *Av Bet Din* of MARAM, during a congregational trip to Israel to discuss the resolution. During the two-hour meeting, we spoke about the different situations of North American and Israeli Reform Movements as well as the upcoming resolution and how MARAM might find a way to support the resolution. My conversation with them paved the way for further discussion in February when the first WRN trip to Israel—with over fifty women rabbis—met with the leadership of the Israeli Reform rabbis. Prior to this meeting, the strategy that MARAM was going to follow was that they were going to absent themselves from the floor of the convention during the debate and discussion. While many individual Israeli Reform rabbis do support gays and lesbians in their quest for a religious ceremony honoring their relationships, the official policy of MARAM remained firm. By massaging the language of the resolution, given their suggestions, we were able to create language that could weave their reality and ours into the WRN resolution and avoid the scenario of an exodus during the convention.

As the convention drew closer and the Internet debates grew heated, the idea of a possible compromise began to be floated. Some of the opposition to the WRN resolution had submitted an "alternative resolution" that was strong in supporting gay and lesbian civil rights. Yet it omitted any reference to gay and lesbian commitment ceremonies. The alternative resolution merely repeated many of the stands that the CCAR and the UAHC had previously endorsed. Not wanting a pyrrhic victory or a vicious floor fight, those of us who authored the resolution agreed to slightly soften some other parts of the language of the resolution. This allowed for the greatest majority to support the document, even those rabbis not yet ready to officiate at gay and lesbian weddings or commitment ceremonies. Under the leadership of Rabbi Shira Stern and Rabbi Susan Stone, co-chairs of the WRN, and Rabbi Kroloff, CCAR president, Rabbi Paul Menitoff, executive vice president of the CCAR, and Rabbi Elliot Stevens, executive secretary of the CCAR, a compromise was fashioned.

By entering into discussion with those who opposed the WRN resolution, the authors of the "alternative resolution" agreed to withdraw their resolution if there were changes made in the text of the officiation resolution. The resolution that was overwhelmingly passed at the Greensboro 2000 CCAR Convention was the product of this compromise.

However, the compromise was a good one, because the new WRN resolution allowed for the truth to be recognized: that there are rabbis who do officiate at same-gender ceremonies and rabbis who do not. Further, the improved WRN resolution allowed for near-unanimous support and allowed for the CCAR to go on record as supporting the dignity of gay and lesbian Jewish same-gender couples.

During the plenum, many questions came up from the floor.

Some supporters of the WRN resolution were very disappointed and felt a stronger resolution could have passed. Many of the amendments from the floor actually made the resolution stronger. In particular, one question from the floor specifically asked, "What can we in good faith call these ceremonies?" It was affirmed from the floor—by the CCAR president, Rabbi Charles Kroloff—that we could call gay and lesbian commitment ceremonies "weddings," even by the ritual name *kiddushin*. This is the brilliance of the resolution. By affirming Reform Jewish principles of rabbinic autonomy, we speak the truth and, yet, begin to institutionalize the reality of Jewish rituals for same-gender commitment ceremonies.

While some were disappointed that the language seemed muted, here is what was really achieved. First, the headlines around the world read, "Reform Rabbis Back Blessing of Gay Unions."[18] From San Francisco to Milan, from Tel Aviv to Chicago, a message of support for Jewish gay and lesbian couples and the commitments they wish to make together was visible.

Second, there were five hundred rabbis, all saying yes: saying yes, to gay and lesbian families, gay and lesbian lives. Rabbis with Jewish traditions behind them were saying yes, there is sanctity and holiness about gay and lesbian commitments in the face of the often dehumanizing portraits that are painted about gay people. Those dehumanizing portraits are often made by people who claim moral and religious authority. It was powerful to hear the ayes go up with such unity.

There were only two speakers against the resolution and perhaps less than ten nays. But the room vibrated with spiritual energy. It really felt that we were standing on historic ground. People, gay and straight, were crying tears of relief and joy. People felt good about what had been achieved, even those rabbis who do not yet officiate. The feeling in the large convention hall was electric. There was a tremendous spiritual sense that we were living in a moment of *tikkun olam*. Spontaneously everyone broke out into the *Shehecheyanu* prayer that says, "Thank You, God, for giving us life, for sustaining us, and for bringing us to this time."

Another important outcome of the vote in favor of the WRN resolution was that the CCAR created a model for coming together even in our differences. This is a strength of our Movement.

A third outcome of the vote in favor of the WRN resolution was the hope and comfort that those who still remain closeted will feel in having the largest group of Jewish clergy acknowledge and celebrate gay and lesbian lives. The vote sent a positive message. The institution of marriage is used as a way to legitimize who is family and even who is human. This was certainly true when African slaves were brought to the United States and forbidden from marrying, and it is true today for gay and lesbian people. Thus, the message sent by the CCAR was a victory for all those who believe in the human dignity of all people, including gay men and lesbians.

A fourth outcome—and perhaps the most important—is the institutionalization of gay and lesbian life-cycle events. The WRN resolution called for educational materials and pastoral materials to be developed. This included gay and lesbian wedding and commitment ceremonies as well as *ketubot* and commitment documents. It is this part of the resolution that will help transform same-sex Jewish ceremonies from mere exotica to regular ritual, from unique occurrences and rarities to expectations and access. Jewish same-gender couples and their weddings and other ceremonies will become part of the normal and, yes, regular life-cycle canon of Jewish life. Will it always be called a wedding? Most people will understand what it means, and many Reform rabbis already do use the term *kiddushin*.

In two short years, through study and dialogue, the CCAR was able to come to a consensus on a difficult issue. This was a consensus that affirmed rabbinic choice but upheld the dignity and sanctity of gay Jewish couples beneath the *chuppah*.

The marriage issue is the final ground of acceptance within the Reform Movement. Reform Judaism in the latter half of the twentieth century became a welcoming haven for gay men and lesbians who wished to be an active part of the Jewish community. Whether in primarily gay and lesbian synagogues or more mainstream synagogues, whether as lay leaders or as rabbis or cantors, gays and lesbians have found a home and place at the Jewish communal table. We can say that Reform Judaism has embraced gay men and lesbians. Certainly there will be no going back into the closet.

The Role of the Individual Congregation

The real work of the inclusion of gay men and lesbians must be realized not just on the political and national scale but also within the individual congregation. As it stands now, each congregation determines its own customs regarding gay and lesbian families. While the UAHC has published a guide for inclusion of gays and lesbians in the congregation, this is a resource that needs leadership in order for it to be utilized. The issues of inclusion of gays and lesbians in the life of the congregation are further reinforced by the position of the rabbi on gay and lesbian issues. Thus, if a rabbi is supportive of including gays and lesbians, he or she can be an advocate at the congregational level, helping to make the individual synagogue a welcoming environment. However, if the rabbi is less than supportive, this can send a strong message of exclusion of gays and lesbians. This is perhaps not an issue in larger cities, where there is more than one Reform congregation. But the consequences in smaller communities, where there is only one Reform synagogue or perhaps one congregation, can be devastating. This is particularly true for young people. Since statistics prove that gay and lesbian teens are one-third more likely to commit suicide than teens who are heterosexual, the issue of inclusion or exclusion can have life-and-death consequences.

Further, the present leadership of the UAHC has seemingly steered away from controversial social issues toward issues of religious education. We can only hope and pray that the commitment to the inclusion of Jewish gay men and lesbians continues to be a priority within the congregational arm of the Movement. It seems clear that when the president of the UAHC speaks out on topics, people do listen and the agenda is set. It is my hope that the present leadership of the UAHC (now URJ) will continue to speak out positively on gay and lesbian Jewish issues and will keep the commitment of the UAHC toward inclusion as a vital linchpin in the social justice agenda for the Movement.

Each time the UAHC or CCAR speaks out and reaches out to include gays and lesbians in the life of the community, its action hammers away at the often dehumanizing myths that are still in circulation about gay men and lesbians. The authority of the Jewish voice with which the Reform Movement speaks sends a positive message both to Jews and to non-Jews who hunger for spiritual leadership on this issue.

Conclusion

The Talmud teaches that if you save one life, it is as if you have saved the whole world (Babylonian Talmud, *Sanhedrin* 37a). The positive and inclusive position of the Reform Movement has certainly saved more than a few lives. The message of reconciliation of gay men and lesbians with the Jewish community has added a wonderful texture to our congregations and to the Jewish people. One can only hope that this vital message of inclusion continues.

Part II: Postscript, 2013—
A Place for All; Continuing LGBT Inclusion in Reform Judaism

It has been almost two decades since the Central Conference of American Rabbis endorsed civil marriage for gay and lesbian couples and more than a decade since the CCAR passed a resolution supporting rabbinic officiation at gay and lesbian Jewish weddings. In the immediate aftermath of the passage of this 2000 resolution on officiation, a CCAR ad hoc task force developed materials to help rabbis prepare gay and lesbian couples for married life. Liturgy was written, counseling handbooks were created, and even a preliminary guide to the ins and outs of the legal situation for gay and lesbian couples, which differed by locale, was compiled. These resources are still posted on the members' section of the CCAR website for use by colleagues. The CCAR has been a leader in publishing materials for gay couples, which includes the groundbreaking wedding book *Beyond Breaking the Glass* (2012), written by Rabbi Nancy Wiener. This is the first wedding preparation book to include as normative wedding counseling, liturgy, and preparation for lesbian, gay, bisexual, and transgender (LGBT) Jewish couples!

But even more significant than the changes and follow-up of the CCAR have been the sweeping changes in society at large regarding civil rights in general and marriage rights in particular for LGBT people. Many states have legalized marriage and/or civil unions. Many nations have legalized gay and lesbian marriage, including Canada, South Africa, the Netherlands, Spain, New Zealand, France, Mexico, Argentina, Belgium, Iceland, Norway, Portugal, Denmark, Uruguay, and Sweden. In every state in the United States and in Canada, in Israel and around the world, Jewish gay men and lesbians have rushed to the chuppah! In each state that has either had a court ruling on or passed marriage legislation, Reform rabbis and Reform Jewish lay leaders have been an essential part of state coalitions to work for marriage equality. Whether in Massachusetts, California, Maryland, or Minnesota, the statewide campaigns for the freedom to marry has had the leadership of Reform rabbis and the support of the Union for Reform Judaism (URJ, formerly UAHC), the Religious Action Center, and the Hebrew Union College–Jewish Institute of Religion.

In the years since the CCAR resolution supporting officiation at same-sex weddings, the URJ issued a new version of *Kulanu* in 2007. This was a handbook for congregational leaders and Jewish professionals to consider LGBT inclusion in their communities. The volume includes samples of programs, sermons, and articles to guide any congregation in opening its tent wide to welcome lesbian and gay couples. The URJ website also has consistently had resources on its website regarding LGBT issues and offers materials for congregation to observe Gay Pride Month in their community.

The Religious Action Center, the joint project of the URJ and the CCAR in Washington, D.C., headed by Rabbi David Saperstein, has been a strong voice for LGBT equality. The RAC has lobbied and filed numerous amici briefs on behalf of our Movement supporting LGBT equality. In the last number of years, there has always been one intern at the RAC who has as her/his portfolio LGBT issues and monitors House and Senate hearings and bills that relate to LGBT concerns. The RAC has been particularly vocal in encouraging a bill to protect employment of gay men and lesbians. In many states in the United States, you can still be fired for just being gay. The RAC has helped local rabbis and congregations fight LGBT discrimination bills in many different states and has played a role in helping Reform rabbis and leaders strategize in their states as well.

Beyond the world of Jewish organizations, Jews have been involved in every corner of the fight for LGBT equality. Many activists in the gay and lesbian community are Jews. Many of the attorneys who have provided pro bono services have been Jews. Their Jewish values of family, *tikkun olam*, and pursuing justice have informed their work. Evan Wolfson, founder of the Freedom to Marry Project and author of the book *Why Marriage Matters*, attributes his dedication to the LGBT fight for equality and equal marriage to his Jewish upbringing. Wolfson stated in an article in the *Jewish Daily Forward* in December 2012, "We had a Jewish consciousness and a Jewish life. . . . I learned the importance of *tikkun olam*, the importance of standing up for what's right, the importance of caring about others."[19]

In every national and local LGBT organization, there are Jewish board members, donors, and professionals who lead the organization in some capacity. The consistent and early support of the Reform and

Reconstructionist Movements has played an important role in modeling for other religious groups LGBT inclusion. I believe this support
also has encouraged all Jews to be involved in the struggle for LGBT
equality. For example, over the last few years the Conservative Movement has finally welcomed LGBT students as rabbinical and cantorial
candidates, and in 2012 produced documents for same-sex weddings
and divorces. In 2006, after much heated debate, the Committee on Law
and Standards of the Rabbinical Assembly finally accepted gay and lesbian students to rabbinical schools at the Jewish Theological Seminary
in New York and the Ziegler School of Rabbinic Studies in California.

This was a monumental marker for the LGBT Jewish community
because now, for most American Jews, the official arms of the three
major liberal denominations welcome LGBT congregants and rabbis. As has happened before, the Conservative Movement eventually
embraced many of the innovations of the Reform Movement. This
becomes important not only in the pew, but also in the voting booth,
as Jews traditionally vote in higher percentages relative to our population size. In 2008 in California, during the Proposition 8 campaign, a
ballot initiative to ban the right to marry of LGBT couples, election
analysis showed that Jews in Los Angeles opposed Proposition 8 by 78
percent.[20] These statistics reflect the continuing shift in the positive
perceptions of LGBT people in the Jewish community in general, and
in particular they demonstrate how the work of the Reform Movement
as a leader in this area has influenced North American Jews.

A rash of gay teen suicides due to bullying raised awareness of the
harassment and pain that still plague young gay, lesbian, and especially
transgender teens. Statistics reveal that 30 to 40 percent of young gay
people contemplate suicide during their teenage years through their
twenties. The Reform Movement has modeled caring and inclusion of
LGBT youth at an institutional level. Through the work of the Campaign for Youth Engagement, our URJ summer camps and the leadership of the North American Federation of Temple Youth (NFTY),
programs, curricula, and other materials and resources have been shared
across the Movement.[21] For example, the NFTY website has multiple

education programs and suggestions for Reform Jewish youth to combat bullying. The national board of NFTY passed the following statement, which appears on the NFTY Initiatives page: "NFTY will not sit idly by regarding all issues relating to bullying, teasing, and harassment. We will continue to add resources for you to use in your TYGs, congregations, and beyond the walls of our Jewish community."

The atmosphere of the Reform seminary, Hebrew Union College–Jewish Institute of Religion, has certainly changed since 1990, when it reversed its long-standing policy and finally began to accept and ordain openly gay and lesbian rabbinical students. On each of the four campuses of HUC-JIR, gay and lesbian students are welcomed, and LGBT issues are addressed. Housed on the Los Angeles campus is the Institute of Judaism and Sexual Orientation (IJSO), whose mission is to study and teach about the intersections of these two areas. The IJSO teaches important seminars to rabbinical and education students and those enrolled in the School of Non-Profit Management. Though housed on the Los Angeles campus, the IJSO does this work at all three of our stateside campuses (New York and Cincinnati). The IJSO is also home to the Jeffrey Herman Virtual Resource Center, named for the son of Rabbi Irv (z"l) and Agnes Herman. This is an online collection of texts, case studies, and liturgies dealing with Jewish LGBT issues. Founded by Dean Lewis Barth and a group of LGBT rabbinic alumni, the IJSO's first full-time director is Dr. Joel Kushner. Dr. Kushner, in addition to his teaching, has made the IJSO a national resource on LGBT Jewish issues for congregations who have been engaged in opening their doors to LGBT Jews and families. He has led board and staff trainings and consulted with other religious denominations on opening the door to LGBT parishioners. The IJSO has sponsored conferences and has begun work to create a template for congregations both within the Reform Movement and without for becoming fully welcoming and accepting of LGBT Jews. In cooperation with the New York campus's Blaustein Center for Pastoral Counseling, headed by Rabbi Nancy Wiener, the IJSO co-sponsored a nearly year-long art show called the Sexuality Spectrum, which offered a groundbreaking exploration of sexual orientation through the creativity of over fifty international contemporary artists.

The Reform Movement must continue to educate on these issues. The work must not stop. There are still many congregations that will not engage a gay or lesbian rabbi as its senior rabbi, let alone deal with transgender rabbis. We still do not publish a *ketubah* suitable for gay couples, nor does our Reform Pension Board work appropriately with gay couples as federal laws have impacted the pension plan. Our Reform Jewish values have been in conflict with the federal laws in terms of inheritance, marriage, and divorce until just recently.

But now in the historic Supreme Court ruling that struck down section 3 of the Defense of Marriage Act in 2013, it was a Jewish lesbian, Edie Windsor, who was the plaintiff. Edie and her partner, Thea Speyer, a refugee from Europe following World War II, were married in Canada in 2006 and had been together forty-two years when Thea died, leaving her estate to Edie. Had their legal marriage been recognized by the federal government, Edie would not have had to pay $363,000 in taxes. On June 26, 2013, the Supreme Court found that the Equal Protection Clause of the United States Constitution protected Edie Windsor as well. And so in a 5–4 decision, the justices struck down the Defense of Marriage Act, a 1996 law signed by then President Bill Clinton, which refused federal recognition of any marriage between gay and lesbian couples.

On the same day, the Supreme Court also struck down California's Proposition 8. The Supreme Court did not issue a sweeping marriage equality statement for the United States, but instead it affirmed that in the states that had marriage equality, including California, same-sex marriages are valid and legal and must be federally recognized. These two rulings show the sea change in the United States on positions toward the humanity and equality of LGBT individuals and their families. Poll after poll shows that attitudes in the United States are increasingly in favor of extending full rights and civil liberties to LGBT people. This is increasingly true around the world as more and more countries have introduced marriage equality legislation. The

Reform Movement can be proud of the role it has played in helping this shift take hold. As it continues to place LGBT equality and issues as a vital part of our spiritual and religious mission, the Reform Jewish Movement educates, challenging Jews within the Movement and without to be radically inclusive. Through example and dialogue, Reform Judaism challenges other faith traditions to examine their perspectives on human sexuality and offers a model to them for welcoming LGBT people into their fold. The Reform Movement, through its advocacy for LGBT people and their equality on the state, national, and international stages, continues to bring healing to LGBT people and their families everywhere and inspires others to work for *tikkun olam*, healing our broken world.

NOTES

1. Gunther Plaut, *The Rise of Reform Judaism* (New York: World Union for Progressive Judaism, 1963), 252–55.

2. From "100 Years before Stonewall" exhibit (University of California, Berkeley, June 1994), as quoted in *Out in All Directions*, ed. Lynn Witt, Sherry Thomas, and Eric Marcus (New York: Warner, 1997), 224–25.

3. On June 26, 1969, following a raid by the New York Police Department on a Greenwich Village gay bar, three days of rioting took place to protest police harassment of gay men and lesbians.

4. Both Herman and Eichberg had gay sons, although both have said to me in private conversation that they did not speak to each other about this at the time.

5. Rabbi Steven B. Jacobs, *National Post and Opinion*, May 3, 1968, as quoted in Albert Vorspan, *Jewish Values and Social Crisis*, rev. ed. (New York: Union of American Hebrew Congregations, 1971), 230.

6. Rabbi Alexander Schindler, address at the UAHC community service in support of people with AIDS (Leo Baeck Temple, Los Angeles, CA, March 12, 1989), 5.

7. Rabbi Alexander Schindler, Presidential Address, Sixtieth General Assembly of the UAHC (New Orleans, LA, November 2–6, 1989), in *Kulanu: All of Us—A Program and Resource Guide for Gay, Lesbian, Bisexual, and Transgender Inclusion* (NY: URJ Press, 2007), 245.

8. Resolution of the Commission on Social Action, 1991. http://urj.org//about/union/governance/reso//?syspage=article&item_id=2065.

9. Ibid.

10. Resolutions of the UAHC and the CCAR in 1993, in *Kulanu: All of Us*, 281–86.

11. Letter from Rabbi Schindler to the Boy Scouts, 1992, and resolutions of the Executive Committee of the CCAR, 1992, and National Federation of Temple Youth, 1992, in *Kulanu: All of Us*, 277–79.

12. Resolution of the Central Conference of American Rabbis Eighty-Eighth Annual Convention, 1977, in *Kulanu: All of Us*, 251.

13. "Report of the Task Force on Jewish Sexual Values," Rabbi Selig Salkowitz, chair, *CCAR Yearbook* 92 (1982), 145–46.

14. "Report of the Ad Hoc Committee on Homosexuality," *CCAR Yearbook* 108 (July 1997–December 1998): 34.

15. "CCAR Responsum on Homosexual Marriage," *CCAR Yearbook* 108 (July 1997–December 1998), 44.

16. Same-sex officiation resolution passed at the 111th Annual Convention of the Central Conference of American Rabbis, March 2000. http://ccarnet.org/rabbis-speak/resolutions/2000/same-gender-officiation/.

17. The rabbinate in Israel is controlled by the Orthodox. Reform rabbis are forbidden by Israeli law from officiating at civil wedding ceremonies. Reform rabbis also may not conduct funerals officially or convert people. Ongoing negotiations with the Chief Rabbinate in Israel, as well as numerous lawsuits in Israeli civil courts, have tried to overturn this situation.

18. *New York Times*, Thursday, March 30, 2000.

19. Michael Kaminer, "Q&A: Evan Wolfson on Marriage Equality Movement," *Jewish Daily Forward*, December 26, 2012, http://blogs.forward.com/forward-thinking/168262/q-and-a-evan-wolfson-on-marriage-equality-movemen/#ixzz2XQdB0IUK.

20. According to exit polling by the Leavey Center for the Study of Los Angeles at Loyola Marymount University, as quoted in the *Los Angeles Times*, November 9, 2008.

21. "Bullying," NFTY, http://www.nfty.org/living/initiatives/bullying/.

20

TO ORDAIN OR NOT TO ORDAIN

The Tale of the CCAR
Committee on Homosexuality
and the Rabbinate

RABBI MICHAL LOVING

Today, openly gay and lesbian rabbis serve congregations all over the country. To the youngest generations, it may seem as though the Reform congregations and institutions have always been open and inclusive, regardless of a rabbi's sexual identity or orientation. Yet, there is always a history behind the status quo, and this is the case regarding the Reform Movement's decision to ordain openly gay and lesbian rabbis. How did the Reform Movement make its decision to ordain men and women who were open about their homosexuality? The decision-making process was long and contentious. At the center of this debate was an ad hoc subcommittee of the Central Conference of American Rabbis (CCAR), the CCAR Ad Hoc Committee on Homosexuality and the Rabbinate. A critical analysis of the work of this committee will shed light on the evolving nature of Reform Jewish ideology in the last decades of the twentieth century.

The Ad Hoc Committee on Homosexuality and the Rabbinate[1] met from 1986 to 1990, and evidence suggests that a gradual change occurred during the four years of its existence. As we will see, some members of the committee felt sure of what stance to take from the beginning of the discussions. These men and women felt the committee must confer complete equality on homosexuals because this was the morally correct position. They wanted the committee to speak out regardless of the consequences. Other members of this body were unsure of their positions, and some were strongly against the idea of ordaining gays and lesbians. Many members expressed great fear over how any resolution would be received by the larger Jewish and non-Jewish public. As the years passed, the committee delved into Jewish law, conducted surveys, held workshops and information-gathering sessions, and fielded letters from rabbis all over the country in an effort to study the potential reactions by the larger Jewish world to the prospect that the Reform Movement would decide to ordain openly gay and lesbian rabbis.

By 1989, those "who had been opposed came to see the injustice of excluding gay men and lesbians from the rabbinate or the harm [that] remaining in the closet caused those gay men and lesbians already ordained."[2] In June 1990, the committee submitted a report to the CCAR recommending that gay and lesbian rabbis be accepted for ordination at Hebrew Union College–Jewish Institute of Religion (HUC-JIR), the Reform Movement's rabbinical seminary. The committee members explored their own moral stances, and they either stayed true to their original beliefs or were swayed by ethical arguments, personal experiences with gay and lesbian rabbis, and the growing momentum of the gay rights movement in the secular world. Surveys, letters, and supportive phone calls at times also influenced the committee, and these testimonies convinced many members that the larger Reform Jewish world believed that this was, at its core, a civil rights and a religious rights issue. They became convinced that inclusion and equal access were central to the teachings of Reform Judaism, and these committee members were ready and willing to accept openly gay and lesbian rabbis.

A Time of Uncertainty: 1977–June 1988

In 1977 the CCAR resolved to uphold civil rights and "civil liberties for all people"[3] and encouraged "legislation which decriminalizes homosexual acts between consenting adults and prohibits discrimination against them as persons."[4] Special outreach was instituted by Reform Jewry to gays and lesbians, and they were increasingly welcomed into the Reform synagogue.[5] Yet, according to Sue Levi Elwell, the Movement was still torn: "Many mainstream organizations, liberal Jewish institutions, and some individual Jews . . . supported the civil rights of gays and lesbians, but [were] still hesitant about the implications of their complete integration as open participants into so-called normative or mainstream Jewish institutions and organizations."[6]

By 1985, Rabbi Margaret Wenig and student rabbi Margaret Holub decided that a paradigm shift was needed. Holub had written her fifth-year HUC-JIR sermon on this topic in March, and in December, Wenig submitted a draft resolution to the CCAR titled "Resolution on Gay and Lesbian Rabbis." This draft quoted the 1977 resolution and endorsed the full inclusion of gays and lesbians in all aspects of rabbinic life, from nondiscriminatory CCAR policies and admission into HUC-JIR, to open ordination of gay and lesbian rabbis.[7] Shortly after the resolution was submitted for official consideration, CCAR president Jack Stern asked Wenig if she would agree to withdraw the draft on the condition that he agreed to convene an ad hoc task force to address the issue.[8]

The newly formed Ad Hoc Committee on Homosexuality and the Rabbinate was created in 1986. Rabbi Selig Salkowitz, who had previously served as the chair of the CCAR's Committee on Human Sexuality, served as the chair of this new committee. Members included official representatives from the CCAR's Rabbinical Placement Commission (RPC), the CCAR, the Union of American Hebrew Congregations (UAHC), and HUC-JIR.[9] Opinions around the table at the first meeting on November 25–26, 1986, were varied. Some felt that a resolution ordaining gay and lesbian rabbis was morally right and should be immediately recommended, regardless of public opinion. Others thought that it would be more helpful to maintain the status quo, fearing that the majority of mainstream Reform Jews were not prepared to accept an "out-of-the-closet" gay rabbi. If the resolution at a CCAR Convention passed, one rabbi argued, it "would trigger a measure of divisiveness internally and in relation to our kindred Movements which would far surpass the impact of patrilineality."[10]

The issues were immense, and although Salkowitz had initially hoped that a decision on whether or not to bring a resolution to the CCAR would take a mere single session,[11] it was quickly decided that the committee would need to reconvene. In the meantime, surveys were sent out to all CCAR members asking for anonymous, personal statements relating to a range of questions regarding homosexuals in the rabbinate.[12] Letters poured in from rabbis and rabbinic students all over the country, mostly very supportive of bringing the resolution to the CCAR. They all cited a deep commitment to Judaism and Jewish values and a wish for inclusion.

One such letter, received by Margaret Wenig on January 27, 1987, begins by stating that being a gay/lesbian person has made the author a better rabbi: "I am much more sensitive to my congregants, to their pain and their need for institutionalized approval. Traditional Jewish themes, such as freedom from slavery, redemption, the courage to be who we are, the experience of being a despised minority, the *Kol Nidre* (being forced to say 'yes,' when we meant 'no') live and resonate in me as a gay/lesbian Jew."[13] An anonymous rabbinic student echoed these same sentiments. She informed the members of the ad hoc committee that her secret identity as a lesbian made her feel "schizophrenic"[14] and ashamed of having to hide. "The proposed resolution sounds much like a dream to me—a fantasy come true,"[15] while at the same time, it also seemed natural, an "extension of both the UAHC's acceptance of congregations with gay and lesbian outreach as well as the CCAR's 1977 resolution."[16] The student hoped that openly gay and lesbian rabbis would be supported by the CCAR during placement and added that openly gay and lesbian rabbis had much to offer to the Jewish community by serving as role models for gay and lesbian youth.

Not *all* of the letters were so positive. One rabbi wrote to committee member Joseph Levine quoting a passage from the 1981 Reform responsa: "We cannot recommend such an individual [a gay or lesbian] as a role model nor should he/she be placed in a position of leadership or guidance for children at any age."[17] The rabbi who wrote this letter felt that he could not accept gay and lesbian leaders who consider themselves a "homosexual first, Jew second," lest the homosexual nature of the rabbi overwhelm or predetermine how he or she will act and with whom he or she will associate.[18]

Many of the letters were read by the committee at their second meeting, on March 4–5, 1987.[19] While the members were "deeply moved by the pain expressed in these testimonies, and shared the pain they felt as a result of what they had learned . . . most realized that while pain is a persuasive argument for compassion, it is not a proper motivation for change within our Movement."[20] Instead, they turned to more scientific means of research: Yoel Kahn presented a paper he had written on the halachic perspective on homosexuality, Margaret Wenig presented psychological and biological material, Harvey Tattelbaum brought to the table a discussion of the legal status of gays and lesbians in the United States, Walter Jacob commented on how other Jewish and Christian institutions had handled the issue, and so on.[21]

The committee "struggled with its process and agenda"[22] and had trouble forming a strategy of how to approach the issue; not all committee members were convinced that the openly gay and lesbian individuals should become rabbis, and many feared the prospect of a negative reaction and a strong backlash if the committee promulgated a resolution that called on Reform Jewry to admit and ordain openly gay and lesbian rabbis. Much attention was garnered in the outside press, and the rabbis on the committee were keenly aware of the fact that everything they said was under close scrutiny.[23] They could not decide if they should maintain the status quo or what, if anything, they should present to the CCAR. The minutes of the meeting clearly reflect the committee members' ambivalence:

> [Rabbi A]: Uncomfortable. Wrestled with this. . . . Feel that we are being rushed, steam rolled. If not for doing something now— you're homophobic. Statements easy. Nervous re statements.

> [Rabbi B]: Afraid of a few things. If we say anything this coming spring that raises false hopes—more harm than good. Say: grappling with issues—to go beyond that raise hope and fears—may not be justified.

> [Rabbi C]: Concerned re reaction of laity. . . . Pragmatic makes us cautious—don't want statements to start fire storms.[24]

The committee ultimately decided *not* to bring a final report to the upcoming CCAR Convention, but to continue its work for another year.[25]

More feedback arrived in the form of letters. Most were pro-ordination, while a few were against. Once again, these documents were reviewed by the members of the Ad Hoc Committee on Homosexuality and the Rabbinate at its next meeting, which took place on December 2–3, 1987. Members of the committee were more open about their positions as they commented on CCAR members' position papers,[26] but the overall question still focused on the nature of the larger Jewish reaction to any formal resolution that the committee might issue.

That said, the directional purpose of this meeting was much more decisive. The question was stated early on: "Where is it we want to go and then how do we get there?"[27] The consensus was that the statement *should* "carry us beyond the status quo."[28] This was agreed upon by everyone, but the specifics of what should go in the statement were still undecided. What should be the model for the statement? Should the focus be on civil rights or addressing people's pain? Should the committee state that heterosexuality is the norm, or should this body compare the debate to inclusivity as it related to women's issues? Should the committee address purely practical issues of ordination and placement, or should it focus on theological themes? How should the topic be approached, and should it be put on the agenda for the next annual meeting of the CCAR? In the end, two committee members volunteered to work on the statement.[29] Their draft, with three dissenting opinions, reaffirmed "monogamous heterosexual relationships"[30] as the Jewish norm, acknowledged the pain and isolation felt by homosexual Jews, and urged that "*all* rabbis be accorded the opportunity to fulfill the sacred vocation to which they had been called."[31]

The next meeting of the Ad Hoc Committee on Homosexuality and the Rabbinate was scheduled for May 1988, and in April, among other correspondence, Selig Salkowitz received a highly supportive letter from Rabbi Randall Falk, who was serving as the chair of the CCAR's Committee on Justice and Peace:

> The members of the Committee [on Justice and Peace] asked that I contact you to inform you of our Committee's endorsement of inclusion in the Resolution on Homosexuality to be submitted to the 1989 Convention in Cincinnati, of the following statement: that sexual preference should not be a factor in recruitment, admission, or ordination at the Hebrew Union College–Jewish Institute of Religion, nor should job placement or job security be affected by an individual's sexual preference.[32]

Falk's committee reflected the voices of others within the Reform Movement, as the few letters received between December and May were highly supportive of the proposed resolution, and all wished Salkowitz luck in passing it. The Ad Hoc Committee on Homosexuality and the Rabbinate itself was also becoming more inclined to draft a statement that embraced the recommendation of the CCAR's Committee on Justice and Peace. This trend was largely due to the forced resignation of a highly respected lesbian rabbi in Minneapolis whose sexual orientation had been made public without her permission in the spring of 1988. Some of the committee members who had previously been opposed to drafting a resolution of this sort had changed their minds. Most of the committee members sympathized with the plight of this rabbi, whom they knew personally. Many members of the committee agreed that this colleague should not have been dismissed from her pulpit purely on the basis of her sexual orientation.[33] The secular gay rights movement, in general, was also gaining momentum at this time, "pushing the debaters. . . . The rabbinical arguments the [rabbis] came up with against them looked pretty feeble."[34]

However, while the May 1988 minutes seemed to imply that the CCAR *would* bring a resolution to the June 1989 CCAR Convention, enough correspondence was received that the committee soon began to think twice. Dr. Alfred Gottschalk, president of HUC-JIR at the time, wrote Selig Salkowitz on June 17, 1988, and proposed a suggested revision to the draft statement.[35] "I realize the true difficulty of your position," stated Gottschalk, "but I strongly urge that we put forward a forthright statement without embellishment."[36] A high-ranking member from the American Jewish Committee's Office of Interreligious Affairs added on June 29, 1988, that "the statement on homosexuality is an important one and will attract a great deal of attention, both within the Conference as well as from the general community. Because of its importance, the resolution should receive enormous care and attention to nuance."[37] These letters and others made the committee pause and reconsider their actions.

At a Standstill: June 1988–1989

Unanimously, and with the concurrence of the CCAR executive board, the committee decided *not* to bring a resolution to the 1989 CCAR Convention.[38] It is unclear at exactly which point this decision took place, but the decision had obviously been made by November 15, 1988, when a committee member wrote to Selig Salkowitz. The author of the letter was one of the resolution's most ardent supporters, and she eloquently expressed her dissatisfaction with the committee's progress: "My feelings about our committee's current position are somewhat negative (albeit I support that position but only because I don't believe we can do "better" at this point—nonetheless I am saddened by that fact). I do not think my negative feelings will help start the session on a positive note.[39] Instead of bringing the resolution to the CCAR Convention, it was decided to "recommend a process of dialogue among the members of the [CCAR Convention], and a Movement-wide process of education."[40] The committee would lead a session at the CCAR Convention and provide its members with background papers and breakout sessions where CCAR members would be able to share their own personal opinions.

In his introduction to the session at the June 1989 CCAR Convention, Rabbi Salkowitz, the chair of the committee, explained the main areas of disagreement among the committee members. One, he noted, was the "nature of homosexuality": is it a personal choice, or an orientation over which a person has no control?[41] The second was halachah: how can it be interpreted? The third was the effect that a resolution would have upon gay and lesbian colleagues. The fourth was the effect it would have on congregational selection committees. The fifth was how this would affect officiation and sanctification of gay and lesbian marriages. And lastly was what the reaction would be of *K'lal Yisrael*, the larger Jewish community.[42]

By the September 1989 meeting of the committee, the members agreed that it was time for action. There was broad agreement that the committee should express strong support for gay and lesbian civil rights and ordination, but many members were still afraid of possible ramifications. "That gays can be good Jews [is obvious]. It's shameful that we haven't made a resolution,"[43] said one rabbi. The conversation moved on to clarifying the committee's goals, and it was decided that educational forums would be set up at every regional *Kallah* (i.e., the CCAR's regional conventions) in the next year in order to receive even more feedback from the members of the CCAR. In the meantime, committee members would keep working on a rubric for a draft resolution.[44]

The letters following this meeting and the regional *Kallot* describe a committee on the defensive. The backlash, and the defensiveness, continued throughout October and November, when Rabbi Alexander Schindler addressed the inclusion of gay and lesbian Jews in his

Biennial Keynote Address. Even the press got involved, as a November 1989 anonymous editorial in the magazine *Tikkun*, entitled "Gay Equality Should Not Be Delayed," delivered a scathing critique of the CCAR's decision not to resolve a formal statement.[45] Due to this negative press, perhaps it should come as no surprise that a revised draft of the "Proposed Statement on Homosexuality" was distributed to the members of the committee on November 16, 1989.[46] Changes from the committee's previous statements were minimal. This statement declared that heterosexuality was still the "Jewish ideal."[47]

Yet, the committee continued to waver. Some members could not reconcile their own personal moral beliefs with what they felt would be best for the Movement. On January 19, 1990, Salkowitz received a compilation of CCAR responses in which it was clear that a large number of CCAR members wanted a resolution in favor of ordaining gays and lesbians.[48] To the statement "HUC-JIR should ordain qualified candidates who are homosexual," forty-four rabbis voted "Strongly agree," twelve "Agree," six "Unsure," two "Disagree," and zero "Strongly Disagree."[49] Likewise, to the statement "The CCAR should take no position at this time concerning ordination of candidates who are homosexual," seventeen responses agreed or strongly agreed, five were unsure, and thirty-four disagreed or strongly disagreed.

The Resolution and Its Aftermath: 1990–2012

On June 25, 1990, the Ad Hoc Committee on Homosexuality and the Rabbinate presented its report to the CCAR's Annual Convention, which was formally adopted as a resolution on the floor of the Convention. Its pages resolved that (1) "all Jews are religiously equal regardless of their sexual orientation"[50] and as such should be integrated fully into the religious life of their community,[51] (2) HUC-JIR would not consider sexual orientation a factor in admitting possible rabbinic candidates,[52] (3) the CCAR would accept all rabbis as members and place rabbinic graduates in jobs without regard to sexual orientation, and (4) while there was "deep concern about the reaction of the other Jewish Movements," Reform Judaism in Israel, and the Reform Movement's relationships with non-Jewish groups, the decision on homosexual ordination "had to make its decision independent of [those] consideration[s]."[53] While a minority report was filed, the majority of the committee still affirmed that "heterosexual, monogamous, procreative marriage is the ideal human relationship . . . [and] heterosexuality is the only appropriate Jewish choice for fulfilling one's covenantal obligations."[54]

While it is beyond the purview of this essay to delve into the various responses received by the CCAR after the adoption of the resolution, suffice it to say that many, many letters were written to Selig Salkowitz and other members of the committee, both ecstatic and enraged. The reactions of the various Jewish Movements were also as the committee had predicted. The Reconstructionist Movement was supportive, and the Conservative Movement took no official stance.[55] The Israeli Progressive Movement agreed with the resolution's stance on ordaining gay and lesbian rabbis, albeit with the caveat that "homosexuality [is] an exceptional phenomenon, which we cannot accept as a norm equivalent to heterosexuality."[56] Unsurprisingly, most of the Orthodox Movement considered the CCAR's resolution to be an affront to halachah.[57]

In 1991, the National Federation of Temple Youth, National Association of Temple Educators, the Women of Reform Judaism, and the American Conference of Cantors all adopted similar resolutions endorsing the principle that openly gay and lesbian individuals should be accepted as bona fide members of their organizations.[58] Numerous resolutions and responsa on gay and lesbian marriage followed in the 1990s,[59] and in 2000 the CCAR resolved that it was acceptable for a rabbi to officiate at a same-gender marriage.[60] The Union for Reform Judaism followed the CCAR's lead and has since published not one, but two editions of its groundbreaking sourcebook *Kulanu: All of Us*, providing program and informational material on how to best integrate gay, lesbian, and transgender rabbis and congregants into mainstream congregations.[61] HUC-JIR offers classes on LGBTQ issues and hosts both the Institute for Judaism, Sexual Orientation, and Gender Identity, as well as the Jeff Herman Virtual Resource Center for Sexual Orientation Issues in the Jewish Community.

All of these resolutions and changing attitudes in the Reform Movement are a reflection of the hard work and dedication of the members of the Ad Hoc Committee on Homosexuality and the Rabbinate, as well as many other activists who preceded them. When Selig Salkowitz called the first meeting to order in 1986, the issue of whether or not to ordain gay and lesbian rabbis was not predetermined. "Some members of the Committee changed their views (or overcame their fears) as a result of letters [they] received. Others . . . held out views on principled grounds not on the basis of public opinion."[62]

By the time the final resolution had been adopted by the CCAR four years later, however, multiple letters from rabbinic leadership, convincing moral arguments, and the personal testimonies of those who had been directly affected by the pain of bigotry and prejudice had convinced all on the committee that the values of justice and Jewish ethics demanded that gays and lesbians be included in all aspects of the Reform Jewish community, including the right to become a rabbi. Members of this committee acknowledged their fears and doubts, but they did not bow to them completely. They brought the debate to the CCAR so that the membership would be able to discuss the issue in depth before making a final decision. Ultimately, the committee's deliberations and discussions played a central role in Reform Judaism's decision to openly embrace gays and lesbians as full-fledged members of its religious community.

NOTES

1. I would like to take this opportunity to thank Dr. Joel Kushner, director of the Institute for Judaism and Sexual Orientation at Hebrew Union College–Jewish Institute of Religion (HUC-JIR), for initiating publication of this paper. Dr. Dana Herman has been an editor extraordinaire, and Mr. Kevin Proffitt and the archival staff of the Jacob Rader Marcus Center of the American Jewish Archives (hereafter AJA) have been helpful

beyond measure. Finally, Dr. Gary P. Zola, executive director of the AJA and professor of the American Jewish Experience at HUC-JIR in Cincinnati, has not only lifted restrictions and granted me access to private committee files, but has been both cheerleader and friend. Without his help, this project would never have come to fruition.

Unless otherwise indicated, all archival material cited is from the AJA in Cincinnati, Ohio. All resolutions are found in *Kulanu: All of Us; A Program and Resource Guide for Gay, Lesbian, Bisexual, and Transgender Inclusion*, edited by Richard F. Address, Joel L. Kushner, and Geoffrey Mitelman (New York: URJ Press, 2007).

2. Interview with committee member, May 11, 2012; MS 725, box 4, folder 8.

3. "Resolution Adopted by the Central Conference of American Rabbis 88th Annual Convention, 1977: Rights of Homosexuals," *Kulanu*, 251.

4. Ibid.

5. Sue Levi Elwell, "The Lesbian and Gay Movement: Jewish Community Responses," in *Twice Blessed: Lesbian, Gay and Jewish*, ed. Christie Balka and Andy Rose (Boston: Beacon Press, 1989), 230.

6. Ibid.

7. Margaret Wenig and Margaret Holub, "Draft Resolution on Gay and Lesbian Rabbis," February 1986; MS 725, box 3, folder 2.

8. Interview with committee member, May 11, 2012. MS 725, box 4, folder 8.

9. Ibid.

10. Letter dated November 12, 1986; MS 725, box 3, folder 2.

11. In his letter to members on the Ad Hoc Committee on Homosexuality and the Rabbinate prior to the meeting, Salkowitz writes that a "second meeting, *if necessary*, would be held in late February or early March"; September 16, 1986; MS 725, box 3, folder 2.

12. Letter from Yoel H. Kahn to Selig Salkowitz, asking that he pass it on to CCAR members, December 17, 1986; MS 725, box 3, folder 2.

13. Letter from anonymous author to Margaret Wenig, January 27, 1987; MS 725, box 3, folder 3.

14. Letter from anonymous author to Joseph Levine, February 2, 1987; MS 725, box 3, folder 3.

15. Ibid.

16. Ibid.

17. Quotation from *CCAR Yearbook* 92 (1981): 71, as cited in letter to Joseph Levine, February 18, 1987; MS 725, box 3, folder 3.

18. Ibid.

19. "Minutes on Meeting of Ad Hoc Committee on Homosexuality, March 3–4, 1987, New York, New York," 1–2; MS 725, box 3, folder 1.

20. "Report of the Committee on Homosexuality in the Rabbinate," 1987; MS 725, box 3, folder 4.

21. CCAR, "Minutes on Meeting of Ad Hoc Committee on Homosexuality, March 4–5, 1987, New York, NY," 1–2; MS 725, box 3, folder 1.

22. Ibid., 3.

23. See article clippings in MS 725, box 3, folder 3 and box 4, folder 1.

24. Ibid., 4–8.

25. "Report of the Committee on Homosexuality in the Rabbinate," 1987; MS 725, box 3, folder 4.

26. For example, "[Rabbi A] opposes ordaining gays and lesbians as rabbis. [Rabbi B] is more ambiguous, distinguishing between responsible and irresponsible sexual relationships," December 2–3, 1987, Meeting of Committee on Homosexuality and the Rabbinate," MS 725, box 3, folder 1.

27. Ibid., 3.

28. Ibid., 13.

29. Ibid., 22.

30. "Draft Statement of the Ad Hoc Committee on Homosexuality, CCAR."

31. Ibid.

32. Letter to Selig Salkowitz from Randall M. Falk, April 22, 1988; MS 725, box 3, folder 5.

33. Interview with committee member, May 11, 2012; MS 725, box 4, folder 8.

34. Interview with committee member, May 23, 2012; MS 725, box 4, folder 8.

35. Letter from Alfred Gottschalk to Selig Salkowitz, June 17, 1988; MS 725, box 3, folder 5.

36. Ibid.

37. Letter to Peter Knobel, June 29, 1988; MS 725, box 3, folder 5.

38. Letter from Selig Salkowitz to members of the Ad Hoc Committee, February 1, 1989; MS 725, box 4, folder 1.

39. Letter to Selig Salkowitz, November 15, 1988; MS 725, box 3, folder 5.

40. Letter from Selig Salkowitz to members of the Ad Hoc Committee, February 1, 1989; MS 725, box 4, folder 1.

41. "Homosexuality and the Rabbinate: Introduction," undated; MS 725, box 4, folder 2.

42. Ibid., 2–3.

43. Notes of the Meeting of the Ad Hoc Committee, September 5, 1989, p. 5; MS 725, box 4, folder 1.

44. Ibid., 6–10.

45. Anonymous, "Gay Equality Should Not Be Delayed," *Tikkun* 4, no. 6 (November 1989): 8–9.

46. "Proposed Statement on Homosexuality," November 16, 1989; MS 725, box 4, folder 2.

47. Ibid.

48. "PARR Survey on Issues Relating to Homosexuality and the Rabbinate," January 19, 1990, enclosed in a letter from Richard A. Block to Selig Salkowitz; MS 725, box 4, folder 3.

49. Ibid.

50. "Report of the Ad Hoc Committee on Homosexuality and the Rabbinate of the CCAR Annual Convention," June 1990; MS 725, box 4, folder 6.

51. Ibid.

52. Ibid.

53. Ibid.

54. Ibid.

55. See various letters and news clippings in MS 725, box 4, folder 8.

56. "Judaism and Sexuality: Position Paper Presented by the Israeli Council of Progressive Rabbis to the 1990 Convention of the CCAR," MS 725, box 4, folder 3.

57. See various letters and news clippings in MS 725, box 4, folder 8.

58. See "Resolution Adopted by the National Federation of Temple Youth, 1991: Homosexuality," *Kulanu*, 265; "Resolution Adopted by the National Association of Temple Educators, 1991," *Kulanu*, 267; "Resolution Adopted by the Women of Reform Judaism National Federation of Temple Sisterhoods 38th Biennial Assembly, 1991," *Kulanu*, 269; "Statement Adopted by the Convention of the American Conference of Cantors: Homosexuality in the Cantorate, 1991," *Kulanu*, 273.

59. See "Resolution Adopted by the 62nd General Assembly of the Union of American Hebrew Congregations Biennial, 1993: Recognition for Lesbian and Gay Partnerships," *Kulanu*, 281; "Resolution Adopted by the Central Conference of American Rabbis 107th Annual Convention, 1996: Gay and Lesbian Marriage," *Kulanu*, 289; "CCAR Responsum on Homosexual Marriage (1996)," *Kulanu*, 301; "Resolution Adopted by the 64th General Assembly of the Union of American Hebrew Congregations Biennial, 1997: Civil Marriage for Gay and Lesbian Jewish Couples," *Kulanu*, 327; etc.

60. "Resolution Adopted by the Central Conference of American Rabbis 111th Annual Convention, 2000: Same-Gender Officiation," *Kulanu*, 329.

61. Richard F. Address, Joel L. Kushner, and Geoffrey Mitelman, eds., *Kulanu: All of Us; A Program and Resource Guide for Gay, Lesbian, Bisexual, and Transgender Inclusion* (New York: URJ Press, 1998 and 2007).

62. Interview with committee member, May 11, 2012; MS 725, box 4, folder 8.

21

ASSESSING LESBIAN, GAY, BISEXUAL, AND TRANSGENDER INCLUSION IN THE REFORM MOVEMENT

A Promise Fulfilled or a Promise in Progress?

JOEL L. KUSHNER, PSYD

At the 2011 URJ Biennial, there were multiple cheers and ovations during the tribute to the legal team of David Boies and Ted Olson. They received the Maurice N. Eisendrath Bearer of Light Award for their arguments that led a U.S. district court chief judge to declare a ballot initiative that had made same-sex marriage illegal in California (Proposition 8), to be unconstitutional.[1] When President Barack Obama addressed that same Biennial, each time he mentioned a justice issue like repealing DADT (Don't Ask, Don't Tell) or promoting the dignity of all people including gays and lesbians, there were loud cheers and a standing ovation from the audience of over six thousand people.

Are these examples the culmination of the inclusive promise that started when five gay and lesbian Jews gathered in the basement of a gay Christian church in 1972 and decided they wanted their own Jewish congregation and to ultimately be part of the Reform Movement? Could those five Jews who founded Beth Chayim Chadashim, the first gay and lesbian congregation in the world and admitted into the Union of American Hebrew Congregations (now the Union for

Reform Judaism) in 1974, ever have imagined a Biennial where support for their rights would be celebrated in such a way? In 2014, has the Reform Movement fully embraced its lesbian, gay, bisexual, and transgender (LGBT) members? Many would say yes and wonder why we still need to talk about these issues. For eight years, as the founding director of an institute on Judaism, sexual orientation, and gender identity, I have had the honor to be part of many aspects of progress on LGBT issues in Reform Judaism. I have also experienced a significant lack of cultural competence in regard to the ongoing daily work of fostering full LGBT inclusion within the Movement. This chapter will address these questions and describe a continuum model to help understand attitudes around inclusion in both individuals and organizations.

The modern history of lesbian, gay, bisexual, and transgender Jews in Reform Judaism has been one of progress over time. There have been many achievements to be proud of, and these successes have been documented in a variety of sources. In 1987 and 1989, the UAHC affirmed resolutions on the full inclusion of gay and lesbian people in the Jewish community. Aaron Cooper (1989) wrote about the successful growth of "congregations with special outreach to lesbian and gay Jews," the progressively larger national and international gay and lesbian Jewish conferences, and the overall slow but growing acceptance of gays and lesbians in the larger Jewish world.[2] In 1990, the Hebrew Union College–Jewish Institute of Religion (HUC-JIR), the Movement's seminary, officially changed its admissions policy so that sexual orientation would no longer be a criterion used to rule out candidates. In 1996, UAHC Press published *Kulanu (All of Us): A Program for Congregations Implementing Gay and Lesbian Inclusion*, to assist its member congregations with specific materials to increase the acceptance and inclusion of gay and lesbian Jews.

In 2000, following several years of a study and review process, the Central Conference of American Rabbis (CCAR) passed a resolution that acknowledged that there is holiness in the relationship between two people of the same gender that is worthy of recognition and that Reform rabbis could choose to conduct or not to conduct marriage ceremonies for same-sex couples.³ Soon after, the CCAR created two officially sanctioned ceremonies—one that was *kiddushin* and one that was a blessing ceremony. Rabbi Denise L. Eger (2001), in "Embracing Lesbians and Gay Men: A Reform Jewish Innovation,"⁴ chronicled the lengthy process that led to the CCAR decision on homosexuality and marriage as well as the path to admitting gay and lesbian students to HUC-JIR (see also chapter 20 in this volume, for an in-depth discussion of the CCAR Ad Hoc Committee on Homosexuality and the Rabbinate). In 2003, the Commission on Social Action of Reform Judaism built on the 1987 and 1989 inclusion resolutions for gays and lesbians, declaring support for the resolution "Inclusion and Acceptance of the Transgender and Bisexual Communities." Later that year, HUC-JIR admitted the first openly transgender rabbinical student. In recent years, LGBT issues have continued to become increasingly mainstream, as seen in a 2009 *Jewish Daily Forward* article by Jay Michaelson entitled "Why Straight People Go to Gay Synagogues—and What We Can Learn from Them."⁵

These achievements represent genuine progress. From this perspective, the state of affairs of LGBT issues in Reform Judaism looks very positive and one that Reform Jews should rightfully celebrate. There has been significant progress and action in the three entities (the URJ, the CCAR, and HUC-JIR) that make up the Reform Movement that have opened up the Movement to LGBT Jews. There has also been rich work in synagogues across the country so that in 2014, LGBT Jews have many more options to find a Jewish home compared to 1972, when the only place they were fully welcomed was a church basement.

Yet there is a concurrent reality in the Reform Movement that reflects the challenges around LGBT inclusion that have been present in our history and, this chapter argues, still exist today. In 2014, while there is much less overt hostility to LGBT issues in our Movement, there is still a significant lack of knowledge around what would be called cultural competence on LGBT issues and how to create inclusive spaces. The concept of cultural competence has been developing for over twenty-five years in the fields of psychology and health care to help practitioners and organizations effectively meet the needs of underserved populations. Being culturally competent in a particular field or with a population means that first, a person or organization has an awareness of their own cultural values and biases toward the targeted group. Once they have that personal awareness and insight into their own attitudes and beliefs toward the group, then they are able to develop an awareness of the targeted group's culture in terms of knowledge of it and the skills needed to work with the population. By mastering these aspects, practitioners and organizations are finally able to develop culturally appropriate intervention strategies that match the needs of the targeted population.

While the overall desire for LGBT inclusion has risen, this chapter proposes that there is now also a wide gap between the desire to be inclusive and taking the everyday actions that are required to manifest that stated desire. It is the underlying attitudes of individuals and the climate of our institutions that have slowed the progress toward full inclusion that previously helped achieve the milestones of seminary admission for gays and lesbians and recognition of same-sex marriage. The idea that as a Movement, we may not be doing as well as we think in terms of LGBT inclusion can be hard to accept, since it challenges a liberal view that many Reform Jews have about themselves and the Movement. Through my experiences training students at HUC-JIR, conducting workshops, lecturing, and consulting around the country, I find that discussing ongoing barriers to LGBT inclusion in many synagogues and organizations often leads to some of the following responses: "Wait, there are gay and lesbian rabbis everywhere." "But we have a gay (fill-in) 'cantor/rabbi/educator' in our congregation." "How can you say we don't support LGBT people? We welcome everyone." Or, "Our rabbi will marry gay people. What more do you want?" When I have probed these statements, I find an underlying perception that the important battles have all been won and things are now fine for LGBT people.

Understanding Climate and Attitude
toward Inclusion in Organizations and People

The climate (in organizations) or attitude (in individuals) toward LGBT inclusion can be mapped on a continuum that contains five points: hostile, indifferent, tolerant, inclusive, and embracing. The Institute for Judaism, Sexual Orientation, and Gender Identity uses a visual illustration (simplified in Figure 1) to help organizations and people recognize where they fall on the continuum, to concretize behaviors that may or may not have been in their awareness, and to provide a guide to future transformation. Research from the field of multicultural organizational development has also provided corresponding action responses to the stages of the continuum.[6]

An organization with a hostile climate is by its nature opposed to homosexuality and is an inhospitable environment for LGBT people. This is usually based on biblical or halachic reasons. A hostile organization may passively or actively oppose anything to do with homosexuality. This may include preaching that homosexuality and homosexuals are an abomination, comparing gay people to animals, and advocating that gay and lesbian people should undergo therapy to change their sexual orientation. An Orthodox organization could oppose homosexuality on halachic grounds but not necessarily maintain a hostile

Hostile	(Oppressing; Denying/Ignoring)
Indifferent	(Denying/Ignoring; Recognizing/Not Acting)
Tolerant	(Recognizing/Not Acting; Educating Self; Recognizing/Acting)
Inclusive	(Educating Self; Recognizing/Acting; Educating Others; Supporting/Encouraging; Initiating/Preventing)
Embracing	(Passionate Supporting/Encouraging; Initiating/Preventing; Championing)

Figure 1. A Climate/Attitude Continuum on Inclusion with Action Responses

climate. Rather, its climate might be indifferent, leading to a sort of "don't ask, don't tell" policy. It might even rise to the level of a tolerant climate within the context of its own community, although this would not hold the same definition as a tolerant or inclusive climate in a Reform organization.

An organization with an indifferent climate is uninterested in the issue either intentionally or due to unawareness resulting from a lack of exposure to or education around issues of sexuality and discrimination. An indifferent climate could also be based on the prejudice of individuals who comprise its members. Individual responses sometimes heard in an indifferent environment include the following: "There aren't any gay kids/families/adults in our congregation, so why would we need to do education?" "Why should we provide special treatment for gay people? Life is hard for everyone." "All kids get bullied; let's do something for everyone." "Things are not really so bad for gay people . . ."

In organizations with a tolerant climate, there may have been some training or discussion about LGBT issues. There is an awareness of the presence of LGBT youth and families, and there can be very positive intentions toward responding to the needs of congregants who are LGBT. Yet, LGBT issues remain a low priority compared to the long list of other issues that preoccupy a synagogue. When pushed to taking more active steps to welcome LGBT people, one hears statements like these: "We welcome everyone, why should we still be talking about this?" "Why do we have to spell it out?" "Everyone is free to worship here, but we don't do targeted outreach." "We're all diverse, we're all different. We all come from a variety of different places. I don't think everyone needs to be subdivided. I think we should be unifying more."

In the tolerant environment, LGBT people can be present but are explicitly or implicitly told not make requests for services or interventions that would help them feel more welcomed in the community. The underlying message is "You can be here, but don't ask for anything more or ask for special treatment." Tolerant organizations sometimes also have double standards in terms of behavior, so that while gay people are "welcome," there can be concerns that they may be too publicly affectionate, that is, hold hands or kiss in the synagogue or in front of children, which leads to discomfort and questions like "How will we explain that to the children?" These concerns coexist with the belief that the organization welcomes everyone equally. Holding two dissonant belief systems is difficult, but it can also lead to growth. When an individual or organization is open to new information and can confront the inequity of their views, they have the potential to move to the next level on the continuum.

After the tolerant climate comes the inclusive climate, and these two stages are often conflated. Using an analogy to help separate them, voting to *not* take away someone else's rights, as in the 78 percent of Jewish Californians who voted against the ballot initiative to make same-sex marriage illegal,[7] is being tolerant. Actively working to defeat that initiative because you want to welcome and support the population it targets is being inclusive. Many Jews and their synagogues volunteered to actively fight against this ballot initiative (being inclusive), but this number is far less than the 78 percent of Jews who simply voted against it (being tolerant).

The inclusive and embracing states sit at the right end of the continuum. When I first put the model together, I was trying to capture a broad range of experiences, and it was based on personal experience and theory. At that time, I saw the final category of embracing as an aspirational stage where all aspects of difference are recognized and celebrated, and it is no longer necessary to do targeted work for a specific group to provide them with the same welcome and inclusiveness that is enjoyed by the mainstream, because all issues are now celebrated equally. Later, based on a field research project that a colleague and I conducted, from looking at survey data, we found that the two stages are related in practice but are differentiated by degree of intensity. An environment with an inclusive climate actively seeks out ways to redress past inequities and make efforts to welcome the previously disenfranchised group. It understands that to create a level playing field, a commitment to education and ongoing work must exist to achieve a space where all people are truly welcomed and can feel at home. The final stage of embracing includes the actions of the inclusive climate but with a higher intensity. There is the belief that the organization actively needs to value the presence and gifts of the population that it is trying to reach. Individuals in the embracing organization are doing the work not just because it will benefit the targeted group but because they believe that having that group as part of the community is essential for everyone in the organization in order for it to be whole, successful, vibrant, and sacred, in terms of a religious community.

Actualizing inclusion is complex work and entails evaluating and addressing multiple levels of an organization's structures, policies, and procedures in terms of what I call the *tachlis* of inclusion—content, language, visibility, and training regarding LGBT issues. These four factors and their presence or absence are tools by which to measure welcoming and inclusion in an environment, and I use them extensively as a training rubric when I consult with organizations. People and organizations are complex and so may contain aspects of more than one attitude/climate on the continuum depending on their own awareness, stage of development, and interest in becoming more welcoming. Some organizations and individuals are comfortable where they are, and it may take significant ongoing effort or sometimes a tragedy to move them forward. Hopefully, like Dr. Martin Luther King's metaphoric arc that bends toward justice, an individual or organization experiencing the constraints and potential harmful effects of their attitude or climate will find opportunities for change and be able to progress to a more evolved point on the continuum.

Research on LGBT Inclusion in Jewish Communities

In their study *We Are You: An Exploration of Lesbian, Gay, Bisexual, and Transgender Issues in Colorado's Jewish Community*, Dr. Caryn Aviv, Gregg Drinkwater, and Dr. David Shneer (2006) conducted a needs assessment using fifty-three face-to-face interviews with Jewish communal professionals and Jewish LGBT individuals. They developed a four-part typology of organizations, similar to the continuum that has already been discussed, which moves from unwelcoming to invisible to tolerant to inclusive. In one finding, they concluded that the professional staff at thirty-four Denver and Boulder organizations generally perceived their organizations to be more welcoming than did the LGBT Jews who either worked in those organizations or utilized their services. Their report found that "in order to make the Jewish community more inclusive, LGBT Jews need to be asked to walk through the open and welcoming doors of community organizations. It is not enough for the Jewish community to expect LGBT Jews themselves to gather up the courage and seek out organizations to meet their needs. It is the task of the professional and lay leadership of the Jewish community to promote structural change by pro-actively and repeatedly inviting LGBT Jews to participate as full and welcomed members of the community."[8] Looking at the thirty-four organizations in the study, the authors also saw great potential for institutional transformation in those that were identified as tolerant organizations.

The Institute for Judaism, Sexual Orientation, and Gender Identity, in conjunction with Jewish Mosaic, commissioned a study for their Welcoming Synagogues Project to explore issues of LGBT inclusion in synagogues of all denominations.[9] Seventy-three percent of all rabbis thought their congregations did a good or excellent job welcoming gays and lesbians. However, when asked what they were actually doing, only 33 percent of all rabbis reported that their congregations had held programs or events related to gay and lesbian people. Content that is related to and of interest to LGBT people has been shown to be one measure of a welcoming and inclusive community of faith.[10] With this finding, the study revealed a large gap between the belief and intention by clergy that their synagogue is welcoming to gay and lesbian Jews and the degree to which the synagogue actually offers programs or services related to that population. While content is only one of the four principles under the *tachlis* of inclusion rubric that the Institute for Judaism, Sexual Orientation, and Gender Identity uses for its trainings, this finding, taken with the work by Aviv, Drinkwater, and

Shneer, suggests that these gaps are crucial to explore so as to better understand their meaning and effect on LGBT inclusion.

Case Studies

The following case examples illustrate different climates and attitudes in organizations and people. A basic assumption is that individuals and organizations can have a sincere intention to be inclusive but can fall short of that goal for a variety of reasons. It is essential to remember that as human beings, we are all subject to blind spots that may prevent us from living up to our highest aspirations. The purpose of sharing these cases is not to find fault but rather to try to understand unexamined forces or behaviors that can be difficult to identify and yet may be preventing movement to greater inclusiveness. If these issues are not examined due to the potential discomfort their examination may cause, then we as individuals may unwittingly collude with factors that ultimately perpetrate oppression rather than repair its damage.

Adrienne Rich eloquently wrote about the impact that can result from a lack of inclusiveness: "When those who have power to name and to socially construct reality choose not to see you or hear you . . . when someone with the authority of a teacher, say, describes the world and you are not in it, there is a moment of psychic disequilibrium, as if you looked into a mirror and saw nothing."[11] According to the minority stress model of health, being ignored and not seen for who you are, in conjunction with the daily microaggressions that minority people experience, can cause long-lasting damage to an individual.[12] The indifferent and tolerant climates both contain elements that erase or diminish LGBT presence and contribute to these types of injuries.

A Transgender Student in Rabbinical School (2003–2010)

In March 2003, HUC-JIR admitted the first openly transgender applicant, Reuben Zellman, into its rabbinic program. It was a progressive and groundbreaking event, and Rabbi Roxanne Schneider Shapiro, the national director of admissions and recruitment at the time, was quoted in several articles praising his qualifications.[13] Nine years later, when asked about the now-ordained Rabbi Zellman, she said, "Reuben was a fantastic candidate. I still remember him after the hundreds of students whom I saw while I was in admissions. . . . There were people on the committee who needed to be educated—but after meeting him, people were so impressed. I would put him as one of the top candidates in five years of doing interviews—his answers and responses—it was because of who he was, not about being transgender."[14]

Rabbi Schneider Shapiro explained that she had gained an education on sexual and gender identity issues as part of a pastoral internship in a university setting while still a rabbinical student in Cincinnati, so from the beginning the issue of gender identity was not strange or scary for her. She saw Zellman as another applicant and not as a transgender applicant. When asked whether there was any consideration to provide training to prepare faculty and students in New York, Rabbi Shapiro said, "No, but there were people who asked that question. I was asked to make sure that he was an appropriate candidate for admission . . . that he had the potential to be successful as a student and ultimately as a rabbi in his rabbinate . . . that if we thought the student is prepared for admission, then faculty would deal. We did think that the LA faculty would deal the best . . . that the LA community could handle it. But no one brought up concerns about other students."

In February 2002, a year prior to Zellman's admission and totally unconnected to it, Rabbi Margaret Wenig had organized what may have been the first seminar on medicine, law, and transgender and intersex issues in any Jewish seminary. The panel included two rabbis, a Jew who had transitioned, and Paisley Currah, PhD, a scholar in the field. Attendance at the seminar was mandatory for all students on the New York campus. For the seminar, Wenig compiled an extensive reader and bibliography on gender identity, which was also added to the New York HUC-JIR library. As Wenig described the seminar, "It blew people's minds. No one or practically no one in attendance had ever thought about these issues before."[15] Several faculty members were present and one of them, Rabbi Carole Balin, developed a class unit on transgender issues that she used for several years. Aside from the seminar in 2002 and Rabbi Balin's class, there were no trainings or workshops for HUC-JIR faculty, students, or staff in preparation for Zellman's arrival that might have addressed understanding of transgender issues or facilitated the development of cultural competence in this area. This sits in contrast to the long deliberations in the 1980s and 1990s around homosexuality and gays and lesbians in the Movement, where members of HUC-JIR, the URJ, and the CCAR all had many opportunities for education and study on that topic.[16]

Being culturally competent in a particular domain means understanding the needs of that domain. People who are transgender frequently encounter problems accessing health care, since their physical bodies do not always match their legal gender. This can result in insurance carriers denying gynecological services to transmen as well as prostate care for transwomen.[17] It also translates into difficulty for people who are transgender to find qualified health-care providers to meet their basic medical needs. Masen Davis, the executive director of the Transgender Law Center and a transman, tells a story about seeking health care for himself. While searching for treatment for bronchitis in a major metropolitan city, the first two clinics that he was sent to under his health plan told him that they could not provide treatment for him because they did not know anything about transgender health care. Finally, a third facility agreed to treat his bronchitis, but when he asked if they could also prescribe his hormone medication, they declined. Instead, he was given a business card and told to seek a referral from the individual on the card. Unfortunately, it was his own business card.

In 2000, the Religious Society of Friends (Quakers) was faced with a transgender staff person who had been denied benefits by their health-care contract. A committee of the denomination began a two-and-a-half-year process to address transgender health care. In 2003, this resulted in the denomination adding trans-inclusive health benefits, including the provision of hormones and surgery coverage.[18] In contrast, it does not appear that HUC-JIR ever considered the health-care implications of their admission of a transgender student. Minimally, this might have included conferring with their health-care insurance carrier to ensure smooth service for all students, including those who may be transgender, and in an inclusive or embracing environment, HUC-JIR might have taken the path of the Religious Society of Friends to develop a fully inclusive transgender heath-care policy.

Discussing their extension of transgender health-care coverage, a Brown University official said that "students had been asking about it, so we'd been looking at it for a couple of years, whether our health plan was in line with our nondiscrimination policy."[19] Following that connection between a health-care plan and an institution's nondiscrimination policy, at the time Zellman was admitted in 2003, HUC-JIR's nondiscrimination policy did not include gender identity and gender expression as a covered category. This would mean that he would not have been legally protected had an issue arisen. Seven years later, Zellman was ordained in May 2010. In October of that year, the HUC-JIR Board of Governors approved the addition of the terms "gender identity and gender expression" into its nondiscrimination policy.[20] Two years later, in December 2012, HUC-JIR added the policy to its website and to its revised employee handbook. Since Zellman, other students who are transgender have considered application to the rabbinical school or have applied, but none have matriculated, and the health-care plan remains unchanged.

Reform Judaism Magazine: "Behind Bullying" (Winter 2010)

Journalists began to write about a sudden rash of gay teen suicides in the summer of 2010. In July, there were three suicides in Utah and then another ten across the country in September. Perhaps the most publicized case was that of Tyler Clementi, a Rutgers University student who jumped off the George Washington Bridge after being secretly filmed by his roommate while being intimate with another man. In reality, there had been no actual rise in the incidence of gay teens committing suicide. The media had merely turned a spotlight onto an issue that had long existed but had been relatively ignored by the mainstream media. For better and for worse, under the media attention, it became a newly discovered tragic phenomenon. Two weeks after Clementi's suicide, the *It Gets Better Project* video project was launched by Dan Savage, an author and LGBT activist, and it quickly had thousands of entries and millions of views. On October 21, 2010, President Barack Obama contributed a video voicing his hope for kids who are bullied, and for several months, there were scores of articles in the media about gay teen suicide as well as on bullying and harassment.[21]

In November 2010, the winter edition of *Reform Judaism* magazine came out with a striking black cover that read "Behind Bullying." The cover story was titled "Behind Bullying: Why Some Adults Act Aggressively toward Others—and What to Do When You Think It's Happening to You." The magazine also included a question-and-answer article titled "When Jack Pushed Jill Down the Hill: Helping Kids—From Tots to Teens—Handle Bullying Behavior." In the two articles, there was no mention of the media storm on gay teen suicide, nor was there a single mention of the bullying of lesbian, gay, bisexual, and transgender youth or adults.

How can this situation be understood in terms of the climate continuum? It is unlikely that this could have occurred in an inclusive or embracing environment. To someone with cultural competence in LGBT issues, the absence of any reference to LGBT youth and bullying and the recent suicides would have been evident and quite troubling. More likely, this speaks to an indifferent or tolerant climate, which, as mentioned in figure 1, includes the action responses of "recognizing but not acting." In these possible climates, there is not necessarily any malice, but rather a lack of interest or perhaps knowledge about LGBT youth, who face higher rates of bullying and whose attempted suicide rate is more than triple that of heterosexual youth. In an environment with these possible climates, the *Reform Judaism* magazine edition on bullying simply took a different path that did not include LGBT issues. On a macro level in recent years, the Reform Movement's climate has run between tolerant and inclusive, so while this case example is surprising, in fact it speaks to the reality of the work that still needs to be done.

Conclusion

In my personal experience of working in the Jewish community, I have seen all types of communities from hostile to embracing. Yet overall, I have encountered far more tolerant communities than inclusive ones. Further, the tolerant climate/attitude in these environments is characterized by a complacency that is difficult, although not impossible, to break through. It feels as if the overall rise of acceptance and tolerance over hostility and indifference, which is real progress, has also led to a plateau for many individuals and organizations. Here, it is easier believe that the work is done, rather than to expend the considerable energy needed to fight for issues that are more nuanced and complicated to resolve. Advances do continue, like the 2007 revision of URJ Press's *Kulanu* into a book that is fully LGBT inclusive. Youth work in NFTY on LGBT issues has taken a strong hold, and there are important beacons of inclusion work in congregations as well as in organizations like the Religious Action Center, which has supported LGBT justice issues like the Employment Non-Discrimination Act (ENDA) and DADT. This progress cannot be overlooked. However, it is also significant that the kind of intra-denominational and semi-autonomous welcoming organizations that have existed for over twenty years in multiple Christian denominations to specifically support congregations to become more LGBT-inclusive do not exist in Judaism. No Jewish denomination, including Reform, has such a program to assist with increasing LGBT inclusion in congregations, and the absence of such a program fits within a predominantly tolerant climate and not one that is fully inclusive.

Despite acknowledged support for the idea of LGBT inclusion by all three bodies that compose the Reform Movement, the actualization of it has become much more complicated. The decision of whether to admit gay and lesbian students to seminary or whether to marry same-sex couples was ultimately a yes-or-no question. The long-term process of inclusion and changing organizational cultures does not operate on that paradigm. Embodied values cannot exist without daily implementation and practice, and this takes a huge commitment of energy. Organizations and people often fail to realize how difficult it is to restore a level playing field for a population that has such an extended history of experiencing discrimination. To ensure the same rights, access, and respect as the mainstream, deep reparative work needs to occur to dispel bias and fear and to redress inequalities in areas like education, health care, language/communication, and worship/ritual. Research has not yet provided all the reasons why some people hold an indifferent or tolerant attitude. While some activists might ascribe it to prejudice or discrimination or bias, the answers remain more complex than that. Similarly, explanations from the mainstream that attribute the problem to questions of limited resources, not enough time, or competing priorities are also missing the complexity of the multifaceted forces at play.

The issue of LGBT inclusion was ignited when those five gay and lesbian Jews gathered in the basement of a gay church and decided that they wanted their own Jewish congregation and to be part of the larger Movement of Reform Judaism. They had a vision that has now spread to the entire Movement and is still calling us. As stated in its resolutions and responsa, the Reform Movement affirms the inclusion of lesbians, gays, bisexuals, and transgender people in the world and in our synagogue communities. This has resulted in policy changes and vibrant work in many synagogues today to create inclusive environments. As director of an institute on Judaism, sexual orientation, and gender identity, I have spent eight years identifying, supporting, and fostering this work to spread best practices throughout our seminary and the denomination. The inclusion continuum is a tool that can start a process of self-assessment by individuals and organizations that desire to become more welcoming to LGBT people. Examining issues around cultural competence can help an organization understand both conscious and unconscious processes that impact their efforts to foster more inclusive and embracing attitudes and climates. Prejudice and even hatred toward the LGBT community exists. It is also true that well-intentioned people may lack the necessary knowledge to implement the positive change they want to create. Yet with reflection and insight into themselves and their community on discrepancies between intent, action, and the true meaning of inclusion, growth is possible. May a growing commitment to understanding the complexity of all of these factors help move the Reform Movement forward toward a full embrace of LGBT people in our Jewish community.

NOTES

1. Union for Reform Judaism, "2011 Biennial Featured Speakers," http://urj. org/biennial11/speakers/; Jessie McKinley, "Two Ideological Foes Unite to Overturn Proposition 8," *New York Times*, January 10, 2010, http://www.nytimes. com/2010/01/11/us/11prop8.html.

2. Aaron Cooper, "No Longer Invisible: Gay and Lesbian Jews Build a Movement," in *Homosexuality and Religion*, ed. Richard Hasbany (Binghamton, NY: Harrington Park Press,1989), 83-94.

3. Resolution on Same Gender Officiation, http://ccarnet.org/rabbis-speak/ resolutions/2000/same-gender-officiation/.

4. Denise L. Eger, "Embracing Lesbians and Gay Men: A Reform Jewish Innovation," in *Contemporary Debates in American Reform Judaism*, ed. Dana Evan Kaplan (New York: Routledge, 2001), 180–92.

5. Jay Michaelson, "Why Straight People Go to Gay Synagogues—and What We Can Learn from Them," *Jewish Daily Forward*, June 3, 2009, http://forward.com/ articles/107069/why-straight-people-go-to-gay-synagogues/.

6. Bailey Jackson and Rita Hardiman, "Multicultural Organization Development," in *The Promise of Diversity: Over 40 Voices Discuss Strategies for Eliminating Discrimination in Organizations*, ed. E. Y. Cross, J. H. Katz, F. A. Miller, and E. W. Seashore (Arlington, VA: NTL Institute, 1994); Bailey Jackson and Evangelina Holvino, *Multicultural Organization Development* (Ann Arbor: University of Michigan, 1988).

7. Shelby Grad, "L.A. Jews Overwhelmingly Opposed Prop. 8, Exit Poll Finds," *Los Angeles Times*, November 8, 2008, http://latimesblogs.latimes.com/ lanow/2008/11/la-jews-overwhe.html.

8. Caryn Aviv, Gregg Drinkwater, and David Shneer, *We Are You: An Exploration of Lesbian, Gay, Bisexual, and Transgender Issues in Colorado's Jewish Community* (Denver: Jewish Mosaic, 2006), http://www.bjpa.org/Publications/downloadPublication. cfm?PublicationID=7454.

9. Steven M. Cohen, Caryn Aviv, and Judith Veinstein, *Welcoming Synagogues Project: Preliminary Results from the 2009 Synagogue Survey on Diversity and LGBT Inclusion* (Jewish Mosaic: The National Center for Sexual and Gender Diversity, The Institute for Judaism and Sexual Orientation at HUC-JIR, 2009), http://www.bjpa. org/Publications/details.cfm?PublicationID=670. The extended project combined qualitative interviews (firty-one phone and in-person interviews) as well as a quantitative survey of over 3,000 synagogues across North America and Canada; 1,221 total respondents representing 997 congregations from across all Movements responded, including 760 rabbis, 109 board presidents, and 39 executive directors.

10. B. Schlager, *With Open Arms: Gay Affirming Ministries in Bay Area Faith Communities* (Berkeley, CA: Center for Lesbian and Gay Studies in Religion and Ministry at Pacific School of Religion, 2004), http://www.clgs.org/resource-library/ open-arms-gay-affirming-ministries-bay-area-faith-communit.

11. Adrienne Rich, "Invisibility in Academe," in *Blood, Bread, and Poetry* (New York: Norton, 1986), 199.

12. Kevin L. Nadal, Marie-Anne Issa, Jayleen Leon, Vanessa Meterko, Michelle Wideman, and Yinglee Wong, "Sexual Orientation Microaggressions: 'Death by a Thousand Cuts' for Lesbian, Gay, and Bisexual Youth," *Journal of LGBT Youth* 8, no. 3 (2011): 234–59.

13. "Gender Bender on the Bimah," *New Voices*, April 9, 2003, http://www. newvoices.org/campus?id=0046; Debra Nussbaum Cohen, "Testing the Borders of Inclusivity," *Jewish Week*, March 14, 2003; Alexandra J. Wall, "Transgender Rabbi-to-Be: Reform Movement Accepts Student from Oakland," *Jewish Bulletin* (San Francisco), March 14, 2003.

14. Rabbi Roxanne Shapiro, personal communication with author, April 26, 2012.

15. Rabbi Margaret Wenig, e-mail communication with author, April 30, 2012.

16. Amy Hertz, "One in Every *Minyan*: Homosexuality and the Reform Movement" (rabbinic thesis, Hebrew Union College–Jewish Institute of Religion, 2007).

17. "Transgender Health and the Law: Identifying and Fighting Healthcare Discrimination" (San Francisco, CA: Transgender Law Center, July 2004), http:// transgenderlawcenter.org/issues/health/transgender-health-and-the-law-identifying-and-fighting-health-care-discrimination.

18. Kay Whitlock, *Workplace Transitions: Effective Advocacy for Transgender-Inclusive Employee Health Benefit Plans* (Philadelphia: American Friends Service Committee, 2005).

19. R. Perez-Pena, "College Health Plans Respond as Transgender Students Gain Visibility, *New York Times*, February 12, 2013.

20. See HUC-JIR Board of Governors Meeting minutes, October 18, 2010, "Report of the Legal Committee," 12–13, and appendix K, "Equal Opportunity and Nondiscrimination Policy," S45.

21. Jesse McKinley, "Suicides Put Light on Pressures of Gay Teenagers," in *New York Times*, October 3, 2010, http://www.nytimes.com/2010/10/04/us/04suicide.html?_ r=1; Jeremy Hubbard, "Fifth Gay Teen Suicide in Three Weeks Sparks Debate," *ABC News*, October 3, 2010, http://abcnews.go.com/US/gay-teen-suicide-sparks-debate/story?id=11788128; Claire Howorth, "Another Gay Teen Suicide," *Newsweek*, October 2, 2010, http://www.thedailybeast.com/articles/2010/10/02/raymond-chase-becomes-fifth-suicide-victim.html

22

INTERVIEW WITH RABBI EUGENE B. BOROWITZ

CONDUCTED BY
RABBI RACHEL M. MAIMIN, DECEMBER 2012

Q: What led you to oppose the ordination of gay and lesbian rabbis initially, and what led you to change your mind?

A: Those are really good questions. There is a particularly complicated answer to the first one so I will begin with that one.

I was proud to be a member of the faculty of the HUC-JIR. I thought a number of the other members of the faculty felt that, before decisions of any considerable significance were made, there should be a rather serious exploration of the questions and the reasons that people took the positions that they did. While that sounds perfectly obvious to me and others, it apparently wasn't in relation to this question. Many members of our New York faculty were satisfied with being quiet and leaving the leaders of the College to settle the issue.

Now remember that "Reform Judaism" back then was not as thoughtfully structured as the Movement we have today. Also, it was not clear that people then wanted to know what the Jewish tradition might have had to say about *how* one should handle the question of making such a controversial decision to begin with. Many normal people don't think that way, but because I'm interested in the reasons for making Jewish decisions, I and some other faculty members were quite concerned.

The CCAR did a sensible thing: it asked four people to state their opinions and then made them available in a pamphlet. I was one of those four authors, and my piece is very much longer than any of the other three. I did not feel that, on the whole, the CCAR would be well served by having had the relatively obvious ethical responses without going into them in some depth. I felt I had to make a substantial effort because I didn't feel my colleagues had at that point done what they needed to do. Writing my piece for the CCAR pamphlet was a difficult task, and overall, I did not think we were served well by the pamphlet.

In any case, it seemed to me that there were reasons for approving the ordination and marriage of homosexuals and reasons against, and I thought they were balanced. That is to say, I didn't see that anybody could clearly say you should do one or the other. What persuaded me under those circumstances to come out with the negative point of view was a series of things.

The major item was that I thought then that the congregations that I knew and had been in would be more—how shall I put it?—I thought they would find it troublesome if rabbis were homosexual. I thought that we should find some way to deal with that, but for the time being one starts saying no and then sees how it might be possible to say yes. I point out that with regard to the ordination of women in the 1920s, there were women who wanted to be ordained and were fit for that, but the College turned down that notion. I believe it was not the faculty but the board of trustees that made the decision, and it was that kind of complexity that led me in the first instance to say for the time being no, that until the community is ready to accept them, I don't think we should go ahead.

What I had not been prepared for was what soon took place. The CCAR was going about this question the right way even though I wished my colleagues had gone into it in greater depth. But while that was going on, it turned out, at least as far as we could tell, that various people in the administration of HUC-JIR were moving ahead with the ordination of homosexuals. Now I didn't write about that at the time, but the truth of the matter is that disturbed me a great deal. I should have thought that the College would want to use all the intellectual power located in the faculty of the College to make a decision out of knowledge and classic understanding. But that was not the case. The case was that the CCAR was going ahead with what seemed to be a decent way of handling it, but the College or, more specifically, some officials at the College, were, so to speak, going around the back door on this matter. It good as made the decision on its own to go ahead with the ordination of homosexuals.

We finally had a meeting in New York at the school, and most of the members of the faculty who came to that meeting had nothing to say. The balance at that meeting was from the few of us who felt particularly negatively because this behavior violated our sense of serious institutional decision making, particularly for a liberal institution. I didn't write anything about that because I didn't want to embarrass the College or make it seem worse than I thought it already was. So I just simply stayed with my negative opinion, now reinforced by the fact that certain people of the administration unknown to me by name had already moved ahead on accepting and therefore preparing for the ordination of homosexuals.

What followed was of some serious interest I think. The question came up from students and within myself about my signing *s'michah*s [certificates of rabbinic ordination]. I adopted a form of handling this question in which any student who wanted me to sign their *s'michah* came to me with the *s'michah* to sign. I would say, "Do you know of any reason why I, by my standards, should not sign your *s'michah*?" At least one student whom I had a high regard for clearly lied to me about that. I didn't know whether it was a lie or not. I signed that *s'michah*, and it was clear in that graduation that this student was homosexual.

I didn't get into any more difficulties with that because an interesting thing took place. For a number of years, as ordination time approached, the ordination class would have a meeting and they would ask for solidarity on the part of all the graduates. That is to say, some students would ask the rest not to come to me to sign their *s'michah* out of solidarity. At any rate, that went on for a number of years.

In the course of those years, it became clear to me that I was probably wrong when this whole thing got started in my understanding that our congregations would largely be offended by having rabbis who were homosexual. It turned out after a number of years that the homosexual students were being accepted in not all congregations but in many congregations. I had misread that situation; you know, I have made errors before, and I'm sure I will make them from time to time again.

And then one day, after a process of some years, a former student [Editor's note: Rabbi David Adelson, see p. 317] appeared in my office with his *s'michah*. He said to me that he wanted me to sign his *s'michah* and asked if I would do so. I said yes I would, now that I saw the change (as I saw it) in our congregations' attitude. The balance of reasons for positive or negative had changed. It was quite fairly clear. So I said yes, I would be glad to sign his *s'michah*. But I asked a favor. The favor that I asked was that he would bring it to the College on the next Thursday after Senior Sermon discussion so that when I did sign it, I would be able to do it in the full presence of the community and be able to explain somewhat about why I was now doing it.

Q: I think this was maybe three years ago? [Editor's note: April 22, 2010.]

A: Yes.

Q: I remember the day very clearly.

A: It was quite a day.

Q: Yes, it was.

A: By the way I don't know whether he's homosexual or not. It didn't make any difference because now signing the *s'michah* had overwritten that former decision of his class. Because now I had come to agree with them. So I did that on that Thursday in the presence of the community, my community, and that was the change. The change, I said, was that I had seen the way in which congregations were accepting homosexuals, which was against what I had anticipated. Well, okay, I wasn't a very good sociologist, but that's not my world.

Some months later I was attending a congregational service at the end of Sukkot. There was a male rabbi in that congregation who had no reason to be friendly with me; he had never taken an elective course with me, and he had found a way around me for the required course I teach. He came over to me at some pause in the service, and he kissed me, which I was very pleased to have him do. (Nice to be able to have good relationships with your clergy!) And I took it that somehow the word had gotten around out into the general community that my position had changed.

And that I think is the tale of my relationship with this issue. But I don't want to leave it there without calling one further thing to your or any reader's attention. Namely, the issue of decision making with regard to Jewish action or responsibility is very important to me. Look at the table of contents of my book *Renewing the Covenant*. That book is a major book of theology, but the point toward which it goes is how you decide what to do or not to do. I mean, that's what the table of contents indicates, and that's what the book is. In the last chapter, the climax of the whole thing is how you make decisions. I think I was following what I had explained to my community in great detail, and when the data was such that I felt it had changed, then I changed.

It caused a great deal of pain to people who were homosexual. It caused pain to people who then by virtue of the class solidarity did not have me sign their *s'michah*s. And it caused me a great deal of pain as well. But that was what I thought needed to be done.

Q: I know that you've written books on this subject, so obviously this is a big question. But in thinking about your decision-making process, I'm wondering if you can talk a little about the role of theology and the role of having interactions with your students and hearing their stories. What role did any or all of those play in your decisions throughout your career?

A: Well, to me the question is, "Do you believe this stuff, or do you not believe this stuff?" If you believe it, well what do you believe and why do you believe it? That's why among other things I wrote that book, which is the key book on the question of decisions. Indeed it's not a book about just God or about the text or anything like that. It is a book that asks, "How do I make decisions?"

It's not that I'm so smart that I figured that out as the key question. You see it also in the fight that developed in the 1920s between [Martin] Buber [1878–1965] and [Franz] Rosenzweig [1886–1929]. They didn't actually fight; they had an exchange of letters. An issue that derives from these letters is that Rosenzweig wanted Buber to perform mitzvot such as lighting candles on Chanukah. Buber said, "I can't tell you whether it's time to light the candles. I can't make that decision because I'm waiting to have some kind of sense from God, an experience that will tell me what I am required to do." (Now, they don't use this particular example, but I am using it because it's today [Chanukah] of course.) Rosenzweig is practically Orthodox (which is why the Conservative Jews gave up on him after a brief love affair), and this illustrates why Buber fails on a critical issue, namely about what it is that you really need to do in advance of experiencing one thing or another. Buber advocates simply waiting for some experience or relationship to come in and give you a foundation for doing something.

Well, I tried to resolve that question in *Renewing the Covenant*, and the whole book is designed to deal with that issue. The theology is the theology of God, who is behind it all. It's theology about the Jewish people and what role they play. For Art Green and certain other people, the Jewish people is secondary, not critical, because he and they only recognize everybody's relationship with God and not any *special* relationships with God. Well, I address that perspective in the end of [my] book as I respond to both the traditional and the liberal (which

I call the loose liberal) ways of making these decisions. I respond to them, and I say what I think needs to be done.

Well since you've given me a chance to talk I'll add one more story. One day I had been asked to go down, I think, to Philadelphia. I thought very highly of the rabbi there; he happened to have a better knowledge of Jewish sources than most of his colleagues, and I looked to him as one of the people who could be counted on to try to take what you needed to do rather seriously. After my presentation and discussion, people came up afterwards to talk with me. The rabbi also came up to me—you know, some little instances of this kind stay in your head—and he looked at me with great unhappiness. He said to me, "You have no idea how much pain it causes me when I see what you have written or said about performing intermarriages." (At that point it was the intermarriage thing before the current flood.) And I looked him in the eye and said, "You have no idea how much pain you have caused me when I see in the *New York Times* that you have officiated with a member of some Christian clergy in a joint marriage ceremony." And he was astonished. He couldn't believe that anybody would say that. But it just happens to be a vaguely related story.

Q: Has your perspective on marriage as a whole shifted?

A: My perspective on marriage as a whole was derived from my mother and father, who had a marvelous relationship. Both of them were immigrants who came to the United States, met in the United States, and had many formative years—no, a number of formative years—in the greater New York area. Then they moved out to Columbus, Ohio, where I grew up. I was six or seven when we moved to Columbus, Ohio, and while I had some memories of Brooklyn and we would go back to visit there once in a while, I saw what my parents did and how they lived. I went through the usual American high school and then university and fraternity activities and held the usual attitudes toward sexuality.

In the early sixties, someone in charge of Hillel on college campuses was trying to get Hillel to be more Jewish. I wrote him a letter and said to him, "What kind of business is this? You don't want to face the key issue. The key issue is whether people can feel free to go around and have sexual relations with other kids. Why don't you get someone to tell them what Judaism has to say on that subject?" And he wrote back and said, "Okay, you do it." Nobody had the guts to do it. It took me three tries before I could figure it out, because I had to think through how liberal Jews should go about making a critical decision. And that book is called *Choosing a Sex Ethic* [1969]. So I'm on the record about the difficulties and problems of sex ethics very early on and try to deal with how one makes such decisions. On the whole, I was pleasantly surprised by the relatively positive sense that I got from what people said about that book.

As to my perspective on marriage: As a whole, as I said, it came from my mother and father. And then from the fact that I had a marvelous wife and we were married—oh, goodness gracious—fifty-seven years. She eventually became a psychotherapist, but if you want a joke, I can give you one: she had to become a psychotherapist because she lived with me. That is to say, she had a case on her hands immediately! Of course that's a joke. We had a wonderful marriage, three marvelous daughters. So as far as I can tell that's it.

Q: To conclude, I'd like to ask you one question about Reform Judaism writ large. Has your understanding of Reform Judaism changed at all throughout your lifetime, especially in thinking about issues of sexuality?

A: Look, I started at Hebrew Union College in 1942. World War II was just coming into being. That world was a prudish world—there was no question about it—and it was very difficult in many ways. Sex was just not a matter that was easy to discuss, and it was certainly equally considered "dirty" by many people to be sexually involved with someone. And, of course, we didn't want the gentiles to hate us.

As a result of all this, there were all kinds of changes, problems. As the century went on, attitudes changed, both in the American community as a whole and the Jewish community in particular. I felt very strongly about freedom and about the right to make decisions that were sensible to you, and those things radically changed over time. All sorts of things did go on. I mean, for heaven's sake, that's how women got to be rabbis!

Editor's note: This interview was edited for style, as well as overall clarity, readability, and length.

PERSONAL REFLECTIONS

PERSONAL REFLECTION

The Difference a Signature Makes

RABBI DAVID ADELSON

I looked up at my *s'michah*. The document that declares me a rabbi hung in its big black-and-gold frame. I remembered with pride the day, over a decade earlier, when it was bestowed upon me at my ordination ceremony. I took it down, tore open the paper backing, rolled it up, and slid it into a cardboard tube. And then I walked out of the temple to the subway.

I was on my way to see my most influential teacher from rabbinical school, Dr. Eugene B. Borowitz. Dr. Borowitz is the Reform Movement's greatest theologian and a revered teacher of generations of rabbis. As a student, I was his teaching assistant and senior thesis advisee, and I even lampooned him, lovingly, in the Purim-spiel.

But there was a problem. Dr. Borowitz had a policy I could not endorse or accept: he would not sign the *s'michah* of gay and lesbian students. If I recall correctly from earlier years, his position was based on the centrality of procreation and family life in Judaism and the role of the rabbi as public exemplar.

Whatever its basis, his position deeply upset me. In my final year of rabbinical school, only two students were writing their theses with Dr. Borowitz: me, and my good friend and study partner Roderick Young, who is gay. When Roderick and I sat at meetings together with Dr. Borowitz, I thought, "How could *I* be entitled to his signature, and Roderick not?"

So I invited Dr. Borowitz out to lunch at some point that year. My goal: convince him to change his policy. I can't recall the specifics of our conversation, but I do recall this: I failed. A few months later, at my ordination, I received the signatures of the rest of the faculty on my *s'michah* certificate. I did not ask Dr. Borowitz for his.

For that reason, my *s'michah* had always stirred in me feelings of both pride and a bit of regret.

Over time, the absence of Dr. Borowitz's signature came to bother me more and more. I quote him regularly when I teach. He has deeply influenced my own thinking about God, Judaism, and life in general. And finally one day, I looked at the *s'michah* and decided that my boycott was helping no one. All it did was cause me pain. Dr. Borowitz was getting older, I reasoned. I might not have much longer. I picked up the phone and called him.

He invited me to come see him later that month. When I arrived that day, cardboard tube in hand, he invited me to join him downstairs for that morning's sermon review. So I took a seat next to him as the room filled up.

It was only then that I learned that the morning's student sermon had been delivered by Molly Kane, on the subject of LGBT rabbis. One after another, students and then faculty praised, prodded, or took issue with points that she'd made. And then, Dr. Borowitz slowly rose to his feet. The room fell to a hush. Dr. Borowitz's teaching is always respected—and everyone also knew about his position on LGBT rabbis. What would he say?

After a pause, Dr. Borowitz launched into a lengthy discourse on the development, over decades, of his policy. "And finally," he said, "we come to the present moment. And I am pleased to announce that as of this year, I will be signing the *s'michah*s of *all* graduating students."

The room burst into applause, and everyone leapt to their feet. After a moment, Dr. Borowitz turned to me. "I have beside me my former student David Adelson," he said. "David, will you please tell all these people why you are here today?"

I rose. I explained that I had indeed declined to ask Dr. Borowitz to sign my *s'michah*. Today, however, I had it with me. I unrolled the document and placed it on the table. I handed Dr. Borowitz a pen. Dean Shirley Idelson rushed over with her camera. Everyone cheered. Of course I had forgotten to identify myself as straight and make clear that what they were witnessing was not in fact Dr. Borowitz knowingly signing the *s'michah* of a gay rabbi. But still: in one dramatic moment, Dr. Borowitz joined the rest of the HUC faculty—and most of the liberal Jewish world—by endorsing LGBT rabbis. And I got my beloved teacher's signature on my *s'michah*. Today it hangs, back in its frame, complete.

PERSONAL REFLECTION

Change Is Possible

RABBI MOLLY G. KANE

The most inspiring sermons I read during my homiletics class in my fourth year of rabbinical school at Hebrew Union College–Jewish Institute of Religion (HUC-JIR), my professor Rabbi Maggie Wenig called "sermons aimed to change a way a person behaved or thought." I read sermons about health-care reform and political change . . . sermons that sought to eradicate homophobia . . . even a speech given by Golda Meir aimed to encourage American Jews to think of themselves as the Jews of Palestine in order to raise money and support. After reading several of this genre, I quickly came to understand that sermons are powerful tools that can call people to action and change people's minds.

That same semester that I was taking homiletics I was scheduled to deliver my senior sermon. The "senior sermon" is a rite of passage and culminating moment in a student's rabbinical school career. All I wanted to do was deliver a sermon like the ones I was reading in homiletics. My Torah portion was *Acharei Mot–K'doshim*, and with the mentorship of my sermon advisor Dr. Carole Balin, I decided to write a sermon about the history of gay liberation and acceptance, and where we still needed to go both in the Jewish community and in American society. As someone who is gay, I believed this topic to be of extreme importance, particularly because while in 2010 it felt like gays had been liberated long ago in the Reform Movement, there were still strides that needed to be made both within and without the Movement.

In 2010, many GLBTQ rabbinical students still felt marginalized by the overall hetero-normative culture at school. While there was never any blatant homophobia, the feeling was that "gay" was still "alternative" in some way. Dr. Eugene B. Borowitz, one of the most highly regarded professors at school, still did not sign the *s'michah*, certificate of ordination, of GLBTQ students. In the more Orthodox Jewish world, being gay and Jewish still felt like two irreconcilable identities. And of course in 2010, marriage equality was only just at the beginning stages of gaining momentum. So as I wrote my senior sermon, it was not enough for me to just examine where we were; I felt an urgency to make an impact.

The week before I was scheduled to deliver my sermon, I sent a draft to my mentor and colleague Rabbi Ellen Lippmann. She called me up after reading it and said, "Where are *you* in this sermon?" And after feeling angry and frustrated that she didn't just say it was amazing, I knew she was absolutely right. I had written a sermon that was completely disconnected from myself. If I did not say why this topic was so important to me, how could I expect others to care? I had not yet written in the sermon that I am gay and this is my history and my future.

On April 22, 2010, I delivered my senior sermon, which began with the following:

> *V'et zachar lo tishkav mishk'vei ishah to'eivah hi.* "Do not lie with a male as one lies with a woman; it is an abhorrence" [Lev. 18:22]. "This section of the Torah stings more than any other," Elliot Dorff once wrote. This text has certainly stung me. When I was younger I wondered, Is it either be gay or be Jewish? And sometimes I thought I should just be gay quietly in order to be the Jew I want to be. But, I don't want to be quiet. And certainly for those of you who know me well—and maybe even those who don't—I am not often quiet. And certainly not this morning.

So there *I* was. From the very beginning of my sermon, I "came out," and not only did I hope to call people to action, but I wanted to make it very clear that full acceptance of gay people and marriage equality in the Jewish world and our country meant full acceptance and marriage equality for me and all the other gay people in the congregation.

When I finished speaking, one of our teachers, a modern Orthodox rabbi, began to applaud, and then the entire congregation joined him. People were in tears. And then later, during the sermon discussion, Dr. Borowitz made the momentous and unexpected announcement that from now on he would be signing anyone's *s'michah* no matter their sexual orientation.

Attending the discussion at Dr. Borowitz's invitation was Rabbi David Adelson, a former advisee. He had brought with him his *s'michah* certificate from eleven years ago, which, in solidarity with his gay classmates, he had refused to have Dr. Borowitz sign. In front of the whole community, Dr. Borowitz signed Rabbi Adelson's certificate. The moment was not just memorable, but historic. It symbolized a shift in consciousness for Dr. Borowitz, and it sent off a ripple effect of energy and possibility throughout the school and the Reform Movement. Change is possible.

My sermon was published online and sent over many electronic mailing lists. I received tons of e-mails for weeks about my words and the experience of that day from classmates, faculty, rabbis in the field, and even some people I had never met. Rabbis from around the country shared the story of my sermon and the experience with Dr. Borowitz with their congregations. Even as I write these words, I am overwhelmed with pride and accomplishment as I look back on that day. The senior sermon that I hoped would "change people's thought and behavior" did just that. It moved people to tears; it celebrated our Reform Movement and all that it had accomplished for gay rights while pushing it to continue moving forward. The sermon made people think and most importantly reminded people that liberation comes in stages and that we are not there yet, but someday soon we could be.

PERSONAL REFLECTION

This Other Eden—Personal Reflections on Sexuality in the UK

RABBI DEBORAH KAHN-HARRIS, PHD

Leo Baeck College, where I trained for the rabbinate, allows final-year rabbinical students to choose the rabbi to ordain them. There is little as nervous and thrilling a moment as asking a rabbi whom you greatly respect to ordain you, and indeed, most of my colleagues agree that one of the greatest privileges of any rabbi is to ordain a new colleague. It was with those feelings in mind that I approached Rabbi Sheila Shulman to ordain me in 1996. In my mind, Sheila is simply one of the finest teachers with whom I have ever studied. I did and still do enormously respect her intellect, her empathy, and her commitment that have always been sensibly tempered by a healthy dose of cynicism. These reasons were why I chose to ask Sheila to ordain me.

But Rabbi Shulman, alongside Rabbi Elizabeth Sarah, were also the first GLBT rabbis ordained at LBC in 1989. It never occurred to me that people would gossip about my sexuality based on Sheila's—that because she was a lesbian, I must be a lesbian, too.

Rewinding, I arrived in the United Kingdom in 1989 to study at Oxford for a year and ended up staying on to train for the rabbinate at LBC. I was newly graduated from Mount Holyoke College, the oldest women's college in the United States. I had a mildly shocking pseudo-punk haircut (shaved up one side, long and falling into my face on the other side with a purple/pink/red streak dyed into a small patch along the front). I was an overweight, young, and somewhat naïve American abroad. I was away from home, from the country of my birth, from friends and family I had known all my life and was busy reinventing myself. First Oxford, then London, gave me the opportunity to discover myself afresh, to become the person I had always wanted to be. My sexuality, however, was never the bit I felt the need to transform.

I was raised for most of my childhood in Houston, Texas, in the 1970s and '80s. Homosexuality was hardly a shocking matter. Though it is perhaps little realized outside of GLBT circles, Houston at this time had a thriving and well-integrated GLBT scene. Moreover, my mother's oldest friend, whom she had appointed my godfather (insofar as Jews have such entities), was gay. My stepmother had close gay friends. And at Mount Holyoke, I knew many lesbians, debated the finer points of whether men should be allowed on campus, and considered whether it was possible to be a straight feminist. All in all, I had the sort of exposure to the GLBT community which enabled me (a) to feel it to be entirely normative and (b) to feel confident that had I wanted/needed to come out, I would have not found it problematic to do so. But as anyone who knew me well in my twenties will testify to, I was largely, very happily, quite straight, but nevertheless wished to remain open and inquisitive.

And yet in the UK I found myself in both a secular and Jewish community with a very problematic relationship to sexuality. Just the year before I arrived in the UK, the infamous Section 28 had been come into law—part of the Local Government Act of 1988, which prevented local authorities, and by extension schools, from promoting homosexuality in any fashion. While homosexuality was (only since 1967 and only since 2000 with a common age of consent) no longer a criminal act, there was still a genuine anxiety about homosexuality in British society. A clear and vocal element of heterosexual society still felt openly threatened by other forms of sexual identity.

The Jewish community I found myself in was no different. Rabbis Shulman and Sarah spent their entire five years at LBC on probation for no other reason than that they were lesbians. During the period just following my ordination, the Assembly of Reform Rabbis UK spent a number of years tearing itself apart over the issue of same-sex commitment ceremonies.* In the end a fudge was issued—conducting a same-sex commitment ceremony would no longer be at odds with membership of the Assembly, but neither would such ceremonies be positively endorsed. Rabbis who found themselves in conflict with their congregations over this matter would not be publicly supported.

It was a curious atmosphere in which to take up my own rabbinate and develop as a human being. I felt anger at the way GLBT members of our Jewish community were treated, but I continued, by and large, to be a straight woman. I really could not have cared less what others thought about my sexuality as a result of my support for the GLBT cause, but it felt strange having to put to rights other people's preconceived notions.

Thankfully time moves many things on, including GLBT equality issues. Things are not completely rosy—transgendered teachers are still hounded by the press and many old prejudices persist. Still, the Assembly now fully endorses same-sex commitment ceremonies and, alongside our sister Movement, Liberal Judaism, has been actively lobbying government in favor of the Gay Marriage Bill currently going through Parliament. Civil partnerships are now legal under UK law, enabling GLBT couples to a range of rights they never previously enjoyed.

And in 2009 when I ordained Rabbi David Mitchell, no one seemed to gossip about either his sexuality or mine. We were what Sheila and I have always been—friends, colleagues, teachers, and pupils—not determiners of each other's sexuality.

---

*This was not true of the UK's Liberal Judaism, another progressive Jewish movement in the UK. The Rabbinic Conference, Liberal Judaism's rabbinic body, and its lay leadership have generally always been welcoming and positive toward the GLBT community, including in the matter of same-sex commitment ceremonies.

Part Four

Beloved Companions:
Jewish Marital Models

As this book is being finalized, decisions have just come down from the United States Supreme Court on landmark cases in favor of marriage equality. In Canada, where I am writing, the issue has been resolved for over a decade, but both countries are part of a larger trajectory toward the recognition of same-sex relationships. For the Reform Movement, civil marriage equality is not a new topic, going back to a 1996 resolution opposing governmental efforts to ban gay and lesbian marriage. From a religious vantage point, in March 2000, the Central Conference of American Rabbis became the first major group of North American clergy to give organizational support to those choosing to perform same-gender ceremonies, even as others chose not to.*

Beyond the impassioned fight for justice that the movement toward marriage equality represents; beyond the often vitriolic attacks that have come in response; beyond the divisions that have come to the fore not only between liberal and conservative political camps but between progressive and fundamentalist religious camps as well; beyond all this, there is the opportunity to ask important questions. What does

---

*Religious Action Center of Reform Judaism, Key Topics: LGBT Equality (www.rac.org).

marriage actually mean? How has it changed over time? What is its significance, both to the individuals who enter into it and to the society in which they live? What are its challenges and its opportunities? How can it be renewed over time, and how might we mark its end? Few other topics draw on issues that are so deeply personal and political, textual and spiritual, contemporary and historical. It is to those issues that this section turns, cognizant of the current debate, and looking at marriage through a Jewish lens. This section intentionally uses the phrase "marital models" instead of "the marital model," in recognition of the diverse ways Jewish marriage has been understood over time.

The first essay, by Rabbi Nancy H. Wiener, is "Jewish Marriage Innovations and Alterations: From Commercial/Legal Transaction to Spiritual Transformation." In it, she frames the conversation by tracing the evolution of Jewish marriage from a world primarily defined by ownership (male) and dependence (female), through Rabbinic and medieval innovations, and into the modern era and specifically the Reform Movement. Among these many transformations, she draws our attention to the new Talmudic description of the wedding couple as "beloved companions," *rei-im ha-ahuvim*, as one of many significant steps in the changing understanding of marriage.

From this historical analysis, we continue with Dr. Eugene B. Borowitz's classic essay "Reading the Jewish Tradition on Marital Sexuality." He employs a relational, covenantal stance to search within Judaism for guidance and develops a thoughtful approach that draws from the tradition. At the same time, he also identifies areas where there is need for reform, both within Judaism and within contemporary secular culture. Above all, Dr. Borowitz argues that "the Jewish teaching on sexuality continues to express with compelling power the mandates of existence under the Covenant."

Next, in "The Ritual Sanctification of Same-Gender Relationships in Reform Judaism: An Eisegetical Approach," Rabbi Jonathan Stein uses the experience of being part of the rabbinic debate on same-gender relationships to elucidate his own eisegetical approach. Recognizing the classic and continued importance of exegesis (deriving our decisions primarily from the textual tradition), he makes the case that "there will be times when we have and will continue to bring values from outside the traditional Jewish textual system and, in an eisegetical manner, insist that they are of such importance and worth that they must be integrated into, imposed upon, or even supersede, what the textual traditional has taught." Like Dr. Borowitz, Rabbi Stein grapples with the appropriate balance between the guidance of Jewish tradition and the liberal Jewish value of openness to new insights and understandings in our ongoing relationship with the Divine.

The remainder of Part Four explores particular issues that emerge within the marital model. From a statement on marital sexual infidelity, reaffirming the value of exclusivity within marriage, we continue with Rabbi Janet R. Marder's incorporation of the human element in her essay "Scenes from a Marriage." Beginning with a case study of Ahasuerus's marriage to Vashti in the Purim story and considering more recent scandals, she turns to the issue of marital infidelity. Above all, her piece is shaped by an understanding of the private story that always coexists alongside the religious issues. With compassion for the challenge of maintaining emotional and sexual intimacy, she speaks to the sacred task of protecting and sustaining marriage.

The two final essays consider issues that once were far removed from the Reform discussion of marriage. In "*Taharat HaMishpachah*: A Renewed Look at the Concept of Family Purity," Rabbi Denise L. Eger discusses the possibility of reinterpreting the traditional laws of family purity as "the concept that allows for maintaining the sanctity, health, and well-being of the family relationship." Then, in "Getting Our *Get* Back: On Restoring the Ritual of Divorce in American Reform Judaism," Rabbi Mark Washofsky considers the restoration of a Jewish divorce ritual, examining the reasons that the requirement for a *get* was eliminated by the early Reformers and suggesting that different perspectives might lead to different decisions today. He argues that our community "can reclaim its voice at a most fateful moment in the lives of its people, acknowledging its deep connection to Jewish tradition and yet realizing its highest moral and ethical commitments."

The personal perspectives close Part Four by relating to two of the issues discussed in the essays. Rabbi Rebecca Einstein Schorr ("Living Waters—Making Mikveh a Regular Practice") reflects on the meaning of mikveh in her marriage, and Rabbi Michael Adam Latz ("Marriage Equality—Thank You God for This Amazing Day") shares his experience of advocating for marriage equality, as a rabbi, a husband, a father, and a gay man. Both Schorr and Latz show us just how much marriage is a profoundly significant relationship, where ancient teachings and modern realities all have their pull, and where protection may be needed both within and without. Above all, the challenge remains the search for *kiddushin*, sanctity, beyond the shelter of the chuppah and within the walls of our homes.

23

JEWISH MARRIAGE INNOVATIONS AND ALTERATIONS

From Commercial/Legal Transaction to Spiritual Transformation

RABBI NANCY H. WIENER, DMIN

Our understanding of why people marry, what the marital bond is or might be, and what constitutes an appropriate and meaningful ceremony have changed significantly over time. Marriages arranged by parents of the bride and groom, or their agents, were still normative among Jews a little more than a century ago. Today, in all but some ultra-Orthodox communities, two individuals choose to make an enduring commitment to each other that is predicated upon mutuality, equality, exclusivity, love, and companionship. Through *kiddushin*, two Jewish adults willingly set each other apart from all others sexually, financially, and emotionally. Publicly, they and those in attendance affirm and celebrate their commitment, as individuals and as a corporate entity—a new household—to contribute to the community and to creation. This recast understanding of *kiddushin* has led Reform, Reconstructionist, and Conservative rabbis to affirm that all Jewish couples, sexual orientation notwithstanding, can celebrate their relationships through appropriate Jewish rituals. How much has changed! The monumental changes liberal Jewish communities have embraced during the last two centuries were not the first, nor will they be the last, wedding innovations our people have adopted. In fact, our wedding customs have evolved and mutated significantly in response to social, political, religious, and philosophical changes within our own communities and in the societies among which we have lived, from the biblical period to today.

The Torah, the product of an ancient Near East milieu, does not speak of mutual, reciprocal, exclusive spousal relationships. Parents or their agents made pacts binding their offspring to each other. Customarily, agreements were confirmed by giving gifts and sharing meals. Finding a woman for a son, thereby ensuring the family line, was a primary goal. At times, intended spouses were attracted to each other; at times, the sentiments and desires of the bride-to-be were solicited. However, attraction and affection were incidental to the binding of two lives together as spouses.

A woman was part of her father's household; she was one of his responsibilities and holdings until another man "took" her. "Taking" was never done by a woman; it was never reciprocal. A woman became an *eishet ish*, *a particular man's woman or wife*; a man never became an *ish ishah*, a particular woman's man or husband. Men "took" women for the purpose of procreation. Eve may have been created for Adam as an *eizer k'negdo* ("helpmate"; Genesis 2:18), but procreation was at the center of that world.

The Levitical laws of permitted and prohibited marriages do not mention love, affection, or commitment. Their concern is to delineate an adult male's proper relationship to things, people, and God. The cultural and conceptual context for these laws understood ownership and responsibility as the purview of two entities: God and adult males. All things in the world were believed to be either part of God's exclusive domain or part of a domain shared by God and men. Knowing to which realm each thing belonged was of utmost importance for men; trespassing clear boundaries meant risking punishment in either the human or the divine sphere. One clear message of Leviticus 18–20 was: Males! To be holy, understand what is yours and what is not yours, and act accordingly.

Women, slaves, and minors belonged to the domain shared by adult males and God. They were dependent entities, cared for by the men of whose households they were a part.[1] Thus, the laws of *arayot* (sexual trangressions) involved women, but assumed that only a man was a fully independent, responsible being, capable of trespassing or violating another man's female property. Marriages were prohibited only if they violated caste (i.e., who might marry a priest) or property boundaries. In this world, where progeny and paternity were of ultimate importance, clearly identifying a woman with a single man, whose children she might bear, was essential.

N'vi-im (Prophets) and *K'tuvim* (Writings) introduced relationship metaphors and images with affectional components. The dominant metaphor focused on God and Israel as spouses who loved each other. The covenant at Sinai was a pledge of steadfast, exclusive, forgiving, eternal love and devotion, which God would uphold, but which Israel was forever breaking. The very metaphor presupposed an imbalance in the relationship; God and Israel were not and would never be equals.

Shir HaShirim (Song of Songs) offered different images: earthly longing and passion and the joy and reality of love as a guiding force in human lives. The stories of Jonathan and David and of Ruth and Naomi showed love as the central element of meaningful human relationships, spousal or otherwise. Neither implied or posited that love and marriage were specifically linked; in fact, they provided clear and powerful examples of loving commitments outside marriage.

And so, in the earliest strata of our tradition, the creation of a new couple had neither a name nor a prescribed ritual. Moreover, love and mutuality were not relevant to such a union. Despite Genesis's reference to Eve, companionship and affection were *perquisites*, not *prerequisites*. Instead, marriage often had financial benefits for a family marrying off a daughter—through the receipt of gifts, and the loss of a dependent from a household. Ultimately, progeny and continuity were the impetus for forming new couples.

Given this as the inherited tradition, the Mishnah provided a remarkable compendium of innovations on, elaborations of, and departures from the scant information about sanctioned relations in the Bible. Where once there was no named marriage ritual, there were now two rituals, *kiddushin/eirusin* and *chuppah/nisuin*, each with legally recognized processes, ascribed meanings, and specific terminology. The Mishnah spoke of *kiddushin*, *eirusin*, *nisuin*, *kinyan*, *ketubah*, *matan* (groom's gift), and *n'dunyah* (bride's price) as interrelated parts of a whole, although they had never been mentioned in the Bible. Elaborating on the Bible's assumptions that females could be transferred from one male's *r'shut* (legal domain) to another's, the Mishnah established parameters for doing it properly. The value of the female, central to this exchange, was based on her virginity, long understood as the best guarantee that she would bear only one man's children.[2]

By the Mishnaic period, *kiddushin/eirusin* was clearly an established social institution, marking a period in which a girl or woman was promised to her husband-to-be, but continued to live in her father's house.[3] A pledge of sale had been made; however, the goods had not yet been transferred.

But what about this arrangement warranted the name it was given, *kiddushin*? The Mishnah offers no explanation of why the term *kiddushin* was applied to this transaction. However, comments in the Babylonian Talmud, *Kiddushin* 2b, shed light on a possible parallel between *kiddushin* and the property category of *hekdeish*. The Talmud states:

> He [the groom, by his act of betrothal] prohibits her [the bride] to the whole world [except himself] like *hekdeish* [an article consecrated to the Holy Temple, which is prohibited for any use other than as an offering to God].

For something to become *hekdeish*, it officially moved from a human *r'shut*, through an oral declaration and a symbolic physical act of transferring possession, to God's exclusive use.[4] So, to make something *hekdeish*, someone could have said, "*Harei zeh, m'kudash l'Adonai, b'davar zu. . . .*" "Behold this [object] is set aside/consecrated for God through this…" Thinking conceptually, those same words, which comprise the traditional affirmation at a Jewish wedding, moved a woman into a man's *r'shut*, setting her aside for his exclusive use, for him to be her *baal* (master).

Another possible explanation for the meaning of *kiddushin* in this context has been offered by Dr. Lawrence Hoffman:

> Seeing the husband's act of betrothal as *kiddushin* implied more than just reserving a woman as his own. It carried the further theological connotation of altering her stance in the covenant from being covenanted through her father to being covenanted through her husband.[5]

Hence, a woman's status as a non-independent entity had implications far beyond the human social and legal spheres; her very relationship to God was related to the man to whose household she belonged.

Once set aside, the woman was free neither to have other sexual partners nor to seek out other husbands—while the groom-to-be was free to do both. Only death or divorce could release her from the promise of exclusivity that her father or other male relative had made on her behalf.

The Mishnah discussed *kinyan* only, the legal means for someone to take possession of property, in relation to two types of humans: marriageable women, and slaves; they were also the two groups of people who had a human *baal*. Side by side in chapter 1 of *Kiddushin*, the modes of acquiring them are enumerated. For a non-Hebrew slave, acquisition was through money, the delivery of a deed of sale, or three years' undisturbed possession.[6] These have striking parallels to the modes the Mishnah required for the *kinyan* of a woman as a wife: *kesef* (monetary exchange), *sh'tar* (written document), and exclusive use, possession, through *biah* (sexual intercourse).[7]

Mishnaic and later Talmudic discussions about *kinyan* struggled to define what constituted each of these three. Giving of a gift seemed to have sufficed in some biblical narratives,[8] but the Mishnah discussed the bride's price and what was defined as *kesef*. All types of *kinyan* achieved through a *sh'tar* detailed the conditions of the transaction. A *ketubah* was no different. A *ketubah*, like every *sh'tar kinyan*, had to bear

the date and place of the transfer (the date of the nuptials); the anticipated condition of the goods (new or used; virgin or not); the amount
of money the new owner would give to the old owner at the time of the
transfer (the bride's price); the types of goods that would move from
one domain to the other (the value of the bride based on virginity and
dowry (in the case of a *ketubah*, ...); and the manner of distributing
goods in the event of a failed deal (*ketubah* upon divorce)—which goods
would stay with the new "owner" permanently and which were his to
use only as long as the deal was in force, and what was to be done with
accrued value or yield during the time the deal was in force.

It was an extraordinary innovation to see part of the goods become
the woman's holdings and safety net in the case of a divorce. Nonetheless, the commercial terms of the agreement had to be mutually
acceptable to the male players in this drama and were a prerequisite
for a marriage. The legal/commercial nature of this transaction is underscored in *Mishnah K'tubot* 1:1:

> A virgin should be married on a Wednesday, for in towns the
> court sits twice in the week, on Mondays and on Thursdays; so
> that if the husband would lodge a virginity suit [goods received
> are not the goods promised], he may forthwith go in the morning
> to the court.

The "taking" of a wife became the last stage of the process, *biah*,
dependent upon all other aspects of the business transaction's having
been completed. The transfer, *chuppah* or *nisuin*, was achieved when,
as with all things acquired, the property moved from the seller's domain to the new owner's domain or, symbolically, when the new owner
carried or lifted it. (The shared root *n-s-a* of "carrying" and *nisuin* underscores the historical context in which these practices originated.)[9]

Although both the Babylonian and the Jerusalem Talmuds retained
the assumptions that the members of the couple were not equals and
that marriage was a legal/commercial transaction,[10] they also introduced new elements into the Jewish understanding of and approaches
to marriage. The two Talmuds provided liturgy for the two-part

process of a woman's becoming a man's wife. Each tradition had its own liturgical formulae for each part. *Birkat Eirusin*, the liturgical centerpiece of *kiddushin/eirusin*, transformed the biblical prohibitions regarding sexual exclusivity for women into a blessing. In this still polygamous world, the betrothed ones who are off-limits and the married ones who are *permitted* are women only.[11]

Interestingly, the two Talmuds offered different forms of *Birkat Nisuin*: the Jerusalem had only three blessings; the Babylonian had six, plus a blessing for wine. The real innovations of these blessings were the meanings they ascribed to marriage. For the first time, marriage was linked to messianic longings, and marriage was seen as a relationship with ideal characteristics such as rejoicing, singing, pleasure and delight, love, companionship, peace, and fellowship. Finally, they introduced a new phrase to describe the couple that was completely separate from the language of ownership—*rei-im ha-ahuvim* (loving companions).

Conceptually, the Babylonian Talmud introduced significant innovations related to marriage. Women fell into distinct legal categories: wives, concubines, prostitutes, and even temporary wives.[12] All were still fundamentally objects used by men to meet their needs. However, the relational, nonmaterial aspects of marriage—for the members of the couple and for the community at large—were now worthy of mention.

Based on *ketubot* found in the Cairo *Genizah*, which followed Palestinian teachings and customs, Mordechai Friedman wrote:

> In antiquity and during the early Middle Ages . . . the *ketubah* was very much a "live" contract between the parties. *Ketubbot* from different localities and periods exhibit various stages of legal development and reflect the historical, social, and economic background of the communities in which they were written, in general, and the circumstances of the bride and groom and their families, in particular.[13]

In fact, Palestinian *ketubot* include the only pre-contemporary *ketubot* in which a wife apparently enjoyed a legal status "approaching equality with the husband's."[14] According to Friedman, "they included a provision which referred to marriage as *shutafut*, 'partnership,' which enabled both parties to initiate divorce proceedings."[15] Some Cairo *Genizah ketubot* require a wife's consent for a man to take an additional wife or wives. Others articulate "mutual obligations." The groom and bride have parallel obligations for each other. Even the concluding formulae reflected mutuality, confirming the consent of both parties to the contents of the *ketubah* and giving instructions for the writing and signing of the document.[16] However, even with these innovations there were still clear and persistent ways in which true parity did not exist. The woman had only one legal sexual partner, her husband, whereas the man could have multiple sexual partners—wives and concubines. The bride's price was still determined by her virginity, and the financial terms of the *ketubah* were determined by the significant males in her life.

Distinct traditions with regard to the legal document coexisted until the Babylonian yeshivot established hegemony over most of the Diaspora in the late eleventh century.[17] Then, the form of the prescribed legal aspects of Jewish marriage rituals gained a heretofore unknown uniformity and fixity.

The next major innovation regarding Jewish marriage came from the nascent Jewish community of Christian Europe. Living in a society in which the dominant religious culture recognized only monogamous marriages, Rabbeinu Gershom pronounced his *takanah* (ruling) banning polygamy in Ashkenaz. Monogamy, which we see as normative and "always" valued by Jews, was a radical legal innovation for Jews in the tenth century. Moreover, given the fact that such a small percentage of Jews lived in Ashkenaz at the time (some estimate that only 10 percent of world Jewry lived outside Muslim countries), the original scope of Rabbeinu Gershom's *takanah* was quite limited. In making this ruling, he consulted rabbis in Ashkenaz, but not rabbis around the world.[18] They felt, in their time and place, this radical change was a necessity. However, this Ashkenazic *takanah* had no significant impact on the lives of many non-Ashkenazic Jews until well into the nineteenth and twentieth centuries.

With the termination of polygamy as a viable and acceptable marriage configuration for the Jews of Ashkenaz, a new set of questions and issues arose. Legal discussions about when a marriage could or should be ended, once focused solely on failures to fulfill obligations, now focused on concerns about the nontangible, noncontractual aspects of a successful marital relationship. Affection, companionship, and *sh'lom bayit* became compelling reasons for maintaining even a nonprocreative marital bond.[19] Interestingly, affectional ties were still not discussed as a viable basis for contracting a marriage, but only as a basis for maintaining one.

In fact, in the West, throughout the Middle Ages and until the modern period, aspects of the original commercial/legal nature of Jewish marriage remained. Details of a *ketubah*, most particularly dowry, were negotiated, often through a hired mediator. The normative understanding of a bride's value was determined by her virginity, the dowry she brought, and her family's *yichus* (lineage), even though the official bride's price of the *ketubah* had become a symbolic two *zuzim*. The exchange of something of value to seal the arrangement was retained in all communities. In the East, the value of the token given to the bride by the groom was stipulated in the *ketubah*; the token itself could take many forms—cloth, coins, jewelry, exotic spices, and fragrances. The ring, which by the Middle Ages was a standard token of *nisuin* in the West, was more than a symbol. Readily discerning its value was still important.[20] Because of the commercial nature of marriage, many communities retained the custom of celebrating *kiddushin/nisuin* on a day immediately prior to the sitting of a *beit din* (rabbinic court), in case the contractual agreement was breached.

By the Middle Ages, Ashkenazic communities adopted another innovation: the fusion of the betrothal and nuptial ceremonies. Although reasons such as economic hardship, the difficulty of ensuring sexual continence during the betrothal period, and the precariousness of Jewish life are the reasons usually cited,[21] an additional, non-Jewish reason influenced the change. The church made no distinction between betrothal and nuptials. So, the merging of two ceremonies probably reflected another way in which Jews assimilated a non-Jewish practice into their marriage celebrations. Slowly, European communities, via *takanot*, adopted this practice.[22] The fusion of *kiddushin/nisuin* did not occur among Jews in Islamic countries until well into the modern era.

While halachah and *minhag* (religious law and custom) focused primarily upon the legal aspects of weddings, communities around the world adopted and adapted a wide range of practices addressing the psychosocial and personal transitions that accompany the formation of a new family. In Central and Eastern Europe, the mothers joined forces to ward off evil as their children's betrothal was established, by breaking earthenware to seal the agreement. In parts of Morocco, the bride, groom, and groom's mother physically acted out the bride's becoming the most significant woman in the groom's life. When the bride approached the home of her husband-to-be's family, where the wedding would take place and where the couple would live, the groom would stand a few feet inside the threshold and his mother would lie down across the threshold so that the bride would have to step over her mother-in-law in order to join her intended on the platform upon which they would be married.[23] Additional practices developed that provided the community at large with an opportunity to acknowledge the significant transition that *kiddushin/nisuin* represented. In Ashkenaz, the gathering preceded the ceremony, during which the groom was given an *aliyah*, called to the Torah for his last time as a bachelor. In many Eastern communities, a celebratory *aliyah* was reserved for the groom on the Shabbat following his nuptials. Throughout the Jewish world, women gathered to fete and prepare the bride-to-be. These customs varied greatly from one region to another.

Despite the variations in practice, little changed regarding the public and private meanings of marriage until the modern era. Influenced by Romanticism, the European Enlightenment, Haskalah, and newly found civic emancipation, new notions about love and marriage gained currency in the Jewish community.[24] Some Jews actively rejected arranged marriages. For them, marriage ceased being a business deal between parents and became a freely contracted relationship between the members of the couple.[25] Gradually, the whole process of entering an enduring relationship was de-commercialized.

The political backdrop for the first institutionalized changes was the appointment by Napoleon of the Assembly of Jewish Notables (1806) and Sanhedrin (1807) to articulate official Jewish positions on a variety of credal and ritual issues that were deemed to have a direct bearing on the Jews' ability to function as citizens. It was under Napoleon that, for the first time, rabbis functioned as representatives of the state at civilly recognized marriages and divorces.

An edict issued by the Royal Westphalian Consistory in 1810 established modern guidelines for Jewish weddings. It specified the place (in the synagogue, in front of an open ark, and under a canopy), the attire worn by the rabbi and groom (no tallit), the language of the ceremony (German), and the content of the ceremony (an address to the couple about marital obligations, followed by the groom's reciting the traditional formula while placing the ring on the bride's finger, a reading of the German *ketubah* word for word, and a recitation of the seven blessings). No glass was to be broken and no questions asked about the ring, because these rituals were deemed inappropriately superstitious and commercial.

By the mid-ninteenth century, all over Europe and in America, thinkers and politicians were measuring societal norms against the Enlightenment notions of inalienable rights, equality, and liberty. The early Reformers mirrored the broader society's burgeoning concerns about the role and status of women. They espoused the emancipation of women as an ethical imperative that outweighed inherited laws and customs, even biblical laws.[26] No longer was a woman chattel or a moveable part of a man's holdings. She was an independent entity, with her own relationship to other human beings and her own relationship to God.

Within a few decades, the Reformers moved from redefining the role of women in worship and education to revisioning the marriage ceremony entirely. At the Brunswick Convention of 1844, they rejected the biblical laws of *chalitzah*, because of the restrictions they imposed upon a young widow. They dispensed with the biblical marriage restrictions for a *kohein* (priest), seeing them as impediments to happiness and a potential cause for someone to leave Judaism. Any detrimental impact that these decisions would have on intra-Jewish relations was deemed less important than the positive impact they would have on the life of contemporary Jews.

Two years later, at the Conference in Breslau, the gap between ideology and practice with regard to women was addressed. A report entitled "For Total Equality" stated:

> The halakhic position of women must undergo a change. . . . A mere theoretical recognition, devoid of all legality, gives them as little satisfaction as, for instance, the Israelites are given in civic matters. . . . For our religious consciousness, which grants all humans an equal degree of natural holiness, it is a sacred duty to express most emphatically the complete religious equality of the female sex. . . . The Rabbinical Conference shall declare the female sex as religiously equal with the male, in its obligations and rights.[27]

With the rhetoric and ideology of inclusion, emancipation, and equality, the Reformers of the mid-nineteenth century overturned attitudes, practices, and customs adhered to by Jews for millennia. The reforms redefined the status of Jewish women from inferior beings with few rights to human beings, equal to men in all respects: legal, religious, and moral. By 1871, this egalitarian principle led the Reformers to adopt additional changes in their marriage practices, overturning many long-standing halachic norms. Women, now equals in the eyes of Reform Judaism, became active participants in the wedding ceremony. Women were allowed to give a token and say a few appropriate words to their husbands, a practice that a growing number of rabbis had adopted in the decades prior to the official resolution. Women, as well as men, could now be counted as witnesses at weddings. The Reform rabbinate decided to allow civil authorities to determine a woman's status as married or widowed in the case of a missing husband, thus opening up options for women that *agunot* (abandoned wives) never had. Civil marriage was considered completely valid and sanctioned in the eyes of the Reform Jewish community, and *kiddushin*, a religious marriage, was required only to consecrate the union.

Through these reforms, marriage was transformed from a legal/ commercial transaction with an inherent religious component into a strictly religious and spiritual ceremony, completely devoid of any legal status within or outside Judaism. A wedding still marked the change of personal status from single to married, but, in its latest form, it celebrated a spiritual transformation. Jews who followed the decisions of the Reformers entered Jewish marriages that were not sanctioned by the entire Jewish community, and the Reformers acknowledged and struggled with this reality. Yet as a group, they made a commitment to the reforms they introduced, at the risk of distancing themselves from more traditional Jews. Reform marriages might not have the requisite witnesses. They might involve people who traditionally were not free to marry. They were likely to include a non-halachic *ketubah*. Yet they were recognized as valid within the Reform Jewish community.

Thereafter, the religious meaning of marriage became a concern of the Reformers. Without its traditional legal definition, what was *kiddushin* when it became a religious adjunct to a civil legal act? This is the question that the Reform Movement has struggled with since the latter decades of the nineteenth century.

The books and articles on marriage written in the twentieth century by members of the Reform Movement (1) embraced the principles of egalitarianism and ethical consistency established by the early Reformers; (2) attempted to convince Jews of the value of a religious ceremony; and (3) introduced readers to liberal Jewish understandings and customs. They put forth the idea that a religious wedding supplemented a civil ceremony with a spiritual and personal dimension. As Doppelt and Polish wrote in the 1950s, "The wedding service is entirely spiritual in character and sacred in procedure as its Hebrew name *qiddushin* (Sanctification) implies."[28] Jewish marriage had become an interpersonal relationship with ethical, social, spiritual, and religious dimensions. Jewish weddings were rituals that celebrated a personal status and spiritual transformation.

And the ceremony itself enunciated the ideals to which the couple should aspire.

Not fundamentally concerned with the parameters of the marital relationship articulated by halachah, liberal Jewish thinkers and writers through the last decades of the twentieth century turned to biblical imagery found in the Book of Proverbs, *Shir HaShirim*, and *N'vi-im*, as well as the midrashic tradition, in their efforts to extricate and explicate the values inherent in Judaism that pertained to the marital relationship. In the last quarter of the twentieth century, discussions about the nature of marital and sexual relations consciously took into account shifting attitudes and mores. The goal has been to engage the minds and hearts of liberal Jews searching for an ethic, a framework—in Gittelsohn's words, "an Extra-Dimension"[29]—for their sexual and marital relations.

The Reform rabbis' manuals of the twentieth century provided wedding ceremonies that radically differed from traditional Jewish wedding ceremonies. First and foremost, there is no required liturgy; the majority of manuals offered liturgical options rather than a single set service. Second, there is an egalitarian assumption; both members of the couple are full participants. The performative and explanatory liturgy states for the couple and those in attendance that the wedding is an act of "mutual consecration." *Kiddushin/ nisuin* is no longer a unidirectional consecration. Even in the 1926 *Rabbi's Manual*, with no particular fanfare, this radical conceptual and liturgical innovation is incorporated into the service.[30] Third, there is an assumption that even Hebrew can be altered to reflect specific aspects of Reform ideology.[31] And fourth, there is an implicit understanding that traditional prayers and symbols of a Jewish wedding can be included, with nontraditional meanings ascribed to them. For example, the chuppah is merely a symbol of the home, not a complex halachic symbol, as contemporary Orthodox rabbis posit.[32] *Birkat Eirusin*, when included, is radically reinterpreted to refer to the expectation of sexual exclusivity for both members of the couple.

Wedding rings can be of any material, including a combination of metal and stone, because their value is irrelevant. *Ketubot* can be of different styles and content, since a traditional *ketubah*'s stipulations of bride price, dowry, and virginity[33] are not part of the *realia* that determine the validity of marriage for us as Reform Jews. How different is the picture of marriage we present in our liturgy and literature from that of traditional Judaism! And how remarkable it is that the innovations related to women and marriage that caused confusion, anger, and derision a little over a century ago have become normative among liberal Jews!

As our sights shifted from the mechanics of adhering to a prescribed set of forms and parameters to analyzing and articulating the content of an ideal marital relationship, once again we found that there were new questions and possibilities to consider. Like the generations that followed Rabbeinu Gershon, we, too, had to consider how to apply our changed understandings. If the essence of liberal *kiddushin* is the content and not the form, then can liberal *kiddushin* be an option for all couples? This question has led to an examination and reexamination of two groups long excluded from Jewishly celebrating their unions: interfaith couples and gay men and lesbians. Thus far, after repeated discussions and debates spanning 150 years, the Reform rabbinate still affirms that *kiddushin*, its symbols and messages, are meaningful within a Jewish context and, therefore, appropriate for use only with a Jewish couple. Today, a growing number of liberal rabbis choose to perform *kiddushin* for intermarried couples, but the official position explicitly rejects this as an option.

The Reform rabbinate struggled with the case of two Jews who understood and affirmed the meanings ascribed to wedding symbols and who sought to establish a Jewish home, but who were not heterosexual. The Reform Movement has affirmed that Jewish gay and lesbian couples whose relationships reflect our stated relationship ideals can celebrate their commitments through appropriate Jewish rituals.[34] For some, this is and will be *kiddushin*; for others, it is not. While this is seen by some within and beyond the liberal Jewish community as an unacceptable, even heretical, innovation, the Reform rabbinate has affirmed it as an expression of our ongoing commitment to the Jewish community and Jewish values. The Conservative Movement has begun to create rituals for same-sex couples, while explicitly stating that the rituals are not *kiddushin*.

In the U.S. and beyond, we have witnessed remarkable shifts regarding same-sex marriage in civil law and in liberal religious communities. In countries where there is a clear separation of church and state, clergy can officiate at weddings whether or not the State recognizes a legal change of status from single to married. In the U.S., where clergy can preside at a civilly recognized marriage, local and national legislatures and judiciaries are grappling with whether or not civil law should acknowledge, honor, and offer the benefits and relationship status that marriage and only marriage can offer to non-heterosexual couples. Viewing the lack of such parity as a breach of civil rights, liberal rabbis continue to be in the vanguard of religious leaders advocating for changes in civil law. Such a change will complement the status changes that their local and national religious communities have already celebrated and honored. New liturgies, *ketubot*, and visual images reflecting the diversity of couples making these commitments are readily available on the internet and in publications from the liberal movements, including rabbi's manuals, educational materials, magazines and official websites. Liberal Jewish weddings in these first decades of the twenty-first century reflect a series of innovations and adaptations that have taken place over many centuries. As a community we rejoice with a couple whose relationship embodies characteristics that imbue it with holiness: respect, truth, emotional health, justice, modesty, covenant, joy, love, exclusivity.[35] We share in the joy as a couple affirms mutual commitments and aspirations personally, spiritually, emotionally, economically, and religiously. With specifically Jewish language and imagery, we and they are reminded of the meaning of the marital relationship and the meaning of the Divine-human relationship. In every new family recognized under the chuppah, we see the promise for devotion, constancy, and faithfulness, and a commitment to Jewish continuity.

NOTES

1. With this framework, Leviticus 18–20 and, in particular, the laws known as *arayot*, sexual transgressions, can be seen in a new light. God said to the Israelite men, with numerous specific examples, that the Egyptians and Canaanites failed to understand the importance of these boundaries, but the Israelites had to understand and observe them if they were to be different and thus holy. The laws that related to the land and what grows on it and feeds on it (livestock) were reminders that all was created by God and ultimately belonged to God. Men could share in the harvest, but ultimately it belonged to God. If a sacrifice was made, a man could partake of it for a limited time, all the while recognizing that it belonged to God. Moreover, by eating it at a non-designated time, he profaned the sacred, by taking what was not rightfully his. Even the laws of social justice and equity can be read as conveying the same message: know what is yours and take only of it.

Men were also told that all women who were not members of their household were off-limits to them. Such women were another man's property/responsibility. This included one's mother, who belonged to one's father (consider the strange turn of phrase used in enumerating the *arayot*: a man reveals his father's nakedness by sleeping with his mother; he reveals his uncle's nakedness by sleeping with his aunt, etc.). In this context, women who were part of another man's household or who had already been pledged to another man were the exclusive property and sexual partner of that person. (Note: The woman had no rights of her own, and she could not make the same claim of exclusivity on any man.) Daughters were not on this list because it was understood that they belonged to their father's household, unless he agreed to transfer them to other men. With every conceivable example, men were told: by taking another man's woman you are violating his exclusive rights; you are challenging or diminishing his status. Men, remember: you can only rightfully have sexual relations with a woman who is a member of your household.

2. In this light, the Mishnaic laws that discuss the fines and damages paid to a woman's male next of kin in the case of a rape are easily understood. Because the value of his property and the price "it" could get on the market (bride's price) had been diminished, he was due compensation for his loss; *Mishnah* 3:1–9.

3. Lawrence A. Hoffman, *The Canonization of the Synagogue Service* (Notre Dame: University of Notre Dame Press, 1979), 140ff.; J. D. Eisenstein, *"Erusin," Ozar Dinim u-Minhagim* (Israel: Shilo, 1975), 29.

4. *Mishnah K'tubot* 1:6.

5. Lawrence A. Hoffman, "Life Cycle Liturgy as Status Transformation," from *Eulogema: Studies in Honor of Robert Taft, S.J.*, ed. E. Carr et al. (Rome: Studia Anselmiana 1993), 161–77.

6. *Mishnah Kiddushin* 1:3; *Mishnah Bava Batra* 3:1.

7. Both continued with the language of commerce—prohibiting *kiddushin* and *nisuin* on Shabbat or *Yom Tov* and discussing the bride's price and dowry; *Mishnah Kiddushin* 1:1.

8. Eliezer negotiating marriage for Isaac and Rebecca (Genesis 24).

9. *Chuppah* was synonymous with a woman's moving into her husband's domain. Babylonian Talmud, *K'tubot* 48a builds on a Mishnaic story from *Mishnah Kiddushin* 1:1 about a bride who did not live near her husband-to-be. If a groom sent an escort to meet her en route, as soon as she was handed over to the groom's escort for the

completion of the journey, she technically entered the *chuppah* and became his wife (*Mishnah Kiddushin* 1:1).

10. Both continued with the language of commerce—prohibiting *kiddushin* and *nisuin* on Shabbat or *Yom Tov* and discussing the bride's price and dowry.

11. *Baruch atah Adonai Eloheinu Melech haolam asher kid'shanu b'mitzvotav v'tzivanu al ha-arayot, v'asar lanu et ha-arusot, v'hitir lanu et han'suot, al y'dei chuppah v'kiddushin.*

12. Babylonian Talmud, *Y'vamot* 37b, 65a–b mention "a wife for the time of your sojourn."

13. Mordechai Friedman, *Jewish Marriage in Palestine: A Cairo Geniza Study*, vol. 1 (Tel Aviv: Jewish Theological Seminary, 1980), 5.

14. Ibid., 19.

15. Ibid.

16. Ibid.

17. Ibid., 19–30.

18. Responsa from Germany in the twelfth century show that, even in Ashkenaz, bigamy continued to be an option considered by those experiencing childlessness. R. Eliezer b. Nathan (*Even HaEizer*, 121c) and R. Eliezer b. Joel Halevi (*mavo L'Sefer Ravaya*, 201).

19. R. Isaac b. Sheshet, in the fifteenth century (*Teshuvot Rivash*, no. 15), counseled acceptance of the situation in which a childless man marries a barren woman. The childless couple who have no desire to divorce may be left undisturbed. In fact, he states there is "nothing immoral or forbidden or even offensive to holiness" in such marriages. Rabbi Jacob Tannenbaum of Hungary explained that the sages of previous generations could not find it in their hearts (*lo m'laam libam*) to permit, in actual practice, a unilateral divorce or the taking of a second wife due to barrenness. In the eighteenth century, R. Israel Lifschutz of Germany wrote (*Or Yisrael*, no. 37) that if a couple is happy and peaceful, a court should not interfere in a childless marriage to remind the husband of his duty. And in the nineteenth century, *Responsa Bigdei K'hunah, Even HaEizer*, no. 1 states that a man who has a "fine, God-fearing" but barren wife may certainly remain with her.

20. Legislation against using anything but a solid metal for the ring referred to the need to be able to assess its actual value, which would become unnecessarily complicated if a stone or anything else was attached to it.

21. Robert Gordis, *Love and Sex* (New York: Farrar, Strauss, Giroux, 1978), 166; Michael Kaufman, *Love, Marriage and Family* in *Jewish Law and Tradition* (Northvale, NJ: Jason Aronson, 1992), 171.

22. Information from Peter Elman, *Jewish Marriage* (London: Jewish Marriage Education Council, 1967), 68: "According to the *Takanot* of Corfu from the year 1642, the existing usage of a marriage comprising two parts separated by an interval of time was formally abolished, except in cases of emergency and even then the maximum interval was limited to one month."

23. All information about Moroccan Jewish customs comes from *Folklore Research Center Studies*, vol. 4, Issachar Ben-Ami and Dov Noy, eds. (Jerusalem: Magnes Press, 1974).

24. See David Biale, "Love, Marriage and the Modernization of the Jews," *Approaches to Modern Judaism*, ed. Marc Lee Raphael (Missoula, MT: Scholars Press, 1983), 1–17.

25. Ibid., 12.

26. Gunther Plaut, *The Rise of Reform Judaism* (New York: WUPJ, 1963), 252. Abraham Geiger wrote in his essay "No Spiritual Minority": "Let there be from now on no distinction between duties for men and women, unless flowing from the natural laws governing the sexes; no assumption of spiritual minority of woman, as though she were incapable of grasping the deep things in religion; no institution of the public service, either in form or content, which shuts the doors of service, and no application of fetters which may destroy woman's happiness." The full text can be found in Plaut, *Rise*, 253–54.

27. The full text can be found in Plaut, *Rise*, 253–54.

28. Frederic A. Doppelt and David Polish, "A Guide for Reform Jewish Practice," *CCAR Journal*, vol. 14, June 1956, 17.

29. Roland Gittelsohn, *The Extra Dimension: A Jewish View of Marriage* (New York: UAHC, 1983).

30. "In mutual self-consecration and in ever-deepening love for one another, may you establish a true home in Israel, a home filled with the spirit of faith, of truth, and of the fear of God."

31. From the 1926 manual focused on the ingathering of the children of Zion, the prayer reads: *"Sameach tisamach reim ha-ahuvim v'yizku livnot bayit yisrael l'shem v'lithila, v'yehi shalom b'veitam v'shalva v'hashkeit b'libotam, v'yiru v'nechmat yisrael uvirshuat olam."*

32. Maurice Lamm, *The Jewish Way in Love and Marriage* (Middle Village, NY: Jonathan David Publishers, 1991), 210: "The *chuppah* is not merely a charming folk custom, a ceremonial object carried over from a primitive past. It serves a definite, though complicated, legal purpose: It is the decisive act that formally permits the couple's new status of marriage to be actualized, and it is the legal conclusion of the marriage process that began with betrothal."

33. CCAR Committee on Responsa, *CCAR Yearbook*, 1984, 164–66, "Virginity and the Ketuba," highlights the non-egalitarianism of the traditional *ketubah* in listing only the status of a woman. "We must also express our modern concern for equal rights for men and women. If we expressly name the status of the female, we should also do so for the male" (p. 165). It goes on to say, "It would be wise either to refrain from any kind of designation of status for the woman in the *ketubah* (for which there is ample precedent) or a [sic] simply to use the designation '*virgin*' as part of a standard formula."

34. For the full resolution, see the 2000 *CCAR Yearbook*.

35. For a full statement of the Reform Movement's current understanding of human relationships and sexual values, see the 1998 Report of the Ad Hoc Committee on Human Sexuality, p. 239 of this volume.

An earlier version of this essay appeared in *CCAR Journal*, Fall 2001, vol. XLVIII/4, 34-50.

24

READING THE JEWISH TRADITION ON MARITAL SEXUALITY

RABBI EUGENE B. BOROWITZ

I have been asked to study what our heritage, particularly the halachah, tells us about the proper sexual values in modern Jewish marriage. The request itself indicates a change in the concerns of many Reform Jews. Once we searched for texts that would show how "the sources of Judaism" supported "the best of modern culture"; today—with authoritative sexual guidance (and observable sexual practices) so varied, contradictory, and often seemingly unethical—we want to know if classic Judaism can help us decide what to accept and what to reject in our society's sexual possibilities.

For the sake of this study, let us quickly bypass the always nettlesome problem of an adequate database by working from the code literature. In Maimonides's *Mishneh Torah*, *Hilchot Nashim* (particularly chaps. 14, 15, 24, and 25) and *Hilchot Kodashim* (particularly chaps. 1, 4, 8, 21, and 22) are relevant; in the *Shulchan Aruch*, see *Even HaEizer*, chapters 21–25 (abridged in the *Kitzur Shulchan Aruch* in chaps. 150–155). But that only brings us to our central problem: It is difficult to determine what texts mean in anything other than the most literal sense. We cannot have the assurance of a Kaufmann Kohler, a

Solomon Schechter, or an Israel Abrahams, that any modern mind reading these documents will arrive at pretty much the same sense of what they once meant, and what they *demand of us today*. What we think the texts meant to their authors will be determined by us as much by *our theory of how history moves*, as by the words in the texts. A historian then is only as useful to us in reading a text as his or her philosophy of history is persuasive.

Another problem then immediately asserts itself. Jewish scholars writing in English find it difficult to deal with classic Jewish legal texts applicable to a contemporary problem without becoming apologetic. Their Jewish readers are generally nonobservant and critical. Besides, non-Jews may consult such works. The authors therefore tend to censor the more unpalatable requirements of Jewish law and practice, and translate its central regulations into as contemporary an idiom as possible.

Thus, Maurice Lamm, when discussing the purposes of marriage in his book *The Jewish Way in Love and Marriage*,[1] puts companionship first and deals with procreation only in that context. That tempts one to misunderstand the traditional Jewish teaching. Even a quick perusal of the relevant legal texts indicates that though the halachah recognizes the importance of and provides for the maintenance of marital companionship, its overwhelming priority in marriage is procreation. Lamm, as a good apologist, wisely stresses that aspect of Jewish tradition that commends companionship, but his presentation no longer yields a properly balanced sense of traditional Jewish law.

Jewish authorities, in their views of marriage (as in many other cases), commend many varied, complex, and partially conflicting values. They subtly balance them with and against each other. One cannot, then, give unqualified descriptions of the Jewish heritage on this topic. As I read the data, it is equally false to say that Judaism teaches that the purpose of marriage is merely procreation or companionship. The Sages treat these values dialectically, trying to give a dynamic hierarchy to certain goods while avoiding a number of evils. Deducing "*the* Jewish view" is then further complicated by some renowned teachers who emphasize one aspect of the tradition, while other equally authoritative halachists emphasize its polar opposite. Citing only one authority or following only one stream of the legal process will not give us the whole view of classic Judaism.

Fortunately, a splendid English work exposes the full subtlety and dialectic of Jewish teaching on marital sexual responsibility. David Feldman's book *Marital Relations, Birth Control and Abortion in Jewish Law*[2] lucidly sets the vast panorama of data before the serious reader. It sets the necessary basis for any responsible Jewish discussion of this topic.

How then shall we approach the classic texts of the Jewish tradition dealing with sexuality and marriage? As I read the variety of contemporary answers to that question, two separate hermeneutic issues tend to divide us. The first has to do with the *authority* we should grant to what we decipher as their meaning. In this regard, I can isolate five distinct positions among Jews. The second issue has to do with the contemporary theory we feel best renders the texts' *substantive* message. Here I find only two functioning major points of view. To some extent, the issues of authority and substance can operate independently of one another, which may explain why our community displays such hermeneutic diversity. And if eclecticism is added to our consideration, the reason we often appear to be anarchic should be clear.

As to authority, for some Jews the traditionalist reading of the law remains fully compelling. That is the Orthodox position, and one that some Conservative Jews share. I do not see how one maintaining such a position could long be comfortable participating in liberal Judaism, so I shall not consider it further.

I find contemporary liberal Jews exhibiting four additional easily identifiable responses to Jewish tradition's behests. One declares the law to be *authoritative*, except for very substantial reason. What constitutes sufficient grounds for change is part of the substantive aspect of hermeneutics. A second view grants Jewish law and tradition *as much* influence upon our decisions as it gives to the insights of modern culture, if not more. A third position considers the Jewish heritage a *valuable guide* to our decisions when its texts are read with the eyes of modern culture (the classic liberal hermeneutic). The fourth attitude holds that Judaism *can often* supply useful resources to motivate Jews to live by the values they have freely selected for themselves.

In sum, we differ as to the suasive power we assign to Jewish tradition and to contemporary culture.

We are also divided as to the *mode of description* we employ in speaking of values. I see only two fairly consistent modes of identifying the enduringly compelling substance of the Jewish tradition. The one describes it in terms of what is ethical; the other speaks from what constitutes a proper interpersonal relationship for Jews, that is, the Covenant.[3]

The ethical interpretation of Judaism is most widely known among us in its neo-Kantian form, as in the work of Hermann Cohen or Leo Baeck. With them, one reads Jewish texts with a Kantian eye for every aspect of freedom, creativity, and universality as employed in the Jewish understandings of law and duty. One might also do this out of another ethical system—a humanistic concern for persons, for example—and get a somewhat different but nonetheless directly ethical appreciation of the Jewish heritage's continuing validity.

The relational position, which I espouse, differs in two important respects. It posits a personalistic rather than a rationalistic mode of interpretation. It also qualifies its universalism in terms of Jewish particularism, that is, it speaks of the *Jewish* relationship, not merely the one in which *all people* relate to one another or to God.

To explain further, I must declare my hermeneutic. I begin with my view of the authority of the Jewish tradition. I have broken with the older liberal practice of subordinating Jewish teaching to general culture, whether that is done rigorously, as by our Reform "Unitarians," or only in considerable measure, as by most American Jews. I have less trust in contemporary wisdom and more in Judaism's independent validity than they do. I am also too critical of the Jewish tradition to accept it as halachah, that is, as heteronomous discipline. Despite this reservation, I understand Judaism to be, at the minimum, as good a guide to living as is our civilization. It therefore is as much a legitimate critic as a beneficiary of today's understanding of the general human condition. For me, Jewish teaching regularly, but not always, functions more significantly in my decision-making than does Western culture, at least as far as values and grounding are concerned. These I interpret in a fundamentally personalistic way. That is, I share Judaism's historic meta-halachah, the Covenant relationship between God and the people of Israel, out of which Torah arises.

Applying this value stance to specific questions, I mediate between the demands of living in Covenant and the socio-historical, personal situation in which I find myself. My decisions and practice are, therefore, characterized by a dialectical flow. They are relatively steady and consistent insofar as my faith and personal integrity remain stable. They are also relatively free and changing insofar as I, at a given moment, detect a need to serve God as part of the people of Israel's historic Covenant in ways previously not utilized by me or the Jewish people. Covenantal personalism makes me more "liberal" than the halachists and less universalistic and anarchic than the pure autonomists. From this stance comes my high commitment to community pluralism and my respect for all interpretations of Jewish living and belief founded on serious concern for the claims of Judaism "however differently perceived" (as the CCAR's *Centenary Perspective*[4] puts it).

This treatment of my liberal Jewish hermeneutic should explain how I have gone about preparing my response to the question put to me: What do you see making up the liberal Jewish ethics of sexuality in marriage today? I have pondered the classic Jewish texts on the subject from my personalistic, Covenantal perspective, and on the basis of a concern with contemporary theories of sexuality going back over a decade to the writing of my book on sex ethics.

I have been able to summarize my thoughts in the form of nine Jewish positions and their dialectical, personalistic counter-concerns. So as to cover many of the questions being raised in this field, I will present these now in truncated fashion. I shall then point to two areas of my continuing perplexity. I will conclude by returning to the systematic task by briefly characterizing the general strengths and weaknesses of the Jewish tradition and of modern culture as they emerge when subjected to this sort of confrontational analysis.

We begin, first, with the fundamental premise of the discussion. For Judaism, marriage is an overwhelmingly important human duty, and spousal sexual intercourse is intimately bound up with its fulfillment. Though the halachah occasionally provides for celibate marriages (as contrasted to non-procreative ones), as in the case of continual menstrual bleeding, it diametrically opposes those tendencies in Christianity, Hinduism, and elsewhere that seek to spiritualize marriage by eliminating intercourse. Our Sages so oppose such a practice of celibacy that their occurrence qualifies women as well as men to demand that the Jewish court effectuate their divorce.

Yet, as the personalist perspective makes plain, the Rabbis, for all their concern about sexual intercourse, give us relatively little instruction as to how we might best engage in it so as to reach its Jewish goals. They do provide us with voluminous, detailed instructions about various sexual prohibitions, most particularly when the wife is halachically a menstruant. By contrast, their positive interpersonal guidance is minimal and marginal. They seem rather inhibited about direct sex-education, fearing *nibul peh* (filthy speech) and immodesty so much that they prefer to err on the side of saying little. And when they do speak, their meaning is somewhat clouded by their addiction to euphemism. Modernity has taught us that we have a better chance of accomplishing our Jewish goals by being less covert about what is so important in our lives. To be better Jews we need to learn directly about human sexuality and to discuss it openly with our spouse so that we can recognize and respond to our individual and mutual needs. We also will benefit by learning how to educate each other about our sexuality as we face the personal and biological changes that continually reshape our marital relationships over the years.

Second, our tradition connects the act of marital intercourse with the highest expressions of holiness of which people are capable. That follows from our having a Covenant with the Most High, and has nothing to do with soil or blood or national destiny. But I do not see much of this tone of sacred sexuality in our early Jewish books. The halachah, precisely as law, is concerned with the legal entailments of betrothal and marriage. *Kiddushin*, despite all our homiletics, is essentially the setting apart of this woman for this man exclusively, just as a sanctuary is set aside from all other places and must not be defiled. Without doubt, elements of spiritual sanctification do enter the relationship, as the blessings under the chuppah indicate. However, when the mystics employed a near-pagan symbolism for God to suggest a mythology of Divine fragmentation and reintegration through human religious behavior—only then did sexual intercourse become directly endowed with sacred overtones. If further evidence is required of the congeniality of this attitude to Rabbinic Judaism, we need not seek far. The Talmudic halachah makes a wife utterly subject to her husband's sexual whims, but by the Middle Ages, the rabbis insist that he has no right to have intercourse with her without her free consent.

Yet, dialectically, by modern standards, the specific rules by which the Rabbis safeguard the sacredness of human sexuality often seem no longer appropriate. The Sages seem frightened of our having fleeting thoughts or images of sexual pleasure (*hirhurim*). They warn us against these dangerous mental intrusions and suggest strategies by which to avoid them. These not succeeding, we should discipline ourselves to repress our sexual imagination. As a result, what might be one of our greatest human fulfillments is associated with what is dirty and defiling. Thus, they instruct us to have intercourse only in the dark and, regardless of our window shades, never during the daytime. By contrast, the modern notion of sexuality as being natural to people seems far more likely to sanctify this drive. Our sexual fantasies usually testify to nothing more than our continuing vitality. How we allow our imaginations to influence our acts, not our day-dreams, is the truer indication of our character. Being creatures of whim and fancy, if we turn to one another in love by day, or enjoy seeing one another as we reach out by night, then surely these acts will only enhance the personal and, potentially, the sacred aspects of our sexual union.

Third, for all its insistence upon sexuality, Rabbinic tradition felt it had only a limited place in marriage. The Covenant is for all of life, not merely to express our sexuality. In Judaism, the marital relationship encompasses far more than sexual satisfaction, because the sex act symbolizes the unique bond between the spouses. So much has been said about Rabbinic Judaism being a worldly religion and having a positive attitude toward sex that we forget its countervailing tendency to sexual self-denial. The laws concerning marital separation during menstruation, most notably the insistence of seven clean days beyond the four-plus days of actual flow, and the heavy condemnation of adultery, radically subordinate the sexual drive to a greater purpose. Moreover, males are often cautioned to limit their sexual activity to rather modest rates of intercourse. The modern world, by contrast, seems obsessed with sexuality and compulsive about better and more frequent sexual performance. It tends to subordinate the personal to the biological, and the relationship turns into an idolatry of sensuality and orgasm. Restoring a Covenantal context to our sex lives would give us a more human sense of its virtues and limits.

Yet it must also be acknowledged that the contemporary preoccupation with sex arose in reaction to the heavy repression that all the religious traditions directed toward it. Thus, modern Hebrew writers of the turn of the century (such as Tchernichovski and Berdichevsky) welcomed the modern understanding of life, for they felt their people had long been deprived of adequate love and sexuality. We may well attribute the morbidity with which much of ghetto Judaism invested sex to the stark dualism of body and spirit that medieval Jewish thought brought into our tradition. Nonetheless, we cannot deny that a similar negative note appears early on in Judaism. The Bible declares a man ritually impure until evening after he has had an ejaculation, and the Rabbis regularly use repressive terms like *kof et yitzreinu* (sublimate our urges) and *koveish et yitzro* (conquer his urge) to describe how we should deal with our sexual urges. The Rabbis' rules and attitudes seem unduly restrictive when we view sexuality as central to human personality. Less fear of our libido and more ease with the free-flowing nature of the personal life need to be infused into our contemporary Jewish sexual style.

Fourth, the Jewish writings consider the goals of intercourse to be far broader than sensual satisfaction. The Covenant between the partners is not founded on their facility in giving each other pleasure but in living together in sanctity. By contrast, Americans have come to value highly their technical know-how in producing and varying sexual pleasure. Often, then, what was once touted as an act of love becomes another test of our capacity to produce results. Not only does the relationship wither in the objectification, but the sex itself finally cannot live up to the anticipated ideal. The hedonistic paradox reasserts itself—directly pursuing happiness only makes it more elusive.

Although they occasionally acknowledged the human playfulness we so easily associate with personal sexual activity, the Rabbis did not give it very much scope or recognition. Some silliness and foolishness is often a most delightful accompaniment to our sexuality. To deny it in the name of human dignity is to miss much of the positive reality of what it is to be a person.

Fifth, our tradition proclaims procreation to be the primary, though not the exclusive, goal of marriage. The Covenant is made not only between the present partners but also with the generations that were and with the generations yet to come. Infertility is thus a terrible calamity to a loving Jewish couple. We gladly summon every resource of medical science to make it possible for the spouses to have a child. And our community rejoices with happiness when we hear of a new pregnancy or the birth of a new child. Surely some special wisdom was attached to propagation since it was the first commandment recorded in the Torah, and it is one in whose fulfillment Jews have regularly known the *simchah shel mitzvah* (joy of a mitzvah).

Yet here too Jewish tradition interpreted a worthy value to the extent that the personal welfare of the partners was subordinated to the law and its communal-historical ends. Should the mother's life be threatened, contraception might or must be used. But severe economic hardship or human deterioration as a result of bearing many children were not halachically acceptable reasons for thwarting conception. Rabbinic literature has many discussions of the evils of wasting male seed and strategies to avoid this abominable occurrence. The modern mind is far more concerned with the human waste produced in the lives of the parents, the infant, and the siblings by insisting that mothers bear children even when the parents responsibly determine it is not to their or their family's best interest to do so. For us, companionship is a far more significant goal than procreation—though one wondrous aim of a true Jewish marital friendship is the genetic blending of persons to produce a totally new individual.

Sixth, from its earliest days, Judaism taught that marriage was the only acceptable social setting for the sexual relationship. It required some advancement beyond the common conventions of the ancient Middle East to reach the monogamous marriage. The logic of the Covenant, as exemplified in this most intimate of human relationships, led Judaism to insist that it involve but two partners. In marriage, the spouses undertook ultimate responsibility for one another, and for the possibility of producing a new life together and nurturing it to maturity. In the Divine model, God occasionally threatens the wayward Covenant partner, Israel, with a divorce, but their relationship was established for all time. Human beings, in all their fallibility, ought to strive for permanence as the ideal of Covenant life. Should they not be able to manage it, our tradition accepts the necessity of divorce, though it considers the dissolution of a marriage a tragedy.

But the stability of the Jewish marriage was procured at the cost of subordinating a woman's life to that of her husband. The idea of a wife as a full personality in her own right, entitled to pursue her individual goals as her husband pursues his, is a recent possibility indeed. Yet can we call the Covenant life between husband and wife humanly complete unless two equal partners bring it into being and maintain it? And that must hold true for the wife's sexual drives and aspirations as well as for her husband's. The flow of initiation, action, and reaction needs to be as open to the wife as to the husband, allowing her to act in ways previously considered unseemly for a Jew. What the ideal of equality will eventually do to transform the Jewish covenant of marriage, I do not think anyone can now know.

Seventh, sexual faithfulness is a cardinal sign of a good Jewish marriage, and adultery is a most heinous sin. The Covenant bespeaks a unique relationship. Performing its unique marital privilege with other partners seriously damages the ties that once existed between the spouses when the intimacy they shared was unique to one another. On the Divine level, the prophets frequently denounce the people of Israel for its marital unfaithfulness. So too, though sexual loyalty requires abstention from other exciting sexual relationships and is a species of Jewish asceticism, nothing can take its place in a Jewish marriage. Our pledge to one another carries special weight when you and I know only each other as sexual partners. Should one of us break that vow of exclusivity, particularly if we do so willfully and self-consciously, we will damage our relationship most seriously. Indeed, even if we find a way to restore it, what we mean to one another cannot ever be quite the same. Some Jews today, fearing this disappointment, agree in advance to allow for occasional acts of adultery. In so deciding they practically invite the Evil *Yetzer* to live with them and never can savor the hope and fulfillment of true Covenant. Their "open marriage" testifies to the diminished standards of human integrity common in our time.

Yet it is also true that the Rabbinic laws of adultery are notoriously one-sided. Classic halachah does not apply them in the same way to men as to women. Moreover, in the so-called "laws of jealousy" it gives husbands preemptive rights over their wives' acts so that mere suspicion of misbehavior becomes grounds for divorce. And shall we agree to the law that after adultery a husband may never take his wife back, ignoring every human consideration as to what brought the act about? Here the law peaks with implacable, impersonal rigor. In the name of community standards of sanctity it calls for depriving the people in the relationship of the right to a positive decision as to what might now best become of it. I do not see that it is a fatal mitigation of the seriousness of adultery to suggest that our modern understanding of persons requires us to introduce more compassion in dealing with a transgressor in this area than the halachah did.

Eighth, incest is a major violation of Jewish marriage. The generations each have their place in the historical progression from creation to the Messiah. We do not mix our obligations to our generation with those that apply to the generations that came before us or the ones that follow us in turn. And the betrayal of exclusiveness found in adultery takes on special pain when we confuse those who are close enough to be loved uniquely with the one we love so dearly that ours is a bond of unique sexual sharing. The infidelity of incest not only breaches our special tie with them but does not allow our family relationships to function in that unparalleled Covenantal mix of high intimacy without genitality.

Here too, by personalist standards, the halachah's impersonal specification of forbidden partners seems unduly extended. It specifies in great detail those whom we may not marry and does so without regard for age, needs, or other personal considerations. Incest may require a definition in largely impersonal terms so as to place an objective limit to our polymorphous sexual cravings. Nonetheless, the Rabbinic extensions of the prohibited list of marriage partners (and perhaps even the far reaches of the biblical list) might, depending on the personal circumstances, warrant suspension in our ethics of marital sexuality.

Ninth, Judaism insists upon the communal context of our private sexual activity. What we do does not merely affect us alone but is an important part of the way the Covenant people seeks to live out its responsibilities to God. Being concerned with modesty, the Sages directed that intercourse be quite a private matter. They not only barred the presence of all other adults and insisted on the seclusion of the spouses, they were also concerned about the possible presence of their children. At the same time they did not consider Jews isolates who, when away from others, may conduct themselves in whatever fashion they might agree to. Being Jews, they should share in the high human standards and messianic aspirations of their people's Covenant wherever they are and whatever they do. Without its members living to

Israel's historic hopes, how can our people ever fulfill its responsibilities for bringing the Messiah? And the Evil *Yetzer* being so strong and human will being so frail, are we long likely to remember the sanctity of our sexuality without keeping in mind the communal dimension of our private sexual life?

This social aspect of our sexuality can be conceded by the personalist without thereby vitiating the bite of the counterbalancing criticism, that is, though the Jewish tradition richly informs us about our common human and Covenantal Jewish sexual goals, it offers us little help in learning how to express sexually just what two people mean to one another. Consider a problem that has grown with our new knowledge and openness toward sex. How shall we continually transform the exclusivity of the Jewish marital pact in relation to the differing rates and paths of the partners' personal sexual development over the many years of an enduring marriage? Our Sages have had little to say about keeping our sexual life fresh over the years. They either did not know about this problem or did not consider it worthy of their attention. Caring more directly about persons, we have a greater range of spiritual needs. Therefore, alongside static communal standards we need a sense of what enriches a modern Jewish marriage as the spouses age.

I realize that in this presentation of nine Jewish theses and their personalist counterpoises I have sacrificed depth analysis to comprehensive sweep. I am also conscious of not having touched on many other vital matters and of possibly suggesting that I have formed a focused judgment on all other issues. Permit me to remedy at least the latter failing by testifying to my—and perhaps our—continuing confusion in this area by saying a word about two perplexing matters, one raised by the halachah, the other by personalism.

I doubt that any category of Jewish law more seriously affects marital sexual life than the regulations concerning menstruation and separation. If we take our tradition seriously, we must acknowledge that these meticulously elaborated rules and their high emotional overtones cannot be censored out of the Rabbis' understanding of how to consecrate a Jewish marriage. But what shall we liberal Jews make of them?

Perhaps we can all agree on one step: the sexually proscribed seven clean days after the cessation of menstruation and the high fastidiousness of the Sages about any later show of blood seem obsessive and ought summarily to be abandoned for a more humanistic, interpersonal evaluation of when sexual activity is fitting. But we are still left with endless, detailed regulations about the onset of the period, taboos during the flow, and what constitutes its proper conclusion. Does all this say anything to us? Here we most certainly need the help of our female colleagues and of Jewish women generally. They need to take the leadership in helping us rethink our old, often archaic feelings about blood and menstruation. Perhaps then we can find an appropriately personalized way for modern Jews to sanctify this significant aspect of female sexuality and thus of Jewish marriage.

The other problem arises from our contemporary culture. We liberal Jews have welcomed women's liberation and have taken some few but important steps toward making it a reality. But how will the presence of a fully self-determining, demanding as well as acquiescent wife change the old tacit arrangements of Jewish marriage under which most Jews still operate? Consider as one aspect of the problem what the modern world has done to damage the male libido by harnessing it to economic or career-oriented ends. Our home lives have suffered, and the marketplace has become foul with our displaced sexuality. If women should now similarly channel much of their sexual drive into the pursuit of success and power, what will become of the sexual primacy of the marital bed? How, we must now wonder, can liberal Judaism today combat the destructive power of a society bent on exploiting the new sexual freedom for women?

In sum, the Jewish teaching on sexuality continues to express with compelling power the mandates of existence under the Covenant. It provides us with a ground of value, standards of practice, and ideals to which to aspire. It directs us to structure our existence so that our lives are not a random sequence of events or experiences. It puts us in a historic context so that the present moment takes its place not only within our personal history but that of our family, our people, and thus of humankind slowly moving toward God's sovereignty. It invests our sexual lives with sanctity, raising our animality beyond the human to where something of the divine image may be seen in us.

Despite this incomparable service, Judaism's sexual teaching shows three major areas in need of reform. First, its historical communal-institutional objectivity causes it to be relatively impersonalistic. We need to balance Judaism's preoccupation with abstract standards by a strong commitment to the individuality we consider basic to our mature existence. Second, its fearful understanding of the relationship between God and our genital activity easily can enshroud sexual activity with a heavy cloak of shame. We now recognize that exacerbating sexual fears and anxieties can cripple our humanity. Connecting our sex life with the transcendent needs to be done without making our sexual guidance damagingly repressive rather than therapeutically liberating. Third, and most obvious these days, classic Jewish texts are almost entirely concerned with male sexuality and male religious responsibility. A complete reworking of all these materials in terms of women's equality must now be undertaken. That cannot be done by males alone. The equal partner must have an equal voice. Indeed, considering the continuing prejudices of most of us men, leadership in this as in many other areas should be in the hands of women.

A similar dialectical evaluation of contemporary culture's view of sexuality is in order. Its weaknesses and strengths are largely the obverse of what I have just said about traditional Judaism. Too often our civilization is amoral about sex and not infrequently teaches shamelessness and the abolition of all guilt. It considers immediate pleasure the highest goal and has little sense of personal integrity through a lifetime' and almost no concern for the individual as the channel for historic human destiny. By glorifying genitality and exploiting our repressions, contemporary society has largely stripped sexuality of its mysterious power to expose us to transcendence. Much of secular sexual attitudes so revulses people with a biblical sense of human dignity that it has sent them back to their Covenantal roots. We draw from them now to provide us with an elemental appreciation of the good so that we can discern and appropriate it when we discover it in modern sexuality.

For there is much that we have learned from our culture. The intimate relationship between sexuality and personality, the devious ways in which excessive repression ultimately expresses itself in pathology, the spiritual possibilities of a liberated but not libertine sex life, the technical and emotional therapies that revitalize our sexual functioning—all must be precious to liberal Jews. But above all, modernity has taught us what it means to be a person, living in full individuality and self-determination, yet paradoxically finding oneself most fully in a projected lifelong covenant of the highest intimacy and responsibility with one specific human being. An unmodernized Judaism may seem authentic, but that is only an appearance; the faithful Jewish continuity we seek is not captured in mere recapitulation but equally in a fresh, if daring, Covenant response to "the words which I, *Adonai*, command you this day."

NOTES

1. Maurice Lamm, *The Jewish Way in Love and Marriage* (New York: Jonathan David, 2008).

2. David Feldman, *Marital Relations, Birth Control, and Abortion in Jewish Law* (New York: Schocken, 1987).

3. When capitalized, the reference is to the particular covenant between God and the people of Israel. Theologically, it serves as the paradigm of Jewish marriage.

4. http://www.ccarnet.org/rabbis-speak/platforms/reform-judaism-centenary-perspective/

This is a revised version of a presentation made to the CCAR Conference on Sexual Values, November 1981. Copyright, 1982, by Eugene B. Borowitz. Originally printed in *CCAR Journal*, Summer 1982, vol. XXIX/3, 1-15.

25

THE RITUAL SANCTIFICATION OF SAME-GENDER RELATIONSHIPS IN REFORM JUDAISM

An Eisegetical Approach

RABBI JONATHAN STEIN

During the CCAR Convention in Miami in 1997, there was a special late-night session designed to give members of the CCAR the opportunity to react to the interim report of the Ad Hoc Committee on Human Sexuality and especially its intended position on the question of the ritual sanctification of same-gender relationships. At one point during that meeting, a certain colleague took the floor and requested that "the committee not make a decision and then dress it up with traditional texts." I was struck by that statement. It helped me to crystallize something that had been nagging at me about our deliberations and the process that the committee had undertaken. That colleague, not really knowing it, was right. We had, indeed, already reached a conclusion about what we intended to recommend concerning ritual sanctification, namely, that we would encourage the CCAR to affirm such ceremonies and to support those colleagues who chose to conduct them. However, we had not reached that decision by extrapolating it from within the Jewish textual tradition. Quite the contrary. As of that moment, those of us who serve on the Ad Hoc Committee had not

quite admitted to ourselves officially the consequences of the fact that
the teachings of the Torah, the classical Rabbinic tradition, and the
later ongoing interpretations of those teachings are virtually unanimous in their condemnation of homosexuality and, as such, that they
allow precious little or no room to reason out the possibility of such
ceremonies from within a traditional framework.

It is true that some members of the Ad Hoc Committee, because
of their serious scholarship and personal facility with the traditional
texts, had volunteered to prepare scholarly papers that would attempt
to justify our position in a textual, if not halachic, framework. I admire
and respect the learning that motivates my colleagues on the committee. Indeed, I yearn to learn from them that it is possible to make such
an argument; it would set my rabbinic mind more at ease. However,
at that late-night moment in Miami, it became incredibly clear to me
that such an exercise would turn out to be exactly what our colleague
was asking us not to do: we would be taking our previously formulated
position, a viewpoint informed by many important considerations, but
not by traditional textual argument, and then we would "dress it up."

As the meeting continued, my mind flashed back to one of the earliest teachings I learned in my first homiletics class at Hebrew Union
College–Jewish Institute of Religion, namely, the difference between
exegesis and eisegesis. I remembered being taught that there are two
essential types of sermons: those that the *darshan* derives "out" of the
text (*ex* in Greek), and those that the *darshan* imposes "onto" the text
(*eis* in Greek). The former, known as exegesis, means letting the text
speak its message directly to the listener, whether in its simplest, literal
form, or in a more complex meaning; the sermon that you preach is
taught to you by the text you choose to explore. Eisegesis means that
you come to the text with a preconceived idea that you want to preach,
and then find a way to make the text "prove" your point. In class we
practiced both methods of textual explication; both were considered
legitimate; both, I was taught, could lead to good sermons. And in some
cases it was possible to preach the same sermon using either approach
on the same text.

As you are well aware, the CCAR Responsa Committee recently issued its negative opinion on the issue of rabbinic officiation at the ritual sanctification of same-gender relationships. The members of that committee wrote that they found it impossible to reach a unanimous conclusion or even a tentative consensus. In fact, the responsum itself acknowledges the basic difficulty of finding a common language for discourse concerning this issue. I believe that this is because we have these two classic worldviews in the Reform rabbinate: one seriously committed to validating change from within a framework of exegesis and, therefore, more tied to the traditional texts; the other using an eisegetical approach and, therefore, open to argumentation from outside the textual tradition. At least one of our more exegetically oriented colleagues has recently characterized this division in political terms, calling it the "culture wars" within the Reform rabbinate. I prefer to consider it an essential difference of approach in methodology with *eilu va-eilu divrei Elohim chayim.*

As I listen to the reasoning of colleagues who have decided that they *will* consider officiating at the ritual sanctification of same-gender relationships, it is clear that they almost always derive the substance of their positions in an eisegetical manner. It is equally clear that those who are *not* comfortable officiating almost always make an exegetical argument based on the classic texts that inform this area of Jewish conversation.

My personal approach to Reform Jewish decision-making prefers the textual tradition and always gives it the first chance to influence my choices. I believe it is a preferable method. Without some grounding in the classical sources, we lose our anchor to the past and our rootedness in the thought system that has historically differentiated Jews from other religious traditions. But, as a Reform rabbi, I also believe, in the now classic formulation of Mordecai Kaplan, that tradition, which always gets a vote, rarely, if ever, gets a veto. The inherent dynamic and genius of Reform Judaism is our openness to new revelations of truth and understanding in our own generation, our openness to hearing the voice of morality and ethics with a contemporary aesthetic, our openness to allowing the values of modernity, carefully sifted, to inform and influence our decisions. This means that there will be times when we have and will continue to bring values from outside the traditional Jewish textual system and, in an eisegetical manner, insist that they are of such importance and worth that they must be integrated into, imposed upon, or even supersede, what the textual tradition has taught.

I believe that we did this in the case of the equality of women. My personal reading of the traditional texts alone leads me to the conclusion that women should be excluded from the rabbinate and cantorate as well as from various mitzvot. We Reform Jews have unanimously chosen, however, to expand our hermeneutic to include the value of the complete and total religious and moral equality of men and women. Though we might reason this out on the basis of some Jewish texts and values (e.g., *b'tzelem Elohim, mishpat*), we do not need those texts and values to "dress up" our decision that the value of gender equality is so powerful and so compelling that we are willing to break with previous generations of our people and move in a totally new and creative direction.

Reform Judaism has long been essentially an eisegetical movement. This is shown in the way we change our liturgy. Although one can certainly find justification within the tradition for liturgical modification, there is no precedent for completely obliterating entire concepts like ritual sacrifice, the Messiah, and bodily resurrection. We have done so based upon our belief that such ideas are no longer acceptable to the minds and hearts of Reform Jews. Surely our reasoning was eisegetical.

This methodology of change has been one of the hallmarks of Reform and a characteristic that has differentiated us from Conservative Judaism. The Conservative Movement still considers itself halachic. In theory, all change in Conservative Judaism must be derived from textual argument. I think that is why it took them so long to approve the ordination of women as rabbis and cantors—it is simply not very easy to find such affirmation within the exegetical tradition. (I believe that the Conservative Movement actually did do eisegesis here, just as we did, but took a long time to "dress it up" with an appropriate textual garment. At least we admit to what our methodology is.)

There have been certain categories of reasoning that Reform Judaism has employed as we have debated whether to institute various changes through our essentially eisegetical methodology. I can identify at least three such considerations: (1) practical realities; (2) the priority we assign to certain values; and (3) the obtaining of new information. For example, in the first area, I believe that our new attitudes toward intermarriage are not motivated so much by principle as by our perceived need to respond to the "practical realities" of living in a society in which so many of our young people marry non-Jews. This has led us to change our attitudes and, in the case of many rabbis and congregations, their practices. Our egalitarian approach to women (and its subsequent impact on our understanding of liturgy) is an example of how our Movement decided to change based upon the second category, namely "the priority of a value." And in the third area, that of "obtaining new information," our Reform predecessors eliminated all references to "the resurrection of the dead" in our liturgy in deference to the reasoning of science, which teaches that the reanimation of dead matter is a physical impossibility.

Among the arguments in favor of affirming the ritual sanctification of same-gender relationships, there are those that fall into all three of these categories. For example, there are "practical" arguments. Many Reform rabbis and laypeople have been influenced by the fact that as more and more gay and lesbian Jews publicly acknowledge their sexual orientation, we have encountered these people as our colleagues, our friends, and our families. Homosexuality has taken on a human face. In addition, the CCAR's 1990 decision concerning the acceptability of homosexual Jews for the purposes of rabbinic ordination has led us on a very pragmatic path that culminated, in part, in the overwhelming acceptance at the 1996 CCAR Convention in Philadelphia of the resolution in favor of the right of homosexual couples to obtain a civil marriage. As this practical Reform Jewish agenda concerning homosexuality has moved forward, we have encountered some limited resistance among our laypeople and our clergy colleagues. But the fact is that the pragmatic issue of the acceptance of homosexuals in our Movement and our support of civil rights for gays and lesbians is basically a nonissue. UAHC resolutions, congregational constitutional changes, rabbinic and lay openness, and programmatic outreach—all these have moved us into a new era.

In the area of "the priority of values," various Jewish ideals have been put forward for consideration as possible ways to trump the traditional texts concerning homosexuality. These include *b'tzelem Elohim* (in the image of God), *mishpat* (law), *chesed* (loving kindness), and *ahavah* (love). The Ad Hoc Committee on Human Sexuality cites them in its list of Reform Jewish sexual values and, by implication, calls upon them as support for its argument.

I believe, however, that the engine of this machine is really fueled by the value of "inclusiveness" that has been articulated most eloquently and forcefully by our colleague Rabbi Alexander Schindler, *z"l*, during his tenure as president of the UAHC. This is, I believe, the true driving force behind the mounting-values argument that presses us forward on this issue. Reform Judaism has already expressed its will to reach out to the intermarried, the disabled, those not yet or formerly married, and the unaffiliated, as well as the gay and lesbian community. Having determined that it is imperative to reach out to Jewish homosexuals, it becomes difficult, if not impossible, to avoid the final steps toward true religious affirmation.

It is in the third area of eisegetical consideration, however, that of "obtaining new information," that we have the most important and compelling argument in favor of a new approach toward gay and lesbian couples.

Our ancestors considered homosexuality to be a particular type of behavior. To the authors of the Torah and the rabbis of later ages, all people were essentially and naturally heterosexual; some people, for whatever reason, chose, of their own free will, to engage in what was, therefore, considered to be sinful homosexual activity. It is this basic assumption that has undergone a serious reconsideration. Testimony from gay and lesbian people and, just as importantly, any number of recent studies conducted by researchers in the area of human sexuality, now point us in a new direction: homosexuality may not be an aberrant human behavior choice, but rather an integral part of the identity of certain human beings. This is to say that homosexuality may be, in fact, an irreducible combination of human genetic predisposition and societal opportunity. Another way of putting this, in theological terms, is that it is entirely possible that God has created gay and lesbian people to be, in terms of their sexuality, exactly whom they profess to be. While there is, to be sure, continuing debate about this, there appears to be an emerging consensus in this area, a consensus that points us into uncharted territory.

We live in a time when we have new information concerning the etiology of homosexuality. We live in a time of a total paradigm shift in the way we understand gay and lesbian people. As we move away from thinking about homosexuality as "what people do" (behavior) toward "what people are" (identity), we undergo, by necessity, an ontological change of category. It is exactly this type of "obtaining of new information" that demands a radical rethinking of a Reform Jewish approach to this issue. Assuming that gay and lesbian people are naturally predisposed to find sexual satisfaction in a relationship with a partner of the same gender, then it is incumbent upon us, as Reform Jews, to rethink the traditional ways in which we have understood homosexuality. We are compelled not only to accept, but, indeed, to affirm these relationships as physically and emotionally satisfying and spiritually fulfilling in the same way that we understand heterosexual relationships. This reasoning leads me, at least, to the conclusion that gay and lesbian relationships are worthy of Jewish religious ritual sanctification.

In conclusion, while it seems clear that there are at least two basic worldviews in the Reform rabbinate, worldviews that find both rootedness and authority in the Rabbinic tradition, for those of us who choose an eisegetical approach, there are, indeed, serious arguments to be put forward in favor of the ritual sanctification of stable, monogamous, committed, loving same-gender relationships.

We live in a time when "pluralism" has become a value near and dear to our Reform Jewish hearts and minds. As we strive to find a way to affirm that there are many ways to be a Jew, so may we continue to recognize that there are many ways to be a Reform Jew. May the ongoing discussion of this important topic continue to be conducted in a spirit and atmosphere that exemplify the values of reason, acceptance, respect, and mutual affirmation that have been and should continue to be among the hallmarks of our glorious Reform Jewish tradition.

This paper was delivered at the CCAR Convention, Anaheim, California, June 23, 1998, and was originally published in *CCAR Journal*, Fall 2001, vol. XLVIII/4, 51-57.

26

MARITAL SEXUAL INFIDELITY

CENTRAL CONFERENCE OF AMERICAN RABBIS
AD HOC COMMITTEE ON HUMAN SEXUALITY

Marital sexual infidelity is a growing phenomenon that threatens the very fabric of society. Its victims extend beyond the immediate circle of husband and wife. Often children are emotionally and psychologically injured, too. Every one of our communities has been shaken by the damage caused by divorce resulting from adultery. Rabbis spend ever-increasing amounts of time counseling the victims of adultery and their families. So too, our Reform Jewish community has had to respond to incidents of adultery committed by rabbis and lay leaders, those who have pledged to serve as exemplars of the highest values our tradition teaches.

This paper addresses the problem of marital sexual infidelity from a Reform Jewish perspective and attempts to place judgments regarding various manifestations of adultery within the value system developed by the CCAR Ad Hoc Committee on Human Sexuality. Our work is a response to three questions: (1) How have traditional Jewish sources defined adultery? (2) How can we frame our Reform Jewish response to adultery in accordance with the guiding principles articulated by the

Ad Hoc Committee? (3) What language can we employ to express our condemnation of adultery and our commitment to the sacred obligation of fidelity of marriage within a Reform Jewish context?

At the Central Conference of American Rabbis' June 1998 annual convention, the CCAR Ad Hoc Committee on Human Sexuality presented a paper that sought to frame a Reform Jewish value system to evaluate the broadest spectrum of human sexual conduct. This value system is defined by three guiding principles: *B'riah* (The Created Universe), which grounds human sexuality within the Divine plan, *Am B'rit* (People of the Covenant), which grants our Jewish tradition a voice in the determination of appropriate sexual conduct, and *Daat* (Contemporary Knowledge), which balances the voice of tradition with the insights gained from the secular world.[1] It is with this paradigm of values in mind that we begin our discussion of marital sexual infidelity.

A View from Tradition

What does our Jewish tradition teach us concerning marital fidelity? At first glance, it might seem that the tradition offers little in the way of useful guidance. Indeed, the concept of "marital fidelity" as we recognize it today does not exist in the eyes of biblical law. The Bible does condemn the sin of adultery and punishes it with death. Yet "adultery" in the Bible refers to sexual intercourse between a man and the wife of another man. The word is never applied to the opposite case, that is, sexual intercourse between a married man and an unmarried woman.[2] Although biblical law thus prohibits a married woman from engaging in any sexual relationship outside marriage, it places no such limitation upon her husband. A man may marry more than one woman,[3] and a married man may take one or more concubines in addition to his wife or wives.[4] In other words, the Bible does not hold the husband to the same requirement of strict monogamous fidelity that it demands of his wife.

Yet over the many centuries of its history, Jewish tradition has moved beyond this unfortunate double standard toward an expectation of marital fidelity that encompasses the husband as well as the wife. This development is expressed in a number of ways.

First, Jewish law has long since done away with the practice of polygyny. Already in the days of the Talmud, at least one rabbi held that a wife had valid grounds for divorce should her husband marry a second wife.[5] This point of view became authoritative Jewish law with the ordinance (*takanah* or *cheirem*) ascribed to Rabbi Gershom ben Y'hudah ("The Light of the Exile," d. 1028) that forbids a husband from marrying a second wife so long as his current marriage continues in force.[6] Rabbi Gershom's edict applies only to Jews of Ashkenazic extraction, that is, to those whose ancestors lived in Germany, northern France, and Eastern Europe. Sephardic Jews, whose roots lie in Spain, the Arabic-speaking world, Asia Minor, and Persia, developed their own legal means for ensuring that a husband marries one and only one wife.[7] In Israel today, Sephardic Jewish men are prohibited from marrying a second wife on the basis of local custom (*minhag*) and rabbinical ordinance (*takanah*).[8]

Second, Jewish tradition has also done away with the institution of the concubine (*pilegesh*), a woman linked in an exclusive, stable relationship with a man but who has benefit of neither *kiddushin* (marriage) nor *ketubah* (the debt undertaken by the husband at the time of marriage, payable to his wife at the time of his death or their divorce).[9] The Bible does speak frequently of concubines. Yet some rabbinical authorities assert that, now that the laws of *kiddushin* have been established, concubines are permitted to no Jewish men other than the king of Israel.[10] Others hold that, whereas it may be permissible under Torah law for a man to take a concubine, he is prohibited from doing so on moral grounds: concubinage encourages licentious behavior and threatens the institution of marriage.[11] The accepted view is that no man is allowed to take a concubine.[12]

Third, the Rabbis strengthened the bonds of marital fidelity by making divorce more difficult, though not impossible, to achieve. In so doing, they drastically modified the standard of biblical law, according to which a husband can divorce his wife virtually at will and for little cause.[13] For its part, Rabbinic tradition instituted the *ketubah*, a set of financial obligations undertaken by the husband and payable upon the dissolution of the marriage, "so that it would not be easy for him to divorce his wife."[14] The halachah insists, as well, that a man not divorce his first wife in the absence of substantial cause.[15] Moreover, a *takanah* (ordinance) issued in the eleventh century by Rabbi Gershom ben Y'hudah forbids the husband to issue a divorce to his wife without her consent.[16] Although these measures did not quite succeed in establishing equality between husband and wife in cases of marriage and divorce, they did strengthen the wife's legal position; far from being helpless in the face of her husband's conduct, the wife could exercise real power and command respect. And by making divorce more difficult for the husband to carry out, the Rabbis underscored their concern for the stability of the marriage and the fidelity of the partners to it.

Reform Judaism's Definition

Whereas a Reform Jewish response to marital sexual infidelity would contain condemnation of any sexual relationship that involves an explicit violation of the marital vow and causes pain or injury to the perpetrator's partner, how must we frame our condemnation? What language within Reform Jewish ideology most effectively conveys our denunciation? In order to respond best to these questions, we have formulated our answers according to three objectives: (1) defining different manifestations of marital sexual infidelity; (2) framing our condemnation of adultery; and (3) applying the Ad Hoc Committee's Statement of Values to marital sexual infidelity.

Defining Different Manifestations of Marital Sexual Infidelity

In order to include certain limited distinctions in our definition of adultery, which will then condition our various communal responses, we turn to Rabbi Daniel Schiff's helpful essay "Separating the Adult from Adultery."[17] Rabbi Schiff asserts that "not all forms of adultery are alike." He identifies five different types of adultery: (1) "technical" adultery—when a couple is separated preliminary to divorce, and one or both partners engage in sexual activity with another partner. Even though the new sexual relationship is technically adulterous, the emotional and spiritual commitment between husband and wife has already been terminated; (2) "circumstantial" adultery—when one partner is so impaired (e.g., Alzheimer's disease) that he or she is incapable of feeling betrayed by what may be the other partner's sexual connection outside the marriage. The healthy spouse, meanwhile, continues to assume responsibility and affectionate concern for the disabled partner; (3) "unknowing" adultery—when a married person pretends to be single and consciously deceives a single person into an act of adultery. The single person is unaware that the relationship is adulterous. The traditional halachah also took such "mistakes" into account; (4) "consenting" adultery—when both partners in a marriage, with each other's knowledge and consent, engage in sexual activity with a partner other than the spouse; (5) "classic" adultery—as Rabbi Schiff observes, "the form of adultery most widely embarked upon and also the one usually thought of when the term 'adultery' is mentioned." In most instances of classic adultery, the adulterous relationship is conducted in secret from the partner. If the secret were to be known by the spouse (and it is often discovered as the affair progresses), it would be perceived as a hurtful violation of the marriage covenant, both because of the infidelity itself and because of the lies and deceit that usually accompany it.

Framing Our Condemnation of Adultery

Rabbi Jonathan Stein, current co-chair of the Ad Hoc Committee on Human Sexuality, has prepared a hierarchical taxonomy of sexual behaviors for evaluation against the Ad Hoc Committee's "Reform Jewish Sexual Values," (see pages 241–246).[18] According to this taxonomy, each sexual behavior will fall into one of the following six categories:

Kadosh ("holy"): a relationship that is both ritually sanctified and in consonance with Reform Jewish sexual values. A married monogamous couple is an example.

Musar ("ethical"): a relationship that is in consonance with Reform Jewish values or that exhibits commitment to specific aspects of those values but that has not been ritually sanctified. A monogamous couple living together without benefit of a wedding or commitment ceremony is an example.

Mutar ("permitted"): a sexual behavior that does not violate Reform Jewish sexual values and that includes emotional involvement but not yet a permanent commitment. Mutually consensual sex within a monogamous and developing relationship is an example.

Lo kasher ("not proper"): a behavior or relationship that does not conform to Reform Jewish sexual values but that is performed between two consenting adults. Consensual sex between two people who are not in the process of developing a committed relationship is an example.

Cheit ("sinful") or *asur* ("prohibited"): a behavior or relationship that violates Reform Jewish sexual values. Promiscuity is an example.

To-eivah ("abhorrent"): a behavior that is both *cheit* and *asur* and that is also abusive, violent, or coercive, or which violates historic Jewish and human societal norms. Rape and pedophilia are two examples.

We place both classic adultery and consenting adultery in the categories of *cheit* and *asur*. We condemn them unequivocally as contrary to the letter and spirit of *kiddushin* and as being outside the pale of acceptable sexual conduct for the following reasons:

1. *Moral Condemnation:* Classic adultery and consenting adultery are violations of a moral commitment that entails trust and responsibility.

2. *Social Condemnation:* Classic adultery and consenting adultery are destabilizing forces within the structure of the family and, therefore, within the structure of the community.

3. *Theological Condemnation:* Since marriage is *kiddushin*, divinely sanctioned, classic adultery and consenting adultery are sins against God and the community that is covenanted with God.

We recognize the ethical and emotional complexity associated with circumstantial, technical, and unknowing adultery. We believe that halachic sources would condemn adultery under any circumstances, but we acknowledge that some expressions of circumstantial, technical, and unknowing adultery require leniency and greater compassion and, therefore, we hesitate to place them in a specific category. We affirm the rabbi's role in assisting such couples in attaining the appropriate spiritual and psychological counseling in order to respond to their specific dilemmas. Finally, we affirm that when any expression of marital infidelity does occur, marriages are capable of being salvaged, often with the help of competent professionals. We affirm the efficacy of professional psychological counseling and the employment of such religious values as *tocheichah* and *t'shuvah*, where appropriate, in order to attempt to repair the damage caused by acts of sexual infidelity. We call upon our rabbis, in their role as pastors, to promote and aid in the attainment of such assistance.

The Ad Hoc Committee's Statement of Values to Marital Sexual Infidelity

Below we offer moral and spiritual arguments for marital fidelity framed by the Statement of Values put forth by the CCAR Ad Hoc Committee on Human Sexuality. We assert that Reform Jewish religious leaders should teach the sacred standards of fidelity and marital commitment embodied in our tradition and in the "Reform Jewish Sexual Values." Such teaching may take place within adult education classes and youth group programming, in rabbis' sermons, and, of course, in the demeanor and behavior of the rabbi himself or herself.

> *B'riah* (The Created Universe), which grounds human sexuality within the Divine Plan—

We affirm the message of the Book of Genesis of our Torah
that asserts that marriage is part of God's plan for humanity. It
is marriage that serves as the foundation of the family, and as
the Ad Hoc Committee's "Reform Jewish Sexual Values" states
under the heading "*Mishpachah*," the family is a cornerstone of
Jewish life. The Torah, through the first mitzvah, *p'ru ur'vu*,
"be fruitful and multiply" (Gen. 1:28), emphasizes the sacred
obligation to bring children into the world through the institution of the family.[19]

Am Brit (People of the Covenant), which grants our Jewish tradition
a voice in the determination of appropriate sexual conduct—

As the prophet Hosea said, "I will betroth you to Me forever;
I will betroth you to Me in righteousness and justice, in love and
compassion; I will betroth you to Me in everlasting faithfulness"
(Hos. 2:21–22). The marital commitment is so central to God's
plan for the Jewish people, that it is likened to the Covenant
itself. Rabbinic tradition places heavy emphasis upon the importance and the exalted nature of the marriage bond. The Talmud
proclaims that "any man who lives without a wife lives without
goodness, without blessing, without a home, without peace."[20]
It further states that "one who has no wife is not truly human."[21]
It is God who assigns each of us a marriage partner,[22] a powerful expression of the Divine intent that marriage be the proper
state of humankind.[23]

We need not read these texts literally, nor are we required
to learn from them that those who are single are somehow less
worthy than those who are married. What they do tell us is
that the marital union is a precious thing in God's sight, that it
must be treated with the utmost concern and respect, and that
any conduct that undermines its stability should be avoided.
The tradition instructs the husband to honor his wife more than
he honors himself and to love her as he loves himself;[24] surely
there is no conduct more destructive of honor and love in marriage than marital infidelity. From all this, we learn that sexual

faithfulness within the bond of marriage is a moral obligation of the highest sanctity.[25]

The word "sanctity," with which we concluded the preceding paragraph, is no mere literary flourish. The traditional Jewish term for marriage is *kiddushin*,[26] derived from the Hebrew word that means "holiness" and "sanctity." This term does not appear in the Bible; it was coined by the Rabbis, who used it to express the ideal of sexual exclusivity in the marital relationship. That which is "sanctified" (*kadosh*; *hekdeish*) is set apart for God;[27] so too, in traditional Jewish thought, the wife is set apart (*m'kudeshet*) for her husband. Transgression against this exclusive sexual relationship is thus much more than a violation of a civil or monetary contract; it is the violation of ritual law, the line by which God and we distinguish the holy from the profane.

Daat (Contemporary Knowledge), which balances the voice of tradition with the insights gained from the secular world—

Sexual fidelity characterizes the holiness of marriage. Reform Judaism has extended this concept to, what we believe to be, its logical conclusion. Since gender equality is a fundamental principle for us, our understanding of marriage requires that its obligations be mutual and reciprocal. In the traditional Jewish wedding the husband "sanctifies" the wife; in our services, each partner "sanctifies" the other.[28] Sexual fidelity is now an expectation that each spouse can expect of and demand from the other.

This expectation is the logical culmination of Jewish religious thought concerning the marital bond. If early Jewish law permitted a man to have multiple sexual partners outside his marriage, our tradition has moved steadily to deny these opportunities to him. It has done so, we believe, not only out of concern for the status and situation of the wife, but also out of the idea that marriage, according to our most deeply held understanding of the nature of that union, requires a commitment by both partners to mutual fidelity. Our teachings on this question, therefore, express not only our own views but also the trend and tendency of our Jewish tradition over many centuries of thought and practice. Both partners are held equally responsible for maintaining that sexual exclusivity and both are held equally responsible for its violation. In accordance with recent resolutions of the Central Conference of American Rabbis, this moral norm would also apply to same-sex couples who have codified their relationships with a sacred ceremony.

We conclude by reiterating the tenth Reform Jewish sexual value articulated in the CCAR Ad Hoc Committee on Human Sexuality Report:[29]

> *K'dushah*, "holiness," is not simply a state of being; rather, it is a continuing process of human striving for increasingly higher levels of moral living. In a Reform Jewish context, a relationship may attain a measure of *k'dushah* when both partners voluntarily set themselves apart exclusively for each other, thereby finding unique emotional, sexual, and spiritual intimacy.

CCAR Ad Hoc Committee on Human Sexuality, 2001

Jonathan Stein, Chair
Richard Address
Donald Berlin
James Bleiberg
Gerald Brieger
Michael Cahana
Denise Eger

Samuel Karff
Jan Katzew
Charles Kroloff
Selig Salkowitz
Eleanor Smith
Mark Washofsky
Michael White

NOTES

1. Central Conference of American Rabbis, "Ad Hoc Committee on Human Sexuality: Report to the CCAR Convention, June 1998," p. 239 of this volume.

2. See Exod. 20:13; Deut. 5:17; Lev. 18:20. The point is most clearly expressed in Lev. 20:10: "If a man commits adultery [Hebrew root *n-a-f*] with a married woman [*eishet ish*], committing adultery with another man's wife, the adulterer [*hano-eif*] and the adulteress [*hano-afet*] shall be put to death." Significantly, Rabbinic and halachic literature routinely refer to "adultery" as *isur eishet ish* or *habaal eishet ish*, i.e., the prohibition of sexual intercourse with a married woman. See Maimonides, *Sefer HaMitzvot*, neg. comm. no. 347, and *Mishneh Torah, Isurei Biah* 1:6 and elsewhere.

3. As the examples of Jacob, Esau, Elkanah, Saul, David, and Solomon (among others) make clear. In the legal texts, we find the permission for polygyny in Exod. 21:8–11 and Deut. 21:15. Talmudic law adheres to this standard: the halachah follows Rava, who rules that "a man may marry any number of wives, provided he has the means to support them all" (Babylonian Talmud, *Y'vamot* 65a). As Maimonides formulates the rule, a man may marry more than one wife "so long as he can provide each one her statutory requirement of food, clothing, and conjugal pleasure" (*Mishneh Torah, Hilchot Ishut* 14:3). That the wife is entitled to the above three "rights" is derived from Exod. 21:10; see Babylonian Talmud, *K'tubot* 47b. Talmudic tradition informs us that the Sages advise a man to marry no more than four wives, so that he do his conjugal duties to all of them; Babylonian Talmud, *Y'vamot* 44a.

4. On the definition of "concubine" (*pilegesh*) in Jewish law, see below in text. The institution of the "slave-wife" (*amah* or *shifchah*; see Exod. 21:8–11, Lev. 19:20, and elsewhere) should be mentioned here as well.

5. This view is attributed to R. Ami, who disputes the position taken by Rava in Babylonian Talmud, *Y'vamot* 65a.

6. *Shulchan Aruch, Even HaEizer* 1:10. On the life and work of R. Gershom and on the question of his role in the creation of this and other *takanot*, see Avraham Grossman, *Hachmei Ashkenaz HaRishonim* (Jerusalem: Magnes, 1981), 106–74.

7. Writes R. Yosef Karo, the Sephardic author of the *Shulchan Aruch:* although the *takanah* of R. Gershom was never accepted in the Sephardic countries, "it is a good thing (for local communities) to enact rules forbidding a husband to marry a second wife"; *Shulchan Aruch, Even HaEizer* 1:10–11. When local custom (*minhag*) holds that a husband may not marry a second wife, he is forbidden to do so; *Shulchan Aruch, Even HaEizer* 1:9 and *Chelkat Mechokek ad loc.*, no. 15. For centuries, it was customary in Sephardic circles for couples to stipulate in their *ketubah* that the husband would not marry an additional wife and to impose severe financial indemnities upon him if he did so; see Mordechai A. Friedman, *Ribui Nashim B'Yisrael* (Jerusalem: Mosad Bialik, 1986).

8. See B. Z. Schereschewsky, *Dinei Mishpachah*, 4th ed. (Jerusalem: Rubin Mass, 1992), 66–67, 452.

9. The relationship is "exclusive," of course, only from the concubine's standpoint; the man is permitted to take wives and other concubines. That a concubine has neither *kiddushin* nor *ketubah* is derived from Babylonian Talmud, *Sanhedrin* 21a; see Maimonides, *Mishneh Torah, Hilchot, M'lachim* 4:4 and Nachmanides to Gen. 25:6.

10. Maimonides, *Mishneh Torah, Hilchot, M'lachim* 4:4.

11. These include Nachmanides, *Resp. Harashba Hameyuhasot Laramban*, no. 284; R. Yitzchak b. Sheshet Perfet, *Resp. Rivash*, no. 398; R. David ibn Zimra, *Resp. Radbaz* 4:225 and 7:33; R. Chaim Ozer Grodzinsky, *Resp. Achiezer* 3:23; R. Moshe Feinstein, *Resp. Ig'rot Moshe*, EHE 1:55.

12. For a discussion of the law on this subject, see CCAR Responsa 5756.10, "Long-Term Non-Marital Relationships," http://www.ccarnet.org/responsa/rr21-no-5756-10/

13. Deut. 24:1; Babylonian Talmud, *Gittin* 90a–b; *Mishneh Torah, Hilchot, Geirushin* 1:2.

14. Babylonian Talmud, *K'tubot* 39b and parallels.

15. Babylonian Talmud, *Gittin* 90b; *Mishneh Torah, Hilchot, Geirushin* 10:21.

16. See *Shulchan Aruch, Even HaEizer* 119:6, Isserles.

17. "Separating the Adult from Adultery," in *Marriage and Its Obstacles in Jewish Law* (Pittsburgh, PA: Solomon Freehof Institute of Progressive Halakhah, 1999).

18. See "Toward a Taxonomy for Reform Jews to Evaluate Sexual Behaviors."

19. Central Conference of American Rabbis, "Ad Hoc Committee on Human Sexuality: Report to the CCAR Convention, June 1998."

20. Babylonian Talmud, *Y'vamot* 62b.

21. Babylonian Talmud, *Y'vamot* 63a.

22. This theme is developed in Babylonian Talmud, *Mo-eid Katan* 18b and *Sotah* 2a. See also the story of R. Yose b. Chalafta and the Roman matron in *Vayikra Rabbah* 8:1.

23. See *Tur, Even HaEizer* 1, deriving this from the verse "it is not good for a man to dwell alone" (Gen. 2:18).

24. Babylonian Talmud, *Y'vamot* 62b; *Mishneh Torah, Hilchot, Ishut* 15:19.

25. See Babylonian Talmud, *Kiddushin* 2b and *Tosafot ad loc., s.v. d'asar.*

26. *Kiddushin* specifically refers to the first of the two stages of the legal process of marriage in Jewish law. That first stage, called *eirusin* ("betrothal"), involves the forging of the marital union, a bond that can be broken only through death or divorce. The couple does not actually live together as husband and wife until they have undergone the second stage of the legal process. This stage is called *nisuin* ("marriage") or *chuppah* (the "wedding canopy," possibly a symbolic representation of the couple's marital home; for a list of the various interpretations of *chuppah*, see *Shulchan Aruch, Even HaEizer* 55:1, Isserles). Although today the entire process takes place in one ceremonial setting, in former centuries the two stages of the process were often performed separately. For this reason, Jewish texts often refer to "marriage" by the compound phrase *chuppah v'kiddushin.*

27. On the interpretation of "sanctity" as separateness, see Lev. 19:2 and Rashi and Nachmanides *ad loc.*

28. See the wedding liturgies in *Rabbi's Manual* (New York: Central Conference of American Rabbis, 1988), 50–84.

29. Central Conference of American Rabbis, "Ad Hoc Committee on Human Sexuality: Report to the CCAR Convention, June 1998."

27

SCENES FROM A MARRIAGE

Rabbi Janet R. Marder

On the surface, it looked like they had everything. They were loaded with money, with a huge, palatial home, richly decorated in the latest style. They had secure and prestigious jobs. They were a popular couple, surrounded by friends; they entertained often and had a lively social life. They knew they were the object of envy among their circle of acquaintances. Their life was easy and pleasant and luxurious. They should have been happy—but something was missing at the core.

The truth was that he was tired of her. She was still a good-looking woman, he supposed, but the bloom was definitely off the rose. He remembered a time when they couldn't get enough of each other. He wondered where all of that passion had gone. He wondered if he would ever feel that way again.

She had her own discontents. Gradually, she'd noticed, a distance had grown between them. Both of them were busy and often tired— that was part of the problem. But more and more, they couldn't seem to find anything to say to each other. When they did talk, it felt perfunctory and superficial. She couldn't remember the last time they'd had a real conversation. She felt lonely, unloved, and unappreciated. He never touched her anymore unless he wanted something from her.

She found him immature, emotionally inexpressive. He found her cold and disapproving.

More and more, it seemed, the two of them went their separate ways and led their own lives, with their own interests and activities. Inside their big, opulent house, they slept apart.

He was restless, wanting something more. She was bored with a marriage that felt empty and dead. But things dragged on for a few years without either of them making a move. Then, all at once, things fell apart. In an effort to inject a little excitement into the marriage, he asked her to try something different—something more daring and adventurous. He asked her to do it for him.

She could tell he was drunk, which infuriated her. She found his request demeaning. She told him so, and flatly refused. He felt angry and humiliated. And that was it: on that very night he decided to dump her. Within a short time he had found someone else—a younger woman, very pretty of course, and much more compliant. The new girl looked up to him and thought he was wonderful. Once again, he felt on top of the world. His middle-aged ex, embittered and resentful, predicted that in time the jerk would get just as tired of her replacement.

The story of Purim, whatever else it is, is also the story of a marriage gone bad. The tale of Esther and Mordechai's triumph begins with a bitter, far-from-civil divorce. Consider the case of King Ahasuerus and Queen Vashti, the discontented pair whose domestic troubles we breeze through impatiently, eager to get to the beauty contest where our heroine will emerge.

Their story, unpleasant as it is, seems somehow familiar. A wealthy man who has everything but feels empty; a powerful man who feels entitled to get what he wants, yearning for a beautiful younger woman; a long relationship that has descended into the doldrums; an angry wife, reeling from the pain of public exposure and shame; marital unhappiness and acrimony put on display for all to see. The tale of Ahasuerus and Vashti seems snatched from the headlines, which often tell of the downfall of rich and powerful leaders undone by their appetites.

We'll never know what was really going on in that Persian marriage two thousand years ago. The Bible isn't interested in telling us, so we're free to spin our own scenarios. So also, the news stories like those about ex-governor Eliot Spitzer of New York or former presidential hopeful John Edwards give us only the most cursory view of what is surely a complicated personal life. Behind the scenes, behind the gossip and the snickers, the shocked recriminations and the moralizing condemnations, lies the private story, which none of us can or should wish to penetrate.

But we can talk about one aspect of those stories, because it is a fact of life today; and we can talk about it in a Jewish context, because it is, for Jews, a religious issue. I mean the painful reality of marital infidelity.

Scarcely had the people of New York put the Spitzer scandal behind them and sworn in a new governor—a different kind of man: low-key, unpretentious, a consensus builder—when familiar words returned to the headlines. Governor Patterson too, it seemed, had some extramarital affairs in his past. So did his wife.

The state of New Jersey chimed in with some provocative headlines of its own, dealing with their previous governor and his very complicated marriage and divorce. Spitzer, Patterson, and McGreevey joined a long line of politicians, including Rudy Giuliani, John McCain, Newt Gingrich, Gavin Newsome, and John Edwards, who have acknowledged episodes of "weakness" in their past. When they broke, these events awakened uncomfortable memories of a time, not too many years ago, when the country was mesmerized by seamy tales emanating from the White House about the private life of the commander in chief.

The *New York Times*, eager to cast an objective, scientific light on these incidents of marital malaise, published an article that examined behavior in the animal kingdom, entitled "In Most Species, Faithfulness Is a Fantasy." Contending that "sexual promiscuity is rampant throughout nature," the article quoted psychologist David P. Barash of the University of Washington, author, with his wife, Judith Eve

Lipton, of *The Myth of Monogamy*. Dr. Barash says that, behaviorally speaking, infidelity is pretty much the norm, stating pithily, "Infants have their infancy; adults, adultery."[1]

So even swans, it turns out, cheat on their spouses, just as people do. Just how common is adultery among humans? One book by Peggy Vaughan, *The Monogamy Myth* (to be distinguished from the earlier-mentioned *The Myth of Monogamy*), claims that 60 percent of American husbands and 40 percent of wives will have an affair at some time in their marriage.[2]

A well-regarded 1994 survey conducted by the University of Chicago puts the number more conservatively, at 25 percent for men and 12 percent for women. These numbers would increase by perhaps 20 percent if they included so-called "emotional affairs" in which the intimacy never becomes physical. There is no reliable evidence that the infidelity rate in this country has increased over the past few decades.

A 1998 Gallup poll found that Americans were quite firm in their disapproval of extramarital sex: 79 percent said it was "always wrong," and another 11 percent said it was "almost always wrong." In a 2006 Gallup poll, Americans said adultery was worse than human cloning.[3]

Our own tradition seems to offer a similarly vehement condemnation. The seventh commandment, "*Lo tinaf*—Do not commit adultery," is an apodictic law: it's an absolute prohibition rather than an instance of case law. The command to refrain from adultery does not include any parenthetical exemptions, such as "except when you fall in love with someone else."

On the other hand, the original biblical understanding of this commandment was far less restrictive than modern interpretations: it applied only to a man having relations with a woman who was married or betrothed to someone else. Adultery seems to have been regarded at the time as a kind of property violation—one man infringing on what belongs to another. The original intent of the commandment was not to legislate monogamy within marriage—at least not for men.

That being said, for at least the past thousand years monogamy has been the legal norm for Jews, and today both Reform and traditional

Judaism views extramarital relations as wrong. Certainly, there are difficult circumstances that require a much more thoughtful and sensitive response. Rabbi Richard Address, a leading scholar on Judaism and aging, published an article in the *Forward* raising the question of whether it would be wrong for a married person whose spouse has Alzheimer's to turn elsewhere for intimacy (see also in this volume, "When Alzheimer's Turns a Spouse into a Stranger," pp. 549–562 below).[4] But setting aside that special case, let's ask where the seventh commandment leaves the average married couple. We know adultery is wrong and faithfulness is the marital ideal. We also know that it can be hard to live up to that ideal. Psychoanalyst Stephen A. Mitchell, in a book called *Can Love Last?*, points out that both men and women have "two fundamental, conflictual needs": a need for security, familiarity, and a reliable anchor; and a need for novelty, adventure, and risk.[5] Both are important. When only one need is met, we feel that something is missing.

Some people, intent on fulfilling the second need, resist making a permanent commitment to anyone. Others devote tremendous energy to satisfying the first drive—searching for the right person, settling down, and building a nest together. But as our sense of safety in a relationship increases, excitement diminishes. One day we discover that the thrill is gone.

Much research shows that marital happiness declines with the transition to parenthood, for reasons most parents can understand. In the years that follow, some couples settle into a comfortable relationship that is loving and respectful, if not passionate; others end up feeling more or less like roommates. It is reminiscent of a line in a film by Ethan Hawke called *Before Sunset*, in which the main character, age thirty-two, confesses that he loves his little boy, but he and his wife have nothing in common anymore except child rearing. He says, "I feel like I'm running a day-care center with someone I used to date."

People who never expected to find themselves in this situation may have an affair or find that their spouse has been unfaithful to them. What follows such betrayal is often a nightmare of shock, anguish, grief, and rage.

Given the dynamics of marriage over time and the myriad stresses upon marriages today, it would be unfortunate if all we had to guide us was the seventh commandment and a shelf of self-help books, many of which contradict one another.

In fact, there's more our tradition can offers us. In addition to the apodictic "thou shalt not," we have in the Talmud several stories that show our Sages wrestling with the real-life tensions of being in a committed relationship. Just reading the stories can open up an interesting conversation. A passage in Tractate *Kiddushin* (81b), the Talmudic tractate dealing with marriage, teaches:

> Whenever Rabbi Chiya bar Ashi fell down prostrate [at the conclusion of his personal prayers], he would say, "May God save me from the *yetzer hara* [a reference to the sexual urge]." One day his wife overheard him. "Let us see," she reflected. "It is so many years that he has held aloof from me; why then does he find it necessary to say this prayer?" One day when her husband was studying in the garden, she adorned herself, disguised herself as a prostitute, and paraded back and forth in front of him.
>
> He asked her, "Who are you?" She answered, "I am Charuta [a name apparently derived from *cheirut*, "freedom"], and I have returned today." He propositioned her. She said to him, "First bring me the pomegranate from the top of the tree." He jumped up and went and got it for her.
>
> When he came home [after his sexual encounter], his wife was lighting the oven. He went and sat inside [or on] it [in order to punish himself]. She said to him, "Why are you doing this?" He told her what had befallen him. "But it was I!" she said. He paid her no attention until she brought [him] proof [the pomegranate]. [But he refused to be comforted.] "Nevertheless," he said, "My intention was wrong."

In just a few lines the world of a married couple opens up before us. There are some things we don't know. How old are these two people? How long have they been together? Are there children? A few things we do know: He has withdrawn from her, and she doesn't know why. Years have gone by while she wonders what's happened. She suspects, perhaps, that her husband is no longer capable of making love. Then she hears him saying that prayer—a prayer he apparently says every day—and she discovers that he is a man tormented by desire. He has apparently never discussed his feelings with her; she has never asked him the question that is so much on her mind. We see here the relationship between emotional intimacy and sexual intimacy—and both are missing from this marriage.

She is probably quite disconcerted and puzzled to learn this secret about her husband. Perhaps she feels rejected. Eventually she takes matters into her own hands and makes an effort to renew the marriage. Remarkably, after she dresses herself up in provocative fashion, her husband doesn't seem to recognize her. "Who are you?" he asks. Maybe she has let herself go for years and he can't believe his eyes. Or maybe he hasn't been looking closely at his wife for a long time. We wonder if he truly has any idea who she is.

After their erotic encounter, he returns home some time later to find his wife "heating up the oven"—perhaps to signify that passion has returned to their relationship. He is depressed and full of guilt. Finally they have an honest conversation—he tells his wife the truth about what happened to him in the garden.

She tries to make him feel better—she doesn't mind that he was living out a fantasy, because, after all, the other woman was really herself. She doesn't mind that he was thinking of someone else when he was with her. But Rabbi Chiya can't accept it. He can't fit his wife into the role of a temptress or a sexual being. His idea of marriage won't allow for this kind of playfulness and daring. It doesn't bode well for their future.

Our Sages lived in the real world. They knew about marriages that felt cold at the center and about temptation and yearning, the ebb and flow of emotion and desire, the tensions that can arise when two people try to make a lifetime commitment. They knew all about the challenges of marriage that Esther Perel describes in her intriguingly titled book *Mating in Captivity*.

Yet our Sages never lost their faith in marriage as an effort to create something beautiful and sacred here on earth. That's why they gave to marriage the Hebrew name *kiddushin*, "holiness."

"So it is that a man will leave his father and mother and cling to his wife, and they become one flesh" (Gen. 2:24). The traditional words from Genesis set before us an ideal of marriage—an exclusive, intimate bond in which two people are closer to each other than to anyone else in the world.

The prophets give us the image of a covenantal union between partners who pledge their best to each other and help each other to reach their best: "I will betroth you to me forever," says Hosea. "I commit myself to you with equity, and with unconditional love. I commit myself to you in faithfulness. Through each other, may we come to know the Eternal" (Hos. 2:21–22).

The chuppah, it is said, is open on all sides. Open to the influence of family, friends, and community. Open to whatever the winds of change may bring to the relationship. And open to enemies of marriage as well: fatigue, inattention and distraction, pervasive negativity, lack of communication, and loss of intimacy. Protecting our precious relationships from all these threats deserves our best efforts. Sustaining a good marriage is a spiritual challenge of the highest import.

NOTES

1. Natalie Angier, "In Most Species, Faithfulness Is a Fantasy," *New York Times*, March 18, 2008.

2. Peggy Vaughan, *The Monogamy Myth*, 3rd ed. (New York: Newmarket Press, 2003), 7.

3. See Pamela Druker, "Our Ready Embrace of Those Cheating Pols," *Washington Post*, July 15, 2007.

4. Richard Address, "Is It Still Adultery If the Spouse Has Alzheimer's?," *Forward*, August 15, 2007.

5. Stephen A. Mitchell, *Can Love Last? The Fate of Romance over Time* (New York: W. W. Norton, 2002), 36–39.

28

TAHARAT HAMISHPACHAH

A Renewed Look at the Concept of Family Purity

RABBI DENISE L. EGER

Traditionally in Jewish life the concept of *taharat hamishpachah*, or the laws of family purity, revolves solely around the halachah of *nidah*. *Nidah* is defined as a menstruating woman or collectively as the laws pertaining to the sexual availability of menstruating women and the process of becoming ritually impure and then ritually pure. This includes the use of the mikveh, ritual immersion, following menstruation and childbirth.

The laws of *nidah* are derived in part from the laws of purity and impurity as described in Leviticus 15:

> [19]When a woman has a discharge, her discharge being blood from her body, she shall remain in her impurity seven days; whoever touches her shall be unclean until evening. [20]Anything that she lies on during her impurity shall be unclean; and anything that she sits on shall be unclean. [21]Anyone who touches her bedding shall wash his clothes, bathe in water, and remain unclean until evening; [22]and anyone who touches any object on which she has sat shall wash his clothes, bathe in water, and remain unclean until evening. [23]Be it the bedding or be it the object on which she has sat, on touching it he shall be unclean until evening. [24]And if a man lies with her, her impurity is communicated to him; he shall be unclean seven days and any bedding on which he lies shall be come unclean.

Further, the Torah describes in Leviticus 18:19 and 20:18 the serious nature of the ritual defilement of having sexual intercourse during a woman's menstruation.

A woman is also considered in a state of *nidah* following childbirth, as described in Leviticus 12:1–8. The length of her ritual defilement depends upon the gender of the child.

As Rachel Biale states in her book *Women and Jewish Law:*

> The laws of *niddah* include innumerable strictures and precautions. Questions about possible violations of these regulations and their exacting details are very prominent in the halakhic literature. The impact of the laws of *niddah* on people's lives was profound since they imposed a set pattern of sexual activity, mandating periods of abstentions and physical distancing between husband and wife. Furthermore, by virtue of the fact that purification and resumption of sex normally coincided with ovulation, the laws of *niddah* favored procreation.[1]

Thus the laws of *nidah* and *taharat hamishpachah* narrowed the sexual availability of wives to their husbands and created a calendar for sexual intercourse that heightened the time of fertility of women and the chance for offspring. This helped husbands fulfill the commandment of *p'ru ur'vu*, procreation.

The Talmud devotes significant discussion to the laws of *taharat hamishpachah* and the laws of *nidah* in Tractate *Nidah*, as well as parts of tractates *Shabbat* and *Sh'vuot*.

In Tractate *Shabbat* 13a-b the following story shows how the Rabbis intensified their attitude toward the observance of *taharat hamishpachah*:

> (It is taught in the) *Tanna D'Vei Eliyahu*: It once happened that a certain scholar who had studied Bible and Mishnah and had unstintingly served scholars died at middle age. His wife took his tefillin and carried them about in the synagogue and schoolhouses and complained to them (the scholars): "It is written in the Torah, for that is your life and the length of your days" (Deut. 30:20). My husband who read much Bible and studied much Mishnah and served scholars a great deal, why did he die at middle age? No one could answer. On one occasion I [Eliyahu, the supposed author

of the *Tanna*] was a guest at her house, and she related the whole story to me. I said to her: "My daughter, how was he to you in the days of your menstruation?" "God forbid," she replied, "he did not even touch me with his little finger." "And how was he in the days of your whites [the seven days following cessation of menstruation]?" "He ate with me, drank with me, and slept with me in bodily contact, and it did not occur to him to do otherwise." I said to her: "Blessed be God for slaying him, for God did not condone this behavior. Therefore, even though the man had much merit on account of his life for the Torah, God punished him, for lo, the Torah has said, 'And you shall not approach a woman as long as she is impure in her menses'" (Lev. 18:19).

With this Talmudic passage it seems that the Rabbis intensified their attitude toward the observance of *nidah* and *taharat hamishpachah*. This story shows how they moved from the prohibition of sexual relations during the impurity of the actual flow of blood to include further restrictions for the seven days after. It not only builds a fence around the Torah restriction but also emphasizes the shift in distinction between the ritual prohibitions and sexual prohibitions. Thus the concept of family purity was extended not only to abstaining from sexual intercourse or contact during menstruation, and then immersion to ritually purify the woman, but also to further abstention of sexual intimacy for a longer time frame. From this example, family purity was not just about menstruation or *nidah*, but further created the window of opportunity for the woman to be at the height of fertility when the husband and wife were once again permitted to each other sexually. Thus the laws of family purity came to take on an enriched meaning beyond the specific Torah prohibitions to include a larger framework of meaning, including the intimate relationship between husband and wife, the rhythm of sexual availability.

While many traditional Jews still observe the details of *taharat hamishpachah*, in the liberal setting the emphasis on ritual impurity and purity has long been cast aside. Especially with Reform Judaism's de-emphasis of the priestly traditions and centrality of the ancient Temple and all associated with it, and with Reform Judaism's emphasis on the equality of men and women, the laws of family purity and ritual immersion in the mikveh were thrown by the wayside. In fact, it was often a symbol of Reform Judaism's modernity that women were no longer subject to these laws of *nidah*, and specifically immersion. These rituals came to be seen as tribal vestiges of the oppression of women and the move to keep them "barefoot and pregnant."

But as the Reform Movement takes the time to reexamine its own teachings on the subject of human sexuality we must also take a look at the notion of family purity. Could there be any way in which to examine this concept, let alone the details, that has application to the Reform Jewish way of life?

The CCAR Committee on Human Sexuality has determined that, indeed, there are important values that guide Reform Jews' approach to human sexuality and its expression. Chief among those values is the concept of *mishpachah*, family. The values state that the family is the cornerstone of Jewish life. For Reform Jews this concept of family is sacred and as such is one of the important ways in which we express our covenantal relationship with God. Our covenantal relationship, *b'rit*, is also one of the important values outlined as critical to understanding the bond between loving partners. In addition we emphasize the value of *ahavah*, love. For love is not merely a feeling, but according to our Reform Jewish values the concrete measure of behaviors we display toward God and human beings. This value, seen in conjunction with those above, weaves a strong fabric of familial responsibility between the adult partners.

When we try to re-imagine the notion of family purity, we can utilize these three values in particular to redefine *taharat hamishpachah* not in a sense of ritual purification, but through the lens of these values. Family purity is no longer synonymous with immersion in the mikveh, or days when sexual relations between husband and wife are prevented. Rather, the test of family purity becomes the way in which we utilize Reform Jewish values within the concept of family. How do we act toward one another? What is our obligation in matters of life changes? What is our responsibility for taking care of our health and that of our sexual partners?

Thus we can understand *taharat hamishpachah* in the broadest of sense. Topics under the heading of *taharat hamishpachah* might include menstruation, menopause, sexually transmitted disease, promiscuity, divorce, or AIDS. We might understand that issues of sexual abuse or domestic violence between partners and the way we deal with these situations might be classified under the topic of family purity. We might understand the concept of *taharat hamishpachah*, family purity, to emphasize the sacred nature of the sexual relationship of spouses and then re-imagine and redefine the Reform Jewish position in light of the Taxonomy of Reform Jewish Values.

The concept of *taharat hamishpachah* is renewed in our Reform Jewish understanding then as the concept that allows for maintaining the sanctity, health, and well-being of the family relationship. *Taharat hamishpachah* as a value is the aim of Reform Jews. Our families' lives and intimate relations require attention, care, and healthful living.

A Word about the Mikveh

The mikveh was the important ritual antidote to ritual impurity, especially in relationship to the menstruating woman. The ritual bath spiritually cleansed the woman following her menses and allowed for the spiritual renewal and the spiritual cleansing of the *nidah*.

All *mikvaot* have similar attributes. They hold forty *se'ahs*[2] of water. Each must have seven steps down. Each must be filled with *mayim chayim*, living waters. Each must be dug out of the earth and be attached to a *bor*, or pit. The pit is filled with rainwater, ice, or other living water (a spring), which mixes with the mikveh through a hole adjoining the two.

The mikveh is also used for purposes other than *nidah*. The mikveh is used in conjunction with conversion. Anyone who chooses to become a part of the Jewish people is immersed in the waters of the mikveh.

This is for both men and women. The mikveh is used to immerse pots, pans, dishes, and other eating utensils manufactured by non-Jews, or to *kasher* plates for Passover. Both men and women use the mikveh at special times: before a wedding and before Yom Kippur or even Shabbat, to heighten the spirituality and connection to God before the holy day or sacred moment. Finally, before scribes write a section of Torah including the name of God, they utilize the mikveh.

In ancient times, the mikveh played an important role in the life of the ancient Jew, and archaeological remains of *mikvaot* remain throughout Israel dating from before the time of the Temple. Of course, for the priesthood and other functionaries of the ancient Temple no sacrifices were made without a daily immersion in the mikveh. The special mikveh ceremony of the high priest on Yom Kippur is described in the Talmud.[3]

Today, the Reform Jewish understanding of mikveh is further expanded to build and deepen our connection to God and our covenant. We continue to advocate for its use in conversion and before a wedding for both men and women. Utilizing the ritual of immersion can heighten the spirituality of those life-cycle moments. But also the mikveh has been reclaimed in recent years to mark other moments and passages. The healing, life-giving waters of the mikveh have been utilized to create ceremonies of healing and renewal following sexual abuse or rape, injury, or illness. In each of these cases the mikveh serves as intended to purify and renew, and spiritually heal and cleanse.

Used in this way, the mikveh still has significant application for family purity. And although we might not share in the same dim view of menstruation that tradition takes, we are now more fully understanding of the anatomical and physical changes that occur in a woman's body. We might indeed reclaim this ancient tradition of immersion and revitalize it for Reform Jewish men and women as a way to re-formulate and renew our spiritual connection to the *b'rit*, the covenant with God. The mikveh still becomes the vehicle for purification, but the purification becomes openness to healing, renewal, and a sense of *d'veikut*, or clinging to God.

Thus there is a place in our Reform Jewish life for both the ritual of mikveh and the notion of *taharat hamishpachah*, family purity.

NOTES

1. Rachel Biale, *Women and Jewish Law* (New York: Schocken Books, 1984), 148–49.

2. This is an ancient biblical measurement equivalent to approximately 200 gallons of water; 1 *se'ah* is equivalent to 5 gallons.

3. *Yoma* 3:3, 4 (30a), and 3:6 (34b).

Originally published in *CCAR Journal*, Fall 2005, vol. LII/4 78-83.

29

GETTING OUR *GET* BACK

On Restoring the Ritual of Divorce in American Reform Judaism

RABBI MARK WASHOFSKY, PHD

One of the trademark features of Reform Jewish religious practice in the United States is our Movement's abandonment of the requirement of Jewish divorce (*geirushin*). For nearly a century and a half, Reform clergy in America have not insisted that a divorcing couple undertake the traditional process leading to the issuance of a divorce document (a *get piturin*, or, more simply, a *get*). Rather, they have accepted civil divorce as sufficient to permit the remarriage of either spouse under religious auspices. This policy has created a curious ritual imbalance. While a Reform Jewish couple will begin their marriage in a distinctly Jewish ceremony (a wedding held under a chuppah, accompanied by the recitation of *b'rachot* and appropriate liturgy),[1] they will end it, should things come to that, in civil court, a secular governmental institution, a place devoid of Jewish ritual and symbolism.

I want to make an argument for righting this imbalance. I contend that our policy does not reflect our understanding of the religious meaning of divorce and that it needlessly separates us from the rest of the Jewish world, including our liberal coreligionists in other countries who continue to require *geirushin*. It is time to restore the *get*, the practice of Jewish divorce, in American Reform Judaism.

Eliminating the *geirushin* requirement was a radical departure from historical Jewish religious practice. You might think our predecessors took that step as an act of protest against the glaring inequities of traditional Jewish divorce law. That law, in all its complexity, is based largely upon a single biblical verse: "A man takes a wife and marries her. She fails to please him because he finds something obnoxious about her, and he writes a bill of divorce, hands it to her, and sends her away from his house" (Deut. 24:1). The text says nothing about the wife's power to initiate a divorce, and its interpreters have construed it accordingly: the husband can divorce his wife, but she cannot divorce him. This unequal power arrangement can lead to abuse. An unscrupulous husband can refuse to grant a divorce, even when the marriage has come to an effective end and it is obvious that he ought to do so. This enables him to render his wife an *agunah*,[2] a woman legally "anchored" to her husband and unable to remarry, and effectively allows him to demand from her painful and unreasonable concessions as the price for his issuing a *get*. The ancient Rabbis responded to this unfairness by empowering the wife to sue for divorce, a right the Bible does not mention. The court (*beit din*), if it found in her favor, could require the husband to issue her a *get*, and it could even resort to coercive measures to secure his cooperation.[3] Traditional halachah (Jewish law), in other words, sought to improve the wife's legal standing by transforming the institution of divorce from a private transaction between two individuals, as Deuteronomy has it, into a public matter, administered and controlled by the community and its legal institutions. Unfortunately, the Rabbis never took the ultimate logical step in this direction. They never created the means for the wife to issue a *get* to her husband, the only sure way to right the imbalance of power that he is currently able to exploit. The inequity remains, a source of suffering that stands as a black mark upon the moral reputation of Jewish law.

Yet that inequity, so offensive to the Reform Movement's historic commitment to gender equality and social justice, is *not* the principal justification our American Reform predecessors offered for their decision. Instead, they raised two different objections to *geirushin*, which they stated formally at the Philadelphia rabbinical conference of 1869. First, adopting a legal theory suggested by Rabbi Samuel Holdheim, the great German Reformer, they maintained that Judaism defines divorce not as a "religious" matter but as an element of civil or monetary law (*dinei mamonot*). In the halachic tradition, monetary law is governed by the principle *dina d'malchuta dina* (the law of the state is valid law), under which Jewish courts accept the validity of certain legal acts promulgated by non-Jewish courts. From this, Holdheim concluded that a civil divorce decree would suffice to dissolve marriage under Jewish law as well. Second, they drew a sharp theological distinction between marriage, which they kept under rabbinical supervision, and divorce. The difference, wrote Rabbi David Einhorn in a paper submitted to the conference, is that marriage is an act of "consecration" that establishes a sacred institution, while divorce destroys that sanctity. Religion therefore has an appropriate role to play at marriage, offering its blessing to the couple as they form their union, but it has no such role when the marriage dissolves. As Einhorn put it, "When two persons unite in community for life, it is the function of religion to offer consecration, sanctification, and blessing. . . . But if the holy bonds are severed, religion can only tolerate the act in sorrow and silence . . . it cannot invest [divorce] with its consecration." Divorce, quite simply, is no longer a matter of religious (that is, ritual) concern. On this basis, the Philadelphia conference in 1869 resolved that "the dissolution of marriage is, on Mosaic and rabbinical grounds, a civil act only which never received religious consecration. It is to be recognized, therefore, as an act emanating altogether from the judicial authorities of the state. The so-called ritual *get* is in all cases declared null and void."[4]

It is no sign of disrespect to our predecessors to ask whether the reasoning they adduced in support of their actions continues to persuade us today. On the contrary: it was they who taught us by their example the importance of examining with a critical eye the doctrines and practices of the Judaism we inherit from the past. And when we do just that, considering *their* decision, we discover at least three points over which we might differ with their understanding of the tradition and with their Jewish religious outlook.

First, the legal theory upon which Holdheim and the Philadelphia Reformers built their argument is faulty at best. It is not quite accurate to classify divorce as an aspect of monetary or "civil" law.[5] While divorce does have monetary ramifications—it severs the financial ties between husband and wife—it also belongs to the realm of *isura*, of ritual law.[6] Most obviously, divorce determines the marital status of the parties, defining the parameters of adultery and incest as well as the legitimacy of offspring born subsequently to the former wife. All these elements of personal status are emphatically *ritual* matters, elements to which, in traditional Jewish law, the principle *dina d'malchuta dina* does not apply.[7]

Second, I doubt that we define the scope of "religion" as narrowly as did our predecessors. We likely disagree with their assertion that religion has no proper function at the time of divorce, that "sorrow and silence" should exhaust the Jewish response to the end of a marriage. It is more probable that we believe the opposite, namely that a marriage originating in a Jewish ritual act deserves Jewish ritual closure at the time of its dissolution. Divorce may well be the end of a sacred union, but it is also most assuredly a dramatic event in the life of two human beings, an experience of trauma and transition, of emotional death and the potential for rebirth. We respond ritually—"religiously"—to all such moments in the cycle of life, from birth to death, to events both happy and sad . . . with the great exception of divorce. Is that exception justified? Our predecessors provided their own answers to that question. But their answer, I would argue, no longer speaks for us.

Third, our contemporary Jewish ritual agenda differs markedly from that of the nineteenth-century Reformers. Their primary goal, as formulated in the 1885 Pittsburgh Platform, was to purge Jewish religious life of outdated observances, "to maintain only such ceremonies as elevate and sanctify our lives, but reject all such as are not adapted to the views and habits of modern civilization."[8] It therefore made perfect sense to them to discard the *get* process, which struck them as a decidedly *non*-modern ceremony, a throwback to a bygone era when Jews, denied the status of citizenship, administered their own marital and divorce law. Ironically, perhaps, our predecessors' very success has brought about a dramatic change in our religious perspective. Having long since achieved their dream of a progressive, dignified form of Judaism that fits quite well with "the views and habits" of the age, we can turn our attention to other goals. Today, we are concerned much more with restoring connections to our Jewish roots. If Reform Jews in earlier times sought to discard rituals, our generation has recovered and nurtured the ritual impulse. Over the last several decades we have restored any number of observances once rejected as outmoded or meaningless. *Geirushin* need be no different. The prospect of its renewal need not strike us as regression to an unenlightened past. We may see it simply but surely as the return of an authentic Jewish practice, a reaffirmation of our desire to participate in the traditions of our people. A ritual process of divorce crafted with care and sensitivity might or might not rise to the level of "consecration." Still, by investing a critical moment of the life cycle with religious significance, it might just achieve the very sort of "elevation" and "sanctity" that the Pittsburgh Platform values so highly.

Such, at any rate, would explain why the current CCAR *Rabbi's Manual* includes a "Ritual of Release" (*Seder P'ridah*).[9] Although the *Manual's* editors acknowledge that "such a ritual and the document attesting it do not have the standing of a *get*,"[10] they nonetheless describe the ritual as "a form of religious divorce." Its presence in an official CCAR publication speaks volumes, testifying that the American Reform rabbinate recognizes the existence within our communities of those "who, having contracted their marriage in a religious setting, now desire the presence of a rabbi in the final act of their separation." To put this differently, the rabbinate understands that the previous situation, which lacked *any* reference to religious divorce, was unsatisfactory and in need of *tikkun*—that is, reform.

In calling for a restoration of *geirushin*, I mean a divorce process that corresponds to our Reform Jewish conceptions of equity and justice. Specifically, our Reform *geirushin* would have to meet two fundamental requirements. First, it must be egalitarian. Both spouses must be active parties in the procedure. Each should be empowered to issue a *get* to the other, so that neither is placed in the passive status of the wife who, under traditional halachah, can only receive a *get* from (but not issue one to) her husband. Second, neither spouse can be entitled to delay or deny the *get* arbitrarily. If either is unable or unwilling to cooperate in the process—for example, if she or he refuses all reasonable requests to participate, either in person or by means of a representative—the *beit din* would have the power to issue the divorce on behalf of that spouse. In so doing, we would arguably bring to completion the Rabbinic project, indicated above, of transforming divorce from a private transaction to a public one. The point is that the phenomenon of the *agunah* can no longer be tolerated. The *get* should never serve as a weapon, a means by which one spouse can score points against the other. The ritual of *geirushin* should rather be an opportunity to bring Jewish religious closure to a Jewish marriage that has reached its legal and effective end, a demonstration that the former spouses are prepared to move on with their lives and determined to relate to each other in an attitude of justice, fairness, and respect.

Thankfully, an equitable divorce process need not be created *yeish mei-ayin* (from scratch). Our colleagues in the Liberal and Progressive Jewish Movements outside the United States have designed procedures for *geirushin* that are egalitarian, efficient, and compassionate. In so doing, they have shown us how a community such as ours can reclaim its voice at a most fateful moment in the lives of its people, acknowledging its deep connection to Jewish tradition and yet realizing its highest moral and ethical commitments. On this issue, it is high time that we American Reform Jews follow their example.

NOTES

1. Not all Jewish couples inaugurate their marriages in such a religious ceremony. There is a long-standing *machloket* (dispute) as to whether Jewish law recognizes a marriage contracted under civil law (say, in the presence of a judge) as valid *kiddushin*. Some authorities say "yes," to the point that they would require either spouse to obtain a *get* prior to remarriage. For extensive discussion, see Elyakim Elinson, *Nisu'in she-lo k'dat Moshe v'Yisrael* (Tel Aviv: D'vir, 1975). At any rate, that issue is of little relevance to our discussion here, which deals with the *l'chat'chilah* standard (what we recommend as ideal or preferred, what individuals *ought* to do) as opposed to the *b'diavad* standard (what we are prepared to accept after the fact as valid).

2. I use the term *agunah* because it is well-known. The more correct designation, however, is *m'surevet get*, that is, a wife whose husband unjustly refuses to divorce her. The term *agunah* is more properly reserved for the wife whose husband for some reason (e.g., disappearance, captivity, illness) is unable to issue a *get*.

3. On the requirement that the husband issue a divorce, see *Mishnah K'tubot* 7:10. For an explanation of how coerced divorce does not contradict the requirement that the husband issue the *get* of his own free will, see Babylonian Talmud, *Bava Batra* 47b–48a; and Maimonides, *Mishneh Torah, Hilchot Geirushin* 2:20.

4. *Protokolle der Rabbiner-Conferenz, abgehalten zu Philadelphia* (New York: S. Hecht, 1870). See M. Mielziner, *The Jewish Law of Marriage and Divorce in Ancient and Modern Times* (Cincinnati: Bloch, 1884), 130–37; Solomon B. Freehof, *Reform Jewish Practice* (New York: UAHC Press, 1963), 1: 99–110; Mark Washofsky, *Jewish Living*, rev. ed. (New York: URJ Press, 2010), 168–69, 412–13.

5. I leave aside here the fundamental question whether Jewish tradition truly supports the Reformers' distinction between "law" and "religion." Yes, the law can be classified into "ritual" and "monetary" categories, but *sof kol sof*, the Jewish tradition—i.e., the Jewish *religion*—encompasses all of human experience, the civil/legal as well as the ritual/religious. The distinction may have reflected the Reformers' own perception of the proper role of "religion" in modern times, but their effort to locate it in the sources themselves is an example of interpretive overreach.

6. This can be seen in the fact that, whereas in matters of monetary law the parties are allowed to draft stipulations and conditions that alter the existing Toraitic and halachic rules (Babylonian Talmud, *K'tubot* 56a and parallels), such freedom does not exist with respect to personal status. The parties cannot stipulate that the wife will be free to remarry during the life of her husband in the absence of a *get*.

7. The tradition is quite clear that divorce is not one of those matters that emanates "from the judicial authority of the state." Jewish law explicitly rejects the validity of divorce documents emanating from non-Jewish courts. See *Mishnah Gittin* 1:5, Babylonian Talmud, *Gittin* 10b; and *Shulchan Aruch, Even HaEizer* 130:19.

8. "Declaration of Principles," Pittsburgh Platform, 1885, http://ccarnet.org/rabbis-speak/platforms/declaration-principles (accessed March 14, 2012).

9. *Maaglei Tzedek: Rabbi's Manual* (New York: CCAR Press, 1988), 97–104. The quotations in the text are found in the *Manual* at pp. 245–46.

10. This is especially true in that, unlike *geirushin*, the ritual is voluntary rather than obligatory in nature. On the other hand, the "Document of Separation" (*Rabbi's Manual*, 103–4) contains language ("I release my former wife/husband"; "she/he is free and responsible for her/his life") reminiscent of the phrase *harei at muteret l'chol adam*, which is considered the "essence of the *get*" (*Mishnah Gittin* 9:3).

PERSONAL REFLECTIONS

PERSONAL REFLECTION

Living Waters—Making Mikveh a Regular Practice

RABBI REBECCA EINSTEIN SCHORR

I think that it was inevitable—my decision to incorporate a regular mikveh practice into my ritual life. But like so many things, it was a gradual acquisition.

My first visit to the mikveh was as a bride. Just days before my wedding, I entered the living waters for the first time. Lillian was my first mikveh lady. She was amazing. Kind, gentle, and with a staid way about her, Lillian guided me in the wonders of immersion. She spoke lovingly about the positive effect monthly immersion could have on the marital relationship. And she told me that the prayers of a bride are heard with special attention by God.

But I was young. And in love. And couldn't imagine a future without the sexual energy that pulsates during those early days. So while I recognized the liminality of the moment, routine mikveh use didn't seem to have a place in my life.

For many years, I viewed mikveh as a powerful vehicle for transition—something to be used to mark momentous occasions rather than a regular activity. I incorporated mikveh into my pre-ordination celebration. I immersed before trying to conceive. I created a mikveh ritual for a family member prior to her kidney donation. However, I still didn't see how mikveh as a regular practice could fit into the life of a liberal Jewish woman.

Somewhere along the way, however, the waters began to call to me. I saw how transformative they were to my conversion candidates. And I yearned for such moments in my own life. The *Yamim Noraim* seemed like a natural entry point. Making time for a pre–High Holy Day immersion became an essential part of my annual preparation.

My soul not yet satisfied, I broached the topic of ritual immersion with my husband. To say that his interest was underwhelming would be an overstatement. The idea that religion would have a place in the marital bedroom was a completely foreign concept to him. No matter how much I tried to reframe it in a spiritual context, having Judaism dictate when we could and could not make love remained an anathema to him. And yet, because he knows and loves me, he recognized that if it had meaning for me, I should explore it. Which is where it was left.

Time passed. Children were conceived and born and filled our waking hours with laughter and needs. The daily grind left scant energy for romance and lovemaking. Lillian's words from long ago flitted through my mind with some regularity as my sexual self seemed to be completely subsumed by my maternal self.

Ironically, it was when my husband took a job on the opposite side of the country that my regular visits to the mikveh commenced. Taking on the mantle of full-time parent became the tipping point that led me to the silken waters.

My husband views these times as something completely apart from him and our sex life. For a while, he even asked me to use a euphemism ("support group") so that he wasn't confronted with something that still reeked of a religious system that he didn't understand. But that became confusing when one month I really did have a support group meeting the very night after an immersion, and he started to wonder just how much support I needed. I wish that he could have found meaning in this ancient practice, but at a certain level, this is an individual journey. There is much value in the routine of regular immersions for my own well-being, spiritual and physical.

The *chafifah* (preparation) is detailed and requires concentrated attention. It is, however, my favorite part, because it is the one time a month that is devoted entirely to me. The scrupulous cleansing requires a set amount of uninterrupted time, a precious commodity for a mother. Focusing on every inch of my body, I am always reminded of the extensive preparations undergone by Esther and the other virgins prior to their introduction to King Ahasuerus. My mikveh bag is filled with luxurious items I use only for this purpose: an expensive hairbrush to capture my stray locks; a huge loofah and my most sensual bath gel to wash away the profane minutiae, leaving only the sacred behind. Then, and only then, it is my most sacred and sensual self that I bring to the waters.

Once. Twice. Three times I immerse in the living waters. The halachah requires one to be completely submerged for the immersion to be a proper one. I take a slight hop in order to get enough height. I imagine the *tzimtzum*—the cosmic moment when God drew within in order to begin Creation. Within myself, my own *tzimtzum*, I come close to that brilliant moment.

I emerge. Up seven steps. God's creation. Full of life and light. And eager for love.

PERSONAL REFLECTION

Marriage Equality—
Thank You God for This Amazing Day

RABBI MICHAEL ADAM LATZ

On May 14, 2013, I stood with my husband and our daughters, ages nine and six, next to Minnesota governor Mark Dayton as he signed marriage equality into law. It was, in every perfect sense, a "*Shehecheyanu* moment"; in the blazing sun with the state capitol as our backdrop, as our daughters smiled and we wept, we thanked God for keeping us alive, for sustaining us, and for enabling us to reach this season.

It wasn't always this way.

Nearly three years ago, after more than a decade in the rabbinate officiating at dozens of weddings, I made the decision along with my colleague Rabbi Melissa B. Simon to refrain from signing legal marriage licenses. As we wrote to our congregation in December 2010, "We will no longer sign civil marriage licenses and serve as agents of the state government that permits some couples to receive a legal marriage license and refuses a license to other couples." It was a decision rooted in our Jewish tradition and in our roles as rabbis.

It was also personal. I was increasingly uncomfortable affording some couples legal rights and denying them to others—and families just like mine.

Then, in May of 2011, our state house and senate voted to place an amendment in the Minnesota constitution that would forever enshrine anti-gay discrimination against same-sex couples. Leaders of the measure proclaimed that they wanted Minnesotans to have a conversation about marriage and enable voters to make the decision, not "activist judges."

Hazor'im b'dimah b'rinah yiktzoru, "Those who sow in tears, reap in joy," proclaimed the Psalmist (126:5).

There was a great deal of weeping in the capitol rotunda as the votes were cast. Thirty states had voted to put discrimination into their constitutions. Could Minnesota stop the tide?

Minnesotans United for All Families was born from those painful spring days. But what blossomed was more beautiful, more majestic, more holy than any of us could have imagined. We organized. We raised dollars. We held rallies and press conferences and meetings and house parties.

But more than that, we listened. We asked people why marriage mattered to them. We shared stories about why marriage matters to us. Courageous stories of binational couples, separated by borders. Enduring couples who had built loving families for decades despite no legal recognitions. Spiritual stories of Jews who proclaimed that denying people marriage assaulted our core values of human dignity and justice. Painful stories about a partner who died and the survivor who was forbidden to attend the funeral, kicked out of the home, and rendered invisible. Sacred stories of families who once rejected their gay children only to realize that God creates with intention and that love is a gift. Funny stories of raising our children. Hopeful stories so that the children of today would believe that love is transformational, that marriage is about commitment.

On election evening in November, in the early hours of the morning, our campaign to defeat the constitutional amendment was victorious. Not simply because we had more votes, but because we offered a new way of doing politics that united heart and soul, that refused to demonize those who disagreed with us, that lifted up the very best of our humanity.

When the state legislature reconvened in January, courageous leaders kept the conversation moving forward. And six months after defeating the constitutional amendment, we stood on the capitol steps to witness history in the stroke of a pen.

We wept tears of joy. We held our children. We sang. It was Erev Shavuot. We brought our faith into the public square, advocating for equality and justice as progressive Jews. The revelation was powerful for us and for the entire state. Shaking the governor's hand was a rabbi, his husband, and their two daughters. Our oldest, Noa, hugged the governor just before the signing.

"Thank you for loving my family," she said.

Our governor, not a very outwardly emotional man, was visibly touched.

"Could you please sign the law now?" she asked precociously.

He smiled, "I need to speak first and then I'll sign it. You can watch me."

"Ok," she replied. "But don't talk too long. These people have been waiting a long time for this."

Touched, he hugged her again. Deep in our bones, in our souls, we all understood the power of this moment.

In the powerful heat of the desert, God opened the heart of the universe to give the gift of Torah.

Standing at the capitol with generations of people who struggled for dignity and equality, who dreamed a new world into being, who proclaimed that love is the law, revealed the very best of our common humanity. There was thunder in our hearts and exquisite spiritual potential in our souls.

Perhaps this is what it felt like for the mixed multitude of Israelites to witness receiving Torah at Sinai: the place where heaven and earth embrace and for one brief moment love radiates from every living soul.

The day after Shavuot, Rabbi Simon and I sent a letter to the congregation. We celebrated the joy of achieving equality in our lifetime. We remembered those who died who led us here. We acknowledged leaders within the congregation. And we shared a policy change. "With the establishment of marriage equality in Minnesota, we are overjoyed to close this chapter and open the next. We will now sign civil marriage licenses for all couples for whom we officiate."

Shehecheyanu, v'kiy'manu, v'higianu laz'man hazeh.

ee cummings translated it so beautifully: "I thank you God for most this amazing day."

Amen.

Part Five

Ages and Stages: Sexuality throughout Our Lives

The statement of "Reform Jewish Sexual Values" in Part Three of this book explores the ways holiness could be expressed in all aspects of one's sexual encounters. In this section, we explore particular issues that arise at different ages and stages of life, from youth to old age. How are we to educate our youth about sexuality? How do we respond to the expectations and consequences connected with sexuality, including fertility, infertility, and weaning, and how do these physical realities affect our sexual selves? How do we come to older adulthood as sexual beings, recognizing changes that are physical and situational, but also spiritual? All these questions and more are addressed in this section.

We begin with our youth. In "Sexuality Education for Our Youth," Rabbi Laura Novak Winer gives a taste of the curriculum *Sacred Choices: Adolescent Relationships and Sexual Ethics*, which she developed for the Union for Reform Judaism. Giving some of the history of the Reform Movement's activism in comprehensive sex education, she describes the origins of this curriculum for Jewish middle school and high school students, focused on sexual ethics.

Another educational approach is presented by Marcie Schoenberg Lee in "The Magic of Sex-in-Text Education: A Key to Synagogue Relevance for Every Liberal Jew." As opposed to Rabbi Winer, who emphasizes that the *Sacred Choices* curriculum begins with the needs of the learners rather than the transmission of text, Lee emphasizes the ability to draw on the Jewish textual corpus to raise relevant issues. She argues that this approach can be used for all ages, but the focus of the essay is on youth, beginning with preschool. "Text," writes Lee, "instantly and powerfully communicates to schoolchildren (and adults) that in Judaism, it has always been permissible to think and talk about sex."

The next contribution comes from Rabbi Billy Dreskin, whose essay "One Model: A Sexuality Retreat for Teens" describes the sexuality retreat for teens that he and his wife, Cantor Ellen Dreskin, learned from colleague Rabbi Jonathan Stein. One major difference between Rabbi Dreskin's program and the *Sacred Choices* curriculum is that whereas the latter focuses on sexual ethics, the teen sexuality retreat includes actual sex education information as well as values-based conversation. Rabbi Dreskin's essay draws on almost a quarter century of experience to provide a template for education in which, as he writes, "assisting young people in their efforts to come to terms with their emerging sexuality is their right and our responsibility." Like Winer and Lee, Rabbi Dreskin offers his work as a model on which other clergy and educators can draw.

Rabbi Barry H. D. Block's essay "Unplanned Fatherhood" is a bridge between the section on youth and the section on fertility, in its focus on young men who unintentionally impregnate their sexual partners. He explores issues of ethics and responsibility, as well as Jewish identity. As with the essays on sex education, Rabbi Block emphasizes the importance of the synagogue as a safe space for young men as well as young women: "Compassion, openness, and resisting the temptation to judge will keep our doors open to these young men and their families when they need us."

Sometimes the crisis is one of unplanned fertility; sometimes, the crisis is infertility, when there is a deep desire for a child. In "Go and

Learn from Abraham and Sarah: Jewish Responses to Facing Infertility," Daniel Kirzane and Rabbi Julie Pelc Adler examine different biblical models of infertility, weaving those narratives in with contemporary theological and personal struggles. They ask, "If fertility is the most basic seed of God's covenant with Israel, why are so many matriarchs and patriarchs, heroes of our tradition, plagued with a compromised ability to bear children? And what can we learn from them in our own similar struggles?" Their exploration leads to "a renewed understanding of fruitfulness" that can shift our perspective on our sexual, and procreative, selves.

Whereas infertility affects both men and women, the next two essays pertain specifically to how some women in particular experience their bodies as both procreative and sexual beings, through breastfeeding and weaning. In "Blessings of the Breasts and of the Womb: Jewish Perspectives on Breastfeeding and the Female Breast," Rabbi Sharon G. Forman examines the connections between Judaism and breastfeeding. Rabbi Forman argues that as in our secular society, Jewish texts show ambivalence about the dual role of breasts both as a sustaining source of nourishment and as a symbol of overt sexuality. Along the way, she incorporates fascinating Rabbinic stories about breastfeeding, including cases of male lactation—most famously Mordechai nursing Esther, his infant niece. In "Weaning: Personal and Biblical Reflections," Rabbi Deborah Kahn-Harris looks into biblical sources, particularly references to Sarah weaning Isaac and Hannah weaning Samuel, then comes to a close reading of Psalm 131. Throughout, she uses psychoanalytic insights alongside textual ones to find personal and theological meaning.

Next we come to one of the most innovative parts of this book. Sexuality in older adults is a topic that is rarely discussed. Here, we begin with Rabbi Karen L. Fox's essay, "Menopause." Like Rabbi Kahn-Harris, Rabbi Fox looks to Jewish sources for guidance on an often unexplored chapter of women's lives. She explores spiritual and ritual implications and suggests ways that synagogues can play a role. In "With Eyes Undimmed and Vigor Unabated: Sex, Sexuality, and Older

Adults," Rabbi Richard F. Address discusses the "longevity revolution" in which a vital, aging population is not willing to renounce their sexual selves. Rabbi Address raises the difficult issue of a situation in which one spouse remains healthy, while the other is institutionalized with Alzheimer's or dementia. How is one to navigate "between what may actually be two 'rights': the keeping of sacred marriage vows and the need for intimacy and personal sexual expression?" Finally, inspired by Rabbi Address, Rabbis Elliot N. Dorff and Laura Geller focus their attention on this exact question in their essay "When Alzheimer's Turns a Spouse into a Stranger: Jewish Perspectives on Loving and Letting Go." Beginning with a case study, they turn to various halachic possibilities and conclude with a thought-provoking idea. Their vision adds a significant ethical voice to the debate about how to find sexual and emotional intimacy at every stage of our lives.

We have included three personal reflections in Part Five, to include a range of experiences. In "Sexuality on Campus—Notes from the Field," Liya Rechtman contributes a valuable perspective as a college student, connecting her Jewish values with "the SlutWalk revolution." In "Coming Out All Over Again," Rabbi Rachel Gurevitz explores how her decision to be actively open about her sexuality enabled her to be an ally to her congregation's teens. Last but not least, Sarah Tuttle-Singer closes part 5 with her playful piece, "The Rabbi and the Vibrator," reminding us both that pregnancy and new parenthood are not incompatible with sexuality and that Judaism is ultimately a sex-positive religion.

Youth
———

30

SEXUALITY EDUCATION FOR OUR YOUTH

Sacred Choices:
Adolescent Relationships and Sexual Ethics

RABBI LAURA NOVAK WINER, RJE

Snapshot: Fifteen high school juniors and seniors are sitting on couches in the youth lounge at their synagogue discussing which is the holier relationship: a relationship steeped in love and monogamy, but no public, religious, or time commitment; or a marriage, also monogamous, in which the love has dwindled and the partners are considering separating.

Snapshot: Twenty-five Jewish ninth graders are listening to and reading the lyrics of "Don't Funk with My Heart" by the Black Eyed Peas, considering whether this song is about love or lust. Led by their teacher, they then engage in a close reading of Genesis 24:62–67, the story about Isaac meeting Rebekah for the first time. They discuss the same question: was Isaac and Rebekah's relationship founded on love or lust?

Snapshot: Several small groups of seventh graders in a Sunday school classroom are tasked with creating public service announcements about achieving balance and self-control in one's hobbies and activities. One group focuses on playing video games. They discuss what it feels like when they play too much, when they play too little, and when they establish the right balance of time spent on gaming. After sharing their skits with the rest of the class, everyone explores the mishnah "Who is mighty? One who controls one's [natural] urges, as it is said, 'One who is slow to anger is better than the mighty, and one who rules one's spirit than one who conquers a city' [Proverbs 16:32]" (*Pirkei Avot* 4:1). Together, they discuss Judaism's teaching that a person who controls his/her impulses, whatever those impulses are, is a hero. They consider how we can all strive to be heroic.

The Reform Movement's Position on Sexuality Education

Since the mid-1970s the Reform Movement has consistently advocated for comprehensive sex education in our public schools. On numerous occasions, all of the organizational bodies of the Movement, including the Women of Reform Judaism and the Central Conference of American Rabbis, have called for the "inclusion of sex education in the public schools on all levels, and the dissemination of accurate educational materials, and for federal support of funding for comprehensive sex education programs."[1] In 2003, the CCAR reaffirmed its position, calling its members to "support federal, state, provincial, and local legislation to provide for the inclusion of comprehensive and age-appropriate sexuality education in the public schools on all levels (from grade school through high school), while opposing federal, state, provincial, and local funding exclusively for abstinence-only programs."[2] In 2004, the Reform Movement's Commission on Social Action echoed these sentiments and went further by urging that support be given to federal, state, provincial, and local efforts to "assure that sexuality education curricula do not include emotionally charged or biased portrayals of sexual activity, sexual orientation, and sexual health."[3]

Throughout this time, the Reform Movement as a whole has also expressed a strong concern that many current abstinence-only sex education programs represent a religiously biased point of view. The same 2004 Reform Movement's Commission on Social Action "Resolution on Sexuality Education" describes some of the concerns held by the Movement on abstinence-only education. Among those concerns is that "many abstinence-only curricula rely on shame, negative stereotypes about women, and inaccurate statistics to frighten students away from sexual activity. Many endanger at-risk youth by ignoring issues of sexual orientation and sexual abuse and by stigmatizing sexually active students; and many offend the diversity of religious perspectives on human sexuality by presenting a specific religiously-based view as universal."[4] The Movement's position has been that abstinence-only education programs present the kind of morality clearly associated with particular religious faiths, based on values that are not necessarily consonant with Reform Judaism.

In 2005 the staff of the Union for Reform Judaism began conversations about teens and sexuality. The URJ leadership was responding to a call for action issued by the CCAR in their 2003 resolution (mentioned above) as well as the perceived increasing prevalence of reports in the news about adolescents participating in extreme sexual behavior. Additionally, it became clear through conversations with Reform clergy and educators, as well as parents and adolescents in Reform congregations, that while many Jewish youth were receiving varying degrees of information-based sex education in their public schools and synagogues, they were, for the most part, not receiving thoughtful guidance on healthy decision making and Jewish sexual ethics. At the time, Reform congregations were individually responding to this need by filling in the educational gaps for their youth by utilizing curricula from Jewish publishers on such topics as birth control, HIV/AIDS, sexually transmitted infections and diseases, and abortion, striving to incorporate the Jewish response to questions posed by each of these issues.

As an experienced Jewish educator, I too had taken an active role in bring sexuality education into both the summer camp and congregational school settings, particularly with regard to AIDS education. I too had cobbled together curricular materials that would respond to the needs of my students and families. As a lead staff member in the

URJ Youth Programs department, I was called upon to share my experience and perspective on the trends in adolescent sexual behavior and propose a course of action. I proposed the development of a curriculum for youth and parents that would address primary areas of concern for our youth and their parents and frame those in a context of Reform Jewish values and ethics. I was given the great honor and responsibility of heading up the development of a sexual ethics curriculum.

The resulting curriculum, *Sacred Choices: Adolescent Relationships and Sexual Ethics*, for implementation in middle school and high school educational settings, including synagogue schools, day schools, youth groups, and camps, renewed the Movement's commitment to the sexual health of its youth. With the publication of *Sacred Choices* in 2007, the Reform Movement became the first progressive Jewish denomination to articulate in an educational curriculum a position on premarital sex, homosexual relationships, and adolescent sexual behavior.

Crafting the *Sacred Choices* Curriculum

Sacred Choices emerged out of our Movement's continued concern about adolescents and the need to respond to the challenges they face with a Jewish voice. To remain relevant, Jewish moral education must address this critical issue for today's young people. In speaking with Reform Jews and their children, the URJ came to the conclusion that our youth are searching for guidance in thinking critically about the messages they receive from their schools, their peers, the media, the Jewish community, and even their parents. The URJ understood teen pop culture, music, reality TV, movies, fashion, video games, and the Internet to be quite permissive about sexual activity, representing sex as cool, fun, and "the thing to do." This was evidenced by the growth in the number of teen-literature books addressing topics of sexuality and relationships during that time.[5] Messages about gender and gender roles are often stereotyped. Youth are more sexually active at younger ages and experimenting with a greater variety of sexual acts than did previous generations. Even the definitions of what constitutes "sex" have changed. In their 2007 study of university students, Hans, Gillen, and Akande found that only 20 percent of their respondents would classify oral-genital contact as having "had sex," whereas in previous studies 40 percent would have classified similar activity as having "had sex." The authors concluded, "The magnitude of change in the classification of oral-genital contact supports our hypothesis that a shift has occurred in sociocultural conceptualizations of this behavior."[6] This is the world in which our youth are forming their values.

Our youth live in a culture in which the boundaries governing what is sacred and what is not have changed. Our permissive culture of individualism with its frequent focus on success pressures youth to participate in activities and behaviors for which they may not be physically or emotionally ready. The Henry J. Kaiser Family Foundation's *National Survey of Adolescents and Young Adults: Sexual Health Knowledge, Attitudes, and Experiences* found that "young people also feel great pressure to have sex, with a majority saying that while putting off sex might be a 'nice idea, nobody really does.'"[7] *Sacred Choices* was designed to offer a Reform Jewish counterpoint to these messages. Its lessons add a Jewish voice to the messages about sex and sexuality with which youth are grappling.

By design, *Sacred Choices* is not a sex education curriculum. It is a sexual ethics curriculum. The authors are not health or sexuality educators; they are Jewish educators. As mentioned above, there already existed several very fine curricular resources that responded to several sex education–related issues: abortion, birth control, and so on. Many of these curricula look at traditional texts and modern responsa, offering answers to the question "What does Judaism have to say about . . . ?" For those congregations that wanted to continue teaching these traditional topics of sex education, we would recommend that they continue to utilize these fine resources. The URJ did not need to re-create those. Rather we wanted to fill in the gaps on what our youth were missing in their Jewish sexuality education experience: opportunities for learning about the ethical issues specifically related to the adolescents' experience of relationships such as peer pressure, communicating with one's peers and parents, and making personal decisions about one's own sexual behavior. *Sacred Choices* was developed to respond to the ethical challenges youth face and to give a specifically Reform Jewish voice to those challenges. The lessons explore Jewish texts and values that are relevant to this crucial aspect of the human experience, sexual behavior, and relationships. Utilizing backward design, a model of curriculum design developed by Grant Wiggins and Jay McTighe,[8] the curriculum authors translated the notion of enduring understandings into values that have lifelong meaning for all Jews. For youth, these values, or enduring understandings, are central to developing a Jewish worldview and a Jewish response to sexuality and being sexual.

In *Mishneh Torah, Hilchot Choveil Umazik* 5:1, Maimonides teaches that individuals do not have complete ownership of their bodies. God has given us these bodies for safekeeping. Thus, any misuse, abuse, or mutilation of the body is viewed as a breach of God's trust. With this teaching, Maimonides guides us to understand that our bodies and our souls are gifts from God. We need to treat our bodies with the level of respect that God demands of us. Thus the foundational Jewish value of *Sacred Choices* comes to us from Maimonides. The enduring understandings for the *Sacred Choices* curriculum are as follows:

1. My body and my soul—including my sexuality—are gifts from God.
2. Jewish tradition provides guidance in making sacred choices about how I use and care for those gifts and in coping with the consequences of my choices.

Curriculum Structure

The curriculum consists of two modules. The middle school module is geared toward sixth through eighth graders and their parents. The high school module is geared toward ninth through twelfth graders and their parents. In keeping with the backward design model, the lessons in the two modules are linked together by essential questions that are explored throughout the whole curriculum. The essential questions are as follows:

1. What does it mean to view my life—my body, soul, and sexuality—as well as those of others as gifts from God? How does it affect my own thoughts and actions? How does it affect my thoughts and actions toward others?

2. How does the way I treat my body and soul matter to myself, to God, and to others, particularly to other people in my Jewish community?

3. What is the guidance that Jewish tradition provides in this area? Which elements resonate with me, and which do not? How can I incorporate Jewish beliefs and behaviors into my own life as I make these choices?

4. What are the consequences of my choices? How does Judaism help me to cope with those consequences? How does God help me to cope with those consequences? What do I do if I have made or do make a choice that does not treat my life and that of others as a sacred gift? Are all choices with regard to sexuality sacred?

5. How is the guidance that Judaism provides in consonance with the messages I receive from pop culture and society? How is the guidance that Judaism provides at odds with these messages? How can I evaluate that range of messages I receive?

The high school curriculum also includes an additional developmentally appropriate essential question:

6. How do I hear and stay true to my inner voice?

Each module contains its own set of age-appropriate lessons. As they explore and answer the essential questions through their engagement with the lessons, the participants begin to develop an understanding of Judaism's stance on ethical issues about their bodies and behavior, the relevance of these ethical issues to their lives, and the participants' personal connection to them.

The Reform Voice of *Sacred Choices*

Sacred Choices strives to provide uniquely Reform answers to adolescents' questions about their relationships, their behavior, and their emerging sexual ethics. In developing the curriculum, the authors sought first to understand what adolescents were thinking about. What were the challenges they faced in their relationships? What questions did they have about Judaism and its view of relationship-related issues? What did research show our youth needed in terms of healthy direction and skill development for decision making? Once we identified these issues, we turned to our Jewish textual tradition for guidance and answers to the questions. We identified and selected texts and concepts—both traditional and modern—to incorporate into the curriculum to most appropriately and effectively address the questions at hand. These texts were consonant with Reform Jewish thinking in the twenty-first century. They were chosen to be accessible to the learners and to offer relevant guidance about their lives.

This approach is unique to *Sacred Choices*. Rather than looking first to the textual tradition to identify the stories, midrashim, and teachings about sexuality and finding ways to transmit these to our adolescents, we first turned to the learners themselves to understand what guidance they were seeking. As a result, adolescents are able to connect in a very real and relevant manner to the Jewish textual tradition explored in *Sacred Choices*.

The central messages conveyed by the materials include the following:[9]

- Synagogue is a safe and relevant place to talk about sexuality, being sexual, and decision making.
- Judaism has wisdom to contribute to this topic.
- There is something sacred about me, my body, my relationships, my sexuality, and my intimate relationships.

- Lesbian, gay, bisexual, and questioning Jews are accepted in the Reform Jewish community.
- Waiting until I am older to have sexual intercourse is wise because it will keep me safer emotionally and physically.
- There are other ways besides sexual intercourse for me to be intimate with someone special.

At the same time, the material seeks to dispute the following cultural misconceptions:

- If I am not thinking about sex yet, I should be.
- If I have engaged in various forms of sexual behavior, I have transgressed Judaism and no longer belong in the community.
- If I am gay, I do not have a place in the Jewish community.
- If I am in love with my serious boy/girlfriend, this is the kind of relationship in which I should have sexual intercourse.
- Sex is shameful.
- Hooking up is fun, and calling it a "sacred choice" is funny.

Each of the snapshots illustrated in the introduction briefly describes a component of a *Sacred Choices* lesson. The first snapshot, in which a group of high school youth is discussing the respective holiness of various types of relationships, is part of a lesson entitled "Let's Talk about Sex" from the high school module. In the lesson, the participants are introduced to the work of Rabbi Dr. Eugene Borowitz, Jewish philosopher, theologian, and professor of education and Jewish thought at the Hebrew Union College–Jewish Institute of Religion in New York. In his book *Choosing a Sex Ethic*, Dr. Borowitz suggests a continuum of sexual relationships. The five levels of sexual relationships represent a continuum of holiness, the lowest level being the least holy and the highest level being the most holy. The five levels are as follows:[10]

Level 1: Conquest: The decision to have sex has been made by one person and is accompanied by violence. Rape is an example of this.
Level 2: Healthy Orgasm: At this level, the focus is on the individual's pleasure.

Level 3: Mutual Consent: Both partners share in the decision to have sex. There is no emotional commitment to one another, only to each other's pleasure.

Level 4: Love: Here there is a private discussion between two persons who love only each other; to have sex only with each other. There is no time commitment.

Level 5: Marriage: This involves a public commitment between two persons to have sex only with each other, presumably forever.

Instructed that this continuum was developed over forty years ago, the participants are prompted to consider whether they agree with the hierarchy as it stands today and share why or why not. The youth consider whether or not there may be other levels to the continuum. Are there other types of relationships that should be added? How would they define those relationships, and where would they rank in relation to Borowitz's continuum? Following this discussion, the participants are given a set of scenarios to read and place on a continuum from unholy to holy using Dr. Borowitz's five levels of sexual relationships as a guide.

This exercise and others like it throughout the curriculum illustrate Judaism's teaching about appropriate, holy, and ethical behavior in relationships and pushes youth to consider their own ethical stance on these questions. They are urged to question where on the continuum they themselves would like to be in their own relationships.

Each lesson in the curriculum incorporates similar types of exercises in which participants are asked to examine a Jewish text or Jewish value and apply it to their daily lives as adolescents. Through these exercises and the conversations that emerge from them, youth can come to see how Judaism is relevant to and offers meaningful guidance to their daily living, including their relationships and sexual lives.

Sacred Choices also strives to provide Reform answers to parents' questions about their children's development, relationships, behavior, and emerging sexual ethics. Parents are the primary sex educators of their children. Yet, they often flounder in figuring out how to effectively and responsively fulfill the role. Parents explore, in the context of the supportive synagogue community, how to effectively support their child's growth, development, and age-appropriate desire for greater independence in making decisions about friends and relationships. In the *Sacred Choices* parent sessions, adults engage with Jewish texts that help them grapple with questions such as: What Jewish sexual values do I want to teach my child? What is a parent's responsibility to his or her child? How do I help my child navigate his/her way through this stage of his/her life?

As Jewish professionals, we have accepted the responsibility to support the youth in our communities as they grow and develop into strong, ethically minded, Jewishly identified adults. Our responsibility in this regard extends to prompting real and meaningful conversations and offering education about sexuality and sexual ethics for both the youth and the adults in the congregation. To ignore these issues in our congregations is to ignore a central aspect of each individual's humanity. As articulated in the introduction to the *Sacred Choices* curricular guides, our Jewish community settings (synagogues, day schools, camps, youth groups) "provide safe places for adolescents to understand their inherent worth and to find acceptance, whatever their sexual orientation or sexual behavior. These conversations literally save lives."[11] We know from far too many recent incidences in our communities that a leading risk factor for suicide among young people is a feeling of ostracism and shame over sexual identity and sexual behavior. "By being certain to convey our support and loving acceptance, we really may lower the risk of self-harm. By educating our young people to make thoughtful, ethical, Jewish-based decisions, our communities may also be protecting the health and even saving lives of adolescents."[12]

The Impact of *Sacred Choices*

Sacred Choices has been implemented in different learning environments across the Reform Movement: congregational supplementary school classrooms, youth groups, summer camps, and Reform Jewish day schools. Since the *Sacred Choices* lessons employ models of both formal and informal educational learning, educators in those settings have been able to adapt the lessons to meet the specific learning needs of their participants, while being able to maintain the focus on the enduring understandings and the essential questions. The curriculum has been purchased by more than five hundred Reform institutions in five countries (United States, Canada, Australia, Israel, and the United Kingdom).

While a comprehensive evaluation of the impact of *Sacred Choices* has yet to be conducted, anecdotal feedback indicates that *Sacred Choices* is indeed helping adolescents find relevance to their daily lives in sacred texts and guidance to their decision-making processes. Feedback from congregations that have implemented the curriculum has included the following comments from teachers, educators, and clergy:

- My students enjoy the opportunity to speak about sex freely and publicly with adults who aren't their parents. The students want to know what their Torah teaches about sexual relationships. They easily apply the lessons to their own lives. They are surprised to hear religious leaders teach that sex can be sacred.
- One of the parents shared with me that during the car ride home they were able to talk to their child about important issues, such as sex, Jewish commitment, ethics, personal choice, and so on, that they had never been able to discuss before.
- Our community is grateful that the temple is using Jewish values to enable our students to navigate and confront the issues that they are facing as teenagers in the world today.

As the feedback above demonstrates, our children are thirsty for conversations not just about sex but also about sexual ethics and values. Our youth need and want to have these types of conversations in their synagogues. Through both its structure and its content as an ethics-based curriculum, *Sacred Choices* provides youth with opportunities to develop their own sense of personal ethics. They learn to integrate

Jewish values into their thought processes, attitudes, and behaviors. They create a Jewish spiritual framework for their relationships and gain tools for making lifelong decisions.

The essential questions outlined above are eternal. One's personal dialogue with them can, and should, go on for a lifetime. These are questions that go to the heart of who we are as human beings, what we believe about our bodies and our behaviors, and our relationship with God, with Judaism, and with those around us. These are the questions our youth learn to ask themselves when entering into and building relationships. Where else would we want our youth to grapple with these questions if not the synagogue?

Sacred Choices furthers the Reform Movement's long-standing commitment to healthy comprehensive sexuality education. Our Movement has taken a strong and clear stance on sexuality education policy. Now we are actualizing that stance for our own youth and families within our congregations and educational institutions. I am proud to have taken this leadership role in supporting youth and their families through the challenges of adolescence and offering them the skills and ethical foundations they need to build healthy relationships throughout their lives.

NOTES

1. Central Conference of American Rabbis, "On Sex Education in the Schools," 1987, http://ccarnet.org/rabbis-speak/resolutions/1987/sex-education-on-in-the-schools-1987/.

2. Central Conference of American Rabbis, "Sexuality Education," March 2003, http://ccarnet.org/rabbis-speak/resolutions/2003/sexuality-education/.

3. Commission on Social Action of Reform Judaism, "Resolution on Youth Sexuality Education," March 2004, http://urj.org/socialaction/aboutus/reso//?syspage=article&item_id=1870.

4. Ibid.

5. J. Shamlian, "New Trend in Teen Fiction: Racy Reads," *NBC News*, August 15, 2005, http://www.nbcnews.com/id/8962686/ns/nbc_nightly_news_with_brian_williams/t/new-trend-teen-fiction-racy-reads/#.Uh-0yxbDEts.

6. Jason D. Hans, M. Gilllian, and K. Akande, "Sex Re-defined: A Reclassification of Oral-Genital Contact," *Perspectives on Sexual and Reproductive Health* 42, no. 2 (2010): 74–78.

7. Kaiser Family Foundation, *National Survey of Adolescents and Young Adults: Sexual Health Knowledge, Attitudes, and Experiences*, March 2003, http://www.kff.org/youthhivstds/3218-index.cfm.

8. Grant Wiggins and Jay McTighe, *Understanding by Design* (Upper Saddle River, NJ: Prentice Hall, 2001).

9. Union for Reform Judaism, *Sacred Choices: Adolescent Relationships and Sexual Ethics*, High School Module (New York: URJ Press, 2008), 18.

10. Eugene Borowitz, *Choosing a Sex Ethic* (New York: Schocken Books, 1969).

11. Union for Reform Judaism, *Sacred Choices*, 5.

12. Ibid.

31

THE MAGIC OF SEX-IN-TEXT EDUCATION

A Key to Synagogue Relevance for Every Liberal Jew

Marcie Schoenberg Lee, MSW, MAJCS

Q: "If we had more time to study sex and sexuality, what would you want to learn more about?"

A: "Sexy stories from the Bible."

These are the verbatim words of a child participating in "Forgotten Treasures: Discovering Lost Traditions of Jewish Sexuality."[1]

Lesson 1 opened with the students reading the Book of Esther,[2] chapter 2, verses 12–14, from the Bibles each held in her hands:

> When each girl's turn came to go to King Ahasuerus at the end of the twelve months' treatment prescribed for women (for that was the period spent on beautifying them: six months with oil of myrrh and six months with perfumes and women's cosmetics, and it was after that that the girl would go to the king), whatever she asked for would be given to her to take with her from the harem to the king's palace. She would go in the evening and leave in the morning for a second harem in charge of Shaashgaz, the king's eunuch, guardian of the concubines. She would not go again to the king unless the king wanted her, when she would be summoned by name.

Stunned silence, and then time allowed for the children's anticipated, developmentally appropriate giggles and comments, time for them to see each other's faces as it dawned on them that each virgin had intercourse with the king, time for them to realize that this was not a classic beauty pageant after all. Immediately thereafter, charts of female and male anatomy were placed on a big table in the middle of the room.

The second day began with students entering the classroom to find the human sexual response cycle written out on the blackboard. They sat down and opened their Bibles to the Song of Songs.

> How fair you are, how beautiful!
> O Love, with all its rapture!
> Your stately form is like the palm,
> Your breasts are like clusters.
> I say: Let me climb the palm,
> Let me take hold of its branches;
> Let your breasts be like clusters of grapes,
> Your breath like the fragrance of apples,
> And your mouth like choicest wine.
> "Let it flow to my beloved as new wine
> Gliding over the lips of sleepers."
> I am my beloved's,
> And his desire is for me.
> Come, my beloved,
> Let us go into the open;
> Let us lodge among the henna shrubs.
> Let us go early to the vineyards;
> Let us see if the vine has flowered,
> If its blossoms have opened,
> If the pomegranates are in bloom.
> There I will give my love to you.
>
> (Song of Songs 7:7–13)

After each couple of verses, the children were asked where in the human sexual response cycle we just studied the lovers in the Song of Songs might be, what might be happening in their bodies.

The children were fifth and sixth graders, embarking upon sex-in-text education crafted to teach them to simultaneously celebrate themselves as sexual beings, learn skills for making decisions that maximize their physical and psychological health and safety, and study science, all through exploration of Jewish texts addressing and helping them navigate this intimate and fascinating area of life, and inextricably woven together with anatomy and physiology.

Children (and adults) who study sexuality this way do not say, "Religious school is boring" or "Judaism has nothing to offer me." Children who are taught by Jewish teachers properly trained in child development, group dynamics, sex education, and relevant Jewish texts want to stay in religious school reading the rest of these episodes, many other "sexy stories from the Bible," and the innumerable Jewish texts that deal with sex.

And so do seniors. "How the hell did I get to be sixty-three years old and not know this?" "How could I have been so active in my synagogue all these years, without ever being taught this? I attend Purim every year!" "Thirty years volunteering in the Jewish community, and I never learned this. It's infuriating and embarrassing." At one-day and multi-session workshops of "Forgotten Pleasures: Rediscovering Lost Traditions of Jewish Sexuality," these are the consistent unsolicited responses from senior participants when they read those same verses in Esther. I have been asked these appropriate questions and heard this justifiable righteous indignation from participants affiliated with liberal movements, with Orthodox movements, and from participants who are unaffiliated.

People who are angry and embarrassed retreat rather than approach. Thus we need an approach to end their retreat, an approach through which what is rightfully theirs and not ours to withhold, the Hebrew Bible and the sources that continue to flow from it, are crafted into vehicles for celebrating ourselves as sexual beings.

Comprehensive lifelong study of sexuality in synagogue gives integrity to the affirmation that the synagogue is a home in which anything important to our lives can be explored and discussed. Its absence renders absurd that powerful promise.

Jewish writings on sexuality comprise a body of treasures in which our ancient sages and our modern scholars and teachers directly discuss, debate, argue, and write differing opinions on the variety of subjects sexuality encompasses.[3] They speak graphically of the physical aspects of our sexuality—physical maturation, foreplay, sexual arousal, and intercourse. They deal candidly with psychological aspects of our sexuality—quality relationships and the need for nurturing. Ethical aspects of our sexuality—privacy, gossip, and trust—are scrutinized. Political aspects of our sexuality are considered—parental and community expectations, forums for meeting partners, cohabitation, and attitudes toward abortion, extramarital affairs, and pregnancy.

The celebration of ourselves as sexual beings is a glory of Judaism. Having in place a comprehensive sex-in-text education program, a gift for every age—preschoolers to seniors—is to offer modern synagogue relevance to every Jew.

Integrating secular material and people's experiences of sexuality in contemporary culture, with ancient and modern Jewish sources on sexuality—many of which contain heroic and visionary ideas for their times—offers the opportunity to explore sexuality, a highly personal and relevant subject that is of interest to almost everyone, through heretofore unfamiliar sources. This approach goes beyond introducing largely unfamiliar Jewish sources, transforming them into resources for modern daily living that inform the development of mental, physical, spiritual, and sexual health simultaneously. In the process, this approach exposes and models the Jewish traditions of learning and decision making through debate, dissension, and discussion, hallmarks of freedom, and in so doing, highlights the exhortation to be proud of being Jewish.

There is glory in the enduring strain of Judaism that sees sexuality as positive and has remained in concert with modern scientific discoveries about our sexuality. Nonetheless, when it comes to publicizing and celebrating this congruence, there is a profound lack. We Jews have welcomed, and continually emphasize in our programming, our acceptance of the scientific discoveries proving that creativity is an essential part of ourselves. It is disconcerting that we have not welcomed, nor emphasized in our programming, acceptance of the definitive scientific discoveries in multiple fields, including child development, brain research, and chemically enhancing the human sexual response cycle, that sexuality is also an essential part of ourselves. Many who accept that creativity is an essential part of the human being, and consequently design programs to develop, expand, and channel it in healthy ways, will not accept the fact that sexuality is as well. The potential for continually transforming exciting discoveries about our sexual selves into ongoing sex education in synagogues and Jewish schools is largely ignored. Instead, if offered at all, it is generally made available as a one-day special program or a one-time workshop or short course, then cut off as suddenly as it was introduced. Squandering the opportunity to make the ongoing celebration of ourselves as sexual beings a foundation of our Movement by connecting synagogue sex education with the sexual development of children is tragic. Our Movement should cherish our human sexuality as it so successfully cherishes our human creativity.

The precise time when children's bodies are changing is the time to give them the gift of simultaneously studying Jewish views of their changing bodies and the science of those changes. It is a loud statement to be programmatically silent about this foremost concern of their lives. It is often the case that the only formal sex education Jewish children attending public schools get is from tightly scripted curricula, and teachers are often forbidden to address or answer many (or any) questions. Within the walls of our synagogues, we have the luxury of answering every single question children ask. Questioning is the classic and enduring Jewish way to learn. Consigning Jewish children to formal sex education programs that don't allow questions at all, or don't allow certain questions to be answered, or teach only abstinence, are at odds not only in substance but in form with the essentials of Judaism. Whatever the quality of sex education available in public schools, Jewish sex-in-text education affords opportunities to sanctify sexuality for students.

When we promise Jewish kids sex education, the content cannot be texts on ethics without explicit mention of sex. The words "vagina" and "penis" have to appear when you promise sex education. Ironically, the ancient Jewish sources contain them, even if poetically and euphemistically named, whereas modern Jewish curricula and books for children generally don't.

In a Jewish environment that reflects its understanding of child development, sex-in-text education begins when it developmentally should. Over the last thirty years I have yet to hear anyone answer the question "When should Jewish sex education begin?" with the proper answer, "In preschool."[4]

Thus should Jewish sex-in-text education begin, and it should continue for life in our synagogues, day schools, camps, Hebrew high schools, youth groups, and college campus organizations. Following the conventional wisdom to wait to discuss sex until children ask a question about it is *sh'tuyot*, foolishness. We do not wait to discuss sharing until our two- or three-year-old comes to us and asks, "What are the benefits of sharing, Daddy?" We initiate lessons on sharing as early as we can, knowing that practicing and mastering that behavior paves the way for a more satisfying life than one of isolation from others. It seems we Jews pride ourselves on being in concert with scientific discovery, except in this essential part of ourselves, our sexuality—discussions of which we generally do not initiate, and from which we often run when our children finally ask, "Where did I come from?"

We know using a felt board to tell stories to young preschool children is not only for fun but promotes progress on the continuum that leads to successfully reading. Felt board stories develop skills including tracking from left to right, a building block essential to learning to read. Likewise, we know that teaching terms of anatomy and physiology to toddlers and preschool children fits the sexuality continuum. Beginning in preschool to weld secular and sacred building blocks of healthy sexuality through the fire of Jewish texts is to lay down a solid foundation of architectural plans for a sound Jewish future.

What elements would a Jewish preschool classroom in which sex education is embedded contain? Picture books with drawings of the human body and the teachers' willingness to volunteer correct anatomical terms at appropriate times are just the beginning of teaching young Jewish children to appropriately embrace their sexual selves.

In addition to lessons and guidance that directly address sexual anatomy, there are opportunities to suffuse other critical areas of development, including talking instead of hitting and moving from parallel play to sharing, with Jewish wisdom that children can integrate and draw on for a lifetime.[5] Regularly invoking *birchot hahodaah*, blessings expressing gratitude for friends and for special activities, can be early building blocks of later sexual integrity. Jewish teachers effectively trained to teach sex-in-text education would understand that "use your words," a mantra of the preschool years, can be channeled into the ability to effectively communicate later in life with one's sexual partner. Learning to give a classmate a toy as soon as you are done using it can develop eventually into appropriate and responsible sharing of our bodies once sexually active. From the morning blessings, recitation of "Blessed are You, Adonai, who heals all flesh, working wondrously," can be the foundation of a program of calling and of sending cards to sick classmates and would simultaneously be a building block to taking good care of ourselves and assisting in the care of others. Infusing the preschool class with Jewish quotes connected to familiar secular mantras builds Jewish literacy.

When a Jewish child can as readily hear from a teacher, "A healing tongue is a tree of life" (Prov. 15:4) as "Use your words," Jewish literacy and a Jewish view of sexuality are linked in early childhood, even if not yet apparent. Fusing the articulation of Jewish vocabulary words, quotes, and texts to the articulation of secular language and texts creates a Jewish school rather than a school that happens to have Jewish kids in it, a Jewish program rather than a program attended by Jews.

With elementary school children who developmentally are focused on differences between boys and girls, reading the story of Deborah and Barak shows that though men's and women's bodies are different, feelings are relatively similar. "But Barak said to her, 'If you will go with me, I will go; if not, I will not go.' 'Very well, I will go with you,' she answered. 'However, there will be no glory for you in the course you are taking, for then the Eternal will deliver Sisera into the hands of a woman.' So Deborah went with Barak to Kedesh" (Judges 4:8–9). Men lean for support on women as women lean on men. Male roles had exceptions in the tradition as far back as the biblical narrative itself. Loyalty, encouragement, candor, and inspiration come out of the mouths of both women and men. A biblical woman was a respected and inspiring military leader. Learning of these possibilities early in life paves the way for intimacy in later life and shows children concrete examples in their own Bible of the words they so often hear, "You can be whatever you want to be."

Invoking this story additionally provides an opportunity to link biblical military leaders to today's Israel Defense Forces. Studying about the IDF and writing to its soldiers, is a powerful way to help children relate in a personal way to multiple aspects of contemporary Israeli society, something we worry is hard for them to do, and also allows for fuller understanding of and respect for the American military.

The story of Deborah and Barak, in which women initiate and men willingly follow a woman's lead on the battlefield, can provide a model for future sexual interactions. For example, it could lead to feeling comfortable in later years with the idea of women initiating and men following in the bedroom, give permission for a reticent partner to try initiating a sexual encounter, and encourage taking other appropriate risks as well.

Sex-in-text education is critical for *b'nei mitzvah* preparation. During the years in which children prepare for *b'nei mitzvah*, their psychological and physical focus on self and others as sexual beings intensifies. If trope and haftarah, Bible and erotica undergird *b'nei mitzvah* training, preparing to become Jewish adults is congruent with their bodies' transformation from childhood to adulthood. When *b'nei mitzvah* students concurrently study Hebrew and liturgy, sex and sexuality, there is no need to plead the case that bar or bat mitzvah should be a beginning and not an end.

> *Mishnah*: The Sages spoke of [the physical development of] a woman in figurative speech: an unripe fig, a fig in its early ripening stage, and a ripe fig. She is like "an unripe fig" while she is yet a child; "a fig in its early ripening stage" when she is in the age of her maidenhood. During both the latter and the former stages, they ruled, her father is entitled to anything she finds and to her handiwork and to the right of invalidating her vows. "A ripe fig"— as soon as she becomes a *bogeret* and her father no longer has any right over her.
>
> What are the marks [of a *bogeret*]? Rabbi Yosei the Galilean says, "The appearance of the wrinkle beneath the breast." Rabbi Akiva says, "The hanging down of the breasts." Ben Azai says, "The darkening of the ring around the nipple." Rabbi Yosei says, "[The development of the breast to a stage] when one's hand being put on the nipple, it sinks and only slowly rises again."
>
> (Babylonian Talmud, *Nidah* 48a)

This text instantly and powerfully communicates to schoolchildren (and adults) that in Judaism, it has always been permissible to think about and talk about sex. The text, rather than the teacher's talking, communicates that truth. Like so many other biblical, Rabbinic, and later sacred texts, though the context may be troubling, the content is nonetheless highly relevant and can be extracted and applied to different contexts and a changed world. This dynamic has characterized Reform Judaism and has been among its great strengths. Engaging troubling texts not only allows for the mining and reappropriation of the wisdom such texts have to offer, but also creates exciting opportunities to simultaneously discuss with learners the very reasons they are troubling. "The ripe fig" above is a troubling text because men defined "girl" and "woman" and then determined their roles and circumscribed their actions and freedoms, even as the text demonstrates the permissibility of discussing sex in graphic terms.

Such is also the case with Exodus 21:10, which acknowledges women's sexual needs. Sexual satisfaction as a woman's right is clearly established even as that right is embedded in a discussion of slavery, redeemed slaves, and multiple wives! Not teaching a text that establishes a woman's right to sexual satisfaction simply because its original context was biblical slavery is not only to miss opportunities to find the glory in Judaism in every possible place, but also to abandon the process by which many mitzvot were established: a behavioral commandment was extracted from a seemingly unrelated, ancient, or obsolete context. Multiple opportunities for children's intellectual and spiritual growth exist when they are allowed to tackle and are taught to navigate troubling texts, along with those texts that are in concert with modern liberal Jewish sensibilities.

Knowing that study of a variety of texts on sex awaits children upon their return to religious school the week after *b'nei mitzvah* is an exciting prospect and one that also decreases the likelihood that they will want to avail themselves of a parent's promise that "you can quit religious school right after your bar/bat mitzvah." Anxious to continue learning about their sexual selves in synagogue, they may now well be additionally motivated by the confidence garnered from having accomplished all that was necessary to celebrate becoming a bar or bat mitzvah. As their bodies continue changing, they are more entitled to study their changing bodies. They learn through studying texts on sex that the responsibility everyone has talked about as linked to *b'nei mitzvah* can be realized in responsibility for their developing sexuality and sexual behavior.

Many high school and college students watch *Criminal Minds* and *CSI: Crime Scene Investigation*, but have never heard of COG, the concubine of Gibeah. In this, the most horrifying story of the Hebrew Bible (Judges 19), arguably a story of criminal minds, the concubine's husband and father-in-law deliver her up to an angry mob bent on rape. Though echoing the mob scene in Sodom, alas, in this story, the woman is not pulled back inside the house. She is shoved outside by her own relatives, gang raped, and then cut into pieces by her husband—all this in a text that never establishes with certainty that she is dead when dismembered. This story illustrates the depths of human depravity and the steps in the inhumane process of objectifying a human being. This story, which closes the Book of Judges, gives way immediately to its polar opposite, the story of Hannah and Elkanah.

Elkanah is a husband who exhibits both faith in his wife's powers of reason and trust in her desires. "Do as you think best" (I Sam. 1:23), Elkanah declares to Hannah, even after he does not receive the answers he had hoped for to the loving questions he had just posed: "Her husband Elkanah said to her, 'Hannah, why are you crying and why aren't you eating? Why are you so sad? Am I not more devoted to you than ten sons?'" (I Sam. 1:8). This episode models the wide range of feelings and respectful interactions present in loving relationships.

What an amazing opportunity for Jewish college students—whose schools often offer self-defense and rape prevention classes, but whose synagogues, in all their years of religious school and youth group, likely never mentioned the rape of the concubine—to use a story more shocking than most *CSI* plots to connect an immediate secular concern with their Jewish identity. College students discuss at length hooking up, romantic socializing, and the kind of lifetime partners they want to find, but few if any have had the opportunity to closely examine the respectful relationship between Hannah and Elkanah. Taking on these two stories, taught together, helps reinforce the critical distinction between violence perpetrated using the sex organs and expressing love through sex in sanctified relationships.

Those postgraduate singles who have chosen to actively seek a Jewish partner often find that bars are a common venue for events that have Jewish sponsorship. Jewish sponsorship notwithstanding, there is rarely anything Jewish about these events, other than that they are attended by Jews. The case has long been made[6] that participants who do not meet someone may well feel their attendance has been a waste of their time because the only goal of the event was unrealized for them. If sharing some Jewish knowledge was an additional goal of each event—if even a small part of the program included sitting around the table studying, over drinks, the text and/

or art of biblical couples such as Moses and Zipporah, or Rachel and Jacob meeting at various ancient wells—the event could be a success regardless of whether a date or mate is found. Additionally, if two singles do meet at the modern well, a bar, they can come back to the group and develop other kinds of friendships through sharing Jewish knowledge and interests. There is success to be had and continuity to be developed by structuring the potential for these to be successful events for every single, whether or not a date or mate is secured. No one's attendance need be a "waste of time" or a failure. All who attend learn something about biblical texts, biblical art, and some pretty famous Jewish couples even if they don't become part of one that evening.

Contemporary young couples, courting or married, heterosexual or homosexual, can engage texts and art of the Song of Songs, a biblical book in which there is no evidence the lovers are married. This erotic love poetry can be a mirror in which couples see their own beauty and the beauty of an actual or potential lover reflected. Coming to see themselves as a gift to another, talking about the fact that though Judaism sees sexuality as a gift from God, sex is most graphically described in a book that does not mention God, is a special opportunity for a group of couples to engage a biblical text that explores the range of feelings ancient and modern lovers experience, its highly poetic language notwithstanding.

Revisiting biblical characters mentioned earlier, turning and turning and turning them again, young couples can also study about King David's taking of Bathsheba in a program on challenges to love and relationships. In confronting difficult issues, such as temptations to have an affair, this story can be explored by engaging not only David's desire for Bathsheba and his political power to acquire her, and not only Nathan's lesson to David, but also the rarely studied episode of the death of the child he conceives with Bathsheba.

Enlightened Jewish sex education for seniors would mine and explore the many Jewish sources that precede by over two thousand years contemporary "jokes" and debates about the use of Viagra:

> King David was now old, advanced in years; and though they covered him with bedclothes, he never felt warm. His courtiers said to him, "Let a young virgin be sought for my lord the king, to wait upon Your Majesty and be his attendant; and let her lie in your bosom, and my lord the king will be warm." So they looked for a beautiful girl throughout the territory of Israel. They found Abishag the Shunammite and brought her to the king. The girl was exceedingly beautiful. She became the king's attendant and waited upon him; but the king was not intimate with her.
>
> (I Kings 1:1–4)

Exploring in a safe, nurturing environment the texts and art of King David with Abishag would likely tap into deeply held views and experiences about older men with younger women, and older women with younger men. Studying Rembrandt's Adam and Eve, portrayed as senior citizens, can be the centerpiece of a program on beauty and aging or a discussion on the relationship of inner and outer beauty. These are opportunities to expand biblical[7] and artistic horizons,[8] beyond David's harp and harping about Bathsheba—critically important stories, but far from the only ones directly relevant to the lives of those assembled in the room.

Not to envision and not to make these connections is to squander what may be among the most powerful opportunities to make and keep Jewish institutions relevant to the lives of each and every Jew. Crafting these links allows us to activate our power to allow healthy sexuality to flower in synagogues that are safe and unafraid. Where Judaism, science, and experience of the secular world are woven together, Jews are given something they can get nowhere else.

At the end of the two-week block program "Forgotten Treasures: Discovering Lost Traditions of Jewish Sexuality," a program inserted into, but alas, not consciously connected at either end to the school-wide curriculum, I asked the students to anonymously write their answers to the question that opens this essay. Throughout the course, the children had been allowed to hear and utter every proper term and every slang word imaginable in the lexicon of sex. What they asked for at the end was the opportunity to study more of those "sexy stories from the Bible." Once they knew they could hear and say "penis," "vagina," and "intercourse" and all of their derivatives, they wanted to learn about and celebrate themselves as sexual beings who were Jews. They did not want to separate their Judaism from their sexuality. Such an approach to Jewish sex education can transform Judaism into the vehicle that shows us and teaches our children how and why good and bad relationships affect sex, and how sex affects good and bad relationships. The point of departure for this approach emphasizes sexuality as an extension of human relationships and demonstrates, through consistent linkage of Jewish texts with anatomy, physiology, psychology, and sociology, the potential of sexuality to reflect desirable ways for people to view and treat themselves and each other.

We have infinitely more power to usher in a world in which the contemporary synagogue is a center of Jewish learning about sexuality than we do to usher in a world without violence, even as we work for and pray for peace. And we can immediately remodel contemporary synagogues even as we recite within them the *Amidah* prayer's wish for rebuilding that world at peace. With lifelong sex-in-text education we have a promising way to gather in Jews who have voluntarily or involuntarily been exiled from synagogue life, even as we pray for both the literal and figurative ingathering of exiles to Israel. How do we do it?

We precede activation of any section of a lifelong sex-in-text Jewish education curriculum with expert teacher training. We can train our accomplished synagogue staff of rabbis, educators, and Jewish professionals who desire to teach sexuality through a preparatory year of continuing education that is dedicated to adding competencies in child development, group dynamics, geriatrics, marriage, and Jewish sex texts to their existing good instincts. Continuing education opportunities can include daylong study retreats, weekend workshops, and portions of every staff meeting.

Teachers who have not been given training in exactly what to say when kids (or adults) giggle may not know they should expect giggling and consequently bark, "It's not funny," or "Be serious," unwittingly undercutting the best sex-in-text curricula in the world. Teachers without opportunities to study the implications of growing up in a home where sex was never discussed or was treated as dirty are consequently unable to understand why parents may be opposed to sex-in-text education. Teachers trained to be highly aware that statistically at least one in six females in the room has been sexually abused in some way are able to not just deal with the texts, but heal with the texts. Teachers mindful that approximately one in ten participants in the room are homosexual, and may or may not be hiding their sexual orientation, will be inclusive. Teachers who have engaged knowledge of bisexual and transgender identities can create an environment of absolute safety. Teachers who know when and why it is crucial to teach males and females separately will unburden participants and maximize learning. Teachers trained to handle the individuals brave enough, after a program on sex, to come and confess sexual problems in their marriage, can inspire, help heal, appropriately refer, and reassure those brave Jewish souls that life as a sexual being can be better and should be more satisfying.

Properly trained teachers allow the programs they are teaching to not end when the session is over, but to transform into portals that connect and expand the involvement of participants with the institution as a whole and with each other.

Once a vision for sex-in-text education is established and teacher training is underway, institution-wide employee orientations can take place. Orientation for all employees of the institution is essential. Knowing what the place they work in offers and *why* enables them to be both extensions and reflections of the synagogue community, who can clearly articulate synagogue programs and motivate members and non-members to attend. This awareness and outlook of the staff render the institution a Jewish place, and not just a place inhabited by people who happen to be Jewish. Orientation for all employees enables every employee to be congruent, in words and behavior, with the programs being offered. When they are armed with knowledge of the rationale for lifelong sex-in-text education, their demeanor or words can become the reason an individual feels at home in the synagogue, becomes a member, or learns about and comes to a program. All staff members, whether the janitor in the hall or the principal of the day school, have interactions with those who pass through the building and, once trained, can be effective representatives and ambassadors, in and out of the workplace.

Once the synagogue staff feel prepared, parent-child[9] orientations, critical to successful implementation of sex-in-text education for children, can be held. Requiring no more than a couple of hours, such orientations enable parents to become partners with appropriate expectations in the endeavor of celebrating ourselves as sexual beings through sex-in-text education. A synagogue with staff who are sex education teachers and can explain to parents and children, sitting in a room together, what children will be learning delivers the message that children and adults can talk together about sex.

And children want to be able to talk with adults about sex. "When asked from whom they [teenagers] would prefer to learn about sex, they almost invariably reply, 'My parents.'"[10] But there are also boundaries between parents and children that make a combination of sex-in-text education at home and at synagogue such an effective partnership. The field of child development and our own experience with children tell us that what we do not explain to children, they will fill in with their own imaginations.

Sex-in-text education, tightly woven into the fabric of our institutions, is an exciting way to fulfill our age-old Jewish obligation to teach and protect our children.[11] If we are willing to create and effectively teach sex-in-text education programs that reflect ancient Jewish theology, confirmed by modern scientific research, that our sexuality is a fundamental part of who we are over our entire lifetimes, and not just something that spontaneously appears with the onset of puberty, we can celebrate ourselves as sexual beings and see our institutions celebrated for teaching us and reminding us, in the words of Dr. Ruth Westheimer, that "Judaism is intensely sexual."[12]

NOTES

1. Marcie Schoenberg Lee, *Forgotten Treasures: Discovering Lost Traditions of Jewish Sexuality—A Sex Education Curriculum* ©1989.

2. *JPS Hebrew-English Tanakh* (Philadelphia: Jewish Publication Society, 1999) is used for all biblical texts quoted herein.

3. Consider as examples, from diverse time periods and diverse points of view, *Igeret HaKodesh*, ca. 1250; Alan Green, *Sex, God and the Sabbath: The Mystery of Jewish Marriage* (Cleveland: Temple Emanu El, 1979); Dr. Ruth K. Westheimer and Jonathan Mark, *Heavenly Sex: Sexuality in the Jewish Tradition* (New York: New York University Press, 1995); and Sandi Dubowski's film *Trembling before God* (2001).

4. Mayo Clinic staff, in an April 30, 2011 post on their website, assert "Sex education often begins as simple anatomy lessons during the toddler years"; http://www.mayoclinic.com/health/sex-education/CC00076.

5. There is much concern and many questions posed about what to do when preschool-age children touch their own bodies or each other's at school. Though a common occurrence reflective of normal development, it is obviously not appropriate at school. But when it does happen, teachers trained in child development and sexuality education for young children can guide children's natural but often ill-timed touching by simply telling them a penis or vagina is private and that when they are at school is not an appropriate time to touch themselves. Teachers might even note this by quoting from *Kohelet*, "There is a time for every purpose under heaven" (Eccles. 3:1). This information and clearly drawn and expressed boundaries are a building block to achieving respect for privacy and for protection of self and others in the present and for the future. As a consultant called in to preschools to both talk with parents and train teachers when these incidents take place, I have found that in all cases I have encountered, staff shortages or inattention allowed children to be unobserved long enough for these incidents to take place.

6. Marcie Jane Schoenberg, *The Relationship between Jewish Singles and the Organized Jewish Community* (Los Angeles: Hebrew Union College-Jewish Institute of Religion, California School, 1974).

7. Many of these carefully crafted connections also take participants where most have never gone before—to close study of biblical characters beyond the first five books.

8. Jewish artist and art critic Richard McBee explains that Jewish art includes art of Jewish subject matter by Jewish artists, art of Jewish subject matter by non-Jewish artists, and art of non-Jewish subject matter by Jewish artists.

9. It is understood that "parent-child" orientations may be grandparent-child orientation or guardian-child orientation, as family structures dictate.

10. Elisabeth Keiffer, "What Every Teen-ager Wants to Know about Sex (But Is Afraid to Ask)," *Family Circle*, April 17, 1984.

11. See, e.g., *Zohar* 2:93a, "If a man does not teach his son Torah, it is as if he had merely created an image"; or Babylonian Talmud, *Kiddushin* 29a, "The father is bound regarding his son to circumcise him, redeem him, teach him Torah, take a wife for him, and teach him a craft. Some say to teach him to swim too." The instruction to teach swimming may be understood as a form of self-protection.

12. Westheimer and Mark, *Heavenly Sex*, 5.

32

ONE MODEL:

A Sexuality Retreat for Teens

RABBI BILLY DRESKIN

In 1987, Jonathan Stein, then senior rabbi at Indianapolis Hebrew Congregation, asked me and my wife, Ellen, to serve as songleaders for a weekend retreat he was facilitating. When he told us it was a program of sexuality education for ninth graders, we consented to attend but asked that he train us to run the retreat in our own congregation. And so, beginning in 1989 and every year since, one or both of us has facilitated a weekend exploration we call "Judaism Takes an Honest Look at Love and Sexuality."

Nearly a quarter of a century later, I still believe deeply in what this program offers to young people as they make their journey from adolescence to adulthood. Its content is as relevant and important as ever, and I am honored to share it in this publication and to encourage clergy and educators to bring it to their own communities. The program is informative, fun, and engages young people in ways that allow them to truly engage with the material and effectively process the information for themselves. That is no small accomplishment when it comes to teens.

The United Nations Education, Scientific and Cultural Organization (UNESCO) defines sexuality education as "an age-appropriate, culturally relevant approach to teaching about sex and relationships by providing scientifically accurate, realistic, non-judgmental information. Sexuality education provides opportunities to explore one's own values and attitudes and to build decision-making, communication and risk-reduction skills about many aspects of sexuality."[1] The Unitarian Universalist Association, which developed the 1971 groundbreaking curriculum "About Your Sexuality," which serves as the foundation for this retreat, offers a similar set of objectives for its own program: (a) provide accurate information, with which young people can (b) deepen communication skills, so they may (c) build attitudes and values, which will help them to (d) make responsible decisions.

Planned Parenthood has argued consistently and persuasively across the decades that this is precisely what we ought to be offering our young people. Information on sex does not necessarily lead to sex; in fact, it often helps young people satisfy their curiosity about sex and feel comfortable postponing sexual activity.[2] I think this retreat makes a substantive contribution to the body of experiences that will assist our kids in reaching these goals. Year after year, I am impressed by how effective this program is in opening up successful communication between teacher and student and, perhaps even more importantly, the incredibly valuable dialogue that takes place between the students themselves, as they test values-positions and form personal ethics on sexuality. Many of these kids go home at the end of the retreat with a deepened sense of what they want from human relationships and where sexual activities might healthfully fit in for them.

There are so many learning moments we bring to our temple youth throughout their years with us. Whether we are teaching them history, Hebrew, prayer, or values and ethics, the young people in our communities benefit from the time they spend at synagogue. In a world that increasingly emphasizes physical, financial, and even intellectual prowess, strength of spirit and heart is more needed than ever. The study of Judaism and sexuality brings this spiritual curriculum to a realm that includes both the physical and emotional as well. The need to assist parents in providing their children with the tools to manage this essential aspect of human existence is greater and more urgent than ever. We cannot teach everything. Our heritage's great lessons will be conveyed regardless of specific curriculum. With the study of sexuality, we have an opportunity not only to convey the great trajectory of Judaism's human goodness, but we might very well save a life along the way.

While most of the schools our young people attend do provide sexuality education that certainly conveys accurate information, they do not necessarily assist students in processing that information so that they are better able to make wise choices for themselves. In fact, it is doubtful we can even do that in our religious school classrooms. But in the retreat format, we have the environment and the time to foster dialogue between student and teacher and between student and student, to move our teens through the four-part process (noted in the Unitarian goals above) that allows them to begin forming responses to questions about sexuality that, in many circumstances, may not otherwise take shape until the moment when those values will be urgently called upon to decide whether or not "this is the moment" for a given sexual experience. If we want our kids to make good decisions for themselves, I cannot think of a better place than the synagogue for these discussions to take place.

The beauty of this retreat is that it brings our teens together with a caring, knowledgeable Jewish professional, as well as trained, knowledgeable staff, whose number-one agenda item is to provide these young people with the tools they need to take care of themselves and each other. Secondarily, this program provides positive exposure to Jewish learning through texts both ancient and modern that offer thoughtful points of view on this subject. And third, this retreat conveys to our young people that their Jewish community cares about them and their well-being, a message they may never forget and that could serve them well in the years following by a deepened sense of connectedness to Judaism and their Jewish community.

In this retreat program, we deliberately include "sex ed" topics (such as how our reproductive organs work, the nature and treatment of sexually transmitted infections and diseases, and an exploration of contraceptive devices) along with more expected conversations on Jewish values regarding sexuality. We do this for a couple of important reasons. First, some students attending the program are not yet ready to engage in the deep processing of human relationships. Young people mature at different rates, and we want to make sure to meet each student where they are. Some, we find, are only ready to learn "the basics" and sex. If that's where they are, then we should send them home with information that is relevant to them. Second, as mentioned earlier, our young people need accurate, explicit information about sexuality if we want them to be able to engage in constructive dialogue and to form beneficial attitudes and values. Bringing to the table both "sex ed" lessons and deeper conversations about the kind of people we want to be, these two areas of focus work together to shape an experience our students enjoy and appreciate and whose messages find homes inside, which they can then carry home and back into their lives as emerging young adults.

As often as possible, staff is composed of married couples. The purpose is to model our message that sexuality is best expressed within the framework of a lifelong, committed, and loving relationship. We do not beat the students over the head with this, understanding that many relationships may look different from marriage, but the idea of long-term commitment being at the foundation of healthy sexuality is consonant with both the messages of Judaism as well as those of sexuality educators.

This brief essay will try to offer the reader a sense of what takes place during the retreat.[3] It is my hope that every synagogue will offer this program. In a world that sends far too many unhealthy messages to young people about their bodies, their self-esteem, and their sexual involvement, we would do well to add our tradition's intelligent and caring voice to the mix.

The retreat begins with Shabbat dinner and a service entitled "To Be Nobody but Yourself," which emphasizes the core message of the weekend, that "this is a weekend about you, about your body and about your soul, about how you can care for both, and about how you are worth doing that for yourself." The service provides a key opportunity for the Jewish professional to make a powerful, personal appeal to the students about what Judaism wants for them, what their synagogue wants for them, and what we want for them.

Following the service, folders are distributed that contain goals for the weekend, goals for each program, and the Jewish texts that will be studied throughout. As the program continues, additional materials will be placed in these folders so that the student will have one place to keep them for future reference after the weekend concludes.

It is at this early point in the weekend that we address the existence of different gender and sexual orientations. While the material encountered is presented in a predominantly heterosexual framework, our language is always careful to remain open to the probability that any number of students already know that they are gay or lesbian or will discover it in the years ahead. We want them to know that they are welcome and cared for every bit as much as anyone else in the group. As Judaism often speaks in metaphors, we urge the participants to view the examples throughout the weekend as being metaphorical as well. The partners involved could just as easily be two men or two women, and each participant is encouraged to interpret the information as best suits them. For our part, as staff members, we will endeavor to use language that keeps these metaphors open wide.

Two messages are then articulated about what we are teaching. The first is that we do not think anybody in high school should be having sex. The physical and emotional issues are simply too complex and too important for them to resolve so soon. Sexuality educators Sol and Judith Gordon write, "[Teenagers] . . . tend to be impulsive. . . . Also, teenage pregnancy is definitely unsound from medical, moral and psychological points of view."[4] Gordon and Gordon also admit, "While we say no to sex for teenagers, no teenager has ever asked for our consent,"[5] and so the second message we articulate throughout the retreat is that even if a young person is already sexually active, this program is still important because of the information it offers as we strive to make satisfying and healthy choices for ourselves, and the unhurried, unpressured environment the retreat provides is an excellent time and place in which to consider these choices.

Jewish texts explored in the course of the weekend are frequently used to introduce topics. They range from the classic and more likely to be familiar (e.g., Genesis on our having been created in the divine image; Hillel on the questions of being for ourselves or only for ourselves) to surprising Rabbinic texts (Mishnah on the value of regular sex in marriage;[6] Nachmanides on the importance of seeing to our partner's orgasm and sexual satisfaction[7]). More importantly, these texts provide a Jewish framework for the weekend's learning, conveying to our students that sexuality education is Jewishly authentic.

The participants are then divided into same-gender groupings where, for most of the rest of the evening, they will have an opportunity to receive information about more than a hundred questions on sexuality. This part of the program employs a technique known as "the card pass," used frequently throughout the weekend to protect each student's anonymity while permitting them to share personal thoughts and ideas. The technique is a simple one. One card is given to each student. One question is asked, and they write their answer on the card *without* signing their name. The cards are collected, shuffled, and redistributed. All of the cards are then read aloud, allowing each student to answer the question without having to reveal that he/she wrote it.

At the conclusion of the program, the entire group comes back together to share impressions about the evening. Most express surprise at how enjoyable the program is (i.e., disbelief that their synagogue would be so direct and engaging with the topic) and that they have already learned something useful.

Prior to breaking for the night, students are told about the question box, which will be available to them throughout the weekend, to anonymously pose questions for which they would like a response. At periodic intervals, staff will process the questions with the entire group, yet another avenue for our young people to receive the information they are seeking without having to identify themselves. Throughout the weekend, students typically grow more and more comfortable with the dialogue, relying less and less on the opportunities for anonymity. Nevertheless, the methodologies are retained, just in case someone still needs them.

Shabbat morning focuses on language. One of the obstacles to meaningful dialogue can be discomfort and awkwardness with the language of sexuality. Following a bit of text study, the participants are challenged to identify different vocabularies we employ for conveying our thoughts about sex. While not done so exclusively, adults often speak a different "language" than teens. Adults will reference sexual anatomy and activities using either their formal names (e.g., vagina and penis) or infantile euphemisms (hoo-hoo and wee-wee), while young people are likely to employ slang. This program does not judge vocabulary choices but acknowledges the differences in communication styles and seeks to help participants become more comfortable speaking for themselves about sexuality. It also explores why we choose particular terms and how society may be affecting the ways in which we communicate.

Large pieces of newsprint are laid out on the floor, each bearing one sexuality term across the top. Participants are given markers and are asked to add as many alternatives to the terms as they can. When finished, each participant is presented with one of the sheets and reads it aloud to the group. In the course of this, laughter abounds but gradually subsides as the sensational aspect of hearing sexual terminology (in all its conventional forms) diminishes. This very important process clears the way for the group to begin its conversations with fewer awkward feelings and increased ability to focus on the topics being explored.

Referencing the morning prayer *Asher Yatzar*, thanking God for our finely crafted bodies, the point is made that nothing about the human body is either ugly or obscene and that sexuality, appropriately expressed, is a beautiful gift from God.

The rest of the morning focuses on sexual anatomy, understanding that the students have probably studied this in school but that it is important for everyone to have a clear understanding how our bodies work if we are to make value-laden choices about them. In addition to drawings and diagrams, photographs of male and female sexual anatomy are included in this section, because (1) there is nothing either dirty or obscene about the body and (2) young people need honest and accurate information if they are to be able to form responsible positions about sexuality in their lives.

The remainder of the morning and afternoon include a number of videos and activities on sexually transmitted infections (STIs) and diseases (STDs), as well as conception and birth, including a video of a child being born. This last video underscores the message that when the time is right, bringing a baby into our lives—whether by vaginal delivery, cesarean section, or adoption—can be one of the great rewards of human existence.

On Shabbat afternoon, the entire group gathers together around a large, white sheet onto which examples of nearly every contraceptive device have been placed. It is explained that birth control is the shared responsibility of both partners and that communication about contraception is an important indicator of readiness to enter into a sexually active relationship. Pamphlets are distributed that provide information about the pros and cons of each device. Students are then encouraged to open, handle, and even play with each form of contraception as the merits and shortcomings are discussed. If our young people are to use contraception, it behooves us to provide them with accurate and thorough information so that they can make healthy and satisfying choices when the time has arrived.

There is then an open-ended discussion about abortion and Jewish perspectives on it, as well as information regarding Tay-Sachs and other genetic diseases that may or may not impact on an individual's decision to complete or terminate a pregnancy.

Saturday evening, in what are likely the most important and fruitful conversations of the retreat, students explore with one another their hopes for their own relationships in the years ahead. Information acquired throughout the weekend will now be employed to begin to clarify feelings and to test attitudes about love and sex. The goal is to assist our young people in making responsible decisions about sexual behavior and to strengthen them in staying true to their own values rather than, in a moment of passion, adopting someone else's. A video on acquaintance rape is viewed, followed by a discussion of sexual rights, whether we ever lose them, and whether "no" can ever mean "yes." A fun, light-hearted activity, "The No Means No Game," conveys the message that one's sexual rights are never surrendered and that partners ought always be attentive to the other's thoughts and feelings. An exercise entitled "The Intimacy Continuum" invites same-gender groups to assess the level of closeness of different sexual activities and to then engage in dialogue with both genders as to what constitutes intimacy and what is ultimately meaningful in human relationships.

The evening ends with a *Havdalah* ceremony inviting participants to consider what is and is not holy as our lives intersect with one another. Between each blessing, time is given to respond to these questions: "What *havdalah* do you want to make? From what do you want to distance yourself? And what do you want to bring closer?" The ceremony concludes with a reference to Leviticus 19:2, God's commanding us to seek holiness, to see the holiness in ourselves and in others, to not countenance exploitation or hurtfulness, but to be cherishing and protecting of ourselves and of those with whom we would share the love of our hearts.

On Sunday morning, students explore their hopes for what a sexual relationship might emotionally provide to them. Audio recordings of men and women speaking about their first experiences with sexual intercourse challenge the students to consider what they would like the outcome of such experiences to be for themselves. A number of Jewish texts foster additional thought, concluding with an excerpt from the Mishnah that challenges us to integrate into our relationships the highest values we learn about God, so that we each benefit from partnerships with other men and women that offer much more than just physical passion, which can serve as an exciting ingredient but which must also include values such as respect, honor, compassion, trust, and love if these relationships are to be truly fulfilling in our lives.

Before the weekend concludes, each student is given materials that they can read at home, keep around for future reference, and also show to their parent(s). It is our hope that the weekend will provide a basis for productive conversation at home. Parents are our children's primary educators, and it is hoped that programs such as these can offer substantive support for parents as they engage in the holy endeavor of raising children who live value-laden lives of integrity and wholeness.

In the twenty-four years that I have been involved in teaching this program, I have always felt it is among the most worthwhile efforts of my career. Through both student evaluations and parent evaluations (written after speaking with their children following the weekend), I have received consistent and nearly unanimous enthusiasm, as well as notes of gratitude. I have no doubt that these young people, as a result of this retreat, are better equipped to continue their journeys. They have better information, have processed it with caring and knowledgeable role models, have formed more specific and carefully considered positions, and are more likely to talk about these challenges with others. In addition, they have formed stronger bonds with synagogue peers, as well as with synagogue staff. Parents express thanks for our giving their children these gifts. And we feel like we have done something of excellence for our community.

This retreat is not meant to be our only strategy for assisting families in guiding their children's sexual growth. Not only can there be other learning during religious school and youth group, but it would indeed be valuable to begin such programming at younger ages as well and to include parents so that, as Sol and Judith Gordon put it, they might become "more askable parents."[8] Jewish learning on self-esteem, body image, and respect for others provides a strong foundation for young people so that when the time comes for them to begin thinking about sexuality questions in their teens, they will already be equipped to ensure that their responses are grounded in Judaism's time-tested values, as well as a long-cultivated belief in their own personal value and goodness.

It is important here to add a note about same-sex relationships. This curriculum may, in fact, be incomplete in its addressing issues of sexuality between partners of the same gender. There are no specific programs during the retreat that focus on being gay or lesbian. And one could conclude from the number of times the boys study by themselves and the girls by themselves that the retreat is not sensitive to these issues. However, the staff is trained to consider all lessons and conversations to be inclusive of gay/lesbian perspectives and ideas. Even when same-gender groupings discuss a topic, the group leader always remains open to, and encouraging of, the sharing and consideration of same-sex perspectives. This may not be the ideal structure (and suggested revisions are always welcome), but I believe we have been consistently compassionate and supportive of same-sex issues and of students in our groups who are or (not yet knowing for sure) may be gay or lesbian.

This sexuality retreat emphasizes Judaism's insistence upon the equality, dignity, and worth of every human being. Assisting young people in their efforts to come to terms with their emerging sexuality is their right and our responsibility. To provide a setting where they can openly and honestly bring their questions and puzzlements, and explore their thoughts and feelings in a disciplined manner with trusted, responsible leaders, is my privilege as a Jewish professional. To secure our children's physical and emotional well-being in the years ahead, this may very well be the greatest gift we can offer.

NOTES

1. *International Technical Guidance on Sexuality Education, an Evidence-Informed Approach for Schools, Teachers and Health Educators* (United Nations Education, Scientific and Cultural Organization, Dec. 2009), 2.

2. "There is a large body of research showing that high quality, comprehensive and rights-based sexuality education programmes can delay initiation of sexual activity and unprotected intercourse, decrease the number of sexual partners, increase contraceptive and condom use, and therefore decrease unintended pregnancies and sexually transmitted infections among young people" (*From Evidence to Action:*

Advocating for Comprehensive Sexuality Education [International Planned Parenthood Federation, July 2009], 3).

3. "Leader's Guide to Judaism Takes an Honest Look at Love and Sexuality" and all non-copyrighted printed and audiovisual materials used throughout the weekend are available (free of charge, excepting expenses) by contacting Rabbi Billy Dreskin, Woodlands Community Temple, 50 Worthington Road, White Plains, NY, 10607, (914) 592-7070, RabbiBillyDreskin@gmail.com.

4. Sol Gordon and Judith Gordon, *Raising a Child Conservatively in a Sexually Permissive World* (New York: Simon & Schuster, 1989), 53.

5. Ibid.

6. *Mishnah K'tubot* 5:6.

7. Nachmanides, *Igeret HaKodesh* 6.

8. Gordon and Gordon, *Raising a Child*, chap. 4 ("Becoming an Askable Parent").

Fertility

33

UNPLANNED FATHERHOOD

Rabbi Barry H. D. Block

"Rabbi, we have a problem, and we need your help." Bill told a tale that shocked him, but that had become sadly familiar to me. His son Joshua, eighteen years old, had been informed that his girlfriend was pregnant and that Joshua was the father. Like too many young men who had come to me directly or through their parents over the years, Joshua faced fatherhood at a time in his life when he was not eager or prepared to become a parent.

Unplanned pregnancy is a tremendous concern in our society. Women, for better or worse, are generally the focus. In more than two decades as a congregational rabbi, though, I have rarely been called by young women or their parents facing an unplanned pregnancy. Postulating that girls and their parents might be more comfortable talking with a woman rabbi, I nevertheless learned that the female colleague who had served with me for twelve years had heard from no more unhappily pregnant women than I.[1] On the other hand, I have frequently heard from young men facing unplanned fatherhood and from their parents, who often cite my vocal advocacy for reproductive choice and past service as board chair of the local Planned Parenthood as one of the reasons they are comfortable approaching me.

This essay is a reflection on the men, boys, and parents of boys who have contacted me and the questions and concerns they have presented.

Since reproductive choice resides with women, these males often feel, and sometimes are, disempowered. Moreover, because of biology as well as traditional, gender-based parenting roles, men often believe women have greater choices about how and whether to parent a child who results from unplanned pregnancy, and they are often correct. In addition, men sometimes find out they have fathered a child only long after the child is born.

I have long been an outspoken advocate for synagogue-based sexuality education that addresses contraception, including male contraception, but now I wonder if that has been enough.

While we emphasize the male's responsibility to avoid unintended pregnancy, ought we also to address the plethora of questions that arise if and when a male learns that his sexual activity has resulted in an unplanned pregnancy? What role should the prospective father have in the decision to secure an abortion to terminate an unintended pregnancy? If the woman chooses abortion, does financial obligation rest upon the man? When the pregnancy is to be carried to term, what is the prospective father's responsibility to provide for the woman during pregnancy? May he rightly terminate his paternal rights, in favor of adoption or maternal single parenthood? In short, what is the responsibility of a Jewish man toward a child that he never planned to conceive, much less parent?

Bill hoped that the young woman would choose abortion or, failing that, adoption. Bill was relieved, instead, when the young woman and her parents proposed to raise the child themselves and to terminate Joshua's paternal rights and responsibilities.

Abortion: Whose Choice Is It Anyway?

Richard was livid. How could his ex-girlfriend refuse his request that she get an abortion? A lifelong Reform Jew, active in our congregation, Richard cited our Movement's long history of support for a woman's right to choose.[2]

But Richard had made a leap of logic that surprised me. If women have the right to choose, he asked, shouldn't a man have the same right? If the law requires the father to bear the responsibilities of fatherhood, at least financially, shouldn't he have the right to forswear those obligations if the woman will not undergo the abortion he desires?

Jewish tradition is no more apt than American law to grant the prospective father the right to terminate a pregnancy. Instead, Jewish legal permission for abortion is granted only in cases of threat to the mother, with authorities differing only on questions of the basis for this ruling and about the extent of the potential injury to the mother required to justify abortion. The definitive 1985 Reform responsum on abortion does not mention the needs of the father.[3] The omission is neither accidental nor surprising. Traditional Jewish support for abortion is founded on one of two arguments: Rashi's determination that the fetus has the status of "a limb of its mother" or Rambam's insistence that the fetus may be destroyed because it is "a pursuer," threatening the mother.[4]

We cannot therefore agree with Richard or others like him who would base their inclination to disclaim responsibility for a child on the lack of a paternal right to terminate the pregnancy. Judaism finds no such right.

Avi's sadness was palpable as he told me that his son Joey, a high school senior, had "gotten his girlfriend pregnant" and that the young woman was going to have an abortion. A temple leader and knowledgeable Reform Jew, Avi was comfortable with the ethics of the young woman's decision to undergo an abortion, even as he confessed his struggle not to let his personal stake in that decision color his judgment. Avi and his wife were also guiding Joey to pay for the abortion and were prepared to loan Joey the money up front.

Avi was also reaching out for help to address Joey's irresponsible behavior: engaging in unprotected sex. Avi and his wife had discussed the matter with their son and invited me to do the same. I counseled Joey, who regretted his behavior and was grateful that he had "dodged the bullet this time," thanks to his former girlfriend's decision to abort. This incident ultimately marked a turning point in Joey's teenage years, which had been marred by impulsive behavior and substance issues. Joey is now a successful adult; Avi and his wife agree that having lived through this experience, and having accepted responsibility for it, contributed significantly to Joey's turnaround.

Before we leave the matter of the potential father's role during pregnancy, we may ask about his financial responsibility for the woman or girl during pregnancy. Mindful that Joey assumed a financial responsibility for his ex-girlfriend's abortion, we may ask whether Joshua, too, has an obligation to provide support to his former partner during pregnancy. Women's claims to pregnancy support may justifiably increase now that paternity can be definitively determined with a simple maternal blood test.[5]

In its most recent responsum on the matter, the CCAR Responsa Committee considers the two cases together, namely the father's responsibility to share the cost of an abortion and the father's obligation to provide for the woman during pregnancy:

> The young man shares financial obligations with respect to pregnancy and childbearing because pregnancy was a foreseeable (if undesired) consequence of their decision to engage in a sexual relationship. In the same way, he can be said to share financial obligation for the abortion procedure, should the young woman decide upon that course, because the abortion is a foreseeable consequence of that same decision.[6]

Joshua is obligated to support his potential child's mother during pregnancy, just as Joey has met his obligation to shoulder financial responsibility for his ex-girlfriend's abortion.

The Father's Obligations

Max's head spun as the woman caller told him about a six-year-old son, a son Max didn't believe was his until paternity tests proved otherwise. Now in his thirties, Max was married; he and his wife had a child of their own. Years earlier, the child's mother had been a "friend with benefits."

The mother was letting Max know that she was seeking child support, which Max would have to pay until the child turned eighteen. She was also offering Max the opportunity to get to know their son and to be his noncustodial father. At the same time, she told Max that she had married shortly after their son was born. Her husband knew of the child's paternity, but the boy had been raised with her husband as his father.

Max agreed to pay child support, but he declined the offer of a relationship.

Later, Max met the woman and her husband at the child support office. They spoke of how well the boy achieved in school. The de facto father handed Max his business card, and Max was impressed by his meaningful employment. "That brief exchange told me a lot," Max wrote. "It appeared that the child was in a stable home, with proud, loving parents who were in a position to provide for his needs (with some financial help from me) and who were focused on his education." Max affirmed his decision that the child would be better off with the parents he had always known, without the intrusion of a stranger-father.

Max told me this story so that I might help him and his wife work through the issues between them that arisen from this new development in their lives. He did not seek my input about what he should do about his biological son. But I wondered: What guidance would our tradition give this man? What obligations does a father have toward his biological offspring? Had Max acted in a way that Judaism would find appropriate?

The Rabbis legislate parental responsibility: "The Mishnah speaks of *mitzvot haben al ha-av*, obligations that the father owes to his son. The Talmud lists these as follows: the requirement to have his son circumcised; to perform the mitzvah of *pidyon ha-ben*; to teach him Torah; to find him a wife; and to teach him a trade."[7] All today would add to this list, while liberal Jews would modify it and would not assign parental roles so narrowly on the basis of gender.

The Rabbis specify that the father is obligated to provide support, whether or not father and child live together. The CCAR Responsa Committee articulates the basis of that requirement: "This duty is expressed . . . in the halachah's rules concerning the custody of children. In a situation where the minor child does not live together with both parents, each parent owes certain personal and financial obligations toward him or her."[8] Seeking to apply this Jewish reasoning to Max's case or to Joshua's, we may conclude that neither can be easily absolved of all obligation toward his biological child. Instead, both are under at least the presumption of accountability for all the responsibilities of a parent.

In its most recent responsum on the issue, "Unexpected Pregnancy and Child Support: A Parent's Rights and Responsibilities," the committee addresses a case like Joshua's: "In our case, the young man is being asked to waive his parental rights by allowing the young woman to adopt their child. And since a parent's financial obligation toward a child stems from his or her standing **as** a parent, by terminating his parental role he effectively terminates as well his financial responsibilities toward the child."[9]

But in what circumstance may a father like Joshua or Max ethically be free of his paternal duties?

Joshua's father Bill, for example, argues that adoption would be in the best interest of the child. Though Bill didn't know it, "the best interest of the child," *tovat hayeled*, is cited in halachah. The Talmud assigns custody of girls to their mothers, while boys are to live with their mothers only until the age of six, when the child goes to live with his father, "who is traditionally responsible for his education."[10] The Rashba later "suggests that the Rabbis based [the Talmudic custody assignments] on the concept of *tovat hayeled*, 'the welfare of the child.'"[11] Modern Israeli religious (Orthodox) courts (*batei din*) have argued that even where halachah would give custody to a particular parent, "if it seems to the *beit din* that the welfare of the child would be better served by living with [the other parent], the *beit din* is authorized to transfer the child" to the other parent.[12] While these texts refer specifically to custody matters between (biological) parents, we may apply the concept more broadly.

Neither Max nor Bill is motivated by *tovat hayeled*. Still, in Max's case, the facts suggest that Max's biological son is best served by remaining with the only parents he has ever known. Max discharges his remaining responsibility by the payment of child support. Max's options, even if he were motivated by the child's best interests, are limited by his having been made aware of the child's existence years after the birth. Joshua, on the other hand, had the opportunity to make a serious assessment of the child's best interest, beginning early in pregnancy, but seems not to have done so. Bill may also be correct that adoption would be in the best interest of the child, but he provides scant evidence.

The CCAR Responsa Committee has examined a case like Joshua's and has concluded that the child's best interests may indeed be served by the young father's severing paternal rights and responsibilities at the request of the mother:

> It is quite arguable that we would frustrate [pursuit of the child's best interests] by forcing this young man to assume the financial and other duties of a father. To do so, against his will and despite what would appear to be the young woman's . . . opposition, may result in tension and strife between the two parents as they struggle over both the child's upbringing and the relationship that will have been forced upon them. That conflict could last for many years, quite possibly to the detriment of the child. By contrast, in terminating his paternal rights and responsibilities, the young man may raise the likelihood that his child will grow up in a stable and cohesive home environment. Put simply, his decision to bow out of the life of his future child may well be in the child's best interest.[13]

On the other hand, the Responsa Committee also emphasizes that such a determination should only be made after a rigorous examination, one that Bill and Joshua did not pursue: "Decisions like this require a careful judgment of the particular situation, one that can be made only by the parties involved, preferably with ample professional counseling."[14]

A Reform Rabbi's Reflections

A separate but related question concerns the Jewish identity of the child. Is the Jewish father obligated to ensure that his biological child is raised Jewish? None of the young women in the cases described above are Jewish, so the answer comes easily to those who regard the child of a Jewish father and non-Jewish mother to be a gentile. For American Reform Jews who accept patrilineal descent, though, the matter is more complicated.

The Jewish parent is required to teach Torah to the child. Naturally, the biological father who is freed and who absolves himself of all paternal duties is in no position to argue that the child should be raised as a Jew. But here we may argue that the opportunity to raise a Jewish child, to strengthen *Am Yisrael*, is a compelling reason for him not to surrender paternal obligations. We may also return to the concept of *tovat hayeled*. The extent to which a father in these situations must press for the child to be raised Jewish is best decided on a case-by-case basis, with the presumption that the father should seek to raise the child Jewish, but with the best interests of the child a compelling reason for him not to do so.[15]

As I consider the cases described here, and others like them, the rabbi's pastoral approach and the synagogue's duties to sex education come into focus.

Our congregations often teach boys how to use condoms, knowing that some will not heed our counsel to delay sexual intercourse until they are prepared to live with all of its natural and foreseeable results. But even the "second choice" of our sex education efforts, that is, the condom, may fail, if only because a student doesn't use one. Therefore, we need to assure our young men that their synagogue home is a safe place to seek counsel if they do one day learn that a sexual encounter has resulted in unplanned pregnancy. Rabbis would do well to tell their young male students stories like Joshua's and Max's and Joey's. We need to be prepared to counsel young men like those three, and parents like Bill and Avi, when they come to our doors. We are blessed with

Reform responsa as our guides. Compassion, openness, and resisting the temptation to judge will keep our doors open to these young men and their families when they need us.

Our efforts will be aided by telling real-life accounts that might have begun with a struggle but that continue to happy endings. Some of those stories are about adoption or successful single parenting. And some of those stories are about mothers and fathers who, despite challenging circumstances, have succeeded in raising happy, well-adjusted Jewish children together.

Like every bar or bat mitzvah parent, Phil[16] was beaming, as were Rebecca and Terry, Zach's Christian mother and stepfather. Phil had not been ready for marriage fourteen years earlier, in his mid-twenties, when Zach was unexpectedly conceived. When Rebecca told Phil that she was pregnant, he drove away for forty-five minutes before turning his car around and agreeing to accept paternal responsibility. Phil credits the Jewish values of his upbringing when he says that he really didn't feel he had a choice. The child was his, and he would step up and be a father, ready or not. Disappointment at unplanned fatherhood did not deter his family from enthusiastically welcoming the child to their family.

When Zach was two years old, Rebecca took a particularly demanding job, and Phil became the primarily present parent, beginning what he now sees as his life's greatest blessing. Ultimately, Rebecca and Phil decided that they were better as friends than as a couple; they would be devoted parents, together and cooperatively, but living apart. Early on, Phil explained to Rebecca that, though he was admittedly not religious or active in any synagogue, he was eager for Zach to be Jewish. Rebecca and Phil amicably reached agreements about shared custody, about finances, and about Zach's entrance to the covenant of Israel. Rebecca and Terry were married when Zach was about four, while Phil remained single much longer.

Zach reports having enjoyed living in both a two-parent household, complete with (Christian) siblings, and a single-parent, Jewish household. He has never known life any other way, and he has never thought of himself as anything other than a Jew. Zach's bar mitzvah was among the happiest days in Phil's life. It was a day that Phil, his father, and his grandmothers would never forget and one that Rebecca and Terry celebrated with the greatest joy.

Phil, like so many men I've encountered, approached his unplanned fatherhood with courage and dedication. These men are in difficult situations, some of which include pain and strife, and some of which result in unforeseen blessing. Drawing on Jewish tradition for inspiration and guidance, men can responsibly and compassionately accept this unexpected role in their lives. And regardless of the circumstances, our communities can embrace young people as they find their way through even the most challenging moments of their lives.

NOTES

1. Conversation with Rabbi Allison Bergman Vann, July 19, 2012.

2. See, *inter alia*, "Abortion Rights," adopted by the CCAR at the 91st Annual Convention of the Central Conference of American Rabbis, Pittsburgh, Pennsylvania, June 23–26, 1980; "Abortion," adopted by the CCAR at the 86th Annual Convention of the Central Conference of American Rabbis, 1975; "On Abortion and the Hyde Amendment," adopted by the CCAR at the 95th Annual Convention of the Central Conference of American Rabbis, New York, June 18–21, 1984; and "Resolution on State Restrictions on Access to Reproductive Health Services," adopted by the 119th Annual Convention of the Central Conference of American Rabbis, Cincinnati, Ohio, April 2008, http://ccarnet.org/rabbis-speak/resolutions/.

3. Walter Jacob, *Contemporary American Reform Responsa* (New York: CCAR Press, 1987), 252–55.

4. Rashi to *Sanhedrin* 72b; Rambam in *Mishneh Torah, Hilchot Rotzei-ach* 1:9.

5. Shari Motro, "Responsibility Begins at Conception," *New York Times*, July 6, 2012.

6. CCAR Responsa Committee, Responsum 5772.3 (unpublished).

7. CCAR Responsa Committee, "Withholding Paternity Information from a Father" (Responsum 5760.8). The Mishnah citation is *Kiddushin* 1:7, and the Talmud citation is *Kiddushin* 29a.

8. Ibid. The responsum cites the following sources: Babylonian Talmud, *K'tubot* 65b; *Mishneh Torah, Hilchot Ishut* 12:14, and *Shulchan Aruch, Even Ha-eizer* 71:1. "The father is obligated under Torah law to provide maintenance for his children until they reach the age of six, even if their mother has the means to support them. From that point on, the obligation is continued under rabbinic law, as an aspect of the general requirement to give *tzedakah*: the *beit din* can coerce the father to provide

maintenance, just as it is empowered to coerce an individual to pay *tzedakah* according to his or her means."

9. CCAR Responsa Committee, Responsum 5772.3 (unpublished).

10. Mark Washofsky, e-mail to this author, July 17, 2012, citing *Eiruvin* 82b and Babylonian Talmud, *K'tubot* 102b.

11. Ibid.

12. *Piskei Din Rabbanim*, 11:366. Source provided in Hebrew by Mark Washofsky; translation mine in consultation with Washofsky.

13. CCAR Responsa Committee, Responsum 5772.3 (unpublished).

14. Ibid.

15. The concepts invoked in this paragraph were developed in e-mail correspondence with Dr. Mark Washofsky, July 16–17, 2012. I am grateful to Dr. Washofsky for his consultation, which assisted immeasurably in the development of this chapter.

16. In this vignette, actual names are used, with permission. The facts are well-known to all who know the family.

34

GO AND LEARN FROM ABRAHAM AND SARAH

Jewish Responses to Facing Infertility

DANIEL KIRZANE AND RABBI JULIE PELC ADLER

God, in love, creates the world.[1]

Then, in love, God shares the power of creation with human beings. Indeed, the Creator even *commands* them, "Be fruitful and multiply" (Gen. 1:28, 9:1, 9:7). God's intention is clear: just as God has brought life into the world, so should human beings.[2]

Before the first couple is able to fulfill this obligation, they eat of the fruit of the Tree of All Knowledge, prompting their expulsion from the Garden of Eden. Their sexuality awakened, they then can embark on their journey of adult responsibility. The man and the woman come together sexually, giving birth to the world's first baby. Eve declares, "I have made a man with the Eternal" (Gen. 4:1). This appears to be the proper course of life. Our God-given sexuality allows us to fulfill our God-given responsibility to populate the next generation.

But what happens when things don't go according to plan?

Despite God's apparent design that human beings should give birth to children, the progenitors of the people of Israel all struggle with infertility. The tragic irony of our story surrounds God's promise to Abraham that he will become "a great nation" (Gen. 12:2). Despite God's assurances of abundance, Abraham and Sarah and generations of their descendants struggle for years to bear children. We are forced to ask: If fertility is the most basic seed of God's covenant with Israel, why are so many matriarchs and patriarchs, heroes of our tradition, plagued with a compromised ability to bear children? And what can we learn from them in our own similar struggles?

Classical Approaches to Infertility

In trying to answer these self-imposed questions, Jewish tradition offers several models for how we might understand the meaning of infertility.

First, there's the challenge model: God puts challenges in our way so that we may overcome them. This is not the same as the prevalent platitude "God doesn't give us anything we can't handle." Rather, this is a teaching that inspires us to find new motivation in our lives, given the difficulties we face. We can see this model at work in the story of Rachel, who is described as "barren" (Gen. 29:31). Her inability to bear children weighs heavily on her, and for years she struggles contentiously with her prodigiously fertile sister (see, e.g., Gen. 30:8). Ever active, Rachel attempts to overcome her situation first by offering her maidservant as her surrogate and later by bargaining for Leah's *dudaim* ("mandrakes," understood by Ibn Ezra as a fertility aid) (Gen. 30:14–16). At last, God "remembers" Rachel and "listens to" her (Gen. 30:22), allowing her to bear a son, Joseph. Having struggled so hard through this challenge, Rachel now catalyzes a major turning point in her family's life. Immediately after Joseph is born, Jacob chooses to leave Haran, inaugurating the next chapter in the history of the people of Israel. The way that Rachel overcomes the challenge of infertility teaches that facing life's trials with fortitude can open up new doors that could not have been imagined before.

There's also the piety model. Not dissimilar from the challenge model, this portrayal suggests that God causes the affliction of infertility in order to inspire a more spiritual life, to urge turning toward the Eternal One with sincere hope of the heart. This is explained in *B'reishit Rabbah* 45:4:

> Why were the matriarchs barren? Rabbi Levi said in R. Shila's name and Rabbi Chelbo in Rabbi Yochanan's name: Because the Holy Blessed One yearns for their prayers and supplications. [Thus it is written,] "O my dove, in the cranny of the rocks [hidden by the cliff]" (Song of Songs 2:14). Why did I make you barren? In order that [you would] "show me your face [and] let me hear your voice" (ibid.).

This is made even more explicit in the midrashic collection *Yalkut Shimoni*:[3]

> Once I [Mar Zutra] was going from one place to another, and I found an old man. He said to me, "Rabbi, why is it that certain heads of households in Israel are prevented from having children of their own?" I said to him, "My son, because the Holy Blessed One loves them with a complete love and rejoices in them and refines them in order that they should supplicate before God. Go and learn from Abraham and Sarah: that they were childless of Isaac for seventy-five years, and they supplicated until Isaac came, and they rejoiced in him. Go and learn from Rebekah: that she was barren for twenty years, and she supplicated until Jacob came, and they rejoiced in him. Go and learn from Rachel: that she was barren fourteen years from her two children [Joseph and Benjamin], and she supplicated until the two of them came, and she rejoiced in them. Go and learn from Hannah: that she was barren for nineteen years and six months until Samuel came, and she rejoiced in him."

These midrashim teach us that God yearns to hear the prayers of those struggling to bring new life into the world. God creates infertility with *ahavah g'murah*, "complete love," in order to inspire heartfelt prayer. In the biblical narrative, we see this model at work especially with Hannah, whose womb God had "shut" (I Sam. 1:5), and of Isaac, whose wife was "barren" (Gen. 25:21) and who is understood by the Rabbis to have been barren himself (Babylonian Talmud, *Y'vamot* 64a). Both of these ancestors turned to God in supplication (I Sam. 1:10–11; Gen. 25:21), and God was pleased by their actions, ultimately granting them children. The Rabbis see both of these figures as emblematic of Jewish prayer: Hannah's prayer serves as the model for *T'filah*, the central component of Jewish worship (Babylonian Talmud, *B'rachot* 31a–b), and Isaac is credited with the creation of *Minchah*, the afternoon prayer (Babylonian Talmud, *B'rachot* 26b), which includes in it the day's most fervent supplications to God. These figures, then, show us that from the agony of childlessness can emerge tremendous religious creativity and spiritual meaning.

A third paradigm for understanding the meaning of infertility is the retribution model, wherein infertility is a punishment for a crime. In this approach, God is recognized not only as the One who can provide children to those who are infertile but also as the One who has the power to afflict infertility on those who otherwise would give birth. Thus, Leviticus 20:20–21 decrees that the consequence for certain unethical sexual relations is to die "childless," a reversal of the intended natural order. Narratively, we see God punish the entire household of Abimelech, who took Sarah away from her husband, by "shutting" their wombs (Gen. 20:18). As well, God may be seen to curse Michal after she criticizes her husband, King David; for after her insult, Michal "had no child until the day of her death" (II Sam. 6:23). The implication in each of these cases is that fulfilling the commandment to "be fruitful and multiply" is a *privilege*, not a right, and it can be taken away for grievous misconduct. The retribution model is a common explanation in today's world even though it contradicts contemporary Jews' understanding of God's role in humans' lives. The ancient roots of this approach lend it a sense of authority, and it is not surprising that many who struggle with infertility struggle also with this message.

Those facing infertility today will likely find in these three interpretations neither satisfaction nor succor. Indeed, we may wonder whether even our biblical forebears themselves would have been consoled by the Rabbis' attempts to explain their suffering. Like our ancestors, those who struggle with infertility feel inadequate, inauthentic, unfulfilled. Complicated questions arise in conversation with Jewish tradition. The Psalmist describes God's partnership with human beings to make life: "For you have made my inner parts; you fashioned me in my mother's womb" (Psalm 139:13); why can't I participate in this marvelous act? God has charged, "Impress [My commandments] upon your children" (Deut. 6:7); why can't I pass on my traditions to my own descendants? God has promised that our people would be blessed with fruitfulness, that we would be "a numerous people" (Gen. 50:20); why am I excluded from this promise? No simple response can fully answer these questions, nor can an easy answer assuage the ache of infertility.

Alternative Approaches in Jewish Tradition

Jewish tradition reaches out to us in our pain. In searching for answers to these profound questions, we may turn to Jewish wisdom to open up what God actually means in commanding, "Be fruitful and multiply." Rabbinic literature offers several ways that individuals can fulfill this mitzvah that are alternatives to childbearing.

A key figure in this conversation is Shimon ben Azai, the rabbi who asserted that the greatest principle of Torah is Genesis 5:1–2, "On the day that God created human beings, they were made in the likeness of God—male and female God created them."[4] In the Babylonian Talmud, *Y'vamot* 63b, Ben Azai recalls this essential doctrine when he teaches that "a person who does not engage in being fruitful and multiplying" is like one who diminishes his or her inborn likeness of God and, indeed, is even like one who sheds blood. Ben Azai clearly avows the central significance of childbearing in Judaism. However, Ben Azai's disciples *immediately* retort to him, "You give a pleasant sermon, but you don't fulfill your own words!" From this we learn that Ben Azai himself had not fathered any children.[5] Ben Azai replies to them, "What can I do, [seeing] that my soul loves Torah? It is possible for the world to be sustained by others." Ben Azai, childless, knows that others will have to propagate new generations. His role will be to teach them Torah so that the world will continue to bear witness to the "likeness of God" that shines forth in the wise and proper conduct of the people of Israel.

This parallel between teaching and parenting is made clear only a few pages earlier in the Talmud. In *Y'vamot* 62a–b, the Rabbis struggle to determine whether one generation of offspring is sufficient to satisfy the commandment to "be fruitful and multiply" or whether those children must also have children. In this context, Rabbi Akiva concludes that the verse from Ecclesiastes 11:6, "In the morning, sow your seed," applies both to having children and to having disciples. Immediately thereafter, we are told that during one period of time, a tragedy befell Akiva's many thousands of disciples and that the world was "desolate" or "empty" (*shameim*) until he was able to train more students. We may infer from this exposition that Akiva—as well as his student, Ben Azai—considered disciples to be as important as children.

Indeed, the Rabbinic tradition is explicit on this count: teaching Torah can substitute for having children. Rabbi Yonatan teaches, "Everyone who teaches Torah to the child of his fellow, Scripture credits him as if it were his own child" (Babylonian Talmud, *Sanhedrin* 19b). This is derived from Numbers 3:1, in which Moses is identified as a forebear of his brother's children. How could this be? As Rashi explains in his commentary on the verse, "Since he taught them Torah." Similarly, Reish Lakish ties this principle to Genesis 12:5, concluding that Abraham and Sarah taught Torah to multitudes, and these disciples counted as their offspring while they were unable to bear children biologically (Babylonian Talmud, *Sanhedrin* 99b). Thus, Jewish tradition affirms that the education of the next generation is the same kind of activity and fulfills the same obligations as giving birth to the next generation. Just as we commonly acknowledge that an author can be "prolific" or a class can be "productive," we assert as well that a teacher can be "fruitful." Just as Rabbi Akiva increased the number of his disciples, so can teachers "multiply" their students. Thus, the commandment "Be fruitful and multiply" is not off-limits to those who cannot bear children.

This applies as well to adoption. In *Tanach*, Sarah, Rebekah, and Rachel all struggle with infertility and agree to adopt the biological children that their husbands bear through their handmaidens.[6] As well, it was mentioned above that Michal, wife of King David, "had no child until the day of her death." Nevertheless, II Samuel 21:8 reports that Michal bears five children with Adriel the Meholathite. Since this same Adriel is identified as the husband of Michal's sister, Merab (I Sam. 18:19), Rabbi Y'hoshua ben Korchah concludes that Merab is the *biological* mother of these children but that Michal raised them (Babylonian Talmud, *Sanhedrin* 19b).[7] Since Michal is their adoptive mother, they carry her name and are counted as her own children. Likewise, Naomi, beyond her childbearing years with no living children,[8] adopts the son of her daughter-in-law, Ruth: "Naomi took the child and held it to her bosom, and she became his foster mother. Her neighbors gave him a name, saying, 'A son is born to Naomi!'" (Ruth 4:16–17). From these examples, the Rabbis conclude that one who adopts a child, raising it as her own, "Scripture credits her as if it were her own child" (Babylonian Talmud, *Sanhedrin* 19b). Indeed, "the one who raises [a child] is a parent, not one who gives birth" (*B'midbar Rabbah* 46:5). Adoption, therefore, is another way of fulfilling the obligation to nurture the next generation.

Jewish tradition thus offers at least three ways that a person may fulfill the commandment to "be fruitful and multiply." One may bear biological children, one may teach Torah to children, or one may adopt as one's own someone else's biological child. We honor the heroes of our tradition who have fulfilled this commandment in all of these ways, including Eve, Shimon ben Azai, and Naomi. Although contemporary Jewish and North American cultures suggest that biological children are the only fulfillment of this central commandment, classical Jewish texts challenge us to consider other possibilities.

The Role of Sexuality

This leads to fundamental questions about sexuality. Our initial reading of the creation of humankind was that their sexuality was created so that they may "be fruitful and multiply." If this commandment does not refer only to having children, we must ask: how can we understand our sexuality outside the context of bearing children? *Tanach* bears witness that sexual relations between Abraham and Sarah and between Isaac and Rebekah were both "pleasurable" (Gen. 18:12) and "fun" (Gen. 26:8) while both of these couples were classically troubled with infertility. Rachel Adler reminds us that the Rabbis permitted sexual intercourse "when women are pregnant or menopausal, when male semen is insufficiently numerous or active to enable procreation, and, in certain cases, when procreation is intentionally prevented."[9] Rabbinic approval of non-procreative sex has also been applied to same-sex sexuality, affirming the value and importance of every individual's sexuality outside the scope of having children. The understanding of sexuality as encompassing more than procreative potential has held true from antiquity through today; sexuality does not exist merely for fertility. What, then, is it for?

We turn once again to Shimon ben Azai, recalling his suggestion for the greatest principle in the Torah: "On the day that God created human beings, they were made in the likeness of God—male and female God created them" (Gen. 5:1–2). This recalls Genesis 1:27, "God created humanity in God's image; in the image of God did God create it. Male and female God created them." Rachel Adler suggests that our sexuality—represented here as "male" and "female"—is "a metaphor for some element of the divine nature."[10] Whatever our sexuality is, we share it on some level with the Holy One.

According to Genesis 2:18, God declares that it is "not good for a person to be alone." Classically, this has been understood as a proof text for the foundational value of lifelong companionship. In short, the Genesis account teaches us that God made human beings with an inherent longing for relationship. Likewise, God longs to be in relationship with *us*. Our liturgy proclaims, "You love us with abundant love." The Psalmist declares, "I know that You delight in me" (Ps. 41:12). God cries out, "Return to Me" (Isa. 44:22), and we reply, "Return us to You, O Eternal, and we shall return" (Lam. 5:21).[11] Our God is a

God of relationship, and we, God's people, embody that yearning for connection.

Nowhere is this clearer than in the Song of Songs. This majestic love song follows the stormy and steamy relationship of a pair of young lovers. Each of the two protagonists proclaims love for the other, describing in erotic and fantastic detail what attracts them to one another. Sexuality infuses the entire text, both explicitly and metaphorically, though the principal characters never consummate their relationship physically. The Rabbis classically understand this text to be a symbol for Israel's relationship with the Eternal, illustrating God as one who yearns for human connection and depicting human beings as people who long for their Creator. At the same time, it is impossible to overlook the poem's focus on human relationship, both exalted and celebrated. Song of Songs is a climactic Jewish text that sanctifies sexuality, honoring it as a divine quality that is rooted in the body while not tethered to physical contact.

Sexuality, therefore, is a holy essence of humanity, reflective of the divine spark in every person. This sexuality is a symbol for attraction toward others, and like God's own relationship with Creation, it can be understood in a wide variety of ways. Relationships with life companions, sexual partners, close friends, dear teachers, and respected students are all emanations of the divine drive to establish lasting relationships and to grow through connection with others.

Seeking Comfort and Understanding

In the face of this focus on relationship, we cannot forget that every person at one time or another faces tragic loss in this realm of sexuality. We are frustrated in our desire to find a life partner, we find ourselves seeking a friend we can trust, or we miss terribly the loved ones who have passed away. And among all these sufferings, one of the most painful is the experience of infertility. We ask why these unfulfilled consummations fill our lives, why God would have created infertility in the first place if God wanted us to "be fruitful and multiply." Jews throughout the ages have spent years, perhaps their entire lives, in the midst of this painful question. And for generations, they have turned for inspiration and support to people and stories held as treasures to the heart.

As we have seen, the sacred texts of Judaism affirm that there are many ways to follow God's commandment "Be fruitful and multiply." *Tanach*, Rabbinic wisdom, and Jewish liturgy all teach that a variety of productive relationships in our lives can fulfill this fundamental mitzvah. They remind us that our sexuality is a profound part of our human nature, reflective of God's own desire to be in relationship. Those who struggle with infertility may turn to our earliest forebears, drawing support from the company of our ancestors who have felt the same pain. We seek the comfort of a renewed understanding of fruitfulness as we take to heart God's promise:

> I will look with favor upon you.
> I will make you fruitful, and I will help you to multiply.
> I will maintain My covenant with you.
> You shall eat old grain long stored,
> And you shall have to clear out the old to make room for the new.
>
> (Leviticus 26:9–10)

NOTES

1. *Chesed* can be understood as God's loving relationship with God's creations. Several sources affirm that God created the world with *chesed*, e.g., *Avot D'Rabbi Natan* 1:37, and *T'hillim Rabbah* on Ps. 119:138. Psalm 89:3 affirms *olam chesed yibaneh*, "Your steadfast love is confirmed forever." These words have been understood through the lens of Kabbalah to mean "the world is built with *chesed*," that God creates through love. Rabbi Jonathan Sacks affirms in various writings and speeches that God "created all in love" (invocation for United States Senate, Nov. 2, 2011) and writes, "[God] creates the world out of no compulsion but as a free act of love" (*To Heal a Fractured World: The Ethics of Responsibility* [New York: Random House, 2007], 136).

2. *Mishnah Y'vamot* 6:6 teaches, "The man is commanded concerning being fruitful and multiplying but not the woman." The Gemara of *Y'vamot* 65b–66a records debate among several rabbis as to whether this reading is accurate or whether this commandment also applies to women. Maimonides, in *Mishneh Torah, Hilchot Ishut* 15:2, confirms that only men and not women are obligated concerning "being fruitful and multiplying." A responsum of the Central Conference of American Rabbis Responsa Committee rejects this distinction between men and women ("Jewish Marriage without Children," 1979).

3. 247:78, commenting on I Samuel 1:20.

4. *Sifra, K'doshim* 2:4.

5. This passage is often understood as indication that Ben Azai was not married. However, the Babylonian Talmud, *K'tubot* 63a, reports that Rabbi Akiva's daughter was engaged to Ben Azai, and the text presumes that they later married. *Sotah* 4b reflects the prevailing attitude that Akiva was unmarried but proposes as well that he may have been married and later divorced. These accounts suggest that Ben Azai may not have been intentionally celibate. Regardless of his marital status, which ultimately is ambiguous, there are no records of Ben Azai having children.

6. Sarah famously abrogates this commitment in Gen. 21:10. After giving birth to Isaac, she says to her husband, "Throw this slave girl and *her* son out. The son of this slave girl is not going to share in the inheritance with *my* son Isaac!" (italics added).

7. Rabbi Y'hoshua ben Korchah holds that it is appropriate for Michal to raise Merab's children because the marriage between Merab and Adriel was a "marriage in error" (Babylonian Talmud, *Sanhedrin* 19b).

8. See above, Babylonian Talmud, *Y'vamot* 62a–b, in which most rabbis conclude that one's children must survive and bear children of their own in order to fulfill the obligation to "be fruitful and multiply."

9. Rachel Adler, *Engendering Judaism* (Boston: Beacon Press, 1999), 131. Adler refers here to David M. Feldman, *Marital Relations, Birth Control and Abortion in Jewish Law* (New York: Schocken, 1987), 81–105.

10. Adler, *Engendering Judaism*, 118.

11. The Masoretic tradition reads *v'nashuvah*, "And let us return." This translation follows the written text *v'nashuv*, "And we shall return."

35

BLESSINGS OF THE BREASTS
AND OF THE WOMB

Jewish Perspectives on Breastfeeding and the Female Breast

RABBI SHARON G. FORMAN

> More than the calf desires to suck, the cow desires to nurse.
> (Babylonian Talmud, *P'sachim* 112a)

One month after giving birth to our daughter, I attended Rosh HaShanah services. Like a harmonic tone previously undetected, the ancient words of *Avinu Malkeinu* ("Our Father, Our Sovereign") transmitted a newly perceived sound, as I recited this prayer for the first time as a mother. "*Avinu Malkeinu*, hear our voice. *Avinu Malkeinu*, have compassion on us and on our children. . . ."[1] Later, the blasts of the shofar reverberated in the sanctuary. "This is the day of the world's birth. . . . As we are Your children, show us a parent's compassion," the liturgy entreated.[2] In broken staccato and then wistful cries, the wails of the shofar shook me on a visceral level, and suddenly I was overflowing with milk.

Scholars from Rabbi Abahu[3] and Saadyah Gaon to Maimonides[4] have explained the significance of the shofar blasts. But, the cells in my body interpreted the shofar calls as cries, whimpers imploring a parental God to nurse, feed, and cradle us. The prayers instruct us to wake up, but perhaps we were the ones trying to rouse God and plead for attention. At that physically tense and emotionally charged moment, I wondered if there were other symbolic and tangible connections between Judaism and breastfeeding.

What does Judaism teach us about breastfeeding and the female breast? What did the ancient Rabbis think of their lactating wives? How are breasts simultaneously extolled for their beauty in Song of Songs (7:4), while they are vilified as sources of inappropriate sexual behavior in the Prophets (Ezek. 23:2–3)? Does the wisdom of the *Tanach*, Talmud, and even Jewish mysticism inform our own attitudes toward nursing and the female body? How authoritative and respected is a mother's decision to either breastfeed or provide alternative feeding arrangements for her child? Could—or should— a Jewish community coerce a mother to breastfeed a child, even if she has made a thoughtful and autonomous decision not to nurse? How might Judaism's mixed messages about breasts reflect our own fears of fatal breast cancer and the desire for a healthy body image? What can traditional and liberal Judaism teach us about our bodies and the desire to nourish offspring?

In our open Western culture, the media floods us with revealing images of women's breasts. Yet, even a cursory Internet search demonstrates that in just the past five years, numerous women across the United States have been asked to leave airplanes, restaurants, buses, museums, and stores when they have attempted to nurse babies in public spaces. Our own society echoes the ambivalence found in Jewish texts equating breastfeeding with a divine action while simultaneously condemning the female breast as a source of depravity.

Breasts in the Bible

While post-Enlightenment European Jews may have attempted to portray Judaism as a cerebral religion and suppress the image of Jews as physical, sexual beings,[5] the topic of female breasts is clearly a lively subject of biblical and Talmudic discussion. In Genesis 49, breasts symbolize the essence of blessing and fertility. On his deathbed, Jacob/ Israel calls his sons together and offers a final benediction. For Joseph, the blessing is rich, as breasts epitomize sustenance and bounty:

> By the God of your father, who helps you,
> Shaddai, who blesses you,
> blessings of heaven above,
> blessings of the deep that lies below,
> blessings of breasts and womb.
>
> (Gen. 49:25)

When despondent Job wishes he had never been born, he muses:

> Why did I not die at birth,
> Expire as I came forth from the womb?
> Why were there knees to receive me,
> Or breasts for me to suck?
>
> (Job 3:11–12)

Even in his despair, Job remembers the loving and nourishing power of the breast. He contrasts the innocence of nursing at his mother's breast with the unbearable misery of his current losses.

Breast Milk in Midrash

In a Rabbinic midrash, breast milk is compared to manna, food from the heavens, which a beneficent creator rains down to sustain the Israelites through their forty years in the wilderness. In Exodus, we learn that "the house of Israel named it manna; it was like coriander seed, white, and it tasted like wafers in honey" (Exod. 16:31). The Rabbis envisioned manna as a magical food, which could assume whatever taste the diner wished. "Just as the breast, which changes to take on many tastes, so too the manna turned into whatever food they wanted" (Babylonian Talmud, *Yoma* 95a). Each mother who offers her own sweet, white nourishment imitates the ultimate Creator, who lovingly provided this life-sustaining food for the Children of Israel.

In a graphic midrash appearing in both *Sh'mot Rabbah* (1:12) and the Babylonian Talmud (*Sotah* 11b), God nurses the Israelite babies who have been condemned to death by the Egyptians. Sending down a heavenly midwife, God arranges for the hidden Israelite newborns to be fed and bathed. When the Egyptians notice the babies, they "want to kill them; but a miracle occurred on their behalf so that they were swallowed in the ground." Even as the Egyptians bring oxen to plough over them, God provides cakes of oil and honey within the rocks, which are then sucked by the Israelite babies. Fortified, the babies break through the earth and spring up like grass in the field. Ultimately these grown children are the first to recognize and honor God by the shores of the Reed Sea. They have not forgotten that the Eternal One had been their wet nurse.

Some midrashim graphically discuss the breastfeeding capabilities of our modest matriarch, Sarah. Encouraging her to announce to the world that even at her advanced age, she was able to give birth to a child, Abraham prods her to "hallow God's name, uncover your breast, that all may be aware of the miracles the Holy One has begun to perform." Sarah exposes her breasts, and "her nipples poured out milk like two jets of water. Noble ladies came forward to have their children nursed by Sarah, saying, 'We do not merit having children suckled on the milk of such a righteous woman'" (*B'reishit Rabbah* 53:9). Sarah provides life-sustaining milk for the first Jewish child as well as the children of every nation.

Breastfeeding in Jewish Mysticism

According to concepts found in the *Zohar*, the thirteenth-century text on which Jewish mysticism is based, the *Shechinah*, or *Matronit*, serves as the feminine aspect of God. In the *Zohar* 3:77b, we are instructed that this lowest of the ten *s'firot*, or cosmic emanations of God's presence, "lovingly suckles all the Children of Israel, thereby providing them not only with nourishment but also with complete well-being."[6]

As the spiritual mother of Israel, the *Shechinah* is exiled when the Temple is destroyed, allowing gentiles to nurse from her.[7] In Raphael Patai's book, *The Hebrew Goddess*, the author explains that the *Shechinah* provided Jews in the fifteenth to eighteenth centuries who followed kabbalism with a kind of goddess, "separate and distinct from the male deity."[8] Patai asserts that this figure possessed the same four traits of many Near Eastern goddesses: "chastity and promiscuity, motherliness and bloodthirstiness."[9] Just as the *Shechinah* embodies these contradictory characteristics, so too do the images of breasts found in many Jewish texts. Yes, breasts enable children to stay alive, but also they are a potentially threatening and powerful component of female sexuality.

Breasts in the Song of Songs

In a whimsical catalog of praise to a lover's body, the poet of the Bible's *Shir HaShirim*, the Song of Songs, describes both female and male breasts when extolling the magnificence of the human form. "My beloved to me is a bag of myrrh / Lodged between my breasts," the appreciative lover muses (Song of Songs 1:13). Arms, necks, chests, eyes, lips, and tongues are conflated with nature. Roses, lilies, wells of fresh water, honey, milk, wine, myrrh, and aloes blossom and emit their aromatic fragrances in this poetic biblical landscape. The female lover's breasts are "are like two fawns, twins of a gazelle" (7:4), while her male companion's breasts "are like clusters" (7:8). Nothing sinister lurks in this perfect garden in which breasts are natural sources of pleasure and wonder for the pair of blissful lovers.

Compilers of *Midrash Rabbah* on the Song of Songs (perhaps created in the sixth century and first published in Pesaro in 1519)[10] provide a slightly different perspective of this unusual book of the Bible. Transporting Leah, Rachel, Adam, Miriam, King David, and other figures from the Torah and Prophets to this idyllic oasis, the Rabbis strive to teach religious lessons, rather than focus on the celebration of human love and pleasure.

In the austere, yet imaginative view of the Rabbis, the two breasts of the lover mentioned in the Song of Songs serve as metaphors for the great leaders, Moses and Aaron. In *Shir HaShirim Rabbah* 4:5:1, the Rabbis explain enthusiastically why it was so vital to describe the lover's symmetrical breasts:

> Just as the breasts are the beauty and the ornament of a woman, so Moses and Aaron were the beauty and ornament of Israel. Just as the breasts are the charm of a woman, so Moses and Aaron were the charm of Israel. Just as the breasts are the glory and pride of a woman, so Moses and Aaron were the glory and pride of Israel. Just as the breasts are full of milk, so Moses and Aaron filled Israel with Torah. Just as whatever a woman eats helps to feed the child at the breast, so all the Torah that Moses our master learned he taught to Aaron, as it is written, "And Moses told Aaron all the words of the [Eternal]" [Exod. 4:28]. The Rabbis say: He revealed to him the ineffable name. Just as one breast is not greater than the other, so it was with Moses and Aaron.[11]

Even if the Rabbis who composed midrash were a bit squeamish about the explicit love scenes in the Song of Songs, they were able to reorient the text to conform with their worldview. Mother's milk equals sweet words of Torah pouring forth from breasts, which are representations of Moses and Aaron. Yes, the body is beautiful, as it reflects the more potent splendor of revelation and the beauty of the first High Priest (Aaron) and the greatest prophet (Moses).

Breasts as a Source of Lewdness in Ezekiel and Hosea

The author of the Song of Songs reveals no embarrassment regarding the human body in general and breasts in particular. How differently the sixth-century-BCE Ezekiel and eighth-century-BCE Hosea, biblical prophets, responded to the female bosom. In these texts, the breasts of the young girls are associated with prostitution. Chastising Israel for lascivious sexual habits, Ezekiel shares the cautionary tale of two girls, the daughters of one mother: They played the whore in Egypt: they played the whore while still young. There their breasts were squeezed, and there their nipples were handled. Their names were: the elder one, Oholah; and her sister, Oholibah. They became Mine, and they bore sons and daughters.

(Ezek. 23:1–4)

God rejects the behavior of the young prostitutes, who represent Samaria and Jerusalem, and punishes them for their "wanton whoring" (Ezek. 23:35). In this prophet's assessment, breasts are not a source of pleasure and beauty, but rather a crime scene. Sharing a grim vision of the future, Ezekiel predicts that the prostitutes will drink and drain a cup of "desolation and horror" and ultimately "tear . . . [their] breasts" (Ezek. 23:33–34).

Hosea's comparison of Israel's behavior to an adulterous wife of a faithful God prompts him to demonize the female breast.

Rebuke your mother, rebuke her—
For she is not My wife
And I am not her husband—
And let her put away her harlotry from her face
And her adultery from between her breasts.

(Hosea 2:4)

As the prophet disparages Israel for her misdeeds, he advocates for a punishment of "a miscarrying womb and dry breasts" (Hosea 9:14). Ezekiel argues that when Israel engages in warped behavior with other nations and gods, she becomes vicious and offers her own children as food to idolatrous fetishes (Ezek. 23:39). The Israelite women desecrate their bodies and their breasts, perverting the natural order and spurning the one true God. Ultimately, Hosea's vision concludes with healing forgiveness from a benevolent God (Hosea 14:5).

Breastfeeding in the Talmud

Moving ahead several centuries into the time of the Talmud (compiled 200–600 CE), the Rabbis legislate rules and also share narratives associated with breastfeeding. Dr. Arthur I. Eidelman, a professor of pediatrics at Shaare Zedek Medical Center in Israel who has studied a flourishing culture of breastfeeding in Orthodox women, observes that "the Talmud reflects a most positive attitude to breastfeeding and the principle that breastfeeding must be sustained for an extended period if one wishes to guarantee the optimal health and development of the newborn infant."[12] In an informative article, he traces Talmudic notions of the contents of breast milk (menstrual blood; Babylonian Talmud, *K'tubot* 60b) and describes foods that breastfeeding women were instructed to avoid (unripe dates, small fish, sour milk, and moldy bread). In the Babylonian Talmud, *K'tubot* 59b–60a, we learn:

> A woman should give suck to her child. . . . The school of Shammai says that if a woman has vowed not to give suck to her child, she must pull the nipple out of the infant's mouth. But the school of Hillel maintains that her husband may compel her to nurse the child. If she has been divorced, he may not compel her. If, however, the infant recognizes her, the husband is to pay his divorced wife a fee and compel her to give suck, in order to avert harm.

Fulfilling her marital obligation, a mother must nurse her child, since her breast milk provides the highest nutrition and protection from *hasakanah* (literally, "the danger"; Babylonian Talmud, *K'tubot* 59b). If a mother is firmly set against nursing her own baby and that baby rejects a wet nurse's milk, the woman can be compelled to nurse the child until the age of two, a typical and minimal time frame for nursing.[13]

In other Talmudic discussions, we learn that Rabbi Eliezer was troubled that a human being could receive milk from a nonkosher animal (his or her human mother), claiming that after the age of two, a child is basically nursing from an unclean animal. His opinion is overruled by that of Rabbi Y'hoshua, who firmly held that children may continue to nurse from their mothers up to the age of four or even five years old if they are sickly.[14]

The Talmudic Rabbis did not only examine legal rulings. They also told incredible tales involving lactation in males. In *Shabbat* 53b, a poor man's wife passes away, leaving him to feed their infant. Since the widower cannot afford to hire a wet nurse, God responds to his prayers and grants him a miracle by opening up his breasts and allowing him to nurse his own child. The natural order of the world is subverted in this unusual tale of miracles and trying economic circumstances.

Mordechai, the hero of the Purim story, can understand many languages, foils a plot to kill a king, and rises to power in a foreign court. Rabbis Berechyah and Abahu in Rabbi Eliezer's name claim that his many talents also include spontaneously being able to nurse orphaned Esther upon the death of her mother. In *B'reishit Rabbah* 30:8, the Rabbis contend that "milk came to him, and he suckled her." In the same story, Mordechai first "went around to all the wet nurses but could not find one for Esther, whereupon he himself suckled her." A less sensational spin on the story, found in *Midrash T'hillim* 22:23, explains that "Mordechai's wife gave suck to Esther, and Mordechai brought her up." No matter who did the nursing or when it occurred, Mordechai's ability to nourish Esther enables her to rescue the Jewish people years later.

Breastfeeding in the Codes of Law

Joseph Caro, in his sixteenth-century Jewish code the *Shulchan Aruch*, discusses the practice of breastfeeding. Breast milk is considered to be kosher and pareve. The mother's lactating breast was not considered to be an unseemly part of the body, as a nursing mother was permitted to study Torah and recite any blessing or prayer (except for the *Sh'moneh Esreih*, which requires standing) while breastfeeding.[15] The nineteenth-century Iraqi scholar Rabbi Joseph Chayim ben Elijah al-Chakam wrote in his code of Jewish law that "since a woman normally exposes her breasts when nursing, her breasts at that time are considered to be like her palms and her face." If someone wishes to recite the *Sh'ma* in her company, it is therefore acceptable in a pressing circumstance, although typically no one should recite the *Sh'ma* in the presence of exposed breasts.[16] Clearly, breasts are not considered erotic organs in this scenario and are the sexually neutral vehicle for feeding a child.

Conclusions

In spite of a few texts containing ambivalent responses to female breasts, Jewish tradition clearly falls into the pro-nursing camp. Breasts are located close to the human heart, infusing milk with wisdom (Babylonian Talmud, *B'chorot* 6b). In I Samuel, Hannah delays sending her beloved child to Eli the priest to serve God. Only after weaning does she release Samuel to the House of *Adonai* at Shiloh (I Samuel 1:24). Nursing a child is a valid excuse for putting off a promise—even a vow to God.

Certainly, no mother should be coerced into nursing a child if this is not her decision. For medical, emotional, or work-related reasons, nursing is not always a sound choice. While unable to replicate breast milk, nutritious formulas provide options unavailable to the women nursing in Talmudic times. But if a mother is searching Jewish texts for guidance about breastfeeding, she will find much support for a choice to nurse. Breastfeeding is celebrated in thousand-year-old rabbinic tales, mandated by the Talmud, and normalized by Jewish codes of daily life. Even Jewish Agency publications in the infant State of Israel advocated agricultural development by conflating tilling the soil with nursing: "In the lands of the exile the Jewish people was denied the privilege and joy of suckling at the breast of the soil, of merging its soul with the soil."[17] Scientists may debate details of the efficacy of breast milk in preventing various diseases in mothers and children. But in Jewish tradition, breastfeeding not only sustains babies, but also can bring us closer to a time of peace and salvation.

NOTES

1. *Avinu Malkeinu*, in Chaim Stern, ed., *Gates of Repentance: The New Union Prayerbook for the Days of Awe*, rev. ed. (New York: CCAR Press, 1996), 121.

2. *HaYom Harat Olam*, in *Gates of Repentance*, 147.

3. Babylonian Talmud, *Rosh HaShanah* 16a.

4. Maimonides, *Mishneh Torah, Hilchot T'shuvah* 3:4.

5. Howard Eilberg-Schwartz, *People of the Body: Jews and Judaism from an Embodied Perspective* (New York: State University of New York Press, 1991), 3.

6. Rahael Patai, *The Hebrew Goddess* (Detroit, MI: Wayne State University Press, 1990), 147.

7. Ibid., 145.

8. Ibid., 139.

9. Ibid., 139.

10. "Song of Songs Rabbah," in *Encyclopaedia Judaica* (Jerusalem: Keter, 1972), 15:154.

11. Ibid., 198.

12. Arthur I. Eidelman, "The Talmud and Human Lactation: The Cultural Basis for Increased Frequency and Duration of Breastfeeding among Orthodox Jewish Women," *Breastfeeding Medicine*, 1, no. 1 (2006).

13. Rambam, *Sefer Nashim, Hilchot Ishut* 21:16; *Shulchan Aruch, Even HaEizer* 82:5.

14. B. Talmud, Niddah:2:3.

15. *Shulchan Aruch, Orach Chayim* 74:4

16. Ariel Picard, "Ben Ish Hai," in *Jewish Women: A Comprehensive Historical Encyclopedia* (Jewish Women's Archive, March 1, 2009), http://jwa.org/encyclopedia/article/ben-ish-hai.

17. Tom Segev, *1949: The First Israelis*, ed. Arlen N. Weinstein (New York: Henry Holt, 1998), 293.

36

WEANING

Personal and Biblical Reflections

RABBI DEBORAH KAHN-HARRIS, PhD

> I wonder, by my troth, what thou and I
> Did, till we loved? were we not weaned till then?
> —*John Donne, "The Good-Morrow"*

My son was just over ten months old when he started refusing the breast. It was not unsurprising. Following a traumatic birth, he was born only notionally full term, and hence very small, effectively being treated as a premature birth. To aid his growth, my husband and I were advised to supplement breastfeeding with bottle-feeding. We were first-time parents trying to overcome a highly medicalized process that had left us both feeling incredibly vulnerable and unsure of ourselves. We accepted supplemental bottle-feeding for fear that if we did not, our son would, in the words of the UK medical establishment, fail to thrive. So after ten months of breast- and bottle-feeding jointly and having started him on solid food at around six months, it was simply no surprise that he was no longer interested in the breast. Bottles and solid food were so much easier and more satiating.

When our second child, a daughter, was born, as second-time parents my husband and I knew so much more. Thankfully her birth was easier, and she took to breastfeeding more easily, too. In fact, she loved breastfeeding, and as a mother I sometimes felt as though she loved it to the exclusion of all else. But I reveled in it, knowing that she was likely our last child and, hence, my only other opportunity to get breastfeeding right and all the bonding that flowed from it. Still, by ten months I was at my wit's end, conflicted, and in pain. I desperately wanted to continue breastfeeding my daughter for as long as she wished to continue, but since she had begun teething, breastfeeding had become physically excruciating for me.

One might imagine that there is a great deal of helpful advice for breastfeeding mothers. My experience was that once you got your child latched on, there was little helpful advice that followed. When I began asking for help as my daughter's incoming teeth began cutting shreds into my nipples, most people were perplexed. Many women suggested I simply stop breastfeeding at once. My doctor suggested nipple guards, but my daughter refused to feed with them on. Some women told me firmly to take her off the breast when she bit me. I had to explain patiently over and over again that my daughter did not bite me. Her incoming teeth were simply very sharp and cut me however gently she latched on. My husband was sympathetic but had no useful advice. I am not sure he has ever fully understood why I simply did not stop breastfeeding at that stage, but to his credit he supported me in my decision to persevere. In the end my sister-in-law, who had breastfed five children, sent me from America the magical paint-on bandages that did not sting. She saved my breasts and my relationship with my infant daughter.

But by fifteen months my daughter and I were struggling. I sensed that she was growing less interested but could not find a way to stop, and I had no experience of guiding a child to wean. So I sought advice. Again, nothing. Lots of enthusiastic groups tried to tell me that it was perfectly acceptable to continue breastfeeding for years, but they had no support to offer me about how to wean when I was ready. Eventually my daughter and I stumbled toward weaning together. While I grieved for the loss of that very deep, visceral connection that breastfeeding provides like no other experience I have ever had, my daughter grew ever more interested in the blueberry bushes in the back garden. Blueberry, not breast milk, would be among her first words.

In my grieving and confusion, I looked for Jewish sources to help me through. Predictably, I found no traditional blessings to say when weaning a child, no ceremonies to conduct, no ritual markers to signify the liminal state in which I found myself. But I am a Bible scholar both by training and inclination, not a liturgist; so I did not sit down to write a contemporary *b'rachah* or create a new ritual. Instead I read *Tanach* and looked for what precious little I could find in the text of the Hebrew Bible on the subject of weaning.

The biblical Hebrew term for weaning comes from the root גמל (*g-m-l*).[1] This root has three distinct meanings (though the second and third meanings clearly are related, as they both refer to the maturation process of living things): (1) repay, deal generously with; (2) wean; (3) ripen, become mature.[2] The root's use in its second meaning, "wean," is less common—employed biblically on only eight occasions: I Samuel 1:23–24; I Kings 11:20; Isaiah 11:8, 28:9; Hosea 1:8; and Psalm 131:2. In addition the *nifal* form of the verb, also meaning "weaning," is found in I Samuel 1:22 and Genesis 21:8.[3] Some of these uses may be familiar to us, the most familiar being Genesis 21:8: "The child grew up and was weaned, and on Isaac's weaning day, Abraham held a great feast."

I had read those lines more times than I could count as congregational rabbi, first on Rosh HaShanah and then often during Shabbat *Vayeira*. Yet never before had I truly heard those words. Why does Genesis not mention the weaning of any other significant figure? Why did Abraham hold a feast? Was this normal practice? If so, why is it not recorded elsewhere in the Bible? Should we understand from the text that weaning marked a distinct phase in the life of an infant/toddler? What age would that likely have been? Should I get my husband to throw a dinner party to mark the weaning of our daughter? So many unanswered questions, so few clues.

A few clues, perhaps, lay in I Samuel 1:22–24, where Hannah resists bringing Samuel to the sanctuary until he is weaned, for as Hannah knows only too well, once Samuel is brought to the sanctuary it is there that he will be obliged to stay and serve for the rest of his life. Clearly she could not bring a child so young that he still required breast milk to survive. So Elkanah allows Hannah to stay at home with her son until he is old enough to be weaned. When Samuel is finally weaned—and the text makes clear that he is still young at this stage—Hannah takes Samuel to the sanctuary, alongside a number of sacrifices, and after slaughtering a bull, she and Elkanah take Samuel to Eli, the priest, and leave Samuel with him. How old could Samuel have been?[4] Elkanah holds no feast to mark Samuel's weaning, and arguably the sacrifices were not to mark the boy's weaning, but his lifetime of servitude to God. Still, read in concert with Isaac's story, a picture begins to emerge.

Both the I Kings and Hosea verses simply make passing reference to the weaning of a child. In Hosea it appears to be linked to the fact that the mother was able to conceive another child only after weaning her first. This phenomenon, while not a reliable form of birth control, is nevertheless a well-documented one. Breastfeeding does provide some protection against conception. The Isaiah verses are both poetic, employing the weaned child as a metaphor for something else, constructed in parallelisms, so that "weaned child" is synonymous with an infant or toddler.

But it was only when I read Psalm 131 that I found myself standing face-to-face with the deeper questions around weaning that called to me to be answered. The psalm is short, a mere three verses, and when first I read it, it so vexed me that I resolved to spend the next year researching it for part of my PhD work. It is worth recounting the psalm here in its entirety:

> The Psalm of Ascent of David
> Eternal One, my heart is not elated and my eyes are not elevated
> and I have not engaged with greatness or wonders beyond me.
> Have I not composed and stilled my breath[5] like a weanling
>   upon his mother?
> Like that weanling is my desire within me.
> Hope, Israel, in the Eternal One, from now until forever.[6]

I was stunned when I first read these words. Foremost was my reaction that here was a biblical text that directly compared the maternal experience of weaning to the Psalmist's relationship with God. In my search for a way to understand the developing relationship between myself and my newly weaned daughter, I discovered that I may also have found a metaphor for my (adult) relationship with God. Might it be that weaning could become a formative theological metaphor in my own thinking?

But when I read this psalm for the first time, I did not read my own translation, but rather the new Jewish Publication Society translation, in which verse 2 reads: "but I have taught myself to be contented / like a weaned child with its mother; / like a weaned child am I in my mind." I was concerned that my own maternal experience of weaning did not resonate with the image portrayed in the psalm. My experience, alongside anecdotal evidence from other women, suggested to me that for many years after the process of weaning is completed, at least some children continue to be anxious or unsettled when near a mother's breast. Some children continue to seek out a sort of closeness to the maternal breast as a means of comfort, suggesting that weaning did not lead to comfort, but quite the opposite—a sort of attachment anxiety.

In this regard, certain psychoanalytical models of mothers and infants may potentially have important implications for the understanding of Psalm 131. In particular Melanie Klein's observations regarding weaning and D. W. Winnicott's ideas about breastfeeding and weaning offer useful insights into possible ways to interpret the image described in verse 2. Klein, for example, believes that infants, even very young infants, engage in "fantasy-building" and that the main object of these fantasies at the outset are the mother's breasts. Breasts are the source of both pleasure (feeding) and pain (withdrawal from feeding). The mother's breasts therefore serve as prototypes for examples of both good, positive life experiences and bad, damaging experiences. According to Klein, the mother's breasts become objects of projection, as described above, but equally objects of introjection.[7] In this latter process the infant sucks the breast into himself, chews it up and swallows it; thus he feels that he has actually got it there, that he possesses the mother's breast within himself, in both its good and bad aspects.[8]

As a child develops, however, he or she should begin to understand the mother as a separate entity, a whole and independent person. As this process takes shape, the child can shift the attachment from the mother's breasts solely to the mother as a whole person. This whole mother will then inhabit the child's view of the breasts—both good and bad. The mother becomes the prototype for both possibilities.[9] Here, then, lies the psychological problem of weaning for the child. It is worth quoting Klein at some length here to explain fully the implications of weaning for the child:

> Coming to our main problem, we find that the child feels, when the breast is wanted but is not there, as if it were lost for ever; since the conception of the breast extends to that of the mother, the feelings of having lost the breast lead to the fear of having lost the loved mother entirely, and this means not only the real mother, but also the good mother within. In my experience this fear of the total loss of the good object (internalized and external) is interwoven with the feelings of guilt at having destroyed her (eaten her up), and then the child feels that her loss is a punishment for his dreadful deed. . . . The actual experience of weaning greatly reinforces these painful feelings or substantiates these fears.[10]

Ultimately for Klein, the experience of weaning is not merely the child's learning to take solid food, but far more importantly, weaning is the means by which the child learns to deal with internal conflicts and to adjust to frustration. Klein states that weaning implies both being weaned from something as well as being weaned onto something else. Proper weaning occurs when the child has learned to replace the mother's breasts with "all those sources of gratification and satisfaction which are needed for building up a full, rich and happy life."[11]

Winnicott in many ways follows on from Klein. He attempts to discover practical ways in which these more theoretical writings can be applied in practice for mothers. He describes a feeding infant as one who is "a bundle of discontent . . . who has raging lions and tigers inside him."[12] He also suggests that satisfactory breastfeeding provides growing infants with the psychological prototype for all instinctive experiences. The process of weaning is one that at some level no child is ever ready for, and hence, a certain amount of anger is always associated with it. The child's desire, based on an internal rage, is to attack the breast. Nevertheless, mother and child are able to come through the process together, partially based on the child's need to protect the loved mother and partially because the mother is able to protect herself.[13] Poor weaning, however, can lead to long-term difficulties.[14]

Even when weaning goes well, the process may lead to a "sadness," which needs to be acknowledged and allowed, not simply glossed over with a few comforting cuddles. After all, the child has a sound basis for this sadness. The process of weaning includes learning about "disillusionment." Ultimately, Winnicott concludes:

> The ordinary good mother and father do not want to be worshipped by their children. They endure the extremes of being idealized and hated, hoping that eventually their children will see them as the ordinary human beings they certainly are.[15]

In relation then to the image of the weaned child in Psalm 131, both Klein and Winnicott offer useful insights. First, both Klein and Winnicott directly address the feelings and experiences of the child. The (presumably) adult Psalmist does not liken himself to the mother in verse 2, but rather to the weaned child. Therefore, in order to grasp the meaning of the image, we, as readers, must understand what the emotions and experiences of a weaned child might be. Moreover, the psychoanalytical model presented by both Klein and Winnicott works well in tandem with the messages readers can glean from verse 1. The language the Psalmist employs to describe himself in verse 1 makes explicit that he does not view himself as god-like. The terms "greatness" and "wonders" (גדולות, *g'dolot*, and נפלאות, *niflaot*), which are far more commonly used in tandem as attributes of God, are utilized by the Psalmist in conjunction with the negative particle, לא (*lo*), to display that the Psalmist understands his separate existence from God. At one level, this linguistic play could be read simply as a means for the Psalmist to express that he is so lowly that all that God is, he is not. But at another level, one that is in keeping with the imagery of the weaned child, the Psalmist may be expressing something far more nuanced—that just as a child during the weaning phase learns to differentiate him- or herself from the mother and to recognize the autonomy that such separation bestows, so, too, the Psalmist, in relating himself to a weaned child, implies that he is also at the stage of spiritual development whereby God is recognized as an external reality beyond the Psalmist's own psyche and that, in turn, the Psalmist recognizes his own individual choice to behave in certain ways. The Psalmist is not humble because God dictates it; the Psalmist is humble through the active choice of an autonomous individual, resulting in a more mature relationship with God. Further, if weaning is indeed about learning about disillusionment and developing a sense of one's parents as "ordinary," then perhaps the Psalmist sees himself at a stage of spiritual development where disillusionment and reconciliation with God enables the achievement of a deeper, more mature relationship. (Whether this process is a conscious or unconscious one remains an open question.)

But where did that leave me, a mother who had not long ago weaned her youngest child? What might the relationship of the metaphor in Psalm 131 be to my own lived experience of weaning my daughter? Did this psalm transform both my own interpersonal relationship as well as my theological one?

I return to the John Donne, which I quote at the beginning of this essay: "I wonder, by my troth, what thou and I / Did, till we loved? were we not weaned till then?" Do we lurch from one attachment to another? Can we be truly weaned of our parental love before we find romantic love? The connection of weaning to adult sexual love is not, to my mind, accidental here. From my perspective, breastfeeding was as intimate an act as sexual intercourse. The infants I breastfed had already been a physical extension of my being pregnant; in infancy, breastfeeding enabled a form of return to that state. My children were again physically attached to me. Latching on and intercourse are to some extent like flip sides of the same coin; the means by which a woman allows another human being to inhabit her and offer that other person more than just sustenance, but, done willingly, also joy. I cannot extrapolate to the experience of all women, but for me breastfeeding was a deeply sensual experience. It attached me to my children, but also back to my own physical body and its potentiality.

If breastfeeding is sensual, the cessation of it, weaning, is no less so. Weaning, too, is a process determined by and rooted in the act of being physically, sexually female. In this sense, weaning cannot but play into all the sorts of attachments, especially those attachments that connect the biological to the emotional and psychological, that shape us as human beings.

There was a moment when I finally realized that I was likely breastfeeding my daughter for the final time. It was not an entirely conscious moment; I knew I was *in the process* of weaning her, but I had not quite worked out when would be the last time. And then it was that final time, and I wondered how I would ever hold her again, how she would be able to be close to me without physical attachment. I wondered if she would ever forgive me leaving her or if I would ever forgive her for leaving me. And then somehow, without knowing the way, we found a path together for her to still her breath against me and rest, for her to know that she would be comforted and loved without the necessity for intimate physical contact. And as I have been with her as she has now grown from infant to toddler to girl, I am only beginning to grasp what real connection might be about, how the maternal metaphor might serve as a determiner of relationships of many types, not the least of which is between myself and God, but the better part of which remains firmly human.

NOTES

1. Not to be confused with the homophone root גמל (*g-m-l*), meaning "camel."
2. David J. A. Clines, ed., *Dictionary of Classical Hebrew* (Sheffield, England: Sheffield Phoenix Press, 1995), 2:363–64. BDB (Francis Brown, S.R. Driver, and Charles

A. Briggs, eds., *Brown-Driver-Biggs Hebrew Lexicon* (Hendrickson: Peabody, MA, 1996)) lists the same range of meanings, see BDB, 168a.

3. By contrast, the primary meaning of "repay, deal generously with" is employed more than twenty times in the Bible.

4. It seems likely that the average age of weaning in the biblical period was between twenty-four and thirty-six months. For a more complete treatment of the age of weaning, see Deena R. Zimmerman, "Duration of Breastfeeding in Jewish Law," in *Jewish Legal Writings by Women*, ed. M. D. Halpern and C. Safrai (Brooklyn: Lambda Publishers, 1998), 52–59; and Mayer I. Gruber, "Breast Feeding Practices in Ancient Israel and Old Babylonian Mesopotamia," *Journal of the Ancient Near Eastern Society* 19 (1989): 61–83.

5. Hebrew, נפש (*nefesh*). The primary definition of נפש (*nefesh*) is not "soul," as is commonly assumed, but rather "throat, neck, or gullet," in short the body's central breathing and eating apparatus. "Breath" is an attested meaning in various verses, including Job 41:13; Genesis 1:30, 35:18; and I Kings 17:21. The usage is also found in the Dead Sea Scrolls in 4QHalakhah^a 13:6.

6. Translation © Rabbi Dr. Deborah Kahn-Harris. Please note that this translation is my own, developed after some time of studying the psalm. It is worth looking at other translations or reading the Hebrew original for some indications of the challenges involved in the translation of this psalm.

7. Melanie Klein, "Weaning," in *Love, Guilt, and Reparation and Other Works 1921–1945* (New York: Delacorte Press, 1975), 290–91.

8. Ibid., 291.

9. Ibid., 294–95.

10. Ibid., 295.

11. Ibid., 304.

12. Donald W. Winnicott, *The Child, the Family, and the Outside World* (London: Penguin Books, 1991), 23. Also see p. 81: "Being hungry is like being possessed by wolves."

13. Ibid., 53–55.

14. Ibid., 82.

15. Ibid., 84.

Older Adulthood

37

MENOPAUSE

Rabbi Karen L. Fox, LMFT

Is it only a hot flash that floods my neck and face as I begin my lecture? Is it the foggy feeling I experience when searching for my keys? Are these simply moments, or are these the indicators of "the change," as menopause is sometimes referred to?

Some women feel that the process of approaching menopause disorders them from a measure of time so deeply ingrained in their body and soul. Some feel off-balance emotionally and unstable physically.

Menopause refers to the cessation of the menses. The terms evolved from the Greek: *meno* for "month," *pauses* for "pause." It is the pause from the monthly cycle that began with early adolescence, the ultimate symbol of femininity, fertility, and hope. Reaching menopause may take a woman six to thirteen years, during which she experiences gradual change in the ovarian cycle. Menopause concludes the childbearing years; it marks the time when a woman has not experienced a menstrual cycle for over a year. She has closed the book on one stage of life. She is moving into a different stage, a stage when aging cannot be denied and the presence of a woman confident in her self cannot be missed. Women today live as much as one-third of their life beyond menopause.

More than forty-three million American women are postmeno-pausal.[1] In developed countries, women are living longer and bet-ter than ever before. Currently our life expectancy is projected to be eighty-four years. This means that women most likely will live thirty-five to forty years following menopause. It is the gateway to the end of life and, as such, has long been a taboo subject. However, Gail Sheehy placed "menopause" in public view when she published her book *The Silent Passage* in 1991.[2]

People have viewed menopause as a deficiency, a disease, and a disorder. Advertisements propose hormones to relieve all these dis-orders. One ad highlights an attractive, fit young woman in dance tights, taking estrogen. In another, a handsome man sips wine and flirts with a woman, with a few gray hairs and little else, as she holds her prescription and states, "I feel like a woman again." If we relied only on pop culture to inform us, we would have to conclude that without hormones our bodies would dry up, our thighs would shrivel, and our minds would rattle. It is as if we are expected to deteriorate with the onset of menopause. Although some women articulate the confidence of entering the stage of the "wise woman," that stage is often presented as less feminine and less dynamic.

Physical Signs

Physical symptoms attributed to menopause are headache and irri-tability, skipped periods, hot flashes, vaginal dryness, osteoporosis, decreased libido, and fuzzy thinking. In actuality, these all may be pre-cursors to menopause itself and may indicate that a woman has entered the six to thirteen years prior to the menopausal stage.[3] Some women slide easily into menopause, and others experience many symptoms. "Fifteen percent of women are symptom free, however 85% experience hot flashes; about 50% of those women concede that they are not tol-erable. In addition, with menopause, thinning of vaginal tissues, heart disease and osteoporosis fracture risk will increase."[4] Some women enter menopause prematurely or artificially as a result of a hysterectomy. With the onset of menopause, women may become more aware of physical disease associated with aging, such as breast cancer, heart disease, osteoporosis, and dementia or Alzheimer's disease.

Because of the significant impact of estrogen on a woman's health and well-being, some women may consider hormone replacement therapy to ease the transition to menopause and sustain health into the future. The use of hormone replacement therapy is quite controversial, and that decision can be made with the resource of an experienced gynecologist, one with both medical and homeopathic training, one who encourages reading and thinking for yourself, one who takes the time to know you as an individual with a unique medical and psychological profile.

Accepting our bodies, at long last, can allow us to pursue *b'riut* (health) in new ways. To preserve and build strength for the later years, exercise and self-care become even more significant. Bone loss increases with estrogen loss; therefore, weight-bearing exercise and calcium intake become important. Healthful eating, sleeping, and stress reduction are significant as well.

Sexual Impact

The capacity to reproduce and the potential of sexual pleasure were considered separate functions for women. Over forty years ago, Masters and Johnson asserted, "Sex drive is not automatically related to estrogen and does not automatically decline with menopause."[5] However, more recent data discredits their view. An Australian study has found that women are likely to experience a dramatic loss of sexual function as a consequence of menopause. The findings are part of the University of Melbourne's Women's Midlife Health Project conducted by the university's Office for Gender and Health, which has been following a large group of Melbourne women for over ten years. "This is the first study worldwide to follow a population-based group of women for more than ten years and record symptoms of menopause as well as physical measurements that include blood samples to record hormone levels, bone density and skin fold thickness," says the project's director, Professor Lorraine Dennerstein. The study found women going through the menopausal transition "experienced a decline in sexual interest, a decrease in arousal and in the frequency of sexual activity, and an increase in vaginal dryness and pain during intercourse."[6] However, the study also acknowledges that "factors like a women's level of sexual responsiveness before menopause, changes in her partner status (gaining or losing a partner) and a woman's feelings for her partner can override hormonal effects. Hormonal effects are most likely to be noted by women in long-term, stable relationships."[7]

The emotional and physical experience of sexuality is dependent on the comfort and the depth of intimacy found in the relationship between partners. The cessation of the menstrual cycle does not automatically determine a loss in sexual desire. However, women may experience a lack of libido due to various menopausal symptoms, such as exhaustion or night sweats, painful intercourse, bladder or urinary tract infections, and mood changes. Other women may experience a heightened sexual desire, liberated from the burdens of birth control, young children, and fear of pregnancy. Today's woman may feel a turning point, which frees her sexually and marks a steady "zest" or sexual energy. For those women who have chosen a new partner, excitement and joy emerge with new love.

Emotional Impact

Menopause affects women in many different ways. Some see menopause as a traumatic time, a time that announces the beginning of the end. For others, it may be seen as a time to complete the major tasks of life. It represents midlife, a phase in which a woman can raise old questions and accept their challenges or be rid of them.

Menopause may be the time to pause and consider the past. Some women may grieve the loss of youth, symbolized by the menstrual cycle. Some may grieve for unborn children and lost relationships and then be able to move forward. Others may grieve for that which is lost and turn it around into that which might yet be. Menopause is an opportunity to ask the most poignant of questions: what kind of life do I want for myself at this stage of life?

Depression is a common disabling disorder affecting more than nineteen million Americans per year, and women are at least twice as likely as men to experience a major depressive episode.[8] We may ask: does menopause cause depression? The *British Medical Journal* reviewed ninety-four articles from thirty years of research examining the relationship between natural menopause and depression. They argue, "There is insufficient evidence at present to maintain that menopause causes depression."[9] The belief that most women suffer depression around the onset of menopause does not appear to be supported by epidemiological data. This fact presents against the stereotype of the expected sadness that a woman might feel at this life transition.

However, the Summit on Women and Depression argues:

> While there is no evidence that menopause is associated with increased depression on a population level, an unanswered question is whether some women may be more vulnerable to mood effects of hormonal changes. Researchers have suggested women with a history of premenstrual mood changes may have increased sensitivity to hormonal changes at perimenopause and women with previously diagnosed mood disorders that are cyclical or related to reproductive events may be at higher risk for depressive symptoms.[10]

Many women report mood swings, agitation, anxiety, and sadness within the months and sometimes years leading to menopause, perhaps due to the hormonal shifts. Additionally, the onset of menopause is complicated by the stress of caring for aged parents and the anxiety of teenaged and adult children not yet established in their own lives. Often, children may have moved on to college and work, and the once bustling home is an "empty nest." These and other emotional stressors abound, and many women experience mood swings as a result.

Jewish Guidance

Scarcely any material exists that even mentions menopause within Jewish tradition. Within the Torah, only Sarah acknowledges that she is beyond the age for childbearing, and the text reads, "Sarah had stopped having the periods of women. Sarah laughed to herself saying 'Now that I am withered, am I to enjoy my husband, in our old age'" (Gen. 18:11–12). However, despite the biological reality, the matriarch Sarah did enjoy Abraham, and Isaac was born. Talmudic searches reveal no resources that mention menopause.[11] Three contemporary Orthodox marriage manuals, which describe the practice of *nidah* (Jewish family purity laws surrounding menstruation) in great detail, do not cite any ritual or concern for menopause.[12] No rites exist to mark this passage/event, which may tell us many things and gives us many opportunities.

For many generations, most women did not reach the age in which menopause occurs. In addition, women's rituals in traditional Jewish practice are few. However, the rituals of *challah* (separating out dough when making challah for the family Shabbat observance), *nerot* (lighting candles to signify the beginning of Shabbat), and *nidah* (observing Jewish family purity laws) are significant personal mitzvot for Orthodox women. It seems unusual that there is no ritual conclusion to the *nidah* years at menopause. A woman who had been a *nidah*-observing Jew and had gone to mikveh at the end of each menstrual cycle during all her married years might miss the routine of sexual separation from her husband, followed by renewal in the mikveh and sexual reunion. The structure of an observant couple's sexual practice is different once she is menopausal. A ritual closure to those years might ease the psychological and spiritual transition. However, because no records of a menopause ritual exist, we now have the opportunity to ease this life transition with new ritual.

Although our tradition did not emphasize aspects of midlife as we perceive it in the twenty-first century, the Rabbis did acknowledge the year fifty as a significant marker in life. According to *Pirkei Avot*, the Ethics of the Sages, age fifty is the stage in which it is appropriate to guide and mentor others: "Fifty is for advice" (*Pirkei Avot* 5:21). The recognition that life experience brings mastery and responsibility to guide and mentor is a value in and of itself.

Yet, advice can be given only when the woman has soothed her own anxieties and is able to reflect on her life experience. A woman can guide, advocate, and mentor when she is content with her own path. Without the distractions of the competition of earlier stages of work and the urgent pull of children and spouse, a woman can experience her own self.

Although our American culture does not conceive of this possibility, moving into menopause requires more quiet and more reflection than previous moments in a woman's life. In learning to be patient with herself during this transition, a woman can hear her own voice enough to acknowledge it and teach from it. She can be "contented with her lot" (*Pirkei Avot* 6:6). Richness is not measured by the money or power we have but how we experience our place in life. Making time for quiet, for reflection, for the spiritual extends the comfort we can feel at midlife. Accepting the realities helps us learn to live with those realities and cherish them as well. Loving the children and friends that are ours, enjoying an article and passing it around, pruning the roses and enjoying their fragrance, making a recipe and sharing it are all moments in which contentment can be ours.

Menopause can also be seen as the stage of embracing the wise woman. In *Women as Ritual Experts*, Susan Starr Sered points to the positive attitude some Jewish women have had about menopause. "One woman expressed her feelings about being too old to have any more children in this way: 'Thank God Who has released me.'"[13] Psychologist David Gutman, in an examination of ethnographic data from Asian, Middle Eastern, and African societies, hypothesizes that "the post parental period of life, in a variety of very disparate cultures, regions and races is a time of enlargement for women. They move into governance roles particularly in the household, but also in the areas of community politics and religion, that were thitherto closed against them."[14]

Many women feel they no longer have to prove themselves intellectually or politically. Many relish the comfort of self-expression. No longer automatically deferential or subservient, a woman with experience is valued at home and at work. She stands with the "Old Girls' Club," an association of experienced women proud, smart, and savvy. She will not retire to the back of the room nor need to wear the gray suit of the upwardly mobile young professional. She may reevaluate spouse and partner and ask: Is this who I want to grow old with? She may no longer retain relationships only because of history. She may scrutinize love, its depth, its power, and its value. She may expect communication, comfort, and companionship from lovers and children. She may feel the confidence of life experience and express herself as she is. She can accept the gifts and the limitations that are hers. She may want to complete goals long left unfinished due to other responsibilities. She may want to study, to paint, to garden, to dance, to explore.

Programmatic Opportunities

Synagogues have the opportunity to step into the vacuum left by our tradition and help ease the passage into this life stage. A "Time to Pause" four-week support group within a synagogue setting will create an emotional and spiritual framework for women. Within the context of such a group, the physical, emotional, and spiritual components of this life transition can be explored. In addition, a "For Men Only" group can complement a partner's experiences of menopause. A quiet woodsy women's retreat in which a community can consider the many endings and new beginnings in life will bring relief to those who have felt alone in this life-span transition.

Ritual

Rabbi Elyse Goldstein acknowledges that women have developed "imitative" rituals to incorporate a feminine aspect into a traditional ritual. She also proposes that at times when no ritual has emerged from the body of our Jewish tradition, "inventive ritual" attempts to ritualize an event to aid in its psychological and spiritual transition.[15]

There is something deeply Jewish about menopause, for Jews often emphasize endings and new beginnings. It marks the physical conclusion of the potential to bear children, which is a key value in Jewish practice. Although women's lives are now full with work and its creativity, the experiences of motherhood are like no other moments in life. I will no longer feel the cramp of the cycle, the headache reminding me of my own time, the excitement of the birth and development of my boys. I am grateful for those moments, moments unique to my life as a woman. Yet, I am ready to step forward, to new creativity found in work and in love. I am also ready to move to a more reflective phase in my life. The postmenopausal phase carries the comfort and confidence of experience, the desire to guide, and the continuing quest for wisdom.

What ritual can capture these emotional and spiritual experiences? Some have suggested a final mikveh visit, both for those who observed *nidah* and for those who did not. A woman might invite her closest women friends to accompany her to the mikveh, and after she has entered into its embracing waters, the women friends can share sweet nuts and raisins as well as their blessings and wishes for the next stages of life.

Others suggest development of a personal *havdalah*, separating years of impending fertility and years of expressing generavity in alternate ways. We might use the same ritual items as mark the separations in time in our tradition: a braided candle, wine, and sweet perfumes, adding cooling herbs like peppermint or lavender. Various liturgies including personal statements, music, and graphic arts are surfacing that acknowledge the transitions that menopause represents. As Sandy Silas, MFT, has said, "There has been no welcome committee for us, but we need to welcome the next generation moving through this change."[16] Rituals develop because of a need to capture and ease a physical, emotional, and spiritual moment, and we are in the midst of that evolutionary process today.

NOTES

1. Christiane Northrup, *Women's Bodies, Women's Wisdom* (New York: Bantam Books, 1998), 533.

2. Gail Sheehy, *The Silent Passage* (New York: Random House, 1991).

3. Northrup, *Women's Bodies*, 533.

4. Ibid., 525.

5. William Masters and Virginia Johnson, *Human Sexual Response* (Boston: Little, Brown, 1966), 117, 238.

6. Jason Major, "Menopause Dashes Sex Life" (press release, University of Melbourne, May 21, 2002).

7. Ibid.

8. C. M. Mazure, G. P. Keita, and M. C. Blehard, "Summit on Women and Depression: Proceedings and Recommendations" (press release, American Psychological Association, March 21, 2001), 10.

9. L. Nicol-Smith, "Causality, Menopause and Depression: A Critical Review of the Literature," *British Medical Journal*, January 7, 1997.

10. Ibid., 27–28.

11. Foremost Israeli halachist Rabbi Avraham Steinberg did not include menopause in his authoritative encyclopedia, for the question does not arise in halachic discussion. Based on conversation with Rabbi Moshe Zemer, Beit Daniel, Tel Aviv, Israel, July 24, 2002.

12. Rabbi Norman Lamm, "A Hedge of Roses" (New York: Feldhiem, 1966); Rabbi Dr. Moshe Tendler, *Pardes Rimonim: A Marriage Manual for the Jewish Family* (New York: Judaica Press, 1977); *Taharat HaMishpacha: A Guide to Jewish Family Laws* (Nanuet, NY: Feldheim, 1974).

13. Susan Starr Sered, *Women as Ritual Experts* (Oxford: Oxford University Press, 1992), 106.

14. David Gutman, *Reclaimed Powers: Toward a New Psychology of Men and Women in Later Life* (New York: Basic Books, 1987).

15. Elyse Goldstein, *ReVisions: Seeing Torah through a Feminist Lens* (Woodstock, VT: Jewish Lights, 1999), 130.

16. Sandy Silas, MFT, facilitator, "A Time to Change" (Wilshire Boulevard Temple, winter 1999).

Adapted with permission from Karen L. Fox from *CCAR Journal*, Fall 2005, vol. LII/4, 68-77.

38

WITH EYES UNDIMMED AND VIGOR UNABATED

Sex, Sexuality, and Older Adults

Rabbi Richard F. Address, DMin

A recent issue of *Modern Maturity* magazine, the official publication of the American Association of Retired Persons (AARP), featured several articles on the role of sex and sexuality in aging, including "Great Sex: What's Age Got to Do with It?"[1] The longevity and health revolution that characterizes the older adult Jewish population provides unique challenges. The impending addition of the "baby boom" generation to the older adult population raises the question of how the Reform Jewish community will approach sex, sexuality, and intimacy in an aging population.

Those who attain old age are held in great esteem in the Jewish tradition, a tradition that is filled with a wide variety of opinions and approaches to the aging process. In a recent Freehof Institute collection on "Aging and the Aged in Jewish Law," Walter Jacob presents a comprehensive overview of the difficulty of defining exactly what "old" is.[2] Jacob argues from tradition that there is great fluidity in the definition of who is old today. Indeed, he reflects the need to see people within their particular contexts, but not segregated into separate classes. The face of the contemporary older Jewish adult reflects this inability to generalize. Economic prosperity and medical technology have combined to create a generation like no other in history. Older adults are living longer and better and, as such, are living witness to an ancient maxim that "some people possess years, others possess old age."[3] Never before has Judaism seen a generation of its elders more attuned to celebrate its years in meaningful ways, while at the same time rejecting cultural stereotypes.

Much knowledge of this emerging phenomenon comes from information gathered from studies of the United States Jewish community conducted in the 1990s. Gerontologist Dr. Allen Glicksman notes that widely held perceptions of Jewish older adults are now outdated. Glicksman comments that members of the current generation of older adults resemble their children and grandchildren more than they resemble their parents. The majority of this generation is American born, as opposed to a 1970 study that saw 60 percent as immigrants. The current Jewish older adult population is now about one-fifth of the total Jewish community and "reflects the lower birthrate of recent generations of American Jews as well as the increased longevity of the elderly."[4] The studies reveal that this population is better educated, more affluent, and more mobile and that it presents a very different picture of "family." Well over half live independently in one- or two-person units, not in care-giving facilities. Care-giving implications are obvious, because those currently over age 75 are growing at a faster rate than others, and "more and more Jews, like elderly in general, will reach the century mark. This means that old age will increasingly span 35 years."[5] Many in our postindustrial age are convinced that age 65 is a meaningless number to fix as an end to an individual's productive work. Given these changes, three-plus decades of post-65 life require rethinking and redefining personal meaning, leisure, health care, economics, family life, political power, and sexuality.

Theodore Roszak termed this new era a "longevity revolution" where the autonomy of the self is in full bloom:

Never before has the population aged seventy, eighty, and even ninety included so many physically and mentally active people. Most obviously, this is because no older generation has ever had so much access to health care. But there is also that fact that no previous generation has been so health and fitness conscious; today's seniors are eager to participate in caring for their own health by exploring alternative medicines and making changes in their habits of living.[6]

This revolution has made it difficult to create vocabulary to describe this older adult cohort. Stereotypes are crumbling. Are they "senior citizens" or "golden-agers," "older adults" or "prime-timers"? "What one more and more finds are hungry minds, physical vitality, keen perception, lively tastes, political know-how, even ambition: people who fully expect to get a lot older before they admit to being old, people not to be dismissed or treated with condescension."[7] The Jewish community must also recognize the need for increased serious adult study, spiritual exploration, and a search for personal meaning and purpose.

What makes this revolution even more exciting is the addition of a new cohort, the post–World War II generation, the oldest of whom are now entering their sixties. This is the generation that was reared in the embrace of exploding suburbia and brought to maturity through the prism of the civil rights movement, Vietnam, Watergate, feminism, and the symbolic trio of autonomy-based social restructuring: sex, drugs, and rock and roll. Many feel that this generation will join the longevity revolution with the same fervor that has marked its movement through other stages of life. Looking around community, congregations, and communal institutions, an observer wonders whether or not there has ever been a generation more unlikely to conform to the stereotypes of aging.

The breakdown of stereotypes and the search to create a meaningful vocabulary have led some commentators to argue for a new life stage—one that reflects this longevity revolution. It is not unusual to meet people well into their sixties and seventies who continue to define themselves as "middle-aged." Gail Sheehey, in *New Passages*, began to look at the need to create a new way of describing the new aging process. She opted to welcome the aging baby boomers to "middlescence."[8] Several years later, Ken Dychtwald picked up on the term, describing it as "a period of high-spirited growth and ascension, not retreat and decline."[9]

With this in mind, society has begun to explore and establish new ideas of what it means to age with meaning and purpose. Given these realities, the role of sex and sexuality will also be viewed in a different light. Autonomy, medical technology, and social history demand a reexamination of sex and sexuality for the older adult population that should begin with the creation of a new sexual ethic for the members of the longevity revolution.

Over a decade ago, Dychtwald cited a series of studies from several universities exposing the myth that older adults and sexuality were mutually exclusive. "Current research is proving that men and women continue to feel sexy and sensual in later life. While the statistics show a slight decrease in sexual activity with increasing age, the facts are far from what the myth would have us believe."[10] The studies showed a healthy interest and appreciation of the role of and the desire for sex as people age. A man in his seventies reported that he experienced a different kind of sexuality, one not associated with having to prove oneself: "It's more loving, more playful, more of a nourishment between two people."[11] These beginning studies led Dychtwald to conclude that "sex and romance, fueled by other changes in relationships, will continue into later years—and may well become deeper, fuller, and more satisfying than ever."[12]

A decade later, the *Modern Maturity* survey confirmed the observations that sexuality is an important part of life by noting that "while frequency drops with age, more than 70 percent of surveyed men and women who have regular partners are sexually active enough to have intercourse at least once a month."[13] What emerges, as well, as we age, is the greater importance of the personal relationship that is involved with sex. "The proportion of those rating their physical relationship with their partner as 'extremely' or 'very' satisfying—67 percent of men, 61 percent of women—is quite close to the percentage who reported high satisfaction with their emotional relationship (70 percent of men, 62 percent of women)."[14] Sexuality, as we age, seems to extend well beyond the physical. In addition to the need for human contact, there exists an equal desire for emotional presence as this longevity generation redefines intimacy. This is also of great importance when considering the realities of disabilities and the expected rise in dementia. "It is a myth that sexual intercourse is the only fulfilling or 'real' sex. A great number of elderly without partners or with very ill partners report pleasure derived from fantasy and self-stimulation. In addition, a number of elderly people derive tremendous sexual satisfaction with their partners from physical intimacies that do not include intercourse."[15]

The *Modern Maturity* survey also examined issues of gender and partner availability. Women continue to outlive men, and as the cohorts of older adults swell, researchers question how sexual intimacy and activity will be played out. Here, the survey indicates that different generational contexts will result in different views on sexuality.

> The generation gap in sexual attitudes between those who came of age in the 1960s and their parents is as apparent today as it was then—especially among women—and may foreshadow a more active sex life for the younger generation as it ages. Women 45 through 59 are much more likely to approve of sex between unmarried partners and to engage in oral sex and masturbation—and less likely to believe that "sex is only for younger people"—than women 60 and older. Older men also espouse more conservative values than younger men, but the gap is much narrower. The gap in attitudes between women over and under 60 suggests that Baby Boomer women, the oldest of whom are in their late 40s and early 50s, will be much less likely than their mothers' generation to accept celibacy as the natural outcome to widowhood. These women came of age believing that they had a right to sexual pleasure and that belief isn't going to evaporate at age 65 or 75.[16]

Recent surveys point to the reality of sexual interest in an aging population, placing increasing importance on the quality of a relationship and the need for intimacy. There is the understanding that personal health, reduced stress, and a caring supportive community contribute greatly to a healthy sexual life. These realities present an opportunity to create environments within synagogues and the Jewish community that provide a forum for the discussion of human sexuality and the sexuality of aging. These discussions are long overdue and include drawing the children of older adults into the conversation in order to understand their parents' need for a healthy sex life, especially after one parent has died. Many rabbis have counseled those who were at a loss to deal with a parent who, after the other spouse's death, is now "carrying on as if he or she were a teenager." Issues of intergenerational care-giving require new thought, patience, and support, as well as guidance from our tradition about how we may best view these new realities. Stein's taxonomy provides the understanding that many situations can be viewed within the framework of his categories of *musar* (ethical) and/or *mutar* (permitted). One of the challenges may be to see how, in certain contexts, these relationships can also take on the notion of *kadosh* (holy).[17] Stein affirms the value of examining the context of situations. He notes that the CCAR Ad Hoc Committee on Human Sexuality struggled to seek a viable middle ground between the tradition's defined categories of sexual behavior and the shifting and evolving realities of our contemporary cultural values. "One way to mediate this tension is to abandon the assumption that sexual behavior can be judged as simply 'right' or 'wrong', 'moral' or 'sinful,' always either 'good' or 'evil.' Rather, it may be preferable to evaluate human sexual behavior on a 'hierarchical scale,' employing a taxonomy of sexual behaviors."[18]

Examples of emerging challenges within the field of older adult sexuality are plentiful. Take, for example, the reality of sexual activity within long-term care facilities. Although most of our older adults live in a situation that finds them caring for themselves, there is a significant population residing in nursing homes. As the older adult population grows, there will be a greater number of people who will seek secure housing options within assisted-living and life-care residences.

The realization that sexual expression is a natural and lifelong part of who we are has led some facilities to formalize a policy of openness and acceptance regarding human sexuality within such facilities. The Hebrew Home for the Aged in Riverdale, New York, for example, has developed a model program that seeks to affirm the sexual expression of its residents:

> Residents have the right to seek out and engage in sexual expression among other residents and visitors. They have the right to obtain materials with sexually explicit content such as books, magazines, videos, and drawings. Access to private space and professional counseling in support of self or others are also defined as resident rights.[19]

Similar policy statements are in place or in development in many Jewish homes for the aged. Such a work in progress is the sexual policy document from the Handmaker Home in Tucson, Arizona, that states: "The residents of the skilled nursing facility and their partners have the right to seek out and engage in sexual expression. Privacy is to be provided to carry on intimate relationships. The environment provided is to be safe and supportive, but must not infringe upon the rights of other residents."[20]

Emerging within the arena of older adult sexuality is the difficulty presented to a healthy spouse whose partner is institutionalized with dementia or Alzheimer's disease (see Dorf and Geller, p. 547, this volume). The longevity revolution has resulted in a rise in the instances of dementia-type afflictions, and there will continue to be situations where the well spouse engages in sexual activity and intimate relationships with a new partner while still married. This reality is not to be taken lightly. One can only imagine the difficult emotional territory that has to be negotiated, the difficult choices between what may actually be two "rights": the keeping of sacred marriage vows and the need for intimacy and personal sexual expression. This opens opportunities for dialogue. Individuals and families should discuss and formalize their wishes in situations where heroic medical care may be needed.

The importance of these advance medical directives (living wills) and durable powers of attorney for health care cannot be stressed enough, given the realities of contemporary medical technology and health care.[21] Perhaps it is time to develop a similar document spelling out a couple's wishes with regard to how personal life may be conducted if the other spouse is institutionalized with Alzheimer's or dementia. Such a document already exists. "An Open Letter to My Spouse Encouraging New Companionship" asks couples to take time and seriously consider the emotional needs that may arise in times of extreme crises. The document assumes the strength of commitment within a relationship, while recognizing that situations may arise that will fundamentally alter the relationship. A key paragraph of this proposed "Open Letter to My Spouse" speaks to concerns that may result from the longevity revolution:

> As medical science, nutrition and exercise, and a host of other factors conspire successfully to allow the average American to live longer, the chances get better and better that I will be "alive" in body, but possibly significantly compromised mentally and/or physically. Loving me as you do, I know that you will care for me to the best of your ability. But if I am compromised, and unable to maybe even recognize you or remember that we are married, you will be faced with a double burden: additional stress of caring for me in my sad state, and the absence of my emotional, physical and intellectual support. I hope that this does not happen, but if it does, I want you to know that I will want you to do the best you can to be supported by a loving companion. Please find someone you like who will be available to provide the emotional, intellectual, and physical support and companionship that I cannot provide to you.[22]

Though such a document may offend some, it may be important to ascertain if such a document, properly drawn from our faith and our values, could be of help. Given the realities that we now face, the case for such a document is worthy of serious discussion within our movement.

Recently there has been discussion regarding the issue of sexual relationships outside marriage brought about by unique circumstances.

Rabbi Daniel Schiff suggests that not all adultery may be thought of as equal. For example, "circumstantial" adultery "takes place under extraordinary conditions, most often in cases of the serious physical or mental impairment of a spouse." Schiff notes that in such situations the person entering into the sexual liaison will be conscious of what he or she is doing. "If the spouse of the comatose patient finds a committed partner with whom a sexual relationship is shared, adultery will be the result, though it is an adultery that arguably might warrant a moral response different from that given to other categories."[23]

Consequently, it is necessary to look at the creation of new categories of relationships that reflect the dynamism that is, and will be, our older adult life. Given the gender and partnership gaps and the need for a life of companionship, intimacy, and sexuality, we can consider developing a way to sanctify relationships between people that may not be formal-ized as a marriage, but is represented as such. This would be a category of relationship for older adults that is comparable to a marriage. Some textual foundation for this may actually exist. A discussion in a recent is-sue of the journal *Tradition* reflects upon a category of relationship called *derech kiddushin* ("in the manner of marriage"). The context for this term derives from marriages arranged for minors by a father who has traveled to distant lands and thereby abandoned his child.

The author of the article traces textual arguments regarding pos-sible alternatives to halachic marriage. The arguments raised in the article speak to circumstances that have little bearing on contemporary Jewish family life. An argument is made that such an alternative cat-egory of relationship "is permissible even if the marriage is not tech-nically valid and moreover, since no marriage has been established, a 'get' is not required for dissolution of the relationship. Any couple may signify that they do not intend to contract a valid marriage and may instead opt for a relationship 'derech kiddushin.'"[24] The value of revis-iting the concept of a relationship that is "in the manner of marriage" can be of great relevance to the real-life situations that now exist. It is time to consider developing a ritual sanctifying such a relationship. Many colleagues have been asked to say a blessing for an older couple who have chosen to commit themselves to each other and who, under certain circumstances, do not seek the legality of marriage. These are people deeply committed to each other, where previous concerns over procreation are now supplanted by legal issues and a deep desire for companionship and intimacy. Given the demographics on the horizon, we must begin a dialogue to address this issue.

To understand and appreciate the changing landscape of sexual relationships between older adults, we need to study the entire range of sexual issues through the filter of historic and/or sacred texts and contemporary personal spiritual search. Underlying all the surveys and statistics is the understanding that increased longevity has raised issues of intimacy, the quality of relationships, and physical and mental health. Congregations can become centers for healthy aging and wellness; such a focus must include permission to discuss the issues of human sexuality. Reform Judaism needs to take part in this dialogue of change and growth.

This dialogue calls upon us to educate for longevity by examining how we can develop programs and supportive environments that consider the role that sex and sexuality play in light of extended life spans and the impact upon those life spans of advances in medical technology and pharmacology. It is important that we are able to look at the context of each individual's life experience regarding his or her need for affirming, nonprocreative, consensual, sexually active relationships that provide intimacy and companionship and that may fall outside formal marriage.

We need to examine the development of rituals and ceremonies that can be used, in the appropriate circumstances, to embrace and support these new realities of life and living. The development of such rituals will challenge us to confront our own views of sex and sexuality, intimacy and spirituality, as they apply to a new category of relationships and contexts. As the ranks of the Jewish older adult population swell, we will meet unique and exciting opportunities to evolve meaningful Jewish responses to new life realities. How we choose to create moments of sacred connection for individuals in such situations will say much about Reform Judaism's ability to respond to the challenges of our changing older adult community.

NOTES

1. Susan Jacoby, "Great Sex: What's Age Got to Do with It?" *Modern Maturity*, September-October 1999.

2. Walter Jacob, "Beyond Methuselah—Who Is Old?" in *Aging and the Aged in Jewish Law: Essays and Responsa*, ed. Walter Jacob and Moshe Zemer (Tel Aviv: Freehof Institute of Progressive Halakhah; Pittsburgh: Rodef Shalom Press, 1998), 1–19.

3. *B'reishit Rabbah* 59:1.

4. Allen Glicksman, *The New Jewish Elderly: A Literature Review* (New York: American Jewish Committee, 1991), 7.

5. Ibid., 8.

6. Theodore Roszak, *America the Wise* (New York: Houghton Mifflin, 1998), 10.

7. Ibid., 13.

8. Gail Sheehy, *New Passages* (New York: Random House, 1995), 63.

9. Ken Dychtwald, *Age Power* (New York: Tarcher Putnam, 1999), 88.

10. Ken Dychtwald, *Age Wave* (New York: Bantam, 1990), 44.

11. Ibid., 46.

12. Ibid., 47.

13. Jacoby, "Great Sex." 41.

14. Ibid., 42.

15. Rachelle Dorfman, *Aging in the 21st Century* (New York: Bruner/Mazel, 1994), 117–18.

16. Jacoby, "Great Sex," 42–43.

17. Jonathan Stein, "Toward a Taxonomy for Reform Jews to Evaluate Sexual Behavior," *CCAR Journal*, Fall 2001, 27–35.

18. Ibid., 30.

19. D. A. Reingold, "Rights of Nursing Home Residents to Sexual Expression," *Clinical Geriatrics*, vol. 5, no. 4, April 1997, 54.

20. Draft of Sexual Policy for Handmaker Home for the Aged, Tucson, AZ.

21. For example, see *A Time to Prepare: A Practical Guide for Individuals and Families in Determining One's Wishes for Extraordinary Medical Treatment and Financial Arrangements*, rev. ed., ed. Richard F. Address (New York: UAHC Press, 2002).

22. "Dementia: Sexual Issues Require Sensitivity," *Paresnt Care Advisor Newsletter*, April 1999, 9.

23. Daniel Schiff, "Separating the Adult from Adultery," in *Marriage and Its Obstacles in Jewish Law*, ed. Walter Jacob and Moshe Zemer (Tel Aviv: Freehof Institute of Progressive Halakhah; Pittsburgh: Rodef Shalom Press, 1999), 80.

24. J. David Bleich, "Can There Be Marriage without Marriage?" *Tradition*, Winter 1999, vol. 33, no. 2, 42.

Adapted with permission from Richard F. Address, *CCAR Journal*, Fall 2001, XLVIII/4, 58-67.

39

WHEN ALZHEIMER'S TURNS A SPOUSE INTO A STRANGER

Jewish Perspectives on Loving and Letting Go

RABBI ELLIOT N. DORFF, PhD,
AND RABBI LAURA GELLER

Sarah, a congregant in her early seventies, comes to her rabbi for counseling. Her husband, Saul, has had Alzheimer's for some time now. He is living in an Alzheimer's unit of a local facility. Theirs has been a good marriage, and she feels responsible for him and his care. She still loves him, but she feels the loss of his ability to reciprocate her love. She feels emotionally alone. She has recently met another man, David, and their friendship has the potential to develop into something more intimate. She is hesitant to discuss this with her children and feels that her friends will be judgmental. Before she allows the relationship to develop further, she wants to be certain that she will not be shunned by her friends and, even more, that there could be some communal recognition and acceptance of her new relationship as well as the blessing of her religious tradition. What insights from Jewish law and Jewish values could help Sarah navigate this stage of her life?

Though a Jewish marriage ceremony does not include the promise "until death do us part," it is based on the commitment to care for each other no matter what challenges emerge. So one Jewish response might be that Sarah ought to live alone until Saul dies. There is, though, a countervailing Jewish value that is reflected in the Adam and Eve story through God's instruction, "It is not good for a person to be alone" (Gen. 2:18). Is there a Jewish way to honor one's commitments to one's spouse in this condition and yet not be alone? What questions or even dangers does creating a new, intimate relationship pose?

One danger is that this a slippery slope. If one may engage in sexual relations with someone other than one's spouse in cases of dementia, what about a situation where the partner has a different illness where he or she is incapable of sexual intimacy but is totally coherent? Is the Alzheimer's situation different?

One might say, in response, that Alzheimer's is indeed different, for having a partner with another kind of illness where sexual intimacy is challenged is not being alone in the same way. A partner who is no longer capable of physical intimacy can still provide emotional intimacy, but an Alzheimer's patient cannot.

Jewish tradition offers an additional way of thinking about why the situation with an Alzheimer's partner is different. It takes into consideration the emotional response of the ill partner to a decision by his or her spouse to become intimate with another person. The Alzheimer's patient would not understand this, but a partner with another kind of illness would almost certainly be aware of what was happening and therefore would feel shame. Judaism has a legal category, *boshet* (shame), that is relevant here. The Mishnah makes assailants liable for the embarrassment they cause their victims as one of the five elements of the crime for which they must pay. The Talmud determines that each of the five elements of assault is legally actionable on its own, so causing one's partner shame, even without physical injury, is a crime (*Mishnah Bava Kama* 8:1, 8:6; and see Babylonian Talmud, *Bava Kama* 85a–86b).

On the other hand, if we distinguish between the Alzheimer's patient and other ill people, are we in danger of minimizing the humanity of the one with Alzheimer's? Is the Alzheimer's patient not still created in the divine image (*b'tzelem Elohim*) and therefore still deserving to be treated like everyone else? Or does one need to be able to distinguish between right and wrong in order to be categorized as having the divine image (or able to engage in intellectual reasoning, as Maimonides defined it)? If so, how does this affect our treatment of people with severe retardation or those in long-term comas?

Given the danger and complexity of this issue, how can Jewish tradition help people in this situation acknowledge their continuing relationship to a spouse of many years, honoring the vision that all human beings are created in the divine image, and yet be free spiritually, morally, and maybe even legally to have intimate relations with someone else? How can Sarah and David describe their new relationship to their children, other family members, or friends? What insights can we glean from Jewish law, Jewish values, and Jewish ritual that can help us navigate this new experience?

We begin by exploring how Jewish law might help us reframe the question. There seem to be four halachic responses: (1) reframing polygamy, (2) reframing concubinage, (3) reframing adultery, and (4) reframing divorce.

Reframing Polygamy

The Bible and Talmud allow a man to marry more than one woman at a time, but in the tenth century Rabbeinu Gershom issued a legislative decree (*takanah*) prohibiting this practice for Ashkenazic Jews. Sephardic Jews continued to permit polygamy. Thus when some Sephardic men immigrated to the State of Israel with more than one wife, the government allowed such men to keep all their wives, but no man could marry more than one woman at a time within the borders of the state.

Would suspending the *takanah* of Rabbeinu Gershom be a halachic solution? If rabbis as a group in our day suspended the enactment of Rabbeinu Gershom in such situations, a man might be free to marry another woman without divorcing his demented but beloved first wife.

The problems with this approach are several. First, it only works if the ill partner is a woman, for women were never permitted by Jewish law to marry more than one man at a time. Second, it undoubtedly will not be an easy matter to convince the authorities of the Reform or Conservative Movements, let alone the Orthodox, to suspend a structural provision of Jewish marriages that has been in place in the Ashkenazic world for over a thousand years. Furthermore, civil law in Western countries prohibits polygamy, and Jews are rightfully wary of violating the laws of the nation in which they live. This last point might be finessed by saying that the ceremony joining the couple is intended exclusively as a religious act and not as an act in civil law, but states might well look askance at such a defense for what looks very much like the kinds of marriages over which states claim jurisdiction. We will return to this question of imagining a ceremony joining a couple without sanction of civil law below.

Reframing Concubinage (*Pilegesh*)

If the healthy person is a man, one might consider the second relationship as concubinage. In the Torah, Abraham had a concubine, Hagar (Genesis 16), in addition to his two wives, Sarah and Keturah (Gen. 25:1). Jacob had two wives, Leah and Rachel, and two concubines, Bilhah and Zilpah (Gen. 30:1–13). Perhaps we could resurrect the legal status of concubinage such that a man with a demented wife could live with, and have intimate relations with, a second woman who would not be a full wife but would have a legal status that would permit intimate relations, both emotionally and physically.

One problem with this, of course, is that this too only works if the healthy person is a man. It does not help women with demented husbands at all. Because it is not egalitarian, and because it creates a clearly secondary status for the new woman in this arrangement, it reinforces the patriarchal dimension of classical Judaism to which most modern Jews object.

Furthermore, the exact duties of the man and woman to each other would have to be worked out in detail, for the ancient rules governing concubines are not clear either in the Bible or in later Jewish law. Rabbi Abraham ben David of Posquiéres (ca. 1125–98) distinguishes between a prostitute and a concubine, in that a prostitute offers herself for sex to any man, while a concubine is part of one man's household and has sexual relations only with him (*Mishneh Torah, Hilchot Ishut* 1:4, gloss), but he does not spell out the duties of the concubine or her lover to each other. Thus reconstructing concubinage would not function in the way proponents of this approach would like—namely, to provide a legal framework for regularizing and even sanctifying such relationships.

It should be noted, though, that Rabbi Arthur Waskow has suggested precisely this legal category for another situation—namely, when singles are living together for a period of time but without marriage—and he maintains that the couple themselves must frame the rules that will govern their relationship:

> Notice of a *pilegesh* relationship is given to a face-to-face Jewish community—not to the state—and is defined by the people entering it (e.g., explicitly monogamous or not, explicitly living together or not, explicitly sharing some financial arrangements or not). In this pattern, the community joins in honoring, acting in accord with, and celebrating such arrangements, and there is an easy public form by which either of the parties may dissolve the relationship.[1]

In other words, this is a relationship that is public and real, but it is does not have legal standing in its creation or dissolution.

In his later book, *Down-to-Earth Judaism*, Waskow changes the name of this relationship to a *zug* (couple) relationship, but the rest remains the same.[2] It is not clear whether he himself would be open to the same framework for a couple consisting of one member who is married to someone else, demented though that person be, but his use of concubinage at least indicates that this is one avenue to explore, despite its problems.

Reframing Adultery

In common parlance, adultery is understood to refer to a married person of either gender engaging in sexual activity of any sort with a person other than his or her spouse. Because adultery is a capital offense in Jewish law, however, and because the Rabbis tried to narrow the application of the death penalty as much as possible, they determined that the category of adultery applies only when a married woman is engaged in sex with a man other than her husband and where there is vaginal penetration (*Mishneh Torah, Hilchot Isurei Biah* 1:10–11). (A married man engaged in sex with a woman other than his wife is not construed as an adulterer because originally he could marry more than one woman at a time.) Thus in our case, a woman married to a mentally incompetent man might have an intimate relationship with another man without vaginal penetration and thus avoid the stigma of violating the prohibition against adultery as it is defined by Jewish law.

In some ways, this is parallel to the responsum in the Conservative Movement that permitted Conservative rabbis to officiate at the unions of gay men.[3] The Talmud defines the ban on homosexual relations to apply only to men engaged in anal sex. Other forms of homosexual activity by either men or women were prohibited by Rabbinic authority. The responsum therefore leaves in place the biblical ban on anal sex by men but removes the Rabbinic additions to that ban in the name of *k'vod hab'riyot*, human dignity, for which reason the Talmud itself gives rabbis the power to override other Rabbinic enactments. Furthermore, in line with this underlying value, the responsum makes clear that what happens in a person's bedroom is private.

In the case of homosexual sex, Rabbis Dorff, Nevins, and Reisner suggested this solution because, short of a *takanah*, there does not appear to be any other legal way to permit gay unions, and the Jewish value of *k'vod hab'riyot* (human dignity) and modern scientific research present compelling reasons to do that. In our situation, however, there seem to be other solutions, as we describe herein, so one may be reticent to invoke this one. After all, this approach involves ignoring the intent, if not the letter, of the Jewish prohibition of adultery. Still, it does offer us another Jewish value to consider, *k'vod hab'riyot*, the human dignity of the partner, which, in this case, would require that Sarah and David need not hide their loving relationship from the larger community.

Reframing Divorce

In traditional Jewish law, only a man can initiate a divorce. The Talmud discusses a case of a man who is demented, making it legally impossible for him to divorce his wife so that she can marry someone else. The Talmud notes that in some cases the man may be mentally lucid on some occasions and not so on others (*"itim halim, itim shoteh"*), and it asserts that anything he does in his lucid moments is considered as if he is always lucid (Babylonian Talmud, *Rosh HaShanah* 28a, *Y'vamot* 113b; *Shulchan Aruch*, *Even HaEizer* 121:3). The accepted practice, then, is to get him to appoint an agent to divorce his wife during one of his lucid moments so that the agent can then complete the divorce proceedings in his name and she can remarry. This presumes what we often find to be the case—namely, that couples who have loved each other for decades continue to want what is best for each other in sickness or old age, even when that means, because of the mental incompetence of one, that the other wants to marry someone else to satisfy his or her needs for companionship when the demented spouse can no longer be an intimate companion.

The Talmud's legal solution to that situation is divorce. It is silent about any further care that the person might offer his or her demented and now divorced spouse. Still, given that we are talking about people who care for each other, some arrangement was probably created whereby the former spouse continued to provide care for the demented partner, either personally or through the agency of others.

This kind of continuing care and even love despite divorce is also evident in another situation common during the Middle Ages, when many Jewish men earned a living through the import/export trade that required them to go on long trips for commercial purposes. Such trips were fraught with danger: ships sometimes sank, some were attacked by pirates, and even on land, men carrying goods or money were prime targets for thieves who might not only steal from them, but kill them. Therefore before leaving on such a trip, or before being drafted into the king's army for a war, a Jewish man who loved his wife and fully wanted to live the rest of his life married to her nevertheless gave her a conditional divorce (*get al t'nai*), such that if he did not return by a specified time, she was divorced and could legally marry someone else (*Shulchan Aruch, Even HaEizer* 143:1, 144:1). Alternatively, he could appoint an agent before he left to give her a writ of divorce if he did not return within a specified period of time (ibid., 144:5–6). Such divorces were clearly acts of love rather than the legal result of discord and a desire for separation.

One major problem with divorce as an option is the patriarchal nature of Jewish divorce: only a man can initiate it. What if the demented partner is the man and he has not made provisions for a conditional *get*?

A possible response might be to consider the healthy woman as "chained" to the mentally incompetent husband. In traditional Jewish law, if a woman's husband cannot give his wife a Jewish writ of divorce (a *get*) because, for example, his whereabouts are unknown or because he is mentally incompetent, or if he refuses to give his wife a *get*, she is an *agunah*, "chained" to her husband and unable to remarry. In our situation, the woman is legally chained to her husband, who lacks the mental capacity to perform any legal act, including divorce; she therefore cannot remarry, and any intimate relationship she has with another man is adultery. Men are never in this category in Jewish law because a man can give his wife a *get*, and if she refuses to accept it or legally cannot accept it due to mental incapacity, he can deliver it to the rabbinic court, which will hold it for her until such time as she chooses to or can accept it, even if that is never. In the meantime, he may remarry.

Since the 1950s, the Conservative rabbinate has devised ways of freeing women from the status of *agunah*. In 1954, Professor Saul Lieberman of the Jewish Theological Seminary of America proposed that a clause be inserted in the marriage contract (the *ketubah*) according to which the couple agrees that if their marriage is dissolved by the civil courts, they will follow the instructions of the rabbinic court to end their Jewish marriage. The rabbinic court, of course, will instruct the man to issue a *get*. This solution, however, depends on the assistance of secular courts to enforce this prenuptial agreement, and some have balked at doing that for fear of violating the separation of church and state. It also inserts into the contract of marriage a clause that anticipates divorce, which may be emotionally jarring to the marrying couple.

Therefore, in response to these problems, in 1969 the Rabbinical Assembly adopted a new document separate from the *ketubah* that both members of the couple sign before being married. The document imposes a condition on their marriage (*t'nai b'kiddushin*), an approach now used by some Orthodox rabbis as well. By signing the document, the couple (and especially the man) agrees that if their marriage is later dissolved by the civil courts and the man issues a *get* to his wife within six months thereafter, then the marriage is a marriage in Jewish law. If he fails to do that, however, then the marriage is annulled from its very beginning. This does not impugn the Jewish legal status of their children; they are not illegitimate (*mamzerim*), because that status applies only to children born of an incestuous or adulterous union. In 1986, the CCAR Responsa Committee dealt with the case of a sixty-three-year-old man with Alzheimer's who was no longer aware of his surroundings. The cost of his care was not covered by insurance, so his wife had been counseled to seek a legal divorce in order to protect her resources so she would not have to turn to her children or to others for charity. Although the responsum acknowledged that there are halachic grounds for divorcing a demented spouse, it maintained that it is still morally wrong to do so. The responsum urged that some way be found not to bankrupt the healthy spouse in the care of the demented one, but it does not suggest how that might be done.[4] Our case is different; the motivation is not financial but rather the need for the healthy partner to have intimacy in her life.

The difficulty, though, with using divorce or annulment as the solution for Saul or Sarah is that divorce is typically the response only when the couple has at least irreconcilable differences and sometimes when the situation between them is much worse. But Saul and Sarah hold no rancor for each other, only sadness, loneliness, and still love. So although divorce settles the legal issues nicely, freeing Sarah to remarry without engaging in adultery—or, if the situation were reversed, freeing Saul to remarry without committing bigamy—it might feel inappropriate emotionally because it misstates the nature of the emotional connections that continue to exist between them, concretized by their mutual promise to continue to provide loving, ongoing care and financial support.

A Ritual Response

This challenge can be addressed through the thoughtful joining of new ritual with sensitivity to Jewish law and tradition. By reframing this kind of divorce as a *get al t'nai*, a healthy couple could proactively make clear what their wishes would be if this situation arose. Ideally, the couple would make this arrangement known to their children long before the document would be applicable so that everyone involved would understand the love that motivates it.

Jewish tradition teaches that God is present in every moment; we acknowledge God's presence by blessing, ritual, and ceremony. These spiritual practices both reflect and reframe the values of our tradition, and they give us direction as to how to think about the transitions we are experiencing. Traditional Jewish life-cycle rituals of *b'rit milah*, bar mitzvah, marriage (sometimes divorce), and funeral reflect the life of a male heterosexual who probably did not live very long. While one could certainly argue that there are many other rituals that our tradition offers connected to other moments of transition that expand the range of the life cycle (e.g., affixing a mezuzah when moving into a new home; expressing gratitude for surviving an illness [*Birkat HaGomeil*]), the modern claim that all of our experiences are Jewish experiences and therefore deserve to be acknowledged through ritual suggests that we turn to creating new rituals to help us think about this transition as well.

There is danger in creating new rituals, as Barbara Myerhoff has pointed out, because they may feel inauthentic or artificial.[5] The most successful and authentic new rituals are ones that echo the power of more familiar rituals and link us to the cosmic narrative of our people reflected in Torah. One new ritual has come to be called "a reaffirmation of vows." Through it the partners in a couple reaffirm their commitment to each other at various stages in their lives. Often these ceremonies are very similar to a traditional wedding, with chuppah, wine, and an exchange of gifts, all in the presence of family and friends. Other times it is a more private reaffirmation, in the quiet of a rabbi's study. Often it involves a restatement of vows in the form of a new *ketubah*, reaffirming earlier commitments and articulating new promises that emerge out of the changing circumstances of their lives.[6]

Our vision is that this kind of ceremony would incorporate a version of a *get al t'nai* into the new covenant or *ketubah*. The couple would explicitly state that should either become so demented as to be unable to recognize their partner as their spouse, a *get* would be enacted, and the healthy spouse would be free to remarry. At the same time, the terms of the *get* would specifically include the requirement of the healthy partner to continue to provide for the ongoing care of the demented partner. This clause would be framed as a reflection of the love they feel for each other—both wanting the healthy person to have a full life and at the same time ensuring the ongoing care and support we appropriately expect from someone who loves us. Because this promise is made in the presence of family, including adult children, should that time ever come the family understands that this is what each partner freely chose.

One might argue that this clause should be part of every *ketubah*. Certainly that too is an option. But in our view, the power of a mature couple who have been together for some time beginning to reflect together and with their families about the changes that might be in store for them as they grow old is somehow more authentic, growing as it does from mature love and the blessing of an important conversation about what may happen in the not-too-distant future.

If that moment should ever come, after a doctor and a rabbi are consulted to determine that the partner really is unable to recognize the spouse, we envision a new ceremony with the rabbi and the immediate family. As the healthy partner removes his or her wedding ring or perhaps moves it to a different finger, he or she might recite words as simple as "We are grateful to You for the blessing of love and for reminding us that it is not good for a person to be alone." In this way, by combining Jewish law, Jewish values, and new ritual, the healthy partner is free not only to enter into a new relationship that may become intimate, but also, once a civil divorce has been completed, legally to marry a new partner as confirmed by both civil and Jewish law.

It is also possible that instead of a new legal marriage with the sanction of civil and Jewish law, some couples might choose instead to create a ceremony that does not represent marriage but rather a different kind of committed relationship. This choice might be emotionally easier, given the ongoing prior commitment of one partner to his or her former spouse. In that case the symbols of a traditional wedding ought not to be employed, so as to make perfectly clear that this new relationship is to be understood not as a marriage but rather as a different kind of partnership, but still one that is worthy of communal recognition and blessing. Depending on what the couple decides to do, there may be problems in both civil and Jewish law with this kind of arrangement. Rabbis in the United States may not participate in a marriage ceremony without a state license. The concern seems to be that the decision not to register the marriage might derive from a desire to avoid changes in their monetary arrangements or in their Social Security status and would therefore constitute fraud against the government. If a couple chooses this option, they should consult a lawyer to make sure that they are not violating civil law.

Sarah and Saul never had this conversation. But in coming to her rabbi, she found the courage to talk with her children, family, and friends about what was really happening in her life. Over time, they came to support her in her decision to open her heart to David, who supported her in her promise to continue to care for Saul.

Although Sarah and Saul never had this conversation, many of us still can. Conversations about the challenges of this next stage of life might well be difficult, but through employing Jewish values, Jewish law, and Jewish ritual in the way we suggest above, we can touch the divinity that is present in all the experiences of our lives and remind ourselves how Judaism brings meaning and purpose to our lives.

NOTES

1. Arthur Waskow, "Down-to-Earth Judaism: Sexuality," *Tikkun* 3, no. 2 (March/April 1988), 46–49; reprinted in Elliot N. Dorff and Louis E. Newman, *Contemporary Jewish Ethics and Morality: A Reader* (New York: Oxford University Press, 1995), 291–92.

2. Arthur Waskow, *Down-to-Earth Judaism* (New York: William Morrow, 1995), 319.

3. *Contemporary American Reform Responsa*, ed. Walter Jacob (New York: Central Conference of American Rabbis, 1987), 144–46. See Elliot N. Dorff, Daniel S. Nevins, and Avram I. Reisner, "Homosexuality, Human Dignity, and Halakhah," http://www.rabbinicalassembly.org/sites/default/files/public/halakhah/teshuvot/20052010/dorff_nevins_reisner_dignity.pdf.

4. *Contemporary American Reform Responsa*, 86.

5. Barbara Myerhoff, *Number Our Days* (New York: Simon and Schuster, 1978), 86.

6. While a traditional wedding ceremony likens the couple to Adam and Eve in the Garden of Eden, a reaffirmation ceremony might liken the couple to Abram and Sarai responding to God's call to "go to a place where I will show you, and you will be a blessing" (Gen. 12:1–2). Notice that Abram and Sarai are older when this call comes to them and that they (or at least Abram) make a covenant with God. So this new ceremony of reaffirmation of vows that could take place around a significant anniversary might involve the couple creating together a new covenant for the next stage of their lives.

We wish to acknowledge our debt to Rabbi Richard Address, who pointed to this dilemma. See his *Seekers of Meaning* (New York: URJ Press, 2012) and his article "Till Death Us Do Part? A Look at Marriage Rituals When a Partner Has Alzheimer's Disease," *Generations: A Journal of the American Society on Aging*, Fall 2011, which has been adapted for inclusion in this volume (see pages 537–47, above). We are also indebted to Professor Emerita Grace Blumberg of the UCLA School of Law for helping us with the aspects of civil law relevant to the various possibilities we discuss.

PERSONAL REFLECTIONS

PERSONAL REFLECTION

Sexuality on Campus—Notes from the Field

LIYA RECHTMAN

I entered college on the eve of the SlutWalk revolution. Only a few months earlier a twelve-year-old girl had been repeatedly assaulted in Texas, and the newspaper reporting on it cited as a possible motive the fact that she was wearing makeup. While I was grappling with how to refuse the boys lining the sweat-infused walls of college parties, women around the world began to organize in a rejection of victim-blaming and woman-shaming. As I was trying to figure out who and what I was as a college student, thousands were holding SlutWalks, mobbing the streets of cities from Toronto to Bhopal in defense of a woman's right to dress and act as she chose. Our mothers invented the Take Back the Night rallies of the 1970s and '80s; for my generation, as I was soon to learn, SlutWalks became the rallying cry of women fighting back against sexual violence.

Sexuality on campus was a complicated terrain, enticing and alluring, but also dangerous. There was a sense that we had all taken health education somewhere along the road, and now we were old enough simultaneously to have completely forgotten what we had learned and to do what we liked. There was a great rush of liberation in knowing that our parents weren't waiting up for us at the end of the night, and in believing that we were immortal and in control of our actions. Walking into a party, trying to breathe in the overwhelming heat of a packed cement box, the trick was to get a glance at a boy's face before he grabbed you from behind and pushed you against a wall, or your friend, or—if you were really unlucky—the speaker system. There wasn't really time to talk about consent, or caring for one's body, or really communicating at all, before you were spun around by your waist and landed with your tongue stuck down the beer-and-punch-encrusted throat of a stranger.

As I tried to navigate the complexity of sexual behavior, culture, and expectations on campus, I was also confronted with the realization that this was the first time that I was not involved in a formal Jewish education program. After a lifetime of religious school leading up to becoming bat mitzvah, I had participated in the confirmation and then post-confirmation programs at my synagogue, in addition to being involved with NFTY and serving on my temple youth group board. Despite the fact that the majority of my high school classmates were Jewish, I alone held the prestigious title of "resident Jew." Up until that point, Judaism had informed every aspect of the way I experienced the world. But college was different. On my first Shabbat, I tried to follow the chalked Jewish stars down the road to the Hillel dinner but was forced to give up once it started to rain. Later, when I finally found my way there, it was a shock to realize that my Jewish community suddenly wasn't composed of friends I had had since third grade and, secondarily, was neither Reform nor feminist. At the time that I arrived, the senior members were debating in earnest whether to put up a *m'chitzah* during prayer; I looked around and realized I was the only woman in the room.

Judaism on campus wasn't feminist enough for me, and the social scene certainly wasn't Jewish or woman-positive. There was a community, though, of which I came to be proud to call myself a member: the on-campus world of sexual respect advocacy. As women on my college campus were going public with stories of rape and sexual violence, and the deplorable lack of support from the college, we fought the administration for more equitable policies; we studied up on everything from male privilege to trauma theory; we wrote treaties and petitions, articles and blog posts about what it meant to be a college-age woman and to be systematically oppressed and limited in our access to education by intimidating and disrespectful classmates and professors alike. And slowly, by writing, petitioning, studying, and arguing, I learned a little about what it meant to be a woman, what it meant to be in college, and what Judaism could offer to the reality I faced.

I found my way to Hillel, eventually. I even started teaching at the local Hebrew school twice a week. At twenty years old I suddenly became responsible for the last frontier of prayer Hebrew education before *b'nei mitzvah* for a classroom full of lively, energetic Jewish sixth graders. Meanwhile, my campus began to boil over with anger toward the administration about sexual assault and identity politics as painful as when they were first introduced in the 1960s. My time was split between meetings on campus climate and writing lessons plans on the Torah service. I felt torn and, subsequently, sought points of connections between the two.

"We cannot stand idly by," I found myself explaining to a physics professor and half of the seniors on the hockey team during a school-wide Day of Dialogue. "We are charged with the maintenance of our bodies and a respect for the bodies of others," I told an open forum on sexual misconduct, muttering to myself "*sh'mirat haguf*" as I sat back down. And finally, in the most personal and intense of conversations when handling these issues, I searched for words and found myself saying to someone, "If you're not for yourself, who will be? And if not now, then when? (*Pirkei Avot*, 1:14) You need to tell someone what happened to you."

SlutWalks are one way that my generation has chosen to fight back against the abuse of women and to regain control over our sexuality. For me, my personal response has found a source in my Judaism, which has taught me to stand up for myself and to pursue justice: *Tzedek, tzedek tirdof* (Deut. 16:20). That is, not just to pursue justice, but to pursue justice and to pursue it twice, over and over again. To repeat, fight, argue, and teach until it makes sense and until I see an impact. I have been in college for nearly three years now and the end—both of unfair policies and my career on campus—is in sight. I am no longer the unconsentingly touched freshman girl lost in the middle of a party while the world outside of campus spins in a feminist, activist haze. I speak, for me, and now, in the pursuit of justice, and I have refused to stand idly by.

PERSONAL REFLECTION

Coming Out All Over Again

RABBI RACHEL GUREVITZ, PHD

"I want to tell you about my son," the father said as he stopped by my office one Sunday morning. "He was just walking down the corridor at school the other day and he saw a girl that he knows from the temple. She had cut off her long hair and had a new, short look. She looked really different, and he noticed that she seemed anxious. So he stopped and said, 'Kim*—you look great! Love the new look!' She gave him such a big smile. She told him that it was a big day for her. Today she was coming out at school. She held her breath. My son gave her a big hug and said, 'That's great. It's just going to get better from here.' Rabbi, I'm telling you this because he shared it with me when I was driving him the other day. And when he'd finished telling me about this exchange at school, he said, 'Dad, I learned that from Rabbi Gurevitz. She helped me see what a difference a friend can make at a time like that.'"

She came up to me in the middle of break one evening at our Hebrew high school. "Rabbi, can I make a time to come and talk to you?" We got together the following week and as she sat down, Jennifer said

* All names have been changed in the vignettes shared.

to me, "So, I'm gay and I have a girlfriend. And that's all fine. But . . . why do I feel like God hates me?"

Two moments from my past few years of congregational life as a rabbi. I'll return to the second moment shortly. But, as I reflect on these experiences, and several others like them, I realize how easily I could have missed them all. And, in doing so, I would have robbed the youth in my community of the pastoral and spiritual support they needed at a crucial turning point in their lives.

I was always "out" in my congregation. I had felt confident enough, during student placement at the end of rabbinical school, that times had changed enough for me to be upfront about that without it impacting my employment prospects. But I wasn't a spokesperson for gay rights. I would gently drop in a reference to my partner during interviews to make it clear that it was just a natural part of the fabric of my life—it wasn't an "issue."

In the first few years of my congregational work, I would choose very carefully when to comment on GLBT-related issues in the context of a sermon or teaching. Often I would let it come from someone else so it didn't appear to be "my issue." But then Tyler Clementi committed suicide at Rutgers University. And the media began to pay more attention to the high proportion of teen suicides who were GLBT youth. And Dan Savage launched the YouTube-based "It Gets Better" campaign to provide opportunities for GLBT adults and their allies to record messages for struggling GLBT youth to show them that there were truly good, wonderful things in life beyond the fears and anxieties they may have been struggling with at any given moment in time.

I realized that I had been doing my community, and especially my teenagers, a disservice. I realized that I had been going out of my way not to bring my sexuality to the attention of my students. So anxious was I not to be regarded by anyone as "promoting homosexuality," I was self-censoring; whereas most heterosexuals wouldn't pause for a moment before saying, "My husband and I just came back from vacation," or "I went to the movies last night with my wife and some friends," I would leave my partner out of my informal conversations.

And the result was that while I was technically "out," most of the youth in my congregation had no idea. And that meant that none of them knew—really knew—that they had an ally and someone who might understand what they were going through. And I needed to change that.

The week after Clementi's death I gave a sermon. I wrote a bulletin article. I wrote a blog piece. And I published an op-ed in the local newspapers. The latter, in particular, was picked up by many of our families and shared with their teenagers. I started to do sessions with our high school students and youth group, speaking about my own journey of coming out, and introducing them to other GLBT members of our congregation. I had students catching me in the corridors, thanking me for the piece that I had written in the papers. And, before long, I had students seeking me out for support or simply to share their story, or a brother or sister's story, with me.

I've stayed connected with many of these young people. Jennifer is now at college, and she is thriving. A year ago she walked into my office wanting to know why it felt like God hated her. We met monthly, and we explored where in society and the media we receive the kinds of messages that make us feel this way. We went on a journey together so that Jennifer could find a personal theology that could enable her to celebrate her uniqueness and truly own her image made *b'tzelem Elohim*—in the image of God—an image that must embrace and include our sexuality too. And how could God hate something that was so essential to our being? Something that, when fully expressed, makes us feel more spiritually whole?

Ten years after I first came out, I found myself coming out all over again. This time around it felt even more profound, even more powerful. This time around it was a *tikkun*—a fixing, a healing, of spirit and of community.

PERSONAL REFLECTION

The Rabbi and the Vibrator

SARAH TUTTLE-SINGER

Ladies, I have some bad news: while it's usually OK to screw your brains out when you're pregnant, using a vibrator may be a little more risky.

It's like this: No matter how incredible and mind-blowing your partner may be in bed (or in the backseat of a car, or in the shower, or on a pool table), orgasms from a vibrator are . . . well . . . more electrifying. It's nothing personal. Anything battery operated that pulsates like one thousand times a second is bound to deliver the goods harder and faster. And this in turn can stimulate uterine contractions.

Well, it was a sad, sad day when I developed uterine irritability during the second trimester of my first pregnancy, and my doctor had to put me on pelvic rest. It was like he had stapled a giant HAZMAT sign to my vag. And so, along with the whole enforced celibacy thing, I was forced to pack up my neon purple iRabbit (and I thought giving up alcohol was hard!) for the sake of my unborn child.

But then, as soon as my doctor gave me the green light, my iRabbit made its triumphant return to my bedside nightstand drawer, where it lived happily ever after . . . until the day of my daughter's *simchat bat*.

My humiliation. Let me tell it to you:

While the guests poured into our home, my daughter and I hung out in the bedroom, waiting to meet with our rabbi to discuss a few things about the ceremony. Now, believe me, our rabbi is *awesome*. I've known him since I was a little girl. He presided over all the services I went to with my family when I was growing up. He told the best Jewish scary stories at sleepaway camp. He officiated at my bat mitzvah. And my mom's funeral.

So, obviously, it seemed fitting that he be part of this rite of passage, as well.

(Can I get a *"L'dor vador,"* people?)

Also? Despite my stint pole dancing at Cat Club in San Francisco when I was twenty-three, and the six weeks I spent dating a guy in the Israeli mafia when I was in high school, I'm basically a nice Jewish girl. I always did the extra-credit assignments during Hebrew school. I never snuck out of my bunk at sleepaway camp. I was even selected to receive a special college scholarship from the synagogue. And the nice Jewish girl in me was happy that my rabbi would see that my then-husband and I were bringing our daughter into the community in such a meaningful way.

("Wait, what does this have to do with vibrators?" I hear you cry. Trust me. I'll tell you.)

The rabbi arrived, greeted us with many *mazal tov*s, and we got down to business. He asked if my daughter was named for anyone special, as is Ashkenazic Jewish custom. And she is. In fact, the poor kid has not one, not two, but *three* names to honor *six* people. Yeah, don't get me started: the birth certificate woman at the hospital wanted to cut me, but whatever—I was still high from the epidural and reeling in melodrama.

Given the long list of family members we chose to honor when naming our baby, the rabbi stood up and said he needed a pen and paper to write it all down. And before I could stop him, he reached over to open the bedside drawer.

Now, let's get something straight: I do not have a pen in my bedside drawer.

Nor do I have paper.

Instead, I have a bottle of K-Y Jelly, enough Trojans to reconquer Troy, and my neon-purple iRabbit vibrator.

As clichéd as it may sound, it really was like the whole thing happened in slow motion. I tried to block him, but I was still a little unstable with the baby in my arms. And so, I had to make a split-second decision: either I drop my daughter on the floor and keep my secrets safe in the bedside drawer, or I sacrifice my dignity while keeping my baby girl safe and sound. Well, shalom, dignity. *Vaya con dios*, and don't let the door hit your ass on the way out.

To make matters worse, I'm pretty much a slam-bam-thank-you-iRabbit kind of gal, so I'm not always careful when I put my vibrator away. When the rabbi grabbed the knob and pulled, the drawer stuck.

At first, I thought I was saved.

But then, with a mighty hand and an outstretched arm, the rabbi yanked the drawer open, and in the process activated the iRabbit's on-switch. Whirring, buzzing, and gyrating, this vibrator, unlike so many smaller, more discreet models, leaves very little to the imagination. It comes complete with a fairly girthy shaft and a well-formed glans, and why yes, it does appear to be circumcised.

The rabbi slammed the drawer shut and we both pretended that we couldn't hear the rhythmic buzzing as we continued to discuss the upcoming ceremony.

"So, her first name is in honor of your mother, may she be of blessed memory?" He shouted, taking on his yarmulke's festive shade of burgundy as the vibrator bumped in the drawer, and the entire bedside table shook.

"Yes!" I yelled back.

And as the vibrator did a bump and grind against the drawer, my entire Jewish life flashed before my eyes. Sunday school story time in the synagogue sanctuary. Reciting the *alef-bet* at Hebrew school. Singing "Hineih Mah Tov" around the campfire at sleepaway camp in Malibu. Reading from the Torah during my bat mitzvah. Singing in the choir on Chanukah.

But still, even though I was mortified, I reveled in the complexity of the moment. Because guess what: you can be a nice Jewish girl and a mother and still have a vibrator.

Just ask my rabbi.

Part Six

There Be Dragons:
Issues, Ethics, and Boundaries

In medieval maps, the edges of the known world were sometimes marked, "There be dragons." Our ancestors did not know what would await them in the areas that remained unmapped. In exploring Jewish perspectives on sexuality, we too are making a map. Some boundaries are clear, delineating permitted from forbidden, right from wrong. Others are more permeable, stretching us to the limits of our understanding. Part 6 brings us to the complex cartography of sexuality, mapping out power and pleasure—territories known and unknown.

We begin with the assertion that certain boundaries can be transgressed, with egregious consequences and the need for response. Rabbi Stephen J. Einstein discusses the possibility of repentance, with special attention to rabbinic boundary crossing, in his essay "The Role of *T'shuvah* in Sexual Transgressions." Next, in "I Do? Consent and Coercion in Sexual Relations," Rabbi Mark Dratch shares his comprehensive study of marital rape and sexual violence. "While respect and dignity should define all human dealings," he writes, "they are essential in sexual interactions." Rabbi Leigh Lerner continues this theme in his sobering and fascinating essay, "Sex Trafficking and Sex Slavery: History, Halachah, and Current Issues," including characters such as the early Reform rabbinic campaigner against sex trafficking known as "Alphabet Browne." Rabbi Lerner also touches on some of the debate around this issue, through his discussion of statements from various arms of the Reform Movement, as well as the situation in Israel, Canada, and the United States.

The next two essays present case studies of sexuality in radically different milieus. In "The Impact of Catastrophe on Jewish Sexuality: Jewish Displaced Persons in Occupied Germany, 1945–1950," Dr. Margarete Myers Feinstein brings together original accounts of postwar sexual encounters between Jewish women and Allied military personnel, Jewish men and German women, and same-sex encounters—some of which were consensual, and some of which were not. She also brings to light issues of premarital sex and pregnancy, family purity, and divorce. In this complicated landscape, "sex after the Shoah was fraught with meaning: freedom and revenge, victimhood and survival, corruption and continuity." From here, we turn to Rabbi Dana Evan Kaplan and Dr. Karen Carpenter's essay, "Questioning Sexuality in Reform Carribean Judaism: Two Perspectives," presenting a rabbi and a sexologist's perspectives. They compare the varied models of sexuality in Caribbean culture and ask what contributions the Jewish Jamaican community might make. The single similarity between these two essays is the question of how Jewish values play out in previously uncharted territory.

Closer to home, my essay, "What Not to Wear: Synagogue Edition," struggles with the question of whether the traditional Jewish value of modesty can be applied to what people wear in Reform congregations. Acutely aware of the restrictive and misogynistic ways in which these rules have been applied (as per Rabbi Dalia Marx's personal reflection earlier in the book), I try to find guidance for contemporary liberal concerns. The remainder of the essays in part 6 explore other boundary issues for which there are more questions than answers. In "Sex and Technology: Creating Sacred Space in Cyberspace," Rabbi Elizabeth S. Wood and Dr. Debby Herbenick explore this issue with an awareness of the opportunities and challenges posed by modern technology. Rabbi Jonathan K. Crane's essay, "Judaism and Pornography," shows the extent to which the Jewish textual tradition contains "diverse legal positions and moral opinions about sexually explicit speech," sometimes permitting and even encouraging various forms of erotic expression. Rabbi Edythe Held Mencher continues the discussion with her essay, "Jewish Views on Sexual Fantasy and Desire," which explores sexual desire in writings from Genesis to *Fifty Shades of Grey* and probes the line between fantasy and reality.

In one of the most thought-provoking pieces in the book, "Release from Bondage: Sex, Suffering, and Sanctity," Rabbi Daniel A. Lehrman also touches on *Fifty Shades of Grey*, not because it is timeless literature but because as a best seller it raises bondage/discipline sadism/masochism (BDSM) as a "frontier of sexuality" in our contemporary culture. Rabbi Lehrman challenges us to approach this frontier "from a perspective in which good and bad are not the primary categories." Moreover, he suggests that the notion of surrender and the dissolution of boundaries in BDSM can be connected to mystical teachings about surrender of the boundaries of selfhood for the sake of spiritual union with God. From biblical sacrifice to children and grandchildren of survivors taking on their concentration camp numbers as tattoos, Rabbi Lehrman explores the paradoxical intersection of suffering and sanctity.

Like this section as a whole, the personal reflections represent a wide range of issues and approaches. In "Queering *T'shuvah* for Everyone," Dr. Jay Michaelson argues that "Queer spiritual consciousness is inherently distrustful because it has seen how rules, codes, and even the operation of conscience itself can be tools of oppression and self-repression." In other words, the existence of oppressive religious boundaries leads to skepticism about boundaries as a whole. He suggests a model of grounded discernment and spiritual practice to distinguish right from wrong. In creative tension with this approach, Rabbi David Dunn Bauer shows how Jewish texts can in fact be a meaningful guide, even in the wake of the damage done by the traditional use, and abuse, of religious teachings. In his aptly titled essay, "Choose Life (and

Be Not a Skunk)!" Rabbi Bauer quotes authorities from the Torah to Pépé Le Pew on desire, to examine how "the same impulse propels us both to achieve and to run amok." How do we recognize the pull of our hearts and our eyes in a way that empowers us but does not endanger us? How do we explore the edges of the map without getting too close to the dragons? These are some of the many questions with which we go forth from the pages of this book, to the landscape of our lives.

40

THE ROLE OF *T'SHUVAH* IN SEXUAL TRANSGRESSIONS

RABBI STEPHEN J. EINSTEIN, DHL, DD

> Return to Me, and I will return to you.
> (Malachi 3:7)

More Jews attend synagogue services on Yom Kippur than on any other day of the year. It is, therefore, a safe assumption that the concept of *t'shuvah*, repentance, as a key religious teaching of Judaism is well known.

Western culture often seems to equate *sin* with *sex*. So, one would expect that the list of sins that comprise our Yom Kippur confession would be heavily weighted toward sexual transgressions. In actuality, they make up a very small number.

Yet, the choice that our Sages, of blessed memory, selected as the Torah reading for Yom Kippur afternoon is Leviticus 18, which outlines forbidden sexual relations. In the *Koren Sacks Yom Kippur Mahzor*, Rabbi Jonathan Sacks notes that—commenting on this choice—Rashi declares, "Sexual sins are common and the desire to commit them is part of the human condition." Sacks further cites Maimonides's teaching that "sexual desire is, for most people and in all eras, the strongest of all inclinations to sin."[1]

We certainly understand that misdeeds in this arena can wreak havoc on our own lives and on the lives of our families, friends, and communities. So, it behooves us to pay close attention to any such misbehavior on our part.

I am writing this chapter from a particular perspective. For the past six years, I have served as chair of the Ethics Committee of the Central Conference of American Rabbis. While I understand that readers are not limited to rabbis or synagogue members, I am basing my approach on the experience I have had in dealing with rabbinic boundary crossing—an action that every human has the potential of committing. I must note how seriously the CCAR considers the matter of rabbinic boundary crossing. Such egregious behavior on the part of a rabbi undermines a congregant's relationship with Judaism . . . and, possibly, even to God.

Maimonides, in his *Mishneh Torah: Sefer HaMada—Hilchot T'shuvah*, outlines the process of repentance. One must be truly sorry for the misbehavior, confess it to God, and vow not to repeat it. Forgiveness must be sought from the person harmed, and restitution made. The process can be understood to have been successful if one is faced with a similar set of circumstances and does not repeat the wrong action.

The CCAR Code of Ethics for Rabbis is based on the Maimonidean approach. It calls for a fundamental change in behavior and understanding. Rabbis who have been disciplined for serious breaches must unequivocally acknowledge their responsibility for harm done and must show remorse to those who have been harmed. They must resolve never to repeat such an offense and are to make restitution. All of this is done under the guidance of a team of rabbinic *t'shuvah*-rehabilitation counselors. An appropriate course of therapy or remediation by a specialized professional is also part of the program.

Of course, a fundamental question needs to be raised: Is *t'shuvah* really possible? While it may be true that a leopard cannot change its spots, human beings are not leopards! Judaism asserts that true repentance *is* possible . . . possible, but not automatic. Saying the words and going through the motions is not enough. A real change of heart is necessary—necessary, but not sufficient. The change of heart must lead to a change in behavior. Failing that, *t'shuvah* has not occurred.

I will cite three specific cases that illustrate the effectiveness—or ineffectiveness—of *t'shuvah*. To protect confidentiality, details will—of necessity—be minimal.

Case 1: There had been rumors of prior indiscretions on the part of this rabbi, but no ethics charges had ever been filed. Finally, a complaint was received and found to be valid. The rabbi completed the prescribed work with the rabbinic *t'shuvah* counselors, as well as regularly scheduled psychotherapy. As a result, he was considered rehabilitated. Not long thereafter, another complaint was filed against him. Though the two complainants did not know one another, the specific actions described were nearly identical. Of great concern was the timing. This misbehavior occurred precisely during the period the rabbi was being mentored by his *t'shuvah* counselors. Very clearly, no real *t'shuvah* had taken place. This individual is no longer a member of the CCAR.

Case 2: There had never been a suspicion of sexual misconduct by this rabbi. However, when a charge of boundary crossing was lodged against him, he readily—and with great remorse—admitted to his wrongful behavior. He chose not to go through the formal process of rehabilitation, but rather to resign from the CCAR. He has told me that he is in therapy. Had he remained a member, a team of rabbinic colleagues could have guided him to full repentance. Should he request reinstatement in the CCAR, such a mentoring team would be assigned. The rabbi would have to be recommended by those mentors before he could regain membership.

Case 3: This rabbi was what might be termed a serial womanizer. Faithfulness to his spouse had not been part of his lifestyle. When this came to light, there was serious questioning as to whether he could really change. A decision was made to assist him to do so. For five years, a dedicated team of rabbinic mentors guided him. This individual truly understood the pain he had caused and was committed to ending his destructive behavior. After half-a-decade of concentrated effort, with the approval of his *t'shuvah* counselors and therapist, he returned to rabbinic service. He has expressed his sincere gratitude for the help he was provided to do *t'shuvah*.

My years on the Ethics Committee have taught me that the Rabbinic notion of *yetzer hara*—the inclination to do wrong—is more than a homiletical device. It is a reality in the life of every person. I worry about anyone who believes that he or she has conquered this inclination. Temptations face us every day, and our sexual desires can be powerful, indeed. If we do not channel them appropriately, we can cause great pain.

The Torah teaches that we were created by God. The day on which humans were created is designated in Genesis as *tov m'od*—very good. As humans, we have the potential to live up to that description. We will not be perfect, but we can become *very good*. When we fail, in any area—but certainly in one so central as sexual standards—we can redirect our actions.

T'shuvah is possible. Indeed it is necessary if we are to become the people we are meant to be.

NOTE

1. *Koren Sacks Yom Kippur Mahzor*, with translation and commentary by Jonathan Sacks (Jerusalem: Koren Publishers, 2012), 993.

41

I DO? CONSENT AND COERCION
IN SEXUAL RELATIONS

Rabbi Mark Dratch

Millions of people a year are the victims of sexual violence. The National Center for Injury Prevention and Control of the Centers for Disease Control reports the following statistics:[1]

About 2 out of 1,000 children in the United States were confirmed by child protective service agencies as having experienced sexual assault in 2003.

Among high school youth nationwide, about 9 percent of students reported that they had been forced to have sexual intercourse.

Among college students nationwide, between 20 and 25 percent of women reported experiencing completed or attempted rape.

Among adults nationwide, more than 300,000 women and over 90,000 men reported being raped in the previous twelve months; one in six women and one in thirty-three men reported experiencing an attempted or completed rape at some time in their lives.

Marital rape, a common form of sexual violence, accounts for approximately 25 percent of all rapes and is experienced by 10 to 14 percent of married women. Shockingly, it was not until July 5, 1993, that marital rape became a crime in all fifty states. In seventeen states and the District of Columbia there are no exemptions from rape prosecution granted to husbands. However, in thirty-three states there are still some exemptions given to husbands from rape prosecution.[2]

How could it be that throughout most of world history, even in countries founded on principles of morality and justice, a husband could rape his wife with impunity? How could it have taken so long for marital rape to become a crime? Chief Justice Sir Matthew Hale of mid-seventeenth-century England explains the position: "The husband cannot be guilty of a rape committed by himself upon his lawful wife, for by their mutual matrimonial consent and contract, the wife hath given up herself in this kind unto her husband, which she cannot retract."

How does Jewish law define the violations of rape, marital rape, and other forms of sexual assault?

The Wrongs of Rape

Rape is forbidden for many reasons.[3] This article will consider a number of explanations: sex, violence, emotional distress, and lack of consent, and then analyze issues of marital rape and sexual violence in a domestic setting.

1. Rape as a Sex Crime

Any sexual or sexualized activity in which nonmarried partners engage, even if it is consensual, is forbidden by Jewish law. According to most authorities, these activities are biblically prohibited. Rambam bases this prohibition on the verse, "There shall not be prostitutes among the daughters of Israel" (Lev. 23:18), explaining that all nonmarital intercourse is, by definition, promiscuous and therefore licentious.[4] Others maintain that only casual promiscuous sex is included in this prohibition; a monogamous relationship between unmarried partners is rabbinically forbidden.[5] Other sources for this proscription include: "Do not prostitute your daughter, to cause her to be a harlot; lest the land fall to harlotry, and the land become full of wickedness" (Lev.

19:29);[6] "When a man marries a woman and has relations with her" (Deut. 24:1), thus positing that marriage is a prerequisite for cohabitation;[7] "You shall not bring the hire of a harlot . . . into the house of the Lord your God for any vow; for these are abominations to the Lord your God" (Deut. 23:19);[8] and the prohibition for contemporaries to have concubines,[9] despite the biblical precedent.[10]

In addition to sexual intercourse, any form of sexual intimacy or sexualized touch between nonmarried partners is forbidden,[11] as is being secluded with most members of the opposite sex.[12]

The words of Rabbi Joseph B. Soloveitchik describe the consequence of inappropriate sexual activity:

> If the sexual impulse is not redeemed and is left in its crudity, the participants in the drama are guilty of an act of mutual exploitation and vulgarization. The corruptions are interlaced and compounded with enslaving a human being, with denying him the most elementary right of personal existence. The person is depersonalized, desensitized and deemotionalized. The climax of the hedonic sexual union is ipso facto an act of objectification of the personal, intimate, and unique.[13]

Notwithstanding the broad prohibition forbidding even consensual relations, there are a number of reasons to discuss the issue of rape: (1) to serve as a backdrop to better understand our subject of sexual violence in marriage; (2) to acknowledge that there is a qualitative difference between consensual and forced sex, even if both are prohibited, and to explore the nature and consequences of this distinction; and (3) to articulate an appropriate Jewish response to rape in a society in which most sexual practices do not conform to Jewish law.

The Talmud describes the psychological dysfunction that may motivate a person to desire illicit sex as "stolen waters [that to him] are sweet, and bread eaten in secret [which to him] is pleasant" (Prov. 9:17). This *yetzer hara* (evil inclination) is a drive that may overwhelm him into feeling that he is unable to control his passions. This is no excuse. There is no justification for engaging in any form of forbidden sexual activity and no license is ever granted to do so:

> Rav Yehudah said in Rav's name: A man once conceived a passion for a certain woman and his heart was consumed by his burning desire (even to the point of his life being endangered). When the doctors were consulted, they said, "His only cure is that she shall submit [to him sexually]." Thereupon the Sages said: "Let him die rather than that she should yield." Then [the doctors said], "Let her stand nude before him." [The Sages answered,] "Sooner let him die." Said the doctors, "Let her (at least) converse with him from behind a fence." The Sages replied, "Let him die rather than she should converse with him from behind a fence."[14]

In one's understanding this Talmudic passage, there is a difference of opinion as to whether the Sages were considering a case in which a married woman or a single woman was the subject of this wanton lust. All agree that any sexualization of a married woman is subsumed under the prohibition of adultery. Those who apply this prohibition to the objectification of a single woman do so in order to protect her welfare and security, as well as to maintain the dignity and honor of all women and to promote a proper societal sexual ethic.[15]

The obligation to prevent a man from raping a married woman,[16] committing incest, or molesting a child stems from the would-be perpetrator's designation as a *rodeif* (pursuer). This designation of the abuser as *rodeif* mandates doing anything necessary to prevent the offense—even killing him if that is the only way to prevent him from committing a sexual assault.[17] Although one who sexually assaults another without genital penetration technically does not come under the category of *rodeif*,[18] he is considered a *rodeif* because of our concern for the victim, in this instance, specifically the psychological trauma and depression she suffers.[19]

2. Rape as Violence

The Torah explicitly compares rape to murder, "for as when a man rises against his neighbor and slays him, so is this matter" (Deut. 22:26).[20] Simply put, rape is a physical and emotional assault on a woman that has a devastating impact on her physical, psychological, and sexual well-being.

The comparison to murder also defines rape as a form of violent assault and battery. Now, while all physical assaults can be located on a continuum which begins with relatively minor physical attacks such as slapping and which culminates in the extreme of murder, there are clear differences between battery and murder. Lesser acts of violence differ not only in the severity of the damage they cause but also in the punishment they invoke. Murder results in the death penalty; assault engenders payments in five areas: damage, pain, healing, lost wages, and shame.[21]

Rape is a form of *chabalah* (assault)[22] which, like other forms of *chabalah*, invokes financial liabilty. Not only must the rapist pay the fifty silver-piece fine mentioned in the Torah,[23] but he must also pay for the pain, shame, and character degradation that he caused.[24] These additional payments make no distinction between the rape of a virgin and the rape of a nonvirgin.[25]

In defining the nature of the physical pain cased by rape, the Talmud rejects the suggestion that it refers to any accompanying brutality[26] and focuses on what it cites as the essential difference between forced and unforced intercourse: *pisuk raglayim* (the spreading of the legs).[27] *Pisuk raglayim* refers to more than a woman's position during sexual intercourse; otherwise one might come to the absurd conclusion that every sexual act is an act of violence. It refers to the coerced and violent physical assault perpetrated by forced genital penetration.

By the defining of the act of rape as violence and assault, rape is removed from the category of sex altogether. In other words, rape is not sex that happens to be perpetrated by force. Rape is assault. And the act of imposed penetration is itself a violent act regardless of the nature of the circumstances that accompany it, that is, whether or not the rapist hit her or held a gun to her head.[28]

While this definition of rape is useful from both legal and political perspectives—it has helped rally communities to pass stricter rape laws and helped the masses understand the horrendous nature of rape—many argue that it is insufficient and problematic as well. While the "rape as violence" theory places the blame where it belongs—on the rapist—it ignores the fact that even if it is not a sexual act, it is an act of sex, and it ignores the impact of this unique violation on the victim. It does not distinguish between sexual violence and nonsexual violence. And it should. For the victim, being sexually molested is qualitatively different from being punched in the nose. And for the perpetrator, the difference is that he chose to act in a sexual manner, in addition to being physically hostile and coercive.

3. Rape as Emotional Distress

Victims of rape are impacted in many ways. In addition to suffering physical injury, they suffer great distress living with the memory of what happened to them, worrying about the risk of pregnancy and disease, and living with feelings of guilt, shame, and self-loathing. Victims often blame themselves for succumbing to the rape. And there is a high rate of Post-Traumatic Distress Syndrome, 49 percent higher than victims of other forms of violence.[29]

Ann Cahill describes the emotional impact of rape:

> In the act of rape, the assailant reduces the victim to a non-person. He (for the overwhelming majority of rapists are male, another aspect of the sexually differentiated nature of the act) denies the victim the specificity of her (for the overwhelming majority of rape victims are female) own being and constructs her sexuality as a mere means by which his own purposes, be they primarily sexual or primarily motivated by the need for power, are achieved. . . . The victim's difference from the assailant—her ontological, ethical, and personal distinctness—is stamped out, erased, annihilated.[30]

Jewish law prohibits emotional assault and abuse. As noted above, in the case of rape, it prescribes payment by the attacker for the shame he caused. In addition, the verse, "You shall not wrong one another; but you shall fear your God; for I am the Lord your God" (Lev. 25:17) prohibits emotional distress.[31] This is referred to as *onaat d'varim* (verbal wronging) and includes any speech or activity that maliciously attacks another's sense of self [32] or causes emotional or psychological pain.[33]

Essentially, *onaah* refers to any form of emotional harm that is brought about by any kind of physical or psychological coercion or oppression.[34]

In addition, rapists also violate "And you shall love your neighbor as yourself" (Lev. 19:18) and "What is hateful to you, do not do to your neighbor."[35]

4. Rape as Lack of Consent

A person who lacks the capacity to give informed consent is considered an *anoos* (one compelled to act unwillingly); he is not liable for his actions, and his contracts are invalid. A person must have the opportunity to choose freely without "any feeling of constraint interfering with the freedom of his will."[36]

Likewise, consent is an essential element in all sexual activity. Judaism insists that all intimacy between husband and wife be consensual.[37]

What constitutes consent? An initial glance at the Bible seems to suggest that lack of protest implies consent. Deuteronomy 22:23–27 states:

> If a girl who is a virgin is betrothed to a husband, and a [different] man finds her in the city, and lies with her; then you shall bring them both out to the gate of that city, and you shall stone them with stones that they die; the girl, because she cried not, being in the city; and the man, because he has afflicted his neighbor's wife; so you shall put away evil from among you.
> But if a man finds a betrothed girl in the field, and the man forces her, and lies with her; then only the man who lay with her shall die; but to the girl you shall do nothing; there is in the girl no sin deserving death; for as when a man rises against his neighbor, and slays him, so is this matter; for he found her in the field, and the betrothed girl cried, and there was no one to save her.

The Torah distinguishes between the responsibility of the victim to cry out in the city and the field, assuming that in the city her pleas will be worthwhile because help is available, while in the field they are not. This distinction is important in understanding the expectations of protest in proving nonconsent. In an unpopulated area a woman need not cry out for help; the cry will not be heard anyway and thus absence of protest is immaterial. In the city, a populated area, it is expected that someone will hear her cry and intervene. Therefore if she does not protest, she must have consented. But this differentiation is not absolute. Even if she is in a populated area, if she suspects that her cries will be ineffective, literally falling on deaf ears because no one will come to her assistance no matter what, then her lack of crying out implies nothing about consent.[38]

In fact, the Talmudic sages castigated those societies that are deaf to the cries of those in need and do not protect their victims. The Sages ascribed moral causes even to natural events and suggested that one of the causes of a solar eclipse is the lack of response by everyone in the city to the screams of a raped woman.[39] The reason is apparently this: the darkness of the night is a time when everyone in the city is sleeping, the windows are closed and the shades are drawn, and no one is aware of her screams. But if, in the middle of the day, no one pays any attention to her cry for help and everyone is as inattentive and unhelpful as they would be in the middle of the night, the city will be stricken with darkness and plunged into the shadows of night. This type of indifference was most grossly expressed on March 13, 1964, when no fewer than thirty-eight neighbors saw or heard Kitty Genovese being attacked in New York City; not one came to her aid. The Genovese Syndrome describes people who were too indifferent, uncaring, or apathetic to get involved and help a fellow human in distress.[40]

While one opinion holds that a rape victim's protest must be continuous from the beginning to the end of the attack, the authoritative position is that an initial protest alone is sufficient to establish nonconsent.[41]

Despite their differences, both of these approaches places the onus of proving lack of consent on the victim herself, a burden that many contemporaries argue is unfair and inappropriate. For one thing, it ignores the responsibility of the rapist. For another, there may be times when a woman is unable to protest or is ineffective in communicating her dissent. Ann Cahill, in her *Rethinking Rape*, argued:

Specifically with regard to rape, consent theory falters on locating the ethical wrong of rape in the absence of the victim's consent. To approach the wrong of rape as embedded in the nonconsensual nature of the act is inevitably to place the ethical burden on the victim. The ethical question that courts must pursue becomes whether the victim sufficiently communicated her nonconsent, or whether that nonconsent was likely given the history of the victim.[42]

Yet, evaluating the presence of any protest may be the only way for judges who, in order to decide the legal consequences of the rape, must determine whether or not the victim consented to the sexual encounter.

Nevertheless, Jewish law understands that there may be times that a woman is unable to protest, and that lack of protest is not necessarily a signal of consent. Rambam writes, for example, that if she was threatened to remain silent while a sword was being held to her throat, absence of protest is not an indication of consent.[43] There are other limitations on her ability to refuse sexual activity and to withstand coercion as well.

What Is Coercion?

Coercion is an act of an agent (the coercer), who aims to secure complying action or activity from another (the coercee), and who does so either by using force or violence to directly alter the behavior of the coercee, or else by imposing a practical necessity upon the coercee by showing a willingness and ability to use force or violence to undermine the coercee's ability to satisfy his or her basic needs.[44]

How does Jewish law define coercion? What are its parameters? Is it coercion if a rapist has no gun or knife but threatens a woman with bodily harm? What if her boss threatens to fire her from her job unless she has sex with him? What if the threats are not made explicitly but she has reasonable grounds to fear retaliation that are implicit in what appears to be a simple request? What if he makes false promises or engages in other deceptions so that she consents without being properly informed of the true circumstances? What if she is seduced by her therapist or physician or teacher or rabbi?

At first glance it appears that threats are not deemed coercive in Jewish law. Sources indicate that an agreement, even if reached under pressure, is valid and effective. For example, the Talmud states that one is not liable for destruction of property based only upon prior threats to do so because "a person often boasts and does not follow through."[45] Elsewhere it is asserted that if a person consents to sell something, even if he consents through fear of physical violence, the sale is valid. This is so because the Talmud views all sales as taking place under compulsion—the seller needs the money; otherwise he would not sell the object.[46]

However, most authorities do not accept this opinion as authoritative and claim that all agreements occasioned by threat or intimidation are invalid.[47] And *Tosafot* rule that the assumption that people do not always follow through on threats does not apply if they are made by those who usually do follow through on them, making them as real and menacing as a knife held to one's throat.[48]

Is it rape if a woman submits because of threats or intimidation that she believes a would-be assailant will carry out? Do the previous arguments that dealt mainly with monetary matters apply to rape?

The Talmud[49] recognizes the coercive nature of threats when it comes to rape. It lists nine categories of objectionable intercourse, one[50] of which includes all forms of coerced sex, whether it is "consented" to out of fear (*eimah*) or whether it is forced upon the victim in an aggressive manner (*anusah*).[51] When subject to pressure, intimidation, and fear, a person is afraid to say no and loses the ability to express any meaningful consent.

Consensual Intercourse, Coerced Intercourse, and Forced Intercourse

Thus Jewish law recognizes three major categories of sexual relations: consensual intercourse, coerced intercourse, and forced intercourse.

1. Consensual Intercourse

It is forbidden for a man to force his wife to have intercourse.[52] Even if she is not forced outright, as long as she is not amenable to intercourse, sexual relations are prohibited.[53] Rambam rules, "[Her husband] should not coerce her [to have relations] when she does not desire to do so. Rather, [they should engage in intercourse only] when there is mutual desire and pleasure."[54] Even if she is ambivalent about her desire, relations are forbidden.[55]

Igeret HaKodesh, chapter 6, ascribed to Ramban, offers the following guidance:

> When a man has relations [with his wife] he should not do so against her will and he should not rape her; the Divine Presence does not abide in such unions in as much as his intentions are in opposition to hers, and she does not consent to his desire. He should not quarrel with her or strike her concerning marital relations. Behold, the Sages said (*P'sachim* 49b), "Just as a lion tears [his prey] and devours it and has no shame, so an *am haaretz* (ignorant boor) strikes and cohabits and has no shame." Instead, he should entice her with kind and alluring words and other appropriate and reputable things. He should not have relations with her while she is sleeping, because their intentions are not united and they are not of the same mind. Rather, he should wake her and arouse her with conversation. The bottom line is this: when a man is sexually aroused, he should make sure that his wife is aroused as well [before having intercourse].

Reasonable words and acts of enticement that attempt to woo another person and seduce her into consensual relations are permitted and are not considered coercive. However, if these advances are rebuffed, they must be stopped.

2. Forced and Coerced Intercourse

While all coerced sex is forbidden, there are various forms and degrees of coercion. At the extreme end of the spectrum is threat of physical, emotional, or financial harm. Realistic fear for one's safety and well-being, apprehension that one's future may be seriously jeopardized if one refuses to submit, concern over threats to the welfare of one's children or family, and the like render the act coercive. A woman really has no viable choice in these situations because the only other option is suffering, harm, or great sacrifice. In such cases, the perpetrator is guilty of rape.

At the other end of the spectrum is marginal consent. Reverend Marie Fortune points out that "acquiescence may pose as 'consent,' but it is not the same."[56] She is referring to what some call "altruistic" sex which is undertaken in order to keep a partner satisfied. Here there are no threats of violence and she is not terrorized. In this situation a woman agrees to sex for what she perceives to be *sh'lom bayit*, perhaps to keep her husband sexually satisfied, perhaps to avoid a fight. While this is not ideal and while, as is stated above, a husband should not have relations with his wife unless she is aroused and willing, such situations may occur during long-term relationships and, if they do not define the totality of their sexual relationship, they are not sufficiently coercive to qualify as rape according to Jewish law.

There are other degrees of coercion as well. A responsum by Rabbi Jacob Ettlinger (1798–1871) recorded in his *Binyan Tziyon*[57] will be helpful in defining two intermediate places on the continuum. R. Ettlinger was asked to rule on the status of a pious, yet naïve, woman who submitted sexually to a guest who stayed at her home. After a while she was taken in by his claims that he was Elijah the Prophet and that her destiny was to become the mother of the Messiah, to be fathered, of course, by this guest.

Of concern to R. Ettlinger was the woman's status pertaining to her husband. Jewish law forbids a couple to remain together after a wife has consensual intercourse with a man other than her husband; it permits them to remain together if she was raped. In this case, was her submission consensual, making it forbidden for her to remain with her husband, or was she raped?

After outlining and dismissing the approach of Maharik (Joseph Colon Ben Solomon Trabotto), R. Ettlinger outlined his own approach. He began his discussion by citing an opinion of Maharik: In deciding a case in which a woman incorrectly believed that she was not doing anything wrong when she was having an affair, Maharik ruled that engaging in extramarital intercourse even if done *b'shogeig* (inadvertently, in error) is still considered adultery and the woman is forbidden to her husband.[58] He brought proof for this position from the actions of Queen Esther. According to rabbinic tradition, Esther was actually a married woman, the wife of Mordecai.[59] But because she engaged in intercourse with Ahasuerus only when summoned by him, a summons she could not refuse on pain of death, each act of intercourse was rape and Esther was not an adulteress. However, when it became necessary to plead with Ahasuerus for the lives of the Jewish people, it was she who initiated that meeting—and that meeting was more than a simple tête-à-tête—for she willingly submitted to the king.[60] As a result of this consensual act, Esther was afraid that she would no longer be able to remain Mordecai's wife.[61] Thus, even though the encounter was occasioned by duress, that is, the danger to the Jewish people, and even though her intention was not to sin, Maharik considered this a consensual sexual act.[62]

R. Ettlinger disagreed, arguing in defense of Esther and on behalf of the woman in question. According to R. Ettlinger, an essential element of adultery is found in a verse describing the *sotah* ordeal: "And when he has made her drink the water, then it shall come to pass, that, if she is defiled and has trespassed against her husband, that the water that causes the curse shall enter into her and become bitter, and her belly shall swell, and her thigh shall fall; and the woman shall be a curse among her people" (Num. 5:27). Adultery is a "trespass against her husband." Therefore, if she does not engage in extramarital sex for her own pleasure but acts solely for the sake of heaven, it is not a violation of her relationship with her husband and the act does not render her an adulteress. In Esther's case, she hesitatingly acted at the behest of her own husband himself. Rashi puts words into Esther's mouth: "Even though I am going of my own volition [to sleep with the king], it is *ones* (a result of force and coercion).[63]

In the case confronting R. Ettlinger, he felt that this woman was naively coerced by the misrepresentations and manipulations of her guest; she had no intention of rebelling against her husband. Clearly, under normal circumstances a husband has no right to forgive the exclusive nature of his intimate relationship with his wife. The kind of arrangement known as "open marriage" is not a viable halachic or moral option. The *Binyan Tziyon*'s analysis is relevant only with regard to understanding the impact of coercion on a woman's state of mind and the nature of her consent or lack thereof. With the agreement of other respected decisors, R. Ettlinger was willing to dissent from the opinion of Maharik.

He suggests a further distinction that takes into account the object of coercion. The Mishnah, *K'tubot* 26b, states:

> A woman was imprisoned by heathens: if [they took her hostage] for the sake of [procuring ransom] money, she is permitted to her husband [upon her release]. If [they took her hostage] for the purpose of [taking her] life, she is forbidden to her husband [upon her release].[64]

What is the difference between these cases? If the kidnappers have a pecuniary interest in keeping their hostage safe and well protected, it is not suspected that they will engage in intercourse with her—they need to "protect their investment." However, if the hostage's life is in danger, the Mishnah suspected that she may have voluntarily had sex with her kidnappers in order to entice them to release her. Such sex, although resulting from her desperate and ominous situation, is not considered coerced; they did not coerce the sex act. Only if the coercion is for sex itself is whatever ensues considered to be rape. However, when the coercion is for another matter and the sex is "volunteered" for the purpose of saving oneself from those other dire consequences, this is not deemed the kind of coercion that defines that intercourse as rape.[65]

This does not mean that the perpetrator has not committed a sin. On the contrary, he acted appallingly, sinfully, and illegally. It does mean, however, that there was a sufficient level of consent with regard to the sexual act that renders a married woman forbidden to her husband.[66]

Thus there are two more points in the continuum of coerced sex between acquiescence and forced intercourse. One is where the coercion is intrinsic—the intercourse itself was coerced—and is considered rape. The other is where the duress is extrinsic and intercourse was offered as a way of relieving a difficult situation. In this case there are two perspectives. From the perspective of the woman, the law regards the sex as consensual, although it may condone it if it is motivated for a greater good. And from the perspective of the perpetrator, the law regards his act as sinful and coercive.[67]

Sexual relations between a woman and her therapist, physician, clergy, or teacher can fall into these categories as well. If the professional threatens her with what to her are significant consequences—financial, emotional, physical, psychological, or spiritual—and she must submit to intercourse or suffer the consequences, the act is rape. There is an inherent imbalance of power in these relationships that makes full consent impossible. Because she is often vulnerable in the settings in which she interacts with and depends upon these authorities, and because in our society people are conditioned to trust and respect them and to defer to their wisdom and insight, it can become difficult for her to distinguish between appropriate and inappropriate interaction. This is true when patients, students, and congregants may fear losing the attention of that authority figure or when they are unable to withstand inappropriate manipulation and exploitation of their vulnerabilities. The psychological concept of transference, the unconscious redirection of feelings or emotions onto a therapist, may be at play as well. Thus a woman's ability to give informed consent is compromised. Every code of professional ethics forbids such relationships.

Canadian Supreme Court Justice Gérard Vincent La Forest summarizes:

> In my view, this approach to consent in this kind of case is too limited. As Heuston and Buckley [page 247] *Salmond and Heuston on the Law of Torts* (19th ed. 1987), at pp. 564–565, put it: "A man cannot be said to be 'willing' unless he is in a position to choose freely; and freedom of choice predicates the absence from his mind

of any feeling of constraint interfering with the freedom of his will." A "feeling of constraint" so as to "interfere with the freedom of a person's will" can arise in a number of situations not involving force, threats of force, fraud, or incapacity. The concept of consent as it operates in tort law is based on a presumption of individual autonomy and free will. It is presumed that the individual has freedom to consent or not to consent. This presumption, however, is untenable in certain circumstances. A position of relative weakness can, in some circumstances, interfere with the freedom of a person's will. Our notion of consent must, therefore, be modified to appreciate the power relationship between the parties.[68]

He continues:

An ability to "dominate and influence" is not restricted to the student-teacher relationship. Prof. Coleman outlines a number of situations which she calls "power dependency" relationships: see Coleman, "Sex in Power Dependency Relationships: Taking Unfair Advantage of the 'Fair' Sex" (1988), 53 *Alb. L. Rev.* 95. Included in these relationships are parent-child, psychotherapist-patient, physician-patient, clergy-penitent, professor-student, attorney-client, and employer-employee. She asserts that "consent" to a sexual relationship in such relationships is inherently suspect. She notes, at p. 96:

The common element in power dependency relationships is an underlying personal or professional association which creates a significant power imbalance between the parties. . . . Exploitation occurs when the "powerful" person abuses the position of authority by inducing the "dependent" person into a sexual relationship, thereby causing harm.

While the existence of one of these special relationships is not necessarily determinative of an overwhelming power imbalance, it will, at least in the ordinary case, be required.[69]

This issue of the abuse of power imbalance as it relates to teachers, rabbis, and other professionals is a difficult concept for some to accept. At times the sexual relationships between these professionals and their clients appear consensual. It is clear that the rabbi, teacher, or professional is abusing his position and that his client lacks the capacity for full consent.

Marital Rape

Sexual relations are a defining feature of marriage. Every other type of relationship or responsibility that exists between husband and wife can be shared by any two individuals—financial support, household duties, companionship, etc. It is intimacy itself which is uniquely reserved by the Torah for husbands and wives to share with, and only with, each other. That is why, according to most authorities, Jewish law empowers a couple to negotiate almost every aspect of their relationship and, for example, set as a condition of marriage that they will have no financial responsibilities or household obligations to each other. However, they cannot set as a precondition to marriage that they will not engage in intimate relations.[70]

The central importance of sexual intimacy in a marriage was described by Rabbi Joseph B. Soloveitchik:

> A covenantal marriage is a hedonic, pleasure-oriented community. Judaism did not overlook or underestimate the physical aspects of marriage. On the contrary, once sacrificial withdrawal from the sinful erotic paradise of change and variety is completed, the natural element in marriage comes to the fore. The two partners owe each other not only fidelity, but also full gratification of their sexual needs. . . . Each one must observe these laws of consortium with regard to the other. The marriage must not be converted into an exclusively spiritual fellowship. Marriage without carnal enjoyment and erotic love is contrary to human nature and is to be dissolved. The ethic of marriage is hedonistic, not monastic.[71]

A husband is obligated to have intercourse with his wife and he may not spitefully deprive her of sex.[72] This duty is found in the biblical verse, "He shall not reduce her food, her garment, and her duty of marriage [*onah*]" (Exod. 21:10).[73] R. Naftali Zvi Yehudah Berlin explains that it is more than just a legal proscription:

> Reason tells us that [the man] is so bound. It is, as we well know, for this purpose that a bride enters into marriage, and she is forbidden to find her pleasure elsewhere because of her husband. Hence,

if he denies her sexual relations, she is deprived of her right. Even
for denying her the pleasure of bearing children, he may be compelled to divorce her and pay her *ketubah* . . . since she is not to be
deprived of her pleasures.[74]

While a woman has no explicit obligation to cohabit with her husband, many authorities infer from the very nature of the marriage
commitment itself a mutual obligation that husbands and wives will
be available to each other sexually.[75]

But this obligation is not absolute and does not offer uncon-
strained license to a husband to be with his wife whenever he wants.
Thousands of years ago Judaism rejected statements like that of
Chief Justice Sir Matthew Hale that "a husband cannot be guilty
of a rape committed by himself upon his lawful wife, for by their
mutual matrimonial consent and contract, the wife hath given up
herself in this kind unto her husband, which she cannot retract."
Jewish law insists that it is forbidden for a man to force his wife to
have intercourse;[76] all sexual intimacy must be consensual.[77] Rambam rules, "He should not coerce her [to have relations] when she
is not desirous. Rather, [they should engage in intercourse only]
when there is mutual desire and pleasure."[78]

In addition, the Talmud describes the possibilities of marital relations that are categorized as *anusah* (rape) and *eimah* (coerced out of
fear).[79] And Maharit (Joseph Trani) writes that a wife should not be
forced to have sex, because "she is not a captive to be sexually ravished
at her husband's whim."[80]

Does a wife have the right to refuse to have relations with her husband? Rambam writes:

> If a woman prevents her husband from having sexual relations
> with her, she is called a *moredet* (a rebellious wife). [The court] in-
> quires of her as to why she rebelled. If she said, "I am repelled by
> him and cohabitation with him is impossible for me," [the court]
> forces him to divorce her because a wife is not a prisoner who must
> consort with a person whom she despises.[81]

This opinion is confirmed by R. Moshe b. Yosef of Trani, known as Mabit, who states that a woman cannot be compelled to submit to her husband, because "she is unlike a captive woman who can be compelled to submit to sexual relations with a man she does not desire." He compares her conjugal rights to those of food and clothing, which her husband is also obligated to provide, and which she can also reject. He also points out that the Torah speaks of "*her* conjugal rights" (Exod. 21:10) and not simply of "conjugal rights"; those rights are hers and not her husband's.[82]

While a wife has the right to reject cohabitation, there may be consequences to her refusal. The court may pressure her to comply by threatening to reduce the amount she is owed in her *ketubah*.[83] If she persists in her refusal, she may be divorced having lost the financial obligations due to her from her husband.[84]

A wife may refuse excessive sexual demands made by her husband and not be labeled a *moredet*.[85] And a woman may refuse to engage in sexual practices that are unacceptable to her.[86]

Conclusion

Sexual relations are meant to be an expression of love, intimacy, and sanctity. They are an interaction between two people who find themselves at their most vulnerable and exposed—physically and emotionally. It is for these reasons and others that, while respect and dignity should define all human dealings, they are essential in sexual interactions. Judaism came to elevate and sanctify the sexual act with the institutions of marriage and *taharat hamishpachah* (family purity).[87] Nonconsensual and forced relations degrade and defame sexual intimacy as well as the partner whom one is obligated to love and respect.

Adapted from "I Do? Consent and Coercion in Sexual Relations" by Mark Dratch in *Rav Chesed: Essays in Honor of Rabbi Dr. Lookstein*, 2 vols; Jersey City, NJ: Ktav, 2009. Used by permission.

NOTES

1. http://www.cdc.gov/ncipc/factsheets/svfacts.htm.

2. www.vawnet.org/DomesticViolence/ Research/VAWnetDocs/AR_mrape.pdf. When his wife is legally unable to consent because of mental or physical impairment or if she is unconscious or asleep, a husband is exempt from prosecution in many of these thirty-three states.

3. While rape in and of itself is morally repugnant, it is necessary to articulate the reasons and legal arguments that support this position. Nevertheless, by doing this, we run the risk articulated by Rabbi Aharon Lichtenstein, *By His Light: Character and Values in the Service of God* (Jersey City, NJ: Ktav, 2003), 125:

> that one will then think that the only significance of the moral element is that it is part of the divine command. At the end of the war in Lebanon, some cast doubt on the halakhic severity of the prohibition of killing non-Jews. My colleague Rav Yehuda Amital spoke out very forcefully on the issue, and among other things, he quoted the opinion of the Raavan (*Bava Kama* 113a) that it is an *issur de-oraita* (biblical prohibition). I recall that someone was critical of this, and he said, "What kind of education is this? It teaches the student that whether or not he's going to kill a gentile should be dependent upon a Raavan in *Bava Kama*! . . . The Rambam answers that with regard to *mishpatim* (civil law), or areas *bein adam lechavero* (between man and his fellow), certainly a person should not feel constrained solely by the *tzav* (divine command), but rather should feel an inner constraint because of the moral element *per se*.

4. *Mishneh Torah, Hilchot Ishut* 1:4; see also *Shulchan Aruch, Even HaEizer* 26:1.

5. Raavad to *Hilchot Ishut* 1:4; Ramban to Deut. 23:18. See *Teshuvot Ziz Eli'ezer*, I, no. 27.

6. *Teshuvot* Rashba, IV, no. 314.

7. Maimonides, *Sefer ha-Mitzvot*, positive commandment 213.

8. Babylonian Talmud, *Temurah* 29b, "R. Elazar said: If an unmarried man has intercourse with an unmarried woman without the intention thereby of making her his wife, he makes her a harlot." This opinion is rejected, and a single woman who has had intercourse with a Jewish man who is not her husband, while she has engaged in a prohibited act and may be considered promiscuous, is nevertheless permitted to a *kohein*.

9. This, despite *Teshuvot She'eilat Ya'avetz* II, no. 15:

> [Some say] Ramban, who permits a concubine, in our day when men are morally lax, sleeping with maid servants and forbidden sexual partners, would forbid it. . . . It seems to me the opposite. For this reason the master [Ramban] would permit it, so that people would not commit greater offenses involving *kareit* (excision) from the Torah. For a man with bread in his basket will not have the same burning desire to go after forbidden relations. There are similar rulings where the rabbis have permitted even something forbidden by rabbinic law to prevent a Torah transgression.

10. *Kesef Mishneh* to *Hilchot Ishut* 1:4; *Teshuvot Radbaz*, IV, no. 225; and *Teshuvot Rivash* 425. See, however, *She'eilat Ya'avetz* II, no. 15.

11. *Hilchot Issurei Bi'ah* chapter 21.

12. Babylonian Talmud, *Kiddushin* 80b; *Hilchot Issurei Bi'ah* chapter 22; *Shulchan Aruch, Even HaEizer* 22.

13. Joseph B. Soloveitchik, *Family Redeemed: Essays on Family Relationships*. David Shatz and Joel Wolowelsky, eds. (New York: Toras HoRav Foundation, 2000), 93.

14. Babylonian Talmud, *Hilchot Sanhedrin* 75a; *Hilchot Yesodei ha-Torah* 5:9.

15. Babylonian Talmud, *Hilchot Sanhedrin* 75a: "R. Papa said: Because of the disgrace to her family. R. Acha the son of R. Ika said: That the daughters of Israel may not be immorally dissolute."

16. Specifically a married woman, so as to prevent a violation of the prohibition of adultery. Some have suggested that the limitation of adultery to a married woman is to preserve the sanctity of the institution of marriage. (Biblically, a man could take more than one wife, so his sexual relationships were not necessarily exclusive. This practice was later prohibited by the *cherem* [rabbinic edict] of Rabbeinu Gershom in the tenth century.) Others have suggested that adultery was a violation of the husband's exclusive right to his wife, a relationship that was not reciprocal. See Jeffrey H. Togay, "Adultery," *Encyclopedia Judaica*, 2:313. See also Judith Plaskow, *Standing Again at Sinai: Judaism from a Feminist Perspective* (New York: Harper & Row Publishers, 1990), 170–77.

17. Babylonian Talmud, *Hilchot Sanhedrin* 73a; *Hilchot Rotzei-ach* 1:10; *Shulchan Aruch, Chosen Mishpat* 425:3–4.

18. Babylonian Talmud, *Hilchot Sanhedrin* 73a; *Tosafot*, s.v. *chayavei k'ritut*.

19. Similarly, see *Teshuvot Iggerot Moshe, Even HaEizer* IV, no. 68.

20. Regarding the analogy of rape to murder, see Babylonian Talmud, *Hilchot Sanhedrin* 74a:

> Forbidden sexual relations and murder [may not be committed to save one's life], according to the opinion of Rabbi (Y'hudah HaNasi). For it has been taught: Rabbi (Y'hudah HaNasi) said, "For as when a man rises against his neighbor, and slays him, even so is this matter." But what do we learn from this analogy of a murderer? This comes to throw light and is itself illumined. The murderer is compared to a betrothed woman: just as a betrothed woman must be saved [from rape] at the cost of [the ravisher's] life, so in the case of a murderer, he [the victim] must be saved at the cost of his [the attacker's] life. Conversely, a betrothed woman is compared to a murderer: just as one must rather be slain [martyred] than commit murder, so also must the betrothed woman rather be slain than [engage in consensual relations]. And how do we know this of murder itself? It is common sense.

21. Babylonian Talmud, *Bava Kama* 83b.

22. *Teshuvot Divrei Yeziv, Even HaEizer* no. 77.

23. Deut. 22:28–29: "If a man finds a girl who is a virgin, who is not betrothed, and lays hold of her, and lies with her, and they are found; then the man who lay with her shall give to the girl's father fifty shekels of silver, and she shall be his wife; because he has afflicted her, he may not put her away all his days."

A simple reading of this verse seems to indicate that the rapist must marry his victim, even against her will, thus revictimizing her for a lifetime. This is not the case. *Tosefta, K'tubot* 3:7 indicates that the woman has the right to prevent this marriage by withholding her consent.

24. Babylonian Talmud, *K'tubot* 39a.

25. See *Tosefta, K'tubot* 39b, s.v., *i hakhi*. The Torah states, Deut. 22:28–29: "If a man finds a girl who is a virgin, who is not betrothed, and lays hold of her, and lies with her, and they are found; then the man who lay with her shall give to the girl's father fifty shekels of silver, and she shall be his wife; because he has humbled her, he may not divorce all his days."

Two important observations:

    a. The payment is given to the father only if the woman is a *naarah*, a young girl who is economically dependent on her father. An older woman keeps the payment herself. (*Sifrei*; Babylonian Talmud, *K'tubot* 39a)

    b. The rape victim is not forced to marry the rapist. She has the right to refuse the marriage. (Babylonian Talmud, *K'tubot* 39b)

26. Being thrown to the ground, for example.

27. Babylonian Talmud, *K'tubot* 39b.

28. See, for example, Susan Brownmiller, *Against Our Will: Men, Women, and Rape* (New York: Ballantine, 1975).

29. Alan Wertheimer, *Consent to Sexual Relations* (New York: Cambridge University Press, 1975), 104.

30. Ann Cahill, *Rethinking Rape* (Ithaca, NY: Cornell University Press, 2001), 192–93.

31. Babylonian Talmud, *Bava M'tzia* 58a:

> Our Rabbis taught: "You shall not wrong one another" (Lev. 25:17). Scripture refers to verbal wrongs. You say, "verbal wrongs," but perhaps that is not so, [maybe] monetary wrongs is meant? [This cannot be so because] when it is said, "And if you sell anything to your neighbor, or acquire anything from your neighbor [you shall not wrong one another] (Lev. 25:14), monetary wrongs are already dealt with. Then to what can I apply "You shall not wrong each other"? [The verse refers] to verbal wrongs, e.g., if a man is a penitent, one must not say to him, "Remember your former deeds." If he is the son of converts he must not be taunted with, "Remember the deeds of your ancestors." If he is a convert and comes to study the Torah, one must not say to him, "Shall the mouth that ate unclean and forbidden food come to study the Torah which was uttered by the mouth of God!" If he is visited by suffering, afflicted with disease, or has buried his children, one must not speak to him as his companions spoke to Job, "Is not your fear [of God] your confidence, and your hope the integrity of your ways? Remember, I pray you, who ever perished, being innocent?" (Job 4:6–7). If donkey drivers sought grain from a person, one must not say to them, "Go to so and so who sells grain," knowing that [that person] has never sold any. R. Y'hudah said: One may also not feign interest in a purchase when he has no money, since this is known to the heart only, and of everything known only to the heart it is written, "and thou shalt fear thy God" (25:17).

32. See Rashi to Lev. 25:17.

33. See Rashi, *Bava M'tzia* 59b, s.v. *chutz*; Rambam, *Sefer HaMitzvot*, no. 251.

34. *Kol HaRamaz* to Babylonian Talmud, *Bava M'tzia* 58a.

35. Babylonian Talmud, *Shabbat* 31a.

36. *Salmond and Heuston on the Law of Torts* (19th ed. 1987), 564–65.

37. Babylonian Talmud, *Eiruvin* 100b: Rami b. Chama citing R. Assi further ruled: A man is forbidden to compel his wife to the [marital] obligation, since it is said in Scripture: "Without consent the soul is not good; and he that hurries with his feet sins" (Prov. 19:2); *Baalei HaNefesh, Shaar HaK'dushah, Mishneh Torah, Hilchot Dei-ot* 5:4, *Shuchan Aruch, Even HaEiazer* 25:2.

Consensual intercourse with an unmarried woman is prohibited as outlined above. Nonconsensual intercourse is rape. Although nonmarital relations are forbidden by Jewish law, there is a marked difference between consensual and nonconsensual sex. Consensual sex is the responsibility and liability of both parties; nonconsensual sex is the liability of the rapist alone who violates the various prohibitions we are now discussing.

38. *HaK'tav V'haKabbalah* to Deut. 22:23.

39. Babylonian Talmud, *Sukkah* 29a.

40. Michael Dorman, "The Killing of Kitty Genovese," http://www.newsday.com/community/guide/lihistory/ny-history-hs818a,0,7944135.story?coll=ny-lihistory-navigation.

41. The Talmud, *K'tubot* 51b, offers a disturbing example of the lack of continuous protest.

Note that the Talmud often offers extreme scenarios in order to test the limits of the principles it is evaluating:

> Rava said: Any woman, the rape of whom began under compulsion, even if it ended with her consent, and even if she said, "Leave him alone," and that if he had not made the attack upon her she would have hired him to do it, is permitted [to her husband]. What is the reason? He plunged her into an uncontrollable passion. It was taught in agreement with Rava: "And she be not seized" (Num. 5:13) [only if she participates willingly from the beginning] is she forbidden [to her husband], [from which it follows] that if she was seized [i.e., acted under compulsion] she is permitted [to her husband]. But there is another class of woman who is permitted even if she was not seized. And who is that? Any woman who began under compulsion and ended with her consent.

See also *Mishneh Torah, Hilchot Ishut* 24:19.

42. Cahill, 174–75.

43. *Mishneh Torah, Hilchot Na-arah HaB'tulah* 1:2.

44. Scott A. Anderson, *"Towards a Better Theory of Coercion, and a Use for It"* at http://ptw. uchicago.edu/Anderson02.pdf, 12.

45. Babylonian Talmud, *Shevu'ot* 46a.

46. Babylonian Talmud, *Bava Batra* 47b and *Rashbam*, s.v. *kol di-m'zabin inish*.

47. *Shulchan Aruch, Choshen Mishpat* 205:7.

48. *Tosafot, Sh'vuot* 46a s.v., *avid inish de-gazim*; *Teshuvot Ri mi-Gash*, no. 122; *Keneset HaG'dolah, Hilchot Mokher be-O-nes, Bet Yosef, siman* 205, 15–29; *Teshuvot Yabi'a Omer*, iii, *Even HaEizer*, no. 20.

49. *N'darim* 20b. In addition to fear-motivated and forced relations, the other categories include intercourse engaged in (1) when her husband hates her and is

thinking of another woman; (2) when one of the parties is excommunicated; (3) when a husband who has two wives has intercourse thinking that he is with the other wife; (4) when one party is angry with the other; (5) when one party is drunk; (6) after the husband has already decided to divorce her; (7) when she is sleeping with another man; (8) when a woman brazenly demands relations.

50. See Ran, s.v., *b'nei anusah.*

51. *Hilchot Isurei Biah* 21:12–13; *Orach Chayyim* 240:2–3; *Even HaEizer* 25:10.

52. *Eiruvin* 100b: Rami b. Hama, citing R. Assi, further ruled: A man is forbidden to compel his wife to the [marital] obligation, since it is said in Scripture: "Without consent the soul is not good; and he that hurries with his feet sins" (Prov. 19:2); *Ba'ailei ha-Nefesh, Sha'ar ha-Kedushah; Hilchot De'ot* 5:4; *Even HaEizer* 25:2.

53. *Magen Avraham, Orach Chayim* 240, no. 7; *Zohar, B'reishit* 49b, 148b, *Vayikra* 225b.

54. *Mishneh Torah, Hilchot Ishut* 15:17.

55. *Kallah Rabbati* 1:11; *Tur, Orach Chayim* 240 and *Even HaEizer* 25.

56. Marie Fortune, *Sexual Violence: The Sin Revisited* (Cleveland, OH: The Pilgrim Press, 2005), 56.

57. *T'shuvot Binyan Tziyon* no. 154.

58. Maharik, *shoresh* 167, cited by Rema, *Even HaEizer* 178:3.

59. *Tziyyon* 13a: "And when her father and mother died, Mordecai took her for his own daughter" (Esther 2:7). A Tanna taught in the name of R. Meir: Read not "for a daughter" [*l'vat*], but "for a house" [*l'vayit*] (i.e., a wife).

60. Babylonian Talmud, *M'gilah* 15a: "Until now [I have slept with Ahasuerus] under compulsion, but now I will do so of my own will."

61. Babylonian Talmud, *M'gilah* 15a: "And if I perish, I perish" (Esther 4:16): As I am lost to my father's house, so I shall be lost to you.

62. Similarly, *Bet Shmue'l, Even HaEizer* 178, no. 4 rules that a woman who willingly enagages in intercourse even if it is in order to save the lives of others, as was the case of Esther, is forbidden to her husband because the intercourse was consensual.

63. Babylonian Talmud, *M'gilah* 15b: "And stood in the inner court of the king's house" (Esther 5:2): R. Levi said: When she reached the chamber of the idols, the Divine Presence left her. She said, 'My God, my God, why have You forsaken me' (Psalm 22:2). Do You punish the inadvertent offense (*shogeig*) like the presumptuous one (*meizid*), or one done under compulsion (*ones*) like one done willingly (*ratzon*)?

64. There is a dispute as to whether the woman becomes forbidden to her husband only if he is a *kohein* (*Hilchot Isurei Biah* 18:30; *Even HaEizer* 7:11) or if she becomes forbidden even to a non-*kohein* (*Tosafot,* Rosh, *T'rumat HaDeshen* no. 92, Rema to *Even HaEizer* 7:11).

65. *Sh'vut Yaakov,* II, no. 117.

66. *Maharik* no. 167; *T'rumat HaDeshen, p'sakim* no. 92; *T'shuvot Sh'vut Yaakov* II, no. 117. See, however, *T'shuvot Sho-eil UMeishiv, mahadura aleph,* III, no.48.

67. See Ramban to Deut. 22:23.

68. Norberg v. Wynrib, [1992] 2 S.C.R. 226; [1992] Scj. No. 60, par. 27.

69. Norberg v. Wynrib, par. 39.

70. Babylonian Talmud, *K'tubot* 56a; *Mishneh Torah, Hilchot Ishut* 6:10; *Even HaEizer* 38:5 and 69:6. See, however, *T'shuvot Tashbetz* I:94; Ramban to *Bava Batra* 126b; *Chavot Ya-ir* to Rif, *Baba M'tzia* VII, 54a. Nahum Rakover, "Coercion in

Conjugal Relations" in *Jewish Law Association Studies I: The Touro Conference Volume*, B.S. Jackson, ed., 1985, 103–104.

71. Soloveitchik, 50.

72. *Hilchot Ishut* 14:7.

73. See *K'tubot* 47a–48b for other possible sources.

74. *Birkat HaN'tziv* to the *Mekhilta de R. Yishmael, Mishpatim* 3 cited by Rakover, 102–103.

75. Rashba to *N'darim* 15b.

76. *Eiruvin* 100b: Rami b. Hama citing R. Assi further ruled: A man is forbidden to compel his wife to the [marital] obligation, since it is said in Scripture: "Without consent the soul is not good; and he that hurries with his feet sins" (Prov. 19:2); *Ba'ailei ha-Nefesh, Sha'ar ha-Kedushah*; *Hil. De'ot* 5:4; *Even HaEizer* 25:2.

77. See Warren Goldstein, *Defending the Human Spirit: Jewish Law's Vision for a Moral Society* (New York: Feldheim, 2006), 151–220.

78. *Mishneh Torah, Hilchot Ishut* 15:17.

79. Babylonian Talmud, *N'darim* 20b.

80. *T'shuvot* Maharit I, no. 5.

81. *Mishneh Torah, Hilchot Ishut* 14:8.

82. *Kiryat Sefer* to *Mishneh Torah, Hilchot Ishut* 14.

83. Babylonian Talmud, *K'tubot* 63b:

> What is the definition of a "rebellious wife"? Amemar said: [One] who says. "I like [my husband] but wish to torment him." If she said, however, "He is repulsive to me," no pressure is to be brought to bear upon her. Mar Zutra ruled: Pressure is to be brought to bear upon her. Such a case once occurred, and Mar Zutra exercised pressure upon the woman and [as a result of the reconciliation that ensued] R. Chanina of Sura was born from the reunion. This, however, was not [the right thing to do]. [The successful result] was due to the help of Providence.

84. *Even HaEizer* 77:2–3.

85. *T'shuvot Yaskil Avdi*, V, no. 69.

86. Babylonian Talmud, *N'darim* 20b; *Baalei HaNefesh, Sha-ar HaK'dushah*; *Mishneh Torah, Hilchot Isurei Biah* 21:9; *Even HaEizer* 25:2.

87. See Norman Lamm, *Hedge of Roses* (New York: Feldheim, 1966).

This essay was written in honor of Rabbi Haskel Lookstein, my teacher and mentor in rabbinics and social responsibility, with respect and gratitude.

42

SEX TRAFFICKING AND SEX SLAVERY

History, Halachah, and Current Issues

Rabbi Leigh Lerner

History and Halachah

From the biblical record of a daring, brave prostitute, to the reactive but decisive action of an ancient Rabbinic leader, to the courageous interventions of a Reform rabbi in New York City, Jews have confronted sex slavery, sex trafficking, and prostitution from our earliest days into the modern period. A review of this history of both ideas and deeds creates a call to engagement for today's Reform Jews.

There is no question that biblical men considered prostitutes to occupy the lowest rungs of the social ladder. In Genesis 34, Dinah is raped by Hamor. He then falls in love with her and wants to marry her, but our ancestors, Dinah's brothers, say, "Should he have treated our sister like a prostitute?" (Gen. 34:31). From the most ancient of days, everyone knows that a prostitute lives in danger of physical harm and that treating someone "like a prostitute" means to show no respect for their physical person. The notion of human rights begins with the acknowledgment that all people have a right to the physical safety of their person. Perhaps an underlying sense of that fact motivated the

Deuteronomist to write, "There shall be no harlot among the daughters of Israel" (Deut. 23:18).

Still, men in the Torah did not refrain from the use of prostitutes. For example, when Judah sleeps with his daughter-in-law Tamar, mistaking her for a prostitute (Genesis 38), he is never condemned for the sexual act itself, only for avoiding his levirate responsibilities. Because prostitutes were used and taken as part of daily life, there was a market for them. In biblical days, desperate families would sell children or adult daughters into sex slavery, essentially engaging themselves in trafficking for their own profit or survival. Yet the effect of such violence is what Torah views as the degradation of society: "Do not degrade your daughter by making her a prostitute, or the land will turn to prostitution and be filled with wickedness" (Lev. 19:29).

Wherever slavery existed, numerous sources assert that personal slaves were also expected to act as sex slaves. Joseph was kidnapped by his own brothers, who certainly may have had a profit motive beyond their personal vendetta against the lad, whom they hated. They may have thought, "Why let him die when we can sell him to Midianite traders?" When sold into Egyptian slavery, the mistress of the house of Potiphar thought she had a right to do anything she wanted with her spouse's personal slave Joseph, even sexually. Joseph fled, and the dungeon was his reward for self-possession and a circumspect character.

Jews present Queen Esther as a valorous woman who used her regal authority to save the Jewish people. A closer reading of the Book of Esther shows that Esther was entering the harem of Ahasuerus. A woman in a harem must give sexual favors upon demand. Jewish history and law militate against a woman entering such a situation voluntarily, as Esther did. Was she actually lured into her position? Kidnapped? When she agrees to appeal to Ahasuerus to save her people, she says, "I shall go to the king, though it is contrary to the law" (Esther 4:16). Rashi to this verse cites *midrash aggadah*: "'Contrary to the law'—Until now, I was coerced [to cohabit with him], but now [I will do so] willingly." Rashi indicates that Esther was a sex slave, albeit in a luxurious environment, a victim of sex slavery, a trafficked woman.

The biblical background makes the Rabbinic attitude to sex slavery, trafficking, and prostitution all the more understandable. The ancient Rabbis lived in a time when sex trafficking and slavery was commonplace. Of the Roman Empire, Juvenal writes, "Long since has the Syrian Orontes flowed into the Tiber and brought along with it the Syrian tongue and manners and cross-stringed harp and harper and exotic timbrels and girls bidden stand for hire at the circus."[1] Rabbinic Judaism stood in condemnation of the free reign of the male libido. In the Babylonian Talmud, *Sanhedrin* 75a, we find the following:

> Rav Y'hudah said in Rav's name: A man once conceived a passion for a certain woman, and his heart was consumed by his burning desire [his life being endangered thereby]. When the doctors were consulted, they said, "His only cure is that she shall submit." Thereupon the Sages said, "Let him die rather than that she should yield." Then [said the doctors], "Let her stand nude before him"; [they answered,] "Sooner let him die." "Then," said the doctors, "let her converse with him from behind a fence." "Let him die," the Sages replied, "rather than she should converse with him from behind a fence." Now Rabbi Yaakov bar Idi and Rabbi Shmuel bar Nachmani dispute therein. One said that she was a married woman; the other that she was unmarried. Now, this is intelligible on the view that she was a married woman, but on the latter, that she was unmarried, why such severity? Rav Papa said, "Because of the disgrace to her family." Rabbi Acha the son of Rabbi Ika said, "That the daughters of Israel may not be immorally dissolute." Then why not marry her? Marriage would not assuage his passion, even as Rabbi Yitzchak said, "Since the destruction of the Temple, sexual pleasure has been taken [from those who practice it lawfully] and given to sinners, as it is written: 'Stolen waters are sweet, and bread eaten in secret is pleasant' (Prov. 9:17)."

Apparently, as in our own time, some trafficked prostitutes were male. *B'reishit Rabbah* 91:6 is set in the time when Joseph's brothers had sold him into slavery in Egypt, had come down to Egypt for food, and were, according to the midrash, seeking their brother. Joseph was already viceroy of Egypt and was tracing his brothers' steps. We learn that "he [Joseph] sent for them [the brothers who were expected to show up at the one storehouse that Joseph had left open after hearing that his siblings were in Egypt] and found them in the street of harlots. What were they doing there? They thought, maybe since Joseph was of handsome appearance, he was set in a harlot's tent. They were arrested and brought to Joseph." What did they think Joseph's role would be in this tent? To attract females, other Mrs. Potiphars looking for a sexual encounter? Or did they imagine him there to satisfy male libidinal needs? We do not know, but we are made aware that trafficked men or women are in need of redemption, for the midrash pictures the brothers as out to redeem Joseph from slavery.

Maimonides sums up the Rabbinic tradition in his *Mishneh Torah*. He bars all sexual relations outside marriage:

> Before the giving of the Torah, a man would meet a woman in the marketplace, take her home, and she would become his wife. Or he would meet a woman, pay her a fee, and have a sexual encounter with her. Since the giving of the Torah, however, prostitution has become forbidden, and marriage now requires a public ceremony including *ketubah* and *kiddushin* before witnesses. Any other sexual encounter is akin to prostitution, which is forbidden by the Torah.[2]

While there is not total agreement with Rambam, certainly his summary of the law has earned wide respect. A story of Beruryah, the scholarly wife of Rabbi Meir, shows how deeply embedded in Jewish history is this Rabbinic attitude. Beruryah was the daughter of Rabbi Chanina ben Teradyon. When the Roman authorities slew her father for teaching Torah, his persecutors captured another daughter of Chanina who supported her father in his cause. They forced her into the life of a sex slave in a brothel. Beruryah said to her husband, "I am ashamed to have my sister placed in a brothel." So Meir took a double measure of denarii and succeeded in releasing his sister-in-law (Babylonian Talmud, *Avodah Zarah* 18a). He fulfilled the mitzvah of *pidyon sh'vuyim*, "redeeming the captive," but he had to flee the country for a time. Perhaps Meir felt the same shame that his wife did, but it was only because of her urging that he agreed to risk his own life to free his sister-in-law.

At the end of the Middle Ages it was decided that a married man who frequented prostituted women was obliged to give his wife a divorce. By the sixteenth century, Jewish communities began to impose heavy fines on landlords who rented their houses for the purpose of prostitution. Anybody who knew of such a case was obliged to report it, and the bawdy house would be closed.[3] Thus, those who profited from prostitution and sex trafficking even tangentially were held responsible to cease and desist.

Similarly, in modern times, Buenos Aires became a human trafficking capital because of its city-regulated prostitution from 1875 to 1936. Many women were duped into false marriages in Eastern European shtetls by a notorious Jewish gang and were trafficked to South American countries and New York for prostitution. During their ship's passage, they were raped and abused and "prepared" for their new careers. This shameful chapter in the history of Jewish life is documented by the First Jewish International Conference on White Slavery, 1910, which reported that in 1903 Buenos Aires had forty-two known brothels, of which thirty-nine were owned by Russian Jews. (Much of Poland was in Russian hands at this time, so some say they were Polish Jews.) Large bordellos of Buenos Aires housed sixty to eighty sex slaves, many in the Jewish quarter. "As the whorehouses and pimps prospered, the Jewish community rejected them. Articles in the local press condemned them and, in 1885, the community established a Jewish Association for the Protection of Women and Girls."[4]

Ilan Sheinfeld's *Tale of a Ring* documents the Zwi Migdal Organization, a Jewish gang of pimps that at its peak controlled four thousand prostitutes in Argentina, many of whom were Jews trafficked from Eastern Europe on false promises of husbands awaiting them. In the late 1920s, one woman, Rachel Lieberman, heard of an official who would not take bribes from the Migdal Organization and became the voice that led to their prosecution and destruction as a gang.

In the United States in the late nineteenth century, early leadership against sex trafficking was provided by Reform rabbi Dr. Edward B. M. Browne, who had two *s'machot*, as well as LLD, AM, BM, DD, and

MD degrees. To make matters easier for all, he was simply known as Alphabet Browne.

While rabbi at Congregation Gates of Hope in New York City, Alphabet Browne noticed that wealthy, well-known Jews from Temple Emanu-El of the City of New York were giving *tzedakah* to sustain thousands of Jewish immigrants but that the people charged with dispensing the *tzedakah* were mishandling it, using their connections to the immigrants for purposes of white slavery. Upon learning that girls were being sold "for immoral purposes," he and his wife went daily to Castle Garden, the immigrant shelter that preceded Ellis Island, to greet the newcomers. Mrs. Browne frequently brought home single young women to be sheltered and employed until a permanent situation could be found for them.

Alphabet Browne became a whistle-blower, demanding that the men of renown guarantee proper "distribution of the contributed money" and fair "treatment of the strangers." He implicated friends, employees, and even relatives of the wealthy. The "great men" were unhappy with this and stifled it in the press, so Alphabet Browne retaliated by publishing his own newspaper, which named the thieves.

At the Schiff Immigrant Shelter, Browne uncovered extortion, robbery, and prostitution, including the case of a young girl allegedly sent to a brothel in Pittsburgh. Rabbi Browne went to Washington, met with President Chester A. Arthur, and convinced him to provide transport back to Europe for those who wanted to go, with him as escort. But two days later, October 15, 1882, the "tzimmes riot" broke out on Ward's Island when an immigrant at Shabbat dinner was refused an extra dollop of stewed prunes and apples. The unhappy diner seized the ladle from the orderly and hit him on the head with it, which began a melee that turned public opinion against the refugees, causing the transport to be canceled. Regardless, that incident does not take anything away from the bold efforts of the Reform rabbi Alphabet Browne, who ended the fraudulent Emigrant Aid Association and stopped a major sex slavery and human trafficking ring.[5]

In the late nineteenth and early twentieth centuries, sex trafficking, called white slavery, became a central issue in the Jewish community. The German B'nai B'rith, its women's auxiliaries, and Bertha Pappenheim's Juedische Frauenbund (JFB), founded in 1904, worked together to help stop the hijacking of Jewish women travelers in an era of huge emigration from Europe when single women and spouses whose husbands were already in America journeyed from Eastern Europe toward the ships that would carry them to the *Goldene Medina*. JFB organized twenty posts at ports and railway stations where a Star of David bespoke the sponsorship and where women could find advice and a hostel bed. The Union of Rabbis, a group that was overwhelmingly Reform, strongly aided in these efforts.[6]

At the CCAR conference of 1909, Rabbi Stephen Wise charged that the failure of the synagogue to reach the working man was "indirectly to blame for the conditions which made possible the recent accusations about the white-slave traffic." Rabbi David Phillipson, Cincinnati, president of the CCAR, admitted that the charges had a basis in truth and that something needed to be done. CCAR lights such as Henry Berkowitz, Emil Hirsch, and Judah Magnes all were active in fighting white slavery.[7] They leave us a heritage worthy of emulation in our time.

Contemporary Definitions

Before looking at sex trafficking in the current era, it would be useful to understand more precisely what is meant by the term in our time.

The Rome Statute of the International Criminal Court (Article 7[2][c]) states that sexual enslavement is the exercise of any or all of the powers attached to the "right of ownership" over a person. It may comprise repeated sexual abuse or rape by the captor, or forcing the victim to provide sexual services to others, or both. The crime is a continuing offense. The Rome Statute's definition of sexual slavery includes situations where persons are forced into domestic servitude, marriage, or any other forced labor that involves sexual activity, as well as the trafficking of persons for sexual purposes, frequently women and children.[8] (Canada has signed onto the statute but not put it in force. The United States and Israel are not parties to it.[9])

Sex trafficking is a type of human trafficking involving the recruitment, transportation, transfer, harbor, or receipt of persons, by coercive or abusive means, for the purpose of sexual exploitation. People generally think that trafficking involves transportation over substantial distances, but persons can be trafficked within a city. That is why it is possible to assert that much prostitution is, in and of itself, a form of sex trafficking. As Farley et al. put it, "From the perspective of those we interviewed in five countries, prostitution might at best be called a means of survival: if one wants a place to sleep, food to eat and a way to briefly get off the street, one allows oneself to be sexually assaulted. At its worst, prostitution is kidnapping, torture and sale of parts of the person for sex by third parties."[10]

Contemporary Jewish Efforts to End
Sex Trafficking and Sex Slavery

Rahab, the prostitute of Jericho (Joshua 2:1) gave aid to the Israelite spies, and when Joshua led the Israelites into the Land, she was spared. Jewish tradition then credits her with walking away from her past to become a religious Jew. She is considered among those righteous who become Jews with no ulterior motive whatsoever (*Kohelet Rabbah* 8:13), a woman of tremendous strength and leadership.

Despite the glowing Rabbinic opinion of Rahab, we might ask why Rahab the prostitute chose to hide the Israelite spies. Could it have been because she realized the hopelessness of her situation? Unless there was a veritable social revolution, she had no way out of her predicament. People stuck in a repetitive, detrimental rut of behavior usually cannot extricate themselves without help, but some strong and clever individuals like a Rahab devise an exit strategy. Perhaps as Rahab's exit strategy, she backed the Israelite "newcomers" in the hope that when at last they rose to power, she would arise out of her sexual enslavement.

In our time, most of those enslaved as prostituted women see no exit, have no exit strategy. They are often drugged, under surveillance, and deprived of sleep, held against their will. I have walked in the dark of night from nightclub to nightclub with a congregant family, seeking their runaway daughter, proffering her picture to bouncers and staff with, "Do you recognize this girl?" Later I helped them engage a private detective, who discovered her, one young runaway among many picked up at a bus station, taken to a drug party, sheltered, and intimidated into submission. Or prostituted women may be illegal immigrants who fear deportation to an equally degraded life or fear reprisals against their loved ones at home by the gang that kidnapped them. Today's trafficked women need a virtual revolution in law and public values to free them, an exit strategy endorsed by society.

First Sweden, then Norway and Iceland have adopted "the Swedish model" to deal with prostitution and sex trafficking and provide an exit strategy. In short, this model considers prostitution to be oppression of women and children. Therefore, it is the oppressor, the "john," who should be arrested and charged. This is, indeed, the case now in these three countries, where it is illegal to be a john, but not illegal to be a prostituted woman. In the main, johns are fined, their names appearing on police blotters, perhaps to be made public, and notice of fines are sent to the john's home, where it can readily be seen by others who live there. Substantial decreases in the numbers of prostituted women and the numbers of persons trafficked for sex have been reported. Important to the whole effort are the social services offered to prostituted women to make safe exit from their situation. No reports show this to be a perfect approach, only a best practice.

In Israel, Rabbi Levi Lauer, a Hebrew Union College–Jewish Institute of Religion ordinee and director of ATZUM and its Task Force on Human Trafficking (TFHT), has spoken widely about sex trafficking in Israel. Any visitor to Tel Aviv cannot fail to notice the "business cards" strewn across the sidewalks and the magnificent walkway on the strand. These cards picture women and feature their phone numbers, offering sexual services.

Rabbi Lauer states that many, if not most, prostitutes were trafficked into Israel across the Negev border with Egypt. In 2005, the number was estimated at three thousand to five thousand. The border fence being built in 2012 is limiting the human traffic, but the women who are in Israel are sex slaves to those who literally bought them from their transporters. Prostitution may involve up to two billion dollars a year, Lauer estimates.

Rabbi Lauer has organized demonstrations in Jerusalem, New York, London, and Washington, DC, to put international pressure on Israel to criminalize the purchase of sexual services, following the model of Scandinavian countries. A first reading of the Orit Zuaretz (Kadima) bill passed in February 2012. Rabbi Lauer believes that Israel will install social services to support exit strategies for prostituted women, but so many are illegal immigrants that he fears they will simply be deported back to their largely Eastern European countries of origin. Thus Israel would avoid expense in absorption, job training, counseling, and other facets of the social service network required for safe exit from sex slavery.[11]

In the United States and Canada, similar efforts are under way to create a groundswell of legislation that would follow the Swedish model. One organizer and leader, Peggy Sakow, resides in both New York City and Montreal. She organized the Temple Committee against Human Trafficking at Temple Emanu-El-Beth Sholom, Montreal, and her committee's efforts won the Religious Action Center's Fain Award in 2007 for a four-day series to bring awareness of human trafficking to the congregation, Jewish community, general public, and youth. As a part of the program, authorities on the subject provided information to a thousand Montreal high school students, as well as during Shabbat services. The program closed with a powerful film about traffickers and their victims. In a breakthrough, the committee assembled local, provincial, and national law enforcement agencies to consider together for the first time the matter of sex trafficking. The

Temple Committee was recognized as an NGO by the United States Department of State and continues its work with annual seminars, and it also tries to involve other congregations in the Reform Movement.

Involvement in healing society of sex slavery and sex trafficking requires a significant change of attitude among middle-class individuals. Prostitution is not a pleasant matter to consider, and many people believe that, as the "oldest profession," nothing really can be done about it. Others advocate legalizing prostitution. Others call prostituted women "sex workers," as if to make prostitution just one more career in our society. Breaking through these barriers will take some education and thinking about a subject that most would prefer to avoid.

The Swedes have shown that something can be done about prostitution in our time. For the nonce, their approach has substantially diminished the sex trade in that country.

Armed with a resolution of the Central Conference of American Rabbis in 2004, and other less specific statements by the Union for Reform Judaism and Women of Reform Judaism, the Reform Religious Action Center (RAC) in Washington, DC, has worked to end human trafficking, which would, of course, include sex trafficking. The RAC wants to make a distinction between sex trafficking, which is a form of slavery, and sex work, which individuals may voluntarily choose to enter, though it be under duress.

In a memorandum from RAC legislative assistants Jacob Fain and Erin Scharff, dated Spring 2005 regarding Human Trafficking and the Sex Trade, the RAC spells out what it considers to be the difference between "trafficking" and "sex work/prostitution":

> Sex trafficking is a form of slavery, and the Reform Movement has clear policy opposing trafficking.[12] Prostitution, or sex work, the act of engaging in sex acts for hire, is often exploitive and frequently coercive. However, for millions of people around the world, and particularly for young women in poor countries, sex work represents one of the only sources of income. For many . . . the choice is sex work or starvation for themselves and their families.

First, the RAC's use of the term "sex work" invests prostitution with a certain dignity that Jewish tradition really does not afford it—indeed, a dignity that society does not afford it, either. Who among us would want to say, when asked what our adult child does for a living, that our daughter or son is a "sex worker"? "Sex work" seems to be a term that engages in *hasagat g'vul*, moving the landmark of what is acceptable and what is not. That does not mean we fail to understand the desperation of those who enter or who are coerced into prostituting themselves in order to have a morsel to eat for themselves or their families.

Second, the RAC points out that "the act of engaging in sex acts for hire is often exploitive and frequently coercive." The frequency of exploitation and coercion is mitigated by the words "often and frequently." It is probably more accurate to say that those who engage in sex acts for hire are almost always exploited and coerced. The RAC seems to want to leave room for a minority, even a fairly sizable minority, who have chosen prostitution as a profession and consider it "sex work."

The facts don't leave much room for doubt about the exploitation and coercion involved in the life of a prostituted woman. When one hundred prostituted women in Vancouver, British Columbia, were asked what they needed most, only about one-fourth of the native women and one-third of the women from Europe said they needed legalized prostitution. Of the respondents, 88 percent of First Nations women and 75 percent of women from Europe needed drug treatment; 92 percent had been raped in prostitution; 85 percent were homeless; 65 percent had been exploited for pornographic purposes; and 65 percent had been threatened with a weapon.[13]

Further, a Canadian commission found that the death rate of women in prostitution was forty times higher than that of the general population.[14] In a number of communities across Canada, Aboriginal youth constitute "90% of the visible sex trade."[15] In Vancouver, 70 percent first prostituted before age eighteen,[16] indicating that we are speaking of child abuse on a vast scale, an abuse that continues into the age of consent and thus becomes discounted as personal choice. Other studies report even higher percentages of minors' first involvement. Children typically enter prostitution subsequent to abusive treatment by caregivers[17] and subsequent to running away from dangerous home environments.[18] In a study of American prostituted women, Farley et al. found that 92 percent wanted to leave.

Since these data or worse can be replicated time and time again, use of the term "sex work" by the Reform Movement or any other group simply dignifies preying upon and abusing people—largely women and children stuck in a violent, demeaning, dangerous, and self-destructive life. Yes, there are those who choose to enter it; yes, the call girl with her gilt-edged clients does exist; and yes, it will be virtually impossible to end this "oldest profession" in its entirety, but providing a society-approved, workable exit strategy for the vast majority who feel stuck in prostitution, who live daily with post-traumatic stress disorder, deserves the endorsement of the Reform Movement with greater vigor and with more detailed planning. That effort begins by abandoning the term "sex work," which lends dignity to what our tradition has never completely eliminated from our midst, prostitution, but a societal fact that we have always struggled to oppose.

The Exodus from Egypt (*Mitzrayim*) was also an exodus from *mei tzarim*—a place of narrow straits. The Israelites leave for wide-open expanses of physical and spiritual liberation. The biblical prostitute Rahab's name comes from a Hebrew root meaning "wide." The bondage in *Mitzrayim* is fully ended by the liberating and open expanses of redemption in Canaan, which occurs thanks to Rahab's trust in the Israelites and their divinely appointed destiny.

Many who are stuck in the narrow straits of sex slavery depend on society to help them find a way out. What does our freedom as a people mean if we Jews do not release others from the straits of slavery into expansive liberty? One hundred years ago, we were not afraid to fight against "white slavery." In our time, we call it as we see it: sex trafficking and sex slavery. The Jewish imperative for our participation in the struggle against sex trafficking and its concomitant slavery is clear.

Now let us gather the will to help the nations where we live to provide approved and sustainable exit strategies for the enslaved.

NOTES

1. *Satire* 3:6.

2. Maimonides, *Mishneh Torah*, *Hilchot Ishut* 1:4.

3. Max Wurmbrand, http://www.jewishvirtuallibrary.org/jsource/judaica/ejud_0002_0016_0_16127.html.

4. Rona Kupferboim, May 25, 2007, Israel Jewish Scene, posted on Ynet, http://www.ynetnews.com/articles/0,7340,L-3403899,00.html.

5. See Janice Blumberg Rothschild, *Prophet in a Time of Priests* (Baltimore, MD: Apprentice House, 2012).

6. Edward J. Bristow, *Prostitution and Prejudice: The Jewish Fight against White Slavery, 1870–1939* (New York: Schocken Books, 1983), 233ff.

7. Ibid., 272.

8. 1 UN Treaty Database, treaties.un.org/doc/source/events/2005/book-english.pdf.

9. http://www.icc-cpi.int/NetApp/App/MCMSTemplates/StatePartiesIndex.aspx?NRMODE=Published&NRNODEGUID={7A50B016-A0B6-43EB-AFF8-15FCEDC03D02}&NRORIGINALURL=/Menus/ASP/states+parties/&NRCACHEHINT=Guest#U.

10. Melissa Farley, Isin Baral, Merab Kiremire, and Ufuk Sezgin, "Prostitution in Five Countries: Violence and Post-Traumatic Stress Disorder (South Africa, Thailand, Turkey, USA, Zambia)," *Feminism & Psychology* 8, no. 4 (1998): 405–26.

11. Interviews with Rabbi Levi Lauer.

12. CCAR 2004 Resolution on Human Trafficking. http://ccarnet.org/rabbis-speak/resolutions/all/human-trafficking-resolution-on/

13. Melissa Farley et al., "Prostitution in Vancouver: Violence and the Colonization of First Nations Women," *Transcultural Psychiatry*, June 2005.

14. Pornography and Prostitution in Canada: Special Committee on Pornography and Prostitution. (Canadian Government Pub. Centre, 1985), 350.

15. Save the Children Canada, Year One: 1999-2000, Out of the Shadows and Into the Light (Vancouver, BC: Save the Children, Canada, 2000), 7.

16. Violence Against Women in Vancouver's Street-Level Sex Trade and the Police Response, www.pace-society.ca (Cunningham & Christensen, 2001).

17. "Identifying Research Gaps in the Prostitution Literature," John Lowman, Research and Statistics Division, Dept. of Justice, Canada, March 2001, p. 2, www.justice.ga.ca.

18. Federal/Provincial Territorial Working Group on Prostitution: Report and Recommendations in Respect of Legislation, Policy and Practices Concerning Prostitution-Related Activities, Dec. 1998, p. 13. www.walnet.org/csis/reports/consult.rtf.

43

THE IMPACT OF CATASTROPHE ON JEWISH SEXUALITY

Jewish Displaced Persons in Occupied Germany, 1945–1950

MARGARETE MYERS FEINSTEIN, PhD

The Shoah destroyed Jewish communities and ravaged Jewish bodies. Forced from their homes, European Jews found themselves struggling to survive in ghettos, concentration camps, forests, and in hiding. Some non-Jews who hid Jews and some privileged prisoners, Jewish and non-Jewish, used their positions to purchase or extort sex from those under their control. In these extreme circumstances, some Jewish men and women traded sex for food, clothing, and protection. Some sought comfort from others through sexual activity, while many others lost interest in sex and devoted their energy to basic survival. After liberation, survivors initially remained vulnerable to sexual abuse, only this time by their liberators. However, as conditions stabilized in the displaced persons (DP) assembly centers of occupied Germany, nearly three hundred thousand Jewish DPs sought to rebuild their lives while adapting tradition to their needs. The lack of familial and communal protections, which had made survivors vulnerable to exploitation, combined after the war with a decline in rabbinic authority to create opportunities for sexual experimentation.

Wartime conditions had deprived Jewish women and men of some of the physical signifiers of their sex. A British nurse who entered Bergen-Belsen shortly after liberation noted, "At first glance we were unable to define their sex. Several were lying on top of their blankets, their heads shorn."[1] Women suffered from the shaving of their hair, the loss of their feminine roundness and softness, and amenorrhea. Devoid of body fat, women discovered their breasts had all but shrunken to nothingness, and with shorn hair, they had no obvious indicators of their sex.[2] It was difficult for female survivors to recognize themselves as women. Unable to see themselves as sexual beings, women survivors were unprepared for sexual advances from the first men they encountered, the liberating troops.

Women survivors were easy prey for Allied military personnel seeking sexual adventure or reward. Misunderstandings often led to terror for the women survivors. Soldiers in all Allied armies frequently expected sexual rewards in exchange for a ride to the next town, a gift of food, or an evening out. Women survivors often did not realize that the soldiers would expect such payment until after they had accepted the proffered assistance.[3] The unexpected advances from men they had welcomed as liberators intimidated these women, who were very aware of their dependence on the goodwill of Allied troops. Moreover, the Soviet Army pursued a policy of rape that victimized not only enemy nationals but also survivors of the concentration camps and of the forests. One survivor remembered the Russian soldiers saying, "We are your liberators. You have to thank us that we liberated you. You have to go to sleep with us. Go sleep with him!"[4] The Western military commanders did not condone rape and maintained greater control over their troops, so instances of rape by Western Allied soldiers were less common, but sexual exploitation did still occur. Survivors often interpreted these rapes and assaults as betrayals, more hurtful than wartime incidents because they had expected their liberators to treat them better than their oppressors.

Although the experiences of the concentration camps had instilled in survivors a distrust of doctors, the loss of menses and the accompanying fear of infertility compelled women survivors to seek medical assistance even when it meant seeing a German physician.[5] Some had their fears of infertility confirmed, but most were reassured that with proper nutrition their menstrual cycles would resume.[6] At least one DP physician, a survivor of the Kovno ghetto, recognized the connection between "acute psychological trauma" and ghetto amenor-rhea.[7] Without the stress of persecution and with improved rations, many DP women welcomed the return of menses.

While menstruation was a defining physical trait for women, the ability to achieve an erection appears to have served a similar function for men. Medical personnel reported that former concentration camp inmates showed evidence of severe loss or disturbances of sexual func-tion.[8] While survivors themselves have noted that hunger and weak-ness deprived most prisoners of their sex drives in the concentration camps, they have also stated that Germans and privileged prisoners retained an interest in sex and frequently sexually exploited weaker or lower-status inmates.[9] As Elizabeth Heineman has suggested, sex may have been more than a perk for privileged prisoners; their "sexual vitality" may have established and maintained their elevated position in the prisoner hierarchy.[10] Impotence, therefore, could also have had real consequences and significance for a man's status and ultimately his survival.

Men were often traumatized by loss of sex drive, impotence, and their emaciated physiques. Rumors circulated that Jewish men were no longer able to "function as men" due to experiments in the concentra-tion camps.[11] Some Jewish men concerned about their fertility sought out German medical advice despite fear and feelings of shame.[12] One psychoanalyst touring the camps observed, "Until liberation, when the death threat was finally lifted, most of the men were impotent."[13] Sex became a means of asserting that one was alive.[14] Roman Halter told an interviewer of his bartering Ovaltine for the services of a prostitute. "He described his experiences with her, with mesmerizing frankness, as though wishing to convey the physical state he was then in—what it felt like to be safe at last, his body discovering that it had a sex."[15]

The sexual act represented his physical survival and the reassertion of his masculinity.

Men liberated in Germany sometimes had their first postwar sexual encounters with German women. Sex with a Jewish woman carried expectations so that, as Lynn Rapaport observes in her study of Jews in postwar Germany, "Jews who wish to have casual sexual relationships without being involved in any social obligations often date Germans."[16] Also, a gender imbalance within the DP population partially explains why some Jewish men looked outside the Jewish community for female companionship. In late 1945, the vast majority of the survivors were between the ages of eighteen and forty-five, and of that group, two-thirds were male.[17] In Regensburg there were 703 Jewish men and only 480 Jewish women. Of these women, 67 were pregnant and 59 were breastfeeding. In Neunburg vorm Wald, there were 114 men and 49 women. Nine of the women were pregnant, and another 10 were nursing infants.[18] Under these circumstances, many Jewish men were left without the possibility of a Jewish female companion. However, in some places, particularly in the British zone, Jewish women equaled or outnumbered Jewish men, perhaps explaining the involvement there of DP women with British soldiers.[19] Given Nazi racial purity laws of the recent past, sexual relations between Jews and Germans were complicated by symbolic meanings.

Few Jewish DPs committed rape against German women, but those who did were motivated by revenge.[20] More commonly, Jewish men bartered their rations for sex. Years of Nazi propaganda celebrating the German woman as the feminine ideal and denigrating the Eastern European man as a beast had encouraged this form of "revenge and desire to taste the forbidden fruit."[21] At the very least such sexual contact turned the Nazi racial order upside down, demonstrating its defeat. The German woman often represented life,[22] and sex with her affirmed the Jewish DP's new life as a free man.

Many DPs, however, disapproved of sexual relations between Jewish men and German women, viewing them as "coarse" and "undignified."[23] In a proposal to the First Congress of Liberated Jews, religious delegates asked that "in the name of faithful Jewry, treat those Jews who marry German women as traitors and exclude them from the She'erit Hapletah / the remainder of Jewry in Europe."[24] Fraternization between Jewish survivors and Germans also concerned the members of Kibbutz Buchenwald, who agreed in June 1945 to expel any member guilty of "intimate relations" with a German woman.[25] DP newspapers and rabbis also called for the expulsion of Jews who consorted with German women.[26]

Part of the repugnance at Jewish-German liaisons stemmed from the Jewish DPs' association of all Germans with the Nazi murderers of their families, and part of it was the fear of losing what remained of European Jewry to assimilation. In this respect, DP leaders intended the expulsions of a few individuals to serve as deterrents to the further formation of Jewish-German couples. At the same time, it was easier to condemn the sexual activity of some survivors with German women than to confront the reality of near annihilation and the inability of Jewish men to prevent it. By paying attention to these perceived betrayals, survivors could avoid the question of Jewish men's inability to protect their families and communities during the war. This avoidance suggests a Jewish parallel to Dagmar Herzog's argument that postwar German debates about sexual propriety resulted in "the displacement of the discourse of morality away from murder and onto sex."[27] DPs' preoccupation with sexual propriety could mask an inability to cope with the reality of near extermination and its implications for Jewish masculinity.

While some Jewish men sought sexual contact with German women, it seemed unthinkable that Jewish women would consort with German men. None of the authorities attempted to prohibit such contact as they did in the case of Jewish men. In postwar Kovno, Rabbi Ephraim Oshry offered his responsum concerning whether a married man could reunite with his wife who had been forced into a brothel serving the German army. Rabbi Oshry declared it permissible, since the wife had been coerced under a death threat, and "certainly these oppressors were so disgusting, abominable, and detestable in her eyes that it is inconceivable they could have seduced her."[28] German men had been perpetrators, and it was unthinkable that a Jewish woman would voluntarily enter a relationship with one. If a Jewish woman was seen with a German man, other Jews quickly informed her that while Jewish men might choose to fraternize, she could not.[29]

Homosexuality also transgressed traditional community norms, which perhaps explains why it was rarely mentioned in survivor accounts. An index search of Jewish survivor narratives in the Shoah Foundation Institute's Visual History Archive found no mention of homosexuality in the post-liberation period. Most discussion of homosexuality in these records was confined to wartime experiences. Although a few survivors mentioned being aware of homosexual or lesbian activity before the war, most of the survivors indicated that their first awareness of homosexuality or contact with homosexuals came in the concentration camps, where they encountered German prisoners with pink triangles.[30] Some survivors credited German male homosexuals with giving them lifesaving assistance.[31]

Many survivors, however, mentioned block elders and *kapos*, most of them Germans, using their positions of power to select same-sex Jewish children as their servants, called *pipels*, and then sexually abusing them.[32] The privileged prisoners were often heterosexual men and women who sexually abused the weaker prisoners they had chosen as servants. These relationships reinforced the status and privilege of the block elders and *kapos*, while the *pipels* received some material benefits that they presumably could hope would assist them in their struggle for survival.[33] The disparity of status between the individuals in these relationships made them inherently coercive, since to refuse the advances of the privileged prisoners could mean death.

Very few of the survivors recounting these relationships spoke about their own rape or sexual abuse.[34] Most of them recalled witnessing the exploitation of others. One survivor, Michael Honey, had been selected to be a servant to a German prisoner in the Mauthausen camp fire brigade. He recalled the other *pipels* inviting him to join in their homosexual activity. When Honey refused, one boy told him that when his master ran out of credit at the camp brothel, he would sodomize Honey.[35] Honey's narrative implied that the boys' sexual activity was a consequence of their rape, their "initiation" into homosexual acts, by the German prisoners. The notion that homosexual encounters among Jewish boys were the result of their corruption by Germans in the camps found an echo in the few postwar references to survivor homosexual activity.

Relief workers, for example, noted that German men had sexually abused boys during the Nazi period. One observer questioned whether boys protected by SS guards "for the sake of carrying on homosexual relations with them" would be able to build "normal child and then adult relationships."[36] Writing about the Feldafing DP camp, Simon Schochet described homosexuality as a problem among young boys who had survived the camps because of their physical strength and the "special attention" they had received from *kapos* and other privileged prisoners.[37] Schochet attributed the postwar sexual transgressions of the boys to their wartime exploitation. Here the Nazi belief that homosexuality was a Jewish disease is stood on its head: the Nazi regime had instead infected Jewish boys with homosexuality.

In addition to the hostility of traditional Jewish society toward homosexuality, it remained illegal in postwar Germany and elsewhere. Homosexuals would have felt it necessary to hide their orientation, either through passing as heterosexual or through a secret life outside of the overcrowded confines of the DP camps. Military court cases may reveal more information about adult homosexuals, but it is difficult to search the records. One case that I stumbled upon reveals two Jewish DPs convicted of sodomy placed in solitary confinement for fourteen days on a diet of bread and water.[38] If this is representative of treatment meted out to homosexuals, then it is clear why they would remain underground. More remains to be learned about homosexuality among Jewish survivors of the Holocaust, and further examination of the interviews housed in the Shoah Foundation Institute's Visual History Archive may yet yield additional useful evidence.

Just as survivors explained homosexual acts among boys as the result of German corruption, so too the DP community understood that
German oppression had robbed some Jewish women of their sexual
innocence. When it came to matters of survival, concentration camp
inmates had learned that the morality of the normal world had no place
in decision making. Lawrence Langer refers to "choiceless choice" to
describe those decisions made within a context of powerlessness that
negates the meaning of moral categories. Choiceless choice also applied to the immediate postwar situation of survivors.[39] Although many
survivors refrained from judging harshly the exchange of sexual favors
for food or transportation when it was necessary, tolerance appears
to have disappeared once circumstances became more stable.[40] A DP
woman did not need to be sexually untouched, but she was expected
to find a stable relationship with a Jewish man.[41] Some Orthodox men
willingly married sexually experienced women, even those who had
engaged in sex with their wartime protectors.[42]

Given the squalid conditions and lack of privacy in the camps, sexual
encounters between DPs could not meet the romantic expectations
of normal society. Yet, the DPs did manage to find opportunities for
sexual intercourse. Just as we have seen with Jewish men, some DP
women found sexual contact to be a physical manifestation of freedom
and an affirmation of life. One female survivor recalled a friend's explanation of her sexual experience: "For one precious moment she felt
free. . . . Today she felt the urge to do it, to feel free at last. . . . There
was a greater meaning to the intercourse than just sex. Gita knew that
she shared her feelings with another person. She also experienced an
exhilarating emotional high and a release of feelings she had kept tied
in knots for so many years."[43] Sexual activity could serve as an emotional catharsis and as a way to feel connected to another human being.

Understanding the survivors' needs for companionship and sexual
contact, some DP leaders encouraged premarital sex as a means of
gauging the viability of future marriages. Sexual function, fertility,
and general compatibility could be established through cohabitation
prior to marriage.[44] Given that DP courtships occurred outside of the

normal bounds of established community and family supervision, some DPs recognized that new practices were needed to prevent hasty marriages followed by divorces. Premarital sex seems to have been mostly confined to established couples, with promiscuity still frowned upon and marriage the ultimate goal.

In Landsberg, the U.S. military camp commander Irving Heymont observed that many couples lived together without the benefit of marriage, but he was told that if a child resulted from the union, then marriage would follow.[45] Indeed, illegitimacy was virtually unknown among the Jewish DPs.[46] In the rare instance that a man did not marry his pregnant partner, she was likely to seek out an abortion. In Belsen, it was mostly DP women impregnated by married British soldiers having abortions.[47] Since abortion was illegal except for medical reasons, a DP would need to find a doctor willing to perform the procedure for a black-market fee. Without connections or funds, these women often resorted to self-induced abortions.[48]

Most pregnant survivors, however, married their partners and gave birth. The pain and fear of being alone in the world encouraged many to enter what they believed to be permanent bonds of matrimony.[49] Sex and reproduction also enabled survivors to demonstrate their triumph over their oppressors. DP artist Samuel Bak wrote, "Men were looking for women and women for men. Giving birth to a Jewish child was a form of retaliation against the brutal cruelty of the recent past."[50] The birth of a new Jewish generation in the land of Nazism also served as "biological revenge."[51]

Not everyone indulged in premarital sex. Some women abstained from sexual intercourse in order to restrict their fertility so that they could prepare for illegal immigration to Palestine.[52] Other survivors sought to live by their parents' values. For example, Sara Tuvel knew that her Orthodox uncle thought "that as a nonbeliever I would not hesitate to move in with Meyer without benefit of a marriage ceremony. But I was still my mother and father's child; I would never go against what they had taught me."[53] The lessons of the prewar era still held sway for some, even as other young men and women delighted in their healing bodies. For many, heterosexual desire was something to be enjoyed and acted upon.

Most DPs chose to create Jewish marriages and homes. Even secular Jews wanted a religious wedding ceremony as a means of forming links with the past and to ensure family continuity.[54] Marriage and sexual relations raised the issue of family purity laws. Since no functioning mikveh had survived Nazi rule, the building of the mikveh was a top priority for religious DPs. Determined Orthodox DPs successfully enlisted the aid of Jewish chaplains and relief workers in obtaining the property and materials necessary for the construction of ritual baths, although not without controversy. A British rabbi serving Belsen DPs convinced authorities to build a mikveh for prospective brides;[55] however, secular DP leaders questioned the priorities of this rabbi, since the wood used for the mikveh construction could have served as heating fuel in the bitter winter of 1945–46.[56] At Landsberg, DPs built a mikveh on their own initiative. When the military commander discovered it, it was declared a health hazard. A compromise was reached that permitted women to use the mikveh provided that they shower afterward.

With sexual activity on the rise, the religious leaders sought to educate young couples in proper Jewish relations. Despite the severe paper shortage, rabbis managed to publish information on Jewish marital law, instructing women and men about such things as the proper timing of marital relations and use of the mikveh after menstruation.[57] These attempts to persuade Jewish DPs, the women in particular, to follow religious law indicated the religious leaders' concern that young survivors were ignorant of the traditions and not particularly interested in learning about them. Indeed the majority of survivors came from non-observant backgrounds. But it was not only secular Jews who ignored the directives of the religious authorities. Even more traditional Jews occasionally found it difficult to abide by the policies of Orthodox rabbis.

At Belsen DP camp the initial absence of a mikveh led to a mini-revolt against rabbinic authority. A couple engaged before the war found themselves reunited as DPs. A British rabbi had agreed to officiate at the Sunday wedding in June 1945. On Friday afternoon, however, the rabbi decided that the marriage could not take place because there was no mikveh available for the bride. A camp leader, Hadassah Bimko (later Rosensaft), retorted that Jewish law permitted any Jew to perform a marriage ceremony and that the wedding would go on with or without him. In the end the rabbi presided over the nuptials. As Rosensaft recalled, "It turned out to be an anti-*mikvah* wedding that took place on Freedom Square in Belsen, under a blue sky. It was the beginning of life."[58] The difficult material conditions of the early months following liberation required religiously observant survivors to make compromises and innovations in their adherence to Jewish law and tradition. The DPs' determination to marry and create Jewish families often overrode obedience to rabbinic decisions. It also points to the loss of rabbinic authority brought about by the dissolution of established communities and the wartime struggle for survival that often forced individuals to rely on their own judgments.

The resolve of DPs to marry and the sympathy of Jewish chaplains meant that rules were often bent. Problems arose for those DPs who could not prove the death of a spouse before remarriage. Since the Nazis did not issue death certificates for the vast majority of their victims in the ghettos and concentration camps, many widows and widowers had to rely on eyewitness accounts and rumors for information on the fate of their spouses. When rabbis demanded further proof before solemnizing a second marriage, survivors searched for authorities who were willing to accept their testimony as proof. Frequently non-Orthodox Jewish military chaplains would take pity on these people. Some survivors in postwar Europe would not examine too closely the credentials of a man claiming to be a rabbi, if he consented to officiate at the wedding.[59] The inability of DPs to procure official documents combined with their drive to create new families led them to disregard the strictures of rabbis. This resulted in ceremonies of questionable validity in Jewish law and in conflict between various rabbinical movements.[60] If no accommodating rabbi were to be found, some DPs would proclaim their intent to marry before witnesses and enter into a common law marriage.[61] Other DPs chose to live with their new partners without the benefit of marriage while they awaited further evidence of their spouses' fates.[62]

The question of *agunot* was such an important issue that one of the first acts of the DP rabbinate in the American Zone was to send a request for guidance on the issue to Palestine.[63] In August 1946, the Rabbinic Council created a committee dedicated to the problem of *agunot*. It resolved that only a rabbi who was part of a *beit din* of three rabbis or a rabbi appointed by the *agunot* committee could hear evidence in such cases.[64] In 1948, a rabbinic responsum from Palestine, recognizing the unusual circumstances of the Shoah, eased the requirements of proof in order to allow more remarriages. On the question of whether to accept testimony from witnesses who may be repeating rumors or may have profaned the Sabbath, Rabbi Shlomo David Kahana wrote, "But in our time, a time of general annihilation, a time when many of the martyrs submitted to death for the sanctification of God's name . . . we should not worry about such suspicions."[65] The unprecedented circumstances following the destruction of European Jewry required innovation and adaptation for Jewish family life to continue.

Sex after the Shoah was fraught with meaning: freedom and revenge, victimhood and survival, corruption and continuity. Even as survivors reveled in their mending bodies and burgeoning sexuality as evidence of their freedom, they adhered to a moral code that distinguished between the acceptable sexual relations between Jews and the tainted relationships between Jews and Germans. Revenge could be taken through pimping or sex with German women but also through Jewish procreation. Jews found postwar rapes and sexual assaults especially difficult to bear because they violated the survivors' expectations that the world would protect them after liberation. At the same time, consensual sex confirmed that one was alive, that one had indeed survived. The DPs' acceptance of premarital heterosexual sex did not extend to tolerance of homosexual activity, viewing the former as a permissible means of gauging the long-term prospects of a Jewish relationship and the latter as a Nazi abomination afflicting Jewish boys. For all of the sexual activity, DPs valued Jewish marriages as an important step in re-creating the family life that Nazi persecution had destroyed. The tensions between DPs and rabbis over family purity laws reflected a loss of rabbinic authority but also the creativity of the survivors in adapting religious ritual and law to their unusual circumstances. In the DP camps, the survivors' sexual relationships affirmed their Jewish identity and rebuilt Jewish life, blending tradition and innovation.

NOTES

1. Quoted in Jo Reilly, "Cleaner, Carer, and Occasional Dance Partner? Writing Women Back into the Liberation of Bergen-Belsen," in *Belsen in History and Memory*, ed. Jo Reilly et al. (London: Frank Cass, 1997), 152.

2. Erna F. Rubinstein, *After the Holocaust: The Long Road to Freedom* (North Haven, CT: Archon Books, 1995), 20–21; Eva Torres, "Videotaped interview, by the University of Southern California Shoah Foundation Institute for Visual History and Education," Interview Code [IC] 6094, segment 49, Visual History Archive [VHA] [online at subscribing institutions]; www.usc.edu/vhi.VHA. The only objection to exhibiting women's hair from Auschwitz at the U.S. Holocaust Memorial Museum came from two female survivors, "perhaps because men do not feel about hair the same way women do. Men are used to shaving daily, while for a woman the shaving of her head is a violation of her womanhood" (Hadassah Rosensaft, *Yesterday: My Story* [Washington, D.C.: United States Holocaust Memorial Museum, 2004], 197). See also Pascale Bos, "Women and the Holocaust: Analyzing Gender Difference," in *Experience and Expression: Women, the Nazis, and the Holocaust*, ed. Elizabeth R. Baer and Myrna Goldenberg (Detroit, MI: Wayne State University Press, 2003), 33–34.

3. Georgia M. Gabor, *My Destiny: Survivor of the Holocaust* (Arcadia, CA: Amen Publishing, 1981), 142–44; Helen Farkas, *Remember the Holocaust* (Santa Barbara: Fithian Press, 1995), 111; Fanya Gottesfeld Heller, *Strange and Unexpected Love: A Teenage Girl's Holocaust Memoirs* (Hoboken, NJ: Ktav, 1993), 272; Sara Zyskind, *Stolen Years* (Minneapolis: Lerner Publication Group, 1981), 262. Some Jewish women had experienced similar situations in the concentration camps and in hiding; see Joan Ringelheim, "The Split between Gender and the Holocaust," in *Women in the Holocaust*, ed. Dalia Ofer and Lenore J. Weitzman (New Haven, CT: Yale University Press, 1998), 341–42.

4. Tamara Freitag, "Videotaped interview," VHA, IC 4182, seg. 70. See also Ruth Krol, "Videotaped interview," VHA 7273, seg. 128; and Gabor, *My Destiny*, 142–44.

5. Helen Waterford, *Commitment to the Dead* (Frederick, CO: Renaissance House, 1987), 97. See also Rubinstein, *After the Holocaust*, 84; Eva Slomovits, "Videotaped interview," VHA, IC 24130, seg. 211.

6. See Alicia Appleman-Jurman, *Alicia: My Story* (New York: Bantam Books, 1988), 356; Gabor, *My Destiny*, 177. See also Ruth Minsky Sender, *To Life* (New York: Macmillan Publishing, 1988), 51.

7. See J. Nochimowski, "Die Ghettoamenorrhoe," *Medizinische Klinik: Wochenschrift für Klinik und Praxis* 41 (August 1946), Yad Vashem (YV), M-1/P-53.

8. Leib Szfman and W. M. Schmidt, "Jewish Health and Medical Work in Europe," *Jewish Social Service Quarterly* 25 (June 1949): 425.

9. Mayer Hersh, "Videotaped interview," VHA, IC 30624, segs. 324–26; Samuel Pisar, *Of Blood and Hope* (New York: Macmillan Publishing, 1979), 65–66; Rubinstein, *After the Holocaust*, 40; Ruth Bondy, "Women in Theresienstadt and the Family Camp in Birkenau," in Ofer and Weitzman, *Women in the Holocaust*, 320; Sybil Milton, "Women and the Holocaust: The Case of German and German-Jewish Women," in *Different Voices: Women and the Holocaust*, ed. Carol Rittner and John K. Roth (New York: Paragon House, 1993), 231.

10. Elizabeth D. Heineman, "Sexuality and Nazism: The Doubly Unspeakable?" *Journal of the History of Sexuality* 11 (January–April 2002): 59.

11. Jacob Biber, *Risen from the Ashes: A Story of the Jewish Displaced Persons in the Aftermath of World War II* (San Bernardino, CA: Borgo Press, 1990), 36; Atina Grossmann, "Victims, Villains, and Survivors: Gendered Perceptions and Self-Perceptions of Jewish Displaced Persons in Occupied Postwar Germany," *Journal of the History of Sexuality* 11 (January–April 2002): 305.

12. Jane Borenstein, "Videotaped interview," VHA, IC 10534, segs. 105–8.

13. Paul Friedman, "The Road Back for the DP's: Healing the Psychological Scars of Nazism," *Commentary* 6 (December 1948): 506.

14. During the war, a partisan man asking a woman for sex would say, "Let me check if I am alive." Nechama Tec, *Resilience and Courage: Women, Men, and the Holocaust* (New Haven: Yale University Press, 2003), 320.

15. Neil Belton, *The Good Listener: Helen Bamber; A Life Against Cruelty* (New York: Pantheon Books, 1998), 138.

16. Lynn Rapaport, *Jews in Germany after the Holocaust: Memory, Identity, and Jewish-German Relations* (New York: Cambridge University Press, 1997), 231. See also Simon Schochet, *Feldafing* (Vancouver, BC: November House, 1983), 161.

17. Zeev W. Mankowitz, *Life between Memory and Hope: The Survivors of the Holocaust in Occupied Germany* (Cambridge: Cambridge University Press, 2002), 19. A few Jewish men sought and found romantic love with German women (Biber, *Risen from the Ashes*, 22–25).

18. "Population in Oberpfalz," YIVO, RG 294.2, MK 483, microfilm reel 63, folder 888.

19. By 1946 there were nearly as many women as men at Foehrenwald DP camp, and from the time of liberation, women outnumbered men in Bergen-Belsen at almost 65 percent to 35 percent. Judith Tydor Baumel, *Double Jeopardy: Gender and the Holocaust* (London: Vallentine Mitchell, 1998), 31; Yehuda Bauer, *A History of the Holocaust*, rev. ed. (New York: Franklin Watts, 2001), 359; Hagit Lavsky, "A Community of Survivors: Bergen-Belsen as a Jewish Centre after 1945," in Reilly et al., *Belsen*, 164.

20. See Judith Tydor Baumel, *Kibbutz Buchenwald: Survivors and Pioneers*, trans. Dena Ordan (New Brunswick: Rutgers University Press, 1997), 20–21.

21. Schochet, *Feldafing*, 161–62; Lucy S. Dawidowicz, *From That Time and Place: A Memoir, 1938–1947* (New York: W.W. Norton, 1989), 302; Shamai Davidson, "Surviving During the Holocaust and Afterwards: The Post-Liberation Experience," in *Holding on to Humanity—The Message of Holocaust Survivors: The Shamai Davidson Papers*, ed. Israel W. Charny (New York: New York University Press, 1992), 72.

22. Pisar, *Of Blood and Hope*, 92.

23. Josef Warscher, "From Buchenwald to Stuttgart," in Michael Brenner, *After the Holocaust: Rebuilding Jewish Lives in Postwar Germany*, trans. Barbara Harshav (Princeton, NJ: Princeton University Press, 1997), 112; Avraham Ahuria, Personal Diary, April 25, 1945, quoted in Baumel, *Kibbutz Buchenwald*, 21.

24. "Die Konferenz beschliesst," YIVO microfilm read at YV, JM/10263, folder 44.

25. "Homecoming in Israel: Journal of Kibbutz Buchenwald," in *The Root and the Bough*, ed. Leo W. Schwarz (New York: Rinehart, 1949), 316.

26. W. Henriques, "Resolution of the Central Rabbinate at the 2nd Congress of the She'erit Hapletah in the British Zone" (in Yiddish), July 22, 1947, YV O-70/29; *Undzer Moment*, quoted in Brenner, *After the Holocaust*, 49.

27. Dagmar Herzog, *Sex after Fascism: Memory and Morality in Twentieth-Century Germany* (Princeton, NJ: Princeton University Press, 2005), 140.

28. Quoted in Irving J. Rosenbaum, *The Holocaust and Halakhah* (New York: Ktav, 1976), 146. For more on brothels in the Holocaust, see Heineman, "Sexuality and Nazism," 54, 56–59.

29. Ruth Kluger, *Still Alive: A Holocaust Girlhood Remembered* (New York: Feminist Press at the City University of New York, 2001), 166.

30. Kitty Fischer, "Videotaped interview," VHA, IC 1677, seg. 17; Stephanie Heller, "Videotaped interview," VHA, IC 21978, seg. 24; David Mandl, "Videotaped interview," VHA, IC 46684, seg. 161; Nikola Hamburg, "Videotaped interview," VHA, IC 51476, seg. 128.

31. Fischer, "Videotaped interview," seg. 18; Francis Joseph Philips, "Videotaped interview," VHA, IC 35849, seg. 67; Herman Schlesinger, "Videotaped interview," VHA, IC 27770, seg. 123; Henry Wermuth, "Videotaped interview," VHA, IC 15694, seg. 262.

32. Lucia Amato, "Videotaped interview," VHA, IC 14682, seg. 70; Stephanie Heller, "Videotaped interview," VHA IC 21978, seg. 24; Michael Honey, "Videotaped interview," VHA, IC 25651, seg. 55; Rudy Kennedy, "Videotaped interview," VHA, IC 35935, segs. 315–18; Nathan Offen, "Videotaped interview," VHA, IC 20084, seg. 21; Mayer Hersh, "Videotaped interview," VHA, IC 30624, segs. 324–26.

33. A study of African men in the South African gold mines suggests that senior miners selected boys to be their servants and passive sexual partners ("wives") as a means of performing their status, while the boys accepted their submissive roles in exchange for material benefits. To a limited extent this is parallel to the *kapo-pipel* transactions. The significant difference lies in the far greater coercive nature of the concentration camps and the *kapos'* unrestrained power over life and death. T. Dunbar Moodie with Vivienne Ndatshe, *Going for Gold: Men, Mines, and Migration* (Berkeley: University of California Press, 1994), chap. 4. I thank Kathleen Sheldon for bringing this to my attention.

34. For two exceptions, see Nathan Offen, "Videotaped interview," VHA, IC 20084, seg. 21; Kenneth Roman, "Videotaped interview," VHA, IC 40310, segs. 167–75.

35. Honey, "Videotaped interview," seg. 55. Honey said that he volunteered for a transport out of the camp in order to avoid being raped.

36. Ralph Segalman, "The Psychology of Jewish Displaced Persons," *Jewish Social Services Quarterly* 24 (June 1947): 364.

37. Schochet, *Feldafing*, 24.

38. Arthur A. Thue, Prison Officer, 1st U.S. Infantry Division to Summary Court Officer, Co D, 3rd MG Regt., "Offense of Sodomy of Jewish DP Prisoners," November 14, 1946; Correspondence—General—1946–47; General Records of Weiden-Neustadt Resident Liaison and Security Office 1945–49; Records of the Field Operations Division; Records of United States Occupation Headquarters, World War II (OMGUS), Record Group (RG) 260, Entry: Bavaria; National Archives at College Park, MD (NACP).

39. Lawrence Langer, *Holocaust Testimonies: The Ruins of Memory* (New Haven: Yale University Press, 1991), 26.

40. Rubinstein, *After the Holocaust*, 35.

41. Schochet, *Feldafing*, 158.

42. Heller, *Strange and Unexpected Love*, 278. This immediate postwar understanding of survivors did not protect Heller from censure when she published her memoir in 1990. See Sara R. Horowitz, "The Gender of Good and Evil: Women and Holocaust Memory," in *Gray Zones: Ambiguity and Compromise in the Holocaust and Its Aftermath*, ed. Jonathan Petropoulos and John K. Roth (New York: Berghahn Books, 2005), 173–75.

43. Rubinstein, *After the Holocaust*, 63. See also Lala Fishman and Steven Weingartner, *Lala's Story: A Memoir of the Holocaust* (Evanston, IL: Northwestern University Press, 1997), 318. Similar feelings of sexual awakening are reflected in the diary of Kibbutz Buchenwald (*Geringshof Diary: December 1945–July 1946*, quoted in Baumel, *Kibbutz Buchenwald*, 107).

44. Biber, *Risen from the Ashes*, 38; Rosensaft, *Yesterday*, 109.

45. Irving Heymont, *Among the Survivors of the Holocaust—1945: The Landsberg DP Camp Letters of Major Irving Heymont, United States Army* (Cincinnati: American Jewish Archives, 1982), 45.

46. Rabbi Philip S. Bernstein, "Status of Jewish Displaced Persons," in U.S. Department of State, *The Displaced-Persons Problem: A Collection of Recent Official Statements* (Washington, DC: U.S. Government Printing Office, 1947), 1309.

47. Laurie A. Whitcomb, "Life behind the Baby Carriage: Reassessing the Life Reborn Narrative of Jewish Displaced Persons through Survivor Testimony" (paper presented at the annual meeting of the German Studies Association, San Diego, CA, October 2007), 12.

48. The number of abortions caught the attention of DP religious leaders. A tragic case of an unmarried Jewish DP dying from complications after an abortion is reported in Joseph Soski, "Memories of a Vanished World" (1992), 95, USHMM, RG 02.072.

49. Hannah Modenstein, telephone interview with the author, tape recording, July 18, 1995. Also, Baumel writes, "Marriages were inspired more by the desire to

escape loneliness and to have children than by love and emotional intimacy" (Baumel, *Kibbutz Buchenwald*, 106).

50. Samuel Bak, "Landsberg Revisited," *Dimensions* 13 (1999): 33.

51. Atina Grossmann, "Trauma, Memory, and Motherhood: Germans and Jewish Displaced Persons in Post-Nazi Germany, 1945–1949," *Archiv für Sozialgeschichte* 38 (1998): 215–39.

52. Baumel, *Kibbutz Buchenwald*, 107.

53. Sara Tuvel Bernstein, *The Seamstress: A Memoir of Survival* (New York: Berkley Books, 1997), 305.

54. Hagit Lavsky, *New Beginnings: Holocaust Survivors in Bergen-Belsen and the British Zone in Germany, 1945–1950* (Detroit, MI: Wayne State University Press, 2002), 149; Rubinstein, *After the Holocaust*, 98.

55. Isaac Levy, "Belsen Testimonies," in Reilly et al., *Belsen*, 240.

56. Lavsky, *New Beginnings*, 114.

57. N. Z. Friedmann, *Taharat Hamischpacha: Von di jidische Ehe-Gesetze* (Föhrenwald, Germany: 1945/46), YV M-1/P-65; Agudat Israel, "Jewish Wife! Jewish Mother!" (in Yiddish), YV M-1/P-65.

58. Rosensaft, *Yesterday*, 79.

59. Bertha Ferderber-Salz, *And the Sun Kept Shining . . .* (New York: Holocaust Library, 1980), 213.

60. Yehuda Bauer, *Out of the Ashes: The Impact of American Jews on Post-Holocaust European Jewry* (New York: Pergamon, 1989), 96.

61. Levy, "Belsen Testimonies," in Reilly et al., *Belsen*, 240.

62. Rosensaft, *Yesterday*, 109.

63. "Council Meeting of Jews in Bavaria" (in Yiddish), *Unzer Weg*, October 19, 1946, 4.

64. Alex Grobman, *Battling for Souls: The Vaad Hatzala Rescue Committee in Post-War Europe* (Jersey City, NJ: Ktav, 2004), 168.

65. Rabbi Shlomo David Kahana, responsum on permission for *agunot* to remarry (after the war), in *Rabbinic Responsa of the Holocaust Era*, ed. Robert Kirschner (New York: Schocken Books, 1985), 139–47, esp. 144f.

44

QUESTIONING SEXUALITY IN CARIBBEAN REFORM JUDAISM

Two Perspectives

RABBI DANA EVAN KAPLAN, PhD,
AND DR. KAREN CARPENTER PhD, CST, PGCHE

> I agree with the theory that people who are sexually repressed
> are those most likely to repress others. This has happened
> with predictable regularity in the modern era. It applies to
> the English in the Victorian era, the Boers in South Africa,
> and in equal measure to the Religious Right in America.
>
> *(Rabbi Eric Yoffie, 2010)*

This chapter explores the lived experiences of two professionals, a rabbi and a sexologist, working in the Caribbean island of Jamaica. Famous for its tourism products of sun, sea, and sex, the island has a small Jewish community that had been without a rabbi for thirty-three years. Kaplan, an American by birth, has studied and worked in a variety of countries and regions including Israel, South Africa, South America, the United States, and now the Caribbean. Carpenter, a native Jamaican also with a multicultural background, is a psychologist and clinical sexologist. Together they question the lived experiences of the larger culture and how this might be interpreted for the individual who is both fully sexual and fully Jewish. In a small community, as is the current Jewish Jamaican population, the extent to which people present themselves as having partners depends very much on the impression congregants feel they will create by attending services together. The willingness to do so revolves around certain key factors such as (1) whether common-law marriages are accepted by the congregation, (2) whether partners from non-Jewish backgrounds feel welcome, and (3) the extent to which teachings are shared on the meaning of marriage for the community. In the absence of any clarity on these questions, the community reflects the behavior of the larger traditional society, with only those in registered marriages attending with their partners. The remaining pairings stay underground.

The phenomenology follows the issues raised by a culture that professes to be Christian yet glorifies sexuality in its dress, music, and daily living. Christianity, like the inhabitants who now call themselves Jamaicans, has been part of the legacy of centuries of slavery. Over ten thousand Africans were transplanted to the islands against their will, followed by the recruitment of indentured Indian and Chinese laborers. The original Taino population was obliterated through overwork and foreign diseases, which the colonizers brought with them. The island's name was changed from Xamaca to Jamaica by the Spanish. During the British reign in the region, Christianity was introduced as a political tool of control, which extended to the control of the sexual expression of the African slaves, who could be both sired and used at the masters' whim. The attitude of the church toward sexuality outside of marriage then and now has generally been repressive and condemnatory. The Christian church has spent more than four hundred years in the islands in its mission of repressing sexual behavior, with little success, as is evidenced by the popular culture.

The music and dance of the island are recognized internationally as two of the most vibrant cultural expressions. These reflect the daily experiences of the society in general, which include multiple partnerships. Approximately half the population of children is born out of wedlock, with visiting "baby fathers" and their multiple "baby mothers." Women in the broader society occupy three main roles for the

Jamaican man: *wifey* (informal wife), *baby mother* (the mother of one or more children but not necessarily a live-in partner), and *maties* (lovers in addition to the wifey or baby mothers). These three titles signal not only levels of attachment but also sexual engagement between a man and his women. It is largely accepted that a man will have more than one woman even if he professes to be monogamous, in which instance he is referred to colloquially as a *one-burner stove*. Couplings often last for short periods of time, and one man may have children with several informal wives or "baby mothers" without living with any of them. Others live together in a pattern of serial monogamy and may take a woman as a "wifey" in a common-law union. Elsa Leo-Rhynie describes the various couplings as "visiting unions."[1]

The result is a kind of sexual schizophrenia that creates two Jamaicas—one of a small, traditional, largely Eurocentric ruling class; and that of the larger Afro-Caribbean majority, with some Indian and Chinese pockets of influence, who see sexual desires and expression as natural and healthy. To prove their respectability, therefore, the majority must outwardly appear to conform to the moirés of the ruling classes, even if it is only an empty gesture.

In more recent years, the retentions of British colonial sexuality have been further diluted by the influence of black American popular culture, first through the technology of cable television and second through the Internet and social networking groups. It is not hard to understand how this has come about when you witness the proliferation of cable channels streaming into the living rooms and bars of the most remote areas of the country. Hip-hop music, MTV, and BET are staples of the last two decades, and Jamaica's own music has had a tremendous influence on the American popular music culture. The two-way exchange between these cultures has not only been through music, as Jamaicans have a long history of temporary employment in farm work programs in the United States as well as the migration of whole families to America. We can easily identify some of the same British colonial overtones spoken of earlier in the American approach to sexuality. When we consider Rabbi Eric Yoffie's critique of

American repression of sexuality and its Victorian origins, cited above, we could easily replace the word "American" with "Jamaican" and arrive at similar conclusions.[2]

Other writers, like Carr, argue that a kind of sexual schizophrenia is to be expected because of how far we have come in divorcing our mental life from our physical selves:

> Few live up to the contradictory ideas about sex in circulation in contemporary culture. . . . It is an issue of having multiple cultural-religious ideals that are not reconciled with each other or our bodies. We are alienated from our erotic selves. As a result, our sexuality and spirituality are sharply separated. Both are harmed.[3]

What Carr points out in his critique of the way in which society generally treats "natural desires" is that contemporary ideals of sexuality are impossible to live up to if that ideal includes a single path that renders sexual desires *uncomplicated*. Carr rejects this notion and argues instead for a multiplicity of expressions that allows for many paths to sexual satisfaction and to the sexual self-concept of the individual. The traditional social need for achieving sexual purity has effectively alienated us from our sexual desires and reduced sex to a manageable nonessential. In general, sexual variety is suspect in Western thinking. Within small geographic spaces such as Jamaica, and most of the Caribbean islands, the Christian ethic dictates that sex should remain in the back room, sexual desire is heterosexual, sexual diversity is bad, and where sex is not productive, it should also be seen as sin. Too much sex or too much pleasure derived from sexual contact is considered both harmful and undesirable for spiritual growth. This is certainly true for any type of gay or lesbian activity. A recent public outcry was raised over a text exploring same-sex behavior in a health and family life curriculum manual. The three pages, which were seen as too explicitly supportive of sexual diversity, were withdrawn by the Jamaican minister of education on the grounds that "the family life values espoused by the Ministry of Education are those based on the Christian principles of sexual morality as well as compassion and tolerance for all persons."[4]

The controversial text was withdrawn from all schools, and the Ministry of Education officer in charge of the project was fired. The Christian doctrine with its sexual prohibitions and Victorian ideals that were imported to the colonies is still in active contention with the African heritage of polyamorous family relationships and centuries-old East Indian and Chinese practices of the *Kama Sutra*, the *devadasi* (Indian "prostitutes of God"),[5] geisha courtesan training, and any other sexual expressions that fall outside the Christian norm. The combination of African and Asian cultural norms and the colonizers' greed for human property has been deeply engrained into the mass culture of the islands. Having more children is seen as better, and contraception is seen as a threat to reproductive wealth.

On the other end of the spectrum, polite society upholds the Victorian myth of sexual chastity and purity, which it imbues with social respectability. This Victorian ideal has rarely been practiced by the masses of the Afro-Caribbean population. This "face card," as the local population would call it, is largely a symbolic respectability preached by the traditional conservatives who describe Jamaica as a Christian society. Forms of sexual expression that deviate from the prescribed forms are publicly decried as sinful and degenerate. Newspaper articles expressing more liberal views are often relegated to the working man's paper and the XNews, but rarely are allowed on the pages of respectable newspapers without vehement opposition. The effect is usually one of shock, followed by the expected moral outcry, usually disproportionate to the views expressed.

We appreciate that while religion plays an important role in setting boundaries for social behavior, what Jamaicans publicly declare they do and what they actually engage in privately differ greatly, as can be seen by the 2008 National Knowledge Attitude Practise and Belief (KAPB) study conducted by the Ministry of Health, Jamaica. The statistics show that of the total sample approximately 75 percent was sexually active in the last year. More women than men reported being in a cohabiting relationship, and almost half the men (49 percent) and 40 percent of the women in the sample reported being sexually active but not living with their partner. In addition, 62 percent of men and 17 percent of women reported having multiple sexual partners. No distinction is made in the Jamaican Ministry of Health data reporting between the categories of "cohabiting" and "married," as this is an artificial distinction in the Jamaican context except as it confers social status and respectability. The same legal rights of state and church marriage are now conferred upon common-law marriages after six years of cohabitation. Children born outside of wedlock enjoy equal legal rights as those within marriage. The results of the 2008 KAPB describe some of the realities of the Jamaican sociosexual context.

How then are we meant to understand the role of sexuality within the community of Jews in Jamaica? A brief glimpse of the historical role of Jews in Jamaica shows us that their involvement dates back to the beginning of the sugar plantations. While Jews did not enjoy the legal rights of the colonial slave masters, their engineering ability was to set them apart as the architects of the sugar industry. Without the influx of Sephardic Jews to the Caribbean and Latin America, it is safe to say the sugar industry as we now know it could not have been born. The Jewish people, while adept at thriving on the margins, found an essential role for themselves within the slave economies of the New World:

> Marranos [secret Jews] played a leading role in introducing sugarcane cultivation to the Atlantic islands of Madeira, the Azores, the Cape Verde Islands, and Sao Tome and Principe in the Gulf of Guinea, and in the 16th century to the Caribbean Islands. They also brought the civilization of sugarcane from Madeira to America, and the first great proprietor of plantations and sugar mills, Duarte Coelho Pereira, allowed numerous Jewish experts on sugar processing to come to Brazil.[6]

The original Jewish community has changed over time, and as the current congregation seeks to solidify its identity, it may be useful to examine what it means to operate as fully Jewish, fully Jamaican, and fully sexual as separate identities as well as components of a single, integrated self. A phenomenological approach to the issue affords us the opportunity to explore the subjective responses of both researchers in their capacities as spiritual and psychological care professionals along with the lived experiences of their community.

While modern Jamaica is a relatively advanced country with multiple universities and various newspapers and other outlets for intellectual expression, there are very few Jewish voices who attempt to have an impact on the broader society. This was certainly not true in the past, when many of the great cultural and social trendsetters were from Jewish backgrounds. But from the time of the mass emigration of the mid-to late 1970s due to political unrest, there have been few prominent Jewish voices who are not only Jewish by origin but speak as active and committed Jews. Ainsley Henriques has been the only one who comes to mind. Over the past three decades or longer, he has been the voice of the Jewish community, speaking to local media when requested and foreign media when visited. In addition, he has become intensely interested in Jewish genealogy and has become an expert in Jamaican Jewish family origins.

This leaves a tremendous amount of territory open for exploration. For the approximately 2.8 million Jamaicans, there have been relatively few religious perspectives available to inform contemporary issues. Many of these voices have been fairly monochromal, projecting similar or identical perspectives on complex issues, usually taking what many might see as simplistic and even fundamentalist positions on various controversies that became important at specific points in time. The opportunity for a rabbi to present a distinctly Jewish and yet influential perspective is thus enormous.

One of the central opportunities of being a rabbi in Jamaica is that of having an impact on the broader society. Any rabbi coming to Jamaica today is aware that they are following in the footsteps of illustrious predecessors. Jamaicans of a certain age all listened to the very first popular radio talk show host, Rabbi Bernard Hooker, who served the United Congregation of Israelites for about nine years in the late 1960s and early 1970s. Rabbi Hooker had a tremendous following because of his entertaining and yet helpful commentary in response to Jamaicans of all backgrounds who called in to his show. This was a time in which there were limited opportunities for entertainment, and so his show was one of a very few options, thereby adding to its following.

The rabbinic writer of this article had the opportunity to participate in the program "Rabbis Without Borders" sponsored by Clal during the 2011–12 year. One of the central arguments made by this program is that rabbis should reconceptualize their role to see as clients not only members of their own congregations, but also broader social circles of whatever sort. The program did not attempt to define what these broader circles might consist of but rather made suggestions that might prove fruitful.

Being in a position to present Jewish perspectives on issues of societal concern is a tremendous opportunity. It needs to be done rather carefully, however. For example, there are certain hot-button issues that are almost guaranteed to result in the advocate being labeled deviant if particular liberal positions are taken. A new rabbi needs to cautiously navigate through these potential minefields if he or she wants to have a positive impact on society without creating a negative backlash or generating hostility toward the Jewish community.

Historically, the Jamaican Jewish community has looked inward. They did not see their role as advocating for Jewish values outside of their community—with the exception of Rabbi Hooker. So this outward-looking approach is a radical departure from established norms over a more than 360-year span. Nevertheless, we believe that the time has come for such an approach. Judaism needs to take responsibility for making a positive impact on Jamaican society. Many people believe that fundamentalist Christianity, which has become the dominant form of Christian religion in Jamaica, has failed as a value system that can realistically assist mature people in making balanced and thoughtful decisions as they relate to non-heterosexual conduct, sexual conduct outside of marriage, or sexual variety within marriage. There is therefore tremendous room for Judaism to have a positive impact on Jamaican civil culture.

This impact can be achieved in numerous ways, whether through the media or actual live events. The key premise is the goal to provide an alternative conceptual framework for understanding how to analyze a particular social problem without proselytizing. In other words, our goal is to help Jamaicans use Jewish wisdom to add richness to the public discourse without pushing them to formally adopt Judaism as their religion. Judaism does not believe that one needs to believe in Judaism in order go to heaven; there is thus no necessity for non-Jews to convert to our religion. Equally, the Christian belief in Messiah need not be threatened by Jewish thought. Rather, we see a huge lacuna in the public discourse and believe that it can benefit Jamaican society to provide a voice that can rationally and logically explain alternative perspectives to pressing problems.

Jamaican, Jewish, and Sexual

There are three possibilities as to what sex is about: pleasure, procreation, or oneness. Judaism, believing that the path to holiness is always found in the "golden middle," rejects the extreme far-right view that sex is only for making babies. Neither does Judaism embrace the extreme secular view that sex is only for fun and pleasure. Rather Judaism says that the purpose of sex is to synchronize and orchestrate two strangers together as one. Sex is the ultimate bonding process.[7]

When Rabbi Shmuley Boteach speaks of the purpose of sex as existing in the "golden middle" for pleasure, procreation, and bonding, he is of course referring to sex within marriage, and he makes this clear in his book *Kosher Sex*. Yet for a great number of Jamaicans, Jewish or otherwise, sex and childbearing outside of marriage is not only common, it is accepted. So too is having children with multiple partners. Boteach speaks primarily to sex within marriage and affirms the idea that Judaism takes the more moderate, balanced approach to sexual relations by viewing it as both pleasurable and reproductive. Many of the teachings on sexuality as they relate to issues of a woman's sexual rights would seem very radical to the larger Christian population; for example, "Marital sexual relations are the woman's right, not the man's."[8] The same might apply to tolerance toward same-sex relations and what Boteach refers to as the spiritual connection that is established through the bodily act of sex. Where Christian views would converge with Boteach's is in the matter of sex remaining within marriage. The Jamaican Jewish community appears to be looking for answers as to how best to incorporate their partners and families into the congregation and how this might be received by long-standing members of the community. In very small communities and groups, the behaviors of members come under closer scrutiny than in larger groups where individuals can remain fairly anonymous. The pointed absence of partners in nontraditional units within the congregation speaks to this silence around what constitutes appropriate sexual unions.

Other perspectives on the Caribbean experience include the psychoanalytic response of persons like Frantz Fanon. He describes the psychological health of the society as a direct reflection of the family structure. Fanon's *Black Skin, White Masks* seeks to provide a psychoanalytic approach to the questions of race and cultural identity in the West Indies. His focus in particular is on the notion of the "black man," which Fanon outright rejects as racist, because for him it describes nothing and reduces a whole race of people to a fictitious stereotyped identity that cannot be understood. We accept that even Fanon's use of the word "race" is problematic. Notwithstanding this, what is interesting about Fanon's treatment of the transplanted African, who is an alien in the West Indies, imprinted with an alien identity, such as British, French, or Dutch, is his constant comparison throughout his work between the experiences of the black man and the Jew. Fanon's task as a black, Martiniquen psychiatrist working in France is to present a clear analysis of what it means to be labeled in this way. He asserts that both Jew and black man present a threat to hegemonic society. The Jew is seen as an intellectual and financial threat and is described as having unusual capacities in these areas. The black man, Fanon argues, poses a sexual threat. It is not hard to see how a black Jew poses both an intellectual and sexual threat to those who believe in these stereotypes. Not only is there the suspicion that these black

Jews can think deeply, but they are also sexual suspects and must be kept poor and ignorant if they are to be properly controlled.

> Two realms: the intellectual and the sexual. An erection on Rodin's Thinker is a shocking thought. One cannot decently have a hard-on everywhere. The Negro symbolises the biological danger; the Jew the intellectual danger.[9]

The fear is that not only will they reproduce quickly but in so doing will require more resources and therefore seek also to acquire more wealth. In his attempt at providing a psychoanalysis of the Antillean, Fanon asserts that the Negro's psychosis is only ever fully apparent in the face of the colonizer. Whether the colonizer is in reality the literal European or exists in the stamps of European approval left behind by the past colonizers is not important for the purpose of this chapter, as the effect is the same. The sexual behavior and practices of Jamaican Jews are likely to be no different from those of the larger population. Many of those attending services on a regular basis have been assimilated into the congregation as adults, bringing with them familial and partnership patterns that predate their assimilation. How should they behave sexually? This is obviously a delicate issue that has to be handled carefully.

What can we draw on? Deliberations on the proper sexual conduct of the Reform Jew have come out of the Central Conference of American Rabbis. In 1998, the Ad Hoc Committee on Human Sexuality of the CCAR set out what it termed "Reform Jewish Sexual Values." They enunciated ten values for relationships, which for the most part support the existing relationship pattern in Jamaica, with the exception of number seven, *b'rit*, which would certainly exclude the majority of Jamaican adult interactions. These values include sexual interactions that reflect (1) *b'tzelem Elohim* (in the image of God); (2) *emet* (truth); (3) *b'riut* (health); (4) *mishpat* (justice); (5) *mishpachah* (family); (6) *tz'niut* (modesty); (7) *b'rit* (covenantal relationship); (8) *simchah* (joy); (9) *ahavah* (love); and (10) *k'dushah* ("holiness").[10]

Relationships are expected to embody the mutuality of the spiritual relationship with God while partners are expected to be honest about what gives them sexual pleasure, sharing honestly both the joys and the challenges facing the relationship. The connection between our sexual behavior and our well-being is to be maintained as well as the concern for the physical and emotional suffering of others. The values expand to include not only heterosexual couples but also same-sex couples, who are all encouraged to preserve and support the next generation. The values encourage couples to demonstrate modesty in their deportment and language. Partners are expected to make a covenant of faithfulness to each other, making the relationship exclusive. Up to this point the values have been easy to apply to most Jamaican partnerships; however, the exclusivity expected of Reform Jews elsewhere may not be reasonable to expect of some members of the community locally. It would not be seen as out of the ordinary for Jamaicans to enjoy more than one relationship simultaneously, even if polite society frowns on the practice. Joy, love, and holiness are the three final values that Reform Jews are encouraged to incorporate in their relationships. The joy is that of giving of oneself in sexual activity that is consensual; the love is that which begins with self-love and regard of self and which extends to others. Holiness or *k'dushah* is achieved in part by the regard we have for each other and the act of setting ourselves apart and remaining special to our partners. The document concludes, "It is hoped that the sexual values described in this statement serve as a source of guidance that leads us to a life of holiness."[11] With the exception of those values that encourage exclusive, monogamous relationships, all others may be achieved through healthy intimate relationships between consenting adults in the local community. What, if any, is our obligation to those members of the community who may subscribe to the Jamaican practice of "visiting unions"? We can hardly exclude whole groups of people with legitimate claims to being Jewish on the ground that they have not followed all of the suggested sexual and relational practices included here.

Integrating the Three

> What is peculiar to modern societies, in fact, is not that they
> consigned sex to the shadow existence, but that they dedicated
> themselves to speaking of it ad infinitum, while exploiting it as
> the secret.[12]

Michel Foucault, contemporary French philosopher, in his ground-breaking work *The History of Sexuality*, traces the chronology of modern sexuality. He looks at the origins of sexual repression, prohibition, and regulation to the point where we have repressed sexual expression to such an extent that we now spend inordinate amounts of time both feeling guilty and confessing our sexual crimes and misdemeanors. For Foucault, this obsession with sexual regulation is in itself a form of modern psychosis, an unnatural obsession with the private lives of others. Foucault would argue for individual self-regulation.

In the synagogue in Jamaica, there is a tacit agreement not to discuss sex directly, which exists alongside the clear understanding that Jews—unlike Christians—do not see sex as dirty, something to be stigmatized as transgressive. Tensions exist between the desire to be seen as upholding the core sexual values of traditional, respectable society and appearing too libertarian, too Bohemian, too laissez-faire. In private, congregants may express incredulity at what they may see as the puritanism of many of their Christian peers, but there have been no public declarations that support this position.

What is particularly remarkable is that the Jamaican Jewish view toward sexual behavior is much closer to the actual sexual practices of the larger population and might provide a more useful ethical lesson, as opposed to the fundamentalist Christianity so prevalent in the country, a Christianity that creates a dichotomy between good and bad, moral and immoral, angels and devils. This uncompromising moralistic preaching drives much sexual behavior underground, thereby making it harder to address and perhaps correct. If something is no longer talked about, it is then taken off the agenda. We have already mentioned the contribution of persons such as Rabbi Hooker, who also described himself as a rabbi for all Jamaica and embodied this principle. We believe he can serve as a model for the future rabbinate in Jamaica.

Despite all that has been said here about the need to recognize and appreciate the existing sexual culture of the island, it would be disingenuous to suggest that some of the local sexual practices should be encouraged. The compromise has to be made between freedom of sexual expression on the one hand and some of the cultural mores and taboos that guide sexual behavior, on the other. For example, young men and women in Jamaica believe that early pregnancy is a means of proving their manhood or womanhood. There is also the practice among the poorest of women of having multiple baby fathers, who do not necessarily provide support for their offspring, and a general intolerance of same-sex behavior. These are not cultural practices that benefit us, and while we may not be able to eradicate them, much has to be done to educate the population to make choices that benefit the public good. The ten values addressed by the CCAR Ad Hoc Committee certainly provide a starting point for both discussion and action among the community as it seeks to play a role in Jamaican sexual and cultural life. This requires us to be able to explain and advocate for a liberal Jewish sexual ethic that supports those values that reflect *mishpachah*. It appears, however, that the last monograph written on the subject of Reform Jewish sexual ethics was Eugene Borowitz's *Choosing a Sex Ethic: A Jewish Inquiry*, originally published in 1969. Therefore, Borowitz's book is useful primarily to give a historical perspective on where Reform Jewish thinking was, at this crucial turning point in history. While much of it may remain relevant, there needs to be much more recent and methodologically more sophisticated approaches that take into account the tremendous development that has occurred in Western society and particularly in Reform Jewish thought in the intervening decades.

Of course, any ethical teachings that might be useful for a society have to be transmitted in a form that is culturally appropriate and easily understandable. Rabbi Hooker, for example, is still remembered by virtually all Jamaicans of a certain age because of his radio call-in show, which was considered to be a pioneering programming effort. There is a popular story about a man who called in one day, expressing dismay that he believed his wife was cheating on him, which in the local expression is called "giving him bun." Rabbi Hooker was completely unaware of this expression, but he did know that bun is a Jamaican sweet bread that people generally eat with cheese. So, entirely innocently, he suggested to the man that he buy cheese and give it to his wife to serve together with the bun! People still laugh about this response forty years after the fact.

It does highlight the reality that viewing Judaism as a religion that has lessons for everyone is an important religious value, but in order to be effective, it has to be explained in the context of a given culture. The Jewish community needs to enunciate a clear set of values that can provide a thoughtful, non-fundamentalist methodology for dealing with the difficult issues that Jamaicans face. Whether we choose to take a descriptive or prescriptive approach to sexual ethics, the result is the same; it must be culturally relevant if it is to impact a people in their personal lives, or "livity," as Jamaicans call it.

NOTES

1. Elsa Leo-Rhynie, *The Jamaican Family: Continuity and Change* (Kingston, Jamaica: Grace Kennedy Foundation, 1993).

2. Eric H. Yoffie, "Sexual Obsession and the Fall of the Religious Right," *Huffington Post*, December 1, 2010, http://www.huffingtonpost.com/rabbi-eric-h-yoffie/sexual-obsession-and-the-_b_785785.html.

3. D. M. Carr, *The Erotic Word: Sexuality, Spirituality, and the Bible* (New York: Oxford University Press, 2003), 8.

4. Anastasia Cunningham, "Sex Text Scrapped—Ministry Pulls Controversial Book from High Schools," *Gleaner* (Jamaica, WI), September 15, 2012, http://jamaica-gleaner.com/gleaner/20120915/lead/lead1.html.

5. Leah Hyslop, "India's 'Prostitutes of God,'" *Telegraph*, September 20, 2010, http://www.telegraph.co.uk/expat/expatlife/8008562/Indias-prostitutes-of-God.html.

6. *Encyclopaedia Judaica*, 2nd ed., s.v. "Sugar Industry and Trade," vol. 15, 487–88.

7. Shmuley Boteach, *Kosher Sex: A Recipe for Passion and Intimacy* (New York: Broadway Books, 1999), 28.

8. "Kosher Sex," *Judaism 101*, http://www.jewfaq.org/sex.htm.

9. Frantz Fanon, *Black Skin, White Masks*, trans. Charles Lam Markmann (New York: Grove Press, 1967), 165.

10. Central Conference of American Rabbis Ad Hoc Committee on Jewish Sexual Values, "Reform Jewish Sexual Values," *CCAR Journal*, Fall 2001, vol. 48, no. 4, 9–13.

11. Ibid., 13.

12. Michel Foucault, *The History of Sexuality: An Introduction*, vol. 1, trans. Robert Hurley (New York: Vintage Books, 1990), 35.

45

WHAT NOT TO WEAR

Synagogue Edition

RABBI LISA J. GRUSHCOW, DPHIL

"Now the two of them were naked, the man and his wife, and they were not ashamed" (Gen. 2:25). Very soon after this verse, Adam and Eve find themselves hiding from God's presence because they have realized—their first realization after eating the fruit—that they are in need of clothes.

Ever since the Garden of Eden, human clothing has been an issue; after we realize we need to wear something, the question becomes, what to wear, and what not to wear? One might expect that the Reform Movement would be silent on this question, leaving it in the realm of individual choice. However, clothing is not merely in the realm of individual choice. Above all, this is apparent in synagogue life. When we come together to pray and to celebrate, should there be any guide? Many Reform congregations have policies, formal or informal, regarding appropriate dress. Rarely, however, are these policies explicitly grounded in Reform Jewish values. This essay is an attempt to explore what values might inform our discussions.

In March 1976, a question was asked of the CCAR Responsa Committee regarding dress code for religious schools and proper attire in the Jewish tradition.[1] In the response, the issue of modesty was conspicuously absent—perhaps because it was not an issue at the time or perhaps because of liberal Jewish discomfort with the discourse of modesty. This discomfort is not unfounded: as liberal Jews, we have rejected religious differentiation on the basis of gender,[2] and the concept of modesty often is directed exclusively against women's dress and comportment, based on the concern that men not be tempted.[3]

That being said, anecdotal evidence strongly attests to concerns about appropriate dress, especially at the primary juncture of life-cycle celebrations and synagogue life—namely, *b'nei mitzvah*. The conversation is indubitably gendered: in a decade in the congregational rabbinate, I have heard frequent concerns about what the bat mitzvah girl—or her mother—is wearing, and I have never heard a word about the bar mitzvah boy or his father. But just because an issue is problematic is not a reason to avoid it. Moreover, the traditional discussion of modest dress contains diverse perspectives, some of which can still be applied. This essay will begin by considering traditional approaches and then turn to a Reform analysis and response.

Traditional Approaches

The first major Rabbinic category that is relevant to our discussion is *ervah*, "nakedness." *Ervah* sometimes refers to the genital area alone but often has a broader connotation. The word usually is connected with the following biblical verse:

> Since the Eternal your God moves about in your camp to protect you and to deliver your enemies to you, let your camp be holy; let [God] not find anything unseemly among you and turn away from you.
>
> (Deut. 23:15)

The Hebrew phrase that is translated as "anything unseemly" is *ervat davar*, which can be translated more literally as "any nakedness," but is perhaps best translated as "any indecency." In the commentaries, Ibn Ezra specifies that it includes both acts and utterances, while

Sforno writes that it denotes impurity, filth, or semen-based defilement. The reference is sexual but not exclusively so.

The key Rabbinic statement interpreting *ervah* is found in the Babylonian Talmud, *B'rachot* 24a: "A *tefach* [handbreath] that is exposed on a woman is nakedness." This then leads to the statement that a man cannot recite the *Sh'ma* in sight of his wife if a handbreath of her skin is exposed, but it is taken to have broader implications for what parts of a woman's body need to be covered in order for someone else to pray.[4]

The commentators on the Talmud (Rashba, Ritva, Rosh) and the codifiers of Jewish law (*Tur* and *Shulchan Aruch, Orach Chayim* 75:1) understand this statement in a way that opens up new meanings. According to their interpretation, for exposed skin to constitute *ervah*, it must be skin that is normally covered. Once this interpretation has been made, cultural standards of dress become very important; for example, if one is in a culture where wrists are not covered, then exposed wrists are not considered nakedness. Similarly, although a married woman's hair also is *ervah* (Babylonian Talmud, *B'rachot* 24a), Rav Moshe Feinstein rules that the *Sh'ma* can still be said in the presence of a married woman with uncovered hair, because many married women now keep their hair uncovered, and so it no longer qualifies as *ervah* that prevents prayer.[5] At the same time, prohibitions traditionally understood to come from the Torah—like the prohibition against bare shoulders—remain in force, and the *Sh'ma* and *T'filah* cannot be recited, even if uncovered shoulders are commonly seen.[6] Another way of understanding these categories is that some practices fall under *dat Moshe*, Mosaic law, while others are *dat Y'hudit*, Jewish law.[7] The practices that fall in the latter category have more flexibility; for instance, a woman leaving her house with uncovered hair is *dat Y'hudit*. These acts are still halachically forbidden, but not from the direct authority of the Torah.

These interpretations suggest that two factors have traditionally shaped Jewish decision making around modesty: first, the issue of cultural norms that can lead to flexibility, and second, the idea that there are restrictions that cannot be changed and have implications for the life of the community. There is room to change, but there are limits. Whether this model is a feasible or desirable one for Reform Jewish synagogues will be treated in the last section of this essay.

Beyond the issue of how one's *ervah* impacts on others, the traditional discussions of appropriate attire and prayer ask how dress impacts on the person praying, on God, and on the synagogue community. Each of these three issues is associated with different halachic concepts, which will emerge from the discussion below.

In the *Shulchan Aruch* (*Orach Chayim* 75:1), the Rama cites the Rosh, who states that an exposed handbreath of skin in a woman can also keep other women from reciting the *Sh'ma* in her presence. According to this position, a woman who is exposed in this way can pray only on her own. The Rashba disagrees, arguing that if she can pray on her own, there is no problem of nakedness, and other women can pray in her presence; the issue is only *hirhur*, the distraction of men. Although most decisors side with the Rashba here,[8] the Rosh's position suggests that the woman's immodest dress is problematic, even in the absence of men.[9] This points to another meaning of *ervah*: indecent exposure that is in itself forbidden, regardless of its effect on others.[10]

Although the Rosh's position is that an immodestly dressed or naked woman can recite the *Sh'ma*, there is another set of rulings related to saying the *Sh'ma* by which the *Sh'ma* cannot be recited if the person reciting it is naked. Rather, she or he must not be able to see their own nakedness with either their eyes or their heart. The reference to the heart seeing nakedness leads to the idea that even a blind person cannot pray naked.[11] A separation must be made, and the genitals must be covered, even if only by opaque water.[12] Moreover, if one also wants to recite the *T'filah*, one's chest must be covered as well.[13] In these passages, the references to *ervah* are more directed: exposed genitalia are being discussed, not the inappropriate exposure of a handbreath of skin. At the same time, the central issue of dress and prayer is shared by all these discussions.

The rulings on nakedness suggest that there is something inherently problematic about *ervah* in the context of prayer, even if a person is alone. One reason for this is the possibility of distraction, which is mentioned as a factor in the prohibition against having any body part touch one's genitals, even when they are covered.[14] Another possibility arises from the explanation of why one's chest must be covered for the *T'filah* (but not the *Sh'ma*). The reason for this can be found in Rashi's commentary on *B'rachot* 25a, where he writes that the one who says the *T'filah* is like one standing before a king. Just as one does not stand before a king improperly dressed, so too does one not stand before God with one's chest uncovered.[15] Here, the issue is not that the one praying might distract him- or herself or others and thereby keep them from prayer. Rather, a new halachic concept is introduced: praying without sufficient clothing to cover oneself shows disrespect to God, because standing before God is like standing before a king. This has implications for formality in dress as well as modesty, but the scope of this essay does not permit a fuller discussion.

So far, we have discovered three problems caused by nakedness and immodest dress of different degrees. First, it can distract the person him- or herself and distract him or her from saying the *Sh'ma* or *T'filah*. Second, it can distract others and have the same effect on them. Third, it is an offense to the honor due to God. A fourth set of issues is added when we consider the context of our communal prayer: the synagogue.

There are many Rabbinic teachings on the sanctity of the synagogue and its importance to prayer. In the Talmud, *B'rachot* 6a, we find the statement that "one's prayer is heard only in the synagogue." In *M'gilah* 29a, the synagogue is defined as *mikdash m'at* (a small Temple, mentioned in Ezek. 11:16) and as the dwelling place of God (Ps. 105:1), a place of both study and prayer. In the *Tur* and *Shulchan Aruch*, it is stated that a person should pray only in the synagogue with the congregation,[16] and the commentators add that the sanctity of the synagogue is so strong that it is better to pray there than anywhere else even if the community is not gathered for prayer.[17]

This sanctity has certain implications for synagogue dress and behavior.[18] For instance, Rav Yosef writes that the reason one should not conduct a wedding in a synagogue where women are dressed immodestly is that one must honor the holy place in which God's presence, the *Shechinah*, rests.[19] One major issue that will not be explored here is the requirement for men to cover their heads.[20] Another issue that pertains more directly to the issue is that there should not be *kalut rosh*, "frivolity."[21] The *Mishnah B'rurah* connects the prohibition of *kalut rosh* with the definition of a synagogue as a small sanctuary and the commandment that we are to be in awe of God's sanctuary.[22]

Rav Feinstein has written a responsum in which he cites *kalut rosh*, and not *ervah*, as being the reason behind a *m'chitzah*, the division between women and men in prayer. According to this argument, the *m'chitzah* can be made of glass (if the women are dressed modestly)[23]— the concern is not to prevent seeing one another, but mingling with one another (an equal sin for both women and men).[24] *Kalut rosh* is a useful category insofar as it is applied not on the basis of gender but of appropriate and inappropriate synagogue behavior, based on the sanctity of the place. As mentioned above, here the only issue cited that is related to dress is that of covering one's head. Although this is too large a topic to be discussed here, it does indicate that dress can be used to express respect for the synagogue. We have come full circle back to Deuteronomy 23:15, which condemns *ervah* as being inconsistent with a relationship with God and holiness in the camp.

Reform Approaches

From a liberal Jewish perspective, the most problematic category is *ervah*, nakedness, as it affects other people. On a fundamental level, we need to ask whether we can accept an approach to determining appropriate dress that focuses on how women's bodies affect men's prayers. The discussion of the Talmud, *B'rachot* 24a, is overwhelmingly focused on the impact of women's immodest dress on men, as shown by the issues raised: Is the man looking to obtain pleasure, or is the woman merely in his line of vision? Even if he is not looking, is he affected? Does it matter if the woman is his wife or another woman? It is clear that the primary concern is with the impact on men. Given that perspective, we must ask whether the traditional discussions of this matter are at all applicable to us as Reform Jews.

Our first and strongest response to this question is that in keeping with the principles of Reform Judaism, we do not discriminate on the basis of gender.[25] Moreover, we believe strongly in individual autonomy and responsibility for one's own religious life—if we are distracted by someone else's attire, it is our responsibility to do everything in our power to avoid or control this distraction, without impinging on the rights and freedoms of others. These principles should undermine the assumptions whereby women are held responsible to modify their behavior for the sake of men's prayer. At the same time, we cannot ignore the reality that when we discuss appropriate synagogue attire, the vast majority of the time the issue arises from how women, and not men, are dressed. We might argue that in our congregations, women who are immodestly dressed distract not only men, but also other women. Recognizing that not everyone is heterosexual, both genders may be distracted sexually. Alternatively, sexual orientation aside, both genders may experience personal discomfort with revealing dress. Still, the focus remains on how women dress, and not men.

Many of the traditional respondents who address this issue ask why women dress immodestly. Classic approaches attributed immodest dress to sexual licentiousness (*z'nut*) or the desire to imitate gentiles (*chukot hagoyim*).[26] More recent traditional answers range from the idea that it is a result of the sins of our generation[27] to the idea that women are not intending to be promiscuous, but that they do not know better, are used to behaving in a modern way, or do not want to be different from their friends.[28]

Our own answers might reject the condescension of the above approaches but acknowledge the role of society and culture in shaping expectations for the attire of women and girls. To the extent that our synagogues have their own culture and try to influence the culture outside of our synagogue walls, we have a role to play in this debate. Our concern is not with the direct impact of women's immodest dress on men but rather with the impact of societal expectations on both women and men. From this perspective, we cannot help but notice that there is an imbalance in societal expectations based on gender and that, for the most part, the weight of this imbalance falls on women. In the world as it is, women's clothing remains a source of distraction.

For ideological reasons, whether or not how someone is dressed distracts others cannot be the primary factor in our response, but we do acknowledge it as an issue. The traditional halachah gives guidance insofar as it takes into consideration cultural norms. Parts of the body that are not normally exposed in most secular situations should not be exposed in the synagogue, but each congregation must determine these standards based on their community.

At the same time, the category of traditional prohibitions that are *not* said to be culturally contingent (e.g., covering shoulders) have limited relevance for our situation, given that this category too has been shaped by cultural forces, which are not acknowledged in the traditional texts. Nevertheless, there is value in maintaining the idea that some things are not acceptable regardless of the cultural code; for instance, we would almost certainly object to a synagogue where no one was clothed, even if that was the cultural norm of that community. This suggests not only that communal standards should be considered, but that the norms of the broader Jewish community or denomination also are relevant to the conversation.

Ervah that distracts the person praying must be left to the discretion of that person, but the concept is an important one to introduce to communal discussion. It is especially important in the situation of *b'nei mitzvah*, where the individual involved may be strongly influenced by parental and peer pressures. It is worth asking our young adults whether they themselves will be distracted by what they wear; for instance, if a strapless dress or a short skirt will lead to their own concerns about exposing more than is comfortable. This is an area where our tradition can guide us in developing a countercultural voice, insisting that our young women—alongside our young men—are to be valued for what they learn and how they lead, rather than what they wear.

Another significant issue raised by the halachic literature is the question of how we must be dressed to appear before God. The traditional sources indicate that the *T'filah* has more stringent requirements for attire than does the *Sh'ma* and that only the former is seen to be equivalent to standing before a king. Although the halachists were stricter with the requirements for reciting the *T'filah* than for the *Sh'ma*, we have reason today to be equally strict with both. If anything, the *Sh'ma* is more central to our individual and communal prayer than is the *T'filah*, as shown by the normative Reform practice of standing for the *Sh'ma*. For us, then, there is the possibility that *all* prayer, and certainly not only the *T'filah*, has the significance of standing before a king. If that is the case, then immodest dress does not simply prevent us or those around us from praying; it also is an inappropriate way to approach God in prayer.

Here, we must ask whether the metaphor holds. Most Reform Jews do not approach prayer thinking that they are standing before the King of kings. As a metaphor, it is both hierarchical and patriarchal. However, we would argue that it also is significant and salvageable. Our ancestors did not go to synagogue every day dressed to meet a king. But the idea that when we pray we approach One who is greater than ourselves was relevant then and is relevant now. If we take this metaphor seriously, it calls for some modicum of modesty and formality. This pertains not only to attire, but also comportment and synagogue etiquette. In these areas, our Classical Reform predecessors were far more exacting than we are today. Nevertheless, for many of us there is a certain informality and sense of comfort that we value in our synagogues and, indeed, that many people feel brings them closer to the Divine Presence.[29]

The essential element to this concept seems to be the idea that we should be conscious that when we pray, we are approaching God, and that consciousness should be somehow reflected in our dress.

The traditional literature thus considers the impact of our dress on our human relationships (both with ourselves and with others) and our relationship with the Divine. The sanctity of the synagogue itself also is a factor. The synagogue is sanctified both by God's presence and by the prayers of the community. As such, one should not enter it in dirty or overly revealing clothes. Conversely, it also is not a place to adjust one's clothing, jewelry, or makeup. It is not a place to preen.

This principle is very similar to the previous principle of standing before royalty. Entering a synagogue requires a particular consciousness of holiness that should be reflected in both dress and comportment. This too seems to be a concept that translates across the ages and into our own congregations.

The question remains: What to wear, and what not to wear? Should these values be translated into communal decisions? There are Jewish historical precedents for dress codes, although for the most part community norms seem to have rendered them unnecessary. In our times, when communal norms are more varied, an argument can be made for a dress code in a Reform synagogue. When one joins a synagogue, one already surrenders some autonomy; for instance, Hebrew school must be attended for a certain amount of time if a child is to become bar or bat mitzvah, and many communities have standards for what food may and may not be brought into a synagogue. Distinct from these other examples, however, a dress code poses particularly difficult problems of enforcement and risks embarrassment of members and guests who are unaware—thereby conflicting with other Jewish values. At the same time, given that communal expectations and standards do exist, it can help to make them explicit (here we are speaking of guidelines communicated to families, rather than signs on the sanctuary door!).

In keeping with Reform Jewish ideology, when it comes to appropriate dress, the emphasis should be on education, over and above enforcement. We encourage communities to study and develop their own customs in this area and to articulate them in the context of Jewish values. Moreover, this educational process should be part of the required preparations for bar and bat mitzvah, so families can be made aware of expectations in the area of appropriate dress.

The word "appropriate" is key. Definitive community standards must originate from the communities concerned. Our tradition contains considerable guidance in this area, centered on three major principles: avoiding distraction for oneself and for others, approaching God with awe, and respecting the sanctity of the synagogue. The community will have succeeded when a guest or member enters and can see these values manifest in the dress and comportment of those at prayer. Then we will know that our camp is holy (Deut. 23:15).

NOTES

1. Walter Jacob, ed., *Contemporary American Reform Responsa* (New York: CCAR Press, 1987), 27.

2. Pittsburgh Principles (1999): "We pledge to fulfill Reform Judaism's historic commitment to the complete equality of women and men in Jewish life." http://ccarnet.org/rabbis-speak/platforms/statement-principles-reform-judaism/.

3. E.g., *Yabia Omer* 6, *Yoreh Dei-ah* 14:1. Rav Ovadia Yosef, in a *t'shuvah* on mini-skirts, begins by saying that he is writing because of "the great stumbling block that it creates for men who look at girls dressed in mini-skirts which reveal the leg and thigh . . . and the eye sees and the heart desires, and wakes the evil impulse in men, and what can that boy do that he might not sin? For the evil impulse only rules over what his eyes see (*Sotah* 8)." Interestingly, here Yosef is making an argument for stringency, and using a Talmudic statement that, in context, is lenient (saying that a man will desire the exposed woman that he sees, but will not go on from there to act improperly toward women whom he has not seen). Yosef's opening argument has one central point: that immodest dress creates a difficulty for men that they will not be able to control.

4. The *Sh'ma* is not the only prayer affected by indecent exposure; the *T'filah* also may not be recited. See Maimonides, *Mishneh Torah, Hilchot T'filah* 4:7; and *Tur* and *Shulchan Aruch, Orach Chayim* 90–91.

5. *Igeret Moshe, Orach Chayim* 1:43 and 3:23, based on the Rif, Rambam, and *Aruch HaShulchan*. On Feinstein's responsa on hair and worship, see the comprehensive article by Norma Baumel Joseph, "Hair Distractions: Women and Worship in the Responsa of Rabbi Moshe Feinstein," in *Jewish Legal Writings by Women*, Micah Halperin and Hannah Safrai, eds. (Jerusalem: Urim Press, 1998), 9–22. Joseph notes that Feinstein supports his argument for leniency on exposed hair by understanding the prohibition to be from Song of Songs (as per Babylonian Talmud, *B'rachot* 24a), and not the Torah (Num. 5:18, in the context of *sotah*). He still argues that married women should cover their hair and that not to do so is prohibited, but he keeps this prohibited act from interfering with prayer. From his perspective, the societal change

is overwhelmingly negative and the result of our sins. In this, he uses the same language as *Aruch HaShulchan, Orach Chayim* 75:1.

6. *Igeret Moshe, Orach Chayim* 3:24; and *Yabia Omer* 6, *Orach Chayim* 14:3.

7. *Mishnah K'tubot* 7:6, regarding which women are to be divorced without receiving the financial compensation of their marriage contract.

8. See *Mishnah B'rurah, Orach Chayim* 75:1.

9. Clearly, the halachists are not imagining a situation in which women are attracted to other women.

10. *Mishnah B'rurah, Orach Chayim* 75:1 notes that the Rosh must be assuming that the naked woman is sitting down, because if she is standing up her *ervah* would in fact be exposed. The assumption is that, for anatomical reasons, men's *ervah* is exposed whether they are sitting or standing.

11. *Yabia Omer* 3, *Orach Chayim* 7:1.

12. *Tur* and *Shulchan Aruch, Orach Chayim* 74:2.

13. *Mishneh Torah, Hilchot T'filah* 4:7; *Tur* and *Shulchan Aruch, Orach Chayim* 91:1. The reference to the chest refers to men reciting the *T'filah*.

14. *Mishneh Torah, Hilchot K'riat Sh'ma* 3:17; *Tur, Orach Chayim* 74:5. Ravad, in his commentary, justifies this prohibition by saying that the man might excite and distract himself.

15. Rashi, s.v. *aval l'tefilah*. See also *Mishneh Torah, Hilchot T'filah* 5:5.

16. *Tur* and *Shulchan Aruch, Orach Chayim* 90:9.

17. *Beit Yosef* and *Bayit Chadash*, ad loc.

18. *Mishnah B'rachot* 9:5; *Mishneh Torah, Hilchot T'filah* 8; and *Tur* and *Shulchan Aruch, Orach Chayim* 151.

19. *Yabia Omer* 3, *Even HaEizer* 10:8.

20. *Mishnah B'rachot* 9:5; *Tur* and *Shulchan Aruch, Orach Chayim* 91:3, 151:6.

21. *Tur* and *Shulchan Aruch, Orach Chayim* 151:1.

22. *Mishnah B'rurah, Orach Chayim* 151:1.

23. Feinstein actually proposes a *m'chitzah* made of one-way glass, which women can see through and men cannot, because of the issue of *ervah*. This makes the issue abundantly clear: women are not in danger of being distracted by men, but men are in danger of being distracted by women.

24. *Igerot Moshe, Orach Chayim* 1:43. See Joseph, "Hair Distractions,"12–13.

25. Pittsburgh Principles (1999). See above, n. 2.

26. Cf. the discussion in *Yabia Omer* 4, *Yoreh Dei-ah* 1, where he mentions both possibilities.

27. *Igeret Moshe, Orach Chayim* 4:112; and *Aruch HaShulchan, Orach Chayim* 75:7, discussed in Joseph "Hair Distractions," 13.

28. *Yabia Omer* 4, *Yoreh Dei-ah* 1, cites these reasons in his argument that immodest dress in these times is not a sufficient reason for a divorce.

29. This feeling is articulated in Syd Lieberman's poem "A Short Amidah," which has appeared in many creative services. In that poem, she rejects the traditional idea that the *T'filah* involves meeting God in a palace, with prescribed formalities. Instead, she writes: "Mine's not a fancy place, / no jewels, no throne, / certainly not fit for a king. / But in that small chamber, / for just a few moments on Sabbath, / God and I can roll up our sleeves, / put some schnapps on the table, / sit down together and finally talk. / That's palace enough for me."

46

SEX AND TECHNOLOGY

Creating Sacred Space in Cyberspace

RABBI ELIZABETH S. WOOD
AND DEBBY HERBENICK, PhD, MPH

Are you reading this on a printed page? Or are you reading this on your Kindle, your iPad, or your computer? Whatever the answer, in a few years all of these technologies will once again change and we will have new systems with which to gather data, read articles, and disseminate information. Technology is defined as the knowledge or study of new industrial or scientific skills.[1] While this may not be what first comes to mind when we think of technology in the twenty-first century, with all of our fancy gadgets and toys, it helps to remind us that technology is defined as that which is new, innovative, and ever changing in our technical and scientific world. Over the last few decades technology has changed not only the way in which our world operates, creates, and relates but also the pace with which we function, the availability of resources, and the various forms of entertainment that engage us. Technology helps humans achieve more, work faster, and play harder. It provides a world of possibilities, both personally and professionally, and there is something exciting and tantalizing about that which is, by definition, always changing and evolving. Let's face it—technology is sexy.

Throughout history, expressions of sex and sexuality have been hugely influenced by technology because of the intimate relationship between the creation of sexual content and avenues of distribution through available technologies.[2] This connection of sex and technology is so basic and so historic that it can be seen as early as in the walls of a brothel in Pompeii or in the carvings of the temples of Khajuraho and Konarak, India, where sex and sexuality were expressed using the available forms of technology of the day.[3] However, technology not only influences cultural norms, it is also highly influenced by the changing needs of a society. Technology is not created or changed in a vacuum; it fulfills a particular need by granting more access, better services, and more widespread understanding on a particular topic. With the invention of the printing press, technology easily allowed for the spread of sexually explicit materials to a much wider audience, bringing the product to the consumer. The confluence of the printing press, its resultant products, and the Enlightenment propelled the immense increase in the circulation of these materials and their increasing political role in society. Increased circulation meant greater access and decreased costs, and thus these materials moved from being restricted to the elite to being available for a growing literate population.[4]

Before the Enlightenment, many of the early attacks on the notion of sexuality as subversive to the well-being of the state and society came from its association with radical political literature. As Lynn Hunt states, "Pornography was most often a vehicle for using the shock of sex to criticize religious and political authorities."[5] Two generations later, in the Victorian era, despite growing legal restrictions, the information revolution continued to transform the dissemination of sexually explicit ideas and images through cheaper means of content production and faster methods of transportation and communication. The production of and representation of sex and sexuality were further changed with the invention of still photography in the mid-nineteenth century, "the single most important event in the history of pornography."[6] The photographic image offered greater realism than before, removed the barrier of literacy, and was more powerful and accessible than words or prints, thereby greatly expanding the audience. The movie industry, which developed in the late nineteenth century, expanded the possibilities of sex and technology by adding sensory experiences such as movement and sound.[7] The computer revolution of the twentieth century further changed the notion of sex and technology. Computer networks erased the differences between production, distribution, and consumption, while also greatly reducing barriers of geographically separate communities and practitioners.[8] Perhaps the most visible aspect of the influence of sex on communication technologies is on the Internet. Apart from images, movies, and written stories, Internet chat rooms and bulletin boards allow for personal sexual expression and an exchange of ideas and views toward sex and sexuality at an increasingly rapid pace. With the explosive growth of the Internet and computers in businesses and homes, along with improved pictures and higher speeds of transmission, ideas and images of sex and sexuality have moved from being the secretive habit of the few to the enjoyment of the many, removing "the biggest obstacles to selling pornography and sexual services: shame and ignorance."[9]

As sexually explicit materials and information have become more widely available throughout history, so too has the influence of technology been felt deeply within society in relation to behavior, practices, and awareness of sexual topics. Ultimately, the question is not whether technology has an influence on sexual norms and practices or whether sexual culture is defined by technological direction. History has shown that there is a symbiotic relationship. The real question is: how do we navigate the current challenges, both religiously and ethically, that the confluence of sexuality and technology present to us in the twenty-first century?

The ease and anonymity that technology, social media, and the Internet provide can often make it difficult to decipher the boundaries between healthy exploration, functional use, and harmful abuse in relation to sexuality and sexual expression. Questions of technology and sexuality are no longer relegated to the realms of history and science but now also involve those of appropriate usage, ethical choices, and religious perspectives. Judaism, Jewish values, and halachah can offer guidance on these issues. The stability and longevity of halachah and Jewish wisdom on issues of ethical and moral behavior, in juxtaposition to the changing nature of technology, has remained applicable throughout history. Jewish wisdom literature seeks to lift up the Jewish people and remind us that in every act of life there is a way to find, create, and maintain a level of happiness and holiness. Technology, in this day and age, has become another medium for living. And while that medium is new and different, the rules and guidelines of the virtual world are still the same as the ones that apply to the real world.

Personal Use of Pornography

Sexually explicit materials, including the depiction of erotic images through sexually explicit magazines, film, and video, popularly called "erotica" or "pornography," are important media to consider. Pornographic films are part of a billion-dollar industry, employing actors, producers, directors, and crew members. Hugh Hefner, Larry Flynt, and Bob Guccione have turned the combination of written words and pictures into huge money-making empires through their respective magazines *Playboy*, *Hustler*, and *Penthouse*. These magazines and movies became more popular and widespread throughout the latter half of the twentieth century as the culture in America became more open about sex and sexuality than ever before in history. A few films in the 1970s made the transition to the mainstream theaters and earned great profit. *Deep Throat* cost only $25,000 to make but earned over $50 million.[10] As production levels of pornographic media increased and attitudes slowly changed, so too did the demand for these industries. As the Internet successfully boomed and spread from business to personal use, a new industry of websites made accessing sexually explicit images, in their many forms (e.g., still images, video, webcam, the selling/buying of vintage erotica), more convenient than ever before. As the way in which information is received has changed, so too have the means by which people share and receive that information. Videos, images, and written erotica and pornography have changed with the times. But with this change in technology, and increased personal accessibility, also comes choice and responsibility.

Judaism and Jewish sources can be used to navigate our ethical understanding of the personal use of pornography. For example, a modern Reform responsum addressed this issue through Jewish wisdom literature and texts:

> The chief source is Deuteronomy 23:15. In discussing the duty to keep the camp of the Hebrew army sanitary, the verse in Deuteronomy expresses itself as follows: "For God walketh in the midst of thy camp. Therefore shall thy camp be holy, that He see no unseemly thing in thee." The phrase translated "unseemly thing" in Hebrew is *"ervas dovor,"* and so "unseemly thing" can be translated as "unseemly word." In fact the *Targum* used the word *"pisgom,"* which means "word," and Ibn Ezra explains the phrase to mean "nothing unseemly in deed or word.". . . There are a number of more direct statements about pornographic speech. The Talmud in Shabbat 33a says that misfortunes come to us and young men die prematurely because of unseemly speech. . . . Actually the whole matter of the avoidance of pornography, although it is more ethical than strictly legal, is organized as a series of legal regulations for self-control in speech (*Even HaEizer* 25:1, etc., and *Orach Chayim* 200:9).[11]

Even though this responsum does not directly address pornography in its current technological form, it serves as a useful foundation to approach the issues of sexually explicit images or words as part of a means of sexual expression. The legal nature of these sources helps explain the importance of societal rules and boundaries at the time they were written. The idea of an "unseemly thing" being done or an "unseemly word" being spoken implies that which might cause harm to the giver or the receiver and would therefore not be acceptable in the eyes of God. Therefore, it is understandable that this would be viewed negatively and, ultimately, be forbidden. Legally, the easiest way to keep order in an ancient society was to prevent something that could cause harm or damage. It was framed within a legal context rather than addressing the real ethical issues on the subject such as what it means to create something "unseemly." When language is unseemly, it can often be seen as doing harm to those who may not want to hear it, whether on sexual matters or other topics. It involves both the speaker and the listener. Pornography involves two parties as well: those who create and those who consume. If both of these parties engage in this activity of their own free will, it does not seem likely that harm is occurring between the two parties.[12] Furthermore, modern sexual research in America indicates that personal pornographic use is not only widespread, it is considered healthy as a means of fantasy, exploration, and even education. Most men report having watched sexually explicit images, and some studies suggest that an increasing number of women and couples do as well. Sexually explicit books, photographs, and film/videos are sometimes even used as part of a complementary approach to sex therapy so that clients can learn how to better communicate their thoughts about sex, sexual positions, sexual technique, and/or the role of sexually explicit materials in their own desire, arousal, or sexual enhancement. If pornography is being used in a healthy way and not as an "unseemly thing," it is likely not causing harm to the individual or to society. Thus, the personal use of pornography is not inherently unethical. Rather, it must be considered in the context in which it is being used, the ethical standards for which it is being produced and distributed, and the healthfulness of its use to the individual as a means of sexual expression.

What Is Healthy? What Is Holy?

What, then, might be healthy personal practices of sex and sexuality in connection with sexually explicit materials? Consider the intersection of masturbation and technology. Research indicates that men, for example, commonly incorporate sexually explicit materials, such as magazines and/or videos, into their masturbation; women do too, though less often than men.[13] Women frequently incorporate the use of sex toys, such as vibrators, another technological innovation that arose in the past hundred years, into their masturbation; in fact a recent nationally representative study found that 53 percent of women ages eighteen to sixty in the United States had used a vibrator[14] (in the same study, nearly one in five men had reported using a vibrator alone[15]). Masturbation in and of itself is not a harmful practice. It can be and often is part of a healthy expression of a person's sexuality, as we have the opportunity to pleasure ourselves, to learn about our bodies, and possibly to later share information with our partner about how we enjoy being touched. Sexually explicit images and vibrators or other sex toys can thus be part of a healthy expression of masturbation or partnered sexual activities. However, when they are used in ways to distance oneself from a partner, such as to avoid intimacy or to make one's partner feel badly for not engaging in certain sexual behaviors or for not being able to be a pleasing partner, then one has to question the health of the behavior. Ultimately, however, masturbation and technological uses involved in masturbation are not inherently harmful.

The Jewish value of *sh'mirat haguf* (taking care of one's body) fully supports the notion that our bodies were created with wisdom by God and that it is our responsibility to take care of our bodies. Part of that responsibility is recognizing the holiness of our health and well-being, in all forms. Proverbs 11:17 states, "He who does good to his own person is a man of piety." Being given the ability to experience sexual pleasure in our bodies is a part of what God gave to us when we were created. Technology, when used ethically and properly, helps to further our ability to explore healthy sexual fantasies and ideas. Judaism, with its emphasis on procreation, has historically taken a dim view of masturbation, though there is debate about how and under what circumstances. However, at their core and removed from the concern about procreation, masturbation, sex toys, and the use of technology for sexual gratification are healthy forms of experiencing sexual pleasure that are not necessarily antithetical to the Jewish values embedded in the idea of *sh'mirat haguf*.

The real issue comes down to God and holiness. If we read the verse in Deuteronomy 23:15 exegetically, we might be able to interpret "our camps" as our homes and communities and "no unseemly thing in you" as our actions relating to unhealthy sexual expression. If we treat our homes and personal lives as a place where God is able to dwell and holiness can be achieved, we should monitor our behavior to be sure that it is always acceptable before the Divine. This means engaging in healthy personal practices of sex and sexuality, whether in reality or in the virtual world. It means not causing harm to family or friends by engaging in a personal practice of pornography that involves deceit, excessive use, or abuse. The ease, accessibility, and use of sexually explicit images in the twenty-first century does not reduce or eliminate the ability for us to create sacred personal space that is healthy, holy, loving, exciting, and filled with God's presence. Rather, it means that we must translate our understanding of creating sacred and healthy spaces and sexual practices to our personal spheres at all times, whether online or offline. As long as we are consciously creating healthy means of sexual expression, whether through the use of technology or not, holiness can be achieved in these spaces.

Sacred Connections

Technology in the twenty-first century has the ability to create and maintain a true sense of community and connection. Social media is a key example of virtual communities that can provide attachment around a common interest, strengthen existing friendships, or introduce new people into relationship with one another. As society and communities have shifted further and further into the realm of the virtual, so too have personal needs for community and relationship shifted toward that medium as well.

Dating online is no longer a joke or a source of embarrassment. When the Internet first gained popularity, couples might have been reluctant to admit that they met in a chat room, on a gaming site, or through e-mail. But as technology changed and personal use of technology increased, so too did the social norms and practices related to meeting others. As entrepreneurs recognized the possibilities and convenience of online meeting and dating, an industry was born. Websites like match.com, eHarmony, or OKCupid promise to find matches through a series of questions that collect your personal data, preferences, and habits. In essence, these websites aim to take the guesswork out of meeting strangers by engaging in a modern form of matchmaking. With Judaism's long-standing history of matchmaking, it is no wonder that JDate, the most popular current Jewish dating website, boasts the ability to connect tens of thousands of Jews all together in one place—every single day. Their goal, very clearly stated, is to foster and maintain Jewish community in future years:

> JDate's mission is to strengthen the Jewish community and ensure that Jewish traditions are sustained for generations to come. To accomplish this mission, we provide a global network where Jewish singles can meet to find friendship, romance and life-long partners within the Jewish faith. . . . Since 1997, JDate has been growing the Jewish community one success story at a time, forming countless relationships and ultimately, creating Jewish families. The most gratifying part of our jobs here at JDate are the thousands of phone calls, emails and letters we receive every year from JDate success stories thanking us for connecting them with their *beshert*. We never tire of hearing stories and testimonies from Jews all over the world about how JDate has influenced their lives and, in the process, helped build the Jewish community.[16]

JDate is a virtual space that works toward creating real and sustained Jewish community by tapping into the needs of a technologically based society. Dating has moved into the online world in a serious way over the last decade. Single Jews are benefiting from the existence of JDate and other websites that let them connect with Jews around the world similarly looking to create and sustain meaningful relationships.

Although JDate's mission is positive and community affirming, users on websites also have the ability to create relationships that are romantic and sexual in nature, but are not intended to be serious or long-term. Some people use dating websites for the sole purpose of setting up casual sexual encounters; in fact, some websites like adultfriendfinder.com, apps on smart phones like Grindr, and sections of websites like craigslist.com are set up specifically to connect individuals who are looking for more casual encounters, or "no strings attached" sex. Before technology and the Internet made it easy and accessible, the old-fashioned way to "pick someone up" was at a bar, nightclub, or party, and these certainly remain common ways that men and women meet their sexual partners. But it is important to note that the same ethics and choices that are made in the real world can and do apply to the virtual world as well.

Unlike the healthy usage of pornography or masturbation, it can be more difficult to find sanctity in a casual sexual encounter. In Judaism, marriage is the ideal sexual relationship embodied by a process of separation and elevation through a serious and long-term commitment called *kiddushin*. Based on the description in Genesis 2:24, which states, "So it is that a man will leave his father and mother and cling to his wife, and they become one flesh," human sexual relationships that are not characterized by marriage or long-term commitment are viewed as antithetical to the Jewish values of *kiddushin*.[17] Casual sexual encounters often tend to serve the most carnal of human needs, forgoing the emotional aspects of being in relationship with another, and are brief and limited. While it is possible to sustain a casual sexual relationship devoid of emotion with another for an extended period of time, it is often rare, though not impossible, that these result in healthy emotions and outcomes for both parties involved, thereby negating any real sense of holiness in the relationship. That is not to say that Judaism views all casual sexual relationships as unethical or immoral. The Torah allows a man to engage in sexual relationships with partners other than his wife, and there are numerous examples of men taking on concubines throughout Torah, though nowadays that practice is no longer accepted. But we learn from this that the absence of *k'dushah* does not automatically translate to immorality. Even though these relationships will not likely result in marriage, they can still be viewed as ethical so long as they are free of manipulation, deceit, and foreseeable harm.[18] Marriage (or long-term commitment), however, embodies the highest level of holiness that can be achieved in a relationship within Judaism, so it is easier to understand it as the holiest way to create a sexual relationship, even through technological means.

While technology in the twenty-first century certainly makes dating and casual sexual encounters more convenient and easier than ever before, there still needs to be a sense of ethical responsibility for the choices and challenges that are presented by these options. Judaism provides a framework within which to address these issues, even in the online world: If there is a healthy sense of commitment and dedication to building a romantic and sexual relationship with the intention for long-term possibilities of love, partnership, or marriage, then a sense of holiness is possible. However, if the only intention in contacting and connecting with another is to fulfill an immediate sexual need, without the purpose of creating any kind of sustained, healthy, or meaningful relationship, or if it causes harm and pain to another, it is more difficult to ascribe traditional notions of *k'dushah* to these encounters.

Technology helps to shape, create, and influence culture and society. But it also responds to the needs of society in order to advance it further. As sex and sexuality have changed within society and throughout history, technology has adapted to the changing needs. With these changes, there also come questions of ethical choices, responsibility, and religious perspective. Judaism is clear that it supports and lifts up men and women who engage in healthy and holy sexual practices. There is room for God to dwell in a relationship and space where trust, love, and commitment exist. And, in this day and age of modernity where sexuality is viewed as healthy and natural, it is also possible for God to dwell in relationships and spaces of exploration, fantasy, excitement, and pleasure, even with oneself. The key to fusing our understanding of Jewish tradition with the confluence of sex and technology in the twenty-first century is through our understanding of that which is healthy, safe, and without harm to others involved. When all of these factors are achieved, the holiness that we seek in our everyday lives is real, tangible, and—most importantly—accessible.

NOTES

1. *Webster's Concise Desk Dictionary*, ed. P. H. Collin (New York: Barnes & Noble Books, 2001).

2. Stephen Kinzer, "A Curator Who Doesn't Blush Easily," *New York Times*, January 30, 1996, A4.

3. Walter Kendrick, *The Secret Museum: Pornography in Modern Culture* (New York: Viking, 1987), 6–10.

4. Jonathan Coopersmith, "Pornography, Technology, and Progress," *Icon* 4 (1998): 94–125.

5. Lynn Hunt, ed., "Introduction," in *The Invention of Pornography: Obscenity and the Origins of Modernity, 1500–1800* (New York: Zone Books, 1993), 10

6. Department of Justice, *Attorney General's Commission on Pornography: Final Report*, 2 vols. (Washington, DC: U.S. Department of Justice, 1986), 242.

7. Coopersmith, "Pornography," 99.

8. Ibid., 108–9.

9. "Giving the Customer What He Wants," *The Economist*, February 12, 1998, 22.

10. Department of Justice, *Attorney General's Commission*, 1365.

11. Joshua O. Haberman, "Pornographic Literature," in *Current Reform Responsa*, ed. Solomon B. Freehof (New York: CCAR Press, 1969), 242.

12. Some question the extent to which individuals may feel coerced into sex work as part of an abusive or illegal relationship; however, this essay considers the likely large proportion of individuals who participate in making sexually explicit images out of their own volition.

13. D. Herbenick et al., "Prevalence and Characteristics of Vibrator Use by Women in the United States: Results from a Nationally Representative Study," *Journal of Sexual Medicine* 6 (2009): 1857–66.

14. Ibid.

15. Ibid., 1867–74.

16. JDate, www.jdate.com.

17. Mark Washofsky, *Jewish Living: A Guide to Contemporary Reform Practice* (New York: URJ Press, 2001), 318.

18. Ibid., 319.

47

JUDAISM AND PORNOGRAPHY

Rabbi Jonathan K. Crane, PhD

It would be easy to dismiss the subject of pornography altogether.[1] One easily could take recourse to those few rabbinic and scholarly pieces that speak explicitly about pornography and, upon quickly perusing their relatively scant treatment of the subject, rule as they do: pornography is a genre both obscene and illegal and thus must be abhorred, proscribed, if not destroyed.[2] This approach may make some of us today comfortable because it is simple; it provides unequivocal and unambiguous guidance on how we should view and treat this kind of speech. And its conservative unanimity that spans many streams of contemporary Jewry may reinforce our own opinions about pornography generally. Though attractive, this approach is more disingenuous and damaging than helpful.

Its disservice happens at many levels. First, the existing essays on pornography give short shrift to the Judaic textual tradition. Vast swaths of the tradition are silenced, and of the few pieces that are brought forth to weigh in on the subject, they are invariably mistreated. Snippets of classical sources are magnified and enhanced by being ascribed extraordinary suggestive and normative power—without any explanation as to why these tiny pieces merit unusual stature. Second, sources that were never consulted offer countervailing—and compelling—positions to the ones proffered by the ruling modern rabbi or scholar. This raises critical methodological questions about how and why certain pieces of the Judaic textual tradition are championed while others are sidelined, silenced, and dismissed.[3] It is no accident that this kind of twisting of and violence toward the textual tradition echoes some of the criticisms lobbied at certain segments of the porn industry.[4] And third, these pieces preclude an honest assessment of whether pornography actually *is* obscene. By definition, either the obscene is subjectively considered perverse or it is objectively what the law prohibits. Current writings on this topic hold one or both of these opinions to be true—and then they read the textual tradition through that lens. But in that very conviction they disallow the possibility of reading the Judaic textual tradition *as it is*. They cannot see, much less uncover, the textual tradition's diverse range of opinions on erotic speech.[5] As will be seen, the textual tradition is not as unambiguous about sexually explicit speech as contemporary authors might desire.

A more robust and honest approach to this subject suspends prejudging pornography morally or politically. That is, I assume neither that sexually explicit expressions are inherently perverse and degrading, nor that they are or should be legally, that is halachically, proscribed. This more neutral stance enables the modern reader of the textual tradition the opportunity to see in this variegated library diverse legal positions and moral opinions about sexually explicit speech.[6] It may surprise some to learn that such speech enjoys some protections in the Judaic textual tradition and that it is in fact invited as a stratagem to further enhance certain values and practices.

Visual Expressions

There are, of course, several ways to communicate sexually explicit content, the two most common being visual and verbal. The Judaic textual tradition contemplates each, and just as with many other issues debated by the ancient Sages, it expresses ambivalence about each kind of expression. Ambivalence does not mean indifference, however; it means holding two seemingly opposite or apposite strong convictions. To be ambivalent about something is to hold both approval and repugnance for it or to be simultaneously attracted to and dismissive of it. Ambivalence may be the antithesis of indifference, and it should not be misconstrued in favor of one's own strongly held conviction about pornography. Discerning the concerns of the ancient Sages when it comes to sexually explicit communication may help us clarify our own opinions on the matter.

In regard to visual expressions, it is possible to see sexually explicit content directly, or bodily in front of one, as well as indirectly, as in when viewing depictions of content. Take Adam and Eve as an example. They saw each other's naked bodies and felt no shame (Gen. 2:25), and even when they became aware of their nakedness (Gen. 3:7) they still felt no shame.[7] When ruddy and handsome King David viewed Bathsheba bathing naked on a nearby roof, he also felt no shame (II Sam. 11:2). Indeed, noticing the physical beauty of another person is a common biblical detail: Sarah, Rebekah, Rachel, and Esther were shapely and beautiful, and no one could compare with the stunning beauty of Job's daughters, Jemimah, Keziah, and Keren-happuch.[8] Joseph, too, was an attractive youth so full of sexual vigor that he distracted women much older than he.[9] Such details suggest that it is neither morally degrading nor a crime to acknowledge visually witnessed human beauty—female or male, clothed or not.

On the other hand, seeing nakedness is in some instances a morally fraught experience. Ham observed his drunken father's naked genitals, and for this his son was cursed (Gen. 9:22–25). Similarly, uncovering the genitals of certain close relatives is biblically proscribed (Exodus 18). Priests were instructed to wear breeches so as not to unwittingly expose themselves to those below when ascending the altar (Exodus 28:42–43).

The Rabbis expand on these biblical impulses. On the one hand, they instituted a prayer one should utter when seeing an unusually beautiful person.[10] According to Maimonides, it is permissible for men to look upon one's naked wife—though not during her menses—as long as it is done in the privacy of one's home.[11] A medieval Germanic kabbalistic text considered observing one's scantily clad wife to be an appropriate sexual stimulant.[12] As for women, the Talmud relates that Rabbi Yochanan situated himself prominently outside the women's mikveh so that when they viewed him, they would beget children as handsome as he.[13] The medieval mystical tract *Igeret HaKodesh* reinforced the notion that viewing a partner's physical form enhances the quality of sexual union, in part because it stimulates the imagination.[14]

The Rabbis also expressed anxiety about viewing naked bodies, however. Though some rabbis assert that it is far better to observe a naked woman than engage with her bodily, others warn against this kind of activity, for it could produce degenerate or even blind children.[15] Another classic source avows that looking intently upon a beautiful unmarried woman or at a married ugly woman is impermissible.[16] It goes on to say that this restriction also extends to looking at her gaudy garments as well as to observing asses, pigs, and fowl when they copulate. Certainly this text expresses negative attitudes about noticing a woman's body, but it also betrays the authors' misogyny by joining that restriction to a rule motivated by fear of arousal from observing animals sexually engaging each other.[17]

If seeing human (and animal) bodies in the flesh is morally ambiguous, what about viewing depictions of human bodies? It would be easy to point to the central command prohibiting the construction of engraved images (Exod. 20:4; Deut. 5:8) as a warning against making such expressions. Yet there is a Rabbinic text demonstrating that depicting sexy human bodies is a proven way to arouse a partner. The Talmud relates that Queen Jezebel made (painted?) two real harlots on the chariot of King Ahab so that when he viewed them his usual frigidness would dissipate and he would become aroused.[18] It is far from clear whether these two harlots were merely nude portraits or if they were arrayed in explicitly sexual acts.

So what about viewing sex itself? The classic textual tradition instructs sexual partners to engage in their intimate affairs under the cover of darkness, though some permit light as long as its source is covered by a screen.[19] The Talmud twice records the story of Rav Kahana hiding beneath the bed of his teacher, Rav, so as to observe Rav's interactions with his wife. Kahana justified witnessing Rav's intimate relations with her as necessary for his Torah learning.[20] Insofar as it is permissible to engage a partner sexually in most any position, it is plausible Kahana witnessed a great deal.[21] Might we then conclude that proper moral instruction includes witnessing firsthand (good) sex, and conversely, teachers should expect that even their most intimate behaviors are rightful subjects for student observation? A countervailing opinion is expressed by Rabbi Shimon bar Yochai. Both he and God despise those who have sex in front of their slaves, though he does not articulate what, if any, punishment they merit for so doing.[22]

Verbal Expressions

Judaic ambivalence also emerges regarding speaking, hearing, and reading sexually explicit words. The earliest source for this ambivalence is the biblical command to keep military camps scrupulously clean of *ervat davar*, "indecent things," because God moves within them (Deut. 23:15). *Targum Onkelos* translates *ervat davar* as *ervat pitgom*, which means "indecent words." A midrash understands *ervat pitgom* as *nibul peh*, "lascivious talk."[23] Thus, anyone who speaks lasciviously about a bride entering the wedding canopy deserves to be stripped of happiness; moreover, the jaws of *Geihinom* gape wide for both the speaker of such *nibul peh* as well as any silent listener of it.[24]

Not all sexual speech is dangerous, however. Though Maimonides observes that the usual topic of men's conversation revolves around sex and therefore rules that it would be better not to have extended conversations with women, Joseph Karo thought that sexually explicit conversations are acceptable with one's spouse. Indeed, Karo encouraged talking with a spouse about sexual issues so as to arouse and inspire the partner's willingness to engage sexually.[25] Maimonides agrees that insofar as a man must secure a wife's consent before sexual intimacy, the best means to achieve this is through conversing with her and intensifying her joy.[26] Jacob ben Asher points to the story of Rav Kahana overhearing his teacher Rav verbally seduce his wife before engaging with her as a source permitting sexually explicit speech whose purpose is to arouse a partner.[27] And Ima Shalom, the wife of the great sage Eliezer ben Hyrcanus, admitted that the secret of their children's beauty was her husband's practice of speaking with her just before sexually engaging with her.[28]

If it is lawful, ethically desirable, and even genetically advantageous to use words to arouse a partner, what precisely should one say? The Song of Songs offers lush and lusty phrases that both extol and perhaps excite a partner; for example, "Your lips are like a crimson thread, your mouth is lovely. . . . Your breasts are like two fawns, twins of a gazelle, browsing among the lilies. . . . Sweetness drops from your lips, O bride, honey and milk are under your tongue, and the scent of your robes is like the scent of Lebanon" (Song of Songs 4:3, 4:5, 4:11). It also offers descriptions of sexual scenes that could be shared with a partner to arouse desire: "His left hand was under my head, his right hand caressed me" (Song of Songs 8:3). The *Igeret HaKodesh* stipulates that a husband must "begin by speaking to her in a manner that will draw her heart to you, calm her spirits and make her happy. . . . Speak to her so that your words will provoke desire, love, will, and passion, as well as words leading to reverence for God, piety, and modesty."[29] Proper verbal foreplay must be a mixture: "some of erotic passion, some words of fear for the Eternal."[30] Warm her heart, it teaches, "by speaking to her charming and seductive words."[31] Sexually explicit speech has a proper place, it would seem, in Jewish sexual ethics.

Fantasy

Sexually explicit communication stirs human bodies and minds. Indeed, this kind of speech stimulates minds by sparking fantasies. No doubt the tenth commandment, which prohibits lusting after a neighbor's wife, is given to curtail fantasies and, more importantly, engaging bodily with people not legally permitted to one, for such couplings would generate bastard children, perhaps disease, and certainly disgrace.[32] It is not surprising, then, that for the polygamous world in which they lived, the Rabbis ruled that men should think only of the wife currently engaged with, lest their children suffer congenital and moral problems.[33] On the other hand, sexual fantasies can be advantageous. According to a Chasidic source, they can enhance spiritual experiences: a man is permitted to visualize a naked woman in front of him so as to reach higher spiritual planes, and he is even permitted to ejaculate during prayer from such arousal.[34] Fantasies also help in the bedroom, according to another Chasidic text: "When a woman fantasizes about a man, a fantasy about the woman arises in the man."[35] Indeed, the whole of the *Igeret HaKodesh* was given in part because of fantasy's power in and for sexual relations: "Know this well and see how far the power of fantasy and thought extend, whether it be for good or evil. Even though this is not the intent of the work, it will help you completely. You will know the power of fantasy, and you will understand the mystery of thought and how powerful it is at the time of union."[36] Authors of the Judaic textual tradition thereby express appreciation of sexy communication for its stimulating capacities and enhancement of liturgical and intimate experiences.

Location of Sexy Speech

The Judaic textual tradition also notes a proper location for the production and consumption of sexually explicit communication. As is well-known, auto-arousal for the purpose of ejaculation is frowned upon, especially outside the confines of marriage.[37] It thus makes sense that consumption of sexually explicit materials for this purpose would also be discouraged. And the Talmud expresses nervousness about supplying sexually stimulating conversation and visuals in a medicinal setting; indeed, it could be dangerous for a certain patient.[38] So Lawrence Grossman—the only other scholar who has written at length on this subject—is not altogether wrong when he says, "Jewish legal literature manifests disapproval of erotic stimulation outside marriage."[39] What he does not reflect upon is the legal approval of erotic communication, especially verbal kinds, *within* marriage. But then he does err when he assumes he can generalize and encapsulate "*the* position of the classical Jewish sources," which, according to him, holds that "since sexual stimulation outside marriage is forbidden, so is pornography."[40] As shown above, such grand statements about the totality of the Judaic textual tradition are undermined when that textual tradition is read broadly and on its own terms.

It is difficult to maintain Grossman's or any similar conclusion that all forms of sexually explicit communication are categorically prohibited to Jews, that Jews may neither produce nor consume this genre. A more nuanced appreciation of the role of sexually stimulating expressions is, I think, supported by the Judaic textual tradition. It would seem that the tonal thrust of the textual tradition favors permitting, if not encouraging, Jews to produce and consume some forms of erotic expressions for the purpose of invigorating marital relations, with perhaps more freedom in the verbal than visual arena. To be sure, this does not mean that producing or consuming pornography is a requirement for sexual intimacy within a marriage. Rather, it means that as long as the people involved are mutually consenting adults in a religiously sanctioned relationship, sexual expression, arousal, and fantasy are theirs to create, share, and enjoy.

NOTES

1. Many books exist on Jewish sexuality generally, yet scant few discuss pornography implicitly much less explicitly. Though Rachel Shtier's piece of historical sociology examines the role of Jews in the porn industry, it does not attend to sources in the Judaic textual library. See Rachel Shtier, "Jews and Pornography," in *Jews*

and American Popular Culture, ed. Paul Buhle (Santa Barbara, CA: Praeger, 2006), 3:201–10. See the bibliography for a partial list of other books on Jewish attitudes about sex and Jewish sex ethics.

2. Lawrence Grossman, "A Jewish Approach to the Pornography Issue," in *The Jewish Family and Jewish Continuity*, ed. Steven Bayme and Gladys Rosen (Hoboken, NJ: Ktav, 1994), 181–99; Solomon B. Freehof, "Pornographic Literature," in *Current Reform Responsa* (Cincinnati: Hebrew Union College Press, 1969), 240–42; Diana Villa, "Judaism on Pornography and Drinking," Schechter on Judaism: Ask the Rabbi, http://www.schechter.edu/AskTheRabbi.aspx?ID=133; E. Gurkow, "Is Pornography a Sin?," AskMoses.com, http://www.askmoses.com/en/article/237,2233031/Is-pornography-a-sin.html.

3. This is not to say that robust Jewish ethical discourse does not employ similar methods. Rather, it is to say that text selection and amplification demand justification.

4. This paper does not address child porn or violent porn. On the former, the Bible instructs that if a man has sex with a virginal and unbetrothed maiden, he is to pay her father a dowry and may not divorce her (Exod. 22:15–16; Deut. 22:28–29). Since the act of having sex with a minor receives only a pecuniary punishment, it would be difficult to say that merely speaking about or visually depicting such acts would be categorically prohibited. That said, there is an overriding concern to protect young children and young adults from sexual encroachment; speech promoting such activity would similarly be discouraged. Regarding violent porn, insofar as a husband and wife may have sex in any position they mutually desire, it is conceivable that sadomasochistic sex would be permissible, and as will be shown, it is therefore plausible the expressions depicting such kinds of sex would also be permissible—but only in certain circumstances. On the other hand, many classic sources bespeak the need to ensure a partner's willing participation, and without such consent any sexual encounters would be considered illegal and immoral (see discussion below). Insofar as marital rape, for example, is impermissible, logic would have it that pornography—whose purpose is sexual arousal—may not have that as its subject matter. The line between consensual sadomasochism and rape is nebulous, however, especially from an outsider's vantage point. No doubt these are troubling observations; more research into these sub-genres is obviously necessary.

5. For a more thorough analysis of extant scholarship on this topic, see Jonathan K. Crane, "Judaic Perspectives on Pornography," *Theology & Sexuality* 16, no. 2 (2010): 127–42. This essay draws heavily on that piece.

6. Several scholars of course define pornography by fiat and then use that definition to study and assess classic sources against that modern definition. See, e.g., Fokkelien van Dijk-Hemmes, "The Metamorphization of Woman in Prophetic Speech: An Analysis of Ezekiel 23," in Athalya Brenner and Fokkelien van Dijk-Hemmes, *On Gendering Texts* (New York: Brill, 1993), 167–76; Athalya Brenner, "On 'Jeremiah' and the Poetics of (Prophetic?) Pornography," in Brenner and Dijk-Hemmes, *On Gendering Texts*, 177–93; Marty Klein, *America's War on Sex: The Attack on Law, Lust and Liberty* (Westport, CT: Praeger, 2006).

7. The fear Adam feels in Gen. 3:10 does not relate to his nakedness as much as it does to the fact that he has compromised his relationship with God. After meting out punishment for disobedience to the serpent, to the woman, and to Adam, God becomes a tailor and sews clothes of skin for Adam and his wife in Gen. 3:21 before

evicting them from the Garden of Eden. Some rabbis construed Edenic Adam as already clothed and not naked. See Jerusalem Talmud, *B'rachot* 2:14.

8. Gen. 12:11, 12:14, 24:16, 29:17; Esther 2:7; Job 42:13–15.

9. *B'reishit Rabbah* 84:7; Rashi on Gen. 37:2; *Midrash Tanchuma* (Warsaw), *Vayeishev* 5, 8; Babylonian Talmud, *Yoma* 35b; *B'reishit Rabbah* 87:6. Compare with Qur'an 12:22–32.

10. Jerusalem Talmud, *B'rachot* 6:4, 7:7. See also Babylonian Talmud, *Avodah Zarah* 20a.

11. *Mishneh Torah, Hilchot Isurei Biah* 21:4; *Shulchan Aruch, Even HaEizer* 20:4, 25:2.

12. *Sefer Chasidim* (Parma), 1084, p. 275; found in David Biale, *Eros and the Jews: From Biblical Israel to Contemporary America* (New York: Basic Books, 1992), 78.

13. Babylonian Talmud, *B'rachot* 20a. See also Babylonian Talmud, *Bava M'tzia* 84a.

14. *Igeret HaKodesh*, 140, 162. Usually ascribed to Nachmanides, it was possibly written by another Spaniard a generation later, Joseph ben Abraham Gikatilla. See Rachel Biale, *Women and Jewish Law: The Essential Texts, Their History, and Their Relevance for Today* (New York: Schocken Books, 1995), 140. A contemporary translation is by Seymour J. Cohen, *The Holy Letter: A Study in Jewish Sexual Morality* (Northvale, NJ: Jason Aronson, 1993). All page citations come from the Cohen edition.

15. Babylonian Talmud, *Yoma* 74b; Babylonian Talmud, *N'darim* 20a. A Chasidic text claims that viewing intently upon a naked woman—but not engaging with her sexually—and contemplating her will enable him to pass a test and ascend to great spiritual heights. See *Shever Poshim*, 34b–35a, found in Biale, *Eros and the Jews*, 126.

16. Babylonian Talmud, *Avodah Zarah* 20a–20b.

17. It was not uncommon, however, to compare a woman's beauty to animals. See, e.g., Song of Songs 4:1–2, 6:5–6.

18. Babylonian Talmud, *Sanhedrin* 39b. Grossman asserts that this is the sole text in the whole of Talmud that references pornography explicitly. He goes on to say that since the subject of this brief passage are two biblical villains, "the intent is clearly to mock the wicked royal pair." That is, insofar as he deems pornography morally bad ab initio, it makes sense that anyone associated with it—as are Jezebel and Ahab—would and should be even more degraded than they already are. See Grossman, "A Jewish Approach to the Pornography Issue," 183.

19. Babylonian Talmud, *Nidah* 16b; *Shulchan Aruch, Even HaEizer* 25:5; *Beit Sh'muel* on *Shulchan Aruch, Even HaEizer* 25:5.

20. Babylonian Talmud, *B'rachot* 62a; Babylonian Talmud, *Chagigah* 5b. See also *Tur, Orach Chayim* 240.

21. Babylonian Talmud, *N'darim* 20b; *Mishneh Torah, Hilchot Isurei Biah* 21:9.

22. Babylonian Talmud, *Nidah* 16b–17a.

23. *Vayikra Rabbah* 24:7. Ibn Ezra, at Deuteronomy 23:15, thinks *ervat davar* means both "words" and "deeds."

24. Babylonian Talmud, *Shabbat* 33a. See also Babylonian Talmud, *K'tubot* 8b; Maimonides, *Guide for the Perplexed* 3:8.

25. Rambam's Commentary on *Avot* 1:5; *Shulchan Aruch, Even HaEizer* 25:2.

26. *Mishneh Torah, Hilchot Ishut* 15:17. The rule against marital rape arcs back to Babylonian Talmud, *Eiruvin* 100b, which also understands that men must use speech to solicit sex from their wives.

27. *Tur, Orach Chayim* 240.

28. Babylonian Talmud, *N'darim* 20a–b.

29. *Igeret HaKodesh*, 172.

30. *Igeret HaKodesh*, 174.

31. *Igeret HaKodesh*, 174; see also p. 176. On verbal foreplay, see Rabbi Jacob Emden's *Siddur Beit Yaakov*, 158a–159a. On early modern erotic poetry, see the work of Judah Leib Ben-Ze'ev, as discussed in Biale, *Eros and the Jews*, 161–62. Here is but one example: "She closed her hand around me and squeezed / So that my beloved could not spring free / She thrust her thighs, down and up, / Racing, racing the horse of her war / For her heart was stormy with the flame of her love."

32. Exod. 20:14; Deut. 5:18; Prov. 6:25–35; *Mishnah Avot* 4:21.

33. Babylonian Talmud, *N'darim* 20a–b; Babylonian Talmud, Kallah 1:1; Babylonian Talmud, Kallah Rabbati 1:15; *Igeret HaKodesh*, 146, 162.

34. *Shever Poshim*, 37b–38a. Found in Biale, *Eros and the Jews*, 126.

35. *K'tonet Pasim* (Lvov, 1866), 33a, by Jacob Joseph of Polonnye, though attributed to the Baal Shem Tov. Found in Biale, *Eros and the Jews*, 132.

36. *Igeret HaKodesh*, 168.

37. Babylonian Talmud, *Nidah* 13b. The *Zohar, Emor* 90a, explores the permissibility of extra-vaginal ejaculation. See also Rambam's commentary on *Mishnah Sanhedrin* 7:4, about the vitiation experienced from ejaculation.

38. Babylonian Talmud, *Sanhedrin* 75a.

39. Grossman, "A Jewish Approach to the Pornography Issue," 187.

40. Ibid., 189 (emphasis added). For a more robust critique of Grossman's essay, see Crane, "Jewish Perspectives on Pornography," 131–32.

48

JEWISH VIEWS ON
SEXUAL FANTASY AND DESIRE

Rabbi Edythe Held Mencher, LCSW

> Eat, lovers, and drink: Drink deep of love!
>
> *(Song of Songs 5:1)*

Sex forges kingdoms and incites war. It can make gentle lovers of warriors and makes poets of ordinary men and women. Sexuality is powerful and dangerous, beautiful and sacred, essential to the stories of our people and our own lives. It is no wonder, then, that sexual desire was a keen interest of the Rabbis and remains a topic of both interest and concern today.

Is sexual desire subject to moral judgment? Does it matter what we fantasize about? What's the relationship between our thoughts and our acts? In seeking to address these questions, we will explore the only three instances of the word "desire" (תְּשׁוּקָה, *t'shukah*) in *Tanach*, the Hebrew Bible, and consider them in light of Rabbinic interpretation and modern psychology. Our inquiry will take us from the cursed desire of Eve to the exalted desire of the Song of Songs, stopping at the complex desire of the contemporary *Fifty Shades of Grey* along the way. Ultimately, this study will both encourage and caution us about sexuality in the eyes of Jewish wisdom.

First, a word of prelude. These sources, and the Rabbis and the psychologists who comment on them here, address primarily heterosexual sexuality. While the general principles of sexual behavior and desire we will explore apply to many forms and expressions of sexuality, our sources operate with many hetero-normative presumptions, such as the presumption that men and women are created to mate naturally with one another. This study does not endorse the hetero-normative; rather, it seeks to uncover from the ongoing Jewish discourse on sexuality guidelines about sexual desire and behavior for the lives of all people today.

Desire in Genesis

The first occurrence of the word "desire" in Genesis refers to the curse of Eve.[1] Following the events of the Garden, in which Eve is convinced by the serpent to eat the fruit of the Tree of All Knowledge and then gives the fruit to Adam to eat, God punishes the guilty parties. Eve's punishment is, "I am doubling and redoubling your pains of pregnancy; with pain shall you bear children, yet your desire [תְּשׁוּקָתֵךְ, *t'shukateich*] shall be for your man, and he shall govern you" (Gen. 3:16). The punishing aspects of most of this curse are clear—multiplied pains of childbirth and subjugation are indisputably negative ascriptions. But what about "your desire shall be for your man"? Why is this considered a curse?

Like the other aspects of Eve's punishment, "your desire shall be for your man" is a reversal of the order of Creation. The presumption of the text is that human beings were always intended to procreate: immediately upon their creation, God blesses humankind and commands them, "Be fruitful and multiply" (Gen. 1:28). However, it stands to reason that God did not always intend for this procreation to be painful and difficult. Thus, God's decree that childbirth will be painful is a reversal of God's intended order. As well, it is clear that male and female human beings were created equally: "God created the human beings in [the divine] image, creating [them] in the image of God, creating them male and female" (Gen. 1:27; cf. Gen. 5:1–2). Again, Eve's punishment that her husband shall rule her is therefore a reversal of this original state.

Eve's desire follows this pattern as well. The more detailed account of God's creation of humanity in the second chapter of Genesis depicts this creation as one of sexual mutuality. God determines that it is not good for Adam (*adam* is also the Hebrew word for "human being") to be "alone" (Gen. 2:18) and therefore puts the first person to sleep. From this "man," "woman" is drawn, an act that is seen by some early rabbis as the separation of an androgynous male-female into two separate beings, male and female.[2] Following this separation, the text teaches, "So it is that a man will leave his father and his mother and cling to his wife, and they become one flesh" (Gen. 2:24). This may be understood once again as God's intended order: the sexual union between man and woman is mutual, an event of "clinging" from which the two become one, united in their sexual act. However, following the events in the Garden, this paradigm is broken. Eve is cursed to "desire" her husband in a submissive way, to tip the balance of power in his favor. Not only shall men rule their wives, but Adam also claims the power to name (and therefore possess) his wife, for it is only *after* the curse that "the man called his wife's name Eve" (Gen. 3:20). Eve's desire is a symbol for that imbalance in the sexual relationship.

This text screams out for interpretation: Why does God punish Eve—and all women who follow her—with sexual submission? As modern readers analyzing the text with modern tools, we may untangle this question by understanding this text not as *prescriptive* but rather as *descriptive*. In other words, the narrative passed down to us in Genesis is our ancestors' sacred attempt to understand the nature of reality as they saw it. Those who told the stories of our ancient beginnings and who later wrote them down into the texts that would become the Torah were seeking answers to the situations they experienced in their own lives. They asked why childbirth was so arduous and why women would consent to have sex at all given how agonizing, even life-threatening, childbirth could be. As well, our ancient ancestors may have witnessed what we also see today, that there are women who repeatedly find themselves submitting to men who dominate them, who even seek to possess them. This ancient text is an ever-living symbol of the troubling manifestation of sexual relations between men and women from antiquity until today.

This first instance of "desire," as we have seen, concerns a woman's desire for a man despite his dominance over her. Two chapters later, Genesis provides another dimension of desire: its capacity to grab hold of a man and not let him go. Cain, disturbed that his offering has not been accepted by God, is overcome with anger. God speaks to him: "Why are you so angry? Why your fallen face? Would you not do well to lift it? For if you do not do well—sin is a demon at the door; you are the one it desires [תְּשׁוּקָתוֹ, t'shukato], and yet you can govern it" (Gen. 4:6–7). Here, it is not a woman but rather a personified sin whose desire is for man. And in this instance as in the former, the man is expected to "rule" the one who desires him.

The first instance of desire, in which man's control of woman is considered a punishment, records the earliest enactment of injustice. Through this second instance of desire, God exhorts man to control sin and thereby to achieve victory over injustice. These early chapters of Genesis thus show both God's sanction of and disapproval of injustice through desire. What are we to make of these seeming contradictions? One option, as mentioned above, is to conclude that our sacred texts reveal to us a social imbalance that our ancestors hoped we would be able to overcome. According to this approach, God does not "really" curse Eve with the desire to be subjugated; rather, our text simply displays the reality that humans perceive in their regular lives. A second interpretation is that injustice is planted so that ultimate redemption can be experienced. As the Psalmist teaches, "Those who sow in tears, in rejoicing shall they reap" (Ps. 126:5). Joseph, sold into slavery and subject to tragic humiliations before earning his reward, tells his brothers, "It was to save lives that God sent me ahead of you" (Gen. 45:5); and Mordecai, facing the utter annihilation of all Jews, says to Esther, "Who knows? Perhaps you have come to a royal position for just such a time [of crisis]" (Esther 4:14). God even tells Abraham directly that his descendants "shall be enslaved and afflicted" (Gen.15:13) before their deliverance. These biblical accounts all affirm the power of redemption that follows suffering. Perhaps God witnesses injustice, allowing for the pain it produces, as part of a grander narrative of salvation. Perhaps it is the voice of Eve or Cain that we hear in the words of Micah:

> I must bear the anger of the Eternal,
> Since I have sinned against God,
> Until God champions my cause
> And upholds my claim.
> God will let me out into the light;
> I will enjoy vindication by God.
>
> (Micah 7:9)

The Genesis accounts of Eve and Cain show us that desire leads to injustice. Perhaps these accounts are human attempts to understand the suffering we too frequently witness, and perhaps they are seeds of humanity's ultimate liberation. In both cases, we learn that the mission of humankind is to overcome the harmful impulses of desire in order to assert justice in human relationships.

Desire in Contemporary Society

Contemporary society—like that of our ancestors—is plagued with pervasive male domination of women. Indeed, according to Sherry Ortner, the submission of women to men is present in every single culture on earth, "within every type of social and economic arrangement, in societies of every degree of complexity."[3] Where did this domination come from? Psychoanalyst and sociologist Jessica Benjamin has proposed that "cultural myths" like those in Genesis do not *generate* this pervasive phenomenon but rather reflect a pattern that emerges from the basic act of mothering. The "essence of trained femininity" emerges from "the mother's lack of subjectivity" vis-à-vis her children. Because mothers tend to the needs of their children, they are perceived universally—by men, women, and children—as existing for the sustenance and pleasure of others, thus creating "an internal propensity toward feminine masochism and male sadism."[4] This may explain the Genesis account's linkage of Eve's childbearing with the curse that her passion will be for her husband, and it also shows that the desire to dominate is not created in men by God (as shown in the story of Cain) but rather develops in response to the conditions of human life outside the Garden.

Throughout much of human history, the dominance of men over women has been expected, even celebrated. Feminist scholarship and activism have accomplished much in combating this hierarchy, challenging modern society to recognize and remove patterns of male control. Intricately intertwined with both of these contexts is a thoughtful approach to contemporary sexual fantasy. In particular, we may explore "one of the fastest-selling book series for any publisher ever,"[5] *Fifty Shades of Grey* by Erika Mitchell (pen name E. L. James).

"I gasp, and I'm Eve in the Garden of Eden, and he's the serpent, and I cannot resist,"[6] says protagonist Anastasia Steele, surprising herself at her willingness to go along with her lover's taboo sexual suggestions. Ana, as her friends call her, is a college senior who finds herself enchanted by Christian Grey, a wealthy and charismatic businessman. In their first meeting, an interview for the college newspaper, Grey tells Anastasia, "I don't have a philosophy as such. . . . I like control—of myself and those around me."[7] At first, Ana considers Grey a "control freak," though later she comes to discover the thrill of sexualized physical punishment administered for not submitting to his authority. Grey delights in sexual practices of control and punishment, which both surprise and seduce Anastasia. For his part, Grey learns to tolerate Ana's gentle touch as he recognizes the significance of his feelings for her. Transformed through one another, Ana and Grey diversify their sexual relationship, engaging in both sadomasochism and tenderness.

The massive popularity among women of *Fifty Shades of Grey* and its two sequels reveals a telling characteristic of our society. Many acknowledge that the fantasies recounted in *Fifty Shades of Grey* stir their own sexual arousal. Some admit that they would actually like to have Anastasia's experience of being whipped during sex, and more reveal that they might like to be restrained and play at being forced to submit to some sexual act.[8] As well, some women insist that the most compelling part of the story is Ana's own control over Grey through his attraction to her; she is desirable and, therefore, powerful. Surprising many with its extraordinary success, *Fifty Shades of Grey* seems to have tapped into an important undercurrent in sexual fantasy in today's English-speaking society.

Rabbinic Voices on Sexual Desire

Jewish wisdom brings valuable perspectives to our attempt to understand what these sexual fantasies can mean. Jewish tradition suggests both that sexual fantasy is dangerous and that such passion is necessary and good. Thus, there are multiple avenues for interpreting what a novel like *Fifty Shades of Grey* may mean to today's Jewish readership.

While Judaism is noted for caring more about the righteousness and holiness of our actions than about our fantasies, the Rabbis were concerned about thoughts connected to particularly unsavory behaviors. The phrase *hirhur halev*, "thought of the heart" refers to thoughts about sins such as idolatry, violence, and sexual impropriety.[9] The Rabbis' fear of sexual thoughts in particular comes in part from Numbers 15:39, which instructs, "Do not follow your heart and eyes in your lustful urge." The explication of this verse in the Babylonian Talmud interprets "following your eyes" as "thoughts of a transgression" (*hirhurei aveirah*), a more pointed form of "thoughts of the heart" (*B'rachot* 12b). In his comment on this phrase, Rashi explains that "thoughts of a transgression" refer to "appetite for women" (*taavat nashim*), which is more difficult to constrain than an actual sexual deed (*Yoma* 29a). Further, Rabbi Ami is quoted as asserting, "Everyone who brings himself 'into the hands of [sexual] thoughts' [*lidei hirhur*] will not be entered into the division of the Holy Blessed One" (*Nidah* 13b). Both Maimonides[10] and Joseph Karo[11] make this statement into normative halachah and suggest that if a man "brings himself into the hands of sexual thoughts," he should turn his mind to matters of Torah in order to distract himself from his baser impulses. Thus, rabbis' disapproval of sexual thoughts is widespread, persisting through the centuries.

On the other hand, the Rabbis also argued that sexual passion is a necessary component of human life. This perspective comes about in a discussion of the nature of human creation. In the Babylonian Talmud (*B'rachot* 61a), Rav Nachman bar Rav Chisda teaches that God created human beings with two inclinations, a "good desire" (*yetzer hatov*) and an "evil desire" (*yetzer hara*).[12] In other words, we were created with two sides to our nature. The evil inclination, *yetzer hara*, is the force within us that leads us toward fulfilling desires without regard for consequences. The good inclination, *yetzer hatov*, is the force of containment that channels *yetzer hara* and that leads us to pro-social, spiritually based, and ethical behavior. Both of these inclinations are set in motion while Adam and Eve are in the Garden, and both are necessary for Creation to continue.

The urges to marry, to build, and to be productive are all derived from *yetzer hara* (*B'reishit Rabbah* 9:9). Indeed, *yetzer hara* is necessary for us to exist, for without it, no one would have sex; as Reish Lakish taught, "If [our ancestors] had not sinned, we would not have come into the world" (Babylonian Talmud, *Avodah Zarah* 5a). Thus, while the "evil desire" is dangerous, with the potential to drive us to wanton and violent behavior, it is also essential to human life; indeed, God calls *yetzer hara* "very good" in creating it (*T'hillim Rabbah* on Ps. 9:2). We both honor our base instincts and seek to limit them, acknowledging our sexual drive and holding it back with our desire to do good.

In this light, what might the Rabbis have said about *Fifty Shades of Grey?* In their terms, we might imagine Christian Grey as a personification of *yetzer hara*, an unbridled dynamo lusting after power, success, and sexual conquest. In contrast, Anastasia Steele is in line with *yetzer hatov*, a simple scholar without significant experience of anything bad. Grey on his own is monstrous; Ana on her own is naïve. The story is a wrestling of these forces as Ana comes to realize the thrilling spark of forbidden sex and Grey comes to appreciate the calming touch of tender love. Today's society often displays sexual activity in simplistic terms: sex that isn't frivolous is usually portrayed as either sinful or holy. Mitchell's novel complicates those assumptions, daring to suggest that painful and dominating sex can be healthy.

The fantasies depicted in *Fifty Shades of Grey* are prevalent in today's society. Research has shown that at least a sizable minority—if not a majority—of all women have enjoyable sexual fantasies in which they are forced to have sex, even as they deeply fear and would fight against being raped.[13] Other studies further suggest that women with a high sense of personal agency and confidence in their own "dominance" frequently have sexual fantasies involving forced submission.[14] These studies have suggested that powerful women actively seek powerful mates to aggrandize their own standing. Insecure women as well may tend to have such fantasies, perhaps yearning to connect to someone powerful.[15] This research can be read in at least two ways: on the one hand, perhaps we see here examples of Eve's "desire for [her] man" passed down through the generations. Or perhaps these studies suggest that the *yetzer hara* of women today is both active and healthily in check.

Approaching Consensual Sensuality

The Rabbis would caution us against walking too far down the path of *yetzer hara*, as they devote much of their discourse about this force to adjurations to suppress it.[16] This warning may be especially fitting for fantasies of domination, the reversal of God's intended created order. Nevertheless, the study of psychology may help uncover "how much" sexual fantasy is healthy for people today. In *Love and Hate in the Analytic Setting*,[17] psychoanalyst and psychiatrist Glen Gabbard reviews the observations of his some of his colleagues, adding his own analysis as well:

> [Robert] Stoller observed that even in the most loving relationships, a measure of hostility is an integral part of sexual arousal. [As well, David] Raphling has noted that unselfish concern for one's partner is always competing with aggressive claims of the self to exploit, possess, and dominate the partner. . . . Aggression has unfortunately developed a bad reputation in many quarters. . . . [Indeed,] aggressive forces are instrumental in the bonding of love relationships. [Otto] Kernberg has made the following observation: "A man and woman who discover their attraction and longing for each other, who are able to establish a full sexual relationship that carries with it emotional intimacy and a sense of fulfillment of their ideals in the closeness with the loved other, are expressing their capacity not only to link unconsciously eroticism and tenderness, sexuality and the ego ideal, but also to recruit aggression in the service of love."

For these scholars, the presence of aggressive themes in fantasy or sexual behavior is not necessarily cause for alarm. Dominance and submission can be used to achieve an experience of loving connection in a relationship characterized by respect and mutuality.

Indeed, this hope for healthy desire is inherent as well in *Tanach*. Long after the expulsion from the Garden of Eden and Cain's murder of his brother, two lovers dance through King Solomon's court, flirting with one another and expressing profound sexual desire. The Song of Songs contains *Tanach*'s third and final instance of the word "desire," portraying a redemptive rather than condemnatory view of passion: "I am my beloved's and his desire [תְּשׁוּקָתוֹ, *t'shukato*] is upon me" (Song of Songs 7:11). Here at last is mutual desire, a man and a woman engaged together in sexual passion. But this is not a passion of equality, for no such desire could exist. Rather, the Song of Songs portrays the two lovers pursuing one another. At times, one is in control; at times, the other. The female lover is more vulnerable, subject to the bruises of the city watch (Song of Songs 5:7), while the male lover is enchanted, perhaps held powerless, by her beauty. This is the ideal passion of *Tanach*: one can have a hold over another, and this domination can be desirable on both sides, so long as the power dynamic is mutually consensual.

What for some may be an element of their sexual fantasy and play becomes for others a compulsion that truly limits their capacity to have sexual and intimate lives characterized by tenderness and affection. If any of us is either experiencing such a sense of being driven and limited in our sexual and intimate life or is involved with a person with whom we experience a coercive or predominantly sadistic or masochistic relationship, it is vital to make use of clinical resources available through psychotherapy to address such issues. Our goal would be to experience diminished suffering and to be able to experience the full range of human connection that is the Jewish ideal. Sometimes such a sense of constriction and compulsion reflects traumatic life experiences that we feel forced to relive, and our commitment to freedom and healing ought to lead us and others toward more life-affirming paths.

Feminist theologian Rachel Adler sees in the Song of Songs a hope for a society repaired of its sexual violence. God's curse of Eve is powerful, and its effects have been felt for generations. But God has also given us the ability to overcome this curse and to restore the intended order of Creation. By turning our attention to creating a just society that affirms mutual relationships, sexual fantasy and activity can contribute to healthy sexual lives and strong Jewish communities. Indeed, this Jewish progression into a more egalitarian society is a hallmark of the modern age:

> When childbirth anesthesia was invented some Victorian clergymen saw it as a rebellion against the decree, "In pain shall you bear children," but Jewish law never forbade the alleviation of childbirth pain. . . . Just as we can invent technologies that . . . ease our birthing without seizing control from birthing mothers, we can invent ways of coexisting without dominating one another.[18]

We may have inherited the consequences of Eve's and Cain's passions, but we are not condemned to repeat them. Dominance and submission can be redeemed as healthy and fruitful elements of sexual passion, affirming the tender and the raw sides of our created bodies. Our challenge today is to embrace healthy sexuality, to emphasize mutual respect, and to honor our passions by turning them to acts of justice.

Desire exists in each of us, a *yetzer hara* that drives our sexual thoughts and actions. Our Rabbis teach us, "If you want, you can rule it,"[19] and the Song of Songs gives us a model of this desire as mutual rather than controlling. Sexual fantasies of dominance and submission can be healthy and exciting so long as they are both sensual and consensual. As we embody our tradition's values of love and respect, we create supportive and nurturing relationships that advance God's image in the world.

NOTES

1. In Genesis 3:14, God says to the serpent, "You are under a curse," and in Genesis 3:17, God informs Adam, "The soil is now cursed." While God does not specifically state that the woman (yet to be named "Eve") is cursed, one may infer that she, too, receives this punishment for the events in the Garden.

2. Cf. *B'reishit Rabbah* 8:1; *Vayikra Rabbah* 14:1; Babylonian Talmud, *B'rachot* 61a; and Babylonian Talmud, *Eiruvin* 18a.

3. Sherry Ortner, "Is Female to Male as Nature Is to Culture?," *Feminist Studies* 1, no. 2 (Autumn 1972): 5–31.

4. Jessica Benjamin, *The Bonds of Love: Psychoanalysis, Feminism, and the Problem of Domination* (New York: Pantheon Books, 1988), 81.

5. Jeffrey A. Trachtenberg, "Oh, My! That Dirty Book Has Sold 70 Million Copies," *Wall Street Journal*, March 27, 2013, http://online.wsj.com/article/SB1000 14241278873234662045783847431292941041.html.

6. E. L. James, *Fifty Shades of Grey* (New York: Vintage, 2011), 245.

7. *Ibid.*, 12.

8. Jenny Bivona and Joseph Critelli, "The Nature of Women's Rape Fantasies: An Analysis of Prevalence, Frequency, and Contents," *Journal of Sex Research* 46, no. 1 (2009): 33–45.

9. Cf. Rashi's comment on Numbers 31:50; *Vayikra Rabbah* 7:3; Babylonian Talmud, *B'rachot* 20b; and Maimonides, *Mishneh Torah, Hilchot Avodah Zarah* 2:1.

10. *Mishneh Torah Hilchot, Isurei Biah* 21:19.

11. *Shulchan Aruch, Even HaEizer* 23:3.

12. David Biale and Daniel Boyarin both use the translation "desire" rather than the more common "inclination"; this translation follows them.

13. Cf. Jenny Bivona, "Women's Erotic Rape Fantasies" (doctoral dissertation, University of North Texas, August 2008), http://digital.library.unt.edu/ark:/67531/metadc9118/m2/1/high_res_d/dissertation.pdf; and Michael Castleman, "Women's Rape Fantasies: How Common? What Do They Mean?," *Psychology Today*, Jan. 14, 2010, http://www.psychologytoday.com/blog/all-about-sex/201001/womens-rape-fantasies-how-common-what-do-they-mean.

14. Patricia Hensely Hawley, "Social Dominance and Forceful Submission Fantasies: Feminine Pathology or Power?," *Journal of Sex Research* 46, no. 6 (2009): 568–85.

15. Ibid.

16. Cf. Babylonian Talmud, *B'rachot* 5a; *Avot D'Rabbi Natan* (version A) 16; and *Midrash Tanchuma* on *Parashat Naso*, 8.

17. Glen Gabbard, *Love and Hate in the Analytic Setting* (New York: Jason Aronson, 1977), 44.

18. Rachel Adler, *Engendering Judaism: An Inclusive Theology and Ethics* (Boston: Beacon Press, 1998), 124–25.

19. *Sifrei D'varim* 45.

Thanks to CCAR rabbinic intern Daniel Kirzane for his invaluable help with this essay.

49

RELEASE FROM BONDAGE

Sex, Suffering, and Sanctity

RABBI DANIEL A. LEHRMAN, NCPsyA, LP

Not to laugh, not to lament, not to curse, but to understand.

(Baruch Spinoza, *Theological-Political Treatise* 1:4)

From sex within marriage to premarital sex; from the missionary position to a Kama Sutra variety; from taboos on masturbation to a recognition of it as a natural part of sexual functioning; from intra-racial sex to inter-racial sex; from genital sex to oral and anal sex; from heterosexuality to gay and lesbian, to lesbian, gay, bisexual (LGB), to transgender (LGBT) to queer (LGBTQ), and perhaps now to "intersex," someone whose anatomy is not clearly male or female (LGBTQI)[1]—since the sexual revolution of the 1960s, our culture's openness about the realities of sex has grown both socially and legally, with an uninhibitedness in the public sphere that seems to grow with every year.[2]

What's next? What frontiers of sexuality remain to be brought out of the closet and into the arena of acceptable public discourse, to be depicted in popular movies and sitcoms, discussed on morning television shows, written about in magazines and best sellers, blogged about, tweeted about, joked about?

The series of novels by British author E. L. James called *Fifty Shades of Grey*, first published in 2011, has brought one such frontier of sexuality to mainstream awareness in its path to selling twenty-five million copies in four months alone, discussed in book clubs across the nation and on morning news programs,[3] advertised in metropolitan commuter trains, spawning copycat novels, even giving rise to a new coinage, "mommy porn," and—sure enough—soon to become a major motion picture.[4]

Fifty Shades of Grey centers around a BDSM sexual relationship between the characters Christian and Anastasia. An acronym for bondage/discipline (or sometimes domination), sadism/masochism, BDSM covers a wide range of activity in which partners take on roles of dominant or submissive. Some BDSM practices involve inflicting and suffering physical pain, such as when established rules have been broken, requiring punishment and discipline. Issues of power and authority, vulnerability and helplessness, shame and humiliation, come into play. BDSM encounters are understood by participants, however, to be consensual activity; typically, the partners have agreed on a code word with which the submissive partner has the power at any time to bring any activity to a stop. *Fifty Shades of Grey* contains scenes in which Christian, the dominant, pulls Anastasia's hair "painfully," hits her with his hand, whips her with a riding crop, and binds her in leather cuffs.

It can be disturbing to consider behavior in which one adult controls, dominates, and sometimes inflicts pain on another adult to be consensual behavior, let alone sexually arousing or relationship-enhancing. BDSM occupies a dark space where sex and violence meet, and while it may be seen as a "game," the pain that sometimes occurs is not pretend. It is a game that seems to flirt with the space where brutal crime can take place, where consent and pleasure, if they are possible at all, may understandably be judged perverse—a scandal and an outrage. Indeed, sadomasochism has long been treated as a pathology of interpersonal and sexual relations, associated with early childhood trauma and developmental interferences.[5] Sex therapist Esther Perel notes a common assumption even among colleagues (who might be expected to be particularly nonjudgmental of sexual practices) that some pathology must underlie the acting out of dominant and submissive roles. In a discussion of a BDSM relationship at a professional conference she attended, she observed, "the unspoken subtext," despite the fact that women are not always in the submissive role in such relationships, that "such practices are inherently degrading to women, a rebuke to the very idea of gender equality, and antithetical to a good, healthy marriage."[6]

Other psychotherapists and professionals in human sexuality have weighed in differently, called to comment because the phenomenal popularity of James's novels thrusts important questions to the fore. Are all forms of BDSM unhealthy, damaging, perverse, a sickness in need of treatment? Sex therapist Sari Cooper, for instance, avers in *Psychology Today* that BDSM "is not weird, it is not pathological, it **is** a flavor of erotica, just as chocolate (and vanilla) are flavors of ice cream."[7]

Where sexual practices raise moral issues, Judaism, like many religions, has much to say. So concerned is Judaism with what we should do and what we shouldn't do sexually that the chapter in Torah most extensively enumerating the sexual prohibitions, Leviticus 18, is put front and center as the traditional Torah reading on the afternoon of Yom Kippur. Large sections of the Talmud, moreover, pertain to issues of "family purity," rules regulating sexual relations within marriage. Many resources are available in our textual tradition for evaluating the moral dimensions of sexual practices.

We could pass moral judgment on BDSM right here at the beginning, and it might be a relief, like de-venoming a snake to make it safe to handle. In order to understand something about BDSM more deeply, however, we need to risk handling it without cursing it from the start. In the spirit of Spinoza, we will suspend the urge to declare judgment, not in order to revise our judgment from bad to good, but in order to think about it from a perspective in which good and bad are not the primary categories. In addition—and complicating things still more!—our project here is as much to understand something about Judaism through the lens of BDSM as to understand something about

BDSM from the perspective of Judaism. Therefore our inquiry may be put from these two points of view: (1) What is there about BDSM that Judaism can help us to understand? (2) In exploring BDSM from the perspective of Judaism, what aspects of our tradition come to the fore and reveal themselves with particular clarity?

We begin by turning to a contribution by psychiatrist Emmanuel Ghent called "Masochism, Submission, Surrender: Masochism as a Perversion of Surrender," in which Ghent explores some of the meanings of BDSM behavior as he has come to understand them from his intensive work with patients. Ghent uses the word "surrender" to name an experience for which he believes everyone has a wish or longing. Surrender is "a quality of liberation and expansion of the self." It involves "a letting down of defensive barriers."[8] Surrender for Ghent is not about hoisting a white flag; it is not about defeat. What is surrendered is the armor of the ego, the protective layers that maintain a feeling of subjective isolation. He describes it as "a controlled dissolution of self-boundaries," *which is both sought and feared*, and he identifies other features of surrender:

- Its ultimate direction is the discovery of one's sense of wholeness, even one's sense of unity with other living beings.
- It is not a voluntary activity. One can provide facilitative conditions for surrender, but in the event, it just happens; it cannot be made to happen.
- It is an experience of being "in the moment," totally in the present, where past and future recede from consciousness.
- It is accompanied by feelings of acceptance—of self, of others, perhaps of things as they are.
- There is an absence of domination and control.
- It may be accompanied by feelings of dread and death, and/or clarity, relief, even ecstasy.

Ghent's description of surrender sounds notes that are echoed by mystics of many traditions.[9] Dissolving the normal boundaries of the self is a core theme in the teachings of the Chasidic masters, who speak of being "stripped of selfhood,"[10] of being "no longer aware of [one's] own self," of "overcoming the bonds of self."[11] A name for this is *bitul* or *bitul yeish*, which means nullifying one's "somethingness" or "selfness," or ego; it is even called "self-annihilation."[12] Says Dov Ber of Mezritch, "You need to think of yourself as nothing. Forget yourself entirely."[13] *D'veikut*, an experience of *clinging* or *cleaving* to God, may similarly be seen as involving a "dissolution of self-boundaries" that Ghent describes. In such mystical states of being, "the ego's will is submerged in the divine will so that one's acts serve God rather than a limited self."[14] This is the path to "ultimate unification" with God,[15] an experience Ghent articulates as "sense of unity with other living beings."

Common as well to the two descriptions, Ghent's and the Jewish mystics', is a transformed awareness of time. In surrender as in *bitul yeish*, there is a feeling of "transcending time" such that "past and future have receded from consciousness."[16] Or we might put it positively and say that the three tenses—past, present, and future—are all at once present, which is the meaning of *YHVH*, the name of God that expresses God's timeless being and that is expressed in our song *Adon Olam*: *God was, God is, and God will be*. While liberating, the experience of timelessness is also disorienting, so it is no surprise that "fear" and "dread" (Ghent's terms) would accompany it—"awe," in religious language.

Yet this awe exists in a signal combination with joyous release. "It is joyous in spirit," says Ghent. There is "limitless joy and incomparable delight" among those who stand in the light of God, says a Chasidic master.[17] Celebration and merriment are hallmarks of the Chasidic way of life, and *hitlahavut* is a name for its most impassioned form—a "burning enthusiasm" reached in intensest prayer. The word itself combines the awe and fear with the joy of it, stemming from a Hebrew root for "flame," our earthly portion of the life-supporting, dangerous sun. Or to change the elemental image, a fitting metaphor for this multiform experience of timelessness/dread/awe/joy might be diving into the ocean, into both the freedom and the overwhelm of boundlessness, into a disorienting but enlivening loss of a dependable here-and-now. *Terra firma* is gone, and with it both security and limitations.

Now what does this kind of spiritual experience, described by both Ghent and the Jewish mystics, have to do with bondage, domination, sadism, and masochism?

Focusing on the masochistic pole of a relationship, the provocative thesis Ghent explores is that seeking out submission, pain, and adversity in BDSM sometimes—and he is careful to say sometimes, not always—springs from a spiritual longing. There is another dimension, "often deeply buried," he says, to masochistic erotic desire.[18] The *apparent* wish is to be controlled, dominated, and disciplined by another person, and this wish is enacted physically by allowing oneself to be ordered about and punished, put in restraints, humiliated; even physical pain is not out of bounds. The core desire in this dynamic is the desire to cede control completely. Even the submissive's power to disobey the dominant is exercised only in order to be disciplined back into powerlessness. The submissive acts autonomously in order to abdicate autonomy. And why? Because the desire is for giving oneself over, not for taking oneself back.

This "giving oneself over" is the clue to the link between this masochistic dynamic and ecstatic spiritual experience. The true longing, deeply buried, may be for authentic surrender, *bitul yeish*, a breaking free of the boundaries of individuality. Such experience is hard to come by, however, so a substitute for surrender can be very enticing. In allowing oneself to be dominated and controlled, afflicted and punished, a substitute is found, a shortcut: the normal boundary between self and other is crossed, encroached upon in a way that the survival instinct normally precludes. It is like storming the walled city of the ego so as to smash its ramparts. The resulting breakdown of the boundary between self and other is experienced by some as liberating. It is, as Esther Perel notes, delight in the "abandon that comes with the sense of powerlessness."[19]

Ghent calls such masochistic enactment a "defensive mutant of surrender." This substitute, this ersatz spiritual experience, Ghent calls *submission*, in contrast to surrender. "Submission, losing oneself in the power of the other, becoming enslaved in one or other way to the master, is the ever available lookalike to surrender."[20]

The look-alike nature of submission to surrender is all the more vivid when we consider that similarities between sexual submission and some Jewish mystical states are not limited to the mental-emotional-spiritual levels, but extend to the physical as well. For instance, some mystical experiences include a letting go or even a vanquishing of physical autonomy. "When a man attains to the stage of self-annihilation he can thus be said to have reached the world of the divine Nothingness. Emptied of selfhood his soul has now become attached to the true reality, the divine Nothingness. . . . *All his physical powers are annihilated*."[21] There can be very specific kinds of dissociation from one's physical being. "Sometimes [a] voice emerges from within the mystic, who then is heard speaking in a different voice from his usual one. Another variation of this phenomenon is the belief that a celestial power is guiding the hand of the writing mystic."[22] In other words, physical defeat, spiritual victory. Given these co-occurring phenomena of spiritual openness and physical "annihilation," it is not hard to see how "submission, losing oneself in the power of the other, becoming enslaved in one or other way to the master, is the ever available lookalike to surrender."[23]

This act of substituting one experience for another might be compared to the search for spirit in "spirits"—that is, in alcohol, in recreational drugs, or in other reckless or dangerous behavior, all involving a giving up of control and a concomitant transformation of the feeling state. We speak colloquially of going to a party and "letting go," "letting loose," "losing inhibitions." Ghent notes the wide spectrum of behavior that partakes of some degree of masochism, from unhealthy and self-injuring forms, to others such as running a marathon, riding a roller coaster, or, we might add, even the child's twirling round and round to the point of collapsing in dizziness. However we may judge the activity, Ghent is focusing us away from the pain or self-injuring behavior itself, and instead on what makes the pain feel worthwhile.

We can see in all of these examples the common goal (not the only goal) of changing one's state of consciousness—in a word, getting high. More than one marathon runner speaks of the spiritual high of extreme exertion; it is a common experience among athletes. BDSM, because it occurs in the sexual realm, is in a class of its own, however, because of the special nature of sexuality. "The closest most of us come to the experience of surrender is in the moment of orgasm with a loved one," writes Ghent. "Little surprise it should be then for the sexual scene to be the desired focus for such letting-go." Being "known in one's naked-ness" is the "ultimate longed-for goal of self-surrender."[24]

How Ghent reaches his conclusions from a clinical perspective is outside our scope here, but we have begun to see that the thrust of his insight—the linking of masochistic behaviors with spiritual strivings or, more broadly, the linking of suffering with spirit—is not as bizarre as it might at first appear. BDSM can contain spiritual longings of which Judaism has a profound and highly developed understanding, including a recognition of the dangers of spiritual exploration. The classic story of the perils of the mystic journey tells of the four rabbis, Ben Azzai, Ben Zoma, Acher, and Rabbi Akiva, who entered the *pardes*, the mystic garden. One died, one went insane, and one "cut down the plantings," a puzzling phrase perhaps meaning he became a heretic. Only Rabbi Akiva exited with all his faculties intact—the same Rabbi Akiva, in fact, who so recognized the spiritual core, with all its fearsome majesty, in the erotic poetry of Song of Songs that he declared it the holiest of all books in the *Tanach*.

Sanctity and self-imposed suffering have long been coupled in reli-gious traditions. Christian practices of flagellation, for example (Latin *flagellum* means "whip"), go at least as far back as the fourth century and grew to "a huge scale in the second half of the thirteenth century, after which it spread all over Europe and became endemic."[25] Flagel-lants, sometimes including both men and women, processed through village streets lashing themselves for hours. The word "passion" as in "passion of Christ," encodes the twinship of suffering and spiritual-ity, as does "Muslim," meaning "one who surrenders and submits." In

Zen Buddhism, too, the pain of sitting for extended periods of zazen meditation may be experienced as a gateway or vehicle to a less dualistic state of being, and some forms of Zen include being hit with a switch as a spur to awakening.

In Judaism, the spiritualization of suffering is less overt than in some religions, but it is hardly ancillary.[26] Fasting on Yom Kippur[27] derives from the commandment in Leviticus 23:32, "you shall *afflict* [*v'initem*] your souls." Indeed, the word we translate as "fast," *taanit*, derives from the same root letters—*ayin, nun, hei*—as do a variety of other words with meanings such as "torment," "suffering," "humility," "self-abasement," and "submission."[28] One such word, *inui*, means "torture." The self-mortification (Latin *mors/mortis* means "death") accomplished through the affliction of fasting is part of the enactment of death on Yom Kippur, along with the four other "afflictions" prohibiting washing, anointing with any oils or cosmetics, wearing leather shoes, and sex. On our most solemn day, when we meditate on all the ways we have fallen short of our own standards and ideals and confront the shame of our wrongdoing, we perform a set of rituals that is not meant to buoy us up, but that rather brings us even lower, down into our earthy humble vulnerability. "The antidote to humiliation is not pride, or a reassertion of self-respect or virtues or positive qualities," writes psychotherapist Lyn Cowan. "It is humility. There are occasions of fault, failure, exposures of shameful weakness, which can be borne only by yielding completely to the feeling of them."[29] In Jewish tradition as in others, we descend in order to ascend. *M'chayeih hameitim*: God brings renewed life to that which has touched death.

Perhaps one reason for *choosing* adversity, humiliation, and self-abasement is that we recognize the spiritual power that can be wrested from pain and suffering. Would Nelson Mandela have had the inner fortitude and the world's respect necessary for leading his nation through political and spiritual transformation had he not lived for twenty-seven years as a prisoner on Robben Island? Elie Wiesel's searing works were formed in the earthly hell he lived through. Oprah Winfrey's gracious stature is inseparable from her struggles. Whether we look at the character-building mission of an army boot camp, the collective calamity of centuries in slavery, or the inevitable hardships of negotiating puberty or a first job, trial and tribulation are necessary conditions for reaching some stages of maturity.

One of our tradition's most dramatic tales is of Rabbi Akiva insisting on teaching Torah publicly, against the decree of Hadrian. He was to be executed as punishment, and as the Romans were raking his flesh with iron combs, Akiva recited the *Sh'ma*. His students were amazed. How at this moment could he bring himself to praise God? Akiva said that he had always wondered what loving God "with all your soul" meant in the *V'ahavta*. (BT *B'rachot* 61b) He was grateful now at last to be able to fulfill that mitzvah. In *Midrash Rabbah*, righteous souls are said to endure severe trials, and this is compared with the owner of flax who will beat it often and severely so as to make it more pure.[30] Even the most abject suffering may be occasion for transcendence.

A phenomenon in contemporary Israel sheds unique light on experiences of affliction and responses to them. Some children and grandchildren of Holocaust survivors have chosen to get tattooed with the numbers their relatives had branded on their forearms by the Nazis. This has of course shocked and appalled many people who see it. How could they possibly do *to themselves* what was done so horrifically to their family and their people? Why would anyone choose to replicate and carry into yet another generation such a graphic and permanent sign of what Primo Levi called part of the demolition of a human being?[31] When Oded Ravek, the fifty-six-year-old son of survivor Livia Ravek, first showed his tattoo to his mother, "she was really upset about it. When I explained the reasons for why I did it, we cried together. I said, 'You're always with me.'" Mr. Ravek's son, Daniel Philosoph, also chose to be tattooed with his grandmother's number. All the descendants interviewed by journalist Jodi Rudoren echoed Ravek's sentiments. "They wanted to be intimately, eternally bonded to their survivor-relative."[32] For a documentary film about the survivors and their self-tattooing descendants, filmmaker Dana Doron interviewed about fifty Holocaust survivors. She asked them whether lovers kissed their numbers as they might a scar. "Some of them looked at me like, 'What are you, nuts?' and some of them said, 'Of course.'"[33]

There are clusters and knots of meanings here. Suffering and trauma are not pushed away, covered over with a long-sleeved shirt. They are drawn close and exposed. The grotesqueness of branded human beings, the beauty of family bonds, somehow interwoven. Grief/suffering/intimacy/satisfaction/bad/good: the words are separate but the experiences are not. Reasonable questions seeking reasonable answers—*Why would someone want to do a thing like that?*—presume a level of logic and singular causality better suited to other domains. Such queries are going to the ocean with a thimble. In these areas of the psyche, unlike in the material world, two things and many more do occupy the same space at the same time. Suffering and sanctity appear to be attached by a double-pointed arrow, like the antirational power of biblical sacrifice.[34] *Sacri-fice*: a *making sacred*—through? in? of? with? pain, destruction, death, blood, suffering. A whole burnt offering, a *holocaust*. A *drawing close*, the literal meaning of *korban*, Hebrew for "offering" or "sacrifice." Pain and suffering, chosen and unchosen, one's own or that of another to whom one is bound by love, hold a special susceptibility to sanctity.

In the heart of Jerusalem was the Temple, and in the heart of the Temple, sacrifice was performed. In the heart of Judaism is an extraordinary genius for holding the kinds of clashing meanings we have been exploring. It is a genius for ambivalence—defined not as uncertainty or indecisiveness, but as the coexistence of opposing attitudes or feelings.

Explosions of paradox happen everywhere in Judaism. In ritual: the breaking of the glass at a wedding—burst of joy, remembrance of destruction; Yom Kippur—most solemn day of the year while also a *Shabbat Shabbaton*, "Sabbath of Sabbaths"—the "fast is a feast," in Philo's words.[35] In story: Abraham is breathtakingly *chutzpadik* on behalf of those at Sodom, while infuriatingly submissive in bringing Isaac up the mountain as sacrifice; Moses is the greatest prophet and also a murderer; the tribe he comes from, Levi, savagely brutalizes the Shechemites, then becomes the tribe of priests. In theology: God is immaterial, beyond all picturing, and full of *chesed* and *rachamim*, compassion and loving-kindness, while also a "Warrior" (Exod. 15:3). God is, in the same breath, Isaiah's "Maker of peace and Creator of bad/evil" (*oseh shalom u'vorei ra*, Isa. 45:7). Examples could be multiplied endlessly.

In BDSM, the union of seeming irreconcilables may be pushed to the nth degree. Life-invigorating eros may vibrate to very nearly the same frequency as life-injuring violence. This is terrifying territory. It is like a dark corridor that leads to we know not what—a place we might prefer to believe does not exist. Indeed, walking by a sex shop in the East Village of Manhattan, seeing the dog collars, the gags and muzzles, the hoods and blindfolds, the whips and paddles, it is impossible not to recall the photos of the abuse at Abu Ghraib. No matter how much one may domesticate BDSM and normalize it with bestselling novels and major motion pictures—"it is a flavor of erotica, just as chocolate (and vanilla) are flavors of ice cream"—it cannot be denied that it sits along a continuum of sexualized violence and violent sex that includes the most horrifying of human behavior.[36]

With BDSM, we are looking, then, at a cluster of psychodynamics that may come to life horrifically, in murderous earnest, in torture chambers and concentration camps, and also in consensual sensual play in the privacy of a bedroom. The dissonance is even more shrill if there is any truth at all to the idea we have explored, that there is a spiritual aspiration motivating some BDSM behavior, an actual striving toward an experience of God. These are the clanging, clashing meanings that BDSM challenges us to hold at one and the same time. It reminds us that spiritual zones may be the farthest things from cozy safety. The High Priest on Yom Kippur risked death, so a rope was tied around him just in case, lest somebody else need to enter the Holy of Holies to retrieve his body. When we do encounter God, injury may result: Jacob's becoming Israel left him with a limp.

Looking at BDSM from the point of view of Judaism, it is tempting to take up a seat in a perch of moral judgment.[37] Religion is prone to be used this way, to survey things dangerous and bad from up behind the crenellated safety of the Old City walls. But ancient Jerusalem drew its water, and thus its life, from outside those walls, from a region down below that could be unpredictable and uncontrollable and dangerously violent. Judaism challenges us with the terribly disturbing teaching of monotheism. We may wish to envision it as a grand magnificent harmony, and such it may be on some ultimate level. But closer to earth, it means that if everything is linked up together, then nothing human is alien to any one of us. The *Tanach* is relentless in driving the point home. It looks at the worst of human behavior and says: That is us. It looks at lust and murder and says: That is us (King David). It looks at deceit and fraud and says: That is us (Jacob and Rebekah in league against Esau and Isaac). It looks at berserk, heedless vengefulness and says: That is us (Simeon and Levi at Shechem). It looks even at genocide and says: That is us (the Book of Joshua). If we had judged BDSM from the beginning, we would immediately have set up a contrast between it and us, the result of which is the quiet premise: it is different from us. Are we, instead, willing to think without being scared? Are we brave enough to look at some parts of ourselves that are even crazier than irrational, that are antirational? Torah reminds us each week who we are. We go to it again and again, seeking a vision of what we would like to be, if only we could be, and surely ought to be. And what Torah gives us again and again is not the Ought but the Is—what we really are—and this turns out to sustain us more than what we came for, because it's true.

NOTES

1. A recent article in the *New York Times* adds yet another letter to the growing acronym, LGBTQIA, explaining that "A" means, among some young people in particular, either "ally" (a friend of the cause) or "asexual," characterized by the absence of sexual attraction. "Generation LGBTQIA," *New York Times*, January 10, 2013.

2. While the changes in the sexual ethos have roots at least as far back as the 1920s, the 1960s and '70s brought the changes to new levels, aided in particular by the first birth control pill, Enovid, in 1960 and the passage of *Roe v. Wade* in 1973.

3. E.g., *Today Show*, March 3, 2012.

4. Peter Osnos, "How 'Fifty Shades of Grey' Dominated Publishing," *The Atlantic*, August 28, 2012.

5. For instance, one influential interpretation of masochistic desire sees it as a response to abusive treatment in childhood, during which a person may learn to gravitate toward punishing others because he or she knows intimacy only through punishment and severity, not through tenderness. For an overview of the history of understanding sadomasochism, see Theodore Millon, *Disorders of Personality* (New York: Wiley, 1996), chaps. 13 and 16. A diagnosis of pathological sexual masochism stipulates that over a period of at least six months, the "recurrent, intense sexually arousing fantasies, sexual urges or behaviors involving the act (real, not simulated) of being humiliated, beaten, bound, or otherwise made to suffer" cause "clinically significant distress or impairment in social, occupational, or other important areas of functioning." The diagnosis of sexual sadism stipulates that a person has acted on sexual urges, "with a nonconsenting person, or the sexual urges, or fantasies cause marked distress or interpersonal difficulty." *Diagnostic and Statistical Manual of Mental Disorders*, 4th ed., text revision (DSM-IV-TR) (Washington, DC: American Psychiatric Association, 2000).

6. Esther Perel, *Mating in Captivity: Reconciling the Erotic and the Domestic* (New York: HarperCollins e-books), 86. Perel notes interestingly that "as a relative outsider with regard to American society, I suspected that the attitudes I saw in this meeting reflected deeper cultural assumptions." In discussing this issue with therapists from a variety of cultures, Perel notes a common feeling of being "somewhat out of step with American sexual attitudes, hazarding "one unpolished observation . . . that egalitarianism, directness, and pragmatism are entrenched in American culture and inevitably influence the way we think about and experience love and sex," while "Latin Americans' and Europeans' attitudes toward love, on the other hand, tend to reflect other cultural values, and are more likely to embody the dynamics of seduction, the focus on sensuality, and the idea of complementarity (i.e., being different but equal) rather than absolute sameness" (ibid., 87–88).

7. Sari Cooper, "BDSM: Fifty Shades of Grey Unplugged," *Psychology Today*, March 6, 2012.

8. Emmanuel Ghent, "Masochism, Submission, Surrender: Masochism as a Perversion of Surrender," passim. Privately published; reprinted in *Contemporary Psychoanalysis* 26, no. 1 (January 1990): 108–36.

9. One view of the various approaches to meditation is that all the systems "aim for One or Zero—union with God or emptiness." In this brief description I elide this distinction. Perhaps the two are different more in language than in experience. See Daniel Goleman, *The Meditative Mind* (Los Angeles: Jeremy Tarcher, 1988), xvii.

10. Arthur Green and Barry Holtz, eds., *Your Word Is Fire* (New York: Schocken Books, 1977), 59.

11. Ibid., 55.

12. Louis Jacobs, *Hasidic Prayer* (London: Littman Library of Jewish Civilization, 1993), 32.

13. Rabbi Dov Ber of Mezritch, *Maggid D'varav L'Yaakov*, ed. J. Emanuel Schochet (Kehot Publication Society), section 110.

14. Daniel Goleman, *The Meditative Mind: The Varieties of Meditative Experience* (Los Angeles: Jeremy Tarcher, 1988), 52. While Daniel Goleman is best known for his work on emotional intelligence, his roots as a student of meditation go back to

his graduate school days when he spent time in India with Joseph Goldstein, Ram Dass, and others.

15. Dov Ber of Mezritch, *Maggid D'varav L'Yaakov*, sec. 110.

16. Ibid., 56.

17. Hayyim Tyrer of Tchernowitz, in Louis Jacobs, *Hasidic Thought* (New York: Behrman House, 1976), 165.

18. Ghent, "Masochism," 108–36.

19. Esther Perel, *Mating in Captivity: Unlocking Erotic Intelligence* (New York: HarperCollins, 2006), 57.

20. Ghent, "Masochism," 108–36.

21. Jacobs, *Hasidic Prayer*, 78; italics added.

22. Joseph Dan, *The Heart and the Fountain: An Anthology of Jewish Mystical Experiences* (New York: Oxford University Press, 2002), 176.

23. Ghent, "Masochism," 108–36.

24. Ibid.

25. Paul Johnson, *A History of Christianity* (New York: Atheneum, 1976), 259.

26. Jewish ascetic practices existed among the Chasidei Ashkenaz in the eleventh to thirteenth centuries and among the sixteenth-century mystics of Safed, e.g., Moses Cordovero, who instructed his disciples to fast for three days in each season of the year. See Lawrence Fine, *Safed Spirituality: Rules of Mystical Piety, The Beginning of Wisdom* (New York: Paulist Press, 1984). Regarding ascetic practices in ancient times, see Steven Fraade, "Ascetical Aspects of Ancient Judaism," in *Jewish Spirituality from the Bible through the Middle Ages*, ed. Arthur Green (New York: Crossroad), 1996.

27. Traditional fast days include five others in addition to Yom Kippur: Fast of Esther, Tishah B'Av, the Seventeenth day of Tammuz, the Tenth of Tevet, and the Fast of Gedaliah. In addition, according to Maimonides, "special public fasts were sometimes imposed by the religious authorities in the face of calamities or governmental decrees that threatened the Jewish community." (*Hilchot Taaniot* 1:4) There are also private fasts, e.g., the fast of bride and groom on their wedding day and the fast on the day of a parent's *yahrzeit*. See Isaac Klein, *A Guide to Jewish Religious Practice* (New York: Jewish Theological Seminary of America, 1992), 252.

28. E.g., *enut, anivut, hitanut, hitanvut*.

29. Lyn Cowan, *Masochism: A Jungian View* (Woodstock, CT: Spring Publications, 1982), 65–66.

30. *Shir HaShirim Rabbah* (Vilna) 2:46, *haro-eh bashoshanim* (Song of Songs 2:16b).

31. Primo Levi, *Survival in Auschwitz* (New York: Simon and Schuster, 1996), 26.

32. Jodi Rudoren, "Proudly Bearing Scars, Their Skin Says 'Never Forget.'" *New York Times*, September 30, 2012.

33. *New York Times*, September 30, 2012. Name spellings reflect the corrections made in the web edition of this article.

34. I have adapted the image of the double-pointed arrow from a line in Michael Eigen's *The Psychotic Core* (New Jersey: Jason Aronson, 1993), 73.

35. In S. Y. Agnon, *Days of Awe* (New York: Schocken Books, 1965) 191.

36. Sari Cooper, "Fifty Shades of Grey Unplugged," *Psychology Today*, March 6, 2012.

37. While for the purposes of this exploration we have suspended explicit moral judgment, the legitimate question nonetheless persists: *Is BDSM an acceptable form*

of sexual behavior from a Jewish point of view? Put this way, however, the generality of the question makes it impossible to answer, because BDSM is not a single set of behaviors, but may cover a gamut from playfully chasing a partner upstairs and throwing him or her on the bed, to activities that would appear to stretch the notion of mutual consent to its breaking point in their resemblance to abusive torture. Therefore we cannot simply rule the whole category in or out. Even the cardinal issue of mutual consent, a necessary condition of any moral sexual behavior, provides no foolproof test of acceptability, since consent may be given under duress of many subtle and unsubtle kinds, since a "yes" or a "no" may be open to interpretation, and since consent may be conditioned by powerful factors both internal (e.g., a history of psychopathology [see note 6]) and external (e.g., power dynamics). It is naive, therefore, to hold that mutual consent provides a clear and straightforward guideline for evaluating the moral dimensions of sexual behaviors.

Complicating matters still further, we must remind ourselves of what we have learned as a society since the 1960s about the dangers of judging others' sexual preferences and practices, including how such judgments may stem from our own self-questioning and our unconscious impulses, desires, and fears.

These are some of the factors that should serve as background when exploring important questions such as: Between the two extremes of gentle fun and painful, humiliating force, is it possible to draw a line between play and abuse? To what extent is it healthy to act out our sexual desires in the name of openness and self-expression, and to what extent does our tradition exhort us to restrain or transcend them? Two helpful texts that could be brought to bear are Rambam's *Mishneh Torah* (especially *Hilchot Isurei Biah*) and *Igeret HaKodesh*, a thirteenth-century text traditionally attributed to Ramban, though many scholars have concluded that it is an anonymous work. *Igeret HaKodesh*, a kabbalistic treatise on sex, responds directly to Rambam, casting his views on sexuality as stodgy and body-denying in the supposed Greek rationalist tradition, as opposed to its own exuberant tone celebrating sexual relations as a vehicle toward holiness. On closer inspection, however, the contrast is less clear. Let us here simply offer a taste of the texts available for study by citing one passage from Rambam's *Mishneh Torah* (while the *Igeret HaKodesh* focuses on his *Guide for the Perplexed*), which, while heterocentric and seeing only the male as agent, nonetheless expresses a noteworthy open-minded in its view of the range of acceptable sexual behaviors:

> A man's wife is permitted to him. Therefore a man may do whatever he desires with his wife. He may engage in relations whenever he desires, kiss any organ he desires, engage in vaginal or anal intercourse [translating the bracketed phrase; cf. Rashi on Dina, Genesis 34:2], or engage in physical intimacy without relations, provided he does not release seed in vain. Nevertheless, it is pious conduct for a person not to act frivolously concerning such matters and to sanctify himself at the time of relations, as explained in *Hilchot Dei-ot*. He should not depart from the ordinary pattern of the world. For this act was [given to us] solely for the sake of procreation. (Rambam, *Mishneh Torah, Hilchot Isurei Biah* 21:9)

PERSONAL REFLECTIONS

PERSONAL REFLECTION

Queering *T'shuvah* for Everyone

JAY MICHAELSON, PhD

T'shuvah, the Jewish process of self-reflection and return (usually translated as "repentance"), has long been fraught with ambivalence for many LGBT people. For many queer folks, self-acceptance and self-trust are essential to psychological health. Yet *t'shuvah* is a process of self-questioning and self-doubt. Feel guilty over misdeeds. Feel judged. Feel inadequate. Many gay people have worked for years not to feel these things. And yet on Yom Kippur, it's part of the point.

So LGBT people must either abandon repentance or queer it, by which I mean, question its assumptions, make it our own, make it more complex, set aside its oversimplifications. The good news is that this is a gift we give to everyone.

Queering Tradition

The classic grammar of *t'shuvah* is problematic. First, it doesn't help that on the Day of Atonement, traditional congregations still read the urtext of Jewish homophobia, Leviticus 18. Nor is it useful that the essential message of *t'shuvah* is that "change is possible"—a slogan more recently deployed by advocates of so-called "reparative therapy" designed to turn gays into straights. In reality, some change is possible, but some change isn't. Some isn't even desirable.

Yet to know this to be true—to know that one's capacity to love is not something that should be repressed—is to interpose one's experience between oneself and the text. The text in its traditional reading cannot be correct, because it is incompatible with a notion of a loving God. But that truth is only known by allowing experience, conscience, and discernment to speak. This is a radical break from traditional *t'shuvah*, which requires surrender to the text beyond the self.

Indeed, the situation many religious queers face is like that faced by Huck Finn in Mark Twain's novel. Huck has been taught that if he helps escaped slaves, he will go to hell. But he has befriended Jim, the runaway slave, and cannot turn him in. So, Huck decides at a pivotal moment in the book, "I guess I'll go to hell, then." That moment, of course, is not damnation but salvation. It is the birth of a mature conscience.

Gays and lesbians born into religious communities all face a Huck Finn moment, at which the comforting immaturity of dogma yields to a more complicated, but ultimately redemptive, moral conscience. It is a big deal. For those who reject religion, it may often mean severing ties with family or renouncing a connection that was once beloved. For those who reject their independent desires and side with religion, it means a lifetime of repression and sublimation. And for those who refuse to choose between God and gay, it means having to do just what Huck Finn did: transcend religion in order to save it.

Doing so is a mark of moral maturity. Total surrender to heteronomous ethics is unhealthy, period. It may be prescribed by some, but it is a childish faith which leads to fundamentalism and religious violence. Transcending it is important for all—but it is *necessary* for LGBT religious people. Queer spiritual consciousness is inherently distrustful because it has seen how rules, codes, and even the operation of conscience itself can be tools of oppression and self-repression. Of course, straight people ought to come to this realization also. But religious queer people have to.

Queering Conscience

Yet once we have had our moments, done the work, and cultivated the mistrust, what is next? If it is not libertinism, then what is to be our guide? How do we tell guilt apart from conscience? And how do we tell sincere affirmation apart from mere preference?

Some people say that the truth is what we feel "deep down." I disagree. On the contrary, as we review our "misdeeds," it's inevitable that long-ingrained feelings of unworthiness and homophobia will surface. Those of us who were taught homophobia as children can't just wish it away through therapy and liberation. It contaminates the "repentance" process for years. These feelings may indeed be felt "deep down." But you can be deep down and also be wrong.

The facile belief that "your conscience should be your guide" is simply not true. Your conscience is a social construct, and the feeling of truth may be merely the feeling of a belief held for a long time. If you're raised not to eat pork, the simple act of eating can induce a feeling of guilt "deep down," even if one has long ago ceased to keep kosher. Guilt has nothing to do with substantive merit—as gay people know all too well. The emotive response of guilt remains long after the mind, heart, and spirit have all reconciled themselves to the reality of sexual expression, and of love. Honest and nourishing sexual expression brings us to love, to truth, to holiness. Guilt knows none of this.

This, too, is of use to everyone, and not only as a guide to better ethical reflection. Really, this entire geology of the self is an illusion. What's called "deep down" is just a feeling that accompanies certain ideas, usually those one has held the longest. It's not an indication of truth—just of endurance. Guilt is a conditioned phenomenon like everything else. It isn't a still small voice; it's a meme, installed by years of repetition, that has no particular value one way or the other.

As we recognize the historicity of our consciences, we are liberated from them, and from the tyranny of the separate self, that delusion of ego that stands between us and the Divine. Recognizing the conditioned nature of conscience is thus a gateway to recognizing the Unconditioned.

Queering Introspection

What, though, remains of repentance if the heteronomous text no longer has authority over us and if the contents of one's conscience are likewise to be subjected to interrogation? Is there no source of ethics immune to this deconstruction?

In the practice of queer repentance, new faculties do arise to fill these voids: contemplation, discernment, mindfulness. *Hinei El y'shuati, evtach v'lo efchad,* "Here, God is my salvation; I will trust and not fear" (Isa. 12:2). Here—in this moment, with the mind stilled from running and returning to past and future anxieties. Here, it is possible to discern between trust and fear.

This is, in a sense, a more demanding form of *t'shuvah* than recourse to a foundational text or illusory geography of the self. It takes work to still the mind in this way and notice the quiet stirrings of heart and body. But then it works. When I am acting in accord with my body, mind, and heart, there is a sense of groundedness, of peace, that arises. Whereas, when I'm merely indulging a preference, there may be a pleasant sense of lust, but it's not integrated; it's ungrounded. I know the difference somatically.

The sense of groundedness that is attachment to a text, a tribe, or an instinct depends upon specific norms and behaviors. I am attached *to this.* But the sense of groundedness that arises from contemplation is different. There is no attachment—only quiet watching and listening. I reflect on an action and inquire as to its consequences: whether it led to love or cruelty, pain or comfort. I see myself as objectively as possible, not by judging, but by observing in a way less distorted by the preferences of the ego. Objections, moral reasoning, pros and cons can be seen and held clearly. Authentic reflection can proceed.

Once again, I propose that such discernment is a requirement for anyone living in a post-foundational age, in which taboos no longer hold such power. But it is an essential ingredient of a queered process of repentance and introspection. If we are to navigate between the poles of ignorance and zeal, between "all is permitted" and "I am forbidden," the course must be steadied by the ballast of contemplation. The mind in this condition remains, of course, informed by sacred traditions. But it no longer sinks under their weight.

PERSONAL REFLECTION

Choose Life (and Be Not a Skunk)!

RABBI DAVID DUNN BAUER

Human love and desire energize us and inspire us. Conversely, though, they can completely knock us off track and make us do really stupid, if not hurtful, things.

This is a universal concern to which I want to apply both some canonical Jewish wisdom and the deep wisdom derived from watching cartoons as a child. Yes, really.

The Rabbis of the Talmud identified the double-edged blessing of eros as the *yetzer hara*, the evil impulse that causes chaos in our lives. But they also taught that "without the *yetzer hara*, a human being would never marry, beget children, build a house, or engage in trade" (*B'reishit Rabbah* 9:7). Though I distance my thinking from these male-centered, heteronormative terms (marriage and procreation being the central events of all lives), otherwise I think the Rabbis got it totally right. The same impulse propels us both to achieve and to run amok. To feel desire both empowers and endangers us.

How should we proceed in response? How do we protect ourselves from madness as we move forward with our ambitions?

Traditionally, the risks of an erotic life are addressed morally. We receive the pastel-colored instruction "Be good" and the more vivid admonition "Don't be bad."

Starting with those polarities (Am I *good*? Am I *bad*?) is one big mistake, one very big mistake.

They aren't irrelevant questions, but asking those questions *first* sets up a lifetime supply of pain and oppression, especially for Queer folk, members of erotic minorities in a straight-dominated world. Traditionally we have ventured out into the world imprinted with a sense, a *knowledge* (we were taught) of being bad. For all people, spiritual growth, reliance upon religion, and creating functional relationships with our fellows and with God are challenging tasks. For Queer folk, these have all been made harder by our being taught to question, "Am I good or am I bad?" before being taught the skills of creating safe, pleasant, productive relationships with others and with God. None of this part of life is easy; being haunted with a sense of being bad makes everything unnecessarily harder.

I believe the challenge of the *yetzer hara*—the challenge of using the power of desire productively and constructively—should be met by all people *technically*, not *morally*. Don't start by asking, "Is this impulse good or bad?" Start by checking on one's *shalom/sh'leimut* (peace/wholeness) quotient: "Am I at peace? Am I whole?"

For this teaching I draw on two somewhat contrasting texts.

First, I find guidance (in a surprisingly literal way) through a verse from Torah that is part of the customary liturgy: "Do not stray after your heart or your eyes to whore after them" (Num. 15:39).

I love this verse for its astringent clarity and the palpable physicality of the words. It's all about the life of the spirit, expressed in terms of the body.

Regarding that powerful verb "to whore," I don't read this text as sex-negative. Rather, I see it as sex-respecting and heart-protective. The text teaches us about the limits of our heart and eyes, what we can expect of them or ask of them, and why we need to be careful. In my reading, the text doesn't upbraid sex workers (because I emphatically do not), but it does critique the abusive ways in which they often are treated.

In the *Tanach*, the Hebrew verb *liznot*—to whore—appears in two contexts, sexual and religious, almost exclusively. Often *liznot* refers to both the sexual and religious simultaneously, as the men of Israel are warned against or fall prey to sexual seduction by women of another faith and nation. The biblical context of this verse leads us to think that the mitzvah is solely about loyalty to God, with no sexual implication. A well-known Talmudic narrative (*M'nachot* 44a) tells a story that combines a message of religious piety with a cautionary tale regarding actual prostitution. A man's tzitzit slap him in the face as he approaches a Roman prostitute. With this as a reminder of the values he is supposed to live by, she (rather adorably) eventually converts, and they marry.

In contrast to that charming tale, the hazily figurative employment of *liznot* in the biblical verse carries a very poignant, intimate plea for faithful connection from God. It doesn't sound political (avoid foreign women), nor overtly sexual (be chaste). Rather, God reveals God's feelings, saying, "Love Me, be tied to Me. Do not let your eyes see Me, or your heart sense Me, as a whore from whom you could easily run to another about whom you cared as much or as little." In this verse, God speaks vulnerably from the heart about the heart.

The other striking phrase in Numbers 15:39 is *v'lo taturu*—do not go about, seek out. *Latur* is a rare verb in *Tanach*. Some few instances are benign. The verb appears most famously throughout Numbers 13 to describe the actions of the ten scouts whose fearful report of the Land triggers God's wrath and condemns the Israelites to their forty-year wanderings in the desert. *V'lo taturu* in this verse (only a few chapters later) carries with it the weight of that story. It warns us not to throw away our time, our lives, needlessly.

Our hearts and eyes have the power to lead us forward; they are organs of desire. They have a taste for delight that does not conveniently diminish at the right moment. They don't always know when to say enough and leave the table or quit the chase, which means they can treat the rest of the self roughly, abusively—to use the biblical word—like a whore, like a body we've hired but don't necessarily respect. In contemporary life, sex workers are often treated like trash. All of us are capable of treating ourselves the same way; this verse implies, "Don't treat yourself like a whore."

I turn now to a second source of eternal wisdom, Warner Bros. cartoons. In doing so, I want to put forward a personal rabbinical teaching: Thou shalt not be a snob. Embrace thou truth wherever it be found, Leviticus or Looney Tunes. I'm serious.

Maybe one has to be a TV watcher of a certain age, but I vividly remember Pepé Le Pew, the perpetually romantic French skunk. In the Warner Bros. cartoons, Pepé never falls for another skunk, but always some unfortunate feline whom he mistakes for his skunkly soul mate. (Most often some careless house painter has accidentally swiped a white stripe down the cat's back, and consequently she resembles a skunk. Poor thing.) When suddenly enamored, Pepé's eyes stretch forward out of their sockets, his heart beats visibly out of his chest.

That's us! That's how our hearts and minds physically behave when they feel attraction or desire. They're vulnerable to what they like, what they appreciate, and even when tired (especially when tired!), they want and they wander. They lead us relentlessly forward but don't notice when the rest of us doesn't follow. Our hearts and eyes do not know when to stop. Speaking personally, I find myself physically being dragged by my eyes and unable to locate my heart within my own chest.

And this is what I mean when I say, "Don't first judge desire as good or bad." First, respond to its effect with mindfulness and skill. Second, ask, "Will this lead to *sh'leimut* and *shalom*? Am I treating myself and the person I desire with true respect? Am I throwing away my time, wandering in a wilderness?"

It has become a meditative practice for me to bring my heart and eyes back, to reset them in their proper place within me, rather than allowing them to roam unchecked, dragging me behind them, as the verse in Numbers describes.

Try this practice the next time you experience either a momentary rush or an exhausting marathon of love, lust, desire, or craving for someone or something.

Stop. Physically stop moving, wherever you are. Close your eyes. Breathe. As you gently breathe in and out, *pull your eyes back inside your head. Firmly reset your heart high but enclosed within your rib cage.* I mean those instructions literally. Pull them back inside with the internal musculature of your body in your head and chest. Bring them home. Then place one hand over your heart, another over your eyes. Breathe and feel grounded again. At that moment, it is pointless to ask, "Am I good or am I bad?" What's important is to ask, "Am I whole? Am I safe?"

We *can* love, look around, desire, and feel it safely. We *can* use the energy in our day, without being dragged disrespectfully through the street by our hearts or eyes, without having the feeble self-control of a cartoon skunk (charming zo he may be, chérie!). We maintain loving awareness of our hearts and eyes; we certainly couldn't go through life without them. But we recognize their capacity to run us ragged, and we lovingly say no to that. We breathe, and reassemble ourselves.

I don't know if the biblical author meant the verse as technically as I read it, but I stand by my recommendation, because, *mon dieu*, it works! It's that simple. And that's all, folks.

To Learn More

Jewish Sexual Ethics

Address, Richard, Joel Kushner, and Geoffrey Mitelman, eds. *Kulanu: All of Us; A Program and Resource Guide for GLBT Inclusion*. Rev. ed. New York: URJ Press, 2007.

Adler, Rachel. *Engendering Judaism: An Inclusive Theology and Ethics*. Boston: Beacon Press, 1998.

Plaskow, Judith. *The Coming of Lilith: Essays on Feminism, Judaism, and Sexual Ethics, 1972–2003*. Boston: Beacon Press, 2005.

Waskow, Arthur. *Down-to-Earth Judaism: Food, Money, Sex, and the Rest of Life*. New York: William Morrow, 1995.

GLBTQ Issues in Judaism

Alpert, Rebecca. *Like Bread on the Seder Plate: Jewish Lesbians and the Transformation of Tradition*. New York: Columbia University Press, 1997.

Balka, Christie, and Andy Rose, eds. *Twice Blessed: On Being Lesbian, Gay, and Jewish*. Boston: Beacon Press, 1989.

Beck, Evelyn Torton. *Nice Jewish Girls: A Lesbian Anthology*. Boston: Beacon Press, 1989.

Boyarin, Daniel, Daniel Itzkovitz, and Ann Pelligrini, eds. *Queer Theory and the Jewish Question*. New York: Columbia University Press, 2003.

Drinkwater, Gregg, Joshua Lesser, and David Schneer, eds. *Torah Queeries: Weekly Commentaries on the Hebrew Bible*. New York: New York University Press, 2009.

Dzmura, Noah, ed. *Balancing on the Mechitza: Transgender in the Jewish Community*. Berkeley, CA: North Atlantic Books, 2010.

Greenberg, Steven. *Wrestling With God and Men: Homosexuality in the Jewish Tradition*. Madison: University of Wisconsin Press, 2004.

Hoffman, Warren. *The Passing Game: Queering Jewish American Culture*. Syracuse, NY: Syracuse University Press, 2009.

Kabakov, Miryam, ed. *Keep Your Wives Away from Them: Orthodox Women, Unorthodox Desires*. Berkeley, CA: North Atlantic Books, 2010.

Ladin, Joy. *Through the Door of Life: A Jewish Journey between Genders*. Madison: University of Wisconsin Press, 2012.

Ramer, Andrew. *Queering the Text: Biblical, Medieval, and Modern Jewish Stories*. Maple Shade, NJ: Lethe Press, 2010.

Shneer, David, and Caryn Aviv, eds. *Queer Jews*. New York: Routledge, 2002.

Judaism and Sexuality

Biale, David. *Eros and the Jews: From Biblical Israel to Contemporary America*. Berkeley, CA: University of California Press, 1997.

Boyarin, Daniel. *Carnal Israel: Reading Sex in Talmudic Culture*. Berkeley: University of California Press, 1993.

———. *Unheroic Conduct: The Rise of Heterosexuality and the Invention of the Jewish Man*. Berkeley: University of California Press, 1997.

Dorff, Elliot, and Danya Ruttenberg, eds. *Jewish Choices, Jewish Voices: Sex and Intimacy*. Philadelphia: Jewish Publication Society, 2010.

Eilberg-Schwartz, Howard, ed. *People of the Body: Jews and Judaism from an Embodied Perspective*. Albany: State University of New York Press, 1992.

Gold, Michael. *Does God Belong in the Bedroom?* Philadelphia: Jewish Publication Society, 1992.

Isaacs, Ronald. *Every Person's Guide to Jewish Sexuality*. Northvale, NJ: Jason Aronson, 2000.

Lefkowitz, Lori Hope, ed. *In Scripture: The First Stories of Jewish Sexual Identities*. Lanham, MD: Rowman & Littlefield, 2010.

Magonet, Jonathan, ed. *Jewish Explorations of Sexuality*. Providence, RI: Berghahn Books, 1995.

Ruttenberg, Danya, ed. *The Passionate Torah: Sex and Judaism*. New York: New York University Press, 2010.

Satlow, Michael. *Tasting the Dish: Rabbinic Rhetorics of Sexuality*. Atlanta: Scholars Press, 1995.

Jewish Marriage

Broyde, Michael, and Michael Ausubel, eds. *Marriage, Sex, and Family in Judaism*. Lanham, MD: Rowman & Littlefield, 2005.

Feldman, David. *Marital Relations, Birth Control, and Abortion in Jewish Law*. New York: Schocken Books, 1987.

Fuchs-Kreimer, Nancy, and Nancy Wiener. *Judaism for Two: A Spiritual Guide for Strengthening and Celebrating Your Loving Relationship*. Woodstock, VT: Jewish Lights, 2005.

Lamm, Maurice. *The Jewish Way in Love and Marriage*. Middle Village, NY: Jonathan David, 2008. (Originally published by Harper and Row, 1980.)

Wiener, Nancy. *Beyond Breaking the Glass: A Spiritual Guide to Your Jewish Wedding*. New York: CCAR Press, 2012.

Sexuality and Gender in Rabbinic Literature

Baskin, Judith. *Midrashic Women: Formations of the Feminine in Rabbinic Literature*. Waltham, MA: Brandeis University Press, 2002.

Biale, Rachel. *Women and Jewish Law: The Essential Texts, Their History, and Their Relevance for Today*. New York: Schocken Books, 1995.

Cohen, Shaye, J. D. *Why Aren't Jewish Women Circumcised? Gender and Covenant in Judaism*. Berkeley: University of California Press, 2005.

Davidman, Lynn. *Tradition in a Rootless World: Women Turn to Orthodox Judaism*. Berkeley: University of California Press, 1993.

Hauptman, Judith. *Rereading the Rabbis: A Woman's Voice*. Boulder, CO: Westview Press, 1998.

Ilan, Tal, ed. *A Feminist Commentary on the Babylonian Talmud*. Tübingen, Germany: Mohr Siebeck, 2007.

Irshai, Ronit. *Fertility and Jewish Law: Feminist Perspectives on Orthodox Responsa Literature*. Waltham, MA: Brandeis University Press, 2012.

Millen, Rochelle. *Women, Birth and Death in Jewish Law and Practice*. Waltham, MA: Brandeis University Press, 2004.

Peskowitz, Miriam. *Spinning Fantasies: Rabbis, Gender and History*. Berkeley: University of California Press, 1997.

Wasserfall, Rahel, ed. *Women and Water: Menstruation in Jewish Life and Law*. Waltham, MA: Brandeis University Press, 1999.

Gender in the Bible

Adelman, Penina, ed. *Praise Her Works: Conversations with Biblical Women*. Philadelphia: Jewish Publication Society, 1995.

Frankel, Ellen. *The Five Books of Miriam: A Women's Commentary on the Torah*. New York: HarperCollins, 1998.

Goldstein, Elyse. *ReVisions: Seeing Torah through a Feminist Lens*. Woodstock, VT: Jewish Lights, 2001.

Lerner, Anne Lapidus. *Eternally Eve: Images of Eve in the Hebrew Bible, Midrash, and Modern Jewish Poetry*. Waltham, MA: Brandeis University Press, 2007.

Ochs, Vanessa. *Sarah Laughed: Modern Lessons from the Wisdom and Stories of Biblical Women*. New York: McGraw-Hill, 2005.

Pardes, Ilana. *Countertraditions in the Bible: A Feminist Approach*. Cambridge, MA: Harvard University Press, 1993.

Judaism and Gender

Antler, Joyce. *The Journey Home: How Jewish Women Shaped Modern America*. New York: Schocken Books, 1998.

Baader, Benjamin Maria, Sharon Gillerman, and Paul Lerner, eds. *Jewish Masculinities: German Jews, Gender, and History*. Bloomington: Indiana University Press, 2012.

Baskin, Judith. *Jewish Women in Historical Perspective*. Detroit: Wayne State University Press, 1998.

Diner, Hasia, and Beryl Benderly. *Her Works Praise Her: A History of Jewish Women in America from Colonial Times to the Present*. New York: Basic Books, 2002.

Diner, Hasia, Shira Kohn, and Rachel Kranson, eds. *A Jewish Feminine Mystique? Jewish Women in Postwar America*. New Brunswick, NJ: Rutgers University Press, 2010.

Eilberg-Schwartz, Howard. *God's Phallus and Other Problems for Men and Monotheism*. Boston: Beacon Press, 1994.

Ellenson, Ruth Andrew. *The Modern Jewish Girl's Guide to Guilt*. New York: Penguin Group, 2006.

Feldman, Jan. *Citizenship, Faith & Feminism: Jewish and Muslim Women Reclaim Their Rights*. Waltham, MA: Brandeis University Press, 2011.

Fonrobert, Charlotte Elisheva. *Menstrual Purity: Rabbinic and Christian Reconstructions of Biblical Gender*. Stanford University Press, 2000.

Frankiel, Tamar. *The Voice of Sarah: Feminine Spirituality and Traditional Judaism*. San Francisco: Harper, 1990.

Glenn, Susan. *Daughters of the Shtetl: Life and Labor in the Immigrant Generation*. Ithaca, NY: Cornell University Press, 1991.

Goldman, Karla. *Beyond the Synagogue Gallery: Finding a Place for Women in American Judaism*. Cambridge, MA: Harvard University Press, 2000.

Greenberg, Blu. *On Women and Judaism: A View from Tradition*. Philadelphia: Jewish Publication Society, 1994.

Grossman, Avraham. *Pious and Rebellious: Jewish Women in Medieval Europe*. Waltham, MA: Brandeis University Press, 2004.

Hartman, Harriet, and Moshe Hartman. *Gender and American Jews: Patterns in Work, Education, and Family in Contemporary Life*. Waltham, MA: Brandeis University Press, 2009.

Hartman, Tova. *Feminism Encounters Jewish Tradition: Resistance and Accommodation*. Waltham, MA: Brandeis University Press, 2008.

Heschel, Susannah. *On Being a Jewish Feminist: A Reader*. New York: Schocken Books, 1995.

Hyman, Paula. *Gender and Assimilation in Modern Jewish History: The Roles and Representation of Women*. Seattle: University of Washington Press, 1995.

Joselit, Jenna Weissman. *The Wonders of America: Reinventing Jewish Culture 1880–1950*. New York: Hill and Wang, 1996.

Kaplan, Marion. *The Making of the Jewish Middle Class: Women, Family, and Identity in Imperial Germany*. New York: Oxford University Press, 1994.

Kaplan, Marion, and Deborah Dash Moore, eds. *Gender and Jewish History*. Bloomington: Indiana University Press, 2010.

Labovitz, Gail. *Marriage and Metaphor: Constructions of Gender in Rabbinic Literature*. Lanham, MD: Lexington Books, 2009.

Misra, Kalpana, and Melanie Rich, eds. *Jewish Feminism in Israel: Some Contemporary Perspectives*. Waltham, MA: Brandeis University Press, 2003.

Nadell, Pamela, ed. *American Jewish Women's History: A Reader*. New York: New York University Press, 2003.

———. *Women Who Would Be Rabbis: A History of Women's Ordination 1889–1985*. Boston: Beacon Press, 1999.

Ner-David, Haviva. *Life on the Fringes: A Feminist Journey towards Rabbinic Ordination*. Needham, MA: JFL Books, 2000.

Peskowitz, Miriam, and Laura Levitt. *Judaism Since Gender*. New York: Routledge, 1997.

Plaskow, Judith. *Standing Again at Sinai: Judaism from a Feminist Perspective*. New York: HarperCollins, 1991.

Prell, Riv-Ellen, and David Weinberg, eds. *Women Remaking American Judaism*. Detroit: Wayne State University Press, 2007.

Ross, Tamar. *Expanding the Palace of Torah: Orthodoxy and Feminism*. Waltham, MA: Brandeis University Press, 2004.

Ruttenberg, Danya, ed. *Yentl's Revenge: The Next Wave of Jewish Feminism*. Seattle: Seal Press, 2001.

Sered, Susan. *Women as Ritual Experts: The Religious Lives of Elderly Jewish Women in Jerusalem*. New York: Oxford University Press, 1996.

Sztokman, Elana Maryles. *The Men's Section: Orthodox Jewish Men in an Egalitarian World*. Waltham, MA: Brandeis University Press, 2011.

Umansky, Ellen and Dianne Ashton, eds. *Four Centuries of Jewish Women's Spirituality: A Sourcebook*. Waltham, MA: Brandeis University Press, 2008.

Weissler, Chava. *Voices of the Matriarchs: Listening to the Prayers of Early Modern Jewish Women*. Boston: Beacon Press, 1999.

Contributors

Rabbi Judith Z. Abrams, PhD (Hebrew Union College–Jewish Institute of Religion, Cincinnati, 1985), is the founder and director of Maqom (maqom.com), a school for adult Talmud study, and is a winner of the Covenant Award.

Rabbi Richard F. Address, DMin is a rabbi of Congregation M'kor Shalom in Cherry Hill, New Jersey. Prior to returning to the pulpit, he served as a regional director for the Union for Reform Judaism and founding director of the URJ Department of Jewish Family Concerns. He also is the founder and editor of www.jewishsacredaging.com and teaches at the New York campus of Hebrew Union College–Jewish Institute of Religion.

Rabbi David Adelson is a graduate of Hebrew Union College and has served as rabbi of East End Temple in New York City since 2000. He has also trained as a hospital chaplain and currently serves as a spiritual director to rabbinic and cantorial students at Hebrew Union College–Jewish Institute of Religion. He is a leader in Just

Congregations and Manhattan Together (URJ and IAF community organizing work). He lives in Brooklyn, New York, with his wife, Lynn Harris, and children, Bess and Sam.

Rabbi Julie Pelc Adler works at the Aitz Hayim Center for Jewish Living in Glencoe, Illinois. She also serves as the director of the Berit Mila Program of Reform Judaism. She received master's degrees from the University of Judaism and from Harvard Graduate School of Education and was ordained as a rabbi by Hebrew Union College–Jewish Institute of Religion. She co-edited the anthology *Joining the Sisterhood: Young Jewish Women Write Their Lives*, published by SUNY Press in 2003, and has published essays and articles in *Spirituality and Health*, *Lilith*, and *Reform Judaism* magazines, as well as *The Sacred Table: Creating a Jewish Food Ethic*, *Midrash and Medicine: Healing Body and Soul in the Jewish Interpretive Tradition*, and *Torah Queeries: Weekly Commentaries on the Hebrew Bible*.

Rabbi Camille Shira Angel is celebrating her bat mitzvah year as the rabbi of Congregation Sha'ar Zahav, San Francisco's most inclusive and progressive twenty-first-century Jewish congregation. Ordained by Hebrew Union College–Jewish Institute of Religion, she is an award-winning educator and author, whose contributions include *Siddur Sha'ar Zahav*; *Intimate Connections: A LGBTQ and Jewish Values Curriculum*; and "Aging and Judaism," a special issue of the *Journal of Psychology and Judaism*. She serves on the national advisory board of the Religious Action Center, the Reform Movement's Commission on Social Justice, as well as the Rabbinic Advisory Council for Shalom Bayit. She's a grateful *ima* and co-parent of a beautiful daughter and loves being Jewish.

Rabbi David Dunn Bauer is an alumnus of Yale University, Reconstructionist Rabbinical College, the Conservative Yeshiva, Institute for Jewish Spirituality, and Rabbinic Leadership Program, and is the first Jew to earn the Certificate in Sexuality and Religion from Pacific School of Religion. He is a rabbi, pastoral counselor, Queer activist, scholar, and sex educator, with a background in professional theater and opera. He teaches widely on Queer Theology and Spirituality and on Eros and Jewish Thought. In addition to synagogues and churches around the country, he has for years taught for Nehirim, Easton Mountain Retreat Center, and the Body Electric School. He is the founder of Queer Spiritual Counseling, a private counseling practice based in the knowledge that God is Queer and so is the Universe (www.queerspiritualcounseling.com).

Rabbi Karen Bender grew up in Los Angeles in the home of Israeli parents, members of a Conservative Synagogue. She studied political science at the University of California, Berkeley, and earned her master's in Hebrew letters and rabbinic ordination from Hebrew Union College–Jewish Institute of Religion in 1994. She served as rabbinic intern in Prescott, Arizona, in Boise, Idaho, and at Central Synagogue of New York. She served at Temple Beth-El of Great Neck, New York, from 1994 to 2001 and as associate rabbi of Temple Judea in Tarzana, California, from 2001 to the present. Rabbi Bender has published numerous sermons, poems, and articles. She has three children, Josie, Joshua, and Shoshana.

Rabbi Barry H. D. Block assumed the pulpit of Congregation B'nai Israel in Little Rock, Arkansas, in 2013. He wrote "Unplanned Fatherhood" during a sabbatical at Temple Beth-El in San Antonio, Texas, where he served from 1992 to 2013. A graduate of Amherst College, Rabbi Block was ordained by the Hebrew Union College–Jewish Institute of Religion in New York in 1991. Among a wide variety of regional and national leadership positions in Reform Judaism, he served as rabbinic advisor of URJ Greene Family Camp for over two decades. Rabbi Block is a former board chair of the Planned Parenthood Trust of South Texas.

Rabbi Eugene B. Borowitz received his bachelor's degree from Ohio State University. He was ordained and received the first of his two earned doctor's degrees from Hebrew Union College, the other being from Teachers College Columbia University. He has served congregations in St. Louis, Missouri, and Port Washington, New York, and was a navy chaplain during the Korean War. Prior to his academic position, he was national director of education for Reform Judaism at the Union of American Hebrew Congregations, editing its books, curricula, and educational periodicals. Presently, Rabbi Borowitz serves as the Sigmund L. Falk Distinguished Professor of Education and Jewish Religious Thought at the New York School of Hebrew Union College–Jewish Institute of Religion, where he has taught since 1962. He is a prolific author, having written hundreds of articles and many books on various aspects of Jewish religious thought.

Rabbi Jeffrey Brown serves as the spiritual leader of Scarsdale Synagogue Temples Tremont and Emanu-El in Scarsdale, New York. He was ordained by Hebrew Union College–Jewish Institute of Religion in 2005 and previously served as associate rabbi of Temple Solel in Cardiff, California, from 2005 to 2012. His contribution to this book was originally published in the Spring 2012 issue of the *CCAR Journal: The Reform Jewish Quarterly*.

Dr. Karen Carpenter, PhD, PGCHE is a psychologist, Florida board-certified clinical sexologist, and sex therapist. She is a founding member of the Caribbean Sexuality Research Group at the University of the West Indies and runs a free sexology clinic for the public as well as a private practice. Dr. Carpenter is a weekly guest expert on issues of human sexuality and relationships on various television and radio shows. She is the host of the radio program *Love & Sex with Dr. Karen Carpenter* and has written the "Love & Sex" newspaper column. She is a full-time researcher in the area of human sexuality and conducts research in psycholinguistics, language, and sexuality and in HIV prevention and control. Follow her on Twitter and WordPress: @loveandsexja and loveandsexjamaica.wordpress.com.

Rabbi Jonathan K. Crane, PhD, is the Raymond F. Schinazi Junior Scholar of Bioethics and Jewish Thought at Emory University's Center for Ethics. President of the Society of Jewish Ethics, he co-edited with Rabbi Elliot N. Dorff *The Oxford Handbook of Jewish Ethics and Morality* and authored *Narratives and Jewish Bioethics*.

Rabbi Nikki Lyn DeBlosi, PhD, was ordained in 2013 by Hebrew Union College–Jewish Institute of Religion in New York City and currently serves on the rabbinic staff of the pluralistic Bronfman Center for Jewish Student Life/Hillel of New York University. She holds a BA summa cum laude in women's studies from Harvard University and an MA and PhD in performance studies from New York University. Her academic areas of interest include queer theory, ethics, and gender and sexuality in popular culture. Before pursuing graduate-level study, Rabbi DeBlosi worked as a campus organizer and writer for the Feminist Majority Foundation. She lives in Brooklyn with her wife and son.

Rabbi Geoffrey W. Dennis (Hebrew Union College–Jewish Institute of Religion, C 1996) is rabbi of Congregation Kol Ami in Flower Mound, Texas, as well as adjunct professor of rabbinics in the Jewish Studies Program of the University of North Texas. He is the author of numerous academic and professional articles, as well as one book, *The Encyclopedia of Jewish Myth, Magic, and Mysticism* (2007).

Rabbi Elliot N. Dorff, PhD, is rector and Distinguished Service Professor of Philosophy at American Jewish University and visiting professor at University of California, Los Angeles, School of Law. He has served on four federal commissions, including the Surgeon General's commission to create a Call to Action for Responsible Sexual Behavior in order to diminish the spread of sexually transmitted diseases, and he serves as chair of the Conservative Movement's Committee on Jewish Law and Standards, for which he co-wrote the rabbinic ruling that permitted Conservative rabbis to officiate at the weddings of gay men or lesbians. His "Rabbinic Letter on Human

Intimacy," originally written with and for the Rabbinical Assembly's Commission on Human Intimacy, is now a chapter of his book *Love Your Neighbor and Yourself: A Jewish Approach to Modern Personal Ethics*, which also contains chapters on parent/child relations and family violence, and his book *Matters of Life and Death: A Jewish Approach to Modern Medical Ethics* contains chapters on contraception, abortion, and infertility treatments.

Rabbi Mark Dratch is executive vice president of the Rabbinical Council of America and founder of JSafe: The Jewish Institute Supporting an Abuse-Free Environment.

Rabbi Billy Dreskin grew up in Cincinnati, Ohio, and attended Brandeis University in Waltham, Massachusetts, where he earned a degree in music composition. He later attended and was ordained in 1987 by Hebrew Union College–Jewish Institute of Religion's New York campus. He has served as a rabbi at Woodlands Community Temple in White Plains, New York, since 1995. Rabbi Dreskin is married to Cantor Ellen Dreskin and is the proud father of Katie, Jonah (*z"l*), and Aiden.

Rabbi Denise L. Eger is the founding rabbi of Congregation Kol Ami in West Hollywood, California. She is a noted activist for LGBT equality, working within the Reform Movement, both in Israel, and the United States. She was named by Equality Forum as a gay icon and by the *Huffington Post* as the most influential LGBT clergyperson in America. She is the president elect of the Central Conference of American Rabbis. She is the proud mom of Ben, a college student.

Rabbi Stephen J. Einstein, DHL, DD is the founding rabbi of Congregation B'nai Tzedek in Fountain Valley, California. Having completed six years as chair of the Central Conference of American Rabbis Ethics Committee, he now serves the CCAR as vice president for member services. He is co-editor of *Introduction to Judaism: A Sourcebook* and co-author of *Every Person's Guide to Judaism*, and co-chair of the URJ-CCAR Commission on Outreach, Membership, and Caring Community. A longtime mentor to rabbinical students, he teaches rabbinic practice at Hebrew Union College–Jewish Institute of Religion in Los Angeles.

Margarete Myers Feinstein, PhD, is research scholar at the University of California, Los Angeles, Center for the Study of Women. Feinstein has written extensively about Jewish displaced persons and postwar German national identity. Her recent book *Holocaust Survivors in Postwar Germany, 1945–1957* (Cambridge University Press) tells the remarkable story of survivors reclaiming their lives and forging Jewish community while still on German soil.

Rabbi Sharon G. Forman was raised in Norfolk, Virginia, and was ordained as a Reform rabbi by Hebrew Union College–Jewish Institute of Religion in 1994. A Yale University graduate, she also holds a master's degree from Columbia Teachers College. She served as the director of the religious school at Manhattan's Temple Shaaray Tefila for seven years, where she also served as associate rabbi and director of youth activities. She currently teaches at Westchester Reform Temple and resides in Westchester County, New York, with her husband, Steven, and three children, Abigail, Joshua, and Benjamin. Also she is the author of the Union for Reform Judaism's *Honest Answers to Your Child's Jewish Questions* (URJ Press, 2006).

Rabbi Karen L. Fox, LMFT, a Californian native, graduated from the University of California, Los Angeles, in 1973 and was ordained as a rabbi by the Hebrew Union College–Jewish Institute of Religion, New York, in 1978. She earned an MA in counseling psychology at Pepperdine University in 1990. She maintains her California license as a marriage and family psychotherapist. Rabbi Fox has served Wilshire Boulevard Temple for over twenty years, in various rabbinic capacities.

She served as a regional director for the Union of American Hebrew Congregations (now Union for Reform Judaism) in New York and New Jersey as well as middle school director of Pressman Academy Day School, at Temple Beth Am, in Los Angeles. She has also published a user-friendly guide to Jewish holidays called *Seasons for Celebration* (Putnam, 1992). Rabbi Fox has enjoyed *chevruta* study, ongoing study of Jewish texts with colleagues.

Rabbi Laura Geller is the senior rabbi of Temple Emanuel in Beverly Hills, California. She was the third woman ordained by Hebrew Union College–Jewish Institute of Religion and the first to be selected to lead a major metropolitan synagogue. Among her awards and honors was being named one of *Newsweek*'s fifty most influential rabbis in America for two years and receiving the California State Legislature's Woman of the Year Award 1994. Author of many articles in journals and books, Rabbi Geller is a frequent contributor to the *Huffington Post* and served on the editorial board of *The Torah: A Woman's Commentary*, in which she has two essays. Rabbi Geller is a Fellow of the Corporation of Brown University, from which she graduated in 1971.

Rabbi Steven Greenberg is a senior teaching fellow at CLAL and director of the CLAL Diversity Project. In 2001 he appeared in *Trembling Before G-d*, a documentary about gay and lesbian Orthodox Jews, and joined the filmmaker, Sandi DuBowski, carrying the film across the globe as a tool for dialogue. He is the author of the book *Wrestling with God and Men: Homosexuality in the Jewish Tradition* (University of Wisconsin Press) and currently a founder and co-director of Eshel, an Orthodox LGBT community support and education organization. He lives with his partner Steven Goldstein and daughter Amalia in Boston.

Rabbi David Greenstein, PhD is the rabbi of Congregation Shomrei Emunah in Montclair, New Jersey. He has written essays concerning the renewal of tradition in the realms of Jewish ritual practice, aesthetics, ethics, and social thought. He is the author of *Roads* *to Utopia: The Walking Stories of the Zohar* (Stanford University Press, forthcoming).

Rabbi Lisa J. Grushcow, DPhil is the senior rabbi of Temple Emanu-El-Beth Sholom, Montreal's only Reform congregation. She was ordained by Hebrew Union College–Jewish Institute of Religion (New York) in 2003, where she was a Wexner Graduate Fellow, and holds master's and doctoral degrees from Oxford University, where she studied as a Rhodes Scholar. She is the author of *Writing the Wayward Wife: Rabbinic Interpretations of Sotah* and is a contributor to *The Torah: A Woman's Commentary*, and *Mishkan Moeid: A Guide to the Jewish Seasons.* She serves on the board of the Central Conference of Reform Rabbis.

Rabbi Rachel Gurevitz, PhD, serves Congregation B'nai Shalom in Westborough, Massachusetts. She received her PhD from University College London in cultural geography (sociology), prior to her rabbinic studies. She is a CLAL associate scholar and graduate of their "Rabbis Without Borders" fellowship. She is married to Rabbi Suri Krieger and has four adult stepchildren.

Debby Herbenick, PhD, MPH, is an associate research scientist in Indiana University's School of Public Health–Bloomington, co-director of the Center for Sexual Health Promotion at Indiana University, and sexual health educator for the Kinsey Institute for Research in Sex, Gender and Reproduction. Dr. Herbenick has written five books about sex and love. She has taught human sexuality to thousands of college students and has an active research agenda related to women's sexual health, sexual response, and relationship quality.

Rabbi Lisa Hochberg-Miller has been the spiritual leader of Temple Beth Torah, Ventura, California, since 1997. She is a recognized and respected leader of the interfaith community; her warmth and ability to connect with others makes her as beloved in the interfaith community and with city leadership as she is with adults and young people in Ventura's Jewish community. Ordained from the Hebrew Union College–Jewish Institute of Religion in 1991, along with her husband Rabbi Seth Hochberg-Miller, she earned her MAHL in 1989, her MAJCS with an emphasis in Jewish education at Brandeis University's Hornstein Program in 1986, and a BJ from the University of Missouri–Columbia's prestigious School of Journalism in 1981. She and Seth are parents of three daughters.

Rabbi Deborah Kahn-Harris, PhD, was raised in Houston, Texas and received her BA in art history from Mount Holyoke College in Massachusetts. She came to the United Kingdom in 1989 to study at the Oxford Centre for Postgraduate Hebrew Studies, before entering the *s'michah* program at Leo Baeck College, where she was ordained in 1996. In 2001 she went to live in Jerusalem for a year, where she taught in several places, including the Machon and Ta Shma. After a brief stint at as temporary assistant rabbi at Temple Beth Israel in Melbourne, Australia, she returned to the UK, where she divided her working time between serving on the rabbinic team at Sha'arei Tsedek North London Reform (previously Southgate & District Reform Synagogue), teaching at Leo Baeck College, working on her PhD in Bible at the University of Sheffield, and teaching Bible and Jewish studies at SOAS in 2007–9. Her PhD is entitled "A Hammer for Shattering Rock: Employing Classical Rabbinic Hermeneutics to Fashion Contemporary Feminist Commentary on the Bible" and was completed during the summer of 2011. Rabbi Kahn-Harris is currently principal of Leo Baeck College, where she also teaches Bible.

Rabbi Molly G. Kane currently serves as the rabbi/educator at Brooklyn Heights Synagogue in Brooklyn, New York. Rabbi Kane was ordained in 2011 by Hebrew Union College–Jewish Institute of Religion. While in school, she served as student rabbi at *Kolot Chayeinu* / Voices of Our Lives, also in Brooklyn. Molly completed a graduate degree in nonprofit management at the Milano School of International Affairs,

Management and Urban Policy at The New School for Public Engagement. She did her undergraduate work at Brandeis University. In addition to her work as rabbi, Molly is also a comedic writer and performer.

Rabbi Dana Evan Kaplan, PhD is the rabbi of the United Congregation of Israelites in Kingston, Jamaica, and former rabbi of Temple B'nai Israel in Albany, Georgia. He is the author of *Contemporary American Judaism: Transformation and Renewal* (Columbia University Press), *The Cambridge Companion to American Judaism* (Cambridge University Press), *American Reform Judaism: An Introduction* (Rutgers University Press), *Platforms and Prayer Books* (Rowman & Littlefield), *Contemporary Debates in American Reform Judaism* (Routledge), and the just-released *The New Reform Judaism: Challenges and Reflections* (Jewish Publication Society).

Rabbi Marc Katz is assistant rabbi at Congregation Beth Elohim in Park Slope, Brooklyn. After growing up in Barrington, Rhode Island and attending Tufts University, Marc enrolled in Hebrew Union College–Jewish Institute of Religion and was ordained in 2012. He lives in Park Slope with his wife, Cantor Julia Katz.

Daniel Kirzane is a rabbinical student and Wexner Graduate Fellow at the Hebrew Union College–Jewish Institute of Religion in New York City, where he received an MA in Jewish education and will be ordained in 2014. He has worked for City Year: Washington, D.C.; BIMA and Genesis at Brandeis University; and T'ruah: The Rabbinic Call for Human Rights. He has also served as a student rabbi in Steubenville, Ohio; in Brooklyn, New York; and at Columbia/Barnard Hillel.

Jessica Kirzane is a PhD candidate in Yiddish studies at Columbia University. She holds an MA in Yiddish studies from Columbia University and a BA in English literature and Jewish studies from the University of Virginia. Her research focuses on the representation of Jewishness and gentileness in American Jewish fiction in Yiddish and English.

Rabbi Elliot Kukla is a rabbi at the Bay Area Jewish Healing Center in San Francisco, providing spiritual care to those struggling with illness, grieving, or dying, where he also co-directs the Healing Center's Kol HaNeshama: Jewish End of Life Care volunteer hospice program. His articles are published in numerous magazines and anthologized widely. Elliot has lectured on Jewish perspectives on gender and sexual diversity across the United States and Canada, and his liturgies for new life cycles appear in numerous prayer books. He also has served as adjunct faculty in pastoral care at Starr King School for the Ministry (a part of the Graduate Theological Seminary of University of California, Berkeley). Elliot was ordained by Hebrew Union College–Jewish Institute in Los Angeles in 2006 and trained in chaplaincy at the University of California, San Francisco, Medical Center in 2007.

Joel L. Kushner, PsyD was trained as a clinical and organizational psychologist. He is the founding director of the Institute for Judaism, Sexual Orientation, and Gender Identity at the Hebrew Union College–Jewish Institute of Religion, the Reform Movement's seminary. Internally, the Institute trains students and clergy on LGBT issues and tools of inclusion. Externally, the Institute's mission is to achieve complete inclusion, integration, and welcoming of LGBT people in congregations and communities. Dr. Kushner consults with a variety of Jewish and non-Jewish organizations, locally and nationally, and frequently lectures on LGBT education and inclusion across the country. He sits on the National Religious Leadership Roundtable of the National Gay and Lesbian Task Force and on the boards of California Faith for Equality, a Wider Bridge, and Nehirim. He is the senior editor of *Kulanu: A Lesbian, Gay, Bisexual and Transgender Inclusion Guide for Congregations*, published by URJ Press.

Rabbi Michael Adam Latz has served as the senior rabbi of Shir Tikvah Congregation in Minneapolis, Minnesota, since July 2009. He is recognized as a leader on fair housing, ending gun violence, marriage equality, creating spiritual communities, and progressive social change.

He believes the rabbi's job is to teach and live Torah in the very busy intersection of spirituality and justice. Previously, he was the founding rabbi of Kol HaNeshamah in West Seattle, Washington. Rabbi Latz was ordained by Hebrew Union College–Jewish Institute of Religion in 2000. He has written for socialaction.com, and his sermon "The Unbinding of Isaac" was selected by *Sh'ma* magazine as one of the eighteen best sermons of 1999.

Marcie Schoenberg Lee, MSW, MAJCS, lectures widely on sex and sexuality to diverse religious and secular audiences in the United States and abroad, and she teaches human sexual behavior at Arizona State University. The Warner Brothers Television Network produced an episode of its series *Raising Arizona Kids* that was an interview with Marcie entitled "Teaching Sexuality to Our Children." She has been a consultant on child development and on sexuality to secular and Jewish preschools and elementary schools. She also teaches her ongoing series "Artful Encounters with the Hebrew Bible" (the entire Hebrew Bible and the Apocrypha through art), "The Christian Bible's Inspiration Was the Glorious Bible of the Hebrew Nation," "Biblical Brains and Bombshells: Women in Judaism," "Rhythms of Contemporary Jewish Practice," and "Judaism and Senior Issues: A Jewish Anchor." She recently completed her eighteenth year as director of the Hillel Teaching Scholars Program for the Training of Religious School Teachers and is a proud 1975 graduate of Hebrew Union College–Jewish Institute of Religion's (then) School of Jewish Communal Service.

Rabbi Daniel A. Lehrman, NCPsyA, LP, is a licensed psychoanalyst practicing in Manhattan, Brooklyn, and South Orange, New Jersey. Formerly a synagogue rabbi in Rockland County, New York, he teaches and leads workshops throughout the New York metropolitan area, with special emphasis on the overlap of psychology and Jewish spirituality. He is on the teaching faculty of the Westchester Institute in Bedford Hills, New York, and is at work on a book called *If Brutality*

Is Human, a psycho-spiritual exploration of violence and moral frailty. More information may be found at DanielALehrman.com.

Rabbi Leigh Lerner guided Temple Emanu-El-Beth Sholom of Montreal for twenty-three years before becoming its rabbi emeritus in 2012. His commitment to social justice led to the organization of the Temple Committee against Human Trafficking, which significantly raised awareness of the problem of sex trafficking and prostitution in Quebec, bringing together for the first time federal, provincial, and local police to cooperate in ending trafficking. The congregation's work, including distribution of the rabbi's guide to a Jewish understanding of the issue, as well as large conferences for youth awareness, merited an Irving J. Fain Social Action Award from the Religious Action Center in Washington, D.C.

Rabbi Jane Rachel Litman is a senior congregational consultant for the Reconstructionist Movement. She teaches at the California Institute for Integral Studies and is the co-editor of the award-winning Lifecycle series published by Jewish Lights. She is happy to answer questions about congregational best practices, sexuality and gender expression, gardening, Japanese art, and great hiking trails in Northern California.

Rabbi Michal Loving grew up splitting her time between her mothers' house in Long Beach, California, and her father's home in Holon, Israel. Ordained in 2012 by the Hebrew Union College–Jewish Institute of Religion in Cincinnati, she received her MA in Hebrew letters from HUC-JIR in 2011, her MA in philosophy from California State University, Long Beach, in 2006, and her BA in English and philosophy from Whittier College in 2002. She currently serves as the director of congregational learning at Congregation B'nai Israel in Sacramento, California, and in her spare time loves to read, watch science fiction, and spend time with her husband and two young sons.

Rabbi Rachel M. Maimin serves as an assistant rabbi at Isaac M. Wise Temple in Cincinnati, Ohio. She received her bachelor of arts in psychology and French at the University of Pennsylvania. She was ordained in 2013 by Hebrew Union College–Jewish Institute of Religion in New York.

Rabbi Janet R. Marder was ordained in 1979 by Hebrew Union College–Jewish Institute of Religion. Since 1999 she has been senior rabbi of Congregation Beth Am in Los Altos Hills, California. In 2003 she was elected as the first woman president of the Central Conference of American Rabbis. She is a senior rabbinic fellow of the Shalom Hartman Institute in Jerusalem and is a co-editor of *Mishkan HaNefesh*, the new High Holy Day *machzor* for the Reform Movement. She is married to Rabbi Sheldon Marder, of the Jewish Home in San Francisco, and they have two daughters, Betsy and Rachel.

Rabbi Dalia Marx, PhD, is an associate professor of liturgy and midrash at the Jerusalem campus of Hebrew Union College–Jewish Institute of Religion. She teaches in the "Year in Israel" program, in the Israeli rabbinic program, and in the MA education program. She also teaches in various institutions in Israel and Europe. Rabbi Marx writes for academic and popular journals. Her new book, titled *A Feminist Commentary: Tractates Tamid, Middot, and Qinnim*, was published in 2013.

Rabbi Edythe Held Mencher, LCSW, serves at the Union for Reform Judaism as full-time faculty for Sacred Caring Community and as a member of the adjunct faculty of the Hebrew Union College–Jewish Institute of Religion's Interfaith Doctor of Ministry in Pastoral Counseling program. She also maintains a private psychotherapy practices in Westchester and Manhattan. Rabbi Mencher was ordained by HUC-JIR (New York) in 1999. She received certification from the Westchester Center for the Study of Psychoanalysis and Psychotherapy in 1989 and currently serves on the faculty of their

Training Institute. She earned her master of social work degree from Hunter College School of Social Work.

Dr. Jay Michaelson holds a PhD in Jewish thought from the Hebrew University, a JD from Yale, and a BA from Columbia. He is the author of five books, including the best-selling *God vs. Gay? The Religious Case for Equality* (Beacon Press, 2011). Formerly the founding director of Nehirim, a national LGBT Jewish organization, Jay is currently vice president of social justice programs at the Arcus Foundation, a leading funder of LGBT causes, and a contributing editor of the *Forward* newspaper. Recently included on the *"Forward* 50" list of influential American Jews, Jay has held teaching positions at Boston University Law School, City College of New York, and Yale University.

Rabbi Andrea Myers is the author of *The Choosing: A Rabbi's Journey from Silent Nights to High Holy Days* and has been a columnist for the *Huffington Post*. She was ordained by the Academy for Jewish Religion in 2002, where she was on the faculty and administration. She has served congregations from the Rockies to the borscht belt and is on the national board of Keshet, a national grassroots organization that works for the full equality and inclusion of LGBT Jews in Jewish life.

Liya Rechtman is a student at Amherst College, studying both English, with a concentration in trauma theory, and religion, with a concentration in American Christianity. This year past year she served on the college's Sexual Misconduct Oversight Committee and for a year prior served on the Sexual Respect Task Force. Liya is also the founding editor of the campus's online publication ACVoice.com, where she writes about feminism, queer identity, and sexual respect.

Rabbi Selig Salkowitz, DMin, was born in Brooklyn, New York. He earned his MHL and ordination at Hebrew Union College–Jewish Institute of Religion in Cincinnati. He also possesses a certificate in pastoral counseling from the Postgraduate Center for Mental Health in New York City, and he received his DMin in pastoral care at the New York Theological Seminary. Rabbi Salkowitz served as a congregational rabbi in Fair Lawn, New Jersey, for over thirty years. Afterward, as far as any person or research has indicated, he was the first interim rabbi in contemporary Jewish rabbinic communities, assisting a sequence of thirteen congregations in distress for one-year terms. Additionally he was the chair of the CCAR Ad Hoc Committee on Homosexuality and the Rabbinate, followed by serving as chair of the Committee on Human Sexuality.

Rabbi Amy Scheinerman is a Jewish hospice chaplain, writer, and teacher. She is a member of the Board of Trustees of the Central Conference of American Rabbis, president of the Greater Carolinas Association of Rabbis, and immediate past president of the Baltimore Board of Rabbis. She maintains a popular website that serves as an educational vehicle without borders, as well as a Torah commentary blog and a Talmud blog with her *chevruta*. She has served Conservative, Reform, and unaffiliated congregations and teaches in a wide variety of venues, including as a visiting scholar at congregations around the country.

Rabbi Rebecca Einstein Schorr was ordained by the Hebrew Union College–Jewish Institute of Religion and is the editor of the *CCAR Newsletter*, a CLAL Rabbis Without Borders fellow, and a contributing author to the Rabbis Without Borders blog and the *New Normal: Blogging Disability*. She is also a regular contributor to Kveller.com and RJ.org and is a frequent guest on Huffington Post Live. Writing at her blog, *This Messy Life*, Rebecca finds meaning in the sacred and not-yet-sacred intersections of daily life. Follow her on Twitter @rebeccaschorr.

Rabbi Jonathan Stein served as president of the Central Conference of American Rabbis from 2011 to 2013. Previously he was editor of the *CCAR Journal*, from 2003 to 2009. Having served as rabbi at Indianapolis Hebrew Congregation and Congregation Beth Israel of San Diego, Stein is currently rabbi at Shaaray Tefila in New York City's Upper East Side, since July 2001.

Sarah Tuttle-Singer is an LA expat (reluctantly) growing roots in Israel where she lives with her two kids and a one-eyed cat in a small village with a view of rolling fields and endless sky. Sarah is a Contributing Editor at *Kveller*, the New Media Editor at *Times of Israel*, and has written for *Times of Israel*, *Offbeat Families*, *Huffington Post*, and *Jezebel*. Sarah is dangerous when bored.

Lee Walzer is the author of *Between Sodom and Eden: A Gay Journey through Today's Changing Israel* (Columbia University Press, 2000), *Gay Rights on Trial* (ABC-CLIO, 2002), and *Marriage on Trial* (ABC-CLIO, 2005). A banking attorney during the week, he teaches Modern Hebrew through immersion at Temple Rodef Shalom in Falls Church, Virginia, and is developing a curriculum for post–*b'nei mitzvah* students to maintain Hebrew reading skills and teach about Israeli society and culture through the study of Hebrew pop and rock lyrics. He lives in Arlington, Virginia, with his husband, Kevin, and son, Joshua.

Rabbi Mark Washofsky, PhD, is the Solomon B. Freehof Professor of Jewish Law at Hebrew Union College–Jewish Institute of Religion in Cincinnati. He specializes in the literature of Jewish law (halachah) and the application of legal theory to the understanding of the Jewish legal process. He writes on the history and theory of halachic decision making and issues of medical ethics in Jewish law. He serves as chair of the Responsa Committee of the Central Conference of American Rabbis. His books include *Jewish Living: A Guide to Contemporary Reform Practice* and *Reform Responsa for the Twenty-First Century*, the latest printed collection of Reform responsa.

Rabbi Nancy H. Wiener, DMin, is the clinical director of the Jacob and Hilda Blaustein Center for Pastoral Counseling at Hebrew

Union College–Jewish Institute of Religion in New York, where she holds the Paul and Trudy Steinberg Chair in Human Relations. She is also the rabbi of the Pound Ridge Jewish Community, a Reform *chavurah* in Pound Ridge, New York. She holds a doctor of ministry in pastoral counseling and a master of Hebrew letters from Hebrew Union College, as well as a master's degree in Jewish history from Columbia University. She is a certified member of the National Association of Jewish Chaplains. She and her spouse, Judith, live in New York City.

Rabbi Laura Novak Winer, RJE, is an expert in educating and engaging teens and young adults within institutions of Jewish learning. Prior to founding her own consulting firm, she worked for twelve years at the Union for Reform Judaism, helping to guide their youth programs. Her Sacred Choices series of publications has won praise for sensitively discussing adolescent relationships in pragmatic and moral terms. Rabbi Winer has led education efforts at Jewish schools, synagogues, and camps throughout the United States.

Rabbi Elizabeth S. Wood is the associate rabbi at the Reform Temple of Forest Hills in Queens, New York. She worked with the Kinsey Institute during her undergraduate career at Indiana University, including her time as a teaching assistant to Dr. Debby Herbenick in human sexuality classes. The intersection of health and wellness, sexuality, and religion has always been an area of interest to Rabbi Wood.

ESSENTIAL BOOKS FROM CCAR PRESS

Perfect for personal enrichment, book clubs, adult study groups, and author events. Discussion questions are available.

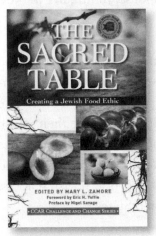

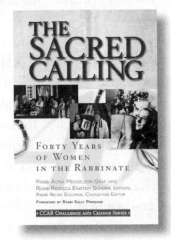

The Sacred Table: Creating A Jewish Food Ethic

Edited by Rabbi Mary L. Zamore
Foreword by Rabbi Eric H. Yoffie
Preface by Nigel Savage

This groundbreaking volume presents the challenge of navigating through choices about eating, while seeking to create a rich dialogue about the intersection of Judaism and food.

The Sacred Calling: Forty Years of Women in the Rabbinate

Edited by Rabbi Alysa Mendelson Graf and Rabbi Rebecca Einstein Schorr
Rabbi Renee Edelman, Consulting Editor

This collection examines the ways in which the reality of women in the rabbinate has impacted on all aspects of Jewish life, including congregational culture, liturgical development, life cycle ritual, the Jewish healing movement, spirituality, theology, and more.

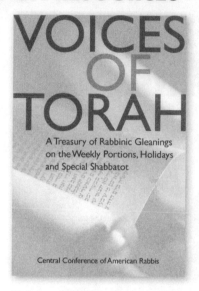

CENTRAL CONFERENCE OF AMERICAN RABBIS

CCAR Press

IMPORTANT JEWISH RESOURCES

Beyond Breaking the Glass:
A Spiritual Guide to Your Jewish Wedding, Revised Edition
Edited by Rabbi Nancy H. Wiener, D.Min.

This is the book for all of today's couples. Explores the rich history of Jewish wedding customs and rituals throughout the centuries while providing contemporary interpretations and creative options.

Mishkan Moeid:
A Guide to the Jewish Seasons
Edited by Rabbi Peter S. Knobel, Ph.D.
Foreword by Rabbi Michael Marmur, Ph.D.

Mishkan Moeid, newly revised and updated from the CCAR classic, *Gates of the Seasons*, this survey of the sacred days of the Jewish yearly cycle provides detailed guidance on observing Shabbat and the Jewish holidays, including historical background, essays, and extensive notes.

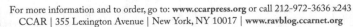

For more information and to order, go to: **www.ccarpress.org** or call 212-972-3636 x243
CCAR | 355 Lexington Avenue | New York, NY 10017 | www.ravblog.ccarnet.org

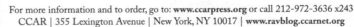